The Metrolink Companion

BEING A LINE-SIDE GUIDE TO THE TRAMWAY SYSTEM
OF GREATER MANCHESTER,
TOGETHER WITH SOME ACCOUNT OF THE PLACES
AND ATTRACTIONS THAT IT SERVES...

TO WHICH IS APPENDED A DESCRIPTIVE ACCOUNT OF THE
EAST LANCASHIRE RAILWAY...

INTENDED FOR THE USE OF BOTH RESIDENTS AND VISITORS
TO THE MANCHESTER AREA...

WRITTEN AND COMPILED BY BARRY WORTHINGTON

SIGMA *Leisure*

Published by Sigma Leisure – an imprint of
Sigma Press, Stobart House, Pontyclerc, Penybanc Road, Ammanford, Carmarthenshire SA18 3HP.

British Library Cataloguing in Publication Data
A CIP record for this book is available from the British Library.

ISBN: 978-1-85058-977-8

Typesetting and Design by: Sigma Press, Ammanford.

Cover photographs: Masthead from an original ELR Timetable c.1850, and a tram on Radcliffe Viaduct, by David Dixon

Maps: Rebecca Terry

Photographs: Barry Worthington, unless otherwise stated

Printed by: TJ International Ltd

Disclaimer: the information in this book is given in good faith and is believed to be correct at the time of publication. No responsibility is accepted by either the author or publisher for errors or omissions, or for any loss or injury howsoever caused. Only you can judge your own fitness, competence and experience. Do not rely soley on sketch maps for nagivation: we strongly recommend the use of appropriate Ordnance Survey (or equivalent) maps.

Preface

The publication of this book coincides with the twenty-second anniversary of the first opening of the Manchester Metrolink tram system, a pioneer of the British light rail revival in recent years. Moreover, it also coincides with the completion and opening of three new routes; namely, the lines to Oldham and Rochdale; Ashton; and East Didsbury. At the time of writing, work is proceeding on a completely new route to Wythenshawe and Manchester Airport. A second cross-city line has commenced, and a new route is projected to serve the Trafford Centre, the new Salford Reds Stadium, and the intended Port Salford container depot. Nevertheless, the expanding Metrolink system is still without a guide or description aimed at the general reader. This book is intended to remedy that omission.

Although it may contain enough technical information and descriptive matter concerning the tramway (and the history of the former railway lines it replaced) to interest the enthusiast, it is really intended to satisfy the curiosity of the ordinary passenger. In so doing, it aims to do two things. Firstly, the book describes what may be seen from the tram window during a journey. Secondly, it will give some account of places and attractions that can be visited from the stations.

In addition, a small number of walks from the Metrolink stations (including such destinations as Prestwich Clough, Ancoats, and Dunham Massey) are also included. After some consideration, it was thought proper to include a description of the East Lancashire Railway. Although not part of the Metrolink system, it is treated as an extension because the journey upon both the Bury tram and steam train constitutes a complete day out.

Consequently, the enthusiast, the resident, and the tourist visitor can use this guide to explore the Metrolink tram system, to organise a day out, or merely as a travelling companion to pass the time on an ordinary journey. As the network expands or updates, so (hopefully) will future editions of the book. The information contained was correct at the time of printing, but, as it is necessarily a work in progress, the author and publisher would appreciate any comments and suggestions from readers with regard to errors, omissions, and changes.

Barry Worthington
Spring, 2014

Acknowledgements

As in the case of detailing sources, it would be difficult to enumerate all the people who have assisted me in researching and compiling a work of this nature. However, I would like to take the opportunity to single out the assistance given by the staff at the Tourist Information Centres in Manchester, Bury, and the Lowry (Salford); the staff at the Local History Library, Manchester, and the Bury Municipal Library; staff at Transport for Greater Manchester; John McCarthy for his comments on the Droylsden/Ashton chapter; Geoffrey Wellans for information about St. Leonard's, Middleton; and my fellow ELR volunteers and 'banana fanciers' for their encouragement. I would also like to mention Jane Evans, my editor, for her advice, assistance and, above all, patience!

Foreword

I am absolutely delighted to lend my support to this publication. Metrolink is a vital and iconic component in Greater Manchester's public transport network. In 1992 Manchester was proud to become the first UK city to bring back trams to the streets, and Metrolink has now gone on to become a huge success with the system ever increasing. The recent expansions are a far cry from its initial Bury and Altrincham services and now serve several parts of the conurbation from South Manchester at Didsbury to Oldham and Rochdale in the North of Greater Manchester, carrying more than 20 million passengers a year in the process. By the time the current expansion programme is complete in 2016 the network will have tripled in size since it first opened over 20 years ago. Metrolink will be by far the largest light rail system in the country and a more comprehensive network than many other European cities who retained their tramway systems. Not only has the network expanded but the signs of Metrolink's on-going evolution are there to be seen every day with more and more of the new and much improved fleet of yellow and silver M5000 running along the tracks. By next year all of the original aquamarine T68 trams will have been retired and Metrolink's bright new future will be fully upon us. In fact, the tracks at the new Trafford Metrolink depot are rather reminiscent of Newton Heath rail depot at the end of steam in 1968 with so many T68 trams now there! It is expected at least one T68 tram will be preserved to add to the growing collection of Manchester's second tramway at Heaton Park where vintage trams run most weekends.

The successful operation and continued growth of Metrolink has had the absolute all party commitment of the former Greater Manchester Transport Authority, Integrated Transport Authority, and now Transport for Greater Manchester Committee and Greater Manchester Combined Authority. It has been our shared desire to have an iconic public transport system which supports the environment, encourages people out of private cars and onto public transport and which supports the economy by helping to regenerate our conurbation getting people to work, shops and using public transport for leisure. All of which will be enhanced by this publication of Barry's book which takes you not only on a journey on a system of public transport which is enjoyable to use but explores some of the magnificent landscape, industrial heritage, a modern city environment and shares with you some of the secrets which Greater Manchester has to offer as well. I hope that using this book will give you many pleasurable hours.

Keith Whitmore
Chairman Heaton Park Tramway Trust
Former Chairman Greater Manchester Integrated Transport Authority and
first Chair of the Transport for Greater Manchester Committee.

Keith Whitmore is an Honorary Alderman of Manchester City Council, a Director of the Royal Exchange Theatre, Manchester, a Director of the People's History Museum, a Director of the Bahamas Locomotive Society and Chairs the Heaton Park Tramway Trust

In loving memory of Harold and Mary Worthington, my parents; who could never understand a small boy's interest in trams...but encouraged him in it, all the same...

Contents

How to use this guide

Apart from the introduction, the section descriptive of an excursion on the East Lancashire Railway, and the chapter relating to Central Manchester, each chapter describes a journey on a Metrolink line that commences in the Central Manchester area. The Central Manchester chapter describing Piccadilly Station, Victoria Station, and the lines within this Central Area is cross referenced with the other chapters to avoid duplication. Each subsequent chapter consists of self-contained sections of route. Consequently, the guide comprises a large jigsaw puzzle, and any journey can be replicated by assembling the appropriate pieces together. This is done by examining the enclosed service map, comparing it with the contents page, and creating an itinerary of appropriate sections. (The one drawback is that, in some cases, sections may have to be read in reverse; as will be the case in most journeys towards the centre of Manchester!)

In order to avoid information overload as the tram rolls along, interesting facts and stories have been added in 'infoboxes'. These may be read or ignored as judged convenient.

Similarly, separate sections have been created for destinations and important towns and areas along the route, usually in the form of a walking 'trail'.

A number of excursions from Metrolink stations have been included, together with a bus excursion to the interesting town of Middleton. As indicated in the preface, a descriptive chapter on the East Lancashire Railway complements the trip on the Metrolink line to Bury.

Lastly, a number of walking excursions commence at Metrolink stations. These explore interesting areas, access the countryside, or lead to historic sites.

Anything important is highlighted in bold type. Commercial premises are placed in italics. Wherever possible, opening times are given, but these are subject to change, so check beforehand if there is anything particular that you wish to see. Although some historic buildings (particularly churches) and museums do not charge admission, it would be courteous to make a purchase or leave a donation towards their upkeep.

Metrolink trams are designed to convey wheelchairs and push-chairs, but not bicycles or mobility scooters. (However, a number of stations, as indicated in the text, have secure facilities for bicycles.) Consequently, the trips outlined in the Guide are usually both wheelchair and family friendly, though it is wise to check access arrangements with regard to some of the older structures, such as churches and historic buildings.

Most children love riding on the trams, and destinations such as Heaton Park, Sale Water Park, Dunham Massey, and the East Lancashire Railway are ideal for a family day out.

Metrolink, Past, Present, and Future

Metrolink is a pioneer in the new generation of British tramways. But what does that mean? What, exactly, is a 'tramway'? The word is an ancient one (and probably Scandinavian in origin), predating the term 'railway'. The root 'traam' originally meant a log or piece of wood. Indeed, the early tramways or wagon-ways in Britain, usually serving collieries, were known as 'tramways', probably because the first rails were made of wood.

The Liverpool and Manchester Railway was the first public 'railway'. It was a new form of transport, linking towns and cities by scheduled steam-hauled passenger trains, and was consequently termed a 'railway' or 'railroad'...no doubt in order to distinguish it in the public imagination from the short, haphazard, colliery line that 'tramway' or 'tram-road' brought to mind. Consequently, over the years, the term 'tramway', acquired a distinct definition. It was a form of rail transport that differed from a railway in permitted speed, axle loadings, gradients, curve radius, and (perhaps) length. Consequently, it was cheaper to build, and far more flexible. Although a 'tramway' could run on a private right of way like a 'railway', it might also run alongside the highway on a reserved track, or down a street or roadway. Although it could be used to serve a rural area where the traffic did not justify a full-scale railway, it soon proved the perfect format for a public transport system intended to serve an urban area. Indeed, in Britain it generally became a term largely used to describe an urban street tramway system. Thus it remained in the popular imagination, until the recent revival, when the original concept, with its amazing flexibility, was once more to the fore. As a result, the term 'light rail' is sometimes used, but when railed vehicles appeared in Manchester town centre, the public immediately called them 'trams'.

Manchester, together with Salford, perhaps saw the first flowering of this new form of transport. John Greenwood (1788-1851) took a lease on the Pendleton toll bar, and was soon impressed by the volume of what we would now call commuter traffic passing through it from fashionable Pendleton and Broughton en route to Manchester. He conceived the idea of a short distance passenger operation, a service that did not require pre booking and charged a low fare, performed by a vehicle that would stop to pick up and set down along the road. Such a vehicle would be open for everybody (the Latin word 'omnibus' can be translated as 'for all'). Greenwood introduced his revolutionary 'omnibus' service in 1824, five years before Shillibeer's London 'bus' (usually thought to be the British pioneer). Greenwood's buses soon became an important part of everyday life, and his son, 'Young' John Greenwood (1818-86) continued to build up the business. Like many others, he realised that haulage would be made much easier (and thus cheaper) by providing a smoother surface for the bus wheels. Consequently, John Haworth, his brother-in-law, invented an early form of guided bus-way. Using a retractable guide wheel running along a slotted centre rail, the bus wheels would be kept engaged with smooth flat metal plates set into the road. In 1861, 'Haworth's Patent Perambulating System' was opened between Pendleton and Albert Bridge, running along the Crescent and Chapel Street. It was not a success and was soon abandoned (the saying 'as useless as a five-wheeled bus' became quite

A surviving Manchester Carriage and Tramway vehicle in Heaton Park
(photograph courtesy of Heaton Park Tramway)

common in the locality). But it was clear that the future lay in some form of railed transport in towns.

That same year, the eccentric George Francis Train opened the first proper street tramway in Britain at Birkenhead. After some false starts, street tramways soon became a popular form of British urban transport, and the first horse tramway line opened in the Manchester area in 1877. It should be noted that both Salford and Manchester Councils insisted upon constructing and maintaining the street tracks and leasing them to an operating company. The Manchester Carriage and Tramway Company was formed in 1880, and soon operated the most extensive horse tramway network in Britain; by 1891 they operated 515 horse trams over 145 miles of track. It was truly regional in scope, with routes extending as far as Ashton, Oldham, and Stockport. Its nearest rival was the Manchester, Bury, Rochdale, and Oldham Steam Tramway Company. Unfortunately, Manchester City Council did not permit the steam trams within their boundary. Moreover, the pioneer of this system, one Henry Osborne O'Hagen, was a colourful rogue who disappeared leaving the company virtually bankrupt. When Parliament finally allowed municipalities to operate their own tramcars, the local councils, led by Manchester, bought out the Carriage Company along with the ailing steam trams, and carved them up into neat little municipal tramways operating the new 'electric cars'. Unfortunately, municipal greed and jealousy sometimes resulted in examples of grave customer dis-service. It took many years to iron out differences and institute through running. Manchester, in particular, was a progressive undertaking. It was the third largest system in Britain, and adopted a modernisation policy in the 1920s, with new routes on reserved or sleeper track. But the death in 1929 of Henry Mattinson (p286), the General Manager, resulted in a change of policy. His successor decided upon a policy of wholesale tramway abandonment that was only held in check by the onset of war. The last Manchester tram ran in 1949. Or so most people thought!

Metrolink Antecedents

The context of most of the early 'light rail' and 'rapid transit' proposals in Manchester was a desire to link the city's fractured railway systems, particularly Piccadilly and Victoria Stations. This resulted in hybrid proposals linking converted railway lines by city centre street track. The first was developed in the 1960s, largely under the auspices of the Manchester branch of the Light Railway Transport League (now the Light Rail Transit Association). Aware of the prejudice associated with the word 'tram' in some quarters at that time, it was called 'Duorail'. Although the proposal came to nothing, the germ of an idea was perhaps planted.

Pic-Vic

This scheme was a conventional rail solution to the problem, similar to the Tyne and Wear Metro. It was proposed by SELNEC PTE (South-East Lancashire and North-East Cheshire Public Transport Executive), the local transport authority which later became GMPTE when Greater Manchester was formed from the SELNEC area in 1974. The new rail link would have been 2.75 miles (4.43 km) long, and run from Ardwick Junction, a

Manchester and Salford Trams in Deansgate
(photograph courtesy of Heaton Park Tramway)

mile south of Piccadilly Station, to Queens Road Junction on the Bury line, about three-quarters of a mile north of Victoria. Just over 2 miles (3.2 km) of the new line would have been in tunnel, most of which situated at 60-70 feet beneath the centre of Manchester. Such a construction project required a large initial outlay of public money, and when Greater Manchester Council took on the project, it was unable to secure the necessary funding from central government. Consequently, the Picc-Vic scheme was eventually abandoned in 1977.

Metrolink Proposals

In the 1980s, light rail (as tramways were then usually called in Britain) was increasingly seen as a more cost-effective solution to the problem of expanding rail transport in urban areas. Inspired by the success of the more conventional Tyne and Wear Metro (opened 1980) and the Docklands Light Railway in London (opened 1987), Manchester transport planners looked to light rail as a way of bridging Manchester's rail transport gap in the city centre. There was also another imperative. By the late 1980s, the power equipment on the electrified suburban railway line from Victoria to Bury (which operated on the unique voltage of 1200 DC by means of a side-contact third-rail power supply) was in need of replacement. Rather than replace the equipment, it was decided to construct a light rail system to connect the Bury line with the Altrincham line via an on-street link, with a branch to Piccadilly Station. The addition of street running as part of the package thus establishes Metrolink's claim to be the first of the new British 'tramway' generation.

This light rail system was first promoted by Greater Manchester Council in 1984. Named simply Light Rapid Transit (LRT), the proposed system was described as "a cross between a tram and a train". The network was planned to begin operation in 1989 pending government approval, and construction costs were estimated at £42.5 million. The proposals outlined a three-line system traversing the Greater Manchester area, linking converted rail lines with an on-street tram system through Manchester city centre. A fleet of two-car "supertrams" with a top speed of 80 km/h would run services at a ten-minute frequency. The lines proposed were Altrincham via Piccadilly to Hadfield/Glossop; Bury via Victoria and Piccadilly to Rose Hill/Marple; and Rochdale via Victoria to Didsbury. Obtaining Government grants towards development was not easy and subject to strict criteria. It was therefore proposed to build the system in phases, beginning with the Altrincham and Bury lines, together with the city centre track as far as Piccadilly Gardens and Station. In 1987, when powers and funding had been secured for the initial phase of the network to go ahead, the brand name Metrolink was first introduced.

Around this time, proposals were put forward by GMPTE for further extensions to the network. In addition to the Bury and Altrincham lines plus the city centre tracks already confirmed, it was envisaged that the network could be extended to include new lines in the regeneration areas along the Manchester Ship Canal in Salford and Trafford. A spur into Rochdale town centre was also first proposed at this time. Of all these early proposals, some parts survived as extension plans. The Rochdale and Didsbury lines came to form the part of the Phase 3 plans; the present-day Eccles line is a modified version of the proposed extension into Salford Quays; and a proposed Barton/Dumplington line has evolved into the Trafford Centre/Port Salford extension scheme. However, the proposals to convert the Marple/Rose Hill and Hadfield/Glossop lines to Metrolink are now in abeyance, and do not feature in the current Phase 3 expansion plans. The Greater Manchester Passenger Transport Authority did, however, commission in 2004 a feasibility study into converting the Marple line for tram-train operation, and in this revised form it remains on the "reserve list" of proposals for future Metrolink expansion. Indeed, it was proposed to the Department for Transport in 2008 as a candidate for the national tram-train pilot. No proposals are current for linking the Hadfield/Glossop services into the Metrolink network.

Construction and Development of the Present system

In 1987 the Government required investment of some private sector capital before authorising Phase 1. Consequently, a tendering process was devised that required bidders to design, build and operate the system. The successful candidate was Greater Manchester Metrolink Ltd. (GMML), a group whose shareholders included GEC Alsthom Transportation Projects Ltd., John Mowlem Plc, Amec Plc and Greater Manchester Passenger Transport Executive (GMPTE). Construction of the on-street section began in March 1990. The first Metrolink lines were formed by converting the electric train lines between Altrincham and Cornbrook Junction and between Bury and Manchester Victoria. The missing section involved restoring the old high-level approach between Cornbrook and the former Central Station. Because much of the Metrolink route was formerly main-line railway with platforms 915 mm above rail level, the new stops in the city centre also have high platforms. This consideration also dictated the choice of high floor vehicles.

Meanwhile, a public demonstration of light rail was held from 9-27 March 1987 at a specially-constructed railway station at Debdale Park, on the site of the former Hyde Road station on the Fallowfield Loop. Entitled Project Light Rail, the demonstration featured a train from the new Docklands Light Railway, which was under construction in London at the time, as a working example of light rail technology.

Phase 1

Conversion of the existing railway lines to Metrolink took far longer than had been planned. The Altrincham line was closed for six months, rather than one month as promised, with bus substitution during that period. On 6 April, 1992, Metrolink services between Bury and Victoria began. They were followed, on 27 April, by the opening of the first street section, between Victoria and G-Mex (now Deansgate-Castlefield). Metrolink vehicle 1007 operated the ceremonial first tram into the city, sporting a special headboard. No. 1007 was chosen as that was the number of the last tram to operate in Manchester on 10 January 1949. Services between G-Mex and Altrincham began on 15 June. Finally, trams started operating into Piccadilly on 20 July the same year, completing Phase 1 of the system. Queen Elizabeth II officially opened the system on 17 July 1992.

Metrolink's new trackwork in Manchester's city centre required reinstalling twice in the first years of operation, caused by allegedly inadequate quality controls and poor design work, such as placing points directly where the blades could be expected to be repeatedly crossed by buses.

The original Market Street stop handled trams to Bury, with High Street handling trams from Bury. When Market Street was closed to road traffic these stops were replaced on 10 August 1998 by a new island platform stop in the centre of Market Street for trams in both directions. Crossover points were installed in the section approaching Piccadilly Station in order to allow inbound trams to access either platform without having first to proceed to the buffer stops at the far end of the undercroft area, resulting in quicker turnaround times. However, this mode of operation was later abandoned. Shudehill interchange opened between Victoria station and Market Street in April 2003. The bus station complementing it opened on 29 January 2006. Cornbrook station on the Altrincham line was opened to provide an interchange with the new line to Eccles. There was initially no public access from the street, but this changed on 3 September 2005 when the original fire exit was opened as a public access route.

Due to the age and condition of most of the track on the Bury and Altrincham routes it was decided that the mostly 1960s trackwork was to be relaid. This construction work included improvements to stations along the lines. The renewals commenced on 29 May 2007 with the cessation of services between Bury and Whitefield. The Bury line re-opened on 13 September that same year. With the possible exception of the section between Stretford and Dane Road, the Altrincham line track was not as worn as that on the Bury line and so not as much work was required. From 2 July various sections of the line were shut down and serviced with a replacement bus service. The Altrincham line re-opened on 28 August 2007.

Phase 2

On 25 April 1997 work began on Phase 2, an extension from Cornbrook on the Altrincham line through Salford Quays to Eccles. Service started as far as Broadway on 6 December 1999 and to Eccles on 21 July 2000. The line was officially opened on 9 January 2001. This was a key factor in the continuing development of Salford Quays, and the creation of Media city in particular. This was a new departure for Metrolink, since the new route did not involve the conversion of an existing railway line but was all 'new build'. It was a mixture of private right of way, reserved track, and street running. In short, a 'tramway' in the fullest sense of the word! The short branch to Media City was left (temporarily) in abeyance.

In 1997 the Metrolink contract or operating franchise was awarded to a new consortium, Altram (Manchester) Limited, a comprising Ansaldo Transport, Serco Investments Limited, Laing Civil Engineering and 3i. Serco Metrolink, a wholly owned subsidiary of Serco Limited, took over the operations and maintenance of the system on 26 May 1997. In March 2003, Serco Investments bought out its partners and Altram (Manchester) Limited became a wholly owned subsidiary of Serco. In July 2007 the contract to operate Metrolink was awarded to Stagecoach Metrolink, a subsidiary of the Scottish transport company, Stagecoach Group plc. Unlike Serco, Stagecoach did not own the concession, but operated it on a fixed-term management contract.

Phase 3

The pioneer Metrolink tramway system was a great success, and a major expansion, referred to as the 'big bang' was now at hand. This involved the conversion of the Oldham and Rochdale loop line from railway use, with new stations, a new section through Oldham town centre, and a street section from Rochdale station into the heart of the town; the creation of a new line to Chorlton and Didsbury on a former railway route; and new lines to Ashton-under-Lyne, and Wythenshawe/Manchester Airport. The proposal ran into both financial and political difficulties, but after energetic lobbying, a successful solution was found. This new 'Phase Three' expansion was split into two phases. Phase 3a utilised existing financial arrangements and funding to finance the Oldham/Rochdale rail loop conversion in a most basic form, without the Oldham or

Metrolink Construction between Droylsden and Audenshaw
(photograph courtesy of John McCarthy)

Rochdale town centre variants; cut back the Ashton line to Droylsden; and reduced the Didsbury, Wythenshawe, and Airport proposals to a short stub of a branch to Chorlton. The existing Media City branch proposal was also included. The remainder, termed Phase 3b, was to be financed by a Congestion Charge. After the failure of the Congestion Charge Referendum, it was largely financed by the Greater Manchester Transport Fund, a judicious pooling of resources by the constituent municipalities of the Greater Manchester area. Upon selecting the M-Pact Thales consortium as preferred bidder, GMPTE went back to the Department for Transport. Final sign off for Phase 3a was received on 16 May 2008 and GMPTE then appointed M-Pact Thales to design, build and maintain the new lines.

Planning permission was granted in October 2007 for a 400 m (440 yard) long extension from a point between Harbour City and Broadway to the central plaza of the new Media City UK development in Salford Quays. The £20m cost for the spur, and four trams to operate it, was entirely met by the MediaCity UK developer, Peel Holdings. Consequently, the branch was included in Phase 3, and Media City UK station opened on 20 September, 2010. It was initially operated as an additional stop on the Eccles line, but a dedicated shuttle service now operates at peak periods. Some have suggested that this short branch was a factor in persuading the BBC to relocate here.

In July, 2011, Stagecoach Metrolink disposed of their interest in the operation of Metrolink to RATP Dev. This French company operates tram services and light rail systems in major cities across the world, from Paris and Florence to Seoul, Hong Kong and Mumbai.

Phase 3a

The lines to Altrincham and Eccles were closed for the whole of August 2009 to allow for the existing lines to be modified ahead of Metrolink Phase 3. On the Altrincham line, the overhead cables were replaced (the original railway line was electrified in the 1930s). The structures were re-used when the line was converted to 25kv in the 1960s, used yet again when converted to Metrolink, and these needed upgrading. A new junction was built near Trafford Bar to allow connections to be built to the Chorlton extension and the new tram depot. Cornbrook station was also closed for re-modelling to allow for the shuttle service to Media City UK. On Saturday 3 October 2009 the last train ran on the Oldham and Rochdale line.

The Chorlton Line opened to the St. Werburgh's Road terminus on 7 July, 2011. Trams began operating to Oldham Mumps (Temporary Station) on 13 June, 2012, and on to Shaw a little later, on 16 December. The Droylsden line opened on 11 February, 2013, followed by the extension from Shaw to Rochdale Station on 28 February.

Phase 3b

Excepting the airport line, work is largely complete at the time of writing (2014) on the extensions that constitute Phase 3b. The East Didsbury extension opened on 23rd May, 2013, and Ashton opened on 9th October, 2013. The planned opening of the Oldham town centre line was advanced, and trams began using the new routing on 27 January, 2014. (The extension to Rochdale town centre was slated for February.)

Although the entire Airport Line is scheduled for completion by Summer, 2016, it will probably open in phases at earlier dates. Work commenced on the first phase of the Airport Line in the Autumn of 2011, and a great deal has already been accomplished, including the two motorway crossings, the crossing of the Mersey and its flood plain, and the bridge across the railway at Baguley. The anticipated completion date means that a fuller account of it can only be given in a future edition of this guide.

Phase 4

Work has commenced on a Second City Crossing, linking Victoria Station (p45) and St. Peter's Square (p38) via Corporation Street, Cross Street, and Princess Street, with a station serving Exchange Square. The first phase will open to St Mary's Gate in 2015, and the remainder the following year.

The Trams

The initial conversion of both the Bury and Altrincham Railway lines presented a problem. The alteration of the stations would have greatly added to the construction costs, and low floor tramcar technology was then in its early stages, so it was decided to use double ended cars which would match British main line platform height. Nevertheless, these vehicles were quickly called trams by people in Manchester. It proved impossible to find a British company to build the first trams, and the unusual requirements of such a hybrid system required a bespoke solution. The first vehicles were built by a consortium. GEC and Alsthom were responsible for the electrics, while the bodies were fabricated by Firema, a division of Fiat. All the trams operate to a nominal overhead current supply of 750 Volts DC.

T68 and T68a

Twenty-six T68 trams, numbered 1001 to 1026, were provided for the Altrincham, Bury and city centre (phase 1) lines, and, in an unmodified state, these vehicles could only run between Altrincham and Bury, direct or via Piccadilly. Six T68a trams (constructed by Ansaldo), numbered 2001 to 2006, were provided for the Eccles (phase 2) line, with retractable couplers and cowling, for use on the street section. The T68 trams are expected to have been withdrawn from service by March, 2014, though the T68a version may be used on the Eccles service at peak times.

'Bananas'

The 'big bang' expansion resulted in an order for 62 new trams; eight for phase one and the two upgrades, four for the Media City branch, twenty-eight for the Phase 3a extensions, eight for the Ashton and Didsbury accelerated extensions, twelve for the Airport line and two for the Oldham and Rochdale town centre lines. This created a total tram fleet of ninety four, and further orders are anticipated. This time, a legitimate tramcar design was available, and the adoption of a striking new colour scheme has led to the new vehicles being christened 'bananas'!

The M5000 is a version of the Flexity Swift high-floor tram, built by the Canadian manufacturer Bombardier Transportation at its factories in Bautzen, Germany and proved on its test facility in Vienna. All the electrical equipment is supplied by Vossloh Keipe of Germany. The first new tram, number 3001, arrived at the Metrolink Queen's Road depot on Monday 13 July 2009, and went into service on 16 December between Piccadilly and Eccles; the official launch event took place on 21 December. The M5000

M5000 Tram (photograph courtesy of John McCarthy)

tramcars are all bi-directional with an articulated centre section and doors on both sides. They are 28.4 metres long, and can carry up to 206 passengers. The units are capable of safely reaching speeds of 80 km/h (50 mph) when running on dedicated lines, and can also be coupled together into trains. They typically weigh between 35 and 40 tonnes. Each tramcar has three bogies. The two outer bogies are powered and the un-motored centre bogie supports the articulation gangway, utilising rubber/metal primary suspension and coil spring secondary suspension. Each powered bogie has two three phase ac 120 kW air-cooled motors. Electrical regenerative braking and mechanical disc brakes are provided, and for emergency use there are six magnetic track brakes.

The new Metrolink colour scheme with yellow ends and yellow and silver sides is used, and these colours are also used inside the trams. There are two wheelchair or child buggy spaces. Tinted glass in the window and door at both ends allow clear through the cab views. Four wide full length glass double doors make the trams feel lighter and brighter, while the door lobbies have a darker floor surface which rises slightly from door sill to centre aisle. A yellow centre grab pole is positioned in the middle of each door lobby, and there is space for wheelchair users to pass.

Signalling and Control Systems

The hybrid origins of Metrolink in Phase 1 initially resulted in two distinct types of signalling system. On the former rail lines, the two aspect red and green signals and track circuit block working was inherited from the railway era. However, the street

Mersey Viaduct (photograph courtesy of John McCarthy)

running sections, where vehicles were driven on 'line of sight', required a white five light signal with geometric aspects at stations and junctions. Phase 2 created a 'new build' route with a large amount of street running, operated entirely on the 'line of sight' principle. Further expansion in Phase 3 saw the system expand far beyond its original hybrid origins, and it was decided to adopt a universal tram control system known as TMS (though sometimes referred to as TOS). At the time of writing, TMS is being 'rolled out' across the system.

Block Section Working

The former heavy rail sections were totally re-signalled, though the original railway signalling principles still applied in the first instance. This meant that both the 'up' and 'down' lines were divided into sections on the basis of 'one vehicle per section' at any one time. Each section was protected by a low voltage electrical circuit which controlled the protective signals. However, block section working restricted the operational frequency. It will all have disappeared by 2015 at the latest. Metrolink controlled all the segregated section signalling except that from just south of Timperley to Altrincham inclusive. Here trams run alongside main line trains and over two level crossings under Network Rail control. This will remain excluded from the new control system.

Vehicle Recognition System (VRS)

Right from the start, this system was used on the street running sections in the centre of Manchester, but was later expanded to 'new build' routes. VRS sent information from the vehicle to both Metrolink Control and the street running signal system. The VRS equipment generated a modulated carrier signal which is transmitted by a pair of coils, mounted one after the other under the un-motored centre bogie. The signal was picked up by cable loop, buried in the road surface or mounted on the sleepers of segregated track. (This cable loop could sometimes be seen between tracks in stations such as Piccadilly Undercroft.) At the start of each journey the driver entered a route code into the VRS control panel. This sets up the description of the tram on the diagram at Metrolink control, and it also, if required, called for the points to change on street running sections.

On street running sections, tram signals were integrated with the road traffic signals. To differentiate between tram and general traffic signals a new form of signal indicator was devised. This consisted of a cluster of white lights, which were lit according to the indication required. A horizontal line indicated "stop"; a vertical line "proceed"; a diagonal line "proceed to left or right"; and a "+" sign cluster "stop if it is safe to do so". The "proceed" indications permitted a driver to pass if the road is clear of obstruction, but they do not indicate it is clear as green signals once did on the segregated sections. As the tram passed over the detection loops buried in the road, the VRS requested a tram "proceed" indication from the road traffic signal Urban Traffic Control System. When ready to depart from a stop and cross a road the "ready to start" request was also sent by the VRS.

Facing points at junctions were called to change position, if required, by a signal from the VRS. The control circuits only allowed point movement when the tram driver can see them move, and they also prevented movement when a tram is moving over the points. Street running signals were not interlocked with facing points at junctions. A separate seven light fibre optic indicator was used to show that the points are set and locked. The indication was a diagonal line of white lights indicating left or right route. If the points were not detected as set in the direction called, then the point indicator showed a horizontal white line for stop.

TMS/TOS

The "Tramway Management System" is a software package creates by Thales, a member of the Phase 3 'design and build' consortium, and capable of adaptation to a variety of circumstances. In effect, it is a far more sophisticated form of VRS (incorporating most of the features described in the VRS section, above) and became the universal means of control for the Metrolink network.

In general, TMS is based on the drive on sight principle, for vehicle movements are under driver's responsibility. When this principle cannot be applied, the system is enhanced with additional modules (like automatic train stop) necessary to reach the required safety level. The TMS system works autonomously at tramway junctions and major road junctions and crossings in the following sequence. As the vehicle approaches a powered junction area or a road crossing area, a command is sent to the track side components. These react by moving and locking the powered point switch (but only if the command can be executed) in the right position, or requesting priority if at a road crossing. At the same time all the movements in the tram network, the status of track side components, and the status of vehicle itself, are displayed in the Operational Control Centre (OCC). This is accomplished by a 'mesh radio' system, which passes data between the tram and the Control Centre, and vice versa. This is the first such application in Britain.

There are a number of key components to TMS/TOS. Firstly, an automatic vehicle localization software packet is installed in the OCC, so that the position of every tram may be monitored by the control staff. Secondly, on-board control units are installed in each vehicle to process inputs and outputs, and provide 'real time' location and operational information to the driver. Last, but not least, the track side components are intended to localize the vehicle position for both public information display at stations and for visualization in the OCC. This function also evaluates the delay and regulates the tram circulation in the network.

Thus, Metrolink is building upon the fine transport heritage of the area, and is set fair to become the largest tram network in Britain.

Central Manchester

Piccadilly Station

The original station opened on 8 May 1842 as Store Street (sometimes called Bank Top), the terminus of the Manchester and Birmingham Railway, which connected with the Grand Junction Railway's line to Birmingham at Crewe. (A journey to the capital city would be reduced to about twelve hours, as opposed to nearly two days by stage coach!) The station was shared later that year with the Sheffield, Ashton-under-Lyne, and Manchester Railway, which was eventually to extend via the infamous Woodhead tunnel to Sheffield and beyond. Store Street was renamed London Road in 1847. By that time the Manchester and Birmingham had become part of the London and North Western Railway, and the Sheffield, Ashton, and Manchester had evolved into the Manchester, Sheffield, and Lincolnshire Railway (later to become the Great Central Railway upon the opening of a line to London in 1899). The Manchester, South Junction, and Altrincham Railway (a jointly owned company, in which both the London and North Western and Great Central were shareholders, see p242) opened its line from Oxford Road Station to London Road on 1 August 1849, and built its own platforms at London Road at the point of junction with the southbound line, the only through platforms in what was otherwise a terminus. During the early 1880s the whole of the station was enlarged (including a handsome main building at the top of the approach), and the through platforms on Fairfield Street bridge were remodeled. Oddly enough for a joint station, the platform areas used by the separate companies were divided by a wrought iron spiked fence in the vicinity of the present platform five! In addition to the owning companies, London Road was used from time to time by other railway concerns, not always with happy results. In the course of a dispute in Victorian times, the ticket clerks employed by one company were forcibly evicted from their ticket office, their tickets being thrown after them! The London and North Western Railway opened Mayfield Station across Fairfield Street in 1910. It was mainly used to accommodate suburban services, and was connected to London Road by a footbridge. After closure, and use as a parcels depot, it is now in a sadly derelict condition.

After 1923, London Road was shared by the London Midland and Scottish Railway, and the London and North Eastern Railway, who also became joint owners of the Altrincham line. Even after nationalisation in 1948, the South side of the station belonged to British Railways London Midland Region and the other to its Eastern Region! Electrification of parts of the station took place in a rather haphazard way. The London, Midland, and Scottish Railway, as a part owner, ensured the electrification of the very busy commuter line to Altrincham in 1931 at 1500 volts DC as far as the through platforms. This resulted in a London and North Eastern proposal to electrify their line to Sheffield, but the war intervened. However, British Railways inherited the plan, and the Sheffield line (including platforms on the North side of the station) was electrified at 1500 volts DC between 1953 and 1955.

London Road station was renamed Manchester Piccadilly when it was rebuilt and reopened on 12 September 1960 for the new London Midland Region electric train services to London. The new West Coast Main Line electric system of 25kV 50HzAC also extended to the through platforms, which, together with the bridges over Fairfield Street, were replaced again at this time. The present island platforms (13 and 14) were built on top of a new pre-stressed concrete slab bridge with cantilevered sides for the tracks. This enabled suburban services from Stockport and Crewe to terminate here (the old Altrincham electric trains continued to run from Oxford Road station until the line was also converted to the new system in 1971). A sad casualty of the modernisation was the magnificent Victorian building, replaced by a functional concourse, similar to that at Euston (witheringly criticised by the late Sir John Betjeman). The Woodhead line controversially closed in 1970, but the section to Dinting and Hadfield remain as an electrified branch. It was converted to 25kV operation in 1984. Piccadilly's island platforms were further rebuilt and lengthened in 1988 in connection with the opening of the Windsor Link, and the glass roof over the terminal platforms was completely replaced in the late 1990s. Part of the station's undercroft was converted to provide two platforms for the Metrolink tram system.

In 2001-2002, as part of preparations for the 2002 Commonwealth Games, a large part of the station was rebuilt, with a new concourse created, together with a new entrance from Fairfield Street.

Situated at the end of a long brick viaduct, the station was built upon a large vaulted undercroft that was extended several times in the course of its history. The undercroft functioned as an underground goods station, complete with its own railway system and stables (using wagon turntables and transverse lines to access the sidings, and reached from viaduct level by a number of wagon hoists). The range of goods included beer barrels from Burton-on-Trent, sometimes unofficially 'tapped' by the shunters! Sunday mornings often resulted in music issuing forth from the cavernous interior as the brass band practiced. The **London Road frontage** of the undercroft repays attention, viewing from left to right. The **station approach** communicates with the station level by crossing **Store Street**. Beyond the iron girder extension, the stone faced **1842 archway** is visible, but note the **Ashton Canal aqueduct** in the distance. A modern shop front is inserted into a **closed arched entrance** to a staircase that once led to the old station building. (This was replaced by a flight of steps from the Store Street archway area, which was closed in the last station alteration.) A modern **pedestrian entrance to the Metrolink 'Ashton' platform** follows. The ensuing corridor is on the site of Birmingham Street, which disappeared in an extension to the undercroft. After the two **modern entrances for the Metrolink tracks** comes one of the great glories of Piccadilly Station; the restored **goods office frontage** of the former London and North Western Railway, dating from the late 19th century. Step back, and read the legend above the shop like ground floor: 'Enquiry, Delivery, Shipping, Cartage, and Goods Agents Offices', with the large finger pointing to a long vanished door. The **elaborate main door** (with a sculptured surround) has been restored, and leads to the **street level** concourse of

The London Road frontage

24

the new entrance, with direct access to the **Metrolink 'Piccadilly' platform**. The **first floor** stone office level, with more ornament, is also worth a glance. Around the corner, in Fairfield Street, is the **new entrance**, once used for goods traffic to and from the undercroft. Notice platform 13 and 14, the **through platforms**, being carried across **Fairfield Street** in the distance. A large part of the former goods station has been converted into an elaborate **taxi rank and car dropping off point**, seen to the right. The entrance to the concourse is directly ahead. There is a handsome wall-mounted **traditional clock** on the left, together with a **wall plaque** commemorating the men of the London Midland and Scottish Railway goods department at London Road who gave their lives in World War Two. The station can be directly accessed by adjacent **lifts**, but most people ascend the **stairs** or **escalator** to the **mezzanine floor** directly ahead. There is an **entrance to the 'Piccadilly' Metrolink platform** to the right of the street level concourse.

The **Metrolink Station** is contained within a large reinforced concrete box in the undercroft, with a screen wall (in which there are 'windows') dividing the tracks. The platforms are connected by a **brick paved pedestrian crossing** at the rear end, from which there is a **view of the Sheffield Street entrance and exit** for the trams. In addition to the access points already mentioned, there is a **lift** to the mezzanine level from the **'Piccadilly' platform**, together with **stairs** and an **escalator**, and a similar arrangement for the **'Ashton' platform**, save that the **lift** also services the main **station concourse**.

The **mezzanine level** is an interesting modern feature, giving a close view of the tops of the great **cast iron columns** that support this part of the undercroft and the **roof**, derived from the brick fire proof floors developed for Lancashire cotton mills. The mezzanine level communicates with a **landing** at the top of the escalators from the Fairfield Street station entrance. **Escalators and stairs** continue to the **station concourse**.

The original main entrance, the **station approach** from the corner of **Ducie Street** and **London Road**, is now reserved for pedestrians and two of the **free bus services** that criss-cross the city centre. The approach used to be flanked by a viaduct level goods warehouse and station on the left hand side, but this has now been replaced by **Gateway House** (Richard Siefert, 1969), a curving office block with shops at pavement level. Amongst these will be found the *Ian Allan* store, replete with a wide range of books and magazines for the military, railway, and other transport enthusiast, together with local history publications and guide books. Model items are to be found upstairs.

The present **station concourse** is a great improvement on the 1960s structure, but notice the tall block of contemporary **railway offices** to the right of the approach entrance, which have also been remodelled. (The concourse is described from this entrance.) The right-hand side is dominated by a large tear-shaped structure, one side of which forms part of a **shopping mall** on the immediate right. The other curves away from the circulating area towards the Southern end of the concourse, containing the **ticket office** and **travel centre**. The structure supports a **gallery** with a **food court** and seating area, accessed by stairs and escalators at either end. The gallery extends, by several links, to a **balcony** that skirts the other side of the mall, passing over the station entrance to access part of the left side of the concourse and communicating with further retail units at that level along the northern wall. There is an **enquiry kiosk** in the middle of the circulating area with a *Virgin Trains* **information office** in an adjacent corner.

Walk past the ticket office, keeping the **platform entrances** on the left. Notice the restored **late 19th century train shed roof**. There is an easily missed **Metrolink lift** on the right. (Passengers for the **Ashton line** should descend to the platform, but those for the City Centre and beyond should alight at the Mezzanine level for the lift opposite.) **Stairs** and **escalators** to the **mezzanine level** are directly ahead with **cash machines** and **toilets** beyond them to the right. **Lifts** to the street level concourse are nearby. **Platform 12** is often used for display purposes and a **left-luggage office** may be found on platform 10. However, the principal feature is the **'travelator'**, situated between platforms 10 and 11. It ascends in two stages to a **high level concourse**, complete with shopping, seating area and **toilets**, accessing a **footbridge** across the end of the station. The bridge also communicates with **platforms 13 and 14**, the through platforms.

Unfortunately, a cast iron plaque, erected by the original Manchester and Birmingham Railway, was removed in the recent remodelling, and it hopefully will be restored to a place of honour.

Piccadilly Station to Piccadilly Gardens
The tram crosses London Road. The extreme width of the thoroughfare reflects its past use as a market for the mill workers and factory operatives. There is a brief glimpse of the **old fire station** building to the left, built 1904-6 as "the finest fire station in this whole round world" in florid Edwardian baroque. This magnificent triangular structure is built round an internal courtyard, once used for drills and cleaning the fire appliances. The thirty-four firemen's married quarters were accessed by verandas. The complex also contained a police station, ambulance station, bank, gas meter testing station (!), and a **Coroners Court**, for inquests into suspicious or sudden deaths. The frontage is a mixture of brick and brown glazed terracotta, now very much the worse for wear. Since the firemen moved out, the place has a semi-derelict and deserted air, and awaits redevelopment, possibly as a hotel and retail centre. A right turn leads to a short section of **reserved track** alongside the roadway. Ahead is the new and impressive bowstring **pedestrian footbridge** linking the station approach with Piccadilly Place and Aytoun Street, but a turn of the head to the right will be rewarded with a view down Store Street **through the archway**, with the stone **Ashton Canal Aqueduct** in the distance. A left turn introduces a short stretch of **private right of way** through the new **Piccadilly Place** development. The office block to the right (No.2, Piccadilly Place) houses **Transport for Greater Manchester**, the body ultimately responsible for the Metrolink system, while the block beyond contains the *City Café,* operated by the ***Double Tree by Hilton*** hotel which is entered from Auburn Street, round the back. On the left, **Nos 3 and 4 Piccadilly Place** surround a rather sterile **little square**. After crossing **Aytoun Street**, the route makes a right turn and runs on a **reservation** alongside the street towards Piccadilly Gardens.

Crown Court, Aytoun Street

The Tale of 'Spanking Roger'

In the course of the seventeenth and eighteenth centuries, the greater part of this area of Manchester was acquired by the Mynshull family. Barbara Nabb, the widow of Thomas Samuel Mynshull, became the sole heiress of this estate upon his death in 1755. One fateful day in 1769, she attended the fashionable Kersal races and met Roger Aytoun. 'Spanking Roger' (after his pugnacious manners, and not a reference to some personal habit!), six foot four inches of a handsome physique in military uniform, swept the lady off her feet. Less than one month after this meeting, the young Scotsman and the sixty-five year old widow were married in the Collegiate Church. Aytoun nourished a military career. With some financial assistance from his wife, he raised his own regiment, the 72nd Regiment of Foot (Manchester Volunteers) to serve in the latter stages of the American War of Independence. He paraded the Manchester streets with a watch pinned to a banner, promising it to the day's first recruit. Other times he would challenge likely candidates to a fight...on the understanding that they would enlist if he won! The local archive still preserves a poster advertising a football match as a recruiting ploy. The Manchester Volunteers never went to America. Instead, they formed part of the garrison of Gibraltar, which was then besieged by the Spanish. The long siege produced conditions of great privation, and members of the regiment were driven to desertion and suicide. Nevertheless, Gibraltar was held. Aytoun returned to Manchester as a hero, but then revealed a dark side to his nature. Barbara died in 1783. Roger had squandered the entire family fortune by 1792, and had mortgaged the landed property. His debts were reduced (!) to over £11,000 by 1797, and finally cleared by the sale of Chorlton Hall. But Aytoun had already left Manchester for pastures new. He married another heiress in his native Scotland in 1794, and died a rich man in 1810! His entangled affairs resulted in land sales that led to a rash of speculative building on the south side of the town.

After crossing the **Rochdale Canal** (p195), note the **Old Crown Court** on the left. It was apparent that the then new Town Hall would have no room for the Police Courts (where prisoners were remanded to higher courts or petty offences such as drunkenness were dealt with). The omission was remedied by holding a competition for the design of a new set of courts, which was won by Thomas Worthington. The winning design had to accommodate the problems associated with a cramped site, the courts being placed in the centre and surrounded by a network of corridors and offices. It is perhaps one of the finest buildings of the period in the popular Venetian style, although financial stringency dictated the use of brick. Nevertheless, the **stonework decoration** is handsomely carved, and includes mythical creatures at the side of the doorways. Inevitably, the eye is drawn to the **great clock and bell tower**. The structure was completed in 1873, at a cost of £81,000. The destruction of the Assize Courts in World War Two resulted in the transfer of the Crown Courts to this building. And here they have stayed, despite the opening of the new Crown Court in Crown Square. Indeed, the interior was refurbished in the 1990s to create four new courts. This works programme also included a **new wing** that incorporates an entrance on Aytoun Street, in a style very much in sympathy with the original.

The building opposite is the **former labour exchange**, a classic example of 1950s Ministry of Works architecture, but now in a very sad condition. Further down the street, on the same side, is the **'Grand'**. It is on the site of the 'House of Recovery', founded in 1796, and later absorbed by the Infirmary. This one hundred bed fever hospital is credited with saving the town from a number of potentially disastrous typhus epidemics in the early stages of the industrial revolution. A warehouse for A. Collie and Co. was built here in 1867, handling over five million 'pieces' of cloth per annum. This warehouse was converted into the Grand Hotel in 1880 and the façade is now incorporated into a luxury flat development. Prices ranged from £50,000 to £300,000 upon opening, and potential customers queued all night! Notice the red granite doorway set into the original frontage of Darley Dale stone. **The adjacent block**, on the corner of Portland Street, was built 1851-2 for Brown and Son and is at the end of a range of warehouses facing Piccadilly Gardens, all designed by Edward Walters, the architect of the Free trade Hall. **Westminster House**, a plain box-like structure that was once the home of the old Greater Manchester Council, is on the opposite corner.

Piccadilly Gardens

We pass over Portland Street and enter Piccadilly Gardens tram station. There is a large **island platform**, accessed by **ramps and steps** at either end. Notice the **stone base of the railings** to the right of the up line. They are all that remains of a boundary wall that belonged to the old Infirmary (see infobox below). To the left is the large **bus station**, with **Piccadilly Plaza** beyond. **The Manchester Tourist Information Centre** is situated on the Portland Street corner in its new incarnation as a rather hip designer information outlet. An **arcade** (open on weekdays in office hours) leads through towards the famous **Chinatown**.

The tall warehouses that stood behind Parker Street were destroyed in the 'Christmas Blitz' of 1940, creating the largest bombsite in Manchester. This was the scene of the first major post-war development in the city. Covell, Matthews, and Partners produced a 'spectacular' design that was to be the first phase in a project that would extend all the way to Oxford Road. Work commenced in 1959, but the entire *Plaza* was not completed until 1965. A **nine storey hotel** is carried upon a concrete cradle, supported by columns and 'piloti'. **Sunley Tower** (twenty four storeys high, together with three floors of plant at the top) is curiously placed so that it is sideways on to the main viewpoint. And **Bernard House** was given an 'experimental roof' that reminded many Mancunians of a Chinese pagoda; 'honky tonk Han', perhaps. Finally, at street level, a shopping complex acted as a base for all these structures. The inhabitants of Manchester do not greatly love Piccadilly Plaza, nor can it be described as a successful building. It constitutes a barrier, blocking off Princess Street and Oxford Street in a way that few other buildings could do. It is surely haunted; blood curdling screams echo at night along the deserted malls, as the shade of Sir John Betjeman throttles the architect. The Hotel did not get off to a good start, for a ceiling collapsed shortly after opening. However, the main problem was design. The architects assumed that everyone would arrive by car, so the main entrance (approached from York Street, round the back!) was placed adjacent to the car park ramp on the top of the shopping areas. They no doubt expected that taxi drivers would welcome an unscheduled tour of part of the complex. Anyone seeking entry on foot had to find a way to the upper mall, and then look for a private escalator. It was thus possible to encounter, in Piccadilly Gardens, an exasperated individual (complete with dinner jacket and en route to a function) plaintively asking all and sundry how you "bloody well get into this place?" Hey presto! There is now a proper entrance at ground level in Portland Street, and the *Mercure Manchester Piccadilly Hotel* can be recommended as one of the best places to stay in Manchester. The Upper Mall 'Piazza' was a failure from the first, as the public stayed away in droves. By 1967,

An Accidental City Centre...

The majority of Mancunians, if asked for the centre of Manchester, will inevitably direct the visitor to Piccadilly. For them, it is the heart of their native city, a place that inevitably comes into the mind of an exile or expatriate. In short, the words Manchester and Piccadilly go together. But it was not always thus. Up to the end of the 18th century, the area was on the outskirts of the town. The foot traveller came to the limit of the Market Stead Lane, and crossed a trickle of water known as the Tib by a large flat stone, the other traffic splashing straight through. Lever Hall stood to the left, and to the right...the 'Daub Holes'. At that time, most of the buildings in Manchester were timber framed with 'wattle' (woven twigs or reeds) filling the spaces between. Since time immemorial, the citizens had dug the clayey earth at this spot to make the 'daub' to be smeared over the 'wattle' filling. The rain had filled the expanding pits to create some rather unwholesome stagnant ponds. It was just the place to erect the new 'Ducking Stool' in the early 17th century! Ahead lay open fields stretching as far as the Derbyshire hills on the horizon. Indeed, witnesses could recall, many years later, a day in 1778 when Squire Trafford and the 'Harriers' killed a hare in the vicinity of the present Portland Street. (It was the Lancashire custom to follow the hounds on foot, and spectators sometimes joined in the chase!) Curiously enough, the daughter of the master of the hunt drowned herself in the largest of the ponds. The construction of the Infirmary proved to be the catalyst that transformed this place into an erstwhile city centre. Doctor Charles White was the inspiration behind the provision of a much needed charity hospital. The subscription list was opened in 1752, and land was purchased (facing the London road across the 'Daub Holes') from Sir Oswald Mosley in 1754. William IV became a patron, and the epithet 'Royal' was added to the title. The 'Manchester Royal Infirmary' was completely reconstructed between 1847 and 1853, when north and south wings were added and the central portion received a dome and a new clock. Part of the cost of the north wing was defrayed by the sum of £3,000, raised by a concert given by Jenny Lind, the 'Swedish Nightingale'. The development of the Infirmary was but one factor in the creation of a fashionable area. The other was the fate of the Lever estate which fell into the hands of property developers after the last owner shot himself (see p71). Market Stead Lane was extended and became known as Piccadilly, possibly derived from the peccadil, a flower that was much used as a vegetable dye in the infant textile industry. The 'Daub Holes' were first converted into a water feature, but then filled in to form an Esplanade in 1853. This was soon populated with public statues. The Infirmary had quite clearly outgrown the limitations of its location by the end of the 19th century. It was removed to a green field site on Oxford Road and the old building was demolished in 1909. Unfortunately, no-one knew quite what to do with the vacant area that remained. There were proposals for a library, an art gallery, even a new town hall, but they all came to nothing. Finally, it was turned into Piccadilly Gardens in the 1930s, a municipal park in miniature, with flower beds, a fountain, and a bandstand. Clearance of the Parker Street area (for a bus station) added to the sense of space (the Luftwaffe did the rest in the 'Christmas Blitz of 1940'). The whole area thus became one of the largest city squares in Britain, to which the name 'Piccadilly' was popularly applied. Sadly, the Gardens were allowed to decline after the 1960s, and the site was often used for fairground rides and the associated fast food stands. Piccadilly Gardens have been extensively remodelled, along with the entire context, though aspects of the design may not be everybody's cup of tea.

only eleven of the forty available shops had been let. Of course, the almost gale force winds that blew through the place (resulting from the down draft created by Sunley Tower) did not help matters. The provision of a fibreglass and perspex overall roof did not solve the problem. Until a few years ago, an exploration of the almost deserted upper Piazza was like an excursion to the former East Berlin. Although many would like to see the place blown up, another fate lay in store. The complex was purchased, for £22 million, by Portfolio Holdings of London and a major refurbishment project commenced. The old Piazza is no more, and a new **arcade** has gone a long way to opening up the shopping area, leading to York Street and acting as a 'gateway' to Chinatown. Bernard House has been replaced by a more conventional structure, but Sunley Tower (mainly occupied by the government departments at the moment) remains.

Sadly, the view of the gardens is somewhat obscured on the right, firstly by the end of a large **brick box of a development** that faces Portland Street, and later by a **concrete barrier** known by some as the **'Berlin Wall'**. The former has a **transport enquiry centre and Travel Shop** (useful for all manner of leaflets and booklets relating to public transport in the area). The **Gardens** themselves (and the spectacular **fountains**) can be glimpsed through a gap in the latter.

If you wish to **explore the Gardens**, leave the station and pass through the gap in the **'Berlin Wall'** at the end of the platforms. This reveals **cafés** on the other side, and leads to the **catwalk** bisecting a central area with the **fountains** to the right. The **jets of water** operate on a timer to a predetermined pattern, and are the delight of small children on sunny days. The **Esplanade**, on the other side of the grassy area, is populated with **statues**. They are, from the Market Street end, **Sir Robert Peel** (p89); **James Watt** (perfector of the steam engine); **Queen Victoria** (sculpted from life, shortly before she died); and the **Duke of Wellington**. The latter was an odd choice for Manchester, for he was a very reactionary Prime Minister. But he died a grand old man, devoted to the Queen, and it was remembered that his victory at Waterloo ushered in an era of peace and progress in Europe.

Peel Statue (Graham Beech)

The range of buildings beyond the Esplanade is interesting. **The former Piccadilly Picture Theatre,** to the left of Oldham Street (with the balaustraded roof), opened in 1922, with a café, restaurant, and a dance hall in the basement, all in the 'beaux art' classical style. Despite a first rate location, the venture closed in 1937. The building stands on the site of the old Mosley hotel. An 'Italianate' office block in York stone (1881) marks the **Oldham Street corner**. The opposite corner used to have a branch of Woolworths, opened in 1928 where the Albion Hotel used to be. It was the scene of a

Piccadilly Statues

Although Queen Victoria is the centerpiece, this monument is the newest. She had come to the throne in 1837, the year that Manchester had been incorporated, and saw the century out by dying in January 1901. Her reign had been one of peace and increasing prosperity. In that time, industrialisation had made Britain a world power with the greatest empire ever known. It was an age of startling progress in virtually every field. The Victorians came to believe that such progress was continuous, and that poverty and ignorance would eventually completely disappear. However, rapid social change had posed immense challenges, but it seemed as if the Queen had presided over a successful transition to a constitutional monarchy and a modern mass democracy. In all this, she had appeared a symbol of stability and assurance; even, at times, a mother figure. Part of the 1897 Jubilee Fund had been earmarked for a statue, and Onslow Ford was selected as the sculptor. The Queen herself had sat for him and pronounced herself delighted with the results. Alas, she died before the monument was completed. Victoria is depicted seated in the imperial robes of state with orb and sceptre (some critics thought she had been made too stiff and formal). To the rear is a figure representing 'Maternity', with a baby in each arm and a faded inscription from Shakespeare. "Let me but bear your love, I'll bear your cares." There is also a small group of 'St. George and the Dragon' on top of the monument. The statue was unveiled in 1901 by Lord Roberts (Kipling's 'Bobs'), the Boer War hero. The behavior of the crowd, who created a crush by straining to get a better view, was such that the V.I.P's. were trapped in their temporary grandstand. The Vice Chancellor of Manchester University was observed removing his academic dress before climbing down the scaffolding!

Victoria is flanked by (for Manchester at the time) two unusual heroes. Sir Robert Peel (p89) is located at the Market street end. William Calder Marshall was selected (after a competition) as sculptor, and rejected the fashion of depicting public men in antique Roman togas. There are, however, two allegorical figures of 'Manchester' (resting her arm on a cotton bale) and 'Arts and Sciences'. Notice that the Manchester coat of arms rests on a sheaf of corn, a coded reference to the town's role in the repeal of the Corn Laws. The statue was unveiled in 1853. It has since been repositioned in connection with the Piccadilly redevelopment.

The Duke of Wellington has stood in the vicinity of Portland Street since 1856, though he used to be nearer the corner. Even so, he is now hidden by the new building. The hero of the Battle of Waterloo in 1815 went on to become a very reactionary Tory prime minister, and his participation in the ill-fated opening ceremony of the Liverpool and Manchester Railway was sufficient to provoke a near riot (iron shutters were fitted to his London home because people kept breaking his windows). However, the Duke lived to an immense age, and gradually became a respected elder statesman, who was clearly devoted to the young Queen. It was also pointed out that his victory had ushered in an unprecedented age of peace and stability in British foreign policy, and that this had underpinned economic expansion and prosperity. His death provoked an outburst of national mourning. "Bury the Great Duke with an Empire's lamentations." The statue stirred immense controversy. Some people wanted Wellington depicted as a martial warrior astride a horse, while others alleged that James Prince Lee (the Bishop of Manchester) had fixed the competition in favour of Matthew Noble, then a comparatively unknown sculptor. Noble produced a Wellington as an 'elder statesman', with four symbolic figures suited to Manchester opinion. They are 'Minerva' (Wisdom); 'Mars' with a sword (Valour); 'Victory' with a wreath; and 'Peace' bearing a cornucopia of plenty. The panels depict the Battle of Assaye (in India); the victory of Waterloo; Wellington receiving the thanks of the House of Commons (in 1814); and the great statesman at the Congress of Vienna (1815), helping to settle the peace of Europe.

Two subsidiary statues once flanked the Infirmary entrance. James Watt (1857) is a copy of the Chantrey statue in Westminster Abbey, and is intended to commemorate the importance of the steam engine in the history of the city (see p159). He has been moved to a new site on the fringe of the water feature, upstaging Victoria a little. Her Majesty would definitely not have been amused! The other statue of John Dalton (1855) was removed in the 1960s to make way for an electricity substation. The old boy would probably have approved!

spectacular and tragic fire in the 1970s, and the refurbished structure became *Nobles Amusements and Piccadilly Disco* (the windows could usually be relied upon to elevate kitsch into an art form). The location will shortly house a new *Travelodge Hotel*. Next door is the **Manchester and County Bank**, also dating from 1928, with ionic pilasters and a row of rather cute lions. The *National Westminster Bank* have now colonised the entire building, but the upper floors once constituted the Imperial Hotel, meant to be one of the finest in the city. However, the B.B.C. took over in the 1930s, making it one of their regional headquarters (complete with studios) until it moved to Oxford Road (now re-housed in Media City, p274). Across **Lever Street**, *Weatherspoons* have opened a branch in 'palazzo' style offices of 1892. Notice the **small brick building** to the left of it, the sole survivor from the late eighteenth or early 19th century of what was the original building scale. **Two buildings**, that appear to be like bookends, box in the *Gardens Hotel*. They were designed by the same architect, and obviously intended to flank a third that somehow never materialised. That to the left (1904) is 'Flemish revival' with tall gables. That to the right (1907) is Clayton House. One floor contains the **library of the Manchester and Lancashire Family History Society**, the ideal port of call if you are cultivating (or pruning?) your family tree. Visitors are welcome by appointment. The *Gardens Hotel* between these two is the structure that stubbornly persisted. It is another 'palazzo' in sandstone from the 1880s, later the headquarters of Manchester Corporation Tramways. The city had the third largest tram system in Britain, but the last 'car' ran in 1949. Fortunately, this mode of transport has been reincarnated in the excellent Metrolink system as Manchester leads the field once again. **St. Margarets Chambers** (1890s) is on the corner of Newton Street. This has a superb 'Elizabethan revival' frontage with huge gables and beautiful panels over the first floor windows.

Piccadilly Gardens to St. Peter's Square

Upon departing the tram station, an area of trees (known as **'The Grove'**) can be seen to the right. Note the track skirting the **Gardens** side of 'The Grove', used by incoming Market Street trams to avoid congesting the main junction. Directly ahead is the façade of the **old Lewis's building** (now *Primark*. see p41). Our tram follows the left-hand curve into **Mosley Street**.

The street was laid out in the last quarter of the 18th century. By 1791, it was a most fashionable address, a street of prestigious schools, places of worship, and public buildings. Nowadays, the banks and offices have taken over, but more than enough survives to interest the visitor. Moreover, it contains Manchester Art Gallery, recently reopened after an extensive refurbishment, and incorporating a new extension.

The Lord of the Manor

The street is named in honour of the Mosley Family, once Lords of the Manor of Manchester. This may conjure up some vision of a feudal knight, feasting his household and guests in the old hall crowning the banks of the Irwell. The truth is rather more prosaic. The Mosleys were minor gentry, who made their money in the 16th century woollen trade. Nicholas Mosley represented the family business in London (he was Lord Mayor in 1599), but returned home to retire. He purchased the manorial rights of Manchester for £30,000, and the family ended up owning property and residences in and around the town. Nicholas was buried in the church at Didsbury (p332), and other family members at the old Collegiate Church (now the Cathedral). Despite supporting the King in the Civil War, their confiscated estates were later restored. Needless to say, another generation supported the Pretender in the 1745 Jacobite rebellion, but this did not affect the family fortunes either. A large part of their income in the 18th century was derived from the market at Manchester, and the subsequent attempts by the family to use the archaic institutions of the town as their personal milch cow became so exasperating that they hastened the cause of municipal incorporation. After a great deal of haggling, the Corporation of Manchester purchased the manorial rights from the Mosleys in 1845. A later descendent of the family, Sir Oswald Mosley, achieved some political notoriety in the 1930s. A gifted and intelligent man, he was influenced by the radical economic ideas of the time. However, his participation as a minor minister in the second Labour government resulted in a complete disillusionment with the British political system. He consequently flirted with fascism, and founded the British Union of Fascists, a decision that exiled him to the political fringe as a figure of ridicule. When visiting Hough Hall (p304), the ancestral Manchester home of the family, he spoke a profound truth. "I wandered through the deserted stables and outhouses...perhaps we should never have left."

At first, the left-hand side is a continuation of the Plaza. In contrast, the opposite side of the street is a riot of architectural invention. The **Betfred** betting shop inhabits a Greek temple, complete with Corinthian fluted columns and a pediment, built for the Manchester and Salford Bank in 1836. **Lloyds Bank** occupies a brick building, with rusticated stone surrounds, and have colonised next door. Number 16, known as **Harvest House**, is an early version of the 'palazzo' style (1839). **Colwyn Chambers** (1898) graces the corner of York Street, once the Mercantile Bank. It is embellished with handsome Ionic columns and fluted pilasters. Crouching figures hold up an arched pediment on the corner door, enabling patrons to enter the hair salon of *Toni and Guy*. None of these can compare with the gorgeous neo-classicism of the place where the **Royal Bank of Scotland** currently dwells. It was constructed for the Manchester and Salford Bank, who moved here from down the road in 1862. This is Edward Walter's swansong; the architect of the Free Trade Hall designed the last flowering of the 'palazzo' style in the city. Two impressive floors of Italianate pedimented windows surmount the tall banking hall, and whole facade is rounded off at the top by an elegant balustrade. You don't have to be in need of funds to take time out and enter it, to enjoy the sumptuous banking hall. Part of the old bank stands on the site of a house (at the York street corner) in which Nathan Meyer Rothschild briefly resided. He was sent by his father from Frankfurt to buy Manchester goods, but departed to London in 1812. He later received news of Napoleon's escape from Elba a full twenty five hours before the British government, a coup that led to the establishment of the family fortune in this country. The later extension to the bank covers the ground once occupied by the Assembly Rooms. Such a new and fashionable street obviously required a select place of assembly, for balls and refined social gatherings. The establishment opened in 1792, admission being restricted to those one hundred gentlemen (and their guests) who had each paid seventy pounds towards the cost of erection. What did they get for their money? A first floor ball room, fifteen glass chandeliers, upholstered seats, Chinese wallpaper, card rooms, a tea room...and, presumably, the very best in female company, as the rules stated that gentlemen had to change partners after every second dance. Fashions change, the select moved out of the street, and the Assembly Room contents ended up being sold at auction. The building itself was demolished in 1850.

Another gem lies at the corner of Charlotte Street to the left. This is the **Portico Library**, so named for its fine neo-classical façade. One Robert Robinson, in the course of a visit to Liverpool, saw an impressive library and newsroom. He was told that it was a private facility, organised by some gentlemen of that town upon the basis of an annual subscription. What was good enough for Liverpool was surely good enough for Manchester. After some initial difficulty, a meeting of prominent townsmen took up the idea, and the library opened in 1806. Thomas Harrison, the celebrated Chester architect, designed the building, producing perhaps one of the finest examples of classicism in the country. The roll call of members and users of the library down the years is illustrious, and includes John Dalton, Thomas De Quincy, and Paul Roget (of 'Thesaurus' fame). The place is still practically run as the founders intended, as it is owned by shareholding members who elect a management committee. (New members

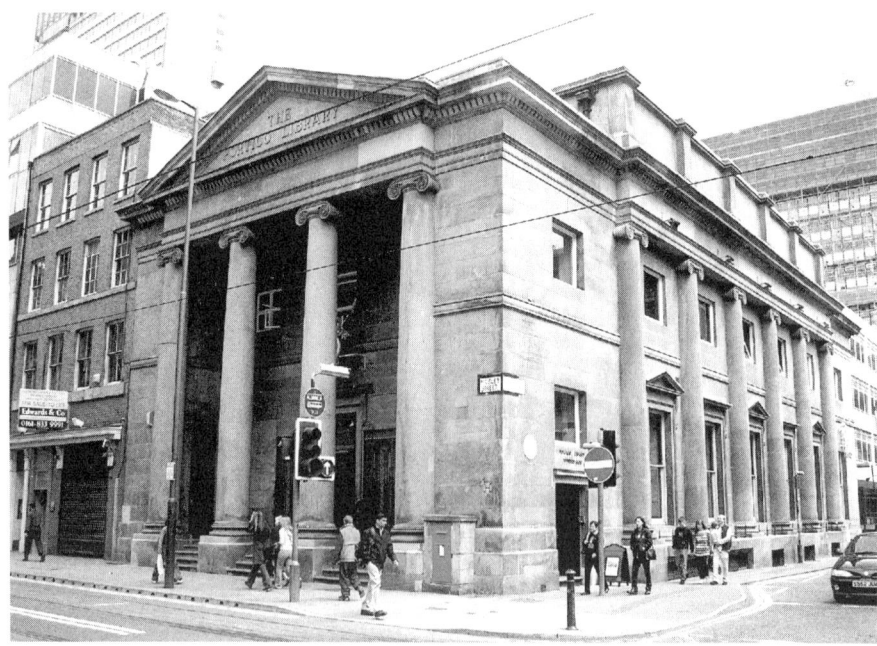

The Portico Library (Graham Beech)

The City Art Gallery

The 'Royal Institution of Manchester' owed its origin to a public meeting, held in 1823, to further the interests of literature, science, and the arts in the town. The organisation it created would construct a venue in which lectures, scientific demonstrations, and exhibitions would take place, in addition to functioning as a school of art and design. Sir Charles Barry (later known as the architect of the Houses of Parliament) was the winner of a competition for the design of the building, proposing an edifice in the best Grecian manner. He had studied classical architecture and absorbed the concept that beauty resulted from mathematical proportion. (His 'nom-de-plume' for the contest was "beauty is nothing without utility.") It was erected between 1825 and 1834, and whatever was left of the original funds were spent on works of art. By the last quarter of the 19th century, the Institution was in difficulties. Fortunately, the Corporation had been stung by criticism that such a progressive city could not provide itself with an art gallery. Manchester had become a laughing stock, and something had to be done. The building and contents were thus purchased from the Royal Institution in 1882, on the understanding that a fixed sum of ratepayer's money would be spent annually, for the next twenty years, on the purchase of works of art for the collection! One cannot imagine the response if this were to happen today.

are proposed and seconded by existing members.) The members have access to newspapers and magazines, private reading rooms, and a service of refreshments. They can also request the purchase of books to add to the collection. Do not be misled. The old bank premises, which fronted on to Mosley Street, are now transformed into a public house! Otherwise, go round the corner into Charlotte Street and ring the bell for admission. (The library is open to visitors Monday-Friday, 9.30 - 4.30.) Walk up the stairs to the **'Portico Gallery'**, a large public room, often used for art exhibitions. Look up at Harrison's **great dome**, before fixing your gaze on the **portrait of Richard Cobden**. Above it is a **wind gauge**, a dial connected to the rooftop weathervane, showing the direction of the gusts of wind. The walls are lined with books, the majority in antique leather bindings. The library's collection reveals much about the literary and academic tastes of past Mancunians, and several rare first editions of novels by Mrs. Gaskell and the Bronte sisters were discovered in a stock check some years ago. Genuine researchers can, of course, use the library on application to the librarian.

Despite the charms of the Portico, the most important building on Mosley Street is undoubtedly the one just beyond it, again on the left; this is the pillared **Manchester Art Gallery**. (The Art Gallery is open daily, 10-5, except on Thursday when it is open until 9; free admission.) The Gallery is a complex of three buildings, with the main (and earliest) structure facing Mosley Street.

(A more detailed description of the Art Gallery and its contents will be found in the author's 'Discovering Manchester', also published by Sigma.) The original **entrance hall** boasts a fine staircase leading to a stone balcony that accesses the principal galleries. The walls above are graced with **casts of the Elgin marbles** (the gift of George IV). There is a spacious **shop** to the rear and a **café and restaurant** to the right. There are two galleries used for temporary exhibitions to the left of the main entrance. It is best to explore the **first floor galleries** in a clockwise manner. Their contents depict the evolving history of British and European art, but the chief glory is the fine collection of **Pre-Raphaelite paintings**, with famous works by Hunt, Rossetti, Millais, and all the usual suspects. Pass through (by means of the **glass bridge**) to the new wing. The Clore

Interactive Gallery is designed to appeal to children. The **two galleries** to the left are devoted to **art in the 20th century**. This wing communicates with the first floor of the **Atheneum Annexe**. The original Atheneum was an institution intended to promote the improvement of young businessmen and managers in a less formal way than the Mechanics Institute. The building (also designed by Barry in the popular Italian Renaissance style) opened in 1839, and contained coffee rooms, lecture halls, a fine library, and a gymnasium. Charles Dickens presided at a 'soiree' in 1843. The building is now incorporated into the Art Gallery complex, and, at this level, **several galleries** depict later artists (including **Vallete**), religious art (**Spencer**

The City Art Gallery and Atheneum Annexe
(Graham Beech)

and **Duccio**), and 'Life and Death in the 17th century' (**English painting** and **Dutch Genre**). The **upper floor**, once the Atheneum's theatre, is devoted to a **Gallery of Craft and Design**.

St. Peter's Square

The tram crosses **Princess Street**. By the time that these lines are in print (2014), the **Cenotaph** will have been relocated to the site of the former Peace Gardens on the right hand corner of Princess Street. This is to enable the whole of St. Peter's Square to be remodelled and allow the Metrolink Station and its track layout to be expanded. Like many British towns and cities, Manchester opted for a cenotaph to commemorate the sacrifice of its citizens in the First World War. (The original, in London, was designed by Lutyens, and was intended to symbolise an empty tomb.) Notice the recumbent effigy of a soldier on the top, like a fallen mediaeval knight, a paladin of chivalry. The memorial now also honours the dead of the Second World War and other conflicts (there are individual memorials to the Manchester Italians, who fought as brothers in arms, 1915-1918; to the dead of the Korean War, 1950-1953; and a special memorial, the gift of the Royal British Legion). On Armistice Sunday, a short service is held, and wreaths are laid. A two minutes silence at eleven (the time the guns stopped in 1918) ends with the sounding of the 'last post' and 'reveille' on the bugles. Afterwards, members of the public place their poppies or crosses of remembrance near the memorial.

> *The garden called Gethsemane,*
> *It held a pretty lass,*
> *But all the time she talked to me*
> *I prayed my cup might pass.*
> *The officer sat on the chair,*
> *The men lay on the grass,*
> *And all the time we halted there,*
> *I prayed my cup might pass.*

It didn't pass – it didn't pass –
It didn't pass from me,
I drank it when we met the gas,
Beyond Gethsemane!

The rear of the **Town Hall**, graced with a **statue of Edward the Elder** (who conquered the Danes and sent men to Manchester "to repair and man it"), can be glimpsed behind the new location of the Cenotaph. The best view of this fine neo-gothic civic building, erected 1868-77 and the masterpiece of Alfred Waterhouse, is from Albert Square. The **Town Hall Extension** (1934-1938), recently refurbished, dominates the background to the left of the resited memorial. The sandstone clad exterior of this building is plain, but rather striking. Colonnades on both the Mount Street and St. Peter's Square sides gave access to gas and electricity showrooms (these municipal departments were very commercially minded) and the passage side, adjacent to Central Library boasted a magnificent curving counter area, where people came to pay their bills. The building is joined to Central Library by a link under the Library Walk between the two structures. Consequently, the undercroft of the Extension now houses the City Library and the Children's Library (in effect, the general lending library of Manchester). The old Rates Hall above the new City Library on the ground floor has been restored and is the main point for residents to obtain information about the city and the way it functions in the form of a 'Welcome Centre'. The courtyard in the middle of the Extension is thrown open to public use by landscaping and the provision of space for the children's play area of the council crèche and nursery. There are public meeting and 'break out rooms'

St. Peter's Square (before alterations) (Graham Beech)

around the courtyard. The upper floors of the Extension retain their current Council functions, but the corridors are opened out to make the floor areas in the offices bigger. The original **Council Chamber**, seating 145 councillors on hog skin upholstery amidst English oak, together with the associated library, ante-room, and panelled committee rooms, remains in situ.

The present **tram station** is destined to be relocated towards Princess Street and will become something of a transport hub. At present, both **platforms** are accessed by **ramps** at either end, where **pedestrian crossings** are located. The **down platform** also communicates directly with the former **cenotaph area**, and a **paved section** of the square that is level with it. However, the Metrolink second cross city link (p18) will enter the square from Princess Street, and there will consequently be two island platforms dealing with trams entering or leaving St. Peter's Square either by Mosley Street or Princess Street.

Central Library redeems the present appearance of the Square. Suffice it to say that the City Fathers decided to make a grand gesture, and build the largest municipal library in Britain. Designed by Vincent Harris, and modelled on the Pantheon, the great steel framed circular structure dates to 1934 (the **foundation stone inscriptions** repay inspection). The lower levels are clad in rusticated stone, the upper storeys are hidden behind Doric columns, and a grand portico fronts the main entrance. The Library has suffered from financial stringency in recent years, and became, in many ways, a shadow of its former self. As a major regional asset, it should not rely on the City council for its upkeep. There really ought to be a levy, to which the other local authorities and the local universities and colleges (whose students seemed to take over the place at term time) contributed. And then there might be balm in Gilead once more.

St. Peter's Church

The Square is named after St. Peter's Church, which once stood in the midst of it. The Reverend Samuel Hall, formerly the curate of St. Anne's, founded the church...and thereby hangs a tale. He was also honorary chaplain to the Volunteers, and omitted the Athanasian Creed at church parades in deference to the nonconformists in the ranks. For this heinous offence, he was refused election as a Fellow of the Collegiate Church when a vacancy occurred. His disgusted supporters rallied round, raised the necessary funds, and built him St. Peter's church. Consecrated in 1794, it was a rather grand affair, with a steeple (added in 1822) and an equally grand and very fashionable congregation. This state of affairs soon changed, and the congregation had all but disappeared by the turn of the century. The building was demolished in 1907. The fine organ, at one time said to be the largest in England, was removed to another church, now also demolished. It was last sighted in a warehouse in Lincolnshire, but its present whereabouts are unknown. (The painting from over the altar is now in St Anne's.) But what were they to do with the large underground vault, crammed full of decaying coffins? It was deemed best to sealed it, and then remodel the site overhead into gardens. A rather tasteful commemorative stone cross with suitable inscriptions, was placed in the gardens in 1908. The Square might have been expanded to make a fine civic space, but the plot of land on the corner of Dickinson Street (occupied by Century House, dating from 1934) was allowed to go to a developer by default of one council vote! But, better late than never, the Square actually is to be transformed into a fine civic space, though the cross will remain as a reminder of its origin.

Central Library (Graham Beech)

The library reopened in March 2014 after the interior was extensively restored and refurbished. The grand **entrance hall**, with its **stained glass windows** (depicting characters from Shakespeare) and **roof** decorated with the arms of Manchester, and other regional heraldic devices, remains. However, the Ryder Architects plan required the removal of the former basement theatre and the antiquated lifts, together with a large part of the stacks. This creates a large **public circulating area** in the floor under the existing domed reading room. The latter, under the **great dome**, once the largest reading room outside the British Museum, has been refurbished, though the original 1930s furniture and fittings (including the **clock** and its **baroque mounting**) remains unchanged. This reverses the original 30% public and 70% private space ratio. The new layout houses all the **archive**, research and study areas and the valuable historic collections, such as the **Henry Watson Music Library**. There are exhibition spaces, the relocated **North West Film Archive,** and **British Film Institute** Mediatheque Viewing Pods. A new **shop** and **café** also features in the new arrangements.

The south side of the Square is now dominated by the thirteen storey **One, St Peter's Square**, scheduled for completion by Spring, 2014. The exit from the Square is guarded by the *Midland Hotel*.

Where Mr. Rolls Met Mr. Royce
The Midland Railway, inspired by William Towle (their very capable hotel chief), decided to build one of the greatest hotels in Europe in the city of Manchester. The hotel opened, to great applause, in 1903, and rapidly became a Manchester institution. It had everything;

400 luxurious bedrooms, a French restaurant, a Turkish bath, winter gardens, a ballroom with a sprung floor, and its own theatre. An orchestra (with vocal renditions) played at dinner, a string quartet at lunch and tea, and there was even music on the famous roof garden (the bass player wore a cloth cap on breezy days), a favourite place to take tea on a fine day. The hotel went through a sticky patch after the last war, and did not really move with the times. (David Hockney, it is said, was refused admission for wearing odd socks.) However, after a thorough restoration programme, the hotel is back where it belongs, and is awash with celebrities once more...see if there are any teens waiting at the entrance to catch sight of their current idol. Charles Trubshaw, the company's architect, produced a rather florid design, combining a variety of styles, but had the good sense to choose glazed terracotta for the exterior surfaces (granite is employed in the lower section). Thus, the building effectively cleans itself. The two large arches were cab entrances and exits. Look for the Wyvern, a mythological beast representing the Saxon kingdom of Mercia, which featured in the railway's coat of arms. There is a memorial tablet, within the entrance on the right, to the historic meeting of Charles Rolls and Henry Royce, an event that took place in 1904. The two were like chalk and cheese. Charles Rolls was a rich playboy, with a passion for fast cars and flying. Henry Royce was a gruff, no nonsense engineer, struggling to build motor cars in a back street in Hulme. But they genuinely hit it off, and Royce was deeply upset when his partner was killed in a flying accident. Enter without fear, for even 'posh' places are friendly enough in this part of the world. Taking tea at the Midland is fun (served between 2.30 and 5.30). The grand entrance hall leads to a restored Winter Garden, situated at the foot of an inner courtyard of glazed white brick. The Octagon Court, to the left, is beneath a light well that was once taller, and capped with a glass dome. On a New Year's Eve, a lavish ball would be held. While the wealthy businessmen and their guests were celebrating at the bar in the Court area, it was the custom for the youngest resident of the hotel (in the days when the staff lived in) to be lowered down to floor level in a basket. These rich men would then pin banknotes to the baby or toddler's blanket as a good luck gesture for the coming year. There are resident ghosts. The 'grey lady' scared the life out of a group of airline cabin crew some years ago. (It made such an impression on them that they always asked to be shown the room in question on subsequent visits.) She is said to have been an elderly guest who made the hotel her home (a common practice before the war). Apparently, the spirit resents her room being let to anyone else, though she is now at peace as the room is now used as a store. A charming small girl also sometimes appears to guests.

Piccadilly Gardens to Victoria Station

We skirt the **Grove**, a group of trees intended to be a focus of interest from both sides. They draw the eye towards the Market Street exit from the Gardens, whilst also providing an interesting feature on the other side by gradually becoming visible from Market Street itself. These trees are rooted in a wide paved area, skirted by tramlines on both sides, which is an extension of the Market Street and Oldham Street pavements. The track snaking in from Market Street on the Gardens side is for incoming trams bound for Piccadilly, and is designed to ease congestion. After a right-hand turn at the junction, the way lies alongside the Piccadilly façade of the **former Lewis's store** (now *Primark*) on the left. You may be able to spot the remains of the **old Lewis's arcade**. In the 1950s, this was the haunt of a battalion of jolly tarts, and thus one of the sights of the city. Before the tram swings left into **Market Street**, there is a view of the **Esplanade**, with its **statues**, on the right. The nearest is **Sir Robert Peel** (p31,89), although **Queen Victoria**, wreathed in white stone, is a prominent feature in the distance. Notice the brightly painted panels and bays of the **delightful conceit** (above *Starbucks Coffee*) of 1879 on the corner of Tib Street.

Metrolink, together with the **Market Street Station** only occupies a short stretch of **Market Street**, between two large department stores. The long **island platform** is accessed by **steps** and **ramps** at both ends.

Market Street was formerly the Market Stead Lane, a narrow twisting way descending to the old Market Place and the Irwell. It was 'improved' by the Victorians (using the

A Tale of Two Stores

The former Lewis's (Primark) became something of a Manchester institution. David Lewis, a Londoner, was enamoured by the concept of a 'department store' (said to have originated in 19th century America or France, but Manchester may have been first in the field), and is credited with pioneering the institution in Britain. He came north and opened his first store in Liverpool in 1856. The firm was always associated with entrepreneurial flair, even showmanship. (Brunel's 'Great Eastern' was chartered, prior to being broken up, and anchored as a floating advertisement in the Mersey.) The original Manchester store, opening in 1877 in the French renaissance style, with a showy corner tower, followed in this tradition. Although intended as a gentleman's drapers, women's clothing, and even food, were soon added. The store's famous 'two shillings and ninepence' (almost 30p) pocket watch was one of its many attractions...along with distorting mirrors, a 'magic lantern' show in the shop windows, and a basement full of slot machines. At one point, the basement was flooded with two feet of water in a recreation of Venice, complete with gondolas! The company negotiated with the Council for room to expand, and exchanged some pavement space for

the right to enclose two inconvenient back streets as an arcade. The new extension, which subsumed the old building, was completed in 1915. It included a great dome, 100 feet high by 36 feet in diameter. This was the centerpiece of the Christmas decorations, and every Manchester child was taken at some time to see it. The extension also boasted the first escalators outside of London, and the 'largest soda fountain in the Empire'. Upstairs might also be found a ballroom sprung on ball bearings, the venue of tea dances. This room was also used for a variety of exhibitions, promotions, and a Christmas toy fair until the 1960s. The final extension, on the Mosley Street side, was completed in 1929. The interior of the store was extensively remodelled in the 1960s, and the dome disappeared. Many people date the start of a long and slow decline from this period. It was painful to witness, for it seemed that the management had some kind of death

Debenhams (formerly Rylands/Pauldens)

wish. When the last tills rang on a sad Saturday in February, 2001, people sensed it was the end of an era. In the midst of the bear garden of the closing down sale, both the shopping public and the staff took photographs for posterity. Lewis's, after some refurbishment, has been reopened by Primark, a discount retailer.

Debenham's, across Market Street, was built in 1929-32 for the Ryland's store company. Although built to the design of P. Garland Fairhurst, Ted Adams (as project architect) should take a lot of the credit for solving the problems on the ground. It is built on an irregular site, and no angle is true. The substantial corner towers are intended to mask this fact, and the vertical mass also offsets the horizontal of six storeys. It is a steel frame building, clad with Portland stone, and intended for adaptation to a multitude of uses. The ground and first floor were originally leased to a number of shops and a bank, while the rest was used as a warehouse. A beacon and revolving searchlight (visible for up to sixty miles) was placed on the roof as a marker for Ringway (now Manchester) Airport. Paulden's store moved here in 1953, shortly before their premises on Stretford Road were destroyed in one of Manchester's most spectacular post-war blazes. This was the making of the site, for Paulden's was just as much an institution as Lewis's. "I know her...if she fell off Paulden's, she'd land in a fur coat..." It is now home to Debenham's.

profits of the municipal gas works), and has become the principal (largely pedestrianized) shopping street.

The tracks turn into High Street, running along a reservation, with the southern façade of the *Arndale Centre* on the left. A little beyond the Mall entrance, opposite Church Street, was the site of Canon Street, now subsumed into the Centre and transformed into a winter garden. Notice the ramped entrance to the **Arndale Market**. Although this cannot compare with the size and character of some of the markets in the surrounding towns, it is well worth a visit. Seek out the *sushi bar* with its life sized

The Arndale Centre

The Arndale Property Trust had been buying up land in the area since 1952, prior to being taken over by Town and City Properties of Bradford (pioneers of the closed shopping mall in Britain) in 1963. The latter submitted a plan for redeveloping a 25 acre site in 1965, the second major post-war development after Piccadilly Plaza. Money proved to be the main problem, but the council was so keen on the project that they advanced loans of over £160 million in 1973. As part of the deal, they purchased the freehold of the site for leaseback to the developers. (The lease later passed to P. and O. Properties, and is now owned by Prudential.) Wilson and Walmersley (who had just masterminded the Educational Precinct on Oxford Road) were chosen as architects, and the whole project was completed in 1980. This massive complex comprised a main two level shopping block astride Cannon Street (originally incorporating a bus station), an extension alongside Cross Street, a multi-storey car park, a tall office block, and a market area. It is often remarked that 'a camel is a horse designed by a committee'. In this case, the infighting between the council, the developers, and the architects (together with the interventions of council engineers who were planning roads that would be never built) produced a veritable dog's dinner. Exterior shop fronts were initially forbidden on Corporation Street and High Street as express roads were intended. The architects wanted internal streets covered with glazed roofs. The developers wanted enclosed malls on the American model, but without any redeeming design features. Consequently, Mancunians have had a love-hate relationship with the Arndale from the first. On the one hand, many people like the idea of a multitude of mainstream shops, well known multiples, department stores, and cafeterias, all enclosed under one roof. In this, the Arndale has a similar appeal to Meadowhall in Sheffield, or the Metrocentre in Gateshead. However, the place can be confusing, the malls are undifferentiated, and people get lost. (As a result of the Market Street slope, enter by the High Street entrance and find yourself eventually on the first floor!) The original managers had some equally quirky ideas, including dressing the first security staff in pith helmets! But it was the tiled exterior that most people objected to. It was truly hideous, resulting in the local joke about 'the largest public lavatory in the world'. "Manchester's Arndale Centre is so castle-like...that any passing medieval army would automatically besiege it rather than shop in it." As in other things, the I.R.A. bomb wrought a transformation. The Corporation Street and Cross Street frontages have been rebuilt, and the second development phase saw Cannon Street transformed into a winter garden (the much disliked bus station closed some years ago). Prudential created a complete revamp of the interior, which saw the introduction of glazed roofs as originally intended.

copy of a Chinese terracotta warrior, *White Eagle*, selling Polish produce to the expatriate community, and the meat and fish stalls.

There are a small number of **market stalls** near the Church Street corner, one of which deals in second hand books. High Street veers off to the right, and the tracks enter **Nicholas Croft**. It once had a flourishing second hand book market, but all this disappeared with road widening. The part of Manchester to the right of the roadway is developing into a **'curry quarter'**, with a variety of restaurants and balti houses, usually much cheaper than the famous 'curry mile' in Rusholme. We now reach **Shudehill**. The name first appeared in 1554, and is something of a mystery. It can be translated as 'the hill of the husking of oats', but what that really means is anybody's guess.

We have a brief view directly along **Withy Grove** to the left. The 'withies' or willows disappeared long ago, but a range of 19th century frontages survives on the right hand side.

The tram crosses Shudehill and enters the **Shudehill tram interchange**, with two **platforms** accessed by **steps** and joined by a **pedestrian crossing** at each end. The **down platform** is paralleled by a **pavement** which rises in the form of a back-to-back ramp to communicate with a platform entrance. The new **bus station** and **multi-storey car park** is located alongside the **up platform** (one of the free cross town bus services connects with the trams here). Again, a parallel **pavement** rises and falls to communicate with an **entrance to the platform** on the level, but there is also a **pathway** from it to the **bus stands**, utilising a **pedestrian crossing**. Another **path**, this time from the Shudehill end, communicates with the bus stands and the main building, protected by a **curving roof**. The **ground floor** of the multi-storey car park contains a **travel centre**, a **shop**, and some useful **toilets**. The station area was called **Bradshaw Street**, after the publisher of the famous railway timetables, whose first offices were round the corner in Withy Grove.

This station is convenient for the nearby *Printworks*, a large entertainment centre (including a multi-screen cinema) located in former newspaper offices. There is a good view of the 400 foot **CIS Tower** (Sir John Burnet Tate Partners), to the right as the tram crosses **Dantzic Street**. It was the tallest office block in Europe when it opened in 1962.

Charity and Conflict

Look at the corner of Nicholas Croft and Shudehill. Withingreave Hall stood somewhere hereabouts, the town residence of the Hulme family. William Hulme (died 1691) left some property to maintain "four of the poorest sort of batchelors of arts taking such degrees in Brazenose College in Oxford." Parliament later authorised the trustees of the charity to grant building leases. As the town expanded and property prices escalated, Hulme's charity became a goldmine. Unfortunately, the clergymen who ran it tended to ...well...use it to provide jobs for other clergy! This scandalous state of affairs ended with the reorganisation of the charity in 1881. The remaining proceeds were sufficient to create and endow grammar schools in Manchester, Bury, and Oldham, together with a hall of residence at Owen's College (now Manchester University). One of the outhouses of the old hall remained until modern times, for, adjacent to Nicholas Croft, stood the 'Rover's Return', a half-timbered building said to date to the medieval period. After a varied career as a pub, dining room, and curio shop, it was demolished in the 1950s. This event must have dispossessed the resident ghost, a Scottish highlander left behind in the course of the 1745 Jacobite Rebellion. Perhaps he haunts the city planning department.

Bradshaw Hall lay across Shudehill, almost alongside the tram lines. John Bradshaw became High Sheriff of Lancashire in 1753, an elevation which resulted in an episode of high drama at his front gate. The harvest failed. On 6 June, 1757, a party of starving men seized the corn from the mills at Clayton and marched to Manchester with the intention of taking the potatoes at the Shudehill market. They encountered a party of soldiers, ordered out by Bradshaw. Faced with a hail of stones, the soldiers opened fire and killed five of the crowd, wounding fifteen. The crowd was so desperate that this was not the end of the matter. They attacked local corn mills and later attempted to free an imprisoned rioter from the Salford Bridge lock up. The authorities, clearly having lost control of events, freed the prisoner, and everything subsided like a summer storm. The event is known in history as 'Shudehill Fight'.

The tracks now continue down **Balloon Street**, the cobbles giving quite a continental feel. It is named in honour of James Sadler (a "pioneer aeronaut"), who made the first manned ascent at Manchester in a hydrogen balloon from a garden that was once here. It runs through the midst of buildings erected by the Co-operative Movement, and it is no surprise to see a modern **statue of Robert Owen** on the left hand corner of **Corporation Street**. Owen came to Manchester from Newtown in Wales. He later became an important mill owner, but a benevolent one. An interest in the effect of the working environment upon his employees led him to formulate theories, which he published in 'A New View of Society.' This earned him the title of 'the father of British socialism.' He was also the first to suggest the idea of co-operation, and is seen as the founder of the co-operative movement (see p190).

Corporation Street, which is now crossed, was another Victorian 'improvement', intending to replace the winding and narrow **Long Millgate** as the entrance to the town from the Bury direction. The near-side of the street is the **stronghold of the co-operative movement**. It is best viewed when travelling in the opposite direction from the railway station, and, from left to right, comprises a 'streamlined' **classical building** of 1928, followed by a fine **Edwardian centrepiece** (faced with red and grey granite) in the 'baroque revival' style of 1905, and ending with a nondescript **brick rectangle**, built to house the bankers in 1980. (The area will be sensitively redeveloped by the Co-operative Movement as part of the NOMA initiative, see p55). The way to the station crosses **Long Millgate**, where the 'Manchester Arms' stood. The pub had once been the starting point for a coach to Bury, but was really a converted 18th century house. In the 1970s, it was one of the first Manchester pubs to introduce strippers, who performed to an audience of bored travellers and goggle eyed railway porters. And all this was lost to make way for a road that was never built. We must all have been mad! The tram enters **Victoria Station** alongside the **pedestrian entrance** from Corporation Street and Long Millgate, and curves to the right before pausing at **Victoria Metrolink Station**.

The station was formed of a large island platform, accessed by a pedestrian crossing and ramp from the railway station concourse. It straddled the site of a number of former bay platforms, so a large part of its platform was sheltered by the remains of the original 1904-5

Robert Owen statue (Graham Beech)

extension roof, damaged in the 1940 'Christmas Blitz'. However, by the time these lines are published, all will have changed. Work will be in progress on the reconstruction and redevelopment of this part of the old station. There will be three tracks instead of the present two, and the new Metrolink Station will consist of two island platforms. On the Long Millgate side, the first platform facing will be used by inbound trams from Bury, Oldham, and Rochdale, but the other two tracks, one running between the two island platforms, and the other round the opposite side of the second platform will be unidirectional. Trams bound for Wythenshawe and Manchester Airport will probably begin and terminate their journey here. The whole will be covered by a new roof, and a mezzanine floor will connect Long Millgate with the Arena (p48). Of course, the junction for the second city crossing will be located at the Corporation Street Crossing.

Please note that Victoria Metrolink Station will be closed for a large part of 2014 to permit construction work. Although trams will continue to pass through, passengers are advised to use Shudehill instead. Passengers travelling between Piccadilly and Victoria stations should change at St. Peter's Square. The following temporary service alterations will apply. Trams from Bury to Ashton will terminate at Abraham Moss, and a new Ashton-Eccles service will operate via Piccadilly.

Victoria Station

Early railways in Manchester were constructed in a somewhat haphazard manner. The historic Liverpool and Manchester Railway established its terminus at Liverpool Road, amidst the canal basins and warehouses, as its promoters thought freight traffic would be its main source of income. The resulting growth in passenger traffic took them by surprise, and they were left with a station on the then outskirts of the town in an insalubrious district. In a similar fashion, the Manchester and Leeds Railway terminated by St. George's church near Oldham Road on the east side of town. The Manchester and Bolton Railway never even made it into Manchester, for its station lay in Salford, across the Irwell! As early as 1838, before their line opened, the Leeds Company realised their mistake. Samuel Brooks, the company vice-chairman, bought a piece of land at Hunt's Bank close to Manchester Cathedral (then the Collegiate Church), and presented it to the company for the purpose of creating a new station to replace the inconveniently located Oldham Road Station. The new station site was a rather tricky location, as it partly intruded upon land originally consecrated as a burial ground. A branch was constructed from a junction with the original line at Miles Platting to Hunts Bank, descending down an incline. Meanwhile, public pressure was exerted

Victoria Station (Graham Beech)

upon the Liverpool and Manchester directors to extend their line to join with the Manchester and Leeds, creating a central station for Manchester and a continuous line of rails between Liverpool and Hull. Consequently, a branch was constructed from Ordsall Lane to link with the Bolton Company's station at Salford. From there, a joint line continued to join the Manchester and Leeds station, which would now be shared by both the Liverpool and Leeds Companies. This station was initially a long low single-storey building designed by George Stephenson, and constructed by John Brogden the contractor, opening to the public on 1 January 1844. It was named 'Victoria Station' "by permission of Her Majesty". The platform handled Manchester and Leeds Railway trains to Leeds and elsewhere at its eastern end. The Liverpool and Manchester Railway commenced operations at Victoria's western end from 4 May 1844. The station was accessed by Hunts Bank itself and a new approach from Long Millgate (and later Corporation Street), crossing the Irk by a wooden footbridge. Victoria Station came to dominate the Long Millgate area and was one of the biggest passenger stations in Britain.

Traffic soon outgrew the original station's capacity. In 1865, the Lancashire and Yorkshire Railway (which the Manchester and Leeds had become in 1846) constructed a number of bay platforms on the south side to accommodate trains arriving and departing on the east. New platforms were constructed on the site of former workhouse land on the north side, opening in 1884. Victoria was again enlarged by William Dawes between 1904 and 1909, and eventually boasted seventeen platforms. The principal feature of the new extension was the provision of bay platforms extending to Long Millgate over a culverted River Irk. 'T'owd Lanky' may not have been the largest railway company, but the 'business line' was certainly one of the busiest. It retains the affections of local enthusiasts to this day. The cast-iron train sheds behind the façade ran back for some 700 yards (640 metres). The Bury line was electrified using a third rail system in 1916. In 1923, the Lancashire and Yorkshire became one of the main constituents of the London, Midland, and Scottish Railway. From 1884, the London and North Western railway (the successors of the Liverpool Company) had transferred their services to Exchange Station, a close neighbour of Victoria. This company also became part of the London, Midland, and Scottish, and, from 1929, a single passenger platform linked them; this was the longest passenger platform in Europe at 2,194 feet (669 metres). (Exchange Station was closed in 1969 and its services were transferred to Victoria. Its site, opposite the Cathedral, is now a car park.) Victoria Station was seriously damaged in the Manchester Blitz, and presented a very sorry appearance for much of the postwar period. However, it has been transformed by the construction of the Arena, which subsumed the northern platforms and resulted in some refurbishment. The site of the southern bay platforms has been utilised by Metrolink. The future seems bright; the Liverpool line will be electrified, and the Long Millgate end of the station is being re-developed.

Hunts Bank is perhaps the best place to begin an exploration of the station (the name recalls the hunting kennels of the largely absentee medieval manorial lords). The enormous **flight of steps** is used as an exit from performances at the 'Manchester Evening News Arena' (see below), and will probably disappear in future re-development. The street falls away to the left towards the **approach bridge** spanning the Irwell and the **site of the former Exchange Station** on the far bank. There is a fine view at that end of the **Cathedral** and (alongside the cobbles of Walkers Croft, constructed over the Irk) the adjacent medieval wing of **Chethams College** (dating from 1422). The new **Chetham's extension**, though simplistic and severe in tone, is not out of harmony with the medieval stonework. But the principal sight is the **original Victoria Station façade of 1844**...it still has the original **mounting for the clock**, which ought to be replaced. The **single story wing** to the left was the part used by the Liverpool and Manchester Railway. Turn right, and follow the **Edwardian facade**, completed in 1909 and 160 yards (146m) long, alongside the **Station Approach** (which, for all its intensive use, is still a private road). Notice the gap where an overall roof spanned the roadway between the station and the now vanished railway offices opposite. The **original part of the canopy** is listed (though the frontage is not!), and contains the names in glass of popular destinations at that time. There is Blackpool (the workers' playground), Ireland (by boat from Fleetwood), London (courtesy of the Midland Railway), and Belgium (by boat from Hull to Zeebrugge).

Enter the station itself by the **left-hand archway** of the two entrances. This houses a fine **tile map of the Lancashire and Yorkshire Railway system** (though the rival London and North Western Railway route to Yorkshire, between Stalybridge and Huddersfield, is somehow omitted). This is placed above the impressive **First World War memorial** (with its tableau of St George and the Dragon) commemorating the men of the Lancashire and Yorkshire Railway who made the supreme sacrifice.

A left turn (past a **smaller memorial** to the dead of the goods department staff) reveals a block formerly devoted to passenger services, with **mosaic signs** typical of the period before 1914. The **buffet interior** (complete with dome) has been restored, and should be briefly visited...even if the prospect of railway food is not appetising (the option of a "capital pair of chops, prepared within ten minutes," is no longer available). The

Victoria Station (Canopy with Edwardian destinations) (Graham Beech)

Northern Rail Enquiries Office now occupies the **site of the old bookstall**. The **through platforms** are directly ahead, but broad **flights of steps** to the right (which some people mistake for the footbridge!) lead to the **'City Room'**, which acts as a vestibule to the Arena. Except before and after a performance, it is an empty and soulless place, though there is a _McDonalds_. The **'Manchester Evening News Arena'** (DLA Ellerbie Beckett), Europe's largest multi-purpose indoor sports and events arena (maximum capacity of 20,500), is built over part of the station and the old Manchester Workhouse. Developers and

Victoria Station (former bookstall)
(Graham Beech)

architects ought to have a sense of history. When they accidentally stumbled on the old pauper graveyard, it was obvious that, in this case, they had not. (There is a memorial plaque to the bodies disturbed at the entrance to the remaining bay platforms.) The Arena is used for everything from rock concerts to sporting events, and includes offices and a multi-story car park.

'Shot at Dawn'

Two names on the First World War memorial have a poignant story to tell. Private Albert Ingham and Private Alfred Longshaw had worked together as clerks at Salford Goods Yard. They decided to enlist together in the Third 'Pals' Battalion, and found themselves in No.11 platoon, 'C' Company, 18th Manchesters. As part of the 30th Division, the unit attacked at Montauban, as part of the Somme offensive, on the 1st July 1916, suffering over 3000 casualties. On the 7th July they attacked at Trones Wood and the Battalion was involved in the fighting around Mansell Copse and the attack on Guillemont on the 30th July 1916. The two men were then transferred to the Brigade machine-gun company together. However, the prospect of returning to the Somme proved to be the final straw. On the night of 5-6 October 1916, both disappeared from their unit when they were under orders to go to the front line at short notice. On 1st November 1916 they were found on a Swedish vessel at Dieppe, and tried claiming that they were American citizens. Eventually Longshaw admitted his true name and that he had deserted from the machine-gun company, and Ingham then admitted he belonged to the Manchester Pals. The two men were tried on 20th November 1916 and found guilty and sentenced to death. It is reported that just before they were shot, Longshaw turned to Ingham and said "Well, good-bye Albert." They were buried at Bailleulmont Communal Cemetery. During the War it was reported that the men had died of wounds but at some time later Private Ingham's father discovered the truth. When asked for his choice of inscription to be carved on his son's unusual red sandstone headstone, he defiantly (and accusingly) chose these words:

> *"Shot at dawn.*
> *One of the first to enlist.*
> *A worthy son of his father."*

Albert and Alfred were probably suffering from what we would call Post-Traumatic Stress Disorder. But, even at the time that the memorial was erected, the Railway thought it proper that their names should be included amongst those of their comrades. Remember them all...

Back in **Victoria Station**, the path continues past the **stylish booking offices** and other passenger facilities (including **toilets**) to the right, replete with glazed tiling and curved door frames. The **Metrolink station** is opposite, on the left, with the tracks curving into a central island platform (this area of the station is currently (2014) being re-developed, see p45). The archway on the left of the passage to Long Millgate, formerly the **entrance to the old fish dock**, is one of the saddest places in Manchester, for it forms the **'Soldiers Gate'** or **'the gates of hell'**. The leave trains in the First World War departed from here, and a little bronze plaque (easily missed) records this fact. Read the inscription..."To the memory of the many thousands of men who passed through this door to the Great War 1914-1919 and of those who did not return." This will remain a feature of the re-developed station. The dock was also used for theatrical traffic, with touring companies (with their scenery and impedimenta) constantly arriving and departing at weekends. The passage exiting into Long Millgate was **'cigar alley'**, which once catered (complete with bank) for the needs of busy city 'gents.' Such frock coated and watch-chained gentlemen might have patronised the *Java Bar* that it now contains. Some of them would, however, proceed to the Blackpool Club Train, a rather unique institution. They were taken to and from their seaside homes by what was, in effect, a travelling gentleman's club, with all the facilities (and entry procedure, as one might be 'blackballed') belonging to the same.

This area of the station is undergoing redevelopment (see p45), and it will be covered with a striking new roof, similar to that used in the 'Eden Project' in Cornwall. There will be a new mezzanine level, enabling the Arena to be accessed from Long Millgate.. Indeed, the site between Long Millgate and Corporation Street, together with the surviving buildings on Todd Street, will be known as the 'Fish Dock' development.

Victoria Station Environs

The **tram station** is convenient for **Exchange Square** a short distance down Corporation Street. However, it is also worthwhile to walk along Long Millgate to the **City Park**. The 'Welcome Arm' of the £30m **Urbis** building (Ian Simpson Architects) embraces the Plaza on the left. Its 2,200 glazed units clad a structure that rises like the prow of a ship, thrusting into the City Park. A restaurant and bar occupy the fifth floor, with fine views over the city centre (reached by a separate ground-floor entrance). 'Urbis' means 'of the city' in Latin, and the contents were intended to explore the many sides of the modern metropolis around the world, in the present and the future. It had a rather chequered existence after it opened. The actual purpose of the building seemed lost on most people, the interactive displays did not seem to have been well thought out, and the entrance fee was considered rather high. The result was a major rethink. The internal arrangement was altered, and free admission was introduced (except for special exhibitions). But it was not enough, and the old exhibition was closed, prior to a rethink as to its future.

It now contains the **National Football Museum**, which opened in 2012 (open Mon-Saturday, 10-5, Sunday 11-5, admission free). The contents include the FIFA Collection, the finest single collection of football memorabilia in existence. The **displays** trace the history and development of football in paintings, prints, woodcuts, and early football equipment, together with toys, ceramics and sculptures from around the world. There are **personal items** relating to such famous players as Stanley Matthews, Bobby Moore, and Tom Finney. We enter by the projecting wing, and inspect the **National Football Hall of Fame**. The adjacent café is the ideal place to relax, and the shop is packed full of souvenirs, gifts and mementoes of your visit. (Visitors can use the free wi-fi facilities in the café or museum atrium.)

The **First Floor**, entitled **'First Half: Story of the World's Greatest Game'**, can be accessed by **escalator** or **lift**. The displays illustrate the origins of the

Urbis in 2002
(Now National Football Museum)
(Graham Beech)

game, and relate some of the stories behind our national sport. Notice the **first F.A. Minute Book** (1863) and the **woollen shirt** worn at this time. The subsequent **displays** ask a number of questions. What does it mean to be a true football fan? How do the fans affect the game and what does the game mean to the fan? (Note a **traditional rattle** and a collection of confiscated **weapons**, together with **L.S. Lowry's 'Going to the Match'**.) How did the league and the competitions we know and love begin? (Note the actual **1896 F.A. Cup**. The visitor can select a presentation about football's pioneering days.) How and why did football become the most popular sport on the planet? (Notice the **1966 World Cup Final Ball**, together with the **Jules Rimet Trophy**) Why, for many fans, have stadiums become places of spiritual belonging and memories, both treasured and terrible? (Pause here to witness the presentation of the **Hillsborough Disaster**.) From the early days of radio commentary to today's 24/7 digital access, how has commentary and coverage of the world's most popular game has changed? (John Motson's famous **sheepskin coat** is displayed.) How and why have different clubs formed, and why do fans follow their club through thick and thin? (Notice a **1958 Manchester United Programme**. It was for the first game played after the terrible **Munich disaster**.) What does it take to play the game? From Sunday League to Premier League, different players bring different abilities to their team. What would you offer? (There are a number of **interactive experiences** available for a small charge.) A continuous **film presentation**, 'Our Beautiful Game: From a Kick Around on the Beach to Wembley Stadium', shows the passion, drama, enjoyment and disappointment of the game in stunning immersive fashion. However, it is perhaps the personal items that mean the most to the visitor; **shirts** worn by **Diego Maradona** in 1986 and **Bobby Moore** in 1970; a **crown** given by a supporter to **Colin Bell**; and **Donald Bell's Victoria Cross**.

The Second Floor is entitled **'Second Half: Playing The Game'**. Displays illustrate why football has become the **world's most-played game**; people of all ages, nationalities, beliefs and abilities continue to play the game every day. You can test your knowledge in the **'You Are the Ref!' challenge**. A gallery features **original drawings**, based on the 'The Guardian's cult classic strip, by Paul Trevillion and Keith Hackett. There are also displays concerning **Football Managers**, and **how players past and present train**, eat and mentally prepare themselves to be the best, together with a **display of football toys and games** from 1900s to the 21st century. There is also a place for little ones to enjoy, comprising an interactive, **soft toddler area** with **dressing up** and a **story corner**.

The **Third Floor** contains a gallery for **temporary exhibitions**, and the **Fourth Floor** a **Learning Zone**, intended to cater for school groups and for holiday family events and activities. The top two floors house a **Restaurant & Bar** with a great view of the city.

The **ancient gateway** belonging to **Chetham's College** is located on the opposite side of **Long Millgate**. The College started life as the manor house, carefully positioned in an ideal defensive site on a sandstone bluff in the angle of the Irk and Irwell. The Hanging Ditch and its extension defended the remaining side. Archaeological evidence points to an inner ditch as well. It was the seat of the Lord of the Barony of Manchester, a manor at the head of a loose federation of subordinate manors across a large part of southern Lancashire. A manor did not merely consist of a landed estate, but was also a collection of rights and privileges that could be demanded of the inhabitants, legal rights that would increase the lord's power, status, and income. All this had originally been granted, after the Norman Conquest, to the De Grelle or Grelley family by Roger the Poiteven, in return for military service. In the baronial hall, the Barons would entertain guests, receive rents, and hold their own private court of law. However, they mainly appear to have resided elsewhere, and used the manor house as a hunting lodge. A medieval survey records the kennels for their dogs (the origin of Hunt's Bank).

The present appearance and layout of the building probably dates from 1422, when Thomas de la Warre donated the site to his College of Priests, and it thus forms one of the best examples of a non-monastic medieval religious building in Britain. This institution was dissolved by Edward VI, and re-founded in a Protestant guise by Elizabeth I in 1578. However, the original building was purchased by the Earls of Derby. Lord Strange came to this family property in 1642 with the purpose of seizing the powder and match (fuses) that were kept as part of the county militia magazine. This was seen by the townspeople as a hostile act, for he was rumoured to be collecting an army for the king. The young Lord was invited to dinner in the hope that things would pass off smoothly. Meanwhile, his supporters began parading the streets with a drum, shouting "the town's ours!" Bloodshed ensued and Richard Percival, a linen weaver, became the first recorded casualty in the English Civil War. Lord Strange later unsuccessfully besieged the town.

Humphrey Chetham (1580-1653) was a wealthy local merchant. Although a moderate puritan, he supplemented his income by money lending, and was not averse to holding royal offices in the county. Either from a natural charitable impulse, or from guilt, he purchased the buildings for £400 and left the interest from a sum of £7000 to educate forty poor boys in a school. He also left £1000 to create a library, the first free library in Britain. The school and the library opened in these premises in 1656, and a Royal Charter was obtained in 1665. It was known as a 'bluecoat school' (after the manner of the boys' dress), and continued as such until 1969. The institution was incorporated with Nicholl's Hospital (founded 1881) in that year to form **'Chetham's School of Music'**, catering for musically gifted children. Entry is by competition. One mediaeval tradition is still followed; the school provides the cathedral choir.

The public may visit the **Library** on weekdays (9.00-12.30, 1.30-4.30), and the Baronial **Hall** is often used for free lunchtime concerts (enquire at reception). Intending visitors report to security, and are escorted to the library. The **gateway** front was rebuilt in 1816, but the rear (with the steps) is original work. The College building is 'L' shaped with the main block across the yard, directly ahead, and a wing running between it and the gateway, on the right. The latter contained the 'hospitium' (for receiving visitors), brewery, bakery, and College House, now Chetham's School of Music kitchens. The main block consists of the Baronial Hall, with the Warden's accommodation to the left. Notice the remains of Hyde's Cross in the yard. It formerly stood at the junction of Fennel Street, Hanging Ditch, Withy Grove, and Todd Street, but was removed here when Corporation Street was constructed in the 1840s. It was perhaps erected near property owned by the Hyde family in the 16th century, but parts of it are probably older.

Walk towards the **left-hand side** of the main building, and enter the **door** round the corner. The **entrance corridor** has a view of the lovely **cloister garth**, surrounded by the cells of the former Fellows. Visitors **ring the bell** at the door on the left for entrance to the library, before ascending a flight of stairs. An **old printing press** is in the corner of two wings. The **main wing**, straight ahead, was the dormitory of the clerks (lesser priests) and choristers. Here are the original **17th century bookcases** (the precious books were chained until 1745) and the curious 18th century gates between them. The inscriptions are original. The **right-hand wing** was formerly the College chapel (dedicated to the Virgin), leading to the **reading room**. This was the Warden's upper

College House, Chetham's School of Music (Graham Beech)

room. There is some fine **plasterwork** over the fireplace, containing the arms of Humphrey Chetham flanked by figures of a cockerel and a pelican feeding her chicks with her own blood (a symbol of Christian charity). The **portrait of Chetham** is said to have been painted from life. It is clear that there was once a curved plaster roof, and the eagle's claw and portcullis of the Earls of Derby may be seen along the top of the **wooden panelling**. The **oval table** is Cromwellian in date, and the painting of **'The Reconciliation of Steele and Addison'** is by Kneller. A fine **clock** is the earliest known (1695) gift of a former 'Bluecoat Boy'. Perhaps the most precious object is the **chest** with the inscription "The gift of Humphrey Chetham esquire, 1655." (The staff will usually open it if politely requested.) It contains a small **17th century chained library** of religious books. Chetham donated five of these to local churches, but only this (from Gorton) survives. The lovely little **bay window** was a favourite place of Karl Marx, who used the library when he came to Manchester to visit Engels. The Library now contains over 100,000 volumes (60,000 published before 1851) and many rare manuscripts. Nowadays, it acquires books on the history and topography of Manchester. Anyone may become a reader upon application to the librarian.

We return to the **College Yard**. The **Baronial Hall** is entered (for concerts) by means of a **screen passage**, which ran between it and the kitchens...a typical medieval arrangement. The **screen** is original. The Warden and other important people sat upon the raised **dais**. The original fire would have been in the centre of the room, for the fine **fireplace** was installed in the 17th century. It opens through to the delightful Victorian **'inglenook'**, with views of the cloister. A **'ladies bay'** is on the same level as the dais. It is sometimes possible to view the **'Audit Room'**, which was part of the Warden's residence. Dr. John Dee, 'Queen Elizabeth's Merlin', is cited as a famous occupant. His occult interests and activities (which included raising the dead in a churchyard near

Preston) caused a public scandal, but he had a powerful patron in the Queen. An old table is preserved here. This bears the **'devil's footprint'**, pointed out as Dee's handiwork by generations of Chetham's lads. On the other hand, the room has been used by accountants ... (The Baronial Hall is used for public concerts, and a package of a concert and guided tour of Chetham's can be pre-booked. At other times it can sometimes be seen upon application.)

To the left of the entrance to Chetham's, the large battlemented brick structure, with gothic windows and a tower, is the **old Grammar School** building, erected 1867-1880. (The original schoolhouse was taken down in 1776.) Hugh Oldham, Bishop of Exeter, founded the Grammar School in 1515. As a local man, who had risen to power on the coat tails of the Stanley family, Hugh wanted to found a school in his native Lancashire. He considered that

Chetham's Cloister Garth (Graham Beech)

"children in the same county, having pregnant wit, have been most part brought up rudely and idly and not in virtue, cunning, erudition, literature, and in good manners." Some things never change! The school moved to a new site in Fallowfield in 1931, and the building is now part of the Chetham's complex. Thomas De Quincy was a grammar school pupil, and his schooldays here are recounted in his 'Confessions of an English Opium Eater.'

Manchester Cathedral (open daily) is nearby. There is a full description in the author's 'Discovering Manchester', issued by the publisher of this volume.

The Bury Line

Piccadilly Station to Victoria Station

Piccadilly Station to Piccadilly Gardens is described on pp26-28; Piccadilly Gardens to Victoria Station on pp40-45; and there is a description of Victoria Station on pp45-50.

Victoria Station to Irk Valley Junction

The tram departs from **Victoria Station**, passes under the **Ducie Road Bridge** at the station throat, crosses **Aspin Lane** by a barely noticed **bridge**, and follows the main railway line on the left, as it ascends **Miles Platting Bank**. (Look out for one of the few links between Metrolink and the rail network!) When the Manchester and Leeds Railway opened this section, in 1844, the trains ascended by rope haulage, and descended by gravity, locomotives being coupled and uncoupled at the company's locomotive shed and works at Miles Platting. More powerful engines soon made this practice redundant, but heavier trains still needed a banking engine. In the late 19th century, the Lancashire and Yorkshire Railway built the alternative **Collyhurst** or **Manchester Loop** line with easier gradients, and both lines came to frame the **Irk Valley**. The loop line diverged to the left at the now defunct Victoria East Junction, by the **Ducie Road Ridge**. This section of the loop is disused and overgrown, but the brow of **Cheetham Hill**, beyond it, has been transformed by the erection of new **apartment blocks** and a **hotel** in recent years.

However, the more interesting views are to the right. (This part of the line is perhaps best viewed from a tram travelling in the opposite direction, when this description should be read in reverse!) The land falls away towards the river valley, and we are on a **brick viaduct** from which there is a good view. Beyond the often flag bedecked *Ashton House* (a budget hotel/hostel), rises the new **Co-operative Headquarters Building**, a large futuristic confection in glass and steel, somewhat reminiscent of a giant 'walnut whip', and the centre piece of the new **NOMA Quarter** (an acronym for 'North of Manchester'). Fronted by the Co-operative Group, NOMA is currently (2014) the largest development project in North-West England, and overall is the largest development outside South East England. The new fifteen storey **Headquarters** building houses more than 3,000 employees working across the Group's family of retailing and financial services businesses. An internal atrium encloses a circular central area, with a glass roof and glazed elevator shafts rising to approximately a dozen floors. **Dantzic Street** is crossed by an iron **girder bridge**, adjacent to a large brick

The new Co-operative Headquarters (photograph courtesy of Co-operative Group Ltd)

building. A red and white sign indicates that this is **Charter Street Mission**. The first so called 'ragged school' opened on this site in 1847; it was re-founded in 1861, and the present building dates to 1866. In 1892 it was renamed as 'Charter Street Ragged School and Working Girls' Home' (inscription over the door). In addition to a diet of scripture and basic literacy, it also provided food, clogs and clothing for children, and a Sunday breakfast for destitute men and women, together with rudimentary medical services. It later taught basic skills such as carpentry to the boys, and home making and cooking to the girls, in order that they might become respectable, useful, and productive citizens. The working girls' home was on the top floor with its own separate entrance on Dantzic Street. Churchill visited in 1906 (and left a £5 donation) and General Gordon is said to have (briefly) taught in the Sunday School. Notice the brief glimpse of **parkland** between the school building and **Irk Street**. This was the site of **St. Michael's Flags**, the heart of **Angel Meadow**.

Note the **Co-operative Tobacco Works** (converted into housing) on the hill and the **former Gas Works site** (now a large car park) before the tram crosses **Bilbrook Street** and **descends an incline** below the level of the original railway line to enter the **Collyhurst Tunnel** (462 yards), curving under it. The tunnel was opened in 1904, to allow suburban trains to access the new extension to Victoria Station. The tram emerges, and passes on to a brick **viaduct**, crossing **Moss Brook** and **Fitzgeorge Street**. The valley can be a strange place, a mixture of the remaining industrial premises and bare stretches of scrub on the slopes. But the surreal survives...see if you can catch a glimpse (on the left) of the **battleship sculpture**, slowly sinking into the ground! **Collyhurst Road** and the **Irk** itself are crossed by a **bow lattice span** of 115 feet on the skew.

Angel Meadow and the Lost Cemetery

The district was once a very fashionable one. In the late 18th century, Manchester merchants and other well-to-do inhabitants began to move here to escape the smoke, noise, and overcrowding in their growing town. To cater for a new congregation, the church of St. Michael's and All Angels was begun in 1788 and consecrated in the following year. Even then, the building was considered plain and ugly, and the surroundings soon grew to match the church. The district began to change, and by the following century it was considered the worst slum in Manchester. Overcrowding (more than 350 per acre) and insanitary conditions led to high mortality and cholera; Engels in his 'The Condition of the Working Class in England' has left a terrible description of the area. In the meantime, a large area of land adjacent to the church had been converted into what was then the largest cemetery in Manchester, catering largely to the poor and destitute, where paupers were buried in what were mass graves. There were perhaps 40,000 interments between 1788 and 1816! The residents were so desperately poor that they dug up the cemetery soil for sale as fertiliser to local farmers. Consequently, the area was paved over in 1855, engendering the name of 'St. Michael's Flags'. The church struggled on. The Reverend Jowett Wilson wore himself out between 1913 and 1927, catering to both the spiritual and physical needs of the remaining poor parishioners. (He was often to be seen wandering around Smithfield Market, collecting pennies in a bucket.) But the last houses disappeared, and church was demolished in 1935. All that remains are a few gravestones near the church site, from the time when it was a pleasant residential area...but the wheel has turned full circle. Well-heeled residents are coming back, and the pauper burying ground is now a pleasant park.

Irk Valley Junction to Prestwich

At **Irk Valley Junction**, the Oldham and Rochdale trams diverge to the right, down the curving **Smedley Viaduct**, to reach the old **Collyhurst Loop** line that later passes underneath us. The junction was the scene of a terrible accident in 1953. The 7 20 am Bury to Manchester electric train plunged 90 feet over the viaduct into the River Irk after it hit the 7 36 steam train out of Manchester Victoria. The engine of the steam train overturned and there were several fatalities in the electric train coaches. After further **brick arches**, we **cross the loop line** by another **iron span**, and there is a fine view of the **Metrolink Depot and Works** on the left, where all the major tram overhauls are carried out.

The tram stops at **Queens Road Station**, which opened on 16 December, 2013. It replaces a staff halt, and drivers are still sometimes changed here. Both **platforms** are linked by a **pedestrian crossing** at the Manchester end. The **Manchester platform** communicates with the end of **Smeaton Street** (where **disabled parking bays** are located) by a **ramp**, and **Queens Road** is accessed from this point by a **stepped incline**. In contrast, the **Bury platform** is linked with **Queens Road** by **steps** and a **lift**. Notice a **gated access point** to the depot on the left.

A left turn at **Queens Road** leads to the new **Irish World Heritage Centre**, situated in the **'Irish Town' quarter** to the left (where a hotel is projected). This overlooks the site of **Angel Meadow** (see p56) in the **Irk Valley**, where a large Irish community was to be found in the industrial revolution. The Centre aims to establish a centre of excellence outside of Ireland which will provide unique visitor facilities, exhibitions, entertainment, sport and accommodation, delivered by advanced multimedia and information technology media, and although open, is still very much a work in progress. For the ordinary visitor, the principal attraction will be the **Irish Diaspora Museum** which will celebrate the Irish diaspora world-wide, where collections, documents and exhibitions will present the history of Irish emigration and the development of the global Irish family. The collections are broad in scope, ranging from fine and decorative arts to Irish social, domestic and industrial history. (The Centre is currently open 10-5 Monday to Friday; free admission, but donation appreciated. For further information about the development of the future Museum, ring 0161 205 4007.) Continue along **Queens Road** to the **former tram depot**, and turn right down **Boyle Street**. The depot was opened (along with the first route) with great ceremony in June 1901. The street is named after Daniel Boyle, the energetic Chairman of the Tramway Committee (the system was known locally as 'Dan Boyle's Railway'). We arrive at the **Museum of Transport** on Boyle Street (open Wednesday, Saturday, Sunday, and Bank Holidays, 10.00-4.30, usually daily in August, admission charge).

Adjacent to the Museum may be found the seeming **ruins of an old church**, of which the tower remains as a local landmark. This is Saint Luke's, consecrated in1839 (when the area was a fashionable residence), where Mendelssohn inaugurated a new organ in 1847. Its present state results from some misguided decisions in the 1980s, and something certainly needs to be done about it Back at **Queens Road**, we reach the junction with **Cheetham Hill Road**. If there is time, turn left and walk towards the **tower of Saint Chad's church** in the distance, beyond *Manchester Fort Shopping Park* on the left. The latter is perhaps the largest open shopping park in Greater Manchester, comprising 37 retail units, including *Next, Boots, Asda Living, Outfit, Peacocks, TK Maxx, Sports Direct, Argos, Clarks, Superdrug,* etc. (late opening on Monday to Friday). The Cheetham Hill area housed the Jewish community in the 19th century, and we soon reach the **Manchester Jewish Museum** (open Monday to Thursday, 10.30-4, Sundays

1-5, closed Jewish holidays; admission charge), housed in the former Sephardic synagogue (designed by Salomans in the Moorish style). There are adjacent buildings (including the **former Town Hall** and the **Free Library** building) also worthy of notice.

After passing beyond the depot junction and under **Queens Road** and **Smedley Lane**, the train reaches the **site of Woodlands Road station**, opened by the Land Y in 1913 to try and fend off tram competition. Now the wheel has again turned full circle!

Beyond the **bridge spanning Woodlands Road**, the tram arrives at **Abraham Moss Station**, with its **staggered platforms**. This is a new Metrolink station, intended to replace Woodlands Road. The **Manchester platform** is linked with the approach to the **Abraham Moss Centre Campus** from **Crescent Road**. There is a **crossing** between the platforms, and the **Bury platform** accesses **Woodlands Road** by a **ramp** and **passage**.

The **Abraham Moss Centre**, visible to the right, commemorates Alderman Abraham Moss (a prominent Jewish former Lord Mayor of Manchester), and

Museum of Transport

The museum is located in Manchester's first bus garage, and rather appropriately contains a large collection of historic buses, once operated by the local authorities (and a few private operators) in the Greater Manchester area. A rare Victorian horse bus is given pride of place in the exhibition, but do not neglect the displays about the evolution of public transport in the Manchester area, which include such things as ticket machines and items of uniform.

Pre-war Manchester bus

provides a range of education, leisure, and cultural services for local residents. In so doing, it comprises a number of elements. **Abraham Moss High School** has just reopened after a major redevelopment, and **Further Education** and **Adult Education** courses are also offered. The school shares a good **library** with the general public. There is a **Theatre**, a smaller **Studio Theatre**, and a **Conference and Exhibition Suite**. The Manchester Sport and Leisure Trust operate a centre that includes **two pools** along with a range of facilities providing a variety of sessions and activities for the individual or the whole family (a wide range of memberships is available). The **former trackbed** of the branch to the ICI plant at Blackley can be traced below the hill upon which the Centre is built, curving away to the right. (An original locomotive, the 'Lady Armadale', is preserved on the Severn Valley Railway.) Notice **St. Anne's Roman Catholic Church**, situated at the top of the slope leading up from the Centre, across **Crescent Road**. It dates from 1957, and is built of brick with a detached **tower** sporting an openwork concrete top.

The tram passes under **Crescent Road**, and soon runs into a **cutting**, spanned by the **Moss Bank** and **Cravenwood Road** over bridges.

The site of **Crumpsall Station** is located within this cutting. It is an original station, but little remains from that period except for elements of the **footbridge** with its **platform**

'The Breezy Northern Heights of Manchester'

At a junction with the depot (formerly a curve leading back to the Collyhurst Loop), we pass from the 1905 extension on to a line constructed by the Lancashire and Yorkshire Railway in 1876-79. It ran to a junction with the original route to Bury at Radcliffe, via Prestwich and Whitefield. Businessmen had flocked to these villages, creating suburban development high above the smoke of Manchester, and the company wanted to tap into this traffic by affording an alternative route between Bury and the city. It opened to Whitefield on 30 July 1879, and trains ran through to Bury on 1 September. In addition to the Bury commuter service, alternate trains continued beyond Bury to Rawtenstall and Bacup. The line to Bury was electrified in 1916 on the third rail system at the unusually high voltage of 1200volts DC. (Bacup trains were diverted to run into Manchester via Heywood and Castleton Junction.) The inter-war period is usually characterised as one of economic depression, but much of the unemployment was structural Some of the new industries (plastics, vehicles, consumer goods etc.) were booming, and low commodity prices increased the disposable income of those in work. The result was a housing boom as new estates began to appear around Manchester full of semi-detached houses retailing at affordable prices (from £350 upwards!). The Lancashire and Yorkshire published a booklet entitled "The Breezy Northern Heights of Manchester" in 1919 in an attempt to promote this line as their own 'Metroland'. The London Midland and Scottish Railway continued the process, opening two new stations to serve new housing developments. The line went through some hard times after the war. The track and stations became very run down and it was almost closed under the iniquitous Beeching proposals. However, it was absorbed into the Metrolink project and is now far busier than ever before.

steps. This is entered from **Station Road**, where the main entrance building was located. Metrolink have added a substantial **ramped approach** to the **footbridge** from the **Manchester platform**, and separate **ramp** and **steps** linking the **Bury platform** with **Station Road**. The latter leads to **Crumpsall Lane**, which spans the line at the north end. You might be able to trace parts of the path of the **former goods siding** that ran behind the **Manchester platform**. It accessed a large goods and coal yard situated beyond the **Crumpsall Lane** road bridge. The site of this yard is now covered in modern housing.

Crumpsall is full of late 19th century **villa style residences** that once belonged to the first commuters. The station is the nearest access point for **North Manchester General Hospital**. Turn right along **Crumpsall Lane** (crossing the Metrolink line) to reach the **road junction** adjacent to the **former Crumpsall Green**. **Westbury Road**, directly ahead, passes along the edge of **Crumpsall Park**. This patch of greenery is all that is left of Crumpsall Hall, a half-timbered sixteenth or 17th century house that was the reputed birthplace of Humphrey Chetham (see p52). It survived as late as the 1880s, when it was demolished and the land acquired as the site of a cemetery. However, it became a park instead, opening in 1890. The **porters lodge** and the **obelisk** are listed. Our way lies slightly to the left along **Delaunays Road**. There are two local legends about the origins of the Delaunay family, both entirely spurious! The first states that they were Huguenot refugees (though the family was Roman Catholic). The second, and more sensational, suggested that they were the family of the ill-fated Governor of the Bastille, fleeing the wrath of the French Revolution! The truth is more prosaic. Angel Delaunay, a master dyer from Rouen, arrived in the district in 1788 (before the Revolution) and introduced Turkey red dyeing to the Manchester area. The road eventually passes **Central Drive** on the right, the main entrance to the **North Manchester General Hospital**. It started life as part of the former Manchester Workhouse Infirmary, relocated here after the original site was acquired for the expansion of Victoria Station. The workhouse was erected in 1855 and the Infirmary followed in 1876. Some parts of the original building still remain.

The line now passes through an area transformed by inter-war and post-war housing developments; before 1914 it was largely open country apart from ribbon development along the principal roads. Beyond **Crumpsall Lane**, we pass under **Wilton Road**, and the surroundings start to open out. The **view** to the right, before the next station, is exceptionally fine. Look out for **Heaton Hall**, the **classical temple**, and the tall concrete **telecommunications tower**, brooding over the scene in the background.

The tram passes onto an embankment, crosses a **bridge spanning Middleton Road**, and arrives at **Bowker Vale Station**. This was a new development, opened by the London, Midland and Scottish Railway in 1938 to serve the growing housing estates in the area. The station's concrete framed and canopied **station buildings** reflected the design of the 1930s London Underground of Frank Pick. Sadly, the bricked up and disused platform buildings were recently demolished, and only part of the **footbridge** (with its **smoke deflectors!**) remains. **Steps** and a convoluted **ramp** lead from the **Manchester platform** to **Middleton Road**, a typical 1930s suburban development. Similar **steps** and a **ramp** link the **Bury platform** to a **path** alongside the station. It also runs in one direction to **Middleton Road**, but links the station to **Windsor Road** in the other direction. After walking either path to Middleton Road, a left turn, followed by a short walk along it, leads to the **Middleton Road Gates** of **Heaton Park**, with the terminus of the **heritage tramway** (see. p61).

After crossing **Windsor Road**, the tram enters **Heaton Park Tunnel** (713 yards), which is something of a cheat. It is not bored through a hill, but was constructed by creating a brick lined trench, arching it over, and restoring the flat parkland on top. This was a condition imposed by Lord Wilton, who did not want his view spoilt!

A similar, but short, 'cut and cover' **tunnel** then takes the line under **Bury Old Road** and into **Heaton Park Station**, located in a short **cutting**. This is another original station, and, again, little survives. **Stairs** and **lifts** at the tunnel end of both **platforms** communicate with the **original forecourt** by the side of **Bury Old Road** (the station building, with its booking hall, has disappeared). The station catered for the residential district and **Heaton Park**. It still does, though police horses are no longer required to control the holiday crowds. Both **Bowker Vale Station** and **Heaton Park Station** were never provided with a goods yard, as passenger traffic pure and simple was their reason for existence. (A separate description of Heaton Park is included below.)

We pass under **Newtown Street**, and run on to the level and then an embankment, passing through somewhat more modern suburbia.

After crossing **Heywood Road**, the tram arrives at **Prestwich Station**. Prestwich is another original station, placed upon an embankment, but little is left of the former structure, save for the **platforms, stairs**, and the street level **subway**, which is entered from the **car park**. The **subway** has been augmented by new **pedestrian access ramps** either side of the line. The one from the **Bury platform** merely leads to the **car park**. However, the **ramp** from the **Manchester platform** accesses both the **subway** and **Poppythorne Lane**, a curious little street that is now pedestrianized. In one direction it runs under the line to the **car park** area, but in the other it connects with **Heys Road** and **Fairfax Road**. (A separate description of Prestwich is included below.)

Heaton Park

'Black Sir John' Egerton was possessed of estates in Cheshire, Staffordshire, and Northamptonshire, but he considered the latter the most important. Consequently, when he died in 1646, his Cheshire estate was left to Rowland, his second son, who was made a baronet by James I in 1617. In 1684, Sir John Egerton married the heiress of the Holland family, obtaining the massive Heaton and Denton estate of over 35,000 acres. His grandson decided to build a new home in this estate on an elevated site in what was then a remote part of the county. Sir Thomas Egerton, the seventh baronet rebuilt this house, leaving us with the fine mansion that we see today. His income from mining rights and rents was calculated, in the last quarter of the 18th century, as more than £5000 per annum, an immense sum. He was created Baron Grey de Wilton in 1784 and Earl of Wilton (in recognition of his contribution to the defence of Britain) in 1800. Sadly, only one of his children, a daughter, survived. She married the Marquess of Westminster, but Royal licence enabled the title to pass to their second son, who became the second Earl of Wilton. The second Earl lived a rather flamboyant lifestyle, and the house parties were legendary. Fanny Kemble, the leading actress of the day, was a frequent guest, often arriving straight from the theatre in Manchester (once going into dinner dressed as Lady Macbeth!). The Earl had been awarded the ribbon of the Guelph Order, which he wore hoping that people would mistake it for the Order of the Garter! When chosen to convey the actual Garter Ribbon to the King of Saxony, he wore it on the journey "for practice!" He began the famous Heaton Park races in 1827, but these terminated in 1839 due to accusations concerning "the partiality of the judges". There were a number of attempts to sell the hall and estate by both himself and his successors. In 1902, Manchester City Council purchased both the house and the extensive 640 acre parkland setting (which the family had originally intended to be sold off as building lots), from the Fifth Earl for £230,000, thus acquiring what is still the largest municipal park in the country. Part of it was used as a reservoir, and some acres were converted into a municipal golf course, but the rest can still be enjoyed by the public (open daily, the gates closing at dusk).

Alight at **Heaton Park Station**, and enter the **park** by the gates across **Bury Old Road**. You could spend all day here, but if time is pressing, the following itinerary is suggested. Take the right-hand path at the fork beyond the gate, noticing the **Papal Monument** to the right. This stone marks the spot where Pope John Paul celebrated mass during his visit to Britain. The pathway leads to the intersection of the main drive and the roadway to the **lake**. Follow the latter by walking straight on, and admire the **frontage of the original Manchester Town Hall**, that forms a backdrop to the sheet of water. (**Rowing boats** can be hired, and the **ducks and geese** appreciate some bread.) The terminus of the **Heaton Park Tramway** may be found adjacent to the **Pavilion** by the lake.

The trams terminate at the **Middleton Road Gate** (see pp60,63) Adjacent may be found **Smithy Lodge**. Sir Thomas Egerton

Heaton Hall

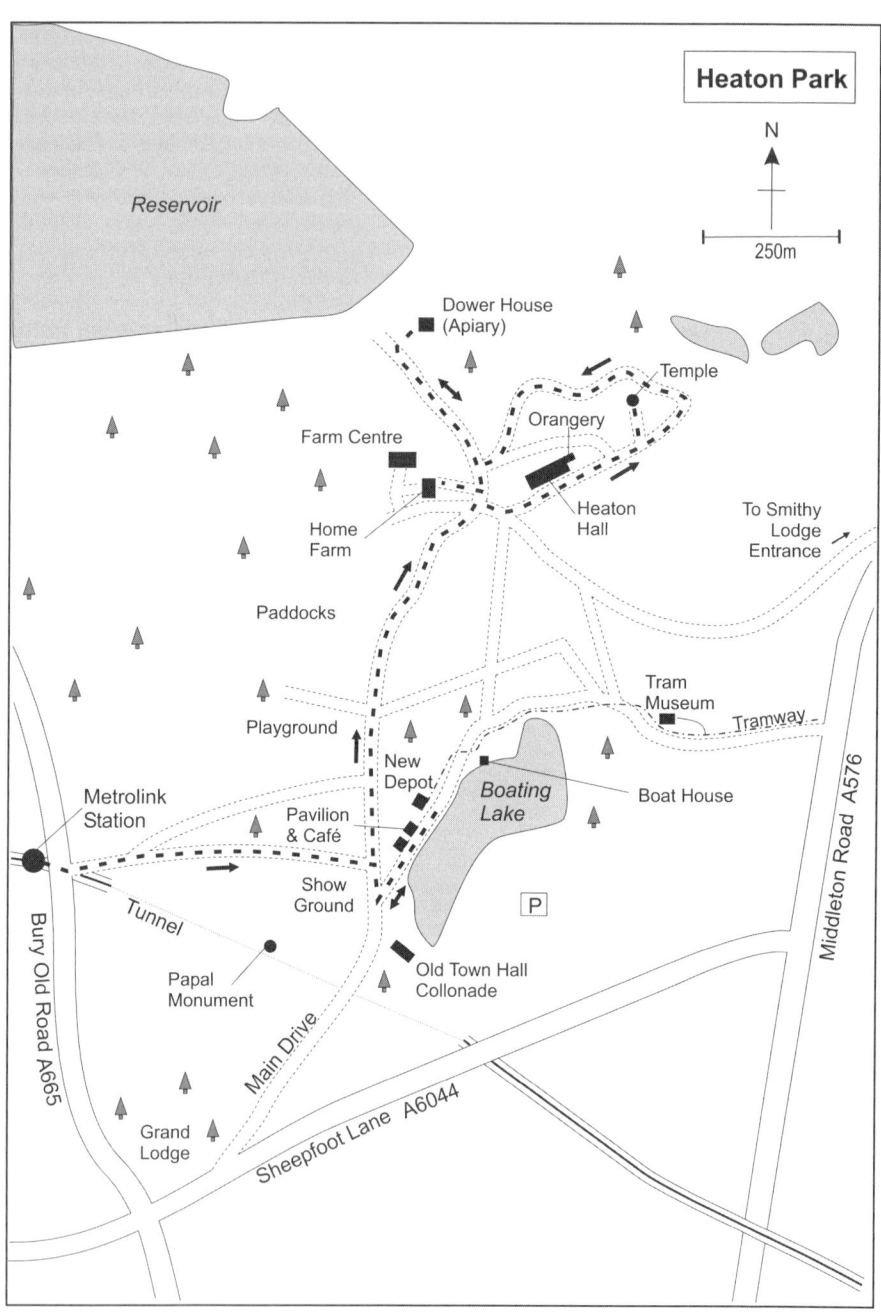

Heaton Park

N

250m

Reservoir

Dower House (Apiary)

Temple

Orangery

Farm Centre

Heaton Hall

To Smithy Lodge Entrance

Home Farm

Paddocks

Tram Museum

Tramway

Playground

New Depot

Boating Lake

Boat House

Metrolink Station

Pavilion & Café

P

Show Ground

Tunnel

Old Town Hall Collonade

Papal Monument

Main Drive

Bury Old Road A665

Middleton Road A576

Grand Lodge

Sheepfoot Lane A6044

Trams in the Park

Manchester Corporation Tramways once had a short terminal siding in the Park (complete with waiting room) at the Middleton Road entrance. The siding was abandoned in the 1930s, but was restored some years ago as a museum tramway, and the original building was converted into a depot and museum. The tracks were later extended to the lakeside. A new extension, to the lakeside pavilion, has been recently completed, and a further one to Bury Old Road Gate, is projected. By the time that these lines are in print, a new depot, by the terminus and behind the lakeside pavilion, will hopefully be complete. Enthusiastic

volunteers operate the trams, and they are always ready to answer questions. The ticket includes admission to the museum, so hop on board! You may be lucky enough to ride on 765, the beautiful single deck Manchester car. Other, double deck, vehicles are in the restoration pipeline, but may have to wait for the new depot to be completed. The latest acquisition is a rare Manchester Horse Tram (with a body that rotates around the truck), that operates on special days (when the specially trained horse is available). The trams usually operate on Sundays and Bank Holidays, 1.30 to 5.30 (and a limited service on Wednesdays in June and July), from Easter to September.

Manchester's famous 'little tram'

was a man of fashion and taste and the design of the lodge shows that he embraced the change towards the romantic landscape. It is the earliest gatehouse into the park and is built in an unusual octagonal shape. It is thought that this was designed by Lewis Wyatt in 1806 as a cottage to be viewed from the house in a romantic, rural setting. Its name derives from a group of blacksmith's shops set close by on Middleton Road, but now demolished. Nowadays, the lodge has been refurbished as accommodation, and it is possible to stay there (ring 0161 773 1085 x211 for more details).

We must now retrace our steps, turn right, and follow the main drive towards the house. The **paddock** on the left can contain anything, from horses to highland cattle. The **old home farm**, on the left, is now is now the **Farm Centre** (daily, 9-6, 3:30 in winter, free), so enter and pass through to the courtyard. Here may be found **stables and pens** for horses, ponies, pigs, goats, and a variety of other animals. You may also catch sight of the **coach**, and there is sometimes a useful **cafeteria**. Proceed through to the adjacent **Animal Centre** (Easter to September 10:30-5 or 7, September to March 10:30-3:30, free) containing a variety of animals including alpacas, guinea pigs, rabbits, and poultry, presided over by some very vain peacocks. A short walk to the **dower house** (signposted) is rewarded with a fascinating display of apiary (beekeeping) with a demonstration hive (usually open Sunday afternoons). However, the main attraction is the nearby **Heaton Hall**. At the time of writing (2014) the Hall is (hopefully) temporarily closed to the public, but a description is included for when it is open once more.

The house is built of sandstone and stuccoed brick, in a traditional Palladian design with the entrance on the north side and the main façade on the south. The west wing housed the kitchens and servant's quarters, and an orangery with loggias fronted a formal garden at the east end. The landscaping was designed to make the most of the uninterrupted views of the rolling hills across to the Pennines. An important feature of this was the **ha-ha** (a kind of ditch), used to keep the grazing animals (so important to the landscaping) away from the formal lawns by means of a barrier that was all-but invisible from the house. Sadly, the Council did not purchase the original contents of the house, but it has been re-furnished in the style of the period.

An inquisitive alpaca!

The **entrance hall** is a room with semi-circular ends with **niches for statues**. Note the **stone flagged floor**. Although one can imagine a bewigged butler receiving guests here, think also of tenants with clogs, waiting to pay their rents on quarter days. There follows a view of the impressive **Grand Staircase**, which divides into two and turns back upon itself to access the top floor. The staircase is complemented with French-polished **bannisters** and an ornate **balustrade**. Note the **candle tripods** of cast iron with brass and lead decorations, and the **imitation marble columns**. Pass along

Wyatt's Masterpiece

The present structure is largely the creation of James Wyatt, added around a far older house after 1772. Wyatt was the son of a Staffordshire timber merchant who became one of the greatest late 18th century architects. After spending six years in Italy, his selection as architect of the proposed Pantheon (a London theatre and promenade) brought him almost unparalleled instant success while still in his twenties. (His brother was one of the principal promoters of the scheme, and it was doubtless due to him that the designs of a young and almost unknown architect were accepted by the Committee.) When the Pantheon was opened in 1772, their choice was at once endorsed by the fashionable public; Horace Walpole pronounced it to be "the most beautiful edifice in England". The design was exhibited at the Royal Academy, private commissions followed, and Wyatt found himself a fashionable domestic architect and an Associate Academician. His polished manners secured him friends as well as patrons among the great, and when it was rumoured that he was about to leave the country to become architect to Catherine the Great, a group of English noblemen is said to have offered him a retaining fee of £1,200 to remain in their service. He became a royal architect, undertaking work at Windsor Castle and elsewhere. Sir Thomas Egerton was far sighted enough to engage Wyatt's services at the very outset of his career, and many people consider Heaton Hall to be his masterpiece.

the **corridor** to the left of the staircase. The **former bedrooms** on the left-hand side are usually used for display purposes. We then turn right and enter an **ante room** which leads to the **library**. Both were remodelled in 1823 by Lewis Wyatt (James's nephew) with **mahogany book cases** by Gillows of Lancaster, said to have originally contained an estimated 4,000 volumes. The library usually contains a fine painting of **Thomas Egerton, the Second Earl**, and a **view of Heaton Park Races**. Proceed into the **Music Room**. It was completed by Samuel Wyatt (another nephew of James) and inaugurated by a concert of the music of Handel and Corelli. The family were talented musicians, and, on this occasion, Lord Wilton played the cello. At one end, resplendent in its green, blue, and gold decorations is a 1790 **Samuel Green Organ** (organ builder to George III). It sports **grisaille paintings** with winged maidens burning incense to the figure appearing in the portrait medallion above; a **picture of Handel** (the noble Lord's favourite composer). The **original music stands** are usually on view. There is a **coved ceiling** and an interesting **chimney piece with bas-relief figures**. We now enter the **billiard room**. The fifteen foot by eight foot **table** is thought to have been supplied by Gillow in the early 19th century, though Heaton Hall had one of the first in England, supplied by the same company in 1771! The game originated in India, and was played outdoors on grass; hence the green baize table. The large **paintings on the wall** are by Michael Novosielski (1750-1795), a Polish artist who worked with Wyatt, and are the only surviving examples of his work. They depict scenes from the life of Oeneus, King of Calydon, and other classical subjects. The next room is the impressive **Saloon**, the centrepiece of the southern frontage. The large circular bay once had a door leading to the outside terrace. The chief glory of this room is the **ornate plasterwork ceiling**, created by the firm of Joseph Rose II of York. He was paid £350 for his work at the Hall. Note the two Georgian **chimney pieces**, with the **oval plaster medallions** including the **crest of the Egerton family**, three crossed arrows. The **sculptures** have stood here since the time of the Fourth Earl. The final room on the ground floor is the **Dining Room**. A huge **Venetian window** highlights this room, as it has done two centuries, but notice the **plaster frieze** and the wonderful apse with a **ceiling decorated with Bacchantes holding musical instruments**. The **main ceiling** incorporates **Greek shield motifs and four oval paintings** depicting the four seasons. Lastly, the **wooden fire surround** has an elaborate decoration of honeysuckle and beasts supporting an urn.

After ascending the staircase, the principal attraction is the **Cupola Room**. This ornate and unusual room, with the large, round dome, was the private sitting room of the Dowager Lady Egerton, the mother of Lord Wilton. It is much more besides, being a **rare survival of the 'Etruscan' style** popularised by discoveries in Italy, and in vogue for a brief period in the 18th century. It was painted by Biagio Rebecca, a friend of Wyatt, and the decoration is oil painted paper, pasted on to the walls and ceiling. The **inner zone of the ceiling** comprises **eight lozenges** painted with representations of **the four elements** of earth, air, fire, and water, each element being painted in pairs. The **outer zone** of the ceiling includes **ovals with figures of the virtues**, including Temperance, Liberality, Fortitude, Meekness, Honour, and Fame. The **walls** are enhanced with semi-circular panels with a fan motif above. These **eight panels depict gods and goddesses in triumph**, including Diana, Venus, Juno, Mercury, Bacchus, and Cupid. There are a **further twenty-four panels** in horizontal strips above the fan motifs. Note the fine, ornate, **chandelier**, and the **painting over the fireplace**. The latter is entitled "Sigismund Weeping over the Ashes of Tancred", which some have suggested was a reference to Lady Egerton's widowhood. The **final two rooms** are something of an anti-climax. The

Yellow Bedroom and its adjoining **dressing room** are thought to have been the private rooms of Lady Eleanor Egerton. The yellow and blue reproduction floral **wallpaper** is a copy of paper discovered in a London house, and date from the 1770s. The **Pink Bedroom**, across the landing, has been decorated in a style fashionable in the period of the Second Earl. There is usually a **pastel portrait of Lady Egerton** on the wall.

A pleasant **circular walk** can be undertaken by following the path from the rear of the house in an anti-clockwise direction. You can make a short detour up to the **Classical Temple**, from where there is a fine view over Manchester.

The 'Manchester Pals'

There is a plaque affixed to the Grand Lodge entrance at the corner of Bury Old Road and Sheepfoot Lane. It commemorates the Manchester Pals who trained in the park in the First World War. As the population enthusiastically responded to Lord Kitchener's call for volunteers, someone came up with a good recruiting ploy...the 'pals' battalion'. Potential recruits who were friends and workmates, it was thought, might be encouraged to enlist if they knew that they could all serve together in the same unit. The movement began in Liverpool, but soon spread to Manchester and its surrounding towns. The proposed 'Manchester Clerk's and Warehousemen's Battalion' was promoted by the principal textile firms and funded by business donations. The response was overwhelming. In all, eight 'service battalions' of the Manchester Regiment were raised in this way, and a complex of hutted camps and training facilities was created in the park to house them. They were the flower of Manchester manhood, and they were squandered on the Somme. Give them a thought as you wander round these beautiful surroundings.

Prestwich

Prestwich was the 'priest's habitation'. The Saxon name has led some to suggest that it was a missionary centre in the conversion of the North West to Christianity. Certainly the ancient church was the heart of an important parish that took in present day Oldham! The manor emerged in the medieval times, and in 1212 it was assessed as four oxgangs of land held by Adam de Prestwich. In the late 18th century, the area was mainly rural with scattered farms and small settlements at Great and Little Heaton and large numbers of the population working on Lord Wilton's estate. The arrival of the railway in 1879-80 encouraged affluent merchants from Manchester to move in and build villas. By 1912, the population had increased to 12,800, and from the 1930s onwards the remaining fields were developed. By 1961 the population soared to 31,000 and Prestwich had become a suburb of Manchester. Prestwich Hospital was built as an asylum in 1851, and by 1900 it had grown into the largest in Europe and had become an important local employer. Changing attitudes to the treatment of mental illness resulted in its closure.

Leave the station and pass though the **car park** (the former goods yard) to the **Longfield Centre** at the entrance to a shopping area. The **library** contains a first floor **Prestwich Heritage Museum** (changing exhibitions of local history) that is worth visiting (library opening hours). Pass beyond the **new square** (with a **fountain**) to **Bury New Road**, turning left at the **Railway and Naturalist** (an amalgam of two former pubs, one of which being the resort of the naturalists, see p71). The centre of Prestwich still has some interesting shops though some of the antique emporiums are no more. Opposite the *Red Lion*, turn right down **Church Lane**. This is the heart of old Prestwich, with several **old houses** and the **tower of the parish church** visible at the bottom. The *Church Inn* is a Grade II listed building. Known as the Ostrich prior to 1823, it has always been the centre of the parish activities, and once had stocks and a bowling green (now the Rectory Lawn). Recent excavations discovered an underground cellar dating to the early 17th century, though there was most likely a tavern on or near this location prior to this date. The pub also has an interesting ghost story. A Monk is said to have been bricked up behind a wall in the building. Friendly though a bit naughty, he has made himself known to people over the years by moving full barrels of beer around the cellar. It is home to the meetings of the Prestwich Heritage Society, and there is a **small display of finds and curios** associated with the pub and the church.

St. Mary's Church is an ancient foundation. The first mention of a Rector of Prestwich, one 'Thomas', dates from 1200, though a place of worship has probably stood on this site for over eight hundred years. The ancient Parish of Prestwich-cum-Oldham (once including Oldham itself) was vast, and forty-one modern parishes have been created from it. (The church is usually closed except for Sunday services, though a Communion service is usually held on Wednesday mornings; ring 0161 773 2912 for enquiries about admission.)

Pass through the **churchyard gate**, flanked by a rare **18th century Mortuary** to the right, and an old stone **mounting block** (dating from 1678 and curiously positioned back to front) to the left. Walk to the western end, and proceed to examine the **ancient tower**, a local landmark (the church is placed upon an eminence, above the river valley). The tower is 86 feet high; greater than the length of the 80 foot long nave (the total length of the church being 120 feet). In 1485, the Wars of the Roses ended, and the newly created Stanley Earl of Derby took over the Pilkington estates in the locality. (The Stanley family had 'assisted' the new king in the final moments of Bosworth Field.) He celebrated this fact by constructing the present **tower** in or about 1500, displaying **his arms as 'Lord of Man'** (incorporating the traditional three legged device) on its east side. The tower was restored in the late 19th century, but it is still largely original in appearance. In addition to the Derby arms, **old carvings and cryptic signs** can be discerned in the walls at various heights. The tower contains **a peal of eight bells** in the key of F. The first bells were mentioned in 1552, and the total weight of the present peal is a little over 69 cwt.

Enter the church by the porch at the north-west end. The **nave** is a surviving piece of medieval work; the irregularity of the height of the **internal arches** in the

The Alamein Peal

The ringing of church bells in Britain was forbidden in 1940. If a peal of bells was heard, it could only mean one thing...the Germans had landed, and everyone was to go to their emergency post. Some were rung in the south of the country in September, 1940, for a few people mistook the receipt of 'Cromwell', the warning code, to mean that the landings had started. But, apart from that incident, they remained silent until 1942. Marvellous news suddenly arrived. Montgomery's Eighth Army had successfully beaten the Afrika Korps at El Alamein, and the latter were in full retreat towards the Egyptian border. There had been victories before, but none had been this decisive. It seemed to be the turning point, and Churchill said so in a broadcast. "Now this is not the end," he concluded. "It is not even the beginning of the end...but it is, perhaps, the end of the beginning." He ordered church bells rung throughout the land, but it was the bells of Prestwich church that were broadcast by the BBC, marked by a plaque right of the tower arch inside the church.

church, and the fact that the pillars are not opposite to one another, indicates different dates of building. The whole body of the church seems to have been rebuilt about the beginning of the 16th century. Between 1485 and 1550 the **roof** was raised, and the **clerestory windows** added. There are **nineteen heraldic shields** under the clerestory windows of local families associated with the church. The handsomely carved **ceiling** (now restored and re-gilded) dates from this time, and is probably the work of the craftsmen responsible for the chancel at Manchester Cathedral (Ralph Langley, the Rector of the church in 1493-1495 was also Warden of the Manchester Collegiate Church, the forerunner of the Cathedral). Special note should be made of the **carving on the roof bosses**. They include a **bearded man** at the east end (the original site of the altar) said to be a representation of Langley himself, and a large **'Jack in the Green' or Green Man'**, perhaps a reference to pagan tree worship or the old fertility religion (the church is probably built on an ancient pagan religious site). The **west wall** contains 18th century **tables of the commandments** formerly surrounding the altar, and the **plaque** to the right of the **tower arch** commemorating the 'Alamein Peal' (see infobox). The **stained glass** is mostly Victorian, though the windows in the West Wall near the North Porch are probably 18th century in origin. The fine **18th century candelabra** were "given by the Pilkington side instead of a garland, 1701" (a reference to the old custom of 'rushbearing'). It bears the Derby Crest of the Eagle and Child.

The **chantry chapels** were completed 1530-1550 (a rather late date as chantries were suppressed in the reign of Edward VI). Here priests were maintained to say masses for the souls of the families who built and endowed them. The **Wilton Chapel** on the north side was originally known as "Hyltons Chantre". It later became the property of the Hollands of Heaton, and passed (by marriage) to the Egerton family of Heaton Hall. (Sir Thomas Egerton became Earl of Wilton in1801.) Consequently, the

St Mary's Church, Prestiwch

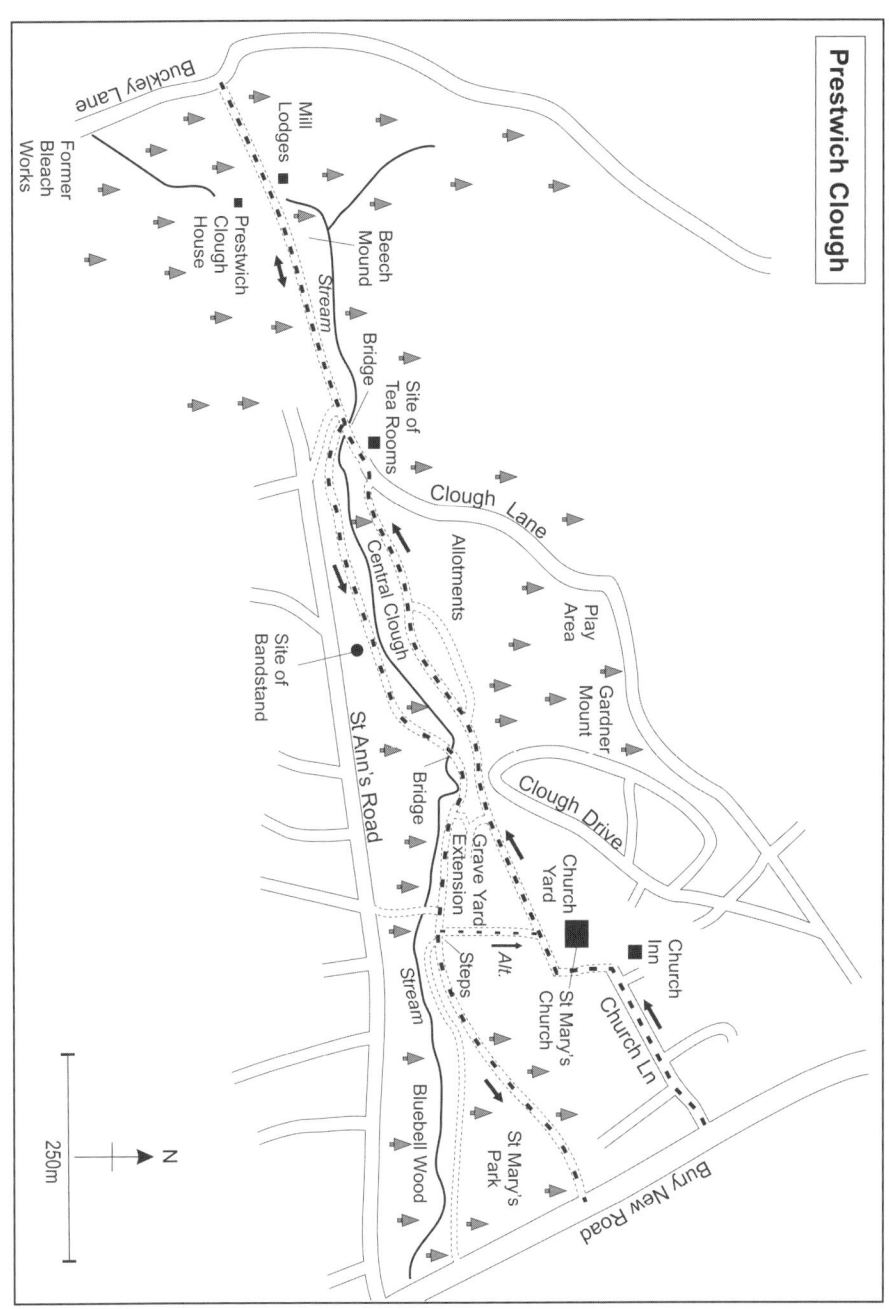

Prestwich Clough

Buckley Lane

Former Bleach Works

Mill Lodges

Beech Mound

Prestwich Clough House

Stream

Bridge

Site of Tea Rooms

Clough Lane

Allotments

Central Clough

Site of Bandstand

St Ann's Road

Bridge

Play Area

Gardner Mount

Clough Drive

Grave Yard Extension

Church Yard

Church Inn

St Mary's Church

Church Ln

Alt.

Steps

Stream

Bluebell Wood

St Mary's Park

Bury New Road

250m

N

69

chapel became the family vault, replete with memorials to the illustrious dead...well, that was the intention, at least. Interments ceased in 1885, as the family began to think of selling up and leaving the area. Unfortunately, during the rebuilding programme of 1888-89 (in connection with the construction of the new chancel) the monuments were removed. In particular, the fine memorial to the first Earl was dismantled, and all that remains is the **black stone sarcophagus** on the north aisle window sill (part of the original inscription has been copied on to it). The marble coat of arms and the memorial stained glass has vanished, but part of the **coiled serpent** (symbolising eternity) was recently discovered. There is, however, a fine marble tablet commemorating **Lord Edward Egerton**, who died in 1743 of smallpox. Its Latin inscription includes a verse adapted from Pope's epitaph on the Duke of Buckingham. Notice, on the south wall of the chapel, the **hatchment** (a heraldic device carried at a funeral), commemorating Mary Margaret, the first wife of the Second Earl, and used at her obsequies in 1858. The chapel is now a **War Memorial Shrine** covering the two great wars of 1914-1918 and 1939-1945. The **centre panel** on the altarpiece depicting the Risen Christ was painted by Professor Tristram. A pre-reformation **aumbry** (a receptacle for mass bread and wine) remains to this day set in the stone of the pillar nearest the altar, preserved behind a glass panel. Pass to the east of the chapel, alongside the **organ**. Directly ahead is a fine **monument commemorating James Lyon** (1783-1836), vicar for fifty years! The work was executed by Seivier in 1836 at a cost of £250. Lyon is shown administering communion to six parishioners.

The present **chancel** (looking rather out of place from the outside) was built in 1889, recognisably designed by Paley & Austin, architects of Lancaster. The **chancel screen and pulpit** date from 1805. The great **East Window** is a memorial to Margaret, Countess of Wilton. Note the fine **reredos** behind the **altar**; it commemorates Henry Arthur Drinkwater, aged eight, who died of scarlet fever in 1863. 'Et in arcadia, ego.' His father, Canon Henry Mildred Birch had been tutor to Edward, Prince of Wales, and was appointed Rector of Prestwich at the behest of Queen Victoria herself.

The **Lever Chapel** on the south side of the nave was originally a chantry chapel containing an Altar dedicated to St. Margaret. It was probably founded by Agnes Langley, and is described as 'new' in the will of Robert Langley, dated 1524. The Langleys were patrons of the living from 1400 to the mid 16th century, and provided an unbroken line of Rectors until 1632. Their family seat was Agecroft Hall (see p289). The chapel passed into the hands of the Lever family of Alkrington Hall in 1630. It has been twice re-built, first in 1731 (**date stone** in west wall), and again in 1874, by Canon Birch. During the course of alterations in 1932, the burial vaults were disturbed. In consequence, a number of burnished **coffin plates** are now affixed to the wall on the left. The oldest is inscribed "Sir Darcy Lever Knight and Doctor of Law Departed this life August 12 1742 In the 39th Year of his Age." His son, Sir Ashton Lever, squandered a large part of the family fortune. (See information box)

There is a rather worn **memorial tablet** on the south wall of the chapel to the Reverend William Assheton, Rector of Prestwich 1685-1731. The **Birch Chapel**, to the right of the chancel, dates from 1875, and now forms a kind of sub-chancel area to the Lever Chapel.

It is well worth taking out some time to explore the **churchyard**, particularly the south side, from which there is a fine view. The **oldest gravestone** lies at the south-east corner of the Church, bearing the date 1641 and naming the children of Thomas Collier. The **grandest tomb** is easily visible in the south-west corner. It commemorates

The Collector

Many gentlemen in the 18th century had a 'cabinet of curiosities'. The contents, usually including fossils, specimens of flora and fauna, minerals, coins and medals, and perhaps small antiquities, reflected the age of enlightenment. Sir Ashton Lever was no different. He was a rich man, receiving the rental of large estates, residing at Alkrington Hall, and owning a town house in the midst of gardens and orchards at the foot of what is now Market Street in Manchester. However, the collecting mania got the better of him, and probably devoured a large part of his inheritance. A visitor in 1773 described a collection requiring 1,300 glass cases in three rooms. It attracted large numbers of local visitors (3,320 on one 'opening day'), so Sir Ashton decided recoup his losses by taking it to London. Unfortunately, it proved to be one attraction among many, and he was reduced to disposing of it by lottery. Even this failed, and the insolvent gentleman committed suicide at the Bull's Head, Manchester Market Place, in 1788. His landed estate in Manchester had been previously sold to a property speculator, who lost no time in dividing it up into building plots. Amongst other things, his demise turned Piccadilly into a fashionable residential area...with a street named after him!

John Brooks, a mill owner and Secretary to the Anti-Corn Law League. Life-size Sicilian **marble figures** representing Charity, Commerce, Integrity, and Industry are set into niches in an open-sided mausoleum with a pedimented top, the work of John Thomas of Paddington. The statue of Charity was exhibited at the Great Exhibition in 1851.

Take the **path** to the left-hand side of the main churchyard entrance, which leads into **Prestwich Clough**. Medieval Lancashire was largely composed of forest, but the word meant something different then. It applied to vast tracts of waste land and moss, interspersed with wooded areas, where the 'forest laws' applied. It was populated by scattered settlements surrounded by islands of cultivation. The 'forest' was used primarily for hunting, but it also provided rough pasture for swine and wood in the form of building timber and fuel. Some tracts of the ancient woodland remain, and Prestwich Clough is reckoned by some to be one of these survivors. The woodland is concentrated in the valley of a stream (the 'clough'), and originally extended as far as the Irwell. By the end of the 19th century, it seemed likely to disappear entirely, and the central part was purchased by the old Prestwich Urban District Council in 1904. It opened to the public in 1906 and more land has been added since then. A long term tree planting programme reversed the decline and produced the landscape that we see today, and Prestwich's most delightful secret.

Continue along the **path**, which curves to the right below the **old churchyard wall**. A sylvan **extension to the burial ground** falls away to the left in the direction of the Clough. We pass the

The Prestwich Naturalists

Prestwich Clough attracted amateur naturalists long before the railway arrived and before the area became a public park. But these men were not middle class idlers with time on their hands. Instead, they were ordinary working men who liked nothing better than to discuss their expeditions over a pint in a local pub (see p66). Typical of these was Richard Buxton (1786-1865), a shoemaker who taught himself to read at the age of sixteen. He compiled 'Flora Mancuniensis' (1840) and published 'A botanical guide to the flowering plants, ferns, mosses and algae found indigenous within sixteen miles of Manchester' (1849). He is buried in the churchyard.

southern gate to the churchyard (usually locked, see below), and the straightened pathway now begins its descent towards the valley bottom. It passes the end of **Clough Drive**, on the right, and there is a **fine view** over the Clough to the left. We continue directly ahead to where the **pathways fork**, following the **left-hand path**. This meanders above the Clough, offering **good views of the wooded stream** through the continuous wooden fence on the left. Look out for the **carved sculpture** to the right, a rugged face suggesting the spirit of the woods. The path descends to the **site of long-vanished tea rooms** on the right, just before the **bridge** across the stream; the Clough was a popular venue at weekends and on bank holidays. Follow the path all the way down to **Buckley Lane**, passing the **beech mound** on the right and the **remains of Prestwich Clough House** to the left. The latter was occupied by the owners of a long vanished **bleach works**, evidenced in the rubble directly ahead to the right of the path. We can exit on to the **main** road, but it is better to retrace your footsteps to where **the paths fork**, just before the **bridge**. From here, the **right-hand path** runs through the **Central Clough** where the poplars, beeches, and horse chestnuts date from the 1904 replanting, and the **stream** trickles to the left. Further on is the **site of the bandstand** near an **oak tree**, with a circular bench round its trunk. The pathway **crosses the stream**, and reaches a **flight of steps** to the left. There are two possibilities here. After **ascending the steps**, continue up the **cobbled path** through the picturesque **churchyard extension** to arrive opposite the **south churchyard gate** (see above). However, the other option is more rewarding. Continue follow the **track that runs beside the stream**, now on the right, through the

Prestwich Clough

Clough below **St. Mary's Flower Park**. The lucky visitor in May will see a carpet of bluebells beneath a canopy of oak. The pathway eventually leads (by curving to the left) directly to **Saint Mary's Park**, from which there is an exit back on to the main road to Prestwich Village and the Metrolink station

Prestwich to Radcliffe

The tram leaves Prestwich Station and continues along an elevated position, passing over **Poppythorne Lane**, **Fairfax Road** and **Willow Road**. There are some good views of the **Pennine Hills** on the right before it enters upon a long and rather unusual modern **concrete bridge**. Formed of an inverted 'T' section, it spans not only the original roadway but the **M60 motorway**; there are two bridges on top of each other! **Besses o'th' Barn Station** is soon reached. This area was open country (apart from development along the main road) until as late as the 1920s. Then the estates of semi-detached houses were built, but the old name for the district survived into the modern era because people associated it with the famous local brass band, formed in 1818.

The London, Midland, and Scottish Railway opened the station in 1933 to cater for this new source of traffic. The station is placed on an **embankment**,

Who Was Bessy?

'Bessy' was a Lancashire lass who once kept the tollgate on the turnpike road here. In Lancashire, at that time, people did not use surnames. Men and women would be given a name to indicate family ("Bill o' Jacks"), circumstance ("John o' God's Sending"), or occupation ("Billy Suet"). In this case it was the latter. But why not call her "Besses o'th' Road?" To the German weavers who had settled in the locality, it was "Bessy of the Bahn (road)," which the Lancashire people soon corrupted into "Besses o'th' Barn!"

with a view of **Bury Old Road** to the left, and has an unusual (for this line) **island platform**. The **original buildings** partly survive. **Stairs**, with a **lift** to the rear, access a

The Besses o'th' Barn rail bridge, crossing a roadway and motorway

subway, which exits on to the main entrance on **Bury Old Road**. A **footpath**, from the opposite side of the **subway**, leads to **Thatch Leach Lane**.

It is worthwhile to turn left out of the main entrance, and wander under the **Metrolink Bridge** to stand on the **road bridge** over the **motorway**. A short distance further, along **Bury Old Road** on the left, are a number of **shops**. *Books 4u* (open daily in the morning) is a mecca for second hand books and comics. The *Locoshed* is an Aladdin's cave of every kind of model, in addition to model railways, and is highly recommended (open Tuesday to Saturday).

The line crosses **Thatch Leach Lane**. To accommodate the splayed track approach to the island platform, to bridge was widened. The **outward track** crosses the original **stone arch**, but the **inward track** is supported by a 1930s **girder bridge** extension. **Victoria Lane** (near to **Victoria Park** on the left), is an **occupation bridge** over a path to the park, and **Westminster Avenue** is crossed, before passing under **Moss Lane** and entering a shallow cutting in which **Whitefield Station** is located.

The original Lancashire and Yorkshire **entrance building** survives at street level (including a **shop**) linking the **platforms** by **steps**, but Metrolink have added a pedestrian **ramp** to the **Bury platform**, accessing (by doubling back) the cobbled former road at the back of the *Natwest Bank*. There is also an entrance to the **Manchester platform** from the **bus interchange** and **car park** to the right. This was the **former goods yard**, and is linked to **Stanley Road**, exiting by the side of the pretty **Whitefield Park**, gifted in 1890 by Alfred Grundy. (Turn left to reach the **station frontage** and **Bury New Road**.) Upon their acquisition of Heaton Park, Manchester Corporation constructed a reservoir on part of their new property. Consequently, an industrial light railway was formed from the goods yard to the reservoir site (utilising a tank engine called the 'Admiral Togo'!), the goods yard being used as exchange sidings for trainloads of puddle clay. The work was interrupted by the First World War, and only completed in the 1920s. The course of the line is now covered with housing.

The name 'Whitefield' is said to be derived from the Flemish weavers who used to lay out their fabrics to bleach in the sun (a process known as tentering). After the battle of Bosworth Field (see p90) most of Whitefeld passed into the hands of the Earls of Derby, who were largely absentee landlords. It remained a village until the 19th century, when Manchester merchants and businessmen settled in the area, a process accelerated by the opening of the railway. It is now, like Prestwich, a dormitory suburb of Manchester. It was the boyhood home of Robert Clive, the conqueror of India.

Leave the station, turn left, and walk to **Bury New Road**. It is worth making a short detour to the right, along the side of *Morrison's* supermarket facing the main road, to examine the aluminium **sculptured panels**. One depicts the famous Besses band (p73), framed by local buildings, including All Saints Church. The other shows the washer women in a 'white field' by a steam laundry, and other local trades. Retrace your steps. The **former bank** (now *Povada*, an Itialian restaurant), to the right on the corner of Church Lane, is a fine essay in brick with a stepped Dutch style gable (Maxwell and Tuke, c.1880-83, for the Bury Banking Company). Cross the road and turn left. The *National Westminster Bank*, opposite, is a grandiose single story stone faced structure with a fine dome, dating from the 1930s. A little further along, to the right, is the fine expanse of **Hamilton Road Park**. It was gifted to Whitefield by Alfred Grundy in 1890 (with a covenant that no public meetings be held in it!). Adjacent is the driveway entrance to **Uplands**, one of Whitefield's grandest houses, though much altered. It is now a health centre. We have now reached *Slattery's*, one of the sights of Whitefield; indeed many visit the place purely to patronise this establishment. The business was started in 1967, and moved into expanded premises in the former one hundred year old 'Mason's Arms' in 2004. After being agreeably detained by the windows, most people are attracted inside. To the left is a wedding cake showroom, with a chocolatier and patissier opposite. There is an elegant dining room and function rooms upstairs (complete with grand piano). Continue and turn right into **Pinfold Lane**, taking time out to admire some of the fine houses. The **library**, on the left, contains part of an **old 15th century oak window frame**, all that remains of Stand Hall. This was a seat of the Pilkington family, and the last surviving portion was demolished in 1966. At the top of the lane, the way leads right along **Higher Lane** past the **cricket ground** to the junction with **Ringley Road** and **Church Lane**. A left turn along the former leads to **Stand** itself. The principal attraction here is the **Unitarian Chapel** to the right of **Ringley Road** (Telephone 0161 766 8036 to arrange admission.) The original chapel was built in 1693 but was destroyed in the 'Christmas Blitz' of December, 1940. It was rebuilt (incorporating some artefacts from the original building) in a pleasing 'New England' style. Stand Grammar School, founded in 1688, used the chapel in its early years. It was attended at this time by Robert Clive, whose mother came from the area. He probably stayed with his uncle at Clifton Hall. Although the celebrated incident of him climbing a church tower is associated with Market Drayton, some locals insist that it was Stand Chapel belfry! Back at the road junction, there are two objects of interest. On one corner is the **War Memorial** (c.1920), with a bronze figure of victory. The opposite corner, between Church Lane and Dales Lane, is the location of **Stand Rectory**. The original 18th century farmhouse was remodelled around 1830 in the Regency style. Walk along **Church Lane** to arrive at **All Saints Church**.

All Saints' Church is one of the many "Waterloo" churches built as an expression of national thanks for victory at the battle of Waterloo in 1815.However, the one million pounds set aside in 1818, was part of the Government's strategy to counteract the possibility of political unrest sparked by the industrial revolution, culminating in the "Peterloo" massacre in Manchester in 1819.The decision to build at Stand, an open pastoral area at the time, was considered necessary to divide the enormous parish of St. Mary's Prestwich, as the local population was growing year by year. Sir John Soane, a distinguished London architect, was approached in 1821 to prepare designs for the church to cost no more than £12,000 and seating some 1,800 people. This he found to be impractical and was passed to the young Charles Barry (who later designed the Houses of Parliament) and the cost limit increased to £20,000. The site was given by the Earl of Derby, and the foundation stone was laid by the Earl of Wilton on the 3 August 1821. The Bishop of Chester consecrated the church for worship on the 8 September, 1826. The **tower** is 186 feet (57 m) in height, and is a prominent object for miles around (see p117). It terminates in an extended **open-arched porch**. Although built in the reign of George IV, whose **coat of arms** is set on the front of the west gallery, the design is based on the 15th century Perpendicular style, slender in construction and crowned by the timber, lath and plaster vaults over the Nave, Aisles and Chancel. Side **galleries** are an important feature of the design as they brace the slender columns supporting the vaults and outer roofs. The re-modelled **east end** dates from 1919. (The church is usually open Monday, Wednesday, and Friday,11am-1pm, and, by arrangement, Saturday 10am-12 noon; telephone 0161 766 2619.) The church forms the centrepiece of the **All Saints conservation area**, designated by the local council in March 2004. Continue down **Church Lane** to arrive back at the station.

All Saints, Stand

The line now passes through a **tunnel** (153 yards) and along a long and **deep cutting**, spanned by **over bridges**, and descending towards the valley of the Irwell. The **bridges** are, in sequence, **Dales Lane, Leicester Road, occupation bridges** leading to a works to the left of the line, and **Radcliffe New Road**. Both the tunnel and the cutting were excavated through treacherous running sand. As a result, the tunnel was provided with an invert (a floor at the base of the walls) and there are **retaining walls** at the foot of the cutting sides. The land falls away so dramatically that the tram runs directly onto an **impressive brick viaduct**, which crosses **Milltown Street**, and the **Irwell**. The **view** is rather fine. The remains of **Pioneer Mill** on the right are all that is left of what was once a forest of chimneys. (Although best spotted on the return journey, see if you can catch a glimpse of the **smallholding** at the south east corner of the viaduct, with its pond, geese, and chickens.) Notice the winding **River Irwell**, and the view towards the modern centre of Radcliffe to the left, with **St. Thomas's Church**.

After crossing **Church Street West**, we now arrive at **Radcliffe Station**. The station, the last original one on this line, once served a junction with four platforms, called 'Radcliffe (Central)' to distinguish it from the other stations in the town. (Radcliffe had no fewer than five stations within its old boundaries, perhaps something of a record!) It is on an embankment, and accessed by **steps** from a **subway**, but little of the original station remains, and that mostly dates from the 1950s (the station was rebuilt after a fire). The **former branch** ran off from the left, crossing the road and passing under the line from Clifton Junction on the Bolton line. Little is left at this point, except for an **abutment** of the road bridge. This branch made a junction with the Bury to Bolton line at Bradley Fold, and was used by a local service between Radcliffe and Bolton known as the 'Dollytub Express'! Exit by means of the **subway** into the **car park** adjacent to **Spring Lane**, part of which was once the approach to the vanished goods yard. A **ramp** from the **Manchester platform**, in addition to the original **stairs**, also accesses the subway. Another, from the **Bury platform** (with a glimpse of the **remains of the former Bolton platform**), accesses the car park. There is also a **ramped path** from the latter, leading to **Church Street West**.

Radcliffe

The name Radcliffe is derived from the Old English words *read* and *clif* meaning "the red cliff or bank", on the River Irwell in the Irwell Valley. The manor belonged to the Pilkington family, who lost it in 1485 after the death of Richard III. By the 18th century, much of the area was part of the estate of the Earl of Wilton. Unlike Prestwich and Whitefield, Radcliffe evolved into an industrial town in the course of the 19th century. At one time it was home to around sixty textile mills and fifteen spinning mills, along with eighteen bleach works. However, the textile industry was not the town's only employer; other industries such as mining and paper making were also important sources of employment. Nearly all of this industry has disappeared, and the town is now more important as a residential satellite to Manchester. Much of the new housing is built on former 'brownfield' sites.

Leave the station and turn right, walking under the **railway bridge** and down **Spring Lane** past the **Memorial Gardens**. This soon becomes **Cross Lane**, which is followed beyond the bend in the road at the junction with **Eton Hill Road**. Look out for **Tithebarn Street** on the right, opposite the **Methodist Church**. The street is named after an easily missed relic of old Radcliffe, for you are now in the old village centre. Here may be found the remains of a 17th century **Tithe Barn**, a single storey stone building of three bays with a wide door and other smaller openings on the gable end. With the exception of a few modifications, the barn has remained largely unaltered since its construction. It is of a single build using composite walling materials and is constructed with an inner and outer leaf or skin with in-fill between, random rubble coursing being common to both skins. This type of construction is common in the Pennine foothills between 1600 and 1720, and these dates have been suggested for the construction of the tithe barn due to the lack of documentary sources. Radcliffe rectory had twenty-four acres of glebe (church) land in the 17th century, but the clergyman was also entitled to an annual 'tithe' (a 'tithe' or tenth of one's income was supposed to be given by parishioners to the church, but this became a valuation of personal income, delivered in the form of agricultural produce, stored in such barns). In 1838, the tithe in Radcliffe was fixed at an annual income of £153 for the Rector. Walk to the parallel **Sandford Street**, turn right, and you will see **Radcliffe Tower** directly ahead. (Enter by one of the two **pedestrian entrances**, to the left of the **barrier**. The tower is situated in an open site, with no restriction on admission.)

Radcliffe Tower is the only surviving part of a medieval manor house, and thus a Grade I listed building and a scheduled monument. Technically, this is a Pele Tower, a strong place of refuge against (usually Scottish) incursions. They are common on the borders but unusual in this part of the world. Like that of the church, the position of

Radcliffe Tower...the only medieval fortification in Greater Manchester

Radcliffe Tower is easily defended, being built in the centre of a bend of the River Irwell. The ground within the bend is flat and low-lying, but the river itself, being on three sides of the house at a distance of only about a quarter of a mile, would afford sufficient protection (the remains of a moat have also been found in a modern excavation). The present stone-built tower probably results from a rebuilding of the house in 1403 by James de Radcliffe, who was lord of the manor. De Radcliffe was given a licence from the king to fortify the site including adding crenellations and battlements, and included a stone-built hall and one or two towers, probably using ashlar stone blocks. It is difficult to reconcile the provisions of the licence with the existing remains, as it seems clear that there was no stone hall (though a contemporary timber building was constructed). It is doubtful whether the second tower was ever built. The former great hall has left its **roof-line** on the ruined tower, and occupied the east part of the main block. According to a 19th century description (when it was still standing and used as a farmhouse), the hall was over forty feet in length, and nearly thirty feet in width. It had an open-timbered roof supported by two massive trusses, which are described as "the most curious specimens of carved oak work I have ever seen." The status of the original manor house declined when the manorial estate was sold in the 16th century. It was even used as a prison, for in 1592 the Earl of Derby sent certain widows, who were catholic recusants, to the tower. This half-timbered wing was demolished in the 19th century, and the tower itself was left to decay. The remains are owned by Bury council, and sited rather incongruously amidst modern housing. As you gaze at it, remember that this is the only **medieval stone fortification** in the Greater Manchester, but (as Michael Caine would say) "not a lot of people know that!"

The remaining stone tower is fifty feet in length and twenty-eight feet in width. The walls are five feet thick all round above the **plinth**, which has a projection of twelve inches. The tower was probably of two stories, with an embattled parapet; but the upper part has now almost entirely disappeared, and only portions of the walls above the level of the first floor are still in situ. The **lower room of the tower** was originally covered by a semicircular **barrel vault**, the **springing** of which may still be seen. Some portion of this vault was standing as late as 1844, when Samuel Bamford (p186), who visited the tower in that year, described it as hanging by a single stone, and "unless it be protected from further wanton outrage must soon share the fate of the hall." The spring of the vault is about five feet from the ground, which would make the height of the apartment about fifteen feet. It was lit at each end by a **window** high up in the wall, and on the **east side** by **two smaller windows** nearer the ground. The **entrance** on the west side is through a **pointed doorway**, four feet wide. The chief feature of this lower room of the tower, however, consists of **three large arched openings** (for fireplaces) about ten feet in width, one at **each end** and the other in the **middle of the east wall** opposite the entrance. They have an inner and outer arch, from the centre of which a **square flue** is carried up in the thickness of the wall. That at the **north end** of the room is still in its **original state**, but the other two have been cut out into **open archways** (that on the south side formed the principal entrance to the tower, when used for farm storage in the 19th century). The presence of three such fireplaces in so comparatively small an apartment would at first sight suggest that the room had been used as a kitchen, but this is unlikely if the tower were used as the part of the house allotted to the family. The **room above** was approached by a **stone staircase** in the thickness of the wall at the south end of the west wall, leading out of the great hall at a height of over seven feet. The **steps are still in position**, along with the sill of a small **two-light**

'Fair Ellen'

The tower is forever associated with the legend of Fair Ellen, the lovely daughter of 'Sir William de Radcliffe'. His first wife had died giving birth to her, but he had married again. The haughty stepmother, Lady Isabella, became insanely jealous of Ellen, and plotted a bizarre revenge. One day, when Sir William had gone hunting, she told her to go to the cook and bid him "dress the white doe for dinner." He told her that she was the white doe that he must kill. In vain she and the scullion boy pleaded for her life, for the deed was soon done.

> *"O then cried out the scullion-boye,*
> *As loud as loud might be –*
> *O, save her life good master-cook,*
> *And make your pyes of mee!"*

Her body was then cut up and made into a pie! When her father returned, he called for his daughter in vain. Lady Isabella said that she had gone into a nunnery, but the brave scullion boy told him the truth. The stepmother was burnt at the stake, the cook boiled alive, and the scullion boy became the heir to all Sir William's possessions! The story is enshrined in 'Lady Isabella's Tragedy', a ballad in the Percy Collection.

window which lit the landing at their head. There is an ordinary **fireplace opening** on the first floor, in the centre of the west wall.

The **pathway** to the left of the tower entrance leads to a gate into the **churchyard**. However, retrace your footsteps down **Sandford Street** to **Cross Lane** and turn right. A little further along, we come to the fenced off **Church Green**, on the right. Turn down the **path** to the right of it, and you will see the **Parish Church** directly ahead. Enter the churchyard by the **Lych Gate**, dating from 1922, and a thank offering for those parishioners who returned safely from the war.

Radcliffe constituted part of the Royal Manor of Salford in Saxon times, and it is reasonable to assume that a church existed at an early date. Some time prior to 1190, William de Radcliffe (formerly known as Fitz Gilbert de Tablois, of a Norman family) built or rebuilt a church close to the manor house. He founded a chantry for Cecelia Montbegon, his wife, in it. A document of 1202 mentions the right of advowson (to appoint the priest). The original church may have been a rectangular 12th century structure, covering the present area of the nave, with a small square ended chancel. The church was rebuilt from the 14th century onwards. The **sandstone exterior**, as a consequence of rebuilding in the 19th century, is largely modern, but the church still preserves its ancient ambience. The greater part of the **tower** is authentic and was rebuilt in 1665 (using the original stones) by Charles Beswick, Rector, Sir Ralph Assheton (Patron) and Mr. Edward Radcliffe, and has a rather stumpy appearance. Over the **west door** may be seen an **ornamental panel** with the date 1665, the arms of the Beswick family and an inscription "Rector Carolus Beswicke." The **north side** has a stone inscribed "Edward Ratcliffe 1665", and the **south side** has the arms of Sir Ralph Assheton. Some details of the **original medieval tower** were preserved, and these include the **outer doorway to the turret** (now sealed up), the **battlemented parapet**, and the **tracery of the window of the west wall**. The clock has faces on the north and west sides. The original was installed in 1785, at a cost of forty guineas. The current mechanism and glass faces date from1908, but one of the original **square stone faces** is set into the pavement outside the **vestry door**. Three **bells** existed in 1552. The present **peal of eight bells** were recast and re-hung in 1923, as a memorial to the war dead. The church has a very active and professional team of bell ringers.

The church is usually entered by the **West Door** under the tower. This was opened through in the 19th century, and its present appearance dates from 1903. (The church is usually closed; ring 0161 724 7879 to enquire about admission.) Notice the **war memorial** (1918) on the north wall and the **list of rectors**. Having entered the **nave**, turn back and look up. Notice the lower part of the (glass fronted) **bell ringers' chamber**, with the bell ropes looped and tied. The **arch in the east wall of the tower** is similar to the chancel arch as it appeared before restoration in 1903, and is possibly 15th century in origin.

The **Nave** is perhaps the oldest complete section of the church. It is separated from the aisles by **two arched arcades** in the 'decorated' style of architecture. They probably belong to the early 15th century, when James de Radliffe (a prolific builder, responsible for Radcliffe Tower) was Lord of the Manor. He probably never saw the Church and Tower completed, as he died in 1408. The arcades support a later **clerestory**, designed to increase the degree of light through twelve widows. It owes its present appearance to a restoration of 1856. The **nave roof** is modern (1870), but quite spectacular. It is supported by four **crossbeams**, each resting on **corbels** projecting from the clerestory walls. At each corbel is a **carved statue** depicting the progress of biblical prophecy of

The approach to Radcliffe Parish Church

the Messiah: from the tower end they are Moses, Isaiah, Jeremiah, and Malachi (south side), and Samuel, Ezekiel, Daniel, and John the Baptist (north side). The **centre of each beam** is marked by a carved octagonal **roof boss**. The most westerly depicts a **sailing ship** (perhaps a reference to the arms of Manchester); then there follows a dove (symbolising the Holy Spirit); the Five Wounds of the crucifixion; and a Hand raised in blessing. On each side (except the most westerly boss, which is flush with the tower wall) is a **winged angel**.

At the west end of the nave, below the tower arch, are two interesting **Churchwarden's Pews**. That on the **south side** contains **panels** from what was probably a 16th/17th century pulpit, one of which is dated 1606. There are the **arms** (a pierced mullet) and **crest** (a boar's head) of the Assheton family; the **arms of the Radcliffe family**; and the **initials** of Leonard Shaw (appointed Rector, 1583/4) and Robert Walkden (appointed Rector, 1624). The back of the **north side** pew is part of Charles Beswicke's furniture, and it contains a **quotation**…"All my Words that I shall speake unto Thee, receive unto Thine Hearte and heare with Thine Eare." Notice the (possibly 13th century) **eastern wall above the chancel arch**. There is evidence here of a former high-pitched roof which predates the clerestory. The two (worn) **inscribed flagstones** are replicas of the originals, which once marked grave sites in the interior of the church (all the remains are now exhumed). The existing **pulpit** dates from 1903, with a **dedication tablet** on the north wall, above it, to the dead of the Great War. However, most eyes will be drawn to the **portrait of Charles Beswicke**. He was Rector from 1662 to 1697, when he died in harness, and was responsible for rebuilding the tower. The glass in the **west windows** is the most recent, depicting 'The Good Samaritan' (1955) and the 'Good Shepherd' (1960).

The **South Aisle** was largely rebuilt in 1872, and the resulting widening virtually effaced the **South Transept**, with which the south wall is now flush. The original entrance to the church also disappeared, though the **font** (1858) marks its site. The **glass** was donated by the Grundy family in 1856. The **South Transept** is now a virtual extension of the aisle, but remains distinct. It was probably once a chantry chapel (where a priest said masses for the souls of the dead) and the **south wall** is probably 15th century in date, along with the surviving **piscina** (for washing the sacred vessels). The **window glass** of the Nativity (1907) was designed by Kempe. The transept leads through to the **Memorial Chapel** dating from the rebuilding in the 1860's and 1870s. The **east windows** depict St. Peter and St. Paul and St. Agnes. The **south wall** has a **sealed door** and its **eastern window** is a representation of the 'Good Samaritan' and the 'Publican and Sinner at Prayer'. Note the **glass in its tracery**; this is the **oldest glass in the church**, and is thought to show Henry IV (who gave James permission to fortify his manor house). The **other window** shows 'Children Coming to Christ' a memorial to a local headmaster. The chapel was converted into a memorial to the dead of World War Two, and was dedicated in 1954.

The main **chancel arch** is reputed to be the **oldest part of the church**, and is perhaps 13th century in origin, though much restored. However, the **small wooden door** by the **prayer desk** accesses the **original base of the south pier**. The **mouldings** on the face of both arch and responds terminate in **modern sculptured heads**. The two heads on the **Nave side** of the arch are (above the pulpit) the Fifth Earl of Wilton (then Patron of the church) and (above the lectern) Adam Crompton Bealey, a local employer and benefactor. The heads on the **south wall** are (next to the chancel arch) the Reverend H.M. Johnson (the curate in 1903), and (above the sanctuary rail) the Reverend Canon Swinburne (the Rector in 1903). Those on the **north wall** are (next to the chancel arch) Archdeacon Price and (above the sanctuary rail) Bishop Knox of Manchester. The chancel was completely rebuilt in 1817, but the **east window tracery** may be original. The present appearance results from the 1903 restoration. The **glass** in the window dates from 1911. Behind the altar is a **worn alabaster slab** (shown if politely requested), said by tradition to mark the resting place of James Radcliffe, the builder of Radcliffe Tower, but probably that of his grandson. The figure of a knight, his lady, and the heads of their children can still be traced.

Retrace your footsteps and proceed to the **north side** of the church. The **North Aisle** was altered and rebuilt in 1870. The stained glass in the **west window** depicts the Resurrection, and that of the **north window** St. Anne, Mary (Martha's sister) and Dorcas's good works in Acts (a memorial to Anne Starkie of Huntroyde, who paid for much of the 19th century alterations). The **North Transept** is modern, but the **three lighted window** may be original. It shows the anointing of Christ's feet. The **Vestry** has been converted into a communal area for the congregation.

Upon leaving the **churchyard**, make a detour to the adjacent **Close Park**, if only to examine **'James and the Ball of Fire'** a recent dinosaur sculpture! There are other sculptures in the park.

The rest of Radcliffe is something of an anti-climax, but still worth exploring if you have the time. Turn left out of the station along **Spring Lane** past the remains of the railway bridge (see p77) to the right, the **bridge abutment** now reduced to a low stone wall. This road leads to a junction with **Water Street**, marked by the fine **Edwardian former town hall** (1911) on the right-hand corner. This is a lavish piece of municipal pride, built of brick and stone in a vaguely baroque style, with domed corner towers and a pillared entrance portico with a curved pediment and wrought iron balcony. **Water Street** leads, to the right, to a section of the **Manchester, Bolton, and Bury Canal** (see p83) that is still 'in water'. The rather fine **Cenotaph**, on the left-hand corner, opposite the town hall, was dedicated in 1922. The bronze

A dinosaur in Close Park!

sculptured figures repay inspection. Turn left, and walk down **Blackburn Street**, passing straight on at the road junction where the **Pilkington Way** by-pass diverges. **St. Thomas's Church**, set back in a grassed over churchyard on the left, is a conspicuous (and impressive) landmark in fashionable Victorian neo-gothic. The first stone was laid in 1862, but it was not consecrated until 1864. Even then, it was not completed, and a tower was added at a later date. Blackburn Street now descends towards the river. **Railway Street**, to the right, once led to Radcliffe Bridge Station. It was opened by the old East Lancashire Railway (see p93) in 1846, and had two platforms with a siding on the west side of the tracks (the station building was on the east platform). It officially closed in 1959, and no trace now remains due to the construction of Pilkington Way, which cuts through the line of the railway. We now reach a charming modern **civic square**, complete with an elegant **clock tower** and **pavilion**. The **market** is situated to the right (open Tuesday, Friday and Saturday, 9-5). The small modern **market hall** contains a variety of stalls and a (recommended) café. **Radcliffe Bridge**, spanning the **River Irwell**, is directly ahead. It is located on the old packhorse route from Manchester to Blackburn (hence the street name), and the original bridge was probably medieval in origin (there are accounts for its repair from 1652 onwards). The **present bridge**, a two arched stone structure, dates from the 19th century. Note the pretty **cast iron lamps**. Beyond the bridge may be found the fine neo-classical **Bridge Methodist Church** (in Milltown Street on the left) and **Radcliffe Library**, built with the aid of the Carnegie Foundation in 1907.

Radcliffe to Bury

The tram departs **Radcliffe Station** by crossing **Spring Lane** on the last leg of this Metrolink journey. The school to the left is on the site of a former goods yard, and is situated in the angle of the Metrolink line and the former line from Clifton Junction (on the Manchester and Bolton line) which joined this line by a **junction** further on. There was also another junction at this point, a Bury facing curve that connected with the branch to Bradley Fold (see p77). Traces of this survived until the Metrolink conversion, as a section of track was used as a negative return feed from the third rail line to an adjacent substation. We are now travelling on a section of the former East Lancashire Railway, which opened in 1846 (see p93). The line passes under **Withins Lane**, the site of an original East Lancashire railway station (replaced when Radcliffe Central opened). Directly ahead is the first sight of **Holcombe Hill** and the **Peel Monument** on top of it (see p103). We pass over **Hagside Crossing** and cross the River Irwell at **Hagside Bridge**. Notice the **embankments** to the left. These contain Elton Reservoir, which fed the water supply to the **Manchester, Bolton, Bury Canal**. There is a long-term project to restore this waterway to navigation by pleasure craft. Look out for the track trailing away to the left. This was the original course of the line, but it now forms a connection to the **Buckley Wells Yard** of the **present East Lancashire Railway** (see p98). As the tram descends into a cutting you may spot items of rolling stock and parts of steam locomotives awaiting restoration. Some days, particularly at weekends in the morning, you may see columns of smoke from locomotives preparing for the day's work. The tram is now travelling on the former 'Loco Curve' (see p116) that connected the Manchester-Bury line with the Rochdale-Bolton line, passing under **Manchester Old Road** and **Manchester Road**. It was formerly used by light engines passing to and from Bury locomotive shed (situated on the former line) and special train workings, such as Yorkshire-North Wales excursions avoiding the centre of Manchester. It was partly reopened to give access to the new Bury Interchange station in 1980. We **diverge from the original route** about half way along to proceed directly ahead across the Rochdale-Bolton line at a right-angle (the excavated spoil from this section was used to backfill the part of the old curve that was not needed). At the time, only a few coal trains used the Castleton-Bury section of the old Rochdale-Bolton line, so a flat crossing sufficed. The advent of Metrolink with its increased frequencies fortunately coincided with the demise of the coal traffic. The consequent reopening of the East Lancashire Railway to Heywood (see p95) necessitated the construction of the present handsome **over bridge** with its plaque.

We now arrive at **Bury Interchange**. The terminal station was opened by British Rail in 1980 as part of a complex that included a new bus station in order to promote interchange facilities between the two modes of transport. Situated in a cutting, partly under a road bridge, it consists of an **island platform** accessed by **stairs**, an **escalator**, and a **lift**. A **waiting room** was provided, but the tram frequency resulted in its removal. The trams access the two platforms by means of a **scissors crossover**. A tiled **concourse** connects with the **bus station** (which is provided with a **travel centre**, **café** and **shop**).

Bury

The name Bury, (also earlier known as "Buri" and "Byri") comes from a Saxon word meaning "castle", "stronghold" or "fort", an early form of modern English borough. The manor originally belonged to the Pilkington family, but passed in 1485 to the Stanleys, Earls of Derby (see p90). At one time, they owned most of the land in the town. Bury was transformed from a small market town by the industrial revolution. Textiles, engineering, paper making, and coal mining constituted the principal industries. In the postwar world, the traditional industries declined, and have been replaced by retail developments, service industries, and the growth of residential estates. The famous market attracts large numbers of visitors.

The first sight that greets our eyes beyond the **bus station** is **Kay Gardens**, its triangular site reflecting a former 19th century market hall. In the centre is a **monument to John Kay**, the inventor of the 'flying shuttle', and one of Bury's famous sons. Broadcloth was a fabric wider than the width of a man's hand, requiring two weavers to pass the shuttle from side to side. Kay's automatic shuttle enabled one man to weave it, accelerating the pace; "a speed which cannot be imagined, so great that the shuttle can only be seen like a tiny cloud which disappears the same instant." The impressive

Bury Black Puddings

Bury and black puddings are synonymous. They are generally sold in the form of a sausage, their black casing containing a mix of pig's blood (these days more likely from another source), pig fat, cereal, plenty of salt, onion, and flavourings. The herbs used vary from one maker's well-guarded recipe to another, but in a Bury black pudding you are likely to find pennyroyal (its best known secret ingredient) along with thyme, marjoram, pepper, and celery seed. Why Lancashire should have retained a love for the black pudding when other areas now largely eschew them is not clear. It was a cheap food for the industrial masses, and easy to prepare in the basic kitchens of the poor, and it was also a street food in the County Palatine long ago (as it still remains today on Bury's famous market). Poles are also fond of 'blood pudding', and the late Pope John Paul lunched on Bury Black Pudding when he visited Heaton Park to say mass.

stone monument has a pillared façade on four sides, each containing bronze plaques (with a portrait medallion on one), the whole surmounted by a dome capped with a sculptured figure bearing a wreath of honour. Enter the **Millgate Shopping Centre** on the right, and pass down the mall to the **paved square** at the entrance to **'Bury's world famous market'**. The market can trace its origins to a charter of 1251, and now comprises two market halls and a largely covered open area of three hundred and seventy stalls. Market days are Wednesdays, Fridays, and Saturdays, when the crowds of shoppers are often augmented by visiting coach parties. The **main hall**, directly ahead, contains a variety of stalls, but the **new hall**, to the right, is reserved for fish and meat. Many people usually make a beeline for the black pudding stalls on the open market.

Market Day in Bury

You can walk through the **Millgate Centre** to **The Rock**, formerly the town's principal shopping street, which leads to a swish **new shopping centre** of the same name, replete with multiples and chain stores. (Oddly enough, the **Millgate** and **Rock** shopping centres are adjacent but not connected to each other, a rather grave planning mistake.) Consequently, retrace your steps to Kay Gardens. A right turn leads to the **Metro Centre** (formerly the Derby Hall) now a theatre and arts centre (with an excellent café and bar). But it it is best to walk between the Bus Station and the Gardens towards **Moss Street. Bury Art Gallery and Museum** may be found to the left (Tuesday - Friday: 10-5, Saturday: 10-4.30, admission free). It is an impressive building with a pillared porch and a façade decorated with **sculptured friezes**. The rather grand entrance is up flights of steps, but there is a modern ramped entrance to the substructure. The **bronze plaque** states that the foundation stone was laid by the son of Thomas Wrigley in 1899, and his famous art collection was opened to the public here in 1901.

Notice the stone **inscription** on the right hand wall of the **entrance hall**, above the **information desk**. A nearby door accesses the **library**. There is a **lift** on the left-hand side, and two sets of **stairs**. One leads down, to the **museum**, but pause at the case in the angle of the stairway. Here are **relics of Sir Robert Peel** (see p89), including his reputed **cradle**, and items relating to the police force of which he was the originator. The **museum displays** are largely temporary themed exhibitions derived from the museum's local history collection, and tend to change twice a year. Note the entrance to the **archive collection**, which may be used by prior arrangement. The other staircase leads to the **art gallery** proper on the first floor. The entrance has an oval balustraded **balcony** overlooking the hall below, and introduces a number of galleries, some of which are used for temporary exhibitions. But the chief glory is the permanent display of the **Wrigley Collection**. There is a **portrait of Wrigley** himself, painted by **G.F. Watts**,

A Victorian Polymath

Thomas Wrigley was one of those multi-faceted larger-than-life Victorians who seemed to have a finger in every pie. The proprietor of Bridge Hall Paper Mills at Heap Bridge, one of the largest and most successful businesses in the North of England, he held forceful views on management (his sons started on the shop floor and worked their way up through every department before he gave them any responsibility), free trade, the taxation of newspapers, and railway management, voicing his views in a stream of pamphlets and letters to the press. He was a director of the East Lancashire Railway (resigning when the board rejected his plan to reorganise the company), a major shareholder in the London and North Western Railway (and a constant critic of its chairman), and a pioneer in the theory and practice of railway signalling. But he also found time to amass a great art collection, and his taste was impeccable. Like many of his time, he was a philanthropist, and he left his collection to the town. This building was created to house what still is one of the finest local collections of art in Britain.

and the **highlights of the collection** can perhaps be enumerated as follows. Firstly, a collection of works by **David Cox**, a specialist in rural landscapes, including 'The Old Mill at Bettwys-y-Coed (1847); 'Funeral at Bettwys-y-Coed'; 'Lane near Rowley Regis'; and 'A Breezy Day'. **John Constable** is represented by 'Hampstead Heath', a typical example of one of the artist's many landscape sketches. 'Calais Sands' is a fine example of the work of **James Turner**, a typical study of the effects of reflected sunlight. Both Constable and Turner influenced the French Impressionists. There is also a good example of the 'Norwich School' of landscape painting in 'Norfolk Landscape' by **John Crome**, the founder of the movement. **Sir Edwin Landseer** was regarded as the most talented animal painter of his day, and 'A Random Shot' clearly demonstrates his skill. There are other fine works by artists, including **Briton Riviere**, and **Daniel Maclise**. The gallery has a good collection of **watercolours**, including work by **de Wint**.

The **Fusilers Museum** (daily: 10-5, admission charge) is on the other side of Moss Street. It is housed in the former Art and Craft School of 1894, another rather fine building with an **impressive frontage** on Broad Street at the rear. The new **entrance hall** (outside the museum area) contains a **Tourist Information Centre**, a well-stocked shop, and some very useful **public toilets**. '*Hero's Café*' is upstairs.

The museum is a model of its kind, with well-presented displays and diorama figures. **Introductory displays** explain the significance of a regiment and the nature of army organisation. There are **relics of the Battle of Minden** and **Colonel Kingsley** (who commanded the regiment in this engagement). Look out for the **mementos of General Wolfe**, the conqueror of Quebec (who had previously been colonel of the regiment). These include his **ruffles** and **ring**, together with a **sash** (reputedly worn at Quebec, where he was mortally wounded in the hour of victory). There are also the **head dress** and **tunic** of **General Ross**. In 1814 he occupied and burnt a large part of Washington. (The President's house had to be whitewashed to hide the scorch marks, and is known as the White House to this day!) The **career of Andrew Robb**, who joined at Preston in 1798, and served throughout the **Napoleonic Wars**, is noted. **Surgeon Major Arnott** attended Napoleon upon his death bed at St. Helena, and relics (including Arnott's **tunic**) are shown. The history of the regiment in the **Victorian age**, in the **Crimean War**, the **Sudan**, and in the **Boer War** at **Spion Kop** is depicted. The **First World War** includes a video presentation of the **landing at Gallipoli** and a **reconstruction of a trench**. There is a moving video about the recent **recovery and reburial of the remains of Private Richard Lancaster**, who died in the first Battle of Ypres. The displays relating to **World War Two** include the regiment's participation in the **Chindit operation** and the rest of the **Burma campaign**, the fighting in **North Africa, Sicily**, and **Italy**, and in **North-West Europe**. This includes the **VC awarded to Fusilier Jefferson**. Note the section devoted to **life on the home front in Bury**, including the **civil defence organisations** and **Home Guard**. There follows a fine **medal collection**, and displays of regimental drums and **silver**. The museum concludes with a look at the **successors of the regiment today**. There is also a good **children's area**, with a tent, helmets, dressing up material, and a selection of toys.

Moss Street leads to **Silver Street**. A quick glance to the left, down **Manchester Road**, reveals the **lantern tower** of **St. Mary's** Roman Catholic Church, dating from 1842. If you have the time, you can stroll down to the 1930s **Town Hall**, cross the **East Lancashire Railway** (with luck, you might see a steam train from the **bridge**), and arrive

'The Lancashire Lads'

The Lancashire Fusiliers have a long and honourable history. It was first raised in 1688 in Devon and soon became a fusilier regiment (fusiliers were used in siege warfare at the time, and were essentially bomb throwers.) However, they later evolved into the 'Twentieth regiment of Foot', and distinguished themselves at the Battle of Minden in 1759. Marching through rose gardens, they stopped to pluck the flowers as emblems for their caps. Due to a misunderstood order, they found themselves in the path of a French cavalry charge. Not only did they stand up to it, but routed the entire cavalry unit, something almost unheard of. 'Minden Day' is still celebrated. The Cardwell army reforms of the 1870s identified each regiment with a locality, and the 'Twentieth Foot' became the 'Lancashire Fusiliers', with Bury as their depot.

> *"Oh it were last Monday morning,*
> *As I have heard men say,*
> *Orders came from Manchester,*
> *We were to march away.*
> *Leaving many a fair pretty maid,*
> *To cry 'what shall I do'?'*
> *For the Lancashire Lads are going abroad,*
> *'Alas what shall I do'?*
>
> *Oh my love is dressed in scarlet,*
> *And breeches of the blue,*
> *And every town that he goes through,*
> *To me he will be true.*
> *Sure, we'll have sweethearts anew me boys,*
> *An' girls to please our minds,*
> *But we'll never forget sweet Bury,*
> *An' the girls we left behind!"*

They are also identified with the Gallipoli campaign in the First World War. One of the beaches became known as 'Lancashire Landing' and the battalion won "six V.C.'s before breakfast." The regiment is now part of the Royal Regiment of Fusiliers, but still maintains a local connection.

The Fusiliers Memorial

at the **Whitehead Gardens**. It contains the **Whitehead Clock Tower**, gifted to the town in 1914, by Henry Whitehead in commemoration of his brother Walter, an eminent surgeon, together with the **Boer War Monument**. A member of the Whitehead family invented the torpedo; hence the model in the gardens! Directly ahead of **Moss Street**, set back in a charming garden, is the modern **Bank Street Unitarian Chapel**. This is the fourth on this site. The first was erected by the Presbyterians in Bury in 1719. It was replaced by a neo-classical structure in 1837, but this was undermined by the excavation of the low-level yard of the East Lancashire Railway. Fortunately, some members of the board belonged to the chapel, and the railway paid generous compensation. The third chapel, a rather ugly Victorian structure, opened in 1852, and lasted until the 1970s, when it was replaced by the present building. It should be noted that Presbyterianism in Lancashire went through a number of changes in the eighteenth and nineteenth centuries. Some groups evolved into Unitarianism, as was the case here. The principle tenet of this creed is the oneness of God and a rejection of the doctrine of the trinity. Turn right down **Silver Street**, passing the former building of the **Bury Banking Company** at the corner of **Bank Street** on the left. (Notice the head of Plutos, the god of wealth, over the door!) Directly opposite, beside the **Fusiliers Museum**, is the **Fusiliers Garden**, containing the **Lancashire Fusiliers Memorial**. Designed by Lutyens, and unveiled in 1922, it formerly stood outside the regimental barracks and depot on Bolton Road. However, it was removed to the present site in 2009, along with a quantity of topsoil where the ashes of veterans had been scattered over the years.

We now arrive at the **old market place**, the centre of the medieval settlement, distinguished by the Victorian **statue of Sir Robert Peel**. (Upon unveiling, it was noticed with horror that the waistcoat buttons were fastened the wrong way!)

The area is overlooked by the great mass of the **parish church** to the right, but do not overlook the interesting **war memorial** on the corner of **The Rock**. It is said that a church has stood on this site for over a thousand years, the first church supposedly founded in 971! Another tradition states that a church was built around 1290, probably the third church in this place. Since then a number of re-constructions took place, and between 1773 and 1780 the whole of the building, apart from the tower, was pulled down and rebuilt. The new structure was said to be 'handsome and spacious', the interior 'well finished' and 'free from gloom'. On the 5th November, 1780, the new church was opened, and the tower was adorned with a new spire in 1842. Unfortunately, it was soon found that the woodwork of the 1780 building had rotted and it was unsafe to hold services there. It was decided to pull down the body of the church but to leave the tower and spire. **Saint Mary the Virgin** (daily except Tuesday; 9.30-4.30) is thus a largely modern structure, built between1871 and 1876.

Bury's Famous Son

Although he left the town at the age of nine, everyone remembered that Peel had been born at nearby Chamber hall, and that his father was a prominent local mill owner. And there were other reasons why the inhabitants would want to claim this famous Prime Minister as one of their own. His father was a staunch 'church and king' man; in other words, a Tory. This was unusual, as the Tory Party was largely dominated by rather reactionary aristocratic landowners, who regarded the new industrialists as dangerous interlopers. The former had introduced the Corn Laws in 1815, a protectionist measure designed to protect grain prices (and thus ensure that farmers could pay high rents). This was directly against the interests of the industrial middle class who wanted free trade. Something would have to give. Peel's great achievement was to persuade the aristocratic Tories to repeal the Corn Laws in 1846. This made him a national hero, especially in the manufacturing districts. There was an important subtext. In reconciling the aristocratic Tory elite to the aspirations of the industrial and mercantile middle class he is regarded by historians as the father of the modern Conservative Party. He also reformed the legal system, reserving capital punishment only for murder and treason. Today, he is mainly remembered as the father of the police force. He introduced police in London when it was his responsibility as Home Secretary, and other towns and cities hastened to follow his precedent. Police in Britain are still known as 'bobbies' to this day. He died, at the height of his fame, as the result of a riding accident, and soon the industrial towns were covered with statues like this one.

Peel statue

J.S. Crowther, the architect, designed a **'narthex'** to connect the church and the tower with its spire. This contains the ornate **south door**, facing The Rock, entered through a **porch** (which now contains a **bookshop**). Viewed from the **inner door**, the design of the **narthex** imitates that of the church itself, complete with a **rounded apse**. The latter was formerly the **baptistery**, with **female saints in stained glass** and stonework depicting **heads of the children of the parish** (it is now converted into the servery of the café). The narthex area was remodelled in 2008, being provided with **oak and glass screens** and new flooring. The base of the tower incorporates some interesting **memorials**, including one to Lieutenant Robert Hood R.N, who accompanied one of Franklin's expeditions and was "assassinated by an Iroquois." The tower itself has a **peal of eight bells**, some dating from 1722.

The exceptionally large **nave** is over seventy-six feet high, eighty-four feet long, and thirty feet wide. The **windows** on the **north side** depict Old Testament figures, and the **south side** New Testament ones. The **west wall** was inspired by Westminster Abbey, and rises in four stages to a great **rose window**. There are over one hundred and fifty **stone heads** at the springing points of the arches, depicting local people, including churchwardens, the architect, and clerk of works (on the **west wall**), and the Earl and Countess of Derby (on the **chancel arch**). The **floor tiles** are by Minton. There is a list of

Rectors from 1189 in the south-west corner. The **pulpit** commemorates Roger Kay (died 1738), who re-founded the grammar school in 1726, and is believed to be buried beneath it. The **font** is derived from the previous church and was formerly in the baptistery. (A **brass plate**, in the middle of the south wall, commemorates the baptism of Sir Robert Peel in 1788.) Notice the **colours of the Lancashire Fusiliers** (this was their garrison church) hung along both side walls; at the east end of the nave, the **colour on the left** was carried by the regiment at the time of the Gallipoli landing, and that **on the right** was laid up when the regiment amalgamated with the King's Liverpool Regiment.

Proceed into the **chancel**. The **sanctuary apse** has five tall **windows** illustrating the life of Christ. Behind the **altar** is an **oak reredos** with the epiphany as its central feature, topped by a pelican feeding her brood with her own blood. The **South Chapel** has an **entrance screen** designed by Sir Charles Gilbert Scott. The reredos features the Virgin and Child surrounded by British saints.

Walk round the back of the church, to the right, to reach the **Blackburn Hall**. Although used as parish rooms, this was the site of Bury Grammar school from 1784 to 1903. The wing with round arched windows dates from the 18th century. Retrace your steps and return to the **Two Tubs**, now on the right. The pub is said to date to the 17th century and it has borne a number of names in its time. Legend has it that a landlord wanted to call it 'The Globe'. He had the bright idea that an old beer barrel,

The Royal Favourite

Time was when Bury had a manor house, where the Lord of the Manor resided and held a Court Leet to enforce his rights over his tenants and villeins. Thus Sir Henry de Bury lived here, a comparatively lowly knight in the medieval pecking order. Unfortunately, he got himself mixed up in a local conflict. In 1315, Sir Adam Banastre organised a revolt against Thomas, Earl of Lancaster because he could not stand the local pretentions of Sir Robert Holland, whom he regarded as the Earl's 'favourite' and an upstart. He sent men to capture Adam Radcliffe (one of Holland's adherents) but he could not be found. The henchmen killed poor old Henry instead. Sir Adam Banastre later came to a rather sticky end, but Henry's successors decided to construct a defensive moat. Many years later, another 'favourite' came on the scene. Ownership of the manor, with much other property in the region, passed to the powerful Pilkington family. Sir Thomas de Pilkington was born about 1425, and his principal residence was the Manor House of Bury. As a reward for his good services, King Edward IV granted him a license on the 2nd May, 1469, " to fortify and castellate" his residence at Bury. Sir Thomas then enlarged and improved the existing moat and constructed a stone curtain wall and a large tower house. What was he afraid of? Well, these were troubled times, and the Stanley family were growing in power and influence in the locality. Sir Thomas transferred his allegiance to Richard III when he ascended the throne and was soon regarded as a royal 'favourite'. He fought for Richard at Bosworth Field, participating in the doomed charge down Ambion Hill. As a result, he lost all his Lancashire estates, including the Manor of Bury. He did not learn his lesson. He joined the rebellion of Lambert Simnel, the pretender, in 1487, and was killed at the battle of Stoke-by-Newark. This must have been seen as a big joke in Bury, for Simnel (whom the king pardoned) was said to be the simple son of a baker, and 'simnel cakes' became a Bury tradition. Thus, most of Bury became the property of the Stanley Earls of Derby, who, although content to collect the rents, did not really want to live there. Consequently, the castle fell into ruin and eventually disappeared.

sawn in half to represent the two hemispheres, would serve as a cheap inn sign. But the locals started to call it the 'Two Tubs', and the name remains! Pass between the pub and the elegant **Castle Buildings** (noting the **castellated columns**) and arrive at the site of **Bury Castle**.

By the 18th century, nothing remained visible above ground. However, in 1865, some workmen digging a sewer trench chanced upon part of the foundations. An enthusiastic local antiquarian financed an excavation that revealed a large part of the castle plan (the site was then mainly open ground) which was recorded. Modern excavations took place in the 1970s and 1999, and it was decided to place a section of the foundations on display in a landscaped setting. Consequently, stand at the railing facing the **Castle Armoury TA Centre**, and inspect the space created for the **moat**. It is clear that Thomas started by cleaning out the moat and cutting the **inner facing** almost vertically into the solid rock. This he **lined with a stone wall**, which shows evidence of repair in places. The excavation revealed a **corner of the moat** to the left. The wall is at a slight angle to form a plinth for a battlemented curtain wall enclosing the site. At some later date, the wall foundations were strengthened with **buttresses**. Look to the left of the last buttress on the right. This is thought to be the foundation of a **garderobe or lavatory**, or rather the shute that descended from it into the moat at this point. The garderobe itself would be probably located in an extension from the **tower house** that extended to the curtain wall here. The 1865 survey revealed a massive tower house forming a rectangle about 82 feet by 63 feet, with walls nearly eight feet thick. Part of the **outline**

The foundations of Bury Castle, with Castle Armoury in the background

of the tower can be seen in the pavement between the castle foundations and the front of the Armoury. Such a huge building would probably require an internal dividing wall and perhaps a double gabled roof. The lower part would be used for storage, but the upper would contain a Great Hall and private apartments. Fragments of **fine window tracery** were found, together with some of the **stone corbels** that supported the battlemented parapet. There is an **artist's impression of the castle** on both of the **interpretation boards**. The discovery of the castle influenced the design of Castle Armoury in the background. The latter was built 1868 to house 8th Lancashire Rifle Volunteers, on the site of Bury Castle, and re-using some building materials. It was extended to provide a drill hall (on the site of the former steam tram depot) in 1907, in some loosely medieval style. It then accommodated the 5th (Territorial) battalion of the Lancashire Fusiliers. The right-hand turret has a portcullis feature which bears the battalion insignia and supporters. Leave the area by the passage to the right of the *Bella Italia* restaurant and arrive at **Bolton Street**, almost opposite the **East Lancashire Railway Station**.

An Excursion on the East Lancashire Railway

Although not part of the Metrolink system, the East Lancashire Railway can be seen as an extension of the Bury line, which it complements. After all, the combination of a tram ride and a trip on a steam train has all the ingredients for a perfect day out. The ELR is an ideal family destination, particularly when events such as 'Thomas the Tank Engine' weekends, the 'Teddy Bears Picnic', the 'Halloween Ghost Train' and the 'Santa Specials' are in full swing. (Trains usually operate at weekends and Bank Holidays throughout the year, with some midweek running in the High Season; for all enquiries about the railway, ring 0161 764 7790.)

The Rose of Lancashire

In September, 1843, alarming news reached Bury. Surveyors had been seen at work between Heywood and Bury; the Manchester and Leeds Railway were clearly intending to extend their existing coal branch to the town. This was not good news, for it promised a round about train journey to Manchester operated by the "Lies and Mancheater Railway", a concern characterised as "the most brutal line in the kingdom." The influential inhabitants met in conclave at the Old Red Lion (on the site of Barclay's Bank, near the Parish Church) and resolved to promote a direct line to Manchester. Almost as an afterthought, this railway would be extended into the Rossendale valley, to terminate at Rawtenstall. Unfortunately, the cost of a separate terminus in Manchester would be prohibitive, so they had their eye on the proposed station at Hunt's Bank (Victoria). This might only be obtained on the back of another railway, so they actually approached the "brutal line" and requested running powers over it from a proposed junction at Collyhurst (assuming that this proposal would induce them to abandon their Bury branch project). The Leeds Board strung them along with the intention of wrecking the 'direct line' scheme, and it was some time before the Bury 'Provisional Committee' realised this. Fortunately, they managed to do a deal with the Manchester and Bolton Railway, reaching Manchester by running powers over their line from a junction at Clifton. The new variant had another advantage, for all of the land between Clifton Junction and Bury was owned either by Lord Wilton or the Earl of Derby, and these noblemen agreed to immediate possession before the conveyances were completed. Consequently, the Manchester, Bury, and Rossendale Railway Act obtained Royal Assent on 4 July, 1844.

The promotion of this railway had aroused the interest of people who wanted the line extended to Accrington, but this could not be included within the original Act. A second Act created the 'Extension Railway', a line from a junction at Stubbins to Accrington, and thence to Blackburn in one direction and Burnley and Colne in another. The two companies immediately amalgamated and took the name of the East Lancashire Railway in 1846. The Blackburn and Preston Railway was absorbed shortly afterwards. The original line opened on a proud day the same year, on 25 September. Two gleaming Stephenson type 2-2-2s hauled a train that eventually comprised no less than sixty

The Railway King

Even amongst his contemporaries, Cornelius Nicholson was a man to be reckoned with. A native of Ambleside, he owned a successful paper mill (which may explain his connections with Bury) and was Mayor of Kendal. He had shrewdly realised the potential of the new railway age, and the benefits that the Lancaster and Carlisle Railway would bring to the vicinity of his town. He wrote the prospectus for the Caledonian Railway (which extended the line to Scotland) and promoted a branch to Kendal that also created the resort of Windermere. But there was much more to this enterprising man. He corresponded with Coleridge, wrote books on history and topography, and was an archaeologist and naturalist. At the opening of the Rawtenstall line, the new managing director of the railway was introduced as someone who knew more about Rossendale than people who had lived there all their lives! Unfortunately, "fired by the demon of territorial aggrandisement," he chose Hudson as his model, and set out to create a railway empire based upon Bury. The company absorbed the Liverpool, Ormskirk, and Preston project, offering a direct route from the East Lancashire towns to Liverpool docks. The Rawtenstall line was extended to Bacup; a separate branch and station served Preston; and branches were undertaken to Southport and Skelmersdale. He even envisaged a more direct Manchester line, an independent route to Scotland (!), and through services to Yorkshire via Colne and Skipton. Most of these fantasies disappeared in the aftermath of the collapse of the 'railway mania', but the Yorkshire project resulted in a bitter dispute with the Lancashire and Yorkshire Railway (as the Manchester and Leeds Railway had become). This was the inspiration for the bizarre 'Battle of Clifton Junction' in 1849, when the rival companies tried to blockade each other's lines with trains! Nicholson discretely departed from the Board, and turned his attention to promoting the Great India Peninsular Railway before retiring to Ventnor.

carriages (including the directors and the band of the 56th Regiment of Foot) from Victoria Station by way of Clifton, Radcliffe, Bury, and Ramsbottom to Rawtenstall.

Meanwhile, the Lancashire and Yorkshire Railway was in the process of constructing its own railway through Bury. A group of Wigan coal owners decided to try and break the monopoly of the original Liverpool and Manchester line by promoting a railway between Liverpool and Bolton, and extending to Bury. The L and Y took over the scheme, with the intention of linking it to an extension from their Heywood branch (opened on 15 April, 1841 to serve Hopwood Colliery), with a station in Bury adjacent to Knowsley Street. The new service from Manchester (via Blue Pitts, as Castleton was then known) to Heywood and Bury commenced on 1 May 1848, without any public ceremony, and the new route to Liverpool opened throughout on 20 November.

Thereafter, the ELR made its peace with the L and Y, both companies amalgamating in 1859. As part of the L and Y system, both lines passed into London, Midland, and Scottish Railway and, ultimately, British Railways ownership. The iniquitous Beeching plan decimated the former ELR in the Bury area. A portion of the original line between Radcliffe and Bury survived as part of the electric line to Manchester (now Metrolink), but the line between Stubbins and Accrington was foolishly closed, as was the section from Rawtenstall to Bacup. Similarly, the old L and Y Liverpool route saw trains disappear between Bolton and Castleton. A limited shuttle service from Bury to Rawtenstall finally succumbed in 1972, and an infrequent service of coal trains between Brewery Sidings, Collyhurst, and Rawtenstall, via Castleton and Bury, constituted all that was left...with a very uncertain future.

But all was not lost. The East Lancashire Railway Preservation Society has a long and complex history. It originated in an abortive attempt to preserve the section of railway between Stubbins and Haslingden, and moved its small collection of locomotives and rolling stock to Bury in 1970. The local authority had acquired the former Castlecroft goods yard (including the goods shed), as part of the land was needed for the construction of a bypass. The authority offered it to the preservation group and the combined rail and road collection opened to the public as 'Bury Transport Museum'. After a scheme to operate on the Rawtenstall line failed, it became clear that nothing could be accomplished until the coal traffic ceased. However, the real turning point had already occurred, though few realised it at the time. In response to a consultation exercise by the Croal-Irwell Authority (a body responsible for the development of a country park along these two rivers) the group had made a detailed submission. It argued that both track and track bed might be purchased and leased to the society's operating company, producing a viable tourist attraction of first rank. The appeal was directed at the (then) Greater Manchester Council's tourist development preoccupations. Here was one of the factors that would act as a catalyst in implementing their strategy. G.M.C. agreed to the proposal, and obtained a great deal of funding from a variety of agencies concerned with derelict land. The line is vested in a Trust (now comprising the local authorities), and leased to the (non-profit making) Operating Company. The Society provides the volunteer labour force.

The restored railway reopened to Ramsbottom on 25 July, 1987, and to Rawtenstall on 27 April, 1991. The advent of Metrolink, although very welcome in other ways, resulted in the loss of a connection with the national rail network. A virtue was made out of a necessity, for local inhabitants elsewhere wanted to replicate the success of the line in the Rossendale Valley. Consequently, the Heywood extension (and the new mainline connection) opened to traffic on 6 September, 2003.

Perhaps the words of the long dead Cornelius Nicholson are still appropriate. "Though much beset by clouds...our emblem is the Rose of Lancashire, unfolding its petals and displaying its blooms."

Playing at Trains?

To many people, the volunteer enthusiasts seem to be merely playing with trains. Therefore, the following details of the impact of the railway in the Rossendale Valley may not be out of place. Over 120 hectares of derelict land have been reclaimed to date. More than 100 specific capital projects have been completed on behalf of the Trust, totalling £12 million, and creating an estimated 300 jobs in the building trade (local firms being mainly employed). The railway presently carries over 130,000 passengers per annum, placing it in the first rank of preserved lines, and resulting in perhaps an additional injection of £1 million per annum, in the form of visitor spending, into the local economy, creating an estimated 250 full and part-time jobs. Surveys have suggested that up to 72% of passengers on the railway patronise local shops and facilities. Moreover, the local authorities believe that the success of the line, with its associated publicity, has played a part in the change in peoples' perceptions of the Irwell Valley as a place to live and work. Indeed, the degree of change is evident in Ramsbottom. Once a quiet place, with closed shops and derelict property, it is now bustling with tea shops, craft shops, antique shops and the like. The line connects with a number of local attractions, and is much used for country walks in the summer months.

Bolton Street Station

The original station opened (in an unfinished state) in September, 1846, and was extensively rebuilt in the last quarter of the 19th century. The street frontage buildings, destroyed by fire shortly after the last war, have been rebuilt and re-sited.

As most people pass the **car park entrance** en route to the booking office, we will begin our explorations at this point. The station itself is situated in a cutting, with a **low-level yard** (now the car park) on the eastern side. Stone gateposts, supporting elaborate wrought iron gates for both carriages and pedestrians, once flanked the sloping approach road from Bolton Street. These have long disappeared, but a stone post can be seen built into the corner of the little shop at the side of the approach entrance. Walk down the approach. These **gates**, the blackened stone **retaining walls**, and the **iron railing** above them, all date from 1846. The **flight of stairs** communicates with Bank Street. Some of the stair risers have been refashioned using used sections of old rail. Some rather curious 'gothic' **openings** may be seen in the retaining wall, and these may be associated with the former Bank Street Unitarian Chapel (p88). The single-storey building containing the **cafeteria** stands on the site of the grand headquarters building, designed in the then popular 'Italianate' style. The usual station accommodation was confined to the ground floor. Upper floors contained the company offices, a palatial boardroom, and spacious attics for storage of papers. The 'great and the good' in the ELR hierarchy had their own side entrance, reached by a fenced off lower section of the yard. Here again were elaborate gates, surmounted by cast iron shields of the ELR coat of arms. (One of these is placed in the entrance concourse.)

A busy day at Bolton Street Station

Sadly, the headquarters building was demolished in the 1970s. Retrace your footsteps to the station entrance. The **entrance building** is rare example of early 1950s British Railways architecture; note the use of varnished wood and tiling. In addition to the **booking hall** and **booking office**, the original **shop** is once again in operation. The wide range of model railway items, books, videos, and magazines, are supplemented by everything that a child could desire, from sweets to souvenirs of 'Thomas' and his friends. The original **enquiry office**, opposite, will give information about local attractions as well as the railway.

After obtaining a ticket, pass through to the **footbridge**. The changing displays concerning events and activities on the railway are worth a glance, but most people are concerned with the excellent **views** from the widows. (Parents are particularly requested not to stand small children on the ledges!) Two flights of **steps** lead down to the **platforms**.

Start with the first set. These stairs lead to **platform two**, sometimes used as the arrival and departure platform for trains in midweek. Turn left to inspect the **modern ornamental gates**. Another left turn leads to a **paved viewing area**, adjacent to the **tunnel mouth**. We are in the North-East corner of the station, directly under the entrance building (supported by concrete columns). The original street entrance was directly over the running line, so this area was once open to the sky. Carriages were (believe it or not!) stored here, as mid Victorian carriages were perhaps no more than thirty feet long. They were rotated from the transverse access track by means of small turntables or 'turn plates' on to three short sidings parallel to the running line. The rusting **fastening points** for the block and tackle employed may still be found on the stonework of the tunnel side wall. Here may also be found the **arches** under the yard approach, still used for storage. However, all this is eclipsed by the view of the **'garter coat of arms'**, carved in the stone pillar to the side of the tunnel entrance. This is the abbreviated version of the company arms that appeared on the locomotives and the carriage doors. Note the motto "Celerite et Utilitate", which may be translated as 'with speed and with service'. An interesting comment on a railway that, at one point, had only five 'luggage (goods) engines' out of fifty considered serviceable, and was paying out more in compensation to aggrieved customers than the profit that the goods operation actually made! (The paved area also contains a good **shop** for second-hand model railway items, railway books, and magazines.)

We retrace our steps back on to **platform two**. It is intended to erect a canopy on this platform, to complement the fine **platform building**. This is a modern pastiche, though it incorporates part of the frontage from the office building at the former Bury tram depot. It contains the **Trackside**, a real ale bar and café that has an entry in 'The Good Beer Guide'. Food is served during the day (and eaten at tables on the platform when it is fine), and accompanied children are welcome while the trains are operating. (Children's parties and other functions are catered for by the railway at competitive rates, and the former can be organised on the train.) There are also **toilet facilities** in this range of buildings. **Platform one** can be found towards the end of the platform, to the left. This platform was formerly used by the Bury 'station pilot' (shunting engine). It was also the starting point for rush hour services to Manchester. Nowadays, it is mainly the head shunt (reversing line) for the tracks leading to the **Standard 4 Group works** erected by a number of society members to house their preservation projects. The current task in hand is the restoration of a 2-6-2 tank engine, the sort of locomotive seen in the Bury area in B.R. days. However there are a number of (restored) wagons, many of which are visible. (You can help their work by patronising the **shop** in the coach.)

Return to the footbridge, and proceed to the **island platform**, on the other side of the station. **Platform three** and **Platform four** usually serve the operating line, though the latter can sometimes be used by the special 'Thomas' trains (hauled by 'Thomas' himself!). Notice the remains of a unique **'bi-directional' signal** on the retaining wall opposite platform four, installed by the Lancashire and Yorkshire Railway. Notice also the remains of the **flight of steps** beside the retaining wall. **Castle Leisure Centre**, above platform four, stands on the **site of the ELR Wagon Works**. Access was obtained by a 'turn plate' on the outermost loop line, which was the starting point of a rope hauled incline to the works! It is not known how long this curious arrangement lasted. The island platform is sheltered by what is left of the **L and Y canopy** (originally twice as long), dating from the reconstruction of the station in the 1870s. The original layout was very different to the present one. The island platform was narrower, accommodating two loop lines instead of one. It was also just above rail height (there was no footbridge, people walked across the tracks). A row of cast iron columns along the centre supported one side of an overall glass and iron train shed roof, spanning the running lines. (The other side was anchored to the headquarters building.) This shed sported a 'Paxton Roof', as used in the Crystal Palace. The roof space extended over the North Eastern and South Eastern corner carriage sidings, but was not well designed; it started to give way a few years after it was finished! Now look at the present canopy. Notice that the **iron columns** are far too short for the roof trusses, for they support spandrels formed (it is thought) of L and Y signal post brackets bolted back to back! Clearly, the original columns have been recycled. Also note that these hollow columns function as drain pipes...very typical of the period. The **waiting room** is often assumed to be original. However, it was an office or mess room from the old Newton Heath Carriage and Wagon Works. Close inspection reveals it to have been originally fashioned from L and Y signal box parts. A recent photograph of the interior produced a mysterious figure that some have claimed was a ghost!

The **largest signal gantry on a preserved railway** graces the southern end of the station, controlling access to and from the Heywood line for all the platforms. It also controls movements to and from Buckley Wells. The **Heywood line** is clearly visible, curving away to the left beyond the **Angouleme Way** road bridge, and **Bury South signal box** is adjacent.

The other line leads to **Buckley Wells works**, beyond Baron Street It is not currently open to the public, but is subject to a long term development programme that will (hopefully) include viewing galleries.

Bury Transport Museum

Bury Transport Museum can be visited before or after a train ride (usually open at weekends and Bank Holidays, and Wednesday to Friday, ring 0161 763 7949; admission included in full line ticket, otherwise admission charge). Leave the station entrance, and cross Bolton Street to the **car park**, opposite, looking for the pathway to the left. This, in turn, leads to the **cobbled path** down to the remains of **Castlecroft goods yard**. (Wheelchair access is via the Castlecroft Road gate.) It was once twice the size, but **Peel Way** occupies the other half. But we still have the old stone **goods shed**, dating from 1849. It is said to be haunted. Certainly, a number of volunteers have had some odd experiences in the place when working late at night.

The museum recently reopened after a refurbishment programme costing £3 million.

The Economical Explorer

John Shae Pering, the company engineer, had an adventurous life. As a young engineer, he was employed by the Khedive of Egypt at Alexandria. He met an eccentric Royal Engineers officer called Howard Vyse, who suggested that they both undertake a systematic survey of the Great Pyramid of Khufru. Pering busied himself in the burial chamber while Vyse worked above it. The latter dislodged a stone that fell down a previously unknown ventilation shaft, landing in the chamber below and almost decapitating Pering! As the company engineer, Pering was methodical, always valuing economy of effort. He designed a standard railway station (with double windows, replicated at Ramsbottom) and a modular section for goods sheds and works that was replicated at Castlecroft, Buckley Wells, and elsewhere. This was a cheap way of doing things; the stone for this shed came from whatever was lying near New Hall Hey cutting, and all the internal carpentry was 'in house'.

The original shed (indeed, the entire yard) operated on a system of turntables, located in each corner. The two wagon roads were thus connected by transverse tracks at either end, so that unloading took place on one staging and loading on the other, the empty wagons and vans being sent across. Note the **cast iron columns** supporting the wooden **roof trusses**. These are hollow and acted as drainpipes, a common feature for industrial buildings of this period. The platform **staging**, on either side of the shed, (accessed by both stairs and lift) host contrasting displays. That to the **left** mainly deals with the **history of transport** in the Bury and Manchester area, while that to the **right** is mainly to do with the **work of the goods** shed and the **work of the East Lancashire Railway**. It includes a **re-creation of a goods office** and a fascinating video of a **day in the life of a goods clerk**. You can also **drive a bus** in a simulator, and children will enjoy **dressing up** as railwaymen and passengers. The **main body of the shed** houses a fascinating **vehicle collection**; mainly **buses**, but also including a **fire engine, traction engines**, and **'Hilda' the steamroller**. Three tracks (the short southerly siding was installed by Society volunteers) are occupied by the **railway collection**. This comprises, amongst other things, a small steam **locomotives from Burnley Gas Works**, a hand-operated **crane**, and one of the few surviving **L and Y vans**.

The modern **shed** at the railway end of the yard is mainly used for the maintenance and servicing of the railway's **diesel locomotives**. It is not open to the public, but a selection of the locomotives can usually be seen over the fence. A path leads to a lineside viewing area.

The River Irwell

Throughout the journey northwards the line affords fine views of the River Irwell. The industrial heritage of the valley included cotton mills, textile printing works, chemical works, brick and wagon works, and coal mining, all of whom had used the river for water in their processes, or in volume for power, and most sadly as an open sewer to dispose of waste. In years gone by it was not uncommon to find the river running orange with the ferrous discharges from the Coal Mining further north. In more recent times, the River has benefited from European development grants through the Mersey Basin Development fund. With input from local authorities, and the Environment Agency, the river now boasts some fine fishing, with coarse fish being available to catch in the rapids around Irwell Vale. The increase in the water quality has encouraged people to visit the river valley, with canoeing undertaken most weekends between Summerseat and Burrs, and even swimming in parts. The areas that used to be impacted by flooding have had new embankments constructed to allow for more flood free development, and through strict regulation, the water quality has improved tremendously.

Bury to Ramsbottom

We depart from Bolton Street Station and immediately pass through the eighty yard long **Bolton Street Tunnel**. (This was constructed using the 'cut and over' method and the ellipse of the arch changes a third of the way through.) The northern facing is battlemented, commemorating the nearby site of Bury Castle. Notice the box shaped area in the retaining wall on the right, the site of Bury North signal box. One of the copings has some crude graffiti of 'Atlas', an ELR locomotive, probably carved in the 1860s by a bored signalman. The curve of the wall into the by-pass embankment indicates the entrance to the former coal and mineral yard. There is a good view of **Castlecroft Yard** opposite, with the diesel shed, diesel locomotives, and a glimpse of the old Goods Shed (Bury Transport Museum). The train passes under **Peel Way** road bridge. Not only has the by-pass obliterated the coal yard, but it also sits on half the goods yard too. The line runs on a wide **embankment**, constructed to accommodate four or more tracks, as far as the former Tottington Junction. The tracks to the left constituted the head shunt and approach to Castlecroft Goods Yard, and an outer siding that ran alongside coal drops (parts of which remain). These serviced the former Corporation coal fired Electricity Generating Station (*California Steel* is now located on this site). Chamber Hall stood somewhere in the vicinity, said to be the birthplace of Sir Robert Peel, Bury's most famous son. (The **'quarter mile sidings'**, currently used for the storage of surplus rolling stock, limits the view in this direction, and the rest is lost under the **industrial estate**.) The new **supermarket complex** is the most prominent object to the right. The construction of the outlying filling station disturbed a former chapel burial ground. An apparition of a soldier in a First World War uniform was allegedly seen shortly afterwards.

We pass the site of Tottington Junction, where the **branch to Holcombe Brook** diverged to the left. Sidings served a mill and a chemical works. The **occupation bridge** once led to the chemical works site, latterly used for reclaiming chemical storage drums. Some remains are visible on the left, amidst a large dump of demolition debris. Try to pick out traces of the **Fernhill Incline** to the right, descending the bank to terminate in long-vanished exchange sidings. Bury Town Yard was situated at the top of the former incline. At one time, in the days before flush toilets were common, 'night soil' (collected by 'honey carts') was brought here and mixed with refuse from the slaughterhouses and stables. When dried, it was bagged as fertiliser and exported by rail to farmers all over the country!

The line now starts to run into open country as the train crosses **two river bridges**. (The cliff to the right has particularly interesting rock strata, undermined by the flowing river.) These two bridges over a bend in the river, not forgetting the embankment in between, offer a fine view over Burrs to the left. **Burrs** is a good example of an early mill settlement. At that stage of the industrial revolution, when the textile machinery was water powered, the first mills were sited in country districts by fast flowing streams or rivers. These particular mills were fed by a stone built mill race sourced from the Irwell. Accommodation was built for the workers who were usually women and children, the latter being pauper 'apprentices' living in a sort of hostel. Such was Burrs, established by the firm of Peel (Sir Robert's father) and Yates. Nowadays, the **remains of the mills** have been preserved in a landscape setting. The Croal-Irwell Warden Service have an office here, but the place is better known for a **Canoeing Centre** (with a café). Look out for the **aqueduct** alongside the road bridge over the Irwell (it carries the feeder for the Manchester, Bolton, and Bury Canal, supplying Elton reservoir); the **Brown Cow** (an 18th century farm house) with its beer garden; and the **camp site** (the only one in Greater Manchester, operated by the Caravan Club) A halt is proposed at a point where the footpath crosses the line. The strange hollow, to the left of the **cutting entrance**, illustrates the former course of the Irwell (it changed direction on the 17th century). It still floods after heavy rain. **Castle Steads**, thought to be a Bronze Age earthwork, is in the vicinity, though not visible.

The train enters **Touch Hill cutting**, over forty feet deep. The steep eastern slope was used as a firing range in World War Two. Photographers use the remains of a vanished wooden occupation bridge, in the form of the **brick abutments**, as a vantage point on event days. The Springside **water meadows** now appear on the left, opposite **Springside Farm**. Notice the flat **wooded area**, also to the left. Incredibly, this was the site of **Olive's Sidings**, serving the associated wagon works. It did a small business in building and repairing railway wagons, in the days when most collieries and many businesses owned their own. This work was replaced by the manufacture of earthenware drainpipes from clay pits on the site! (Artifacts stamped with their trademark can still be found in the area.) The wagon works closed in the 1890s, and nothing remains. The line runs, from this point, along a short ledge at the side of the river. A footpath crosses the railway at **Chest Wheel Crossing**, where the road joins it on the left. There was a bad landslip at this point, but it has been remedied by the installation of a 'land anchor'. The former Summerseat goods yard is visible on the right, just before the bridge. The small stone **goods shed**, in private hands, may be developed as a restaurant. The train passes over the **road bridge** and comes to a halt in **Summerseat Station**.

Alas, the station buildings have disappeared, but the surviving 'up' platform incorporates what is believed to be a section of the **original ELR platform** at its southern end. Platforms at this period were usually of this height, and continental platforms preserve the tradition. This section of the platform was never altered, since it coincided with the threshold of the booking hall entrance. A fine **garden area** now replaces the demolished 'down' platform, opposite. This is appropriate, as Summerseat Station was noted for its gardens in the old days, and won many awards. The old **entrance steps** are still in use (but give onto a blind bend, so beware!). Consequently, the **new entrance** at the north end of the platform communicates with **Miller Street**, in the Brooksbottom direction.

The station serves **Brooksbottom** (easily seen from the railway) to the right, and **Summerseat** itself, on the left. This side of the station overlooks a **reclaimed sewage works**, situated in the bend of the river, now a nature reserve. Exit the station by the new entrance, and pass along **Miller Street** to a right turn by **Victorian Lanterns** (p102). Turn left for the **river bridge** and the **viaduct**. The majority of visitors passed this way for the *Waterside Inn* (p102), though it is currently (2014) closed. There is a pleasant footpath from here to Ramsbottom, by way of **Gollinrod Gorge**, a local beauty spot. However, if it is a fine day, and you are prepared for a short country walk, make another right turn and double back down **Pollards Lane** and **Queens Place**. At the end of the latter, a sharp left leads to **Rowlands Road**, climbing the valley side. A **churchyard** on the right marks the site of the original Rowlands Chapel (demolished in 1975). It contains a **war memorial** and the **mausoleum of John Robinson Kay**, an owner of Brooksbottom Mill and an ELR director. The road becomes an **unadopted path** (very muddy in winter), with a **fine view** to the right, before **Nabbs Farm** is reached. The latter is the home of ***Falshaw's Farm Shop and Ice Cream Parlour*** (complete with picnic and play area, spring lamps, cows, and wandering ducks and chicken!).

Alternatively, exit the platform by the **steps** and (carefully!) pass under the **railway bridge** to explore Summerseat itself. The **garden centre** is a short distance along **Railway Street** on the left. In addition to horticultural items, the centre houses a well-stocked **gift shop** (including toys, fancy goods, and fashion items) and an excellent café. Turn sharp left up **Peel Road**, and left again down **Higher Summerseat**, the location of two historic pubs. Joshua Hoyle, the later mill owner, was a stalwart of the temperance movement (p114) and thought his employees should abstain from alcohol too. Consequently, the two traditional pubs in Summerseat were late arrivals, and the other side of the railway from the family business. The ***Hamers Arms*** and the ***Footballers Inn***, were created out of cottages once owned by the Hamer family, also local mill owners. The latter establishment has a sign depicting Bury FC holding up the (twice won) FA Cup, and was once the haunt of Pat Phoenix, Peter Adamson, and other early *Coronation Street* stars.

We look to the right as the train leaves the station. **Miller Street** is distinguished by a fine row of artisan's dwellings before we pass **Hoyle's Goods Shed** (the railway entrance can be clearly seen). The shed has been converted into flats, and is known by the curious name of 'Victorian Lanterns'. **Brooksbottom Viaduct** is quite spectacular. Originally, the centre spans were wooden, rendered rot proof by the 'kyanisation' (using a solution of arsenic) process. The L and Y rebuilt the bridge in its present form in the 1880s, raising the central stone piers above the level of the springing point of the original timber supports. (This can be easily seen from the roadway.) The view from the viaduct is rather fine. **Brooksbottom Village**, to the right, is full of restored cottage-like houses, but all eyes will focus on the *Waterside Inn* (once the mill canteen) astride the river, with its beer garden and picnic area. Beyond is the stately pile of **Hoyle's Mill**. This company once almost cornered the market in navy blue cloth for the G.P.O., British Railways, and assorted police forces and corporation transport departments. The weaving sheds are gone, but the most impressive part of the mill is now converted into studio flats that changed hands at prices in excess of £100,000. At this point, cast a glance to the left at

the **'Brickhouses'** part of Summerseat. Look down on the pretty gardens and cobbled **Starling Street**, climbing up above the tunnel entrance. A favourite spot for photographers, but few know that they are standing on an ancient pack-horse route.

Brooksbottom Tunnel was bored through a large outcrop of rock (the river flows round it on the eastern side), and is one of the longest tunnels on a preserved railway. After a short length of cutting, the train then runs through the short **Nuttall Tunnel**. There is no reason why this should really be here, but Daniel Grant, the tenant of nearby Nuttall Hall (and one of the famous Grant brothers)

The Waterside Inn, astride the Irwell

Brooksbottom Viaduct with locomotive (A.E. Bayfield)

demanded it. He occupied a fashionable medieval fantasy mansion, and seeing locomotives from his front windows would spoil the illusion. The tunnel was quid pro quo for some land of his that the company wanted urgently and cheaply. Moreover, the **northern tunnel face** is battlemented to chime in with the medieval appearance of his (now demolished) ancestral pile. This is best viewed when travelling in the Bury direction. Try to pick out the heraldic devices and the line of **corbels in the form of grotesque faces**. (Said to be caricatures of the directors of the original ELR!) Again, we cross a bend in the Irwell by means of **two river bridges,** separated by a short shallow embankment. **St.Andrew's** (see p107) is a conspicuous landmark to the left, with a tower reminiscent of a 17th century Scottish castle. **Holcombe Hill** looms in the background, and the eye is drawn to the **Peel Monument** at the top. (Not on the actual top of the hill, as it was carefully positioned so that it could be seen from all angles.) It is the highest point in Greater Manchester, and the view from the top extends as far south as Mow Cop in Staffordshire on a clear day. The pleasant **Nuttall Park,** the grounds of the former Nuttall Hall, is visible through the trees on the right hand side of the line. The train passes over a drained former mill lodge. A short earth embankment replaces a viaduct of stone piers over the lodge area. The *TNT* **lorry park** marks the site of the Square Print Works (printing patterns on woven cloth), which was serviced by the railway. Indeed, it had its own internal railway system, presided over by a series of shunting locomotives, all called 'Archibald'. One of these was described in the 1920s as being "armour plated," a description of a war surplus Simplex military locomotive. There is also a view of the **football and cricket pitches** to the right, before the train enters the station.

Ramsbottom

Ramsbottom Station is considered by many to be the prettiest on the line. The fact that trains cross here, and that it serves an interesting place, meant that all the stops were pulled out. The vanished original buildings have been replaced by a new structure (complete with a traditional waiting room containing a coal fire). Notice the double-headed windows, a Pering design feature that has been recreated. Drink in the other features; the **footbridge, signal box**, **level crossing** gates, a small **shelter** on the opposite platform, the milk churns, and the luggage. A **station canopy** completes the picture. A (closed) **paper mill** stands beside the station, though the sidings have long disappeared. The former station goods yard is now used as a car park. There is a pleasant **line side picnic area** the other side of the level crossing, to the right, with a view of the river (and the leet that once served the paper mill) as well.

Ramsbottom sounds like a music hall joke. Nothing to do with sheep, for it signifies the 'valley of the ransoms' (wild garlic). Actually, at the same time that the Grants were gazing upon the 'Golden Valley' (as the district became known,) Peel and Yates established a calico printing works on the site of the present town centre (known as the 'old ground'). This was purchased in 1806 by the Grants, who later replaced it, in1821, with the Square Works (then the largest and most modern in Europe, see p103). The Ashton Brothers developed a large cotton mill on the eastern side of the town. Large scale industry has disappeared, but Ramsbottom is still a busy place and a very desirable location in which to live. The town centre is a conservation area.

Opposite the station entrance is the *Buddha Lounge*, with a curious statue of the Buddha throwing his hands in the air, as if Lhasa United had scored the winning goal! If you have time, and it is a fine day, turn left upon exiting the station, and keep to the left, until you reach the **path** that crosses under the railway and leads to the attractive **Nuttall Park**. A right turn from the station leads to the foot of Bridge Street, with *The Railway* on the corner. **Bridge Street** largely dates from the 1840s, and is replete with specialist shops. Look out for the **traditional sweet shop** (with delicious ice cream and

The Cheeryble Brothers

Charles Dickens was very much a London writer. But he was also an inveterate traveller, and when he came to the North of England, it was almost as if he had arrived in another country. Preston (which he visited during a bitter strike) became 'Coketown' in 'Hard Times'. But it was Manchester that had the greatest impact. He commenced writing 'A Christmas Carol' there, but was also introduced to the Grant brothers, whose business had an office in the town. The Grants were one of the sights of the place: once seen, never forgotten. They originated from Grantown-on-Spey, and legend has it that they passed this way in 1783 with their father in a party of drovers. Their father had decided to re-locate from Scotland, and the valley seemed a likely spot. They stood up a piece of wood and resolved to choose the place in which direction it fell. It pointed towards Ramsbottom...or so the story goes. The brothers were successful businessmen, but also kindly and philanthropic...if a little eccentric. This combination fascinated Dickens, for it seemed to offer an alternative model to that of the utilitarian ideology satirised in the character of Scrooge. They became the model for the Cheeryble Brothers in Nicholas Nickleby.

Departing Ramsbottom Station

traditional teddy bears); a **delicatessen** selling traditional Lancashire food; *Horsebits* (with a horse mannequin in the window!); a **hat hire** emporium for the ladies; a **leather goods and accessories** shop; a large **pet shop**; and *Memories* antique emporium, with stalls on two floors. These are juxtaposed with a number of **cafés and a tea shop**, and the **fish and chip shop** can be recommended. The 19th century **St. Paul's Church** was consecrated in 1850, on land donated by the Ashton brothers, local mill owners who also defrayed part of the construction costs. St. Paul's is noted for its fine spire, the subject of a recent appeal. About half way along Bridge Street, to the left, is a **passageway with bollards** that leads to an open area behind the shops. A small **market** operates here on Saturdays, and a **farmer's market** is held on the second Sunday of the month. Pick out the **cobbled way** directly ahead, with the row of shops to the right and *Morrisons* supermarket and car park to the left. It runs directly to the *Irwell Works Brewery* with its large blue painted door and frame. It is housed in the former 'Irwell Steam, Tin, Copper, and Iron Works (built 1888) and is one of Ramsbottom's best kept secrets. A window in the entrance hall gives on to the new **micro-brewery**, producing a variety of beers (including one called 'Steam Plate' in honour of the railway). The 'Tap' is to be found upstairs, an atmospheric bar dispensing the brewery's products. The 'Tap' is open most days, and tours of the brewery can be arranged (01706 825019).

There is a **little square** at the junction of **Bridge Street** and **Bolton Street**, distinguished by the **Tilted Vase Fountain** (recalling the joke about "what's a Grecian urn?"). The first residence of the immortal Grant brothers is now the **Grant's Arms** pub in the background (the present frontage, with its clock, was placed on to the original house in 1828). The **Civic Hall**, on the slope to the right of it, was formerly the Conservative Club of 1860. A short detour to the right leads past *Atelier Rose and Gray* (a fine commercial art gallery) and *Ramsons* (a restaurant mentioned in 'The Good Food Guide', and the 'Michelin Guide'), to arrive at the **Weslyan Chapel**, a fine building erected 1873-4 to replace the original chapel of 1825. Retrace your steps and

Romsbottom's Chocolate Festival

seek out the unique *Chocolate Café* (with a shop on the ground floor) to the left of the square, then follow the street up the hill to the **library** and the **Heritage Centre** (weekdays except Wednesdays and Saturday afternoons, entry through library; some Sundays, using separate entrance, ring 01706 821603 to check, admission free).

The niche shopping continues along **Bolton Street**. The **blue plaque** to the right on Number 18 (*Roger Greenlees*) records the residence (in 1842) of Peter Murray McDouall, the Chartist, who practiced medicine in Ramsbottom between 1835 and 1842.

Notice **Number 23** (*Cherry Picked*) on the corner of **Smithy Street**. This was built in 1833 by Peter Hamer, a blacksmith (the smithy was located in the cellar, now *Enchanted*

The Other Famous Son

Born in Wigtownshire in 1815, McDouall became a doctor, and a Chartist National leader, active in Ramsbottom and Ashton-under-Lyne. He advocated a political strategy that advocated linking Chartism with trade unionism, and promoted this as the editor of "The Chartist and Republican Journal." As part of a tour of the Midlands and the North of England, he gave a lecture in Derby's Mechanics Hall (the spy's notes call him `MacDowell'), calling upon the bourgeoisie and the aristocracy to set an example to the lower classes by moderating their life styles. In particular, he suggested that the Queen might give up half a million pounds of her "salary" annually, to relieve the poor. He led the two mile procession to deliver the Chartist Petition to parliament. While residing in Ramsbottom, he gave evidence to a Parliamentary Committee enquiring into the 'truck system'. He stated that the Grants paid their workers with tokens once a week in the Grant's Arms. These could only be used to purchase beer there or exchanged for substandard and overpriced provisions in their 'tommy shop'. A somewhat darker side to the 'Cheeryble Brothers' was thus revealed. Disillusioned with the seeming failure of the Chartist movement, he was lost at sea whilst emigrating to Australia in 1854. In 1867, working men in towns were given the vote.

Cave). A detour along Smithy Street, to the left, accesses the **Theatre Royal**. The theatre (box office 01706 826760) is the second building on the site and owes its existence to the Blakeborough family. In 1912 a cinema was converted from stables, which was later destroyed by fire. E E Blakeborough replaced this in the 1930s with a purpose built cinema. Films ceased around 1968, and the building was used for snooker. It was then acquired by the Summerseat Players, and transformed into a multi-purpose little theatre, able to accommodate conferencing and functions. A thriving local film society also uses it as a cinema.

Bolton Street passes the former **Baptist Chapel** (1861) and **Saint Joseph's R.C. Church** (1880), to arrive at the impressive entrance drive to **St. Andrew's Church** (see p103), on the left. There is a good **view of the west end**, with its fine **tower** incorporating the features of a Scottish baronial castle! (Note the **date stone with the arms of Clan Grant** round the right-hand corner).The church was constructed in 1832-4 by the Grant brothers for use of their workforce, and was heated by the exhaust hot water from their mill engines. Naturally, the founders were true to their roots, as it was originally a Church of Scotland establishment, and most of the mill workers adopted the religious opinions of their bosses. In the late 19th century, long after the brothers had gone to receive their reward, the congregation split into two hostile factions. One wanted to transfer the church to the Anglican confession, while the other wanted to continue as Presbyterians. They promptly demonstrated their Christian principles by brawling for possession of the sacred edifice. The Church of England crowd won the day. Its interior contains nine **memorials** to various members of the Grant family that are worth seeing. (For information about access, ring 01706 826482.) Walk a little further and turn right down **Dundee Lane** to reach **The School House**, dating back to 1664 (note the **date stone** over the door). It was rebuilt in the 19th century, incorporating much of the original masonry. The building was originally used as a Court House, but was then named 'Well House' as its occupants maintained the local well. **Medieval stone** was incorporated in the 19th century rebuilding from Manchester Cathedral (being rebuilt at the same time), hence the second date stone inscribed 1414 and some curious carvings. The **broach spire of Emmanuel Church, Holcombe**, (133feet tall), is visible from this spot. The church was erected in 1853, to replace a Chapel of Ease with a history going back to Tudor times.

If it is a fine day, or you are feeling energetic, you can continue past the **library** (p106), following the signs for the steep **'rake'**, passing **Emmanuel Church**, to reach **Holcombe Hill** (the **tower** is open when the flag is flying, see p103).

Ramsbottom to Rawtenstall

The crossing gates swing open, the signal is 'pulled off', the 'right away' is given, and the train pulls away from the platform and rolls over the crossing, past the **picnic area** to the right. The area of the track bed beyond is surprisingly spacious. But it was once much bigger. Parkland and the local **baths** now replace the former coal and mineral sidings on the left. This area was sometimes used to marshal the empty stock for the 'wakes' holiday excursion trains. In contrast, the **site of the former exchange sidings** is still visible on the right. The railways were 'common carriers' of all manner of goods up to the 1960s, and undertook delivery to most destinations within a twenty-four hour period. This service relied on a complex system of road delivery and pick up, feeder trains, and trunk routes, connected by marshalling yards, sort sidings, and goods yards. These were 'sort sidings'. Every day, a 'pick up goods' would work the line between here and Bacup, the locomotive shunting the station goods yards to deliver and pick up wagons and vans. (Another train would also work the numerous mineral sidings of the quarries, once numerous beyond Rawtenstall.) The wagons would be shunted according to geographical destination, to be forwarded to other yards. (For example, anything bound for a Yorkshire destination would be sent by a goods working from here to Collyhurst sidings.) The area is partly occupied by a **siding, loop, and headshunt**. The northern section has now been appropriated for the use of cellulose sludge tanks connected with the paper works in Stubbins. Beyond the **fire station**, to the left, the train crosses **Stubbins Lane** by means of a **low bridge**. A level crossing had been intended, but the gradients on the Accrington line (added to the original railway project as an afterthought) had to be altered (a rope hauled incline to the summit towards Accrington was originally intended). Of course, this meant that the gradients on the Rawtenstall line had to be altered at the point of junction, hence the very low bridge. The later demands of double decker buses resulted in a substantial lowering of the roadway, and chaotic flooding in bad weather. The closure of the railway should have resulted in the removal of this inconvenient bridge (it is also narrow, with traffic controlled by lights). Instead, the restoration of the line necessitated the provision of storm drains, which seems to have solved the flooding problem. **Stubbins Village** lies to the right of the bridge.

We pass through the remains of **Stubbins Station**. The **junction for the Accrington line** was situated between the bridge and the south end of the station **down platform** (though the station was never a junction itself, and passengers from Bacup and Rawtenstall changed trains at Ramsbottom for Accrington). Consequently, there was barely room for the **down (left-hand) platform**, with the Accrington line running round the back of it. In the course of restoring the line, work began on extending this platform to accommodate larger trains, but the loss of a grant meant a choice between completing the vital Rawtenstall terminus platform and here. The **up platform**, opposite, still survives. The long vanished station buildings were at street level, and there never was a goods yard. Interestingly enough, the main entrance was by subway, and the **railings at the top of the platform steps** are still visible. These steps are sealed off, but the **subway** is still in use: it constitutes part of the Rossendale Way, a long distance footpath. One day the station may reopen...and will be much in demand by walkers as the nearest point to access 'the tops'.

Beyond the station, the track bed of the **former Accrington line** can be seen rapidly ascending on the left. Beyond, there are views of the hilltops. **Chatterton village** lies opposite, across the river. This was once one of the busiest places in the valley...until the mill was attacked by a group of machine breakers in the early 19th century. A neat **row of artisan's houses** to the left precedes a **road bridge**, with a similar (unrestored) bridge on the Accrington route. The hamlet of **Strongstry** is visible on the right, a quiet (and thus desirable) place to live. Part of the area between the railway and the Accrington line has been converted into a **nature trail**. We cross the Irwell by one of the two **Alderbottom Viaducts**. The **high level viaduct**, on the former Accrington line to the left, is a very prominent sight. After a short cutting, notice the Accrington line curving away to the left, crossing the Irwell by the impressive stone **Lumb Viaduct**. The river now runs close to the railway on this side. Cast your eyes to the tops of the grassy slope opposite. You may be able to pick out the **L and Y boundary stones**, set out like little milestones. The sculpture of **Remnant Kings** is much easier to spot.

The train comes to a stop at **Irwell Vale Halt**. This station is used by walkers, local inhabitants (particularly on a Saturday for shopping excursions), and is also the haunt of a select group of railway photographers. The station is built on the site of former railway sidings, protected by an L and Y signal that survived into the 1960s. Line side **picnic facilities** are available. There is a fenced off viewing area on the right, adjacent to the **level crossing and subway**.

A footpath leads from here up to **Edenfield Church**, parts

Pretty Irwell Vale village

of which date to the 16th century. The old stone tower has a curious lean. **Irwell Vale** itself once boasted three mills, two chapels, a post office, and co-operative stores. Now it is a quiet little place, much sought after by house hunters. Note the inscription relating to the former **Primitive Methodist Chapel**, and the **bridges** over the Irwell and the Ogden. The remaining **Methodist Chapel** serves refreshments on Summer Sundays, and hosts talks by the Irwell Vale Railway Photographers. It is a short (and pretty) walk to **Lumb**, where **Lumb Hall** is visible (private property, please respect). This ancient dwelling incorporates mediaeval cruck beams in its construction. For the energetic, there is a charming **walk along the Ogden stream**, leading to **Helmshore** (turn left at the **stile**, beyond the **Ogden bridge**), where the **Helmshore Mills Textile Museum** (with a working water wheel in the basement of the older building) may be visited (open April to October, 12-4 or 5, admission charge), returning to Rawtenstall by bus.

The train passes over the **level crossing** (which is operated by the user), and crosses a great bend in the river by **two bridges**. One of these was recently (2002) damaged by flood water, which undermined its central pier. However, all is now well again. The river bend encloses a large **sewage works** on the left. This mundane location had its moment of fame in the First World War, when it was bombed by a Zeppelin. (The commander was under the impression that he was attacking Derby!) Note the football pitch, and (best seen in winter) the 17th century **Ewood Hall**. This site was once the property of Whalley Abbey, and it is said to be haunted by the chanting of ghostly monks. Before the train passes under the **road bridge**, note the **old turnpike bridge** over the river, to the left. This gives the locality its name, and was constructed by the legendary 'Blind Jack of Knaresborough', the celebrated 18th century road builder.

The **site of Ewood Bridge station** is interesting. The former station was often criticised in the past for its inconvenient location, and the restoration strategy decided against reopening, preferring to replace it with Irwell Vale Halt. The unusual bridge level booking hall and the other facilities are long gone, but the remaining platform structures were cannibalised for re-use elsewhere along the line. (A **small portion of platform** remains as part of the road bridge.) To the left, the area once occupied by the goods yard is in private hands, and it contains a superb **goods shed**, thought to be East Lancashire Railway in origin.

A short distance beyond the station, the train passes under the **motorway bridge**. This was constructed in the declining years of the coal traffic. A few years later and the track bed might have been cut at this point. The valley really opens out at this end of the line and there are some fine views up to the 'tops' on either side. This end of the line was famous for its quarries in the 19th century, though only one was rail connected south of Rawtenstall, the present terminus. Opposite a bend in the river, look out for on old **brick lineside hut** on the right. This is all that remains of the quarry exchange sidings, which connected with a rope-hauled incline (passing under the top road) to **Horncliffe Quarry**. The quarry was, in turn, serviced by a narrow gauge system, with a locomotive driven by "Hellfire Jack," a reference to his other occupation as a Methodist preacher, and not his driving ability! (These quarries supplied the finest flag stones in the world. Lancashire flags were in great demand, and upon the recent renovation of Nelsons Column in London, the flags from this quarry were used to replace damaged flagstones.) As the train approaches **Townsend Fold Crossing**, notice the **railway cottages** on the right. The crossing is manned, and a **B.R. signal box** faces the old stone

The Hardman's Mill chimney

goods shed. In the late 1970s, the crossing was the scene of a terrible accident. A Class Forty diesel locomotive, at the head of a coal train, ploughed into a car that had tried to 'jump' the crossing before it. We pass the gardens of a new housing development to the right, before entering **New Hall Hey Cutting**, with its **occupation bridge**. The "moist laminated folds" described on the opening day in 1846 are still visible. A final crossing of the Irwell presages **Rawtenstall West Crossing**, with its **B.R. box**. **Hardman's Mill** is located to the left with its tall **chimney**. There is a **platform** on the top. This, together with the **ornamental window slits** in the chimney, gave rise to the local legend that there is a staircase in the thickness of the wall! The ***Old Cobblers Inn*** is visible from the crossing. It caters for families, and serves meals.

Rawtenstall

The train finally pulls into **Rawtenstall Station** where the journey terminates. Virtually everything is a recent creation. The original station was situated further to the north, and the line continued over a level crossing to run alongside the river. This section is now a bypass, so the opportunity of returning to Bacup has been lost forever. The **platform** terminates near a **water tower**. It is an island platform for the greater part of its distance, with the principal platform to the left and a siding to the right, containing a **coach** selling refreshments. It can be a bit windswept in winter, and a canopy is proposed for the future, with a screen at the Southern end. The **short section of platform** opposite the head shunt, on the left, is all that remains of the **original down platform**. It contains an **ELR lamp standard**, and there are wagons alongside it, including a low-roofed **gunpowder van**. The **station buildings** are a rather fine pastiche, again using the ELR motif of double-headed windows, and distinguished by a fine **clock tower** over the **booking hall**. To the left side is **Buffer Stops**, a real ale pub, and **toilets**, and to the right a **waiting room**. A great deal remains of the **former goods yard** complex to the right of the station, with a (re-cobbled) **yard** used as a car park. The **ELR Goods Shed** is now used as a car showroom, but a glimpse of the interior reveals the similarities to Buckley Wells and Castlecroft sheds. The **Cotton Warehouse** was probably constructed by the L and Y, and now contains offices and a club.

The earliest settlement at Rawtenstall was probably in the early medieval period, during the time when it formed part of the Forest of Rossendale, and consisted of simple dwellings for forest servants and animals. More substantial buildings may have followed in the 15th and 16th centuries with corn and flour mills. The town entered a major period of growth during the industrial revolution, as new mills were constructed to process cotton. It was incorporated as a borough in 1891.

Taking a short walk from the station up the valley, you can encounter the many interesting sites and attractions of Rawtenstall. Cross the road to the **promenade** alongside the river (the large *Asda* **supermarket** is on the site of Longholme Mill, and the **footbridge** that crosses the Irwell at this point was used by the mill hands), but don't miss the **ice cream shop** to the right of the footbridge. Linger here along the **lower river path** to the left of the footbridge to feed the ducks, perhaps, but notice the odd **metal tree sculpture** (sometimes decorated) towards **Bocholt Way.** This is the way we go, to the junction with the new by-pass, largely constructed on the track of the old railway at this point, which we cross. The **fire station**, to the left, was opened in 1988. The *Café Artisan*, set back beyond a forecourt on the right (daily except Monday and

Rawtenstall's promenade!

Tuesday, late opening Thursday to Saturday), becomes a bar in the evenings, with live music Saturday nights. Across Bacup Road, notice the *Queen's Arms Hotel* on the corner. The building dates to the late 18th century, and was the only establishment with stabling facilities when the nearby turnpike road opened. It was used for the inaugural meeting of the St. Annes on Sea Land and building company in 1874; the resort was a property speculation by local businessmen and quarry owners, and many people removed there upon retirement. (The row of shops beyond Bacup Road contains *Rossendale Models*, specialising in radio-controlled vehicles, boats, and aircraft.) Turn right and walk down **Bacup Road** as far as **Longholme Road** on the right. The latter follows the course of the **old turnpike road**, and forms an interesting diversion. Notice the **Limy Water** as it flows towards the Irwell, and continue along the path beyond the bollard to a **viewing area** with seats. Here you can admire the old **packhorse bridge** over the Irwell. Retrace your steps and continue along **Bacup Road**, walking as far as the **cricket ground** on the left. The **lodge** (1864 date stone) to the right of it originally served the long vanished Greenbank House.

Opposite the cricket ground is the recently renovated stone edifice of **Ilex Mill** (1856), which is followed by the rear of the distinctive **Weavers' Cottage**. The cottage, which appears on a map of 1784, may have been a rebuild of a house dating to 1712, creating a loom shop, a kind of halfway house between a weaver's cottage and a mill. The Bacup Road frontage has been restored by the Rawtenstall Civic Society, who currently occupy the Cottage. Notice the **'takin' in' door and steps**, where the yarn was delivered to the looms on the upper floors. Turn right into **Fall Barn Road** to access the cottage from the rear, but first look up at the magnificent **range of window lights** that illuminated the loom shops from the sunny south side. (Usually open Easter to September, Saturday, Sunday, and Bank Holidays, 2-5, ring 01706 229828 for further information; admission free, but donation or purchase appreciated..) The **two rooms on the ground floor** would have been used for checking and packing the cloth bales before they were sent to market at Rochdale or Halifax Piece Hall. The larger room is the **reception area** and contains a **clogger's shop**. The smaller room is fitted out as a **kitchen**, with a pump and a fine range. On the **landing** are photographs of the cottage and its inhabitants at various periods. There is a **tea room** on the **middle floor**, which is also used for meetings and temporary exhibitions. The **top floor** has been opened up to re-create the full size of an 18th century loom shop. There are a number of examples of looms, including a **table loom**; a **traditional four post loom** (used by cottage weavers for centuries); and a fine example of a **flying shuttle loom**, which enabled broad cloth (wider than the reach of the weaver's arms) to be woven. The latter is fitted with a 'drop box' to enable a complicated pattern to be woven. A modern reconstruction of a **'walk wheel' spinning wheel**, together with a more **traditional wheel**, is placed here, though yarn would not be spun in a loom shop. There are also changing **local history displays**.

Leave the Weaver's Cottage, and continue along **Fall Barn Road**, bearing left towards the end of the **Medical Centre**. Look for the gap in the wall by the side of Bocholt Way.

The Rawtenstall Murderess

Until the 1970s, another cottage backed onto the Weaver's Cottage; one with a notorious history, for it was the home of Maggie Allen. Margaret Allen was a lesbian who dressed in men's clothes and preferred to be called 'Bill'. (During the war she worked as local bus conductor, where trousers were acceptable.) On the 28th August 1948 she battered Nancy Ellen Chadwick to death with a hammer. Mrs Chadwick was an elderly neighbour who had come to borrow a cup of sugar. Although she dressed shabbily, her pockets were often stuffed with wads of banknotes. The neighbours had apparently never enjoyed the best of relationships and Allen found her irritating in the extreme. Allen confessed to the police that she was "... in one of my funny moods." She was convicted after a short trial held on the 8th December 1948 and was hanged on the 12th January 1949 by public executioner Albert Pierrepoint, the first female execution in Britain for 12 years and only the third at Strangeways Prison.

The Weaver's Cottage

Although there is no pedestrian crossing, this point is used as a **crossing for the by-pass**, though great care should be exercised in crossing this very busy road. **Fall Barn Road** continues on the opposite side. Follow the sign for **Lambert's Mill** and walk up the access road to the left. **Lambert's Mill** (Mon-Sat 9-5, Sunday, 10-4) is a complex of factory shops, together with a museum. The **ground floor** contains a wide selection of furniture and furnishings, but the principal attraction is a small but interesting **footwear museum**. It tells the story of the slipper industry in Rossendale, with a **video presentation** and interesting displays (including some curious examples of **Victorian advertising**). The display of historic and modern footwear is noteworthy. The **first floor** contains a **gift shop** with a wide range of items and an excellent **café**.

Retrace your path all the way back to **Longholme Road**, and notice that this street (and the former turnpike road) is continued as a **paved passage** opposite. Cross the road, and follow this route, passing the large **Longholme Chapel** to the right, with its fine neo-classical façade. It was built in 1842 at the cost of £7,000 and could seat 1,300 people. We now reach the lower end of Bank Street, and a number of original buildings survive here. Among them is the former toll house, now the famous *Fitzpatrick's Herbal Health* (open daily, except Sundays).

A section of Bank Street beyond the shop has had the **cobbled surface restored**. It is possible to see the **path of the tram track** (removed in the 1930s), including the site of a passing loop. The street eventually leads to **Rawtenstall Market** (Thursday and Saturday). However, it is perhaps better cross to the other side of **Bank Street** by the adjacent **pedestrian crossing**. The **clock tower** is all that remains of Holly Mount School, erected in 1839 by the Whitehead brothers, local mill owners, for the education of the children of their employees. The adjacent **garden**, opened in 1979, should be

The path of the steam trams!

entered for a view of the original **school date stone**, placed at the foot of the tower. Continue past **St. Mary's Church**. This fine neo-gothic structure was built in 1836, but greatly re-modelled and extended in the 1880s. The **Memorial Gardens**, beyond the church contain a tasteful **war memorial**. We now arrive at the fine **library**, opened in 1907, and the gift of Andrew Carnegie, the great philanthropist. Our way now lies along side of what is now a large **traffic island**. However, this was once a part of the town known as Captain Fold, and the

The 'Sas Shop'

Fitzpatrick's Herbal Health on Bank Street (daily except Sunday), known locally as the 'Sas Shop', is something of a Rossendale institution. Fitzpatrick's Botanical Herbalists has been making soft drinks for the people of Rossendale and Lancashire since 1899. During the Industrial Revolution, Lancashire experienced a massive population influx. The easy availability of ale and gin led to widespread alcoholism, and in response the Temperance Movement began in the Lancashire town of Preston in 1835. Prohibition was never legislated here, but non-alcoholic bars sprang up to promote abstinence from the 'demon drink'. The Fitzpatricks, an Irish family of herbalists, started their business in 1899. At their peak they had around thirty shops. Interest in 'taking the pledge' faded after World War II and today this shop is the sole survivor. The tiny Victorian bar still looks pretty much as it ever did...ceramic tap barrels, with shelves lined with jars of medicinal herbs, roots and extracts. Local people still call in to purchase sarsaparilla cordial, blood tonic, dandelion and burdock, black beer and raisin, and much else besides, to consume in the shop or to make up at home.

The 'Sas Shop'

location of the 17th century New Hall Hey House. Amazingly, it survived in a derelict condition until 1969; its disappearance remains a blot upon the doings of local planners. Fortunately, the former **United Methodist Free Church**, in the guise of a Greek temple, remains to be admired on the right. It dates from 1856. Carry on past the old chapel up **Haslingden Road**, until the entrance to **Whitaker Park** is reached.

The estate was purchased from William Cockerill of Haslingden (who later pioneered industrialisation in Belgium) in 1840 by George Hardman, a local mill owner. He built Oak Hill, the present building, which was considerably enlarged in the 1880s. The house and surrounding parkland was purchased by Richard Whittaker in 1900. He was the archetype of the Lancashire self-made man, having started life as a 'doffer' in a mill (responsible for changing bobbins) at the age of six, and ending it as a director of Howard and Bullough, an Accrington based textile machine manufacturer. He had a good heart, and presented the house to the corporation as a museum (1902) and the grounds as a fine landscaped park (1901) for children to play in and the adults to enjoy. The **Rossendale Museum** (open daily except Monday, 10am to 4pm), admission free) is well worth a visit. From the **entrance hall**, turn left into the former **dining room**. This is now used as a **reception area**, with a **small shop**. A **free audio-guide** is available. Notice that the Hardman family had a fine view of their mill, with its tall chimney, from the **window**. We now explore the **ground floor**. Across the hallway is the **fine and decorative art room**. Next door is a magnificently recreated **Victorian drawing room**. Opposite, across the passage, is the **Natural History Gallery**, a monument to the art of the taxidermist. Children are drawn to the **baby elephant**, and the **tableaux of a Bengal Tiger being attacked by a Boa Constrictor**. The **adjacent room** is used for temporary exhibitions, but notice the **large fossils** displayed in the floor surface. The **upstairs galleries** contain a variety of interesting **local history displays**. If there is time, explore the park, and perhaps venture as far as the **ski-slope**. This artificial slope was one of the first in its field, but has found it hard, in recent years, to compete with newer slopes, some even employing refrigerated snow. In 2011 it was saved by local efforts, and once more caters to a (largely local) clientele. (Ring 01706 226457 for further information.)

Eddie 'the Eagle'

The ski slope is associated by many local people with the man who opened part of the complex...Eddie 'the Eagle'. Eddie was a good downhill skier, but wasn't a good ski jumper when compared to the international competition. However, to realize his Olympic dream he decided to switch to ski jumping for reasons of cost and easier qualification (there were no other competing British ski jumpers). Eddie was informed of his qualification for the Games whilst working as a plasterer and residing temporarily in a Finnish mental hospital due to lack of funds for alternative accommodation (rather than as a patient). Eddie began jumping using his equipment, though he had to wear six layers of socks to make the boots fit. He was also handicapped by his weight and his eyesight, requiring him to wear his glasses at all times, even though when skiing they fogged to such an extent that he could not see. However, his lack of success endeared him to people all across the globe. The worse he did, the more popular he became. He subsequently became a media celebrity and appeared on talk shows around the world. The widespread attention that Edwards received in Calgary turned into a large embarrassment for the ski jumping establishment, and many athletes and officials felt that he was "making a mockery" of the sport Shortly after the Olympics finished, the entry requirements were greatly toughened, making it next to impossible for anyone to follow his example. Nevertheless many thought that he alone embodied the original Olympic spirit. At the closing ceremony, the president of the Organizing Committee, Frank King, seemed to single out Edwards for his contribution: "At this Games, some competitors have won gold, some have broken records, and some of you have even soared like an eagle."

Bury to Heywood

The train leaves Bolton Street Station and almost immediately passes under the **Jubilee Way Bridge** before entering the Heywood line by an inclined curve to the left. This was the connecting curve to the L and Y. line, to enable traffic to be exchanged between the two companies. After the 1916 electrification of the direct Manchester line, the Bacup and Rawtenstall steam service was diverted this way (see p59). **Bury South Box** is situated in the angle of the junction, to the right. You may catch a glimpse of the **Whitehead Memorial Tower** (see p88) in the background. The first **stone bridge** carries **Manchester Road** across the railway, and a second arch on the right once spanned the Land Y line to Bolton. Both this arch and its approach cutting have been backfilled. There is a short area of cutting prior to the **Knowsley Street Bridge.** Bury's **Town Hall** (not visible at this point) is situated at the top of the leftward bank, a rather grand

1930s building whose completion was interrupted by World War Two.

The bridge arch gives on to the **site of Knowsley Street Station**, the Land Y's station in Bury. The original footbridge was adjacent to this arch, and collapsed on 19 January, 1952, taking a number of visiting Blackburn Rovers fans with it. One man was killed and one hundred and seventy-three injured. Nothing now remains; a new **hotel** and **car park** development occupies the site of the main buildings to the left, and **new housing** intrudes to the right. A 'loco curve' (mostly in cutting) was constructed in the last quarter of the 19th century, commencing at the East end of the station site, skirting it to the South (right of the present line), and joining the Manchester line south of Buckley Wells (see p83). It was used for light engine movements to and from Bury shed, but its principal purpose was to route trans-Pennine goods trains (via Radcliffe and 'Black Harry Tunnel' on the Patricroft branch) to and from Liverpool, but avoiding Manchester, and Yorkshire goods trains via Windsor Bridge Junction (where Salford Crescent Station is now located) and a vanished goods branch to Manchester Docks. It closed around 1967. The almost forgotten track bed was later utilised as an approach to a new Bus-Rail Interchange... the Southern part of the curve was retained, but a new right of way was cut through the Knowsley Street site, crossing the original Land Y line at right angles, before terminating in the new Interchange. The resulting spoil was used to fill in the rest of the 'curve'. When the Interchange opened in 1979, the electric trains ran a service that was not much disturbed by the infrequent coal trains at the (signalled) flat crossing. However, when the ELR decided upon the extension to Heywood, the Metrolink trams prove to be an altogether different proposition. It was necessary to cross Metrolink by a bridge. The position of the Knowsley Street Bridge required a very steep approach incline from that direction – the other incline is still steep but less severe. The **Metrolink Bridge** (or the 'ski-jump, as the railway's working members call it) is a unique feature. Operating experience suggests that this incline can be easily negotiated by short trains (and some diesel locomotives with heavier loadings). Otherwise, a 'banker' is required. Of course, it is easy to make a virtue out of such a necessity, and it is expected that large numbers of enthusiasts and photographers (not to mention excursion trains) will be drawn to the railway to witness the 'ski jump' in action. You may be lucky enough to see a Metrolink tram whiz under as you cross, and the **Interchange** is visible to the left.

As the train descends from the bridge, notice the remains of a small park to the left. **Pyramid Park** is so-called because the debris of the old goods yard, large cotton shed, and goods shed that formerly stood on this site was piled up into grassy pyramids. We pass under **Market Street** by a stone arch that once crossed the entrance to the yard throat. The girders of the bridge over the actual line, to the right, were found defective, and it was simpler to slew the line this way and backfill the girder bridge. After passing Townside Fields, with new housing (including sheltered accommodation) on the left, and some parkland to the right, the train runs under **Heywood Street**, and passes through a shallow cutting before **Alfred Street** road bridge. (The junction for the former Bury loop, or loco curve, was situated between these two bridges.)

After falling away towards the **valley of the Roch**, a tributary of the Irwell, the line now starts a continuous climb towards Boadfield at Alfred Street, to avoid a steeper ascent on the far side of the river. The **large mill,** visible to the right, was formerly the CWS Pilot Mill, and is now is the home of *Antler Luggage*. It was rail connected, and the adjacent Gigg Mills sidings served other mills in the vicinity, including the **remains of Beech Mill** on the left. The impressive brick **Roch Viaduct** of seven arches crosses the river and valley; the structure's current appearance dates from an extensive rebuild in 1862. There is a fine view Southwards (on the right) down the river valley, with the turreted tower of **Stand Church**, Whitefield (see p75), a prominent object on the horizon. Almost immediately after the viaduct we cross the **motorway bridge** over the M66, a unique feature in British railway preservation. As in the case of the Rawtenstall section, this bridge was constructed in the dying days of B.R. operation, when the entire line from Castleton was only used by about two or three coal trains a week! Beyond this point, the **branch to Heap Bridge** diverged to the left. It served a factory complex containing the famous Bridge Hall Paper Mills, once owned by Thomas Wrigley, a prominent director of the ELR, and a pioneer in railway signalling. It opened in 1874, and served the Yates Duxbury paper works in its latter years, before closing in 1967. (The company had an extensive private railway system, and one of their locomotives was preserved on the ELR.)

However, the train runs on under an **occupation bridge** to enter a **long cutting** to run along up **Broadfield bank**. The cutting is spanned by a bridge carrying **Moss Hall Road** across the railway. As we emerge from the cutting, note part of the award winning **Heywood Distribution Park** to the right. Many freight forwarding and haulage companies use this large (over 160 acres in extent) site, and there is a long-term proposal to put in a rail connection with the ELR This is appropriate, as extensive sidings (and a private railway system) once served No. 35 Maintenance Unit, R.A.F. Heywood, which once occupied this land. It was not an airfield, but a large distribution depot containing aircraft parts and other stores, employing a largely civilian workforce. It opened in 1938/9, just in time for World War Two, and closed in 1967. Its main gate was graced, in the early 1960s, with a display aircraft; a Gloster Meteor, the first jet fighter to enter service. This example, an F8 dating from 1954, can now be seen at the Yorkshire Air Museum. Housing now appears opposite, including a **new estate** on the site of a demolished cotton mill. The **bridge across Pilsworth Road** is new. The original was taken out to enable vehicle access to the Park, but road alterations have enabled another routing to be employed, much to the relief of local residents. This meant that a handsome new concrete bridge has been constructed for the railway.

Little remains of the **site of Broadfield Station**, save part of the platform on the left where the grass of peoples' gardens have swamped it like the waves of the sea.

The line then passes along a grassy corridor with housing estates on either side, with the spire of **St. Luke's Church** (p118) visible on the left. It passes under **Schofield Street** and **Manchester Road** by substantial original stone bridges, before the present terminus is reached.

Heywood

Heywood Station is a completely new creation. The original was constructed adjacent to Manchester Road, on an inconvenient curve, so the surviving platforms were demolished. (A **gap in the retaining wall**, on the right as the train enters the station, marks the position of the long vanished footbridge at the end of the original platforms.) The new configuration, which utilises part of the old goods yard, results in a **much-improved new platform**, which is equipped with a **shelter**. When funds permit, it is proposed to erect a suitable station building, perhaps including a canopy. The line continues across **Green Lane Crossing**, an automatic barrier operation. The greater part of the track beyond this point is leased by the ELR It extends to the junction (one mile distant) with the national railway system at Castleton, and is used for light engine movements and excursions to and from the railway (see p119). The Heywood station precincts were formerly the home of the Standard Wagon Works, but the company have closed down its Heywood operation. Notice the old stone **Warehouse** and associated yard to the right. This area is scheduled for redevelopment, perhaps including a museum in the old shed. A branch canal once extended from the Rochdale Canal, terminating beyond **Sefton Street** alongside the station and the terminus of the railway branch that pre-dated it. Both served the large coal depot at the canal branch terminus. It, in turn, was connected by a tram road with Hatters Coal Pits near Hopwood Hall. There is a convenient *Il Vecchio* restaurant and pizzeria at the top of the station approach, and the historic *Phoenix Brewery* (1898) is home since 1991to a micro-brewery (a visitor centre and shop is projected).

Heywood (pop. 28,000) is a town within the Metropolitan Borough of Rochdale, and lies on the south bank of the River Roch. It is believed to date from when the Saxons cleared the densely wooded area, and divided it into heys or fenced clearings. During the middle ages, it formed a chapelry centred on Heywood Hall, a manor house owned by a family with the surname Heywood. Farming was the main industry of this sparsely populated rural area, which in the 15th century "consisted of a few cottages". The local population supplemented their incomes by hand loom weaving. The factory system in the town can be traced to a spinning mill in the late 18th century; a period of "extraordinary growth of the cotton-trade" in the mid-19th century was so quick and profound that there was "an influx of strangers causing a very dense population". The town was granted borough status in 1881. Imports of foreign cotton goods during the mid-20th century precipitated the decline of Heywood's textile and mining industries, although this resulted in a more diverse industrial pattern. The whole town is undergoing a major regeneration as part of the government's New Deal for Communities, and New Heart for Heywood are investing around £52 million.

Heywood Station is some distance from the town centre, but do not let this put you off exploring. (A vintage bus service, also connecting with other attractions, is projected.) Turn right at the top of the station approach and walk about half a mile into the comparatively unspoilt **town centre**. The **public library** (1905) is now incorporated into a new leisure complex, and the **Magic Market** (open on Tuesday, Friday, and Saturday), opposite, is worth a visit. After noticing the **war memorial and gardens**, cross the road to admire Heywood's pride, the **Parish Church of St. Luke**. The church is a fine example of Victorian neo-gothic, consecrated in 1862. The tower and spire is detached from the main church building and stands 188 feet (57 m) high, dominating Heywood's townscape. The **interior** is rich and sumptuous, but do not miss the wooden **model** of the church, constructed by two local pensioners. (To arrange a visit to the church, ring 01706 369 324.) The nearby **Queens Park** has recently undergone a multi-million pound facelift,

Monkey Town
You may hear this place referred to as 'Monkey Town', and there are two explanations for the local legend. Locals will tell you that a 'tackler' (mill workers who had a reputation for being gormless) went into a pub and saw the landlord's new set of stools...with holes cut in the seat to allow them to be picked up easily. He was so taken with this that the drinkers convinced him that this was because the locals had tails...a well-known fact! The other explanation is more prosaic. The Irish navvies building the line were lodged in a shanty at Heap Bridge, which in their brogue soon translated into 'Ape Bridge'.

with many of its Victorian attractions restored, such as the old fountain and many of the statues. Further afield, **Ashworth Valley** is a noted beauty spot, where it is possible to spend a pleasant hour or so following the wooded **Cheesden Brook**.

The Future

The railway is to be extended a further mile beyond Heywood to form a junction with the national system at Castleton. There will be a joint station and a major re-development of Castleton itself, to include new housing and office accommodation, a hotel, a re-vamped main street, and new moorings on the canal. Hopefully, by the time these lines are in print, work will have started on this project.

The Oldham Line

Piccadilly Station to Irk Valley Junction

The route from Piccadilly Station to Piccadilly Gardens is described on pp26-28; Piccadilly Gardens to Victoria Station on pp40-45; Victoria Station itself on pp45-50; and Victoria Station to Irk Valley Junction on pp55-56.

Irk Valley Junction to Central Park

The tram diverges to the right, down the curving (and sloping) **Smedley Viaduct**, to join the old **Collyhurst (or Manchester) loop**. (The **River Irk**, for once in a pretty wooded setting, flows to the right of the viaduct, best seen on the return journey.) Although rope haulage had long been abandoned on Platting Bank (p55), the weight of the Lancashire and Yorkshire Railway expresses had increased so much that an easier gradient was sought. The answer was a new loop line, commencing at Victoria Station East Junction, and re-joining the main line at Thorpes Bridge. Not only were the gradients lighter, but a four track layout permitted faster lines for the expresses without a banking engine to impede them! It was opened in 1878, and closed as a result of the Victoria Station remodelling in the 1990s. The tracks joining the loop line by the Smedley viaduct enabled local trains from the new (1904-5) Manchester Victoria bay platforms that were bound for Oldham, Rochdale, Middleton, Royton, and Bury via Heywood to join the 'slow lines' at the point of junction. This junction is now restored, and a quick glance to the left here will reveal that part of the loop is now used for access to and from **Queens Road Depot**, located beyond the **Bury viaduct**. As the tram runs down the Collyhurst loop line towards Thorpes Bridge, notice that the two Metrolink tracks have replaced the old four track layout. We cross **Smedley Road** and the meandering **River Irk**, and, after the **Collyhurst Road** over bridge, enter **Rochdale Road (Queen's Road) tunnel**. This was built on the 'cut and cover' principle, and is 262 yards long. Most of the loop line beyond it is in a **cutting**, partly reinforced in places by stout **brick retaining walls**, and spanned by a number of road bridges. Beyond **Queen's Road**, notice the **Monsall Street** road bridge. This (and the subsequent two bridges) has been reinforced by inserting a corrugated steel arch below the original girders; a special form of concrete was injected between the two.

Monsall Station is located between the **Monsall Street** and the **Jocelyn Street** bridges. The **outward platform** (for Oldham) is connected with **Monsall Street** by a **ramp** and **steps**, but the inward platform is linked to Ruislip Avenue by a **lift** and **steps** on the south side. (Both platforms are connected by a **pedestrian crossing** at the Oldham end.)

Most people associate the district with the former Monsall Isolation Hospital, which opened as the 'Barnes House of Recovery' (a fever hospital) in 1871. After many years of sterling service (which included major contributions to medical research) it closed in 1993. Nowadays, Monsall is largely a residential area, but has plenty of 'green' spaces. Houses in the area are now in demand due to the opening of the Metrolink line.

Beyond **Monsall Road** over-bridge, the tram starts to emerge from the cutting and runs on to an **embankment**. (Notice the large **police station** complex appearing on the left.) The Miles Platting railway line comes in from the right, and we enter **Central Park Station**.

The Ghosts of Trains Past

As we travel along the loop line, we perhaps ought to be aware that this was once a main line. In addition to the local trains on the 'slow lines', crack expresses thundered by on the fast tracks. The Lancashire and Yorkshire Railway's Dining Car Express to Leeds, York, and Newcastle came this way. Some of the expresses conveyed a portion which was detached at Wakefield and conveyed passengers to Hull. Through carriages continued to Riverside Pier in that port, alongside the boats. The railway's steamers 'Duke of Clarence' and 'Duke of Cornwall' operated a summer service to Zebrugge, with connections to Brussels and elsewhere on the continent. For the more adventurous, the Wilson Line steamers plied to Scandinavian and Baltic ports. There were even through carriages via Wakefield to Harwich for the Great Eastern steamers. Then the Kaiser, with other crowned idiots, decided to start a war.

The station has had a rather curious history. It was completed in 2005 in readiness for the Metrolink extension, but due to delays and financial problems, it lay without tracks and looking rather forlorn until almost seven years had elapsed. It forms part of *The Gateway*, a £36.5 million **transport interchange** which will include local bus services as well as the Metrolink tram stop. Nevertheless, although the station lies next to the railway line between Victoria and Rochdale, there is currently no connection, though it is possible that railway platforms may be added in future. The station building features a **striking curved copper and glass canopy** suspended by a cable-tensioned steel structure, designed by architects Aukett Fitzroy Robinson (whose work has included Clapham Common Tube Station). There are **stairs** and **lifts** from both of the **platforms** to a large **paved concourse** under the station, and **ramps** from the Manchester platform ends leading to a **pedestrian crossing**. The impressive canopy does not help in the case of driving rain, so platform shelters have been provided. Speaking of rain, notice that the rainwater runs off the roof at a collection point, and into the curious **vase shaped funnel** of the main drain!

The Gateway passes under the station. To the **south**, it goes under the **railway bridge**, but notice, before reaching **Oldham Road**, the **Sharp Project** on the left. (The greater part of the building fronts Oldham Road, but entry is from Thorp Road.) This is Manchester's independent hub for the **creative and digital industries** and its entrepreneurs, and has been developed by members of the city's creative sector with the support of Manchester City Council (which owns the site). The Sharp Project aims to nurture small businesses, with an emphasis on the specialisms of animation, CGI and visual effects, and offers almost 200,000 square feet of accommodation, from a single shipping container to a 15,000 square foot sound stage. (It also hosts a 4,000 square foot music studio and a motion capture studio.) The existing tenants include web design companies, independent producers, post-production and CGI companies, IT networks and IP lawyers. The *Holiday Inn Central Park* is nearby on **Oldham Road**. Immediately to the **north** of the Metrolink Station are **bus stops** on the left, followed by the junction with **Northampton Road**. The **traffic island** is graced with a **modern sculpture**, and forms the entrance to the **Central Park** development.

Central Park

The south side of the traffic island is the domain of 'Mr. Plod'. The **Greater Manchester Police Divisional Headquarters** is on the western side. This building comprises 125,000 square feet of office space with 357 car parking spaces on the adjacent 5.3 acre plot.

The actual **Greater Manchester Police Force Headquarters** are opposite. Greater Manchester Police required a 'state of the art' **Command Headquarters Building** to provide the most advanced facilities to manage the largest police force outside of London. The six storey building with glass and stone facades sits within a six acre plot (providing over 700 parking spaces) and supports modern day policing by providing accommodation for a smarter more effective workforce. Both buildings accommodate approximately 2,500-3,000 people occupying the area 24 hours a day, 7 days a week. The **three office blocks** across the island, to the north, are allocated to *Fujitsu*. With 175,000 square feet of space across the three buildings, the multinational *Fujitsu Services* has made Central Park home to 900 staff. Immediately to the left of *Fujitsu* may be found **'One, Central Park'**. Manchester is a significant home for science and technology businesses and research, and this campus is intended to become **one of the country's first official 'Science Cities'** and the UK's 'Knowledge Capital'. This expertise is being developed further through a cutting-edge, 100,000 square foot centre for business enterprise, training and academic excellence. In a pioneering collaboration between **Manchester and Salford Universities, Manchester Science Park and Manchester College of Advanced Technology,** One Central Park will hopefully be a place where industry and academia can meet to develop tomorrow's products and services, as well as acting as a base to train people in the skills sought after by many businesses. It provides modern, leading-edge facilities with the potential for **start-up companies** to grow and evolve into their own **bespoke accommodation on Central Park** itself. **Madison Place** is located to the right of the *Fujitsu* blocks. It consists of a

*Central Park Station (*photograph courtesy of John McCarthy*)*

'village' of five new self-contained two and three storey office buildings. The offices provide state-of-the-art air conditioning, full raised access floors, suspended ceilings, double glazing, carpeting, and shower facilities. A group of the **National Health Service** are already in occupation of Unit C. For small and medium sized businesses wanting to make a step up into quality offices, Madison Place provides an opportunity. There is planning consent for 114,000 more square feet of individual customised office space.

Central Park to Freehold

After leaving the station, the tram runs on to an **impressive concrete viaduct** formed of an inverted 'T' shape, very similar in design to the one at Besses o'th' Barn (p73). However, this is curved and far more graceful, constructed in 2005 to carry Metrolink over the main **Calder Valley Railway Line** to Rochdale and Yorkshire. The **former Newton Heath Carriage and Wagon Works** of the Lancashire and Yorkshire Railway were situated beyond the railway line to the left. The viaduct deposits the Metrolink line alongside the railway, and, beyond **Thorpe Road** over-bridge, the tram passes a network of tracks on the left, accessing a **major railway complex**. This was Newton Heath Locomotive Sheds, now the **motive power depot** for servicing *Transpennine* diesel multiple units of all types, together with the odd diesel locomotive. (The main railway line diverges beyond the depot complex far to the left, out of our sight.) Notice that the Metrolink line is now **reduced to single track**, paralleled by a **single railway track** on the left, in a manner reminiscent of the Altrincham line beyond Timperley (p256). After the **Dean Lane** road bridge, the tram enters **Newton Heath and Moston Station**, situated in a **cutting**.

It is on the site of Dean Lane Station, though little remains of the original structures; the platform buildings and street level booking office have long since vanished. (As there was already a Newton Heath station on the adjacent main line, 'Dean Lane' was used in railway days, and remained in use long after the other station had closed. The revived name is more appropriate.) Like Navigation Road Station, the new Metrolink incarnation consists of a **single platform** on the right hand side, used for arrivals and departures in both directions, and connected with Dean Lane by a doubled-back **ramp** and **steps**.

After the **Reliance Street** road bridge we see the reason for this peculiar arrangement, for the railway line services a large **rubbish treatment plant**. This plant was served by a siding from the original railway line, but trains cannot apparently be mixed with trams. Consequently a separate track alongside Metrolink is reserved for the few 'dusty bin' trains that need to use it! The single line (which is used as a run-round loop for the locomotives) continues beyond the **Morton Street** over bridge, but notice the **removable barrier** at the end of the **head-shunt** of the railway line on the left, situated between the **Mill Lane** and **Mill Street** over bridges. The railway line makes a junction with Metrolink beyond this barrier, at the point where the line **becomes double track** once more. (This junction is used for the reception of ballast trains and the like.)

The now double track line continues through a wooded **cutting** and passes under **Failsworth Lodge** (now an occupation bridge leading to playing fields, though once the driveway of a grand house) and **Broadway**. The latter was an inter-war road improvement; it was meant to have trams, but they never materialised due to the change of policy after Mattinson's death (p286). After the **Hulton Street** over bridge (and a **pipe bridge**) the line passes out of the cutting and on to an **embankment**, crossing **Hardman Lane** to arrive at **Failsworth Station**.

The original station opened in 1881 (the last to be completed), but its structures and wooden platforms have long since disappeared. There is a **pedestrian crossing** between

Railways to Oldham

Oldham has never really been on the way to anywhere in particular, but, despite never a main line destination, it was at the centre of a complex network of railways. The Manchester and Leeds Railway (as it then was) opened a branch from their main line at Middleton Junction to Werneth Station in 1842. It ascended the fearsome 1 in 27 incline with the help of rope haulage, and although more powerful engines enabled this to be dispensed with as early as 1851, the working of the line remained problematical till the end of its days. This line was extended (by what had now become the Lancashire and Yorkshire Railway) to Mumps Station in 1847. A new line, from Oldham to Rochdale, opened in 1863, together with a short branch from it to Royton. Oldham Central, sited between Werneth and Mumps, was rebuilt at this time as a consequence of the opening of the Oldham, Ashton, and Guide Bridge Junction Railway (p139) from Guide Bridge to Oldham Clegg Street (adjacent to Oldham Central) in 1861. This became a joint line, owned by the Manchester, Sheffield, and Lincolnshire Railway (later Great Central) and the London and North Western Railway. In addition to local trains, it was used to operate a through carriage between Rochdale and London Euston! Clegg Street station also serviced the London and North Western branch from Oldham (via Glodwick Road Station) to Greenfield, where it joined their line from Manchester to Huddersfield. Nevertheless, these developments still largely depended in some way on the excruciating Werneth incline for communication to and from Manchester! Consequently, the line from Thorpes Bridge Junction to Werneth Junction (the present Metrolink route) opened in 1880-1, and most passenger trains were diverted that way. However, though not as bad as Werneth bank, it still presented a hefty climb. A curious feature of the route after Werneth Junction was the narrowness of the Oldham tunnels; the carriage windows in the dedicated Lancashire and Yorkshire Railway stock were barred! Nowadays, only the line from Thorpes Bridge to Oldham and Rochdale remains, and that is now part of the Metrolink tram system.

the Metrolink **platforms** at the Oldham end, and both **platforms** are linked with **Hardman Lane** by **steps** and **lifts**. (Notice the delightful **owl sculpture** at the foot of the Manchester platform steps!)

Failsworth is worth a visit to see the famous **Failsworth Pole**. After leaving the station, turn left down **Hardman Lane** and then left again along **Old Road**. Look for the **blue plaque** on a cottage to the right. It commemorates Joseph Burgess (1853-1954). an early pioneer in the history of the Labour Party. The roadway curves to the right, by some metal **bollards** stretching across the road. Follow the sharp **right hand bend** to emerge on to **Oldham Road**, opposite the **old library and town hall building**. Originally built in 1880, at a cost of £2,600, Failsworth Town Hall housed a range of council services. It was extended sometime later to provide a home to the new library (opened 1909, **inscription**), gifted to the people of Failsworth by Andrew Carnegie. Failsworth Town Hall closed a few years ago when the last council tenants moved out. An ambitious regeneration scheme saw the old Town Hall refurbished and extended to bring the former Carnegie Library back to life and in use once again. The development boasts a spacious function hall with bar (there are plans to include a café area), and the building is shared between Oldham libraries and Oldham Lifelong Learning service. Turn left into **Oldham Road**, cross the **Rochdale Canal**, and you will soon see the **striped maypole** rising above a **brick tower**.

Following a major restoration of the **Pole, clock tower** and **gardens** in 2006, a bronze **statue of Ben Brierley** (a local Lancashire dialect poet) was erected in the gardens.

Failsworth Pole and Parish Church

Fertility and Freedom

The maypole is an old English folk custom. Children are encouraged to happily dance round it, weaving their strings or ribbons into an intricate pattern. Of course, this is a sanitised version of folklore. In the past, it was the young men and women of the community that danced round what was really a phallic symbol in a spring fertility ritual designed to encourage the regeneration of all living things. Dancing in a circle 'widdershins' (in and out in a clockwise motion) imitated the cycle of life. The 17th century religious extremists tried to stamp the custom out (though it was starting to fade of its own accord) because they thought it superstitious and 'papist', but also because what happened later when everyone had too much to drink. Towards the end of the 18th century, what remained of the custom became politicised. The French revolutionaries took May Day to symbolise political renewal as well as the renewal of nature, and the custom of planting a 'liberty tree' was imported into England from France. Indeed, May Day remains a significant date in the calendar for left-wing political groups and all labouring men and women. In Failsworth, instead of a liberty tree, the local population decided to plant a maypole on the traditional site for such objects as a symbol of loyalty to the king. This might be seen as a reactionary act, but they were actually celebrating a constitutional monarchy that gave liberty to the 'free-born Englishman'. The pole that now stands on the site replaces one blown down in 1950.

Notice the **lower course of the old road** past an original row of cottages in the Manchester direction. Towards Oldham, the tower and spire of **St. John's Parish Church** soars above the *Royal Oak*. The church was designed by E. H. Shellard for the Church Commissioners, and built in 1845-6, of hammer-dressed stone with slate roof. There is

Ben

Benjamin Brierley, often known as *Ben Brierley*, (1825-1896), was a weaver and writer in the Lancashire dialect. He was born in humble circumstances in Failsworth, and started life in a cotton mill, educating himself in his spare time. At about the age of thirty he began to contribute articles to local papers, and the re-publication of some of his sketches of Lancashire character in *A Summer Day in Daisy Nook* (1859) attracted attention. In 1863 he wrote the *Chronicles of Waverlow*, followed by a longer story called *The Layrock of Langley Side* (afterwards dramatized) in 1864. He then began a weekly titled, *Ben Brierley's Journal*, which remained in publication until 1891, and gave public readings from his own writings, visiting America in 1880 and 1884. His various *Ab-o'th'-Yate* sketches (about America, London, etc.), and his pictures of Lancashire common

Ben Brierley statue

life, were very popular, and were collected after his death. In 1884 he lost his savings by the failure of a building society, and a fund was raised for his support.

> *Aw've just mended th' fire wi' a cob;*
> *Owd Swaddle has brought thi new shoon;*
> *There's some nice bacon collops o'th hob,*
> *An' a quart o' ale-posset i'th oon;*
> *Aw've brought thi top cwot, does to know,*
> *For th' rain's comin' deawn very dree;*
> *An' th' har'stone's as white as new snow;*
> *Come whoam to thi chiller an' me.*

a six-bay nave with a clerestory and aisles; the (later) west tower and the chancel is flanked by an organ chamber and vestry. (For further information, ring 0161 681 2995/07581).

The **embankment** continues beyond the station, and the line crosses the **Rochdale Canal**, before passing *Housing Units of Hollinwood* on the right. This retail park sells everything from home furnishings to fireplaces and bathrooms, and there are other retail facilities within the complex. The tram now crosses **Hudson Street** and enters **Hollinwood Station**.

The original station opened with the line in 1881, but nothing of it remains. It lay on the embankment between the bridges spanning Hudson Street and Bower Lane, with a private approach road (Railway Road) between the two streets alongside the goods yard tracks, which looped round the back of the Manchester platform. The station platforms were accessed by a subway from this station approach. The former goods yard and mill sidings, used mainly for coal and cotton traffic, were situated on the up side of the line, beyond Bower Lane/Hollinwood Avenue. All was obliterated by the construction of the motorway. The **Metrolink Station** is on the same site, and has some unusual features. A **pedestrian crossing** links the platforms at the Oldham end and communicates with an **extensive footbridge** across **Hollinwood Avenue** and the **M60 Motorway** to the **Factory Fold** housing estate. (Hollinwood Avenue has replaced the former Bower Lane.) There is also a **ramp** down to **Hollinwood Avenue**. At the opposite end of the platforms, **lifts** and **stairs** access **Hudson Street** (a large 'park and ride' facility is proposed on the south side).

In 1950, *Ferranti* established a large plant for the manufacture of transformers on Hollinwood Avenue, and these were often shipped by rail (in the dead of night!) using the old goods yard. The old **transformer works** can be seen from the Oldham platform; it is now a printing plant. Notice that the old Railway Hotel to the right of the station (a substantial structure, probably dating from the opening of the first station), has obtained a new lease of life as *La Via* (the way), a Spanish restaurant.

The tram leaves the **station** and crosses **Hollinwood Avenue** and the **M60 Motorway**, with the **footbridge** leading to **Factory Fold** on the left. After crossing the **Drury Lane** over bridge, a curious thing occurs. The former railway line continued on an embankment, but now Metrolink **descends an incline** towards **South Chadderton Station**.

The Mummy of Birchen Bower

The Ferranti factory was built on the site of Birchen Bower. Hannah Beswick, who lived at this isolated country spot, had a deep dread of being buried alive. She consequently arranged with her doctor, Charles White, for her body to be kept above ground. She died in 1758, and Doctor White, (a distinguished practitioner and the originator of Manchester Royal Infirmary) embalmed her with tar, leaving the face exposed. Eventually, he removed her to his house in Sale (p318), where she was kept in the case of a grandfather clock! Her face appeared where the dial would be, covered in a velvet cloth. Once a year, as the will instructed, two "witnesses of credit" were procured, the cloth drawn back, and an inspection was made for signs of life. At length, the 'mummy' became an exhibit at the old Natural History Museum in Peter Street, Manchester, alongside the skeleton of 'Billy', a celebrity carthorse that had lived sixty-one years. The old girl was finally laid to rest (presumably quite dead) at Harpurhey Cemetery in 1868. From then on her spirit is said to have manifested itself around her old house, restless because her deathbed wishes were not being fulfilled. She was allegedly seen wandering from a barn near the house to a nearby pond in an agitated state, wearing a black gown and a white lace cap. It became common folklore that on wintry nights the barn would glow with unearthly light, and it became a place to be avoided by the locals, apart from those who were fulfilling a dare or the unnaturally curious. The barn seemed to be a focus for the haunting and there seems to have been reports of poltergeist activity, with a cow being transported into the hayloft by unknown means! She was also said to have been seen wandering through the house, even when it was redeveloped to separate apartments. Local legend eventually suggested that she haunted the area of the barn to protect treasure that she had hidden in life, and the spectre became more and more frightening as time wore on. Eventually the house was demolished and the haunting fell away as people forgot about the ghost. There was to be a reminder of the haunting in 1981 when a ghost was seen inside the Ferranti factory, erected on the site of Birchin Bower.

At the station, notice that a **pedestrian crossing** between the **platforms** (accessed by **ramps** and **steps** on both sides) at the Oldham end has replaced the former subway that once ran under the vanished embankment! In fact, the crossing is now level with **Coalshaw Green Park** on the left, and a **footpath** through the park communicates with **Lancaster Street** and **Coalshaw Green Road**. Another **path** to the right of the **crossing** links **Canal Street**. In the future, a **path** from the **outward platform** may link with the proposed **Rose Mill** residential development.

It is worthwhile exploring the **little park** if you have the time. The **café** (closed Friday) can be recommended, and a full lunch is usually available (except Saturday) between 11.30 and 1pm Like a roller coaster, having descended, we ascend once more by means of a unique **'cutting within an embankment'**! Having attained the appropriate level once more, the tram crosses **Stanley Road** and **Washbrook**, before commencing a **long curve to the right** towards **Werneth**. The line begins to run alongside the edge of a ridge, and there is a **fine panorama** to the left, taking in Chadderton, Royton, the lower flanks of west Oldham, and distant Tandle Hill, with a number of **mills** in the foreground. (There is also a fine view of the **towers of Manchester**, best seen on the return journey.)

The **staggered platforms** of **Freehold Station** straddle **Block Lane**. The **Oldham platform is before the roadway**, and exits by means of **steps** and a **ramp** to a **pedestrian area**. From here, further **steps** and a **lift** communicate with **Robinson Street**. Alternatively, a **footbridge**, alongside the **Metrolink line bridge**, crosses the road and links with a **pedestrian crossing** of the line leading to the **Manchester platform**. This platform is similarly linked by a **ramp** and **steps** to a **pedestrian area**, thence by further **steps** and a **lift** to **Block Lane**. It is proposed to construct a **pathway** from this station exit to **Jammy Lane**. There is **disabled parking** and a **'drop off' point** on **Block Lane** near here.

The scene is dominated by **Hartford Mill** to the right, now (2014) in a very sad condition. It was erected in 1907 and extended in 1920 and 1924 (eventually utilising 120,000 spindles powered by two mill engines), and therefore constitutes a fine example of the final phase of cotton mill design. Spinning ceased in 1959, and after a period as a mail order warehouse, it finally closed in 1992. It is actually owned by Oldham Council, and is a Grade Two listed structure.

An Excursion to Middleton

If you would like an interesting excursion, alight here and walk along **Block Lane** towards the **Dog Inn**, turning left into **Denton Lane**. Catch the meandering 415 (daily) local bus at the stop marked 'F', and alight at **Foxdenton Park**. (See information box)

The journey can be resumed by bus, which crosses the **Rochdale Canal** and passes under the **railway line to Rochdale**. This point was the terminus of the trams coming from the opposite direction (due to the low bridge), and was the **site of Middleton Junction Station**. Here the original branch to Oldham Werneth (p124) diverged from the main line. Later, a short line to Middleton left the railway a brief distance beyond the station. The station opened in 1842 and closed in 1966, though the junction (and part of the Werneth branch) continued to be used by trains to and from a coal depot and power station at Chadderton until the 1980s. The bus now turns left along Greengate (the large former Avro factory, famous for churning out Lancaster bombers during the war, was situated at the far end of this road) before turning off to the right, in order to meander through **Alkrington Garden Village**. Once rolling farmland, it was added to Middleton in 1886 and developed into a premium residential area. **Alkrington** itself is beyond the Manchester Road to the west of here, and is the site of **Alkrington**

Foxdenton Hall and Park

Foxdenton Hall is a two-storey Georgian mansion and former manor house, with an English garden-bond brickwork exterior and its own private gardens. The original Hall was erected in the mid-15th-century as a home for the Radclyffes, who had acquired the title of joint Lords of the Manor with the Asshetons of Chadderton through marriage. The medieval Hall was demolished to make way for a second Hall, built in 1620. The ground floor of that second Hall now forms the basement of the present Hall, built in 1700. The building has been described as "a dignified early Georgian house, particularly rare in this part of the country". The Radclyffe family moved out

Heron sculpture at Foxdenton Hall

of Foxdenton Hall in the late 18th century, favouring properties that they had purchased in Dorset, although still maintaining ownership and leasing it as farm accommodation. The Hall and the adjoining Foxdenton Park were leased to Chadderton Council by the family in 1922, when it was opened to the public. In 1960 the council took over ownership of the Hall, by which time it was in a state of disrepair. Following protest about the funding and the condition of the building, Foxdenton Hall was restored in 1965. The Hall is not usually open to the public, but is available for private functions. Foxdenton Park has an excellent café, a well maintained bowling green, children's play park, sensory garden, and tennis courts. Additionally, a focus for both children and adults is provided by the chainsaw artist, Richard James, who recently tree sculptured the Heron of Aesop's fable. The Park and Hall feature in an annual programme of special events. (For further information, ring 07970674855.)

Hall. The Hall was built in 1736 by Sir Darcy Lever and designed in the Georgian style of the time by Giocomo Leoni. In 1942 the house came into the possession of the local council, and was later bought by developers. They restored and converted the Hall into three luxury private dwellings in the 1990s. (Private property, please respect.) The hall's accompanying **woodland**, comprising some 125 acres (50 ha) is a designated **nature reserve**. We eventually arrive at **Middleton Bus Station**.

Although ignored in the Domesday Book of 1086, Middleton is said to be "of great antiquity," and a community at Middleton is thought to have evolved outwards from a church that existed considerably earlier than the Norman Conquest. The name Middleton first appears in 1194, and derives from the Old English *middel-tūn*, meaning middle farm or settlement, probably a reference to its central position between Rochdale and Manchester. The development of Middleton as a centre of commerce occurred during the 17th and 18th centuries. Lord Suffield obtained a Charter from George III in 1791 to hold a weekly market and three annual fairs in Middleton. Suffield built a market house, warehouses and butcher's shambles in the town at his own expense. Industrial scale textile manufacture came with the industrial revolution. Silk production gave way to cotton spinning, which continued through to the mid-20th-century. **Warwick Mill**, a notable landmark, is a relic from these times.

In the early 1970s, The Arndale Property Trust cleared land adjacent to Middleton Gardens to build a perfectly hideous 'American-style' modern shopping precinct adjacent to a rather complicated bus station. This has, of late, been greatly improved. But never fear, for several consolations are at hand!

Leave the **bus station**, and walk along **Long Street** to the large **traffic island**. Continue along Long Street, now a **main road**. Lying on the left side of the street, opposite the **library** and **Jubilee Park**, the *Olde Boars Head* is a quaint old black and white timber structure, said by some writers to date from 1587. (This date is taken from a fireplace inscription, though the object in question was removed from Middleton Hall. However, a stone lintel in the cellar bears the date 1632). Part of a row of ancient cottages, it operated as a coaching inn on the road between Chester and York. Like many

Old Boars Head

such places, there are countless stories and legends connected with it. Bonnie Prince Charlie is said to have taken refuge at the inn in 1745, though he seems, like Elizabeth I and Cromwell to have had an ambition to stay in every pub and house in the country! Inevitably, Dick Turpin is said to have stopped over on his way to York, though his celebrated ride there only appears in 'Rookwood', a novel by Harrison Ainsworth, a Victorian Manchester writer. Local radical and reformer Samuel Bamford (p186) held many of his meetings at the hostelry. A secret tunnel to the Parish church was supposed to exist. There have been many alterations and additions over the years, and a later extension called **'The Sessions Room'** was added to the right hand side with an **18th century door and window**, all making up the quirky building we see today. The sessions room served as the local courtroom and has seen many 'sessions' of a kind since, as its large size compared to the older cosier parts serves as a great function room for small parties and other events. Middleton Council bought the property in the late 19th century, with a view to building a town hall on the site, but the First World War put paid to this idea, and a Councillor's house was used instead. The inn was again in danger in 1919 when councillors wanted to demolish it to make way for a war memorial. This was sited elsewhere and the old pub remains to this day a favourite and trusty old watering hole for Middleton folk. It is a venue for the musicians of the town, who still pay an annual tribute here to the late Pete Cowap, a popular local music legend of recent years. It comes as no surprise to find that the place is haunted.

The **library**, opposite, dates from 1889 and is a typical example of a public building of its period. Note the **plaque commemorating Jim Allen** (1926-99), the local television playwright who 'educated himself' here. The **old parish school** (1842), a 'National' or Anglican institution, is to the right. The **cobbled area** between them is an entrance to **Jubilee Park**, which runs up the side of the hill. Notice the **old anchor** lying against the end wall of the library. It came from the 'Syrene', a Norwegian three-masted brigantine that ran aground at Blackpool in 1892. Take the **right-hand pathway**. The **stone**, visible on the left, is a memorial to local inhabitants who died in a flood in 1927. The path emerges at the top of **Church Brow**. **St. Leonard's Street** runs directly ahead, past the **south gate of the churchyard**. After admiring the first **view of the church** in its natural setting, ignore the gate (usually locked and rarely used) and turn left down **St. Leonard's Passage**, skirting the **west (tower) end** of the church and leading to the **car park**. Here, there is another **gate** and an **entrance to the church through a modern wing** tacked on to the ancient edifice.

The **Parish Church of St. Leonard** stands in a commanding position on the north side of the town, on high ground overlooking the valley of the Irk. A wooden Saxon church is believed to have occupied the site until probably about 1100, when a Norman church was built. Virtually nothing remains of this second church, though it appears to have stood till the beginning of the 15th century, when Thomas Langley, Bishop of Durham, pulled it down and built an entirely new structure "of well hewn stone, with a roof of wondrous beauty."

Langley's church was consecrated on 22 August 1412, but (until recently) the only structure which could be ascribed to Langley with any certainty was the **tower**. It was thought by 19th century historians that the greater part of the present building dated from 1524, when Richard Assheton reconstructed it. This was perhaps intended as a celebration of the knighthood granted to him by Henry VIII for his part in the Battle of Flodden Field, or a thank offering for his preservation and safe return...perhaps a little bit of both. Recent investigations now suggest that the present church is that predominantly built by Langley with some additions; the **clerestory** above the nave, the north-east **Langley Chapel**, and a **rebuilt chapel** to the south-east probably being added by the Asshetons.

St Leonard's, "a wooden steeple for a stubborn people"

Local Boy Makes Good?

Thomas Langley was born in Middleton, the third son of Alice and William Langley. In 1375 he was sent to St. Mary's Abbey, Thetford; a noted route enabling bright boys to enter Corpus Christi College in Cambridge. He returned to Middleton, and in 1385 was appointed rector of Radcliffe. He soon realised that, in an age when churchmen were usually the only reliable and efficient royal administrators, his future lay with the civil service (and the rewards of church office that came with it). He was soon appointed Dean of York. However, this was blocked by the Pope, because of the little matter of Langley's small part in the deposition and murder of Richard II. In 1401 he was given custody of the privy seal, which office he held until 1405. A grateful king saw that he was elected Bishop of London, but the new Pope vetoed that as well. In 1405 he was appointed Chancellor of England for the first time. From then on until his semi-retirement in 1430, the diligent cleric spent 5,670 days in the service of the crown, mostly living in an Inn of Court in Holborn. After Archbishop Scrope of York rebelled (and was captured and executed after a show trial), Langley was elected in August 1405 as Archbishop in his place. Again, the Pope disapproved and excommunicated both Langley and King Henry IV. They both backed down, and the excommunication was lifted. Instead, Langley was installed as Bishop of Durham as a kind of consolation prize. In 1407 he resigned his Chancellorship and, on the same day, he was appointed what was in effect the first Foreign Minister of England. Even ecclesiastical affairs seemed to be going his way, for there were two rival Popes, one in Rome, and the other in Avignon. Consequently, he was awarded a Cardinal's hat in 1411 by the Pope in Rome, John XXIII, (who presumably wanted English support). In 1412, in his first visit to his birthplace since 1385, he ordered an early rebuilding of the Norman parish church at Middleton, adding a chantry for prayers for the souls of his deceased family (and for himself when the time came). He also founded a school related to the chantry (which later evolved into Middleton Grammar School). Henry IV died the following year, with Langley (his executor) at his side. During the reign of his successor, Henry V, he spent three quarters of his time in the service of the crown (a politician first and churchman second) and, finally, at Windsor on 28 September 1422, he delivered up the gold seal of England in a purse of white leather to the infant Henry VI. He returned to Middleton for the last time in 1424. From 1430 until his death Langley attended to his diocese, something he had, by his own admission, neglected. But he continued with various diplomatic assignments when called upon by the government. He died in 1437.

The **exterior walls of the building** are constructed of rather rough masonry, except those of the **tower**, which still retain the more finely wrought work of Langley's time. The walls of the **aisles** and the **clerestory** are **embattled**, and the external detail of the **north side** of the building has an elaborately **panelled and moulded embattled parapet** to the aisle wall. On the middle of the **parapet of the south aisle** is the **inscription**: ric. assheton et anna uxo. ei. anno d'ni movoxxiii,' and at its east end are two stones with **inscriptions**; the upper one is uncertain, but the lower has the initials SBB STD. The tower is of three stages with diagonal buttresses and a **vice** (staircase) in the south-west corner. The **west window** of the ground story is of two cinquefoiled lights with tracery over, and above this is a window of two trefoiled lights with a quatrefoil in the head. The jambs of both are old, but the mullions and tracery have been renewed. The **upper stage of the tower** contains a **clock** with faces on the north, south, and west sides, above which is a string-course crowned with an **embattled parapet**. The north and south sides of the tower are plain, but there are slits to light the vice in the south-west corner on both faces. In 1709, a further story was added in the shape of a **wooden belfry stage** with a roof gabled on all four sides, giving a curious finish to the tower. It was deemed "a wooden steeple for a stubborn people." There is a **ring of eight bells**. Six were cast by Abraham Rudhall of Gloucester in 1714, and two were added in 1891, by Mears & Stainbank. (The church is usually open on Friday 1pm-4pm in summer, and sometimes Saturday 11.00am-4.00pm, and Sunday 12.00pm-4.00pm.)

Before entering the church, begin by inspecting the **south porch** (sometimes locked off), which projects in front of the south aisle wall at the second bay from the west. It has a low pointed outer **carved** arch, an **embattled parapet**, and the whole of its south face has been **elaborately panelled**, though the detail is now much worn away and its beauty lost. Over the entrance are two shields (one with the Assheton arms) and the **initials** A RA, seeming to imply that it is the work of Richard and Ann Assheton. The **inner doorway** has a moulded arch and retains its **old nail-studded door** with wicket and wooden draw-bar. Inside the church, we enter the **nave**. It is has an **arcade of five bays** with octagonal piers and pointed arches. The **capitals and bases** of the pillars are coarsely moulded, but the **eastern arch on the north side** has a line of **12th century billet ornament**, a piece of detail from the former church. There is nothing to show why this particular arch should have been thus distinguished. The **clerestory** runs the whole length of nave and chancel, and has twelve three-light square-headed **windows** on each side. The **roof** to both nave and chancel is of a flat pitch with brackets carried down the wall resting on **corbels** between the clerestory windows, and is a modern restoration of the original oak roof of the 16th century church. In all probability, the **south arcade** (and some of the south elevation) either collapsed or had to be pulled down, enabling Assheton to make his alterations. Certainly, the present **south arcade** has been moved several feet to the north, making the **tower arch** and apex of the Langley **roof** totally off-centre! (The weathering of a former roof remains in the **east wall of the west tower**, showing the centre line of Langley's nave.) The **tower arch** itself is pointed, but is constructed of **12th century masonry, probably dating from about 1140**. It rests on three 12th century **shafts** at either side, with moulded capitals and bases that were raised some height above the floor in the rebuilding. Above, on the **south side**, is a **door** which formerly led from the upper stage of the tower to the roof. The nave underwent extensive alterations and restorations in 1846-7 and 1868-9. In 1869 a stone coffin containing human remains was found in the north side of the nave in the third bay from the west.

The **south aisle** is 21 feet 6 inches wide, but narrows to 15 feet 6 inches, the width of the Assheton Chapel, near its east end. The **east end of the wider part** is occupied by the **Hopwood Chapel** and **pew** (used by the family who occupied Hopwood Hall), which is enclosed by a **Jacobean oak screen** with **twisted balusters** along the top. The **pew** has four linen pattern panels inserted at its north-east corner. The walls of the chapel on the east and south are likewise **panelled**, hiding a medieval **piscina** (for washing sacred vessels) at the south-east. There is a **moulded bracket** on the east wall eight feet. from the floor. At the **east end** of the south aisle is the **'Langley door'**, which has a square shouldered lintel (a typical Tudor feature) and a two-light window over. The **door** itself is ancient and nail-studded, and the masonry is older than that on either side of it, suggesting that it has been moved. It is just possible that the door way is a part of the 15th century church in its original position. The **font** is at the west end of the south aisle, and was plain till 1846, when it was carved as at present.

The **north aisle** has a narrow pointed door with moulded jambs opposite the second bay from the west, with a **three-lighted window** to each of the other bays, and one at the west end which is entirely new. At the **east end of the north wall**, between the third and fourth windows from the west, is a **recess** in the wall under a **four-centred arched head** raised above the floor. The recess contains a medieval **coffin slab** with a foliated incised cross. Above it was **formerly the indent of a small brass of a hooded female** with inscription under. There is nothing to indicate whom the brass commemorated or whether it had any link with the recess underneath, but the latter was popularly styled the 'founder's tomb,' and there is a tradition that the original north aisle was built by Maud Middleton early in the 14th century, and that she was buried under the north wall. It is possible that the incised slab marked her burial-place, and that (in the rebuilding of 1524) the recess was made to contain it, with a brass placed above to commemorate the lady whose remains it formerly covered. A modern interpretation suggests that the recess may indeed be Langley's work, but that the stone coffin lid may have been removed there from the original chancel. It is a floreat or 'cross of resurrection' (the

The Middleton Archers, a detail from the window in the Parish Church, probably the first English war memorial (photograph courtesy of Geoffrey Wellens)

wooden cross is springing into leaf) design, and may be from the coffin of a priest. There is an **old oak almsbox** (for contributions) at the west end of the north aisle.

The **chancel** preserves none of its ancient ritual arrangements, and probably assumed its present appearance during Assheton's alterations. The **north wall** was still probably

The Middleton Archers

In 1513, Henry VIII took a great army on campaign in France, leaving England in the care of Catherine of Aragon, his wife. James IV of Scotland used the opportunity to invade. A scratch force, composed of the household troops of noblemen and local levies from the Northern Counties, marched forth to meet them commanded by the seventy year old Earl of Surrey, and accompanied by the Banner of St. Cuthbert from Durham Cathedral. Among the Lancashire and Cheshire men commanded by Sir Edward Stanley were a company, mostly archers, raised by Richard Assheton. The battle turned out to be a famous victory. James IV and the flower of the Scots nobility were slain at Flodden Field. Richard Assheton was knighted, and expressed his gratitude to both God and Man by rebuilding the church. But he did more. He created a unique stained glass window that some have described as the first English war memorial. "It contains the figures of some of the principal persons of Middleton and neighbourhood who accompanied Sir Richard Assheton to Flodden, and represents first himself and his lady in scarlet, in long garments, with an attendant squire in blue, his chaplain also in blue kneeling before an altar, and seventeen bowmen . . . also in blue with long hair, and the name of each man originally placed over each figure." In many parts the window is little better than a patchwork of mutilated fragments. The figures of the archers are fairly recognizable, but Sir Richard and Lady Ann are so broken up and mixed with other parts that it is difficult to trace them. Some of the names of the archers can still be read. They include: Henricus Taylyer, Richard Kylw—, Hughe Chetham, James Gerrarde, John Pylkyngton, Philipe Werburton, William [Ste] le, John Scolefede, Wylliam—, James Taylier, Roger Blomeley, Crystofer Smythe, Henry Whitaker, Robart Prestwyche, and Richard Bexwicke. The archers stretch across the upper portion of the two lights, and Sir Richard and other figures are below. These no doubt were originally in a third light, but of the exact disposition of the parts there is unfortunately no record. In 1786 Philip de la Motte visited the church and made an engraving of part of the window, which has preserved the names of the archers and the dedicatory inscription as it was in the latter half of the 18th century. The inscription, which has since been transposed, is given thus: 'Orate pro bono statu Richardi Assheton et eorum qui hanc fenestra[m] fieri fecerunt quoru[m] no[m]ina et imagines ut supra ostenduntur anno d[omin]i mccccv.'

originally solid, being pierced with an arch when the so called **rector's chapel** (now the organ chamber) was built. The **rood screen**, though damaged in the 18th century, and probably also by repairs c. 1835-44, is a good example of 15th century work. The whole was repaired in 1898, when the **rood was set up over it**. It has a wide central opening with double **doors**, and four openings on each side, with traceried heads. Above these are modern canopies with richly carved cornice and cresting. The lower part is filled with panels with carved shields on which are displayed in bad heraldry the arms of the Asshetons and their alliances. The screen formerly extended across the full width of the church, but the parts in front of the two chapels appear to have been demolished when the galleries were erected. These have now been replaced by modern screens in character with the older work. The **screen between the chancel and the north chapel** (organ chamber) is ancient, and has nine openings with traceried heads and a four-centred arched doorway at the west end with carved spandrels. The cornice is carved with the vine trail, but the cresting is broken and mutilated. The **screen opposite**, between the chancel and Assheton Chapel, is modern and very plain, but retains a little old work in a leaf-pattern cornice on the chancel side. There are **four old stalls** at each side of the chancel door, the **misericordes** being very simply carved with leaves, and in the choir are six old **bench-ends**, three on each side, now used as ends to the choir stalls. Otherwise all the fittings, including the font, pulpit, and seating, are modern.

There are several **brasses to the Asshetons** within the altar rails, the most interesting being that of **Sir Ralph Assheton and his wife Margery (Barton) with seven sons and six daughters**, and a shield of Assheton quartering Barton. There is no inscription, but the details point to a date at the end of the 15th century. **Other brasses** are those of Edmund Assheton, rector, 1522, Richard Assheton, 1618, and **Ralph Assheton, 1650, the Parliamentary General** (his monument was removed from the Assheton Chapel in 1889), his sister Alice and her three husbands. This is the only brass in Britain of an English Civil War officer in full armour.

The **chancel glass** is particularly fine. The **east wall** above the window sill was rebuilt in 1847, and the present **five-light window** substituted for a late window of seven lights with transoms, but no tracery. The **window on the north wall** has three trefoiled lights, and is the **original 16th-entury** one. However, the most interesting glass in the church is that known as the **Flodden window** on the south side of the chancel. Up to 1846-7 this glass was in a three-light window in the north aisle, but was at that time removed to its present position, suffering a good deal in the process.

The west half of the chancel has an **arch north and south to the two chapels**. A **doorway on the south side** to the vestry was blocked up in 1872, and the entrance removed to the east end of the Assheton Chapel. The **north chapel**, now used as an **organ chamber**, was probably built at a later date than the north aisle. It was formerly known as the Rector's or Langley's Chapel, presumably from the fact that the altar of the Virgin and St. Cuthbert, endowed by Langley, was on this side of the nave. There is nothing to show, however, that a separate chapel existed on the present site before the existing one was erected. The **east window** is of five and the **north window** of four lights under three-centred heads. To a later date than 1524, too, must be assigned the south-east **vestry**, which is below the level of the floor of the church, probably to avoid blocking the windows of the chancel and south chapel

The **Assheton Chapel**, to the right of the chancel, contains some fragments of 16th century glass in the windows. It includes a shield in the west light (probably the Assheton heraldic device, also the arms of Middleton quartering Barton), and a fragment with the heads of a bishop and a priest in the south light. The three middle lights have each three shields of modern glass with the arms of various families connected with Middleton Church. In the Chapel were once preserved a **crested helmet, sword, banner**, and three **spurs**, popularly associated with Sir Richard Assheton, the soldier of Flodden. The crest (boar's head) and banner were probably carried at the funeral of Sir Ralph Assheton in 1765, and afterwards deposited here (they are placed on top of a screen). The **banner** was cleaned in 1895, and the arms of Assheton impaling Copley, together with the Ulster red hand, were disclosed, proving it to be not earlier than 1739. It is now enclosed between two sheets of glass. The **sword** and **spurs** are now preserved elsewhere for security reasons.

After leaving the church, walk down **the incline** (known as **St. Leonard's Street**) between the churchyard, where **Samuel Bamford** (p186) is buried, and the churchyard extension to the right. Turn left up **Morton Street** at the bottom. A right turn down **Bardsley Street** leads to **Boarshaw Road**. Cross the road towards the **reconstructed brick sign** from 'Middleton Corporation Electricity Works' with a 1900 date. It is the start of a short lane that leads to the Grammar School. The **Old Grammar School** as it is known today was founded in 1572 and was constructed in 1586 as Queen Elizabeth's

Grammar School. It came about as a replacement of Thomas Langley's school in the Parish Church, founded in 1412. Alexander Nowell, Dean of St Pauls Cathedral, who was educated at the church school, funded the project during the reign of Queen Elizabeth I. Constructed in an attractive light sand coloured stone with **mullioned windows** and an adjacent **'schoolmasters house'**, the building fell into disrepair around the turn of the century through dis-use and flood damage. It was purchased by Alfred Butterworth for £400 in 1909 and was donated back to the Parish Church. After use as a Sunday School, it was then leased to the Middleton Operatic and Dramatic Society. In the 1990s, the 'Old Grammar School Trust' was established and funding was obtained from English Heritage and the National Heritage Lottery Board to restore the building. It is now used as a meeting venue for local community groups. The school displays many **artifacts and objects relating to Middleton history** as well as a **gallery of artwork** by the Middleton Art Society. (Usually open Tuesdays and Thursdays 2-4 pm; for more information telephone 0161 643 2693.) Retrace your steps to **Bardsley Street**, but continue across **Morton Street**. Notice the **plaque** on the gable end on the right; the Middleton contingent was assembled here by Samuel Bamford, prior to marching (in their Sunday best) to the demonstration at St. Peter's Fields in Manchester. Little did they suspect what awaited them, and the part that they would play in the history of this country! We reach **Clarke Brow** by bearing left at **Edward Street**, directly ahead. The **Brow** turns into **New Lane**, and we are rewarded with fine views of the north side of the church as we ascend. Opposite the car park, on the left, is the ***Ring O'Bells***, set

The Sad Cavalier

The pub is said to be haunted by a Sad Cavalier, who has been nicknamed Edward. The ghost, dressed in his royalist finery, has been seen on a few occasions, within the pub and outside by various landlords and members of the public. 'Edward' manifests himself in other less visual ways, including footsteps sounding on the stairs, and other strange noises. He was also known to lay a heavy hand on customers, much to their surprise when they turn to find nobody in the vicinity. One of the more frightening incidents was recorded in the Oldham Evening Chronicle, August 18th 1972. Mr. George Barnett, the landlord at that time, was checking barrels in the cellar around midnight. When a stone was thrown at his shoulder, he looked around but no-one was in the room. This was the first time he had been shaken by a strange event within the pub, but he had felt a strange presence before, and had even seen a glass slide along the bar. He thought that someone had perhaps upset the spirit. The traditional story about the Sad Cavalier suggests he was the son of Lord Stannycliffe of Stannycliffe Hall in the 1600's. The Lord and his family were unwavering Royalists during turbulent times of the Civil War. Unfortunately for them Middleton became more staunchly Parliamentarian, with the Old Boar's Head becoming the Roundhead headquarters in the area. The story goes that a pocket of Royalist resistance (including the Lords son) survived in the area, and used the cellars of the Ring o' Bells as a clandestine meeting place. The cellars were linked to Middleton Parish Church by a yet another secret tunnel, by which they could escape if their furtive council was compromised (this passage is said to have been verified by openings which were bricked up within the cellar). One day somebody betrayed the son of Lord Stanycliffe to the Roundheads whilst he was still in the pub. He managed to flee to the cellars and down the dark tunnel, only to be cut to pieces by Roundheads who were waiting at the church by the passage exit. His body is supposed to have been buried under the flagstones of the cellar, where he is said to remain to this day. Helmets and pikes have been discovered under the cellar floor, but no human remains have been found.

back on the right. This is a building of uncertain date. Though much altered down the years, some say that it is the oldest secular structure in Middleton.

Continue along **New Lane** to return to **Long Street**, and thence back to the **Bus Station**.

Freehold to Werneth

The line now crosses **Jammy Lane** and **Suthers Street** before finally negotiating the last of the long, lazy curve into Oldham by means of a sharp right hand bend. The ground level is now rising, and we pass the **site of the junction** with the original Oldham branch (p124) to the left (remains of the track bed can still be seen), which joined after breasting the infamous Werneth Bank. The curious **structure with the domed roof** is said to have housed the winding engine when cable haulage was employed. Notice **Hartford Works**, a nondescript six-storey brick former cotton mill to the right. It dates from circa 1850, but was later taken over by Platt Brothers as their new works. They later substantially altered the interior for use as a warehouse and show rooms. Indeed, you may catch a glimpse of an **adjacent clock tower**. This belongs to **Bath House**, the former company offices (P.B. Alley, 1883) fronting Featherstall Road South in a rather wooden French Renaissance style (best view on the return journey).

The Platt concern opened their 'Hartford New Works in Werneth in 1844, two years after the railway opened. The company sidings were to the left of the line, the location of perhaps the largest part of the complex, comprising the Hartford Iron Works and its associated shops, extending beyond Arkwright Street. The company even installed its own narrow-gauge internal railway system! Apart from Bath House and Hartford Works (both converted

Platt Brothers

In the late 18th century, the Platt family of Dobcross adapted their skills as smiths to commence the manufacture of textile machinery for the woollen industry. In 1821, Henry Platt established himself in Oldham as a manufacturer of cotton spinning machinery. In subsequent partnership with Elijah Hibbert, he founded Hibbert, Platt, & Sons, which developed from an assembler of machine parts to a fully integrated manufacturer in its own right. In 1854, the company changed its name to Platt Brothers and Company and began to manufacture looms, mainly for export. In1868 the company became a limited liability company under the chairmanship of John Platt. Platt Brothers were at the forefront of technological innovation and their plant in Oldham was highly mechanised, employing 15,000 people. (In the 1890s it was estimated that Platt's supported 42% of Oldham's population!) The company was the largest of its kind in the world, with its own iron works and collieries. Platt Brothers systematically improved the technique of cotton spinning and perfected the carding machine, the roving frame, and the self-acting mule. Platt's mules were unrivalled in their length and speed of operation, and in productivity. Members of the family had other industrial interests; Samuel Platt was a principal promoter of the Manchester Ship Canal, and his yacht Norseman headed the opening procession. The Edwardian boom saw Platt Brothers reach its peak levels of production, when the average length of new mules ordered from the firm reached 1,274 spindles. Platt Brothers also supplied plans for mills as well as machinery, and supplied fitters to erect the machines, both at home and abroad. The 1920s and 30s heralded a slump in textile machinery manufacture and Platt Brothers began to lose money as prices for the few orders of machinery were driven down. The result was a series of mergers, in which power and control passed from Oldham and the original company lost something of its identity, though the brand name survives.

into industrial units) it has all gone. The tram passes under **Featherstall Road South** over bridge (the original Oldham Corporation tramway tracks were discovered in situ during refurbishment works to this structure). The **site of the former Werneth Station** in a cutting lies directly ahead. It was the original terminus of the branch, opening in 1842, and became a through station in 1847, being re-modeled between 1880 and 1895. The main entrance was from Railway Road on the south (right) side, accessed by a paved approach which communicated with a building that straddled the tracks. However, many people entered it by a spur from the footbridge at the west end, which linked with Featherstall Road. In addition to a mineral yard on the left, a goods yard was located by Railway Road on the right. In its latter years, the station was sadly reduced to bare platforms with 'bus shelters', and few people used it (one suspects its real users in the past were the employees of Platt Brothers). Consequently, it did not re-open as a tram stop.

Metrolink in Oldham

It was intended to build the Oldham/Rochdale extension 'all of a piece', but financial and political difficulties resulted in a two stage solution. Consequently, the section in Oldham between Featherstall Road South and the former Oldham Way roundabout, together with the original Mumps Metrolink Station was temporary in nature. It was replaced by a new routing through Oldham town centre, on 27 January, 2014. The temporary section then closed. The utmost economy had therefore been exercised in converting this section of railway to Metrolink operation, and a large part of the overhead poles and associated fittings will be reclaimed and re-used elsewhere on the network. The former route can be observed from the Gas Street Bridge (p140), and an account of this section is included as a piece of historical record.

The tram formerly continued along the 1847 extension to Mumps, passing through a ridge to access where the centre of the town lies. It traversed **Werneth Tunnel** (471 yards) and, after a short cutting, **Oldham Central Tunnel** (449 yards). The **site of the former Oldham Central Station** is also located in a cutting, extending to the **Clegg Street** over-bridge. The station was accessed from the corner of **Wellington Street** and **Clegg Street** by means of a brick booking office on the north side of the line, supported by a lower storey built upon the down or Rochdale platform. The footbridge paralleled the road bridge, and canopies stretched from the bridge to just west of the platform buildings on both platforms. Although the station was near to the town centre, it was closed in 1966 and demolished soon afterwards. Beyond the **Clegg Street** over bridge, a surprise was in store, for the cutting dramatically opened out, and another railway line joined the route from the right. After 1861, the Clegg Street Station terminus of the Oldham Ashton and Guide Bridge Junction Railway (see p124) opened adjacent to Central. This station was also accessed by **Clegg Street**, which terminated astride the station running lines (with an incline beyond to the goods yard). Passengers, however, could continue by means of a long footbridge that spanned the large goods yard to reach **Woodstock Street**. The rival stations could flourish for many years, since trains from Clegg Street ran to Guide Bridge (on the Great Central main line to the Midlands and London) and eventually Stockport (on the London and North Western main line to London Euston). Clegg Street, together with the Oldham, Ashton, and Guide Bridge line, closed to passengers in 1959, though the site (including the goods yard) was later used as a parcels depot for local mail order traffic. The whole area is now a **retail park**. Beyond Clegg Street and the junction site, the line crossed **Waterloo Street**. The extensive Waterloo Sidings beyond the bridge have disappeared, but the

Rhodes Bank Footbridge (also called 'Gas Street Bridge') that spanned them still survives. The tram serviced a temporary Mumps Metrolink station the other side of the bridge.

The **Rhodes Bank (Gas Street) Footbridge**, still largely in its Lancashire and Yorkshire Railway condition, can be reached by walking through the car park at the side of the **Library** (p144), and left along **Oldham Way**, crossing the latter by the **ramped footbridge**. (It leads to **Preston Street**, on the **Glodwick** side of town.) There were latterly only two tracks instead of the many that constituted two running lines and Waterloo Sidings. To the west is the site of Central and Clegg Street Stations, beyond **Waterloo Street**. To the east, where the line curved, was the **original Mumps Station site**, with its junction. The station entrance was from Victoria Street, which may be still traced looping alongside **Oldham Way** by the **car park**. **Oldham Way** cut through a tangled district of industrial premises that stretched between the town centre and the north side of the railway. It included the town gas works and (later) the electricity works.

You might be able to spot the **remains of the original station** near the temporary car park. There was a junction just before the western end of the old platforms, though curiously, Mumps was never a junction station. Instead, the Oldham, Ashton and Guide Bridge local trains diverged to the right and terminated about a quarter of a mile along the branch at the now vanished Glodwick Road Station, which opened in 1862 to accommodate the traffic on this new line. The London and North Western Railway (a constituent of the Oldham, Ashton, and Guide Bridge Railway) extended the line beyond this station by means of a branch via Lees to Greenfield, where it made a junction with their Trans-Pennine main line to Huddersfield and Leeds. Glodwick Road Station closed in 1955 when passenger services on the Greenfield branch were withdrawn (the Guide Bridge and Stockport locals were transferred to Mumps). Goods traffic continued until the complete closure of the Greenfield branch in 1964. The original Mumps station was the terminus of the 1847 extension, but after the further extension of the Oldham line to Rochdale in1863, the original structure was rebuilt in 1887. It was modernised in the 1950s, but retained its essential Lancashire and Yorkshire Railway appearance until it closed. The station boasted a large curving island platform accessed by subway from the Victoria Street booking hall. There were single track bay platforms at both ends, and the whole was roofed over by a fine glass and iron canopy. (Metrolink kindly gifted the canopy to the East Lancashire Railway (p95), where parts of it will live on at one or other of their stations.) A large goods yard (used by both railway companies) was located in the angle of the junction between the Rochdale line and the Greenfield branch. Nothing remains of the station and the site of the goods yard and branch line is buried behind an earthen bank on the right.

Nowadays, the trams diverge to the left just beyond **Featherstall Road**, passing northwards through the **site of a former goods yard**, and gaining height to run alongside the above roadway. This is part of *Westwood Business Park*, and many of the original businesses remain. The line crosses **West Street**, adjacent to the new entrance to the Business Park, before passing over an area that has been cleared. The rest of the ground is open land, in which the tracks curve to the right, round a curious structure that happens to be a **covered reservoir**, to run in an easterly direction along the south side of **Middleton Road**.

The tram arrives at **Westwood Station**. Two **platforms** are connected by **steps** to **pedestrian crossings** at both ends. **Ramps** are provided near the west end of the

Rochdale platform, and the east end for the Manchester one. A further ramp from the latter commnicates with a path to Richmond Road.

Westwood is an urban area of Oldham, occupying a hillside known as North Moor, close to its boundary with Royton and Chadderton. Apart from industrial and commercial units, Westwood is "almost entirely" composed of Victorian era terraces, with some small pockets of housing association and council house properties. It is the home of 60% of Oldham's Bangladeshi community, the second largest concentration of Bangladeshis in the United Kingdom. (Most of the community have immigrated from the Sylhet Division of Bangladesh.) Consequently, the district features a replica of the Shaheed Minar national monument, which commemorates those killed in the Bengali Language Movement demonstrations in 1952. The Westwood Moravian Church congregation was founded in 1865. A church building for the congregation dating from 1869 still stands in the locality. After crossing Winterbottom Street, the line turns sharply south to run alongside the Oldham Way slip road on the left. The development of the next section is rather complex. Originally, Oldham Way crossed, by means of a flyover, a large traffic island which intersected Manchester Street, and the slip roads

The Life and Times of a Stationmaster

Thomas Normington, the first stationmaster at Mumps, was a native of Dewsbury, and a classic example of the Victorian self-made man. He was born in comparatively humble circumstances in 1824, leaving school at the age of nine to work in the local woollen trade. He obtained employment at Brighouse station as a parcel porter, and was appointed to Mumps just before the extension opened from Werneth. He has left us with two anecdotes of his time there. In 1848, the new branch to Blackpool opened, and a Sunday excursion from Mumps was advertised at one shilling and sixpence for men and one shilling for ladies. A large crowd of perhaps two thousand turned up at the station, but the superintendent of the line arrived and ordered that they should not be admitted. He explained that he had information that numbers of men were dressed as women to take advantage of the reduced fare! Normington suggested that if this were so, they deserved to travel, but the superintendent ordered that the women be admitted one at a time. Meanwhile, one of his inspectors stood on a chair holding a rod with a notice requesting 'ladies' to hold their tickets high above their heads while the superintendent 'peeped' at them as they passed! This caused the crowd to rush the door, sending both superintendent and inspector flying. "It was very well known on the line that the superintendent was a most eccentric man." In the summer of 1849, Normington was travelling up Werneth bank when the haulage rope broke. "It's all up," the driver told him, "we shall have to stop here all night." Normington recollected that the locomotive was Number 131, a newly built 2-2-2 'Hawkshaw Single', and he judged it powerful enough to ascend the incline unassisted. Consequently, he ordered the driver to set back to the foot of the slope, where three carriages were uncoupled. The train then ran forward only to stall short of the summit. However, the train breasted the incline at the second attempt. The incident encouraged further, more official, experimentation, and rope haulage was later discontinued. Normington ended his career as Superintendent of the Yorkshire District of the Lancashire and Yorkshire Railway, before retiring in 1895. He was a 'company man' in the oldest and best sense of the word: he did not suffer fools gladly, whether the 'fools' were porters or company directors. Consequently, he was perhaps not as generously treated in old age as he should have been. His revenge was the publication of rather colourful memoirs.

on either side of Oldham Way commenced and terminated at the Manchester Street Island. To this arrangement has been added the Metrolink line. It swings to the left, and **crosses the island** through the centre section of the flyover! (Metrolink actually passes through the section to the north of centre of the island, and there are signalled **road crossings** at both ends.) The section beyond presented a few construction problems. The terrain (a ridge) and the obstacle of *The Pennine Way Hotel* dictated a cutting, a diversion, and a small tunnel! However, the hotel was demolished, making the route shorter and straighter. There is a glimpse of **St. Patrick's Church** on the hill, before the tram ascends the **cutting** towards King Street Station, but the tunnel proposal is replaced by a **bridge** under the junction of **John Street** and Foundry Street. It has recently been adorned with the **Oldham Coat of Arms** on both sides! Adjacent to the bridge on the right (but not visible from the line) is an annexe of **Oldham Sixth Form College**. It incorporates the original **entrance arch** of Oldham Royal Infirmary which once stood between 1872 and 1972 on the site. A *Co-operative Funeral Parlour*, which also stood in the way near this point, has been re-located!

The tram now arrives at **King Street Station**. The **Rochdale platform** is connected by **ramp** and **steps** to **King Street**, with **steps** to the **car park** on the left of the station. The **Manchester platform** has a ramp at the Oldham end, and a **stepped terrace** communicating with **Union Street West**. Note the fine **landscaping** to the right! The **stone pillar** on the left at the end of the Rochdale platform, marks the site of King Street Baptist Church (1862-2005).

The line crosses **King Street** and passes the **former Grand Theatre** (p146) on the right hand corner and **'Pocket Park'** and **George Street** (p146) on the left. It is now **street running** for most of the length of **Union Street**. **Brunswick Street**, to the right, leads to the **Oldham Campus of the University of Huddersfield**. Notice the **archway** forming the entrance to *Brunswick Square* (p146) also on the right; it is all that is left of the Methodist chapel that formerly stood on the site.

A **pedestrian area** takes up the whole road between **Peter Street/Hobson Street** and **Clegg Street**, framing **Oldham Central Station**. The **station** itself comprises an **island platform** with **ramps** at both ends.

Look out for **Phoenix House** on the right (opposite the Job Centre) with its **Heron Sculpture** (p146). The **Prudential Assurance Building** on the left is also noteworthy (p146). It should be noted that **Peter Street** leads to an entrance to the *Spindles Shopping Centre*, and the north side of **Clegg Street** to a **bus station**. The tram crosses **Clegg Street** and passes the **Lyceum** (p145) on the left. At the crossing of **Greaves Street**, there is a glimpse of the **tower of the Parish Church** on the left, before noting the **old post office** on the opposite corner, followed by the **garden court** and the **old library building** on the right (p143-4). Beyond **Waterloo Street**, shops and cafés appear, though the area is rather run-down; it is hoped that the trams will bring a much needed regeneration. Notice the former Conservative Club (with its balcony) on the left (p143). Beyond the **newspaper offices** (p144) on the right, we arrive at the junction with **Yorkshire Street**, crossing the **new link road**, and curving slightly to the south of **Mumps** (p145).

Here the line enters the new **Mumps Station**; there are **two platforms** with ramps at the west and steps at the east end, with additional ramps at the rear. The station is intended as a **bus interchange**, and there are **three saw tooth bus stop bays** on each side. There is a **Park and Ride facility** on the land south of the line and north of Oldham Way, entered from the Oldham direction.

Oldham

Much of Oldham's history is concerned with textile manufacture. It has been said that "if ever the industrial revolution placed a town firmly and squarely on the map of the world, that town is Oldham." Local soils were too thin and poor to sustain much arable farming, and so the agricultural economy was largely based upon sheep, which provided the raw material for a local woollen weaving trade. By 1756, Oldham had emerged as centre of the hatting industry in England. The rough felt used in the production process is the origin of the term "Owdham Roughyed" a nickname for local people. In the last quarter of the 18th century, Oldham changed from being associated with cottage industry, producing woollen garments by domestic labour, to a sprawling industrial metropolis of spinning mills, for Oldham became the world's manufacturing centre for cotton spinning in the second half of the 19th century. By 1851, over 30% of Oldham's population was employed within the textile sector, compared to 5% across Great Britain. It overtook other textile manufacturing centres as the result of a mill building boom in the 1860s and 1870s, a period during which Oldham became the most productive cotton-spinning town in the world. In 1871 Oldham alone had more spindles than any country in the world except the United States, and in 1909, was spinning more cotton than France and Germany combined. By 1911 there were 16.4 million spindles in Oldham, compared with a total of 58 million in the United Kingdom and 143.5 million in the world; in 1928, with the construction of the UK's largest textile factory Oldham reached its manufacturing zenith. At its peak, there were over 360 mills, operating night and day. As the importation of cheaper foreign yarns grew during the 20th century, over-reliance upon the textile sector resulted in Oldham's economy declining into a depression, although it was not until 1964 that Oldham ceased to be the largest centre of cotton spinning. In spite of efforts to increase the efficiency and competitiveness of its production, the last cotton was spun in the town in 1998. Engineering, particularly the large concern of Platt Brothers and (latterly) Ferranti's, was important, together with coal mining, but the former has declined, and the latter has disappeared. Since the de-industrialisation of Oldham in the mid-20th century, these industries have been replaced by retail, publishing, healthcare, and food processing sectors, though factory-generated employment still retains a significant presence.

The following walk is commenced at the **new Oldham Mumps Station** (p142). One is struck by two things; the peculiar name of the road that the station is named after, and the distinctive structure with a tower at the street's eastern end. You might think that it belonged to a church or a chapel, but this is the baroque corner tower (topped by a small dome) that marked the **former District Bank** (Mills and Murgatroyed, 1902-3). A genuine temple of mammon! In contrast, a modern **Mosque** (complete with a green dome and a minaret) may be observed opposite, in the distance.

Continue along Union Street, passing the headquarters of the *Oldham Evening Chronicle*. The neo-classical building to the right was the **former Conservative Club**, dating from 1911. Churchill once appeared on its balcony. This part of the street is rather run-down, and it is hoped that the trams will bring urban regeneration in their wake. Indeed, Oldham Council has embarked upon a programme of upgrading and refurbishing the 'Metrolink corridor', in which sculptures, tree planting, and landscaping all feature. After crossing **Waterloo Street**, we arrive at the **old library building** at the corner of **Southgate Street**. It was designed by Thomas Mitchell, a local architect, and opened in 1883 by Sir John Lubbock (the originator of Bank Holidays). It was fitted out as a library, art gallery, and museum in 1885 (note the **inscription** on the Union Street

A temple of mammon! The former bank at Mumps

side), and this second opening was attended by 50,000 people (half the population of the town)! Notice the **female statue surmounting the gable**. The identity of the figure is not known, though the local tradition is that she was nicknamed 'Lady Wrigley', a reference to the colourful local councillor, 'Colonel' William Wrigley, who had been vocal in opposing the idea of spending ratepayers' money on a public library! It is intended to develop the old library as a Heritage Centre in which the town's rich historical collections can be properly displayed. The building will also house the 'front of office' operations of the Oldham Coliseum (p149), for the car park across Southgate Street is earmarked as the site of a new, state of the art theatre which will be the Coliseum's new home. (A detour can be made from here to view the course of the old railway/Metrolink line, see p139.) Notice the **carved wooden owl** at the entrance to the library gardens. Turn left into the **pretty park/garden court**, noting the **carvings on the library wall** (including Raphael, Chaucer, Mozart, and Handel) and the original **town coat of arms** carved on the chimney breast. It is derived from the crest of Hugh de Oldham, Bishop of Exeter. Directly ahead is the modern **Gallery Oldham**, opened in 2002. (Mon. to Sat, 10-5, Sun 10-4; free admission) The **entrance hall** contains an **enquiry desk** (the **tourist information centre** is on the next floor in the reference library), and to the left is *Café Culture*. There is a **large library area** to the rear, from which access is obtained to an **education suite** and first floor **reference library**. However, most visitors will seek out

Mumps

It is not a medical condition, but the name of a nearby street or district, recalling the 'mumpers' that frequented the place. This was a local term for 'alms' or a charitable payment, but could also be applied to beggars. In pre-industrial England, there were two types; the 'aged and impotent' who were perhaps 'deserving' and the 'sturdy rogues and vagabonds' who were not. But ordinary people were more sympathetic. The professional beggars seldom bothered them, for they targeted the rich and well-to-do. These beggars often treated begging as a trade, with their own unofficial guilds and associations, complete with a code of behaviour and recognition signs. They stood more in the tradition of Robin Hood and his Merry Men than anything else, and the jovial vagabonds of the comic opera is all that has come down to us of a vanished way of life.

"Of all the trades in England,
A begging is the best,
For when a beggar he is tired,
He can lay down and rest.

And a begging I will go,
And a begging I will go!

For I've been lame in Duckinfield,
And I've been blind in Shaw,
And many's the bonny country lass,
I've beggar'd in the straw!

And a begging I will go,
And a begging I will go!"

the **stairs** and **lift** to the right before proceeding to the **second floor**. Here are a number of **modern galleries** used for temporary exhibitions. Do not omit the unusual **photographic panorama of the town**, taken in 1875. Amongst other things, it shows the course of the railway through Oldham.

After leaving the Gallery, turn left then right and walk up **Greaves Street**, passing the former **Quaker Meeting House** on the right. The **stone lions** outside the building once graced the Victoria Market Hall, sadly destroyed by fire in 1974. The building on the right hand corner of Union Street was the Post and Telegraph Office, dating from 1877. It now houses the **Local Studies and Archives** (daily, times vary). Glance up the continuation of Greaves Street across the road for a glimpse of the **tower of the Parish Church**. Turn left and continue along **Union Street**, noticing the **Lyceum** to the right. Designed by N.G. Pennington in 1856, this is one of the town's most impressive buildings. It was intended to function as a kind of educational club for working people, but also seems to have doubled up as the local stock exchange! Close inspection reveals that it is built in two halves; that to the left was the original Lyceum, while the right hand portion (distinguished by the insertion of ventilation slats into the decorative laurel wreaths!) was the School of Art and Science. The old Lyceum contains the Lyceum Theatre, situated in the lower ground floor of the building; a varied programme of five main productions is presented each season. The building also contains a music education centre and the former School is a community centre.

The area of **Union Street** between **Clegg Street** and **Hobson Street/Peter Street**, is pedestrianised, and cont-ains **Oldham Central Station** (p142) opposite *Sainsbury's*. Notice the red brick and terracotta of the **Prudential Assurance Building** on the right, built in 1901 and designed by Alfred Water-house. Opposite the Job Centre, look up at the **sculptured bird** on the front of **Phoenix House**. No, it isn't a phoenix, but a heron, symbolic of Heron Develop-ments, the owners! Continue walking until **Brunswick Square** is reached, to the left. The old Methodist Church,

The old library and the new

built in 1875, has dis-appeared, but the **archway** remains, framing the entrance to the **courtyard** of the Brunswick Development (1985). Some of the stone features have been formed into an attractive **fountain**. **Brunswick Street**, to the left, leads to the **Oldham Campus of the University of Huddersfield**. The **Grand Theatre** is found at the road junction at the corner of King Street and Union Street. It is a large theatre built in 1908, with a brick and terracotta façade now much altered, and a corner entrance rebuilt in 1936 with a tower and clock. Originally it was the most prestigious theatre in Oldham, with 'an elaborate interior'; Gracie Fields (before she became famous), and the D'Oyly Carte Opera Company have trodden its boards. The building was internally altered for a pre-war cinema and later converted into a bowling alley and then a nightclub. It is now in a rather sad condition and currently houses the *Oldham Leisure Lounge*, offering a combination of pool, snooker, arcades, and refreshments.

Oldham King Street Station (p142) is directly ahead, but we cross over the **pedestrian crossing** to the right, to continue northwards up **George Street**. But first, have a quick look at **Pocket Park**, on the corner of George Street. Jill Randall created the **steel screen** surrounding the little park to reflect Oldham's ever-changing climate, using **symbols from weather maps**! It is hard to believe that this was once a lane of thatched cottages called Bardsley Brow. Notice the second-hand book shop on the right. The **chapel** on the left is a Grade II listed building dating from 1815. Oldham was an early Methodist centre, and Wesley visited it during his preaching travels. But turn left down **David Street** to explore the **chapel's rear**. This is a small back street called **'Jackson's Pit'**, and is one of the oldest parts of the town. The road from Manchester to Huddersfield once came this way, and gossiping women were ducked in a stagnant pond. All that remains are traces of **cellar dwellings** under the chapel where some of the poorest inhabitants lived. Walk up **Jackson's Pit**, turn right, and then immediately left by the *George Tavern* into **George Square**. Walk through this paved area passing a number of examples of **modern sculpture** and bearing to the left. By the *Three Crowns pub*, turn right into the **Water Street Arcade**, opened in 1989, and said to be on the site of the ancient road to Yorkshire. A left turn brings us on to **West Street** with a view of the **Civic Centre**. Built in two stages between 1964 and 1977, the tower is **201 feet high, standing at 896 feet above sea level**. It cost £6,800,000. The **Spindles Shopping Centre**, with a noted **stained glass roof**, is to the right, but search out the **paved passage** further on the right, between the shops. Turn left into **Henshaw Street**, and follow it to the corner of **Tommyfield Market Hall** and **Albion Street**. Look either side of the shop signs on your left to see **carved stone capitals** representing various tradespeople. We now follow **Albion Street** on the right, alongside the market.

As you pass along **Albion Street**, look out for *Lever's Fish and Chip Shop*, with a **blue plaque** commemorating the origin of Fish and Chips! Nearby is H2O, a large stainless steel drinking fountain. In contrast, at the corner of **Curzon Street**, may be found **Sat-is-Factory**, a seat in the form a mill chimney and roof! A number of tiles, set into the street, commemorate local businesses. Take some time out to explore the **Hilton Arcade** on the right; it contains a historical display. It was built in 1893 by John Hilton, a local tailor, and above the High Street entrance is a fine example of **decorative wrought iron work**. You may be able to pick out the **faces of Gladstone and Disraeli**, either side of the **lamp**. They cannot see eye to eye, but, upon close inspection, it is difficult to tell them apart...save for the fact that Gladstone has a wing collared shirt and Disraeli his well-known kiss curl! Almost opposite across High Street, is the **site of the first Yate's Wine Lodge**, distinguished by a **blue plaque**. Now a forgotten Lancashire institution, they were once full of a strange assortment of vaguely disreputable characters, jolly tarts, and old ladies tippling port and lemon. Turn left and pass along **High Street**, then left into **Lord Street**. To the right of the **bank** is **Church Lane**, one of the town's most elegant and secluded streets. Walk along this street to the **third door on the left**. This was the site of the residence of Captain Chippendale, an officer of the infamous Manchester Yeomanry who employed spies to report on the local radical movement. Not a popular man! Next door is the **former County Court**, designed in 1894 by Sir Henry Tanner. Interestingly enough, a horse powered cotton mill (employing

Tommy's Field

The market traders once congregated, prior to 1830, around what is now the main entrance to the Spindles Shopping Centre. The Watch Committee, to clear the streets, then tried to move them to the site of the old Town Hall, but they were largely ignored. Instead they occupied a plot of vacant land near their old haunt. This was owned by a Sir Nathaniel Curzon, who leased it to a pig breeder called Tommy Whittaker. It was thus known as 'Tommy's Field', later corrupted to 'Tommyfield'. Never just a market, Tommyfield rapidly became the heart and soul of Oldham. It was used for political meetings, fairs and circuses, and was resorted to as a rendezvous for courting couples! The first market hall was erected in 1856, and replaced by the far grander Victoria Market in 1908. This was sadly destroyed in a spectacular fire in 1974. The present market hall is a rather tasteful replacement. Tommyfield Market Hall has over 130 stalls with a wide range of goods including food stalls and cafés, and is open daily. The principal outdoor market days are Monday, Wednesday, Friday, and Saturday. A small flea market is held on Wednesdays, and there is usually a car boot sale on Sundays.

'spinning jennies') was erected here in 1780. At the end of the street are **Church Steps**, leading to the **Parish Church of St. Mary**.

The church of Saint Mary stands on high ground east of the market-place on an ancient site, but is a modern building belonging to the early part of the 19th century. (The church is usually open on the second Saturday of the month, between 9.30 and 12.30; tours of the crypt are given for a small donation. Ring 0161 633 4847 for further information.) In 1476, Ralph Langley, parson of Prestwich, built ' a body of a church' there. The indenture between Rector Langley and the masons he employed sets forth that the building is to be of four arches on each side, of hewn stone, with side aisles. This work, with later

The Oldham Giant

The crypt predates the present church. In the 19th century, someone had the bright idea of heating the church with exhaust steam from an adjacent mill, but it leaked into the crypt, creating such a disgusting stench that matters had to be put in order. Nowadays, the crypt can be visited by a tour when the church is open. It contains two interesting relics. One is a 14th century stone coffin, discovered during alterations. The other is the enormous lead coffin of the 'Oldham Giant'. This is reputed to contain the remains of John Clegg, who was buried in 1823. This market trader weighed forty-three stones, measured sixty-three inches around the waist, and was seven feet six inches high. In later life, he was taken to his place of work in a wheelbarrow.

St. Mary's Parish Church with the War Memorial in front

restorations and additions, apparently lasted till the beginning of the 19th century. Illustrations of the old church as it existed towards the close of the 18th century show a building consisting of chancel with north and south chapels, nave with north and south aisles, south porch, and west tower, and a vestry added at the east end under the chancel window in 1777. An Act of Parliament was obtained in 1824 to replace the church (except for the crypt) with a new structure. Amongst the designs submitted was one by Charles Barry, who planned to utilise parts of the medieval church until money was available to complete what was a rather ambitious scheme. The more modest design of Richard Lane was chosen instead, and a piqued Barry appealed in vain to the Bishop of Chester, who thought an inexpensive church suitable for an industrial location! In later life, Charles Barry was the architect of the Houses of Parliament. The old church was pulled down in 1827, and the present structure erected between that date and 1830 in the Gothic style of the period. It consists of a **chancel** 20 feet wide by 14 feet long, with small north and south **vestries**, a **nave** of six bays 90 feet by 26 feet, with north and south **aisles** each 17 feet wide, and a west **tower** 10 foot square inside with walls 5 foot thick. There are **galleries** on three sides, approached by wide stone **staircases** at the west end of the aisles north and south of the tower. None of the fittings of the old building has been preserved. In the **vestry** is an **old oak chest** with three locks, without date or inscription, but probably belonging to the end of the sixteenth or beginning of the 17th century. The **plate** includes a chalice of 1663, inscribed with the initials G. H. and A. H., and with the maker's mark H N over a bird.

Leave the **churchyard** by the **main gate** and descend the **steps** to the **war memorial**. The memorial was built of bronze and granite in 1922 by Albert Toft, and originally commemorated the local units of the Manchester Regiment. A **Roll of Honour** is set into the base of the memorial. It lists the dead of World War Two, and is changed daily. A short detour eastwards along **Yorkshire Street**, then left up **Fairbottom Street**, leads to the **Oldham Coliseum**. Few towns these days can boast a live theatre, but Oldham can. The Coliseum Theatre dates back to 1885 and began life as the 'Grand American Theatre'. In March 1931 the theatre closed and reopened as a cinema but it only survived until March 1932 when the recession caused complete closure. However, in January, 1938, the Oldham Repertory Theatre Club had opened at the former Temperance Hall in Horsedge Street with its production of Shaw's 'Arms and the Man'. The club was for members only, thus avoiding the need to be licensed. Here they provided weekly rep until 1939. Such was their success that they signed the lease on the now derelict Colosseum, and in July, 1939, they staged their first production in their new home

Nowadays, Oldham Coliseum is a building-based producing theatre. It has a capacity in its main auditorium of 585 seats; in addition the theatre has a studio with a capacity of 50 seats. The company produces eight shows a year on its main stage, offering a balanced programme of drama, comedy, musicals, new writing, and the annual pantomime. In addition to in-house produced work on the main stage the theatre also takes in four weeks of touring theatre as well as around fifteen non-theatre performances including music, dance, and stand-up comedy (to obtain the current programme, telephone 0161 624 1731). Back once more at the **War Memorial**, cross over to the old **Town Hall**. It was on the steps of this building that Winston Churchill was declared Member for Oldham in 1900, the start of his political career. It is a Grade II listed structure in the neo-classical style, built in 1841, eight years before Oldham received its borough status. One of the last purpose built town halls in this style, it has an Ionic portico, copied from the temple of Ceres, near Athens. Long existing as the political centre of the town, complete with courtrooms, the structure has stood empty since the 1980s. It has regularly been earmarked for redevelopment as part of regeneration project proposals. In September 2008, it was reported that "Oldham Town Hall is only months away from a major roof collapse". A tour taken by local Councillors and media concluded with an account that "chunks of masonry are falling from the ceilings on a daily basis...the floors are littered with dead pigeons...revealed that the

The former Oldham Town Hall

The 'Scottish Play'

The Oldham Coliseum was the scene of a tragic accident involving the play that raises the hackles of superstition in many actors...Macbeth. In January 1947, Harold Norman was an actor playing the role of Macbeth. It is said that he did not care for the usual superstitions observed by actors in 'The Scottish Play', referring to the play as 'Macbeth' and rehearsing his lines out loud! During a sword fight scene Harold was accidentally stabbed with a real sword. The wound became infected and he died in Oldham Royal infirmary on the 27th February of peritonitis caused by the sword wound. This unfortunate death was bound to have an effect of people's minds, given the tragic event, the nature of the play, and Harold's lack of superstition. Inevitably Harold was thought to have returned to the theatre in spirit form, and he is said to have been seen several times. His apparition appears most often on Thursdays, as this was the day that he was mortally wounded.

building is literally rotting away". Fortunately, remedial work to stabilise the building is now under way. It is now proposed to re-develop the building as a cinema, with restaurants and cafés. Walk down **Greaves Street,** to the left of the building. From here, **later extensions to the town hall** are visible. Across the street may be seen the **Edgar Wood Building,** constructed in 1901 for Hesketh Booth, the Town Clerk. Never a retiring bureaucrat, he placed a prominent 'H.B.' carved in stone above the door! Wood was influential in the 'Arts and Crafts Movement', and the plans for this building (based on a 16th century Lancashire cottage) were exhibited at the Royal Academy. Continue down **Greaves Street** to return to **Union Street,** near the **Library.**

The Rochdale Line

The section of Metrolink within Oldham is described in the previous chapter; for the convenience of the reader, this chapter continues the previous one by describing the line between Mumps and Rochdale.

Mumps to Newhey

This part of the original line (and the subsequent Metrolink section) once had some of the characteristics of a rural branch, and these still linger in places. The communities that it served were fairly self-contained, being mill settlements where most people worked locally. The through traffic to and from Manchester was largely in the form of raw cotton bales, cloth, and coal, and passenger traffic was secondary. Now all has changed. In the dying days of the railway, the stations served what were, in effect, dormitory suburbs, and the traffic was commuter driven. This state of affairs was inherited by Metrolink.

Upon leaving Mumps Metrolink Station, you might catch a glimpse of the **mosque** (with its elegant green dome) at the top of the slope, but the most eye-catching landmark is the **stone tower** on the left (p143). You might think that it belonged to a church or a chapel, but this is the baroque corner tower (topped by a small dome) that marked the former District Bank (Mills and Murgatroyed, 1902-3)!

Before the tram swings leftwards, notice the remains of the former crossing of Oldham Way. Indeed, the history of this section of the line is rather complicated. It formerly crossed Whitehead Street, which had been widened when the bridge was rebuilt in 1886. In 1960, plans were made to construct Oldham Way, a four lane by-pass to the south of the city centre; it would terminate at its eastern end by the large Mumps Roundabout. Whitehead Street would become part of a re-aligned **Lees Road** (A669), making a junction with the roundabout at this point. Consequently, the bridge was rebuilt in 1968-69. After Lees Road, the line crossed **Back o' th' Moor** by means of a bridge built in 1891 by the Liverpool firm Holme and King, comprising two 11 foot-deep wrought-iron plate girders, each more than 100 feet long and weighing more than 50 tons. (The floor carrying the railway weighed a massive 80 tons.) This road also became linked to the roundabout, but the bridge remained unaltered. It famously proclaimed Oldham as 'the home of the tubular bandage'! The much photographed advertisement was unveiled by local firm Seton in 1996, as a tribute to Oldham's contribution to medical science, and the firm's partnership with the local cotton manufacturers. The bridge was carefully removed one weekend in January, 2011 and the Lees Road Bridge was demolished soon after. The sections of viaduct (actually a kind of elevated stone causeway) remaining were demolished to provide convenient access by **inclines** on both sides to ground level. Finally, the roundabout itself was eliminated by creating an ordinary road junction on its east side that diverted traffic from Back o' th' Moor directly on to Oldham Way.

Consequently, the **temporary tram route** crossed the site of the **former Mumps Roundabout**, and the roadway by a **level crossing**, before attaining the **original level** of the railway line once more beyond **Back o' th' Moor**. Now the crossing has also passed into history, and the line now runs to the north of the by-pass.

A vanished Oldham landmark (photograph courtesy of John McCarthy)

We are now travelling northwards, alongside **Brook Street** on the right, upon the start of the final Lancashire and Yorkshire Railway extension of the circuitous route towards Rochdale. This section of railway, from the original Mumps station to Rochdale, opened in 1863, with the short branch to Royton in the following year. The line soon runs into a **cutting**, and passes under **Shaw Road**, and the surroundings start to open up to the right, the location of **Oldham Central Industrial Estate**. This was the site of the extensive Hartford Sidings (with a cotton warehouse at the Yates Street end), and it was linked by a crossing of nearby Derker Street with the internal railway system belonging to the 'Old' or 'East Works' of Platt Brothers (see p138).

The tram now enters **Derker Station**, situated to the south of **Yates Street**, which spans the line by a low **iron bridge**. The **Rochdale platform** is connected by **lift** and **stairs** with Yates Street, with cycle stands and lockers at the upper level. Both **platforms** are linked by a **pedestrian crossing** at the south end of the station, and passengers exit from the **Manchester platform** through the **car park** to **Cromford Street** and **Yates Street**. Indeed, the station functions as a **'park and ride'** location, with space for 254 vehicles. The Metrolink station stands on the site of a railway station opened as recently as 1985 in a housing area that then lacked rail services. It replaced the poorly situated Royton Junction Station (see p154). At that time, the Passenger Transport Executive had a strategy for developing local railway lines, and devised an inexpensive standard station design. Thus, the original station was provided with timber platforms sporting 'bus shelters'. Everything was demolished and replaced by the present Metrolink structures.

Beyond the **Yates Street** over-bridge, the line now runs on the flat for a short distance, passing a yard mainly used by a steel fabricator on the left. This was the site of storage sidings, and the two running lines (one to Royton and the main line to Rochdale) separated about here. At the **Holyrood Street** bridge (now rebuilt as a footbridge), we pass under the former Royton line span (the main line passed through a former span to the right). The **trackbed of the Royton line** is clearly visible to the left (in a cutting) as the main line starts to curve to the right. It opened in 1864 and was closed under the Beeching proposals in 1966. This, like others made at the time, was an odd decision, as the branch was still quite busy, and future housing development would have made it busier still. But the terminal station was falling apart, and a sensational accident in 1961 (in which a runaway diesel multiple-unit ran through the buffers, crossed High Barn Street, and demolished two houses opposite) did not help matters. A short branch serving Higginshaw Gas Works, which diverged from this line after the junction, continued for some time after.

Royton Junction Station opened at the same time as the branch, an impressive place with four platforms (two on each line). The main building was in the angle of the junction, and a footbridge linked all the platforms. Access was by a private road on the west side which led, via the vanished cotton mills and local streets, to Higginshaw Lane. There was also a pathway which ran from Holyrood Street Bridge between the running line and the sidings to reach the main line Manchester platform. The station survived the closure of the branch, and staggered on in a very sad state indeed until 1987. No trace of it remains. The **wooded area** to the right of the line at this point was the site of extensive sidings, and there were others (known as Woodstock Sidings) to the left beyond the station itself. What were they used for? These were sort sidings, where full and returning empty coal wagons were marshalled in connection with the many mills and industrial premises between here and Rochdale. Of course, other goods, including shipments of raw cotton, were dealt with, but coal always seemed to take pride of place.

The famous **Oldham Edge**, a ridge stretching towards Royton, is situated to the west of the line hereabouts.

> *On Owdham Edge the grass is green,*
> *Reetest view that 'ere tha's seen.*
> *Tha stands on't top an tha looks abeawt,*
> *There's nowt but mills wi' their chimney spouts!*

The **Woodstock Occupation Bridge** is passed. It is linked with **Meek Street**, which may have been named after the railway's civil engineer. The bridge itself accessed the former Woodstock Mill on the left of the line. We are now descending (the site of Royton Junction marked the highest point on the line at 613 feet above sea level) and pass into a fine area of open country. The route has some good **views of the Pennine Hills** in the distance, and passes **Royton Moss**, largely on the right. After the **Bulcote Lane Bridge** (sometimes known as **Cop Road**), notice the three arch **Occupation Bridge**, leading to **Old Bank Farm** on the right. The tram now runs through the valley of the **River Beal**, with the **stream** itself mostly running along the right side. It opens up into **Moss Hey**, and Shaw is announced by **two large mills** on the right. **Lilac Mill** is the first; it was built in 1918 and immediately converted into an aircraft factory in the closing stages of the First World War (the main plant was at Chadderton, and the Lancashire and Yorkshire Railway produced a number of aircraft transporter wagons). The **second mill** (see below), with which it is connected by an overhead bridge, is alongside **Shaw and Crompton Station**.

As in railway days, some services terminate here, but Metrolink wished to avoid unnecessary crossings of **Beal Lane** by siting the new **Shaw and Crompton Station** before the **level crossing**. The latter has seen the former gates replaced by traffic and tram signals! The **platforms** are accessed directly by **ramps from Beal Lane**, though a **pedestrian crossing** is provided at the south end. This station is rather unusual, as it is provided with an **island platform**; the eastern facing of the **Manchester platform** serves a **bay or terminating siding** for trams to and from Manchester. This also explains the provision of a **driver's rest room**! A remodelled **car park** (north of Beal Lane, to the west of the former station site) provides over fifty spaces, and there is also provision for **bicycles**.

This district has always been known by the dual name of **'Shaw and Crompton'**, and was transformed from a collection of farm villages to a major cotton spinning centre in the 19th century. (The *Shay Wake* pub on the corner of the main cross road, refers to 'Shaw Wakes', the annual holiday that the local mill workers once looked forward to.) The few remaining mills are converted to other uses, and it now serves as a dormitory suburb for Oldham and Manchester.

Nowadays, the principal attractions are **Crompton Moor** and **Dunwood Park**, two fine country parks, and both a short bus ride from the station. (Excursions to both these locations are described on p159.) The **centre of Shaw and Crompton** is reached by a left turn from the Metrolink Station, and a walk down **Beal Lane** (*Benons Café*, to the right, can be recommended), soon reaches the main cross road, which intersects with **Market Street**. A short walk along **Rochdale Road**, directly ahead, leads to *Arcadia Rail*, a model railway shop with a fine reputation. (Open daily, except Tuesday and Sunday.) However, a stroll left down **Market Street** (the principal shopping centre), and a right turn down **Greenfield Lane**, leads to **High Street** and one of the finest **war memorials** in Lancashire. Unveiled in 1923, it consists of an animated **bronze group**

The Mills of the Valley

The Metrolink station is dominated to the east by Briar Mill. Built and operated by Briar Mill Ltd., it was later occupied by Courtaulds. Like the rest of the mills, cotton production eventually ceased, and conversion to other uses followed. In this case, it was used for the warehousing and distribution of catalogue items. The company also purchased neighbouring Lilac Mill, and constructed a bridge to join the two. In the 1980s Bolton steeplejack Fred Dibnah was paid £7000 to demolish Briar Mill's chimney one brick at a time. His efforts and dare-devil methods were documented in a television series. Briar Mill is typical of a Lancashire spinning mill in its final maturity. Built around an iron girder frame, with fireproof floors of concrete and brick, and powered by a horizontal steam engine, the water tank (which also supplied a sprinkler system) was usually enclosed in an ornate brick tower. Upon this, the mill or company name was emblazoned.

"These are the mills of the valley,
Shiloh, Monarch, and Tame.
These are the mills of the valley,
We shall not see their like again!"

by Richard Goulden atop a tall stepped granite plinth. A heroic man, clothed only in a cloak, fends off two writhing and snarling panthers with a sword, while protecting a group of children which huddle against him, partly hiding under his cloak. The beasts are a reference to a satanic evil, while the hero clearly suggests Saint Michael.

The railway line between Shaw and Rochdale was single track in later British Rail days, but Metrolink have doubled most of it again. The tram crosses **Beal Lane** and passes through the site of the former station. Its opening, in 1863, coincided with that of this stretch of the line. The main buildings were on the Rochdale platform, and an extensive goods yard was located on the site of the current car park, on the left. There was also once a short branch to the right, crossing the Beal (which runs in a culvert under the crossing, and to the right of the station site). It led to Bank House Colliery, which closed some time before the First World War. There is an area of **industrial premises** to the right of the line, currently occupied by the *Littlewoods Home Shopping Group* as a distribution centre. It is on the site of Ash and Dee Mills, and incorporates the surviving **Newby** and **Lilly No.1** and **No.2** mills. The line passes under **Linney Lane**, which spans the line by a fine panelled steel bridge. Note the space to the left which formerly accommodated the approach to **vanished sidings**.

The tram takes a lazy curve to the left to pass under **Milnrow Road**, followed by the Bridge Street footbridge (see p165). Notice the **playground** and **bowling green** to the left, and the row of cottages forming **Railway Terrace**, to the right. Crompton's siding (actually, a short branch) was formerly situated beyond these. A & A Crompton had mills either side of Milnrow Road at this point. Woodend Mill (burnt down, 1920) was the closest to the railway on the right, and was connected to it by the branch, which ran as far as Park Mill (demolished 1991) across Milnrow Road. This involved a level crossing that was operated by utilising a bell and a red flag! At some stage, an overhead wire was erected to enable an electric loco to work the private line, The locomotive was painted green, had a pantograph on its roof, and was known locally as 'Pharoah's Chariot'! This method of working may have lasted until World War Two. The **bowling green** indicates the start of **Dunwood Park**. The greater part of the pretty wooded

Dunwood Park from Milnrow Road

Country Park (see p165) now appears on the left-hand slope. (See if you can pick out the **sandstone art installation**, looking like a lump of cheese!) The **River Beal**, previously beyond a wooded area on the right, is now crossed again. It is particularly picturesque at this point and follows the line for a short distance. The former Jubilee pub, now sadly closed (2014) is glimpsed to the right, before running under **Milnrow Road** a second time **Jubilee Cottages** (p165) appear on the left, and **Dun Wood** is succeeded by **Jep Wood**. Notice the area between **Milnrow Road** and **Jubilee Crossing**, on the right. Nature has reclaimed a large part of it, so it is difficult to believe that this was an important industrial complex, centring on Jubilee Pit, served by sidings and a short branch. The pit later came into the hands of the ubiquitous Platt Brothers, who used it as a source of coking coal for their iron works at Werneth. (A description of the Jubilee area may be found on p165.) At the **occupation level crossing**, notice the **surviving chimney** with 'Howarth Finisher Mill' picked out in brick. The former Jubilee Mill belonged to Robert Howarth, bleachers, dyers, and finishers. **Jubilee House** (the manager's residence) is adjacent.

The valley sides open out as the line commences a long curve to the left, to run in a north-westerly direction beyond Newhey towards Rochdale. This is the start of perhaps one of the most rural parts of Metrolink, and there are some **beautiful views**. As we approach **Newhey**, notice the **scars of quarrying** beside the line and up on the hillside to the right (the shale sandstone was extracted by the 'New Hey Brick and Terracotta Company').

St. Thomas's Church still stands on the hill top overlooking Newhey, and can be seen for miles around. It is built of white Bath stone, and is a replica of Holy Trinity Church at Weston-Super-Mare in Somerset. The money to build the church was given by James and Benjamin Heap, in memory of their father, Thomas Heap (of Cliff House, New Hey), who was a local mill owner. The foundation stone was laid in 1875, and the church was consecrated on St. Thomas's Day, 21st December 1876. The building has a simple **cruciform plan**, with

The spire of St. Thomas's Church, Newhey

the Holy Table or **Altar** at the East end against the wall, and a **Children's Corner** and a **Memorial Chapel** respectively in the two transepts. The latter is memorial to those who died in the Second World War, and contains an oak case with a Book of Remembrance. The **font** by the West door was given by the teachers and scholars of the Church School in 1876, and dedicated to the name of the Ever Blessed Trinity. It is decorated with **eight carvings** depicting scenes from the Bible, some of which are quite unusual. One of Noah and his family leaving the ark shows elephants and giraffes in the background! Another depicting the baptism of the Ethiopian eunuch shows the mules of his chariot in the background. A panel showing Moses leading the people across the Red Sea also vividly depicts Egyptian soldiers and horses being overwhelmed by the returning sea. Another panel shows a beautiful carving of the blessing of the children. We also see Simeon holding the infant Jesus, Our Lord's baptism, and the Day of Pentecost. Stained glass was put in the **East Window** just after the First World War, the whole of the interior of the **Chancel** was refaced with stone, and **panels** containing the names of all who lost their lives or served in that war were erected above the font. The church has a fine peal of bells, and became a listed building in 1987. (The church was damaged in an arson attack before Christmas, 2007, but is recovering. Contributions towards the restoration fund are still appreciated. For further information, and details of church opening, ring 01706 845677.)

After passing under **Two Bridges Road**, and crossing a **watercourse** that is a tributary of the Beal, the tram arrives at **Newhey Station** (known by the archaic version of 'New Hey' in railway days).

Newhey Station has two **platforms** to the south-east of **Huddersfield Road**, which spans the line. The **Rochdale platform** communicates with this street by a folded-back **ramped path** with some **steps** shortening it if required. There is a similar **ramp** to the street for the **Manchester platform**, although a separate **flight of steps** also directly access the road. There are facilities for **bicycle storage**. Nothing remains of the original 1863 station (the main building was on the Manchester platform) that once stood on this site, though the **brick railway warehouse** still survives (as a carpet business) on the site of the goods yard to the left, still sporting the legend 'Lancashire and Yorkshire Railway Cotton Warehouse'.

This station can be used to access **Jubilee Colliery Country Park** and **Dunwood Park** (p159).

The Lancashire and Yorkshire Railway Cotton Warehouse at Newhey

For a visit to **St. Thomas's Church** (p157), leave the station, turn right up **Huddersfield Road**, and left (at the *Bird in Hand*) along **Church Street**. However, Newhey also has an interesting **steam museum**. After leaving the station, turn left, following **Huddersfield Road** before turning right at the junction (noticing **Cotton Tree Corner**, with its stone commemorating the vanished inn and detailing the textile industry in the area) along **Newhey Road**. This road becomes **Elizabethan Way**. Look for the turning on the left for the industrial premises (**Ellenroad Approach**) and the **250 foot chimney**. This leads to **Ellenroad Engine House Museum**. (Open and in steam the first Sunday of each month except January, 11-4, admission charge; non-steaming days, usually Tuesdays and Sundays, and the Saturday before a steam day, 11-3, free, but donation appreciated. For further information, ring 07789 802632.) Ellenroad Mill was built in 1891-2, and rebuilt in 1921, but everything was demolished in 1985, except for the engine house and chimney, which are now listed. At **Ellenroad Engine House** is the only **fully-working cotton mill engine with its original steam-raising plant**. The 3,000 horsepower *Victoria and Alexandra* Ellenroad mill engine of 1892 was a triple expansion steam engine built by J&W McNaught of St. George's foundry, Rochdale. When the new ring mill was built, the triple expansion engine was converted to a twin tandem compound engine by removing the high pressure and intermediate pressure cylinders and installing two high pressure cylinders. The original coal-fired **Lancashire boiler** still survives. To this has

The Steam Engine

The first practicable steam engine was invented by Thomas Newcomen, a Cornish ironmonger, around 1710. It was a beam engine, and operated by rocking up and down a large beam on a central pivot, rather like a huge see-saw. Its purpose was to pump water out of deep mines, so one end of the beam was attached by a chain to the movable part of the pumping gear at the bottom of the shaft. The weight of this ensured that the piston, attached by a similar chain to the other end of the beam, was always at the top of the cylinder at the start of the working cycle, and would always return there after the power stroke. It was also called an 'atmospheric engine' because the boiler technology of the time could not produce high pressure steam, so low pressure steam was condensed in the cylinder below the piston to create a partial vacuum. Consequently, atmospheric pressure (the top of the cylinder was left open) was responsible for the downward movement of the piston and the beam end in the power stroke. An engine of this type was installed in a coal pit at Dudley in 1712, and its use soon spread throughout the mining districts. Unfortunately, there was not much else that it could be used for; it cost a fortune in fuel (not an issue at a coal mine) and its single power stroke (even regulated by a flywheel) could not be used to power machinery. James Watt began a series of improvements in 1765. He firstly condensed the steam in a separate condenser, sucking it out of the cylinder by an air pump operated by a cam linked to the beam. He then realised that the open end of the cylinder could be enclosed, steam substituted for air pressure, and the process reversed to produce a reciprocal or two stroke cycle. Nevertheless, it remained a low pressure engine, the steam acting upon a partial vacuum. By 1776, these engines had been perfected. They were faster, had a smooth motion and, most importantly, one end of the beam could be used to drive a wheel. Richard Arkwright realised the immense possibilities, and others copied him. By the 1790s, steam powered cotton mills began to appear, particularly in Lancashire. If there was a catalyst to the industrial revolution, this was surely it. Later mill engines abandoned beam technology and evolved into horizontal machines, using high pressure steam and passing it through different sized cylinders as 'compound engines'. And steaming qualities were greatly enhanced through the ubiquitous 'Lancashire Boiler'.

been added other **engines**. There is an example from Whitelees Mill, a **classical Watt-type beam engine** built by John Petrie & Company of Rochdale in 1841, and exhibited in its original condition, still working after more than 160 years! The **Marsden engine** is recognised as the last steam mill engine to have powered the mill for which it was designed and built. It was manufactured in 1907 for Barker's tannery in Otley, which ceased production on 6th July 1988. The latest acquisition is the **Fern Mill engine**, originally installed in the spinning mill of the Fern Cotton Spinning Co, Ltd of Siddall Street, Shaw, Oldham. It is currently in bits, and forms part of an ambitious project to recreate a mill engine similar in size and design to the existing Ellenroad one. There are other, **smaller exhibits**, including engines and historic machines. On steaming days, there is also a display by the **Ellenroad Amateur Radio Club**, and refreshments are available.

Crompton Moor and Dunwood Park

Crompton Moor lies to the north-east of Shaw. Spanning approximately 160 acres (0.6 km²), and reaching an elevation of 1,282 feet (391 m), it is one of the largest open spaces run by Oldham Countryside Service. It is best accessed from **Shaw and Crompton**

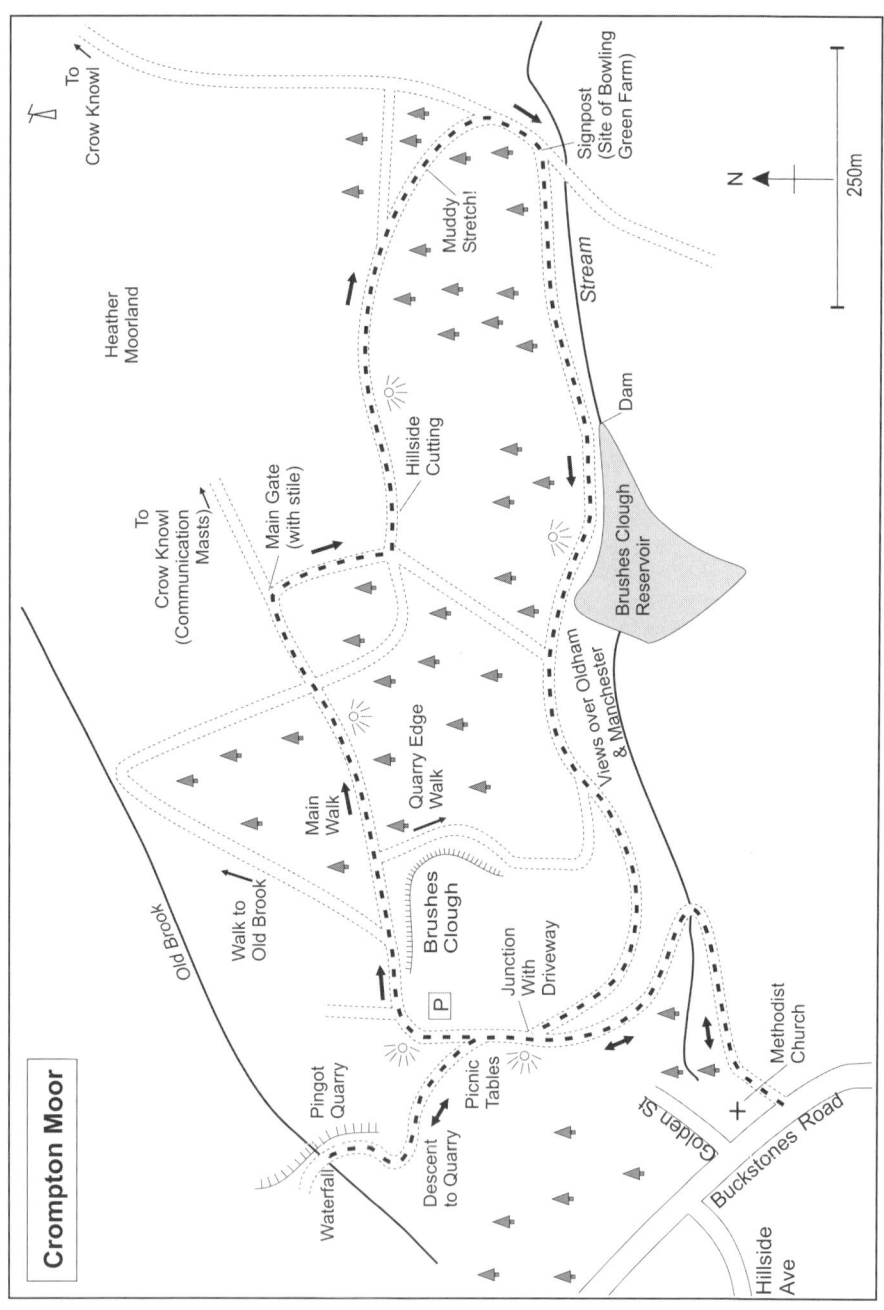

Crompton Moor

To Crow Knowl

Heather Moorland

To Crow Knowl (Communication Masts)

Old Brook

Walk to Old Brook

Main Walk

Quarry Edge Walk

Brushes Clough

Main Gate (with stile)

Hillside Cutting

Muddy Stretch!

Signpost (Site of Bowling Green Farm)

Stream

Dam

Brushes Clough Reservoir

Views over Oldham & Manchester

Junction With Driveway

P

Picnic Tables

Descent to Quarry

Pingot Quarry

Waterfall

Golden St

Methodist Church

Buckstones Road

Hillside Ave

N

250m

160

Station (p155) by two **local bus** services from the stop across **Beal Lane** to the left of the station. Take the 408 (daily and hourly) and alight at the **Hillside Avenue terminus** before walking on to turn right at the junction with **Buckstones Road**, towards the **Methodist Church**. Alternatively, take the 428 (hourly, Monday to Friday only) and alight after turning from **Hillside Avenue** into **Buckstones Road**, walking back along the latter to the **Methodist Church**. Both options require a left turn upon reaching **Shore Edge Methodist Church** (the way is **signposted**) and following the **tarmac road** past the **first car park** to where it terminates at the **main car park** (the stone enclosure wall also includes a small **picnic area**). There is a **magnificent view** from the latter (aided by a **viewing table**) which includes the distant **Beetham Tower** in Manchester (p238).

The walk described can be accomplished in a few hours and is suitable for a family party, though not for wheelchairs or buggies. Parts of the route are rough underfoot and can be a little steep; consequently, suitable footwear is recommended and care should be exercised. Small children, in particular, should be closely supervised. There are (as yet) no toilets or café, but the adjacent Methodist Church Hall is sometimes open for teas at weekends (01706 847393).

The pathway from the car park **forks** beyond the **gateway**. Children, in particular, will want to see the **Crompton Waterfall**, which is reached by the path to the left, which descends towards the former **Pingot Quarry** (dating from the 19th century). The **waterfall** tumbles quite spectacularly over the quarry face, and the path continues almost to the foot. Retrace your steps back to the **fork**, and take the right-hand or **main ascending path**, from which there is a fine **view** backwards, and a view over **Brushes Clough Quarry** to the right. Ignore the **path** to the left, and follow the **main path** (distinguished by blue and yellow markers) to where it **forks**. The left hand path

Waterfall at Pingot Quarry

runs alongside the trees to the **Old Brook** (which feeds the waterfall), from whence it eventually returns. However, we continue on, through the **tree plantation**, to the **next fork** (where the right hand path diverges to run along the quarry edge). The way here is **straight on**, up the slope, with another fine **view** backwards. At the limit of the tree-line, continue on beyond the **crossroads** (where the diversion via the Old Brook rejoins from the left) towards the heather moorland, to reach a **metal gate**. There is a glimpse of the communications **mast** at **Crow Knowl** (391 metres, the summit of the moor), and, if you are feeling energetic and have the time, pass through the **stile** to the left of the gate and continue along the **path** to **Crow Knowl** for a fantastic view. (Another path returns from this viewing point to rejoin our route at Bowling Green Farm, see below.) However, we turn right by the **gate**, and follow the path as it descends to a **crossroads**. Turn left here, following the path that seems to pass through a **little cutting** in the hillside. There are good **views** to the right, and the path passes through a **gate and stile**, beyond which is a **fork;** we take the right-hand path, which descends through **woods**. (Please note that this stretch can be muddy after rain!) The path terminates at a **junction** with the path from Crow Knowl (see above), requiring a sharp right, and another sharp right at the **sign post**. This area is the site of the former Bowling Green Farm, though little remains. The route now follows the **stream**, which can be heard murmuring to the left, in the valley. It seems impossible that such a little thing can be made to create a sheet of water, but we soon come across the stone faced **dam** on the left, followed by **Brushes Clough Reservoir**. The path runs alongside the reservoir, and there is a **fine view** of the steep valley, with the **reservoir overflow** cascading down. There is **evidence of mining** in the remains of former buildings. The **main path** continues downhill; ignore the paths diverging left and right, and enjoy the view over Oldham and Manchester, with the **Beetham Tower** (p238) prominent on the horizon. The pathway eventually joins the **tarmac driveway**, with the **main car-park** clearly visible.

As both **Dunwood Park** and **Jubilee Park** can be accessed from both **Shaw** and **Crompton and Newhey Stations**, it is suggested that they be visited as a walk between the two Metrolink Stations in either direction. In the case of the former

In Dunwood Park

A lump of cheese?

Remains of Jubilee Colliery

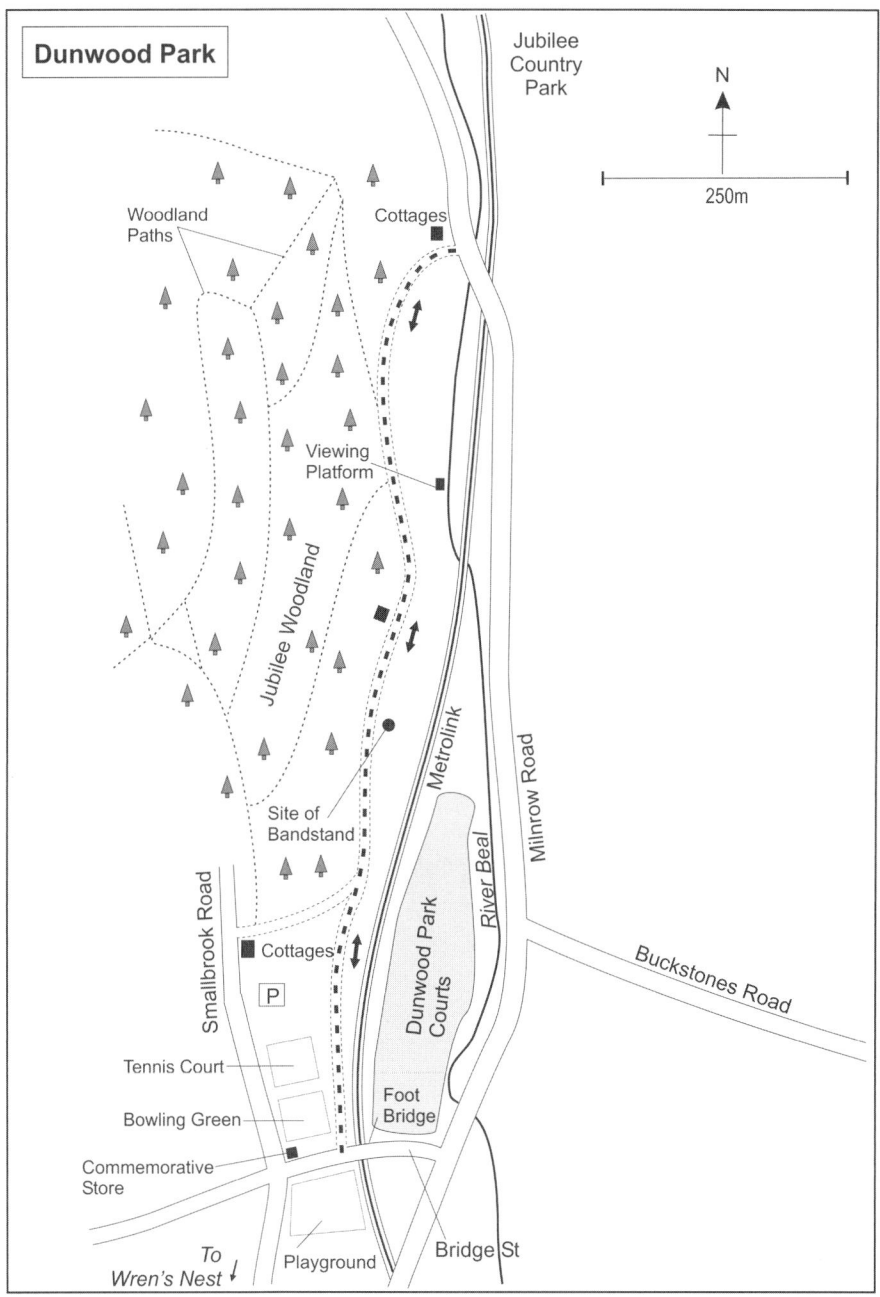

Dunwood Park

Jubilee Country Park

N

250m

Woodland Paths

Cottages

Viewing Platform

Jubilee Woodland

Metrolink

Milnrow Road

River Beal

Site of Bandstand

Smallbrook Road

Cottages

P

Dunwood Park Courts

Buckstones Road

Tennis Court

Bowling Green

Commemorative Store

Foot Bridge

To Wren's Nest

Playground

Bridge St

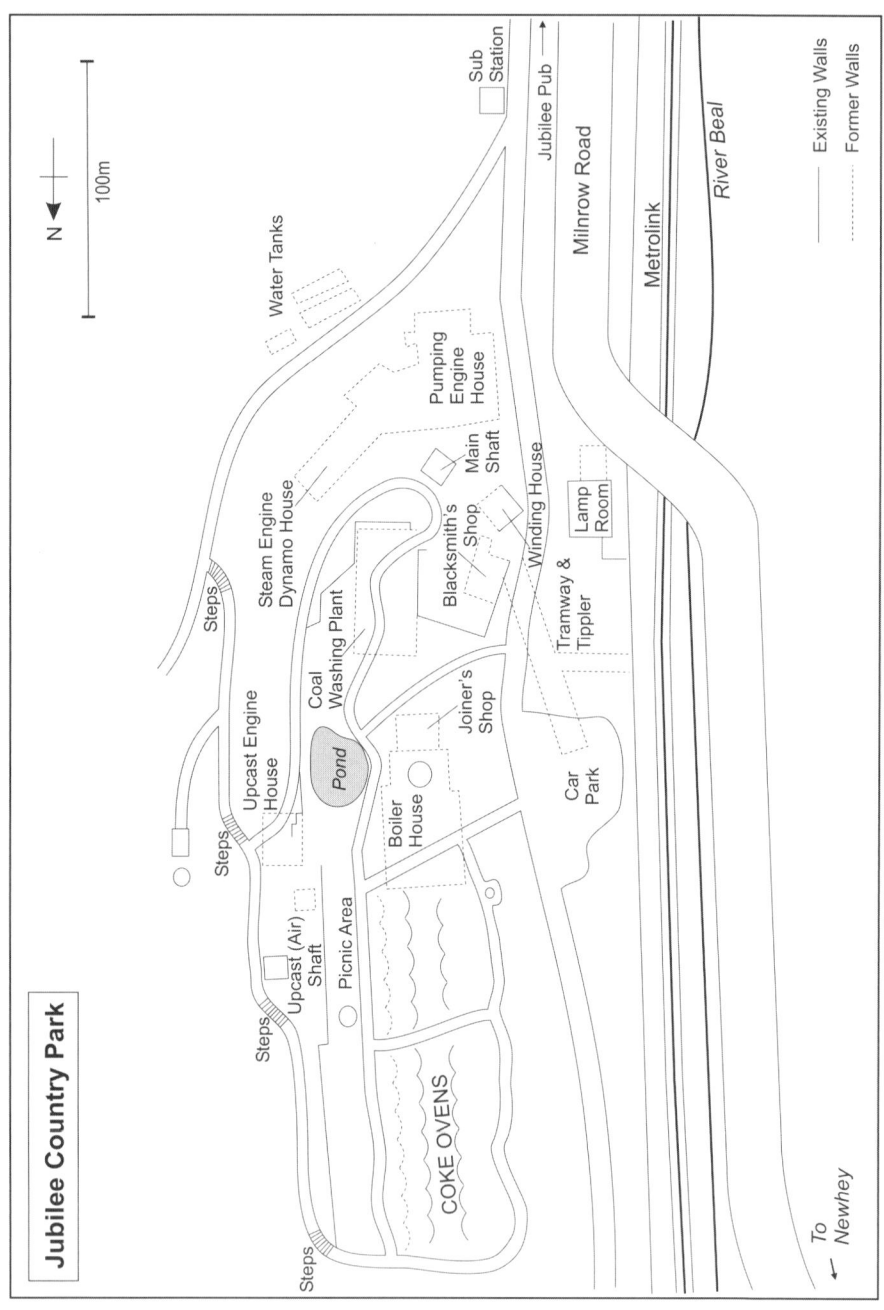

Jubilee Country Park

N

100m

Steps

Upcast (Air) Shaft

Picnic Area

COKE OVENS

Steps

Steps

Steps

Upcast Engine House

Boiler House

Joiner's Shop

Coal Washing Plant

Pond

Steps

Steam Engine Dynamo House

Water Tanks

Blacksmith's Shop

Main Shaft

Pumping Engine House

Winding House

Tramway & Tippler

Lamp Room

Car Park

Sub Station

Jubilee Pub →

Milnrow Road

Metrolink

River Beal

To Newhey ←

—— Existing Walls

······ Former Walls

station, turn left down **Beal Lane**, and right into **Milnrow Road**, catching a **bus** (the 181/182 daily, the 58 Monday to Saturday) outside the *Cricketers* pub. Alight at **Bridge Street**, and turn left up this way, crossing over the **footbridge** spanning the Metrolink line. Dunwood Park is entered by the **path** along the right-hand side of the **bowling green**. Alternatively, the footbridge can be avoided by alighting at the Wren's Nest stop and walking up **Smallbrook Road** and turning right towards the **bowling green**. In the opposite direction, the Park can be reached from **Newhey Station**, by turning left along **Huddersfield Road** and left again at the junction with **Shaw Road** to reach the **bus station**. Travel by bus (the 181/182 daily, the 58 Monday to Saturday) alighting at the **former Jubilee pub**, and walking back. **Jubilee Country Park** (see below) is accessed from the former pub car park on the right. By continuing over the **railway bridge** (which now crosses the Metrolink line), the **entrance to Dunwood Park** is reached by the side of the **row of cottages** (formerly housing the officers of the vanished colliery and their families) on the left.

Jubilee Colliery Country Park (see sketch map) is not as widely known as Dunwood or Crompton Moor, but is worth a visit. The hamlet appeared in 1810 (the year of George III's Jubilee!) as a result of the opening of this road (it was then the Shaw to Rochdale Turnpike). The Inn was relocated in 1863 as a consequence of the opening of the railway. Mining dates from 1845, but the greater part of the former colliery was created in the 1880s, and was developed by Platts (p138). It closed in 1932, and very little is left. However, it is now a rather fine **nature reserve**, though perhaps not as frequently visited as its neighbour, across the road and the railway. Enter the area by the **pub car park**, and follow the **cobbled lane** on the left. It leads to the **site car park**, from which a number of gravelled **paths** run (one completing a circuit of the site). The Park could possibly be better interpreted, but it is fun spotting the **colliery remains**, and, of course, the wildlife! (See sketch map on p164.)

Dunwood Park was opened on the 14 September 1912. The development of the park was undertaken and funded by Crompton Urban District Council on land given to the council by Captain Abram Crompton, a local land and mill owner. Development was in response to the industrialisation and development of Shaw as a major mill town. Detrimental effects of pollution, high density population, disconnection from the countryside, and hard working conditions, provided a need for development of a 'breathing space' which was accessible to all. The initial development was designed and supervised by Manchester architect, Ernest Woodhouse. The Park underwent a major refurbishment in 2011, and this is ongoing. (For further information, ring 0161 620 8202.) This description of Dunwood Park commences at the **Smallbrook Road** end. It should be read in reverse if approaching from **Jubilee**.

Continue past the **bowling-green** (1914/15) and **tennis courts** (1922) on the left, with the Metrolink line on the right. There is a **junction** in the way shortly after, and a pathway to the left leads towards the entrance to the park from an old stone **row of cottages**. This way can be taken to access a path from it to the right through **Jubilee Woods**. It should be noted that these **beautiful woods** dominate the high ground to the left of the main path, and should be explored if time permits. The **woodland paths** parallel both each other and the main path, so it is impossible to get lost! Otherwise, follow the metalled **main path**, which offers views of the **Metrolink line** through the trees to the right, and leads to the former **bandstand green**. The residents of Shaw were wont to gather in this area to listen to local brass bands; it is now transformed into a **new performance arena**. Notice, a little further on, the rather odd **sandstone sculpture**, looking like a giant piece of cheese! Look out for the **steps** to the right, leading down to a **wooden stage** on the **bank of the Beal**. The path eventually curves to the right, and emerges alongside **Jubilee Cottages** (p165).

Newhey to Rochdale

The tram departs from Newhey Station and passes under **Huddersfield Road**. The line is crossed just after the bridge by the **Oldham Corporation Aqueduct**, now a pipe replacing a steel trough erected in 1911, and supported by masonry columns. The line is now curving to the left towards Rochdale, a long curve that started at the previous station. There were generally no heavy engineering works on this section of the original railway, but this **cutting** is an exception. It is spanned by **New Hey Road**, followed by **Milne footbridge**. The latter is adjacent to the *John Milne* pub and restaurant, together with the *Premier Inn* (accessed from **New Hey Road**), glimpsed on the right. This must be the only pub named after a geologist!

Elizabethan Way appears to the left shortly afterwards. This was once open country towards the housing, but the Beal was culverted, and this new road built in the 1960s. The distant **chimney** belongs to Ellenroad Mill (see p158). The tram now passes under a **slip road** prior to the **M62 Motorway**. Just beyond the large road interchange to the left, the line runs under **Ladyhouse Lane** over-bridge, still following **Elizabethan Way** and passing by a **large industrial complex** on the right.

We have now arrived at **Milnrow Station**. Both **platforms** are linked by a **pedestrian crossing** at the Manchester end. The **Rochdale platform** has a zig-zag **ramped path** to

John (Earthquake) Milne

John Milne was born in Liverpool in 1850, but grew up in Rochdale living in Drake Street and at Tunshill, a small hamlet situated to the north-east of Milnrow. (Tunshill House, a former inn called the Kings Arms, still exists. It has the Royal Arms sculpted over the porch). His father was a local man, involved in the wool trade. Milne led a remarkable life and by all accounts was a man abounding with energy and enthusiasm. He was an avid golfer and enjoyed music, literature, photography, anthropology. and natural history. But his passion was earthquakes! Educated at King's College and the Royal School of Mines, he worked as a mining engineer in Newfoundland and Labrador and in 1874 served as a geologist on a mining expedition to N.W. Arabia (in which he also looked for the 'real site' of Mount Sinai!). At the age of 25 he took up the position as professor of Geology and Mining at the Imperial College of Engineering in Tokyo. He founded the Seismological Society of Japan and over the years compiled an extensive catalogue of Japanese earthquakes. In collaboration with Alfred Ewing and Thomas Gray, he invented a revolutionary new seismograph that was used for many years and was known as the Milne-Shaw seismograph. After 20 years in Japan, a fire at his home, on February 17, 1895, destroyed the house, his observatory, library and many of his instruments. Disheartened, he returned to England with his Japanese wife and his assistant Mr. Hirota. Milne's new home was Shide Hill House, near Newport on the Isle of White. With support from the Royal Society, Shide Hill House became the focal point for seismic research world-wide. Milne oversaw the establishment of a seismograph network of 20 observatories located in England, Russia, Canada, the U.S.A. and Antarctica. One of the locals of Newport said of Milne, "He always spoke with a quiet Lancastrian accent which fascinated us lads, as did his nicotine-stained, bushy moustache with a gap burned in it by numerous cigarettes. He died on July 31, 1913 of Bright's disease. He was 63.

Elizabethan Way and also **stepped access** to the end of **Harbour Lane North**. (The old road has been turned into a **pedestrian footbridge** over the line.) The **Manchester platform** is linked by a **stepped path** to **Harbour Lane North** at the other side of the footbridge, a point where a **path** to the **car park** begins. The **car park** itself is situated alongside the **Manchester platform**, and is accessed by both **steps** and the **crossing**. **Station Road** commences from it, and leads to **Dale Street**. A left turn along the latter can be used as an alternative way of reaching **Milnrow Bridge**, via the principal shopping street (see below). Nothing whatever remains of the original station that once stood here. The main buildings were on the Manchester platform, accessed from Station Road, and the goods yard was on the same site, to the south of that street.

As a distinct town, Milnrow appeared in the 19th century as a consequence of industrialisation. (It was the terminus of an electric tram route operated by Rochdale Corporation.) Although heavy textile industries declined during the mid-20th century, the town has continued to grow as a result of a mixture of suburban development and gentrification, and is now a residential suburb. The visitor should follow the twisting **Harbour Lane North** from the **footbridge** to its junction with **Bridge Street**, turning right towards **Milnrow Bridge**. Notice the **plaque** on the parapet, to the right. It records that road widening swept away the site of Tim Bobbin's school, which was near here. Milnrow has been described as "the centre of the south Lancashire dialect". John Collier (who wrote under the pseudonym of

The former Chapel at Milnrow

Tim Bobbin, see p179), an acclaimed 18th century caricaturist and satirical poet who wrote in a broad Lancashire dialect, was from Milnrow. Rochdale-born poet Edwin Waugh was influenced by Collier's work, and wrote an extensive account of Milnrow during the mid-19th century in a tribute to Collier. The main part of the town (with the shopping centre, together with a number of cafés) straggles further along **Dale Street** (see above), but cross Bridge Street to inspect the **picturesque row of cottages** opposite, next to the bridge. The row incorporates medieval masonry, for the cottages were created from the original Milnrow Chapel! Founded as a Chapel of Ease (catering for local people, but reserving lucrative baptisms and marriages to the mother church) in 1496, enlarged in 1537, and rebuilt in 1725, it was abandoned for a newer church in 1799. Notice the classical features of the **former entrance door** and the multiple **mullioned windows**. The chapel's replacement lies up the hill on **Kiln Lane** (accessed by **St. James Street** on the right). The **Parish Church of St. James** was consecrated in 1814, but extensively re-modeled in 1868-9 by G.E. Street at the expense of the Schofield family, local flannel manufacturers.

Described as "solid and serious," it is a good example of the 'gothic revival' style of that period (ring 01706 642988 to arrange a visit).

Milnrow is a good starting point for a visit to **Hollingworth Lake**; there is an hourly 452 bus service (not Sundays) from the stop outside the **cottages** (see p171).

The line now passes under **Harbour Lane North** by a 19th century bridge, followed by **Elizabethan Way** (built in the 1960s) before traversing a pleasant wooded **cutting** crossed by **Buckley Hill Lane** and a three arched **occupation bridge**.

At the end of the cutting, the immediate vicinity is in a state of transition. The **housing** to the right is in contrast to the **open ground** on the left, yet the latter is the site of the developing **Kingsway Business Park**. The Business Park is a £315million mixed use development of 170 hectares (420 acres), and is located adjacent to and with direct access onto the M62 at Junction 21. This is a joint development by The North West Regional Development Agency and Wilson Bowden Developments, with support from the Rochdale Development Agency, Rochdale Council, and the European Regional Development Fund. It is not intended to be a gated, fenced-off, development but is envisaged as an open, welcoming environment that can be enjoyed by employees and visitors alike. Seventy acres of parkland, more than seven miles of purpose built foot and cycle paths, and thousands of shrubs and trees will try to ensure that Kingsway Business Park is both a place to inspire a productive workforce and to encourage a healthy lifestyle too. At the moment (2014), there is little to see, although a large **hangar like building** has been erected (existing occupants include *ASDA, J.D. Sports,* and *E-ON UK*).

Kingsway Business Park Station is already open. It consists of **staggered platforms**, linked by a **pedestrian crossing**. The **Rochdale platform** is the first to be reached, with its **ramp** terminating at the **crossing**. A path to the left runs to **Michael Faraday Avenue**, which passes the entrance to the existing part of the **Business Park**. The opposite side of the **crossing** accesses the **ramped end** of the **Manchester platform** before exiting between the **houses** on the right to reach **Leyfield Road**. Here there are stops for the 462 service to Ladyhouse and Milnrow in one direction, and Rochdale in the other.

After a short section of level ground, the line runs on to an **embankment**, from which there is a **fine view**. Ahead, **tower blocks** mark the site of Rochdale in the distance, while there are panoramic **views of the Pennine Moors**. The tram now passes over the **Rochdale Canal**, before crossing a **bridge** spanning **Kingsway** to arrive at the next station.

Here at **Newbold Station**, as in the case of South Chadderton, the **embankment has been altered** to enable the new Metrolink stop to be nearer ground level alongside *Morrison's* **supermarket** and the **car park** to the left of the line. The station consists of an **island platform**, linked by **foot level crossings** of the down (Rochdale) line at either platform end. Both **crossings** access a fenced **footpath** alongside *Morrison's* Car Park. The **pathway** leads in one direction back to **Kingsway**, and in the other, by a **ramp** and **steps** adjacent to the **crossing** at the Rochdale end, to the **car park entrance** (for the supermarket) and a way to **Witley Road** (which is linked to **Milnrow Road**). **Cycle parking** facilities may be found near the Kingsway end of the new footpath.

(Newbold is the starting point for a delightful walk along the **towpath** of the **Rochdale Canal** to **Smithy Bridge** and **Hollingworth Lake**, see p171.)

When the former level is regained, the Metrolink line is **singled** prior to the **bridge over Milnrow Road**. (The bridge was rebuilt in British Rail days, when the entire line beyond Shaw had been singled.) The original railway line then described a long curve to the left, to join the main line, terminating in a bay platform at the east end of Rochdale Station. Nowadays, the Metrolink line crosses the railway route by means of a new and impressive **flyover viaduct**. It has three sections; first a an **earth embankment** just to the north of the former loop line track; second a **new bridge over the main line**; and third, a **concrete viaduct** which descends towards the main line and the former loop line track bed. The actual crossing of the main line commands a **fine panoramic view**, especially of the **Pennine Range** on the right. The line then **parallels the railway**, crossing **Milnrow Road** once more, and then **Oldham Road**. After crossing **Richard Street**, Metrolink parts company with the railway, and descends **High Level Road** (now closed to other traffic), becoming **double track** once more. It passes in front of the **Railway Station entrance** before turning sharp right (and terminating prior to the extension opening) at one or other of the platform sides of **Rochdale Station Metrolink Station**.

(A walking tour of Rochdale commences at this station, see p176.)

The station is located adjacent to Saint John's Church (p176), with the **roadway** on the right-hand side. It consists of a **central island platform**, with **pedestrian crossings** at both ends communicating with the **paved area** which surrounds the station. There are **steps** at the Rochdale end, and a slightly **curving ramp** towards the railway station.

The actual **Rochdale Railway Station** was opened by the Manchester and Leeds Railway in 1839. It became a rather grand affair under the Lancashire and Yorkshire Railway, comprising two large island platforms, one with a bay platform for terminating Manchester trains, and the other with a bay for terminating Oldham Loop trains. However, the 1972 remodeling reduced it to one large island platform and a (currently disused) bay platform at the east end. It is on a **viaduct** accessed by **stairs** and **lift** from the **street entrance**, adjacent to the Metrolink station. However, the advent of Metrolink will create an important transport hub, and it is intended to re-open (in March, 2014) the **former subway** beyond the street entrance to access a new car park development on the opposite side of the station. There is a frequent service of trains to Manchester Victoria Station in one direction and (via the **picturesque Calder Valley line**) to Bradford and Leeds in the other. Take the train to Smithy Bridge (for Hollingworth Lake) and Hebden Bridge (niche shopping, canal trips, and a connecting bus to Haworth for the Brontes and the Keighley and Worth Valley railway) for a good day out.

The Metrolink extension, scheduled to open in February or March 2014, continues down **Maclure Road** by means of a **reservation** on the left-hand side of it. The tram passes the old fire station (p177), crosses Richard Street and swings to the right running on a short section of **reserved track** alongside **Drake Street**. At this point, a new road (to be called New Wood Street) will run to join Oldham Road to the right, intersecting a water feature. (The area formerly had a canal basin at the terminus of a branch from the Rochdale Canal.) The area between **Moore Street** on the left, and the junction with **School Lane/Milnrow Road**, will hopefully be the **site of the proposed Wet Rake Station**. The decision was taken to abandon this proposal and divert the funding to finance the station at Kingsway Business Park. As this would leave Drake Street without access from Metrolink, the chorus of objections resulted in a re-think. Now (summer, 2012) moves are afoot to restore the station as part of the expansion plans by the Council finding funding from elsewhere. We cross **Milnrow Road**, with **School Lane** (p177) on the left. Notice the triangular **Wet Rake Gardens** to the right (the site of the Union Foundry), in the angle of the junction with **Oldham Road** near the *Cask and Feather* (which has its own brewery). At this point, the track curves to the left to begin the descent down **Drake Street** to the town centre. The tracks on this part of **Drake Street** run very close to the pavements, and the locality is populated by quirky **shops** in which you can purchase suits, telescopes and binoculars, vinyl records, bridal wear, and pianos. (There are also a number of interesting cafés.) The area is the subject of a regeneration programme which will see improved paving and street furniture, together with grants for the renovation of small properties. The **Champness Hall**, on the left, opposite **Water Street**, dates from 1925 and is quite a landmark in the town, housing one of the largest auditoriums in the North West. It bears the name of Thomas Champness, a Methodist pioneer in lay training, and housed the Rochdale Mission. The place contains a children's play and activity centre, offices for community projects, and a large banquet hall (available for private parties and functions) on the top floor known as Rooftops! The auditorium is still used for worship and church purposes, but is also available for concerts and meetings. (For further information, ring 01706 645731.) Notice the black and gold front of Butterworth's Jewellers on the left, dating to 1896.

The track becomes single at the bottom of **Drake Street** before swinging sharply to the right into **Smith Street**. This is because the curve itself crosses the culverted river Roch at the point of the curve, and it was presumably thought that the reconstruction for double track would be too expensive. (It is proposed to open out the course of the river in the town centre to the left at this point in order to make it an attractive feature. The original medieval bridge will be revealed by this operation.) Notice *The Regal Moon* to the left, a pub located in the former Regal Cinema, which opened in 1938. It had been designed for Associated British Cinemas (ABC) by architect Leslie C. Norton in the chain's 'house style', with a total of 1,901 seats (1,208 stalls and 693 in the balcony). It finally closed in October 1992. There is also a fine view of the **19th century town centre** to the left. Notice the *Duke of Wellington's Hotel* on the right hand corner. This 18th century wool merchant's house became an inn by 1810, the leading 'coaching house' in the town. The area outside it became something of a 'speaker's corner', and a crowd of 8,000 celebrated the passing of the Reform Act here in 1832.

The line terminates at **Rochdale Town Centre Metrolink Station**. This is located alongside **Smith Street** and adjacent to the intended **shopping centre**. It comprises an **island platform** (serviced by a **scissors crossover** at the approach). A **ramp** accesses a **pedestrian crossing** at the west end, communicating with **Smith Street** and the **new bus station** on the south side, and the **shopping centre** on the north side. A **ramp** at the opposite end leads to a path to the shopping centre.

The new **bus station** lies across **Smith Street** almost at right angles to the tram terminus, with the eastern side adjacent to the **River Roch**. The **main building**, capped with **overlapping pear shaped roofs**, is situated within in an island, around which the buses manoeuvre and park at **bays**. It contains a **travel centre**, a **café**, and **toilets**, and is provided with a **taxi rank** and **bicycle storage**. (It is the first bus station to be run partly on hydro-electric power.)

The environs of the bus station and tram terminus are interesting. The entrance to the river culvert at the east side or end of both is formed by a **19th century bridge**. A **plaque** on it records the tenth anniversary of Rochdale's twinning with Lviv, called Lvov or Lemberg at other historical periods. (Rochdale has significant Polish and Ukrainian communities.) **Number One, Riverside**, a new iconic building, lies across the river. It houses the new **council offices** (with a **customer information point**) and a **new library** (complete with **coffee shop**). About five minutes' walk beyond this development, along **Smith Street** and its continuation, **Entwistle Road**, may be found the new **Leisure Centre**. Based in the town centre, it features an eight-lane 25 metre swimming pool and a 17 metre learner pool with moveable floor. It also has a sauna and steam rooms, two fitness suites, dance studios, a four-court sports hall and car park. (For further information about the centre, ring 01706 926000.) Last, but not least, the former council offices and bus station site on the north side of the Metrolink Station are scheduled for demolition. They will be replaced by a **new shopping centre**, comprising 300,000 square feet of mixed shopping and leisure uses. The development scheme extends the existing centre down to meet the new Metrolink and bus interchange, creating a pedestrian-friendly gateway into the town centre from the river. A traffic-free **Baillie Street** would form a key part of the scheme and a new entrance into the **Wheatsheaf Centre** from Baillie Street would replace the existing overhead walkways.

The project includes around 30 new shop units, a cinema, and cafés and restaurants to boost the town's evening economy, along with new car parking facilities.

An Excursion to Hollingworth Lake

There are two ways of reaching this popular resort from the Metrolink tram system. The first is by means of a short **bus ride** from **Milnrow**, catching the 452 bus (hourly, not Sundays) from the stop outside the historic **cottages** on **Bridge Street** (see p167). At first, the passenger may wonder where they are going, for after turning left up **Kiln Lane**, the bus turns off and literally 'goes round the houses'! But this is soon remedied, and the way lies along **Wild House Lane** and **Milnrow Road**, running out into open country, with fine **views** (particularly to the left, over Rochdale). After a right turn at **Smithy Bridge**, we arrive opposite the *Beach Hotel* (p174) and turn left into **Lake Bank**, alongside **Hollingworth Lake**, where we alight. (The return stop is on the 'promenade'.)

However, if it is a fine day, and you would like a **country walk**, follow the **towpath** of the **Rochdale Canal** from **Newbold** to **Smithy Bridge**. After alighting at **Newbold Metrolink Station**, walk along the **path to Kingsway** (p168). Cross the road, turn right, and walk a short distance before turning left up **Burnside Road**. Continue along the pathway directly ahead to reach the **swing bridge** across the **canal**. There is a fine **view** at this point, taking in **Kingsway Business Park** (p168) in the foreground and the **Pennine Hills** in the distance. However, we turn left without crossing the bridge, and commence our walk along the **towpath**, noticing that it is wide, gravelled (except under bridges, where it is cobbled), and suitable for buggies. The towpath passes under the former railway bridge (now used by Metrolink) and **Firgrove Bridge (Rochdale Road)**. The towpath enters open country beyond, spanned by two original brick bridges (**Coppy Bridge** and **Belfield Bridge**, the latter accessing an old mill to the right). The canal now bends to the right, and is joined on the left by the **railway line**. This was the Manchester and Leeds Railway, which became the Lancashire and Yorkshire Railway in 1846. This section, between Manchester and Littleborough, was the first to open in 1839, and the railway opened throughout in 1841 with the completion of the Summit Tunnel. There is a fine view beyond the railway. Notice the **clock tower** of Birch Hill Hospital, the old Rochdale Workhouse Infirmary. The canal passes through a curious **shale cutting**, beyond which is the **Clegg Hall Road Bridge** (the best **ramped access** is from the other side, and there is a good view from the top). It leads to the complex surrounding **Clegg Hall**; the surviving features include **weaver's houses**, a dye house, and the mill manager's house. The Hall is clearly visible from the towpath beyond the bridge. **Clegg Hall** is thought to have been built c.1610-18 for Theophilus Assheton, a member of the Middleton family of that name (p131), though a medieval house probably stood on the site. It is constructed of dressed stone, and comprises **three gabled bays** of two storeys (plus attic level), all raised above a full basement. Notice the near-symmetrical elevation with its projecting plinth and the imposing central two-storey **porch** approached by an impressive flight of steps. The neoclassical design and decoration are very advanced for the region at this period, and some have argued for 1640 as an alternative date. The property has had a very chequered history. From 1818 to 1869 it was a public house called the Horse and Hounds, but generally known as the 'Black Sloven', the name of a favourite hunting mare of legendary speed which belonged to a former owner, Mr Charles Turner. After many years in a semi-derelict condition, it has recently been restored. (Private property, please respect.)

Clegg Hall

Continue along the towpath, passing the **Little Clegg Road Swing Bridge** to arrive at **Smithy Bridge**. There is **ramped access** to **Smithy Bridge Road**, and a historical **interpretation board** relating to the Rochdale Canal From the top of the bridge note the level crossing and **railway station** in one direction and our way up the hill in the other. Press on past the **Methodist Church** and the **Library** on the left and **Milnrow Road** on the right. The road curves to the left, and we arrive at **'The Beach' Hotel** (p174) at the start of **Lake Bank**.

The Rochdale Canal was constructed by William Jessop and opened in 1804 (see p195), but after a period of decline it officially closed to navigation in 1952. It was re-opened in 2004 for the use of pleasure boaters, and now forms part of the 'Pennine Ring'. Jessop realised that the nature of the canal (through hilly country, with many locks on some stretches) would result in water shortages. Hollingworth Lake, with its three earth dams, was completed in 1800, four years before the canal. The lake covers an area of 130 acres

The Clegg Hall Boggart

Clegg Hall is reputed to be haunted. The Clegg Hall boggart (as ghosts are called in Lancashire dialect) is usually dated to the 13th century in most versions of the story. There is a fictionalized account written by a local vicar in 1910; in it, the master of the house went off to the wars in France, and while he was away, his wicked brother killed both his nephews, throwing them over the battlements into the moat. When the father returned, his brother crept through a secret passage from a nearby hall (possibly Stubley Old Hall was meant), ready to do away with the distraught man. However, one of the children's voices was heard calling out "Father, beware!" The father suddenly awoke, sending his terrified evil brother running away, to plunge to his death! Ever since, the phantom boy has been heard issuing warnings. 'The Boggart Chamber' became a place to be avoided, although it is not clear if this referred to the pre-1620s house or not. It is alleged that a young girl was playing hide and seek there, and she was found dead behind a wall and a curtain. At various periods, there were hints of counterfeiting activities in the vaults and cellars of Clegg Hall, and it was common for smugglers and counterfeiters to use tales of ghosts to scare off locals.

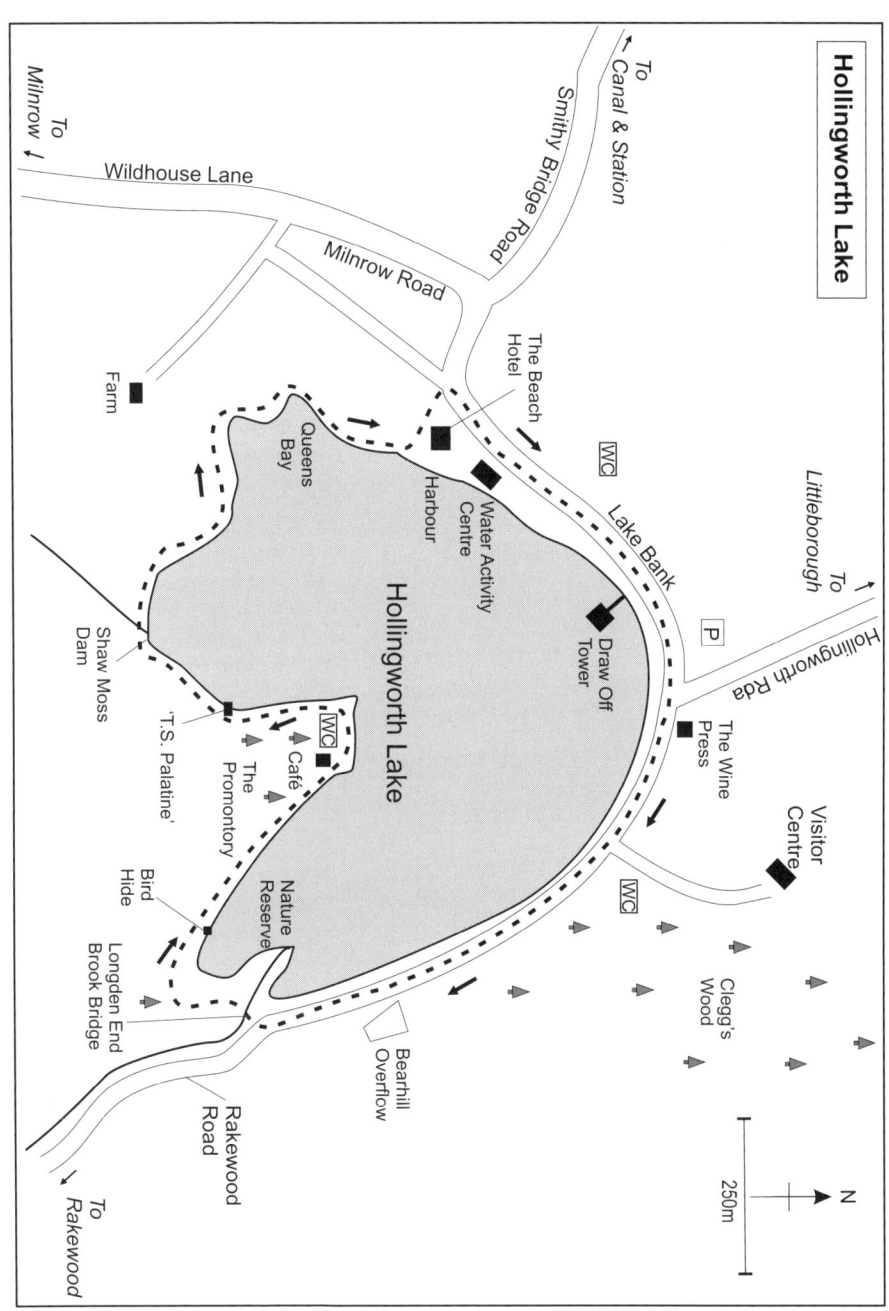

Hollingworth Lake

To Milnrow
To Canal & Station
Smithy Bridge Road
Wildhouse Lane
Milnrow Road
Farm
The Beach Hotel
Queens Bay
Harbour
Water Activity Centre
WC
Lake Bank
To Littleborough
Hollingworth Lake
Draw Off Tower
P
Hollingworth Rd
Shaw Moss Dam
'T.S. Palatine'
The Promontory
Café
WC
The Wine Press
Visitor Centre
Bird Hide
Nature Reserve
WC
Longden End Brook Bridge
Clegg's Wood
Bearhill Overflow
Rakewood Road
To Rakewood
250m
N

(53 ha), and the path around it originally measured 2.5 miles (4 km). In places the lake was originally 25 feet (7.6 m) deep, with the average depth being about 10 feet (3.0 m). Nowadays, the lake supports water sports like sailing, windsurfing, canoeing, swimming, rafting, rowing and fishing. However, the majority of visitors, particularly family groups, are content to stroll along the water's edge, picnic, feed the ducks, walk round the Lake, and patronise the restaurants and cafés. In summer, visitors can also hire rowing boats.

Whether you plan to perambulate the circuit of the Lake, or just potter around on Lake Bank, the following description may prove useful. The present appearance of the **Beach Hotel** largely dates from 1901, when it was rebuilt after a fire. The original establishment provided accommodation, private and public refreshment rooms (wedding breakfasts were provided), and a covered dancing platform nearly four thousand yards in extent and illuminated by gaslight. Since many of the dancers would be wearing their best clogs, the band must have played rather loud to be heard above the racket!

We schottisched and we polkad to the strains the band did play;
We waltzed and we mazurkad till she waltzed my heart away.
I whispered in this manner, as around the room we flew,
And doing the Varsovianna, that: "I love you Dorothy Drew."

She was very fond of dancing, but allow me to remark,
That one fine day she danced away with the calico printer's clerk.

The hostelry is the start of **Lake Bank**, the centre for most of the water based activities, and a fine 'promenade' along this side of the lake shore. (It is the site of a noted Easter Fair.) Notice that the opposite side of **Lake Bank** is an almost continuous line of **cafés** and **eateries**. The **Hollingworth Lake Sailing Club** (largely sailing dinghies) is situated next to the *Beach Hotel*, followed by the **Hollingworth Lake Rowing Club** and the **Water Activity Centre**. Since 1989, Hollingworth Lake Water Activity Centre has offered tuition in outdoor activities, including kayaking, canoeing, power

The Sailing Club boats

boating and sailing. This area is the start of the **promenade walk**, and there is a fine collection of **ducks** for children to feed! There is a fine view across the Lake as we walk. Notice the **Rakewood Viaduct**, which carries the M62 across the valley, with a total span of 840 feet; it opened in 1971. The **Draw off Tower**, on the right, was rebuilt when extensive repairs to the Lake were undertaken in 1985. Up to two million gallons a day can be taken to replenish the Rochdale Canal.

Continuing the perambulation, we now reach, beyond the road junction, the **Wine Press**. Formerly the 'Fisherman's Inn', the white painted structure predates the Lake, as it started life as an 18th century farmhouse. The former barn and stabling now house the restaurant. Look out for the driveway on the left, leading to the **Hollingworth Lake Visitor Centre** (daily in the summer season, 10.30-4.45, admission free). The **driveway passes** a fine **tree sculpture** of the 'Green Man', and a **Sensory Garden**, and accesses

The 'Weighver's Seaport'

In the 1850s, the owner of Harehill Woollen Mill, and his engineer, Mr. Sladen (later the landlord of the Mermaid Inn), saw the potential of the lake as a tourist attraction. They leased the lake from the Canal Company and created novelty amusements and facilities for boating. Despite very cold water and strong undercurrents caused by water entering and leaving the lake, small rowing boats became popular, and two paddle steamers were operated from 1856. Two hotels catered for day trippers and weekend visitors, and 'Pleasure Gardens' appeared on the opposite bank. The facilities were advertised by the Lancashire and Yorkshire Railway, who transported visitors to Smithy Bridge and Littleborough stations. The resort became known as the 'Weighver's Seaport', a cheap alternative to Blackpool! At the height of its popularity in the late 19th century, there were three lake steamers, and a variety of stalls and lock-up shops (many close to the landing stage for the ferry) were soon trading in sweets, snacks and souvenirs. On special holidays, there were fortune tellers, conjurers and tricksters. Although photography was in its infancy there were six businesses taking photographic portraits of visitors. Other attractions included a roundabout with galloping horses, a camera obscura, a steroescopic exhibition, and a gymnasium. Swimming became popular despite the cold water, perhaps inspired by Captain Matthew Webb, who used the lake for training before becoming the first man to swim the English Channel from Dover to Calais in 1875. By the beginning of the 20th century, travel was easier, people took longer holidays, and the lake's attraction started to diminish. The Lake was selected as the camp site for the Manchester Regiment Brigade of the East Lancashire Territorial Division, and family and friends made the journey to visit the tents in the Ealees Valley. Most soldiers from the camp were sent to the Dardanelles, and many did not return. The survivors, and mourning family and friends, often made a pilgrimage to the site after the war. The area was almost forgotten by1950. However, Rochdale Council purchased the boating rights in that year, and the emergence of a new 'leisure society' in the 1960s and 70s resulted in the creation of a Country Park in 1974. Ten years later, it was in a list of the top ten country parks in England.

(beyond the Centre) a **children's playground**. The Centre contains a **shop** and **café**, and houses good **displays** depicting local history (including the Rochdale Canal), landscape and natural history, and the lives of local people. Temporary exhibitions are held in an **upstairs gallery**. We now follow **Rakewood Road**, passing the **reservoir overflow** at **Bear Hill**, and, keeping to the **lakeside road**, arrive at a **fork**. The right-hand path leads to a **bridge** crossing **Longden End Brook**. This is the main source of water for the lake, but notice the silt deposits have created a **marshy area** by the shore, an ideal haven for wildlife. The path curves around a **lagoon**. In 1986, the Country Park staff built a **bird hide** to overlook the lagoons and islands of the **Nature Reserve**; it is used for spotting Great Crested Grebe, Mallard, Coot, Canada Geese, and the occasional Kingfisher. The way now lies along **'The Promontory'**, a tongue of wooded land stretching out into the Lake. It was once the site of the Lake Hotel, which stood within its own 'Pleasure Grounds'. These could only be reached by steamer from the landing stage, opposite, and the two were connected by 'submarine telegraph'! The grounds offered dancing, roller skating, quoits, bowling, and even billiards to its captive audience. There is a modern (seasonal) *'Pavilion Café'* and a **picnic area**. We pass the Sea Cadet Base of **'T.S. Palatine'**, which provides instruction for youths in sailing, navigation and water safety.

It stands on the site of the former ferry terminus. The shore path now crosses **Shaw Moss Dam**, and continues its meandering way past the site of the former Queen's Hotel to return to the ***Beach Hotel***.

Rochdale

Historically a part of Lancashire, Rochdale's recorded history begins with an entry in the Domesday Book of 1086 under *Recedham Manor*. The ancient parish was a division of the Hundred of Salford, and one of the largest ecclesiastical parishes in England, though mostly moorland and 'waste'. By 1251, Rochdale had become important enough to have been granted a Royal charter. Subsequently, Rochdale flourished as a centre of the woollen trade, and by the early 18th century was described as being "remarkable for many wealthy merchants". It rose to prominence during the 19th century as a major mill town, helped by the opening of the Rochdale Canal. The changes brought by the success of Rochdale's textile industry in the 19th century led to its attainment of borough status, and it remained a dominant settlement in its region. However, during the 20th century Rochdale's spinning capacity declined towards an eventual halt. Rochdale today is a predominantly residential town.

Upper Town

This walk starts at the Metrolink **Rochdale Railway Station**. Leave the station, and note the **large domed church** to the left. This is **St. John's R.C. church**, the inspiration of the Reverend Henry Chipp who was Parish Priest from 1897 until 1936. He wanted it designed in the Byzantine Style, based on the Church of Santa Sophia in Istanbul, built by the Roman Emperor Justinian (527-565 AD); in this case, the architects were E. Bower Norris and Oswald Hill. Bishop Casartelli laid the foundation stone on 28 July 1923, and it was completed in 1925 at a cost of £21,000. Bishop Henshaw consecrated the church on 24 September 1930, when it was at last free from debt. St. John's is built in the style of a **Greek cross**, with the **four transepts** forming the arms of the cross. The **concrete dome and barrel vaults** comprise one single slab of concrete, only five inches thick within the dome, with an outer surface faced

St. John's church

with brick, the work of local builders R and T Haworth. The **dome** itself is 68 feet in diameter, and 95 feet from the ground. There are three five light **windows** in the **transept** arms, and thirty-six **small windows** around the **base** of the **dome**. The church has **two side chapels**, the Sacred Heart and the Lady Chapel, and **two chapels at the rear** of the church, one dedicated to St. John the Baptist, and one to St. Anthony of Padua. The **altar, pulpit, organ** and **pews** were transferred from the old church. There are fourteen **Stations of the Cross** that tell the story of the first Good Friday and are used as a Catholic devotion. The unusual **balconies** are probably taken from the style of eastern churches. In these, the **balcony around the upper storey**, a matroneum or gynaeconitis, was an area set-aside for women and children. The **mosaics** are the glory of the church (the cost of the **mosaic** for the apse alone was an estimated £1,000). The **sanctuary mosaic** was designed by Eric Newton, and was completed on 31 October 1933. The **central figure** is that of Christ the King (the associated feast day was established by Pope Pius XI, and his Papal Coat of Arms and the Coat of Arms of Bishop Henshaw are on the side walls). Mosaics in Byzantine times were **zoned**, and the arrangement follows this tradition. The highest, lightest, purest **zone of heaven** contained the **figure of Christ**, with eternal and transcendental scenes from the **Ascension** and/or **Pentecost**. The second zone was usually **scenes from the life of Christ** and the **death of Our Lady**, **salvation** and **resurrection**, the **calendar of the Christian year**, and **Holy Places**, Bethlehem or Golgotha. The third zone, the **terrestrial zone** usually contained **saints**, male saints nearer the apse and female saints further away. The mosaics have recently been repaired and cleaned by Paul Lupton (Alberti Lupton). The western end of the churchis usually open (ring 01706 646877 to check.)

On the opposite side of the road is the **imposing fire station**. This magnificent structure, with its fine **hose tower**, opened in 1933, when it was one of the most up to date and best equipped in Britain. It has been replaced by a new facility, and its future is presently uncertain. However, it is still currently (2014) the home of the **Greater Manchester Fire Service Museum**. (Usually open Fridays and first Sunday of each month, except January, 10-4. Admission is free. Ring 01706 901227 to check these details are still current.) The **collections and displays** in the museum portray the proud record of achievement and development of fire brigades, firefighters, personalities and manu-facturers associated with fire heritage in

The former Fire Station

Greater Manchester. The many and varied exhibits include several **full-size fire appliances**, along with a large collection of **equipment, photographs, uniforms, medals, insignia, models** and **other memorabilia**. Parts of the museum have been laid out to form **period tableaux** so as to portray the exhibits in a more natural setting. This includes a **Victorian street frontage** housing an insurance office, fire equipment supplier's shop and fire station. Inside the station stands a **horse-drawn steam pump** surrounded by various contemporary items and fittings. There is also a **1940s Blitz scene** featuring a trailer fire pump with uniformed personnel and equipment.

Follow the course of the Metrolink extension along **Maclure Road** to the junction with **Drake Street**, then along the latter towards the town centre (see p169). Turn left down **School Lane**, and the imposing **Parish Church of St. Chad** will soon become visible to the right. There are a number of entrances into the **churchyard**. Near one of them may be found the **town stocks**, still in their 1688 condition. They were last used in 1822, when a miscreant with the unfortunate name of Billy Pod was confined to the general amusement of the population! But before inspecting the church and churchyard, take time out to look at the **old vicarage**, beyond the churchyard on the right. In the 18th

St Chad's Parish Church, Rochdale

century, vicars and parsons were country gentlemen (often younger sons of noblemen and gentry). Samuel Dunster, vicar from 1722 to 1754, replaced the original thatched cottage and built this Georgian house (with a fine **Queen Anne porch**) in 1726, modelled upon his London home. (It is now used as offices for voluntary organisations, and the modern vicarage is next door.) Notice the remains of a **dividing wall** between it and the churchyard. This was built in 1760 by Dr. James Tunstall (Vicar 1757-72), and is said to have resulted from the insistence of his wife (who clearly wore the trousers) that their daughters would not mix with the choir boys! Across the road is the entrance to **Broadfield Park**. This is Rochdale's oldest, dating from the 1870s, and well worth a look. There is a fine (1893) **bandstand**, a **statue of Alderman George Leach Ashworth** (the inspiration for the town hall project), and a **jubilee fountain**. The park is landscaped to suit the contours of the hill, and one of the paths is carried over one of the entrances by a pretty **wrought iron bridge**. It is worth realising that the park constitutes an **alternative route to Touchstones** (p185), avoiding the church steps. In this instance, follow **Sparrow Hill**, past the **Broadfield Hotel** (a former nurses home, built in 1904) and turn left into the park, passing the **statue of John Bright** (p186) and exiting on to **Chester Road**. The **Touchstones Gallery** is round the corner, to the right. However, most visitors will wish to return to the **churchyard**. Enter through the Victorian **lych gate**, noting the **war memorial** and the **sundial** (erected in 1783 at a cost of £4 4sh 6d!).

There are **two interesting graves** to the right, at the **east end** of the church. The one surrounded by iron railings is the resting place of **John Collier ('Tim Bobbin')** the dialect writer and satirist, who died in 1786 (see p179). The family grave between the

Tim Bobbin

John Collier (1708-1786) was a caricaturist and satirical poet known by the pseudonym of Tim Bobbin. Born in Urmston, the son of an impoverished curate, he moved to Milnrow at the age of seventeen to work as a schoolmaster. Marriage and nine children meant he needed to supplement his income and he began producing illustrated satirical poetry in Lancashire dialect and a book of dialect terms. His first and most famous work, *A View of the Lancashire Dialect*, or, *Tummus and Mary*, appeared in 1746, and is the earliest significant piece of Lancashire dialect to be published. He regularly travelled to Rochdale to sell his work in the local pubs, where most of the business of Rochdale was conducted as there was no cloth hall at that time.

People in the pubs would ask him to draw portraits of them and their friends and he would charge on the basis of the number of heads in the picture. The Lancashire dialect poetry collection, *Human Passions Delineated*, a work which he both wrote and illustrated, appeared in 1773. In it he savagely lampooned the behaviour of upper and lower classes alike. The etchings were widely reproduced, and some were printed on ceramics of the time, and a coloured reproduction of many of the plates was published in 1810. He died in 1786 leaving the sum of £50. He wrote his own epitaph twenty minutes before he died, "Jack of all trades...left to lie i'th dark" which is inscribed upon his gravestone. He had also written a number of other humorous epitaphs for graves, a number of which can still be seen in the churchyard.

Tim Bobbin's grave

hedge and the boundary wall contains the remains of **Hamlet Nicholson** "patentee and manufacturer of the compound cricket ball."

There are three traditions concerning the founding of the church; two are historical, and the third, involving 'boggarts' is legendary (p183). St. Chad (or Ceadda), consecrated Bishop of Mercia in 669, is a popular saint in the Manchester area. After education by St. Aidan on Lindisfarne, he performed a number of missionary journeys, and it is possible that he founded the first church here (perhaps to exorcise a pagan site) in the course of his wanderings. The second tradition ascribes the founding of the church to his successor in 673. There is no mention of a church in Domesday, but that does not mean that a Saxon church had not existed, for much was destroyed in William the Conqueror's 'harrying of the North'. One Adam de Spotland donated land for a chantry in the 12th century, and a William Stapleton swore on the relics of the holy saints at St. Chad's, Rochdale, around the same time (denoting a church of some importance). The first actual mention of the church occurs in a document of 1194 which refers to Geoffrey the Dean (of Whalley) as Vicar.

Whatever the earliest church may have been, the structure seems to have been entirely rebuilt on a large scale during the 13th century, and the present nave pillars probably date from then and remain in their original position. The tower was rebuilt in the 14th century, and the **Trinity Chapel** on the south side of the **chancel** existed in 1487. The **chapel of St. Katherine** on the **north side** was founded probably about the same time or a little earlier (it is mentioned in 1514). It is likely that many other changes had been effected in the structure before the middle of the 16th century when (c. 1558) the **greater part was rebuilt**. This building stood substantially without change till the beginning of the 19th century, when it was in a ruinous condition, but a proposal to take it down and rebuild it was fortunately abandoned in favour of restoration at various dates.

The **whole of the east end of the church** and **nearly all the work on the exterior** of the building are therefore **modern**, and apart from the **nave arcade** and the **lower part of the tower**, has little antiquarian interest. It is built of wrought stone, the **east gable** has a plain coping with cross and angle pinnacles, and the walls to chancel, nave, and aisles have **embattled parapets**. The **chancel roof** is slightly higher than that of the nave, and both are covered with green slates, while those of the aisles are lean-to roofs covered with lead. The **tower**, considered the oldest part of the church, has stonework dating from the 13th century. It is thirteen feet square inside, with walls five feet thick, and has a vice (staircase) in the south-west corner. Though the original tower was retained in 1873, not very much ancient detail has been left. It was raised in height, but had its chiming clock removed in 1872. However, the old **two-light pointed belfry windows** still remain on each face of the tower, those on the south and west sides being slightly out of the centre, occasioned no doubt by the space occupied by the vice in the south-west angle. On the south side, to the west of a 14th century window, is an **old sculptured stone head** built into the wall. The old tower finished above these windows, but was raised by a **new belfry stage** with two lofty stone louvred windows of three lights on each face. Above this it finishes with a new **embattled parapet** and angle **pinnacles**, and

Naughty Vicars

Richard de Perebald, Vicar between 1302 and 1317, was fined twenty shillings in 1306 for hunting and killing deer. Gilbert Haydock, vicar from about 1522 to 1554, refers in his will to his "bastard children." His successor, Richard Gorstilow, had to be deprived of the parish for pocketing the revenues but not attending to his duties. John Hampson, vicar at Elizabeth's accession, though seemingly a more conscientious man, still did not think it necessary to actually live in the place. Consequently, the people more readily attended to the active puritan minister who was appointed in Hampson's place, and who for nearly thirty-five years laboured among them. For a century, except for a brief interval, the church was in the hands of Puritan clergy. Their successors, after the Restoration in 1660, do not appear to have been men able to counteract this teaching. Hence the power of Nonconformity in the district is readily accounted for. Two other Vicars were perhaps more foolish than anything else. William Hay (Vicar 1819-39) was also a barrister, and a magistrate. He read the Riot Act at St. Peter's Fields in 1819, and the resulting 'Peterloo Massacre' hung like an albatross round his neck for the rest of his life. Dr. John Edward Nassau Molesworth had the laudable ambition of doing something about the ruinous state of the building. Unfortunately, he decided to finance the repairs by levying a 'church rate' upon the parishioners, and it was not just the nonconformists who objected! Opposition was led by the young John Bright, who openly harangued Molesworth at a meeting in the church. This spilled over into the churchyard, where Molesworth and Bright shouted at each other while standing on tombs! Church rates were abolished by parliament in 1858.

has a good 18th century weather vane. There is a **ring of eight bells**, two cast by John Rudhall in 1787, and four in 1752 by Abel Rudhall. The tenor, which bears the motto, 'Success to the town and trade of Rochdale,' was cast in 1719, recast in 1756, and again in 1812. (The church is usually open May-August, Wednesday and Thursday, 2-4; ring 01706 645014 to enquire about admission to the church.)

We enter the church through the modern **South Porch**, with a carved **figure of Saint Chad** (or Ceadda), the Saxon 'apostle to the north', over the door. Note the **list of Vicars of Rochdale**, dating to 1194; three have had nearby streets named after them!

Start your exploration at the west end. The **tower arch** is lofty and open to the nave, but an oak screen was erected after 1900 to create a baptistery. The **arch** and the surrounding masonry is probably 14th century in origin. Note the **carved heads** at the springing points. These seem pagan, and may be a reference to the 'green man' of the old fertility religion. Under the tower may be seen the worn **octagonal stone clock face built into the floor**. The old clock was replaced in 1787 by a new chiming clock manufactured by Mr Barnish for £350 (and removed immediately after his death).There is a **wall tablet** (erected 1807) by a Rochdale man to his ancestor, who may or may not have had a local connection, but did fight at Agincourt and in the Wars of the Roses. Unfortunately, romantic history may not have a place for a chivalrous knight called 'Sir Bertine Entwistle'! The fine **West Window** depicting 'Faith, Hope, and Charity' was designed by Edward Burne Jones and made by William Morris. The font, which stands in the north-west corner of the church, was found buried (perhaps hidden from religious reformers) in the vicarage garden in 1893 by a workman planting a tree. It consists of an octagonal sandstone bowl entirely without ornament and of rough workmanship, and dates apparently from the thirteenth or 14th century. It is very much worn, but the top still shows the holes for fastenings. On 2 February, 1898, Grace Stansfield (Gracie Fields) was christened at it (see p187).

The **nave piers**, as before stated, are of thirteenth or 14th century date, alternately octagonal and round, eighteen inches in diameter, with **moulded capitals and bases**. The details of the capitals and bases are unusually good for Lancashire work, the bases having water-moulding and the capitals a moulded abacus and fillet. Four of the capitals, two on each side, in addition, have carving in the bell. The third pier from the west on the south side has good but rather flat stiff **leaf foliage**, and the first pier on the north side **foliage** of an apparently later date running round the bell. Two other capitals, one on each side, are **carved with small human heads**. (One of these is now very much mutilated.) The **nave clerestory** consists of five square-headed windows upon each side spaced without reference to the arcade beneath, and the **roof** is a good modern one put up a few years after 1855, with rich ornamental tie-beam and curved pieces under, carried down the walls between the windows and resting on brackets, but intersecting both the tower and chancel arches rather awkwardly. The **pulpit**, dated 1907, shows the Sermon on the Mount. The **brass plaque** on the south wall, near St. Chad's Window, commemorates the **visit of the Queen and Prince Philip** in 1994, when the church celebrated its eight hundredth anniversary. The **window** to the right is a **memorial to Sir Clement Royds**, a local banker and MP, and a benefactor to the church.

The **chancel arch** is modern and very lofty, the line of its springing being above the crowns of the arches of the chancel and nave arcades. There is no screen between the chancel and nave, the only division being a low stone wall. The **chancel** itself consists of six bays with an arcade of pointed arches, on clustered shafts open to the north and south aisles. It has a **lofty clerestory** of six square-headed three-light windows on each side, and a rich double **hammer-beam roof** with angel terminations. The **choir stalls** occupy the first four bays from the west, those to the first and second bays being **old**; tradition suggests that they incorporate **15th century work** from Canterbury Cathedral! Other, 16th century, carving on the **pews** includes the **arms of the Byron family**. The sixth bay contains the sanctuary, the fifth being open at each side to the aisles. The **East Window** of 1885 is a fine example of Victorian stained glass. Try and make out the figure of the **pelican**, traditionally thought to feed her offspring with her blood, and therefore a symbol of Christ. There are twenty-eight **angels playing musical instruments** in the windows above the stalls.

The **Chapel of St. Katherine** has been perpetuated to the left of the chancel by the 1886 rebuilding. The screen bears the cross moline and shackbolt, and an inscription: 'In te Domine speravi. Deus Deus meus. In Domino confido.' It probably dates from the restoration of 1558. The **altar rails** have the **carved mouse** trademark of Thompson of York. Note the **laid-up military flags**, including the standard of the Sixth Battalion, **Lancashire Fusiliers**, the local Territorial Army unit, dating from the First World War. The **dark wooden sideboard** is a Byron family heirloom, presented to the first Baron Byron of Rochdale to mark the grant of his peerage for leading royalist troops at Edge Hill and Worcester. (The fact that most of the townsmen probably supported the other side was conveniently forgotten.) The chapel also contains a **plate of copper to the memory of Susanna Gartside** (d. 1668), with a skeleton at each side of the words, 'As you are, so were we; as wee are, so you must be.'

The Trinity Chapel, to the right of the chancel, has a similar **screen**, with the inscription 'Miserere mei Deus. Domine exaudi. Inclina Domine. Parce nobis Domine. Libera nos Domine.'; the chapel itself dates back to 1487, and was a chantry founded by the Butterworth family. The **altar rails** and **table** were in the original chapel, dating from the 16th century. In the second bay of the south wall is a **small door** between two closely-spaced buttresses, which probably served the Trinity Chapel, and was called in the 17th century the 'little door.'

The **oldest plate** consists of a paten of 1698-9, inscribed 'Ex dono Tho. Holden Filii Ric. Holden in usum Ecclesiae Rochdaliens. 1696,' with the maker's mark S.H. under a crown; a chalice presumably

Imaginary Ancestors

The Trinity Chapel passed to the Dearden family (as part of a land purchase) in 1823, and was very much altered in 1847 by James Dearden. Finding himself in possession of the Manorial Title and Rights, he registered his Arms in 1841. The poor gentleman had been cultivating his family tree, and genealogists had found a whole host of rather dubious (but worthy) medieval ancestors. He consequently filled the chapel with imitation 16th century brasses, together with the effigies of a cross-legged knight (supposedly indicating a crusader) and a bishop. One wonders how the congregation kept a straight face! The brasses are still there, together with two worn carved slabs set in the floor.

of 17th century date, without marks and inscription, but with an engraved band under the rim; and a paten of 1702, inscribed 'Ex Dono Sarae Holden Filiae Richd. Holden in usum Ecclesiae Rochdaliensis 1702'.

Upon leaving the church, take a detour around the **west end**. Here is a **wall**, said to be Saxon in origin, though the attribution is dubious. It consists of a series of grooved stone posts, in which vertical stone slabs have been inserted. The wall was discovered in this position, but modern opinion suggests that the grooved posts were re-used at some date, and were originally marker posts, the grooves perhaps originally containing lengths of wattle fence. The **path** to the left leads past an ancient **water source**, and affords a **fine view over the back of the Town Hall**. Return to the east end of the church. Notice that it is finely placed on high ground about eighty feet above the river, on the south side of the town, and is reached on the north side by a flight of 124 **steps**. These steps, derived from Blackstone Edge stone, and reconstructed in 1810, were probably in existence in some form in the 17th century.

Lower Town

Descend towards the **Town Hall Square**, cleared of ancient housing when the Town Hall was built. To the left of the steps is **Packer Spout Gardens**, created in the 1930s. The **spring** that feeds the **ornamental pond** was known as **Packer Spout** (perhaps because the water was used for the pack horses that conveyed the cloth bales in the 18th century). Nearby is the **site of St. Chad's Well**. The church steps terminate by the side of the impressive Town Hall. Opposite are a range of buildings. The first is the *Flying Horse*, dating from 1925. The original 18th century hostelry once boasted the largest assembly room in the town and was the venue of the weekly police courts. Interestingly enough the current

Building Boggarts

Gamel, the Saxon Thane of Rochdale, decided to build a church by the side of the Roch, dedicated to St. Chad. The workmen got so far as putting in the foundations, but when they arrived at work one morning, they found that no trace of their labours could be seen. Then, someone discovered that the foundations had been transported to the top of the hill! Gamel was angry. He thought that his villeins and bondmen were playing a trick. Perhaps it was done to spite him. Or perhaps people were afraid of annoying the old pagan spirits, formerly worshipped here. The locals thought it best to remove the foundations back to the original site as quickly as possible. (But wiser heads had noted that there was no physical evidence of the move; the foundations had been clearly placed on top of the hill by a supernatural agency.) The foundations were put back by the river. And the next morning, they were on top of the hill again! But this time, a watch had been kept by brave men. Some say that they saw goblins transporting the foundation materials. Others say that it was a herd of spectral pigs! But it was clear that the church was destined to be on top of the hill...after all, that was where the boggarts (a Lancashire term for mischievous spirits) wanted it to be!

building retains a separate entrance to the function room, used by the 'gentry' of yesteryear. To the left of it is the former **Empire Hall** (*Dali Bar*) a music hall opened in 1904. The *Litten Tree*, on the corner of **Fleece Street**, was once the Post Office and (later) County Court.

Rochdale was incorporated as a municipal borough in 1856, and the idea of building a suitable **Town Hall** was soon discussed. A small minority of the councillors prevailed, and a site was chosen by the river. The design competition was won by William Henry Crossland of Leeds, who chose the **neo gothic style**, in this case redolent of the cloth halls of medieval Flanders. Crossland planned a building in the shape the letter 'E', with the main range facing north and three wings projecting south. There would be a suite of public rooms in the central section, including an exchange, council chamber, and a large hall for public meetings: all accessed by a central grand entrance to the north and a monumental staircase in a south wing. Rooms for the mayor, administrative offices, and a public library were to be housed in the eastern end, while the police and fire service (including a court room and cell) occupied the western end. John Bright laid the

Rochdale's fine Town Hall

foundation stone in 1866. Construction costs spiralled, and by the time it was opened in 1871, it had cost eight times the original budgeted estimate! But, as George Leach Ashworth, the Mayor, pointed out in his opening day speech; "we cannot have beauty without paying for it!" The Town Hall is very much as Crossland designed it, except for the original tower, which burned down in 1883. The **current tower** was designed by Alfred Waterhouse, and was constructed between 1885 and 1887. It was erected on new foundations, and is linked to the main building by an **arched bridge**. (Guided tours of the town hall are available on the last Friday of each month starting at 2.15 from reception; charge. At other times, ask at the reception what rooms may be open. There is a good restaurant open to the public Mon-Fri 12-1.30)

The **Entrance Hall** was originally intended to be used as an Exchange by the town's woollen merchants. It has a **vaulted ceiling** borne on columns of red and grey granite, with carved capitals. The **stained glass** in the north windows include the arms of nations trading with Rochdale and representations of commercially important plants. The **Minton tiled floor** features the arms of Rochdale, the Duchy of Lancaster, and the Royal Arms. Note the **statue of Jepthah's Daughter**! To the left of the entrance hall is the **Reception Room**, formerly the Council Chamber. The principal features are the striking **pierced stone arches** and two carved **stone fireplaces**. The **painted decoration** includes a frieze depicting technological advances in the textile industry, and illustrations of spinning and weaving. The **Small Exchange** originally served as the vestibule to the Mayor's Suite. The **decoration** consists of a **frieze incorporating**

animals illustrating the sources of clothing before the invention of spinning and weaving. The **ceiling** has **panels depicting the crafts and trades of the town**. The **Mayor's Reception Room** (now used as a Committee Room) has rich **oak panelling** and **decorations on the theme of 'night and day'**. The highlight is a series of corbels that support the beams of the ceiling; they represent **leading councillors and the architect** (Alderman Ashworth is clutching a model of the building). The **Mayor's Parlour** is decorated more simply, but has a fine **ceiling** depicting the Garden of the Hesperides. The **corbels** represent musicians, and the **stained glass** the months of the year and the seasons. The current **Council Chamber** was converted from the Magistrates Retiring Room in 1980. The north side **windows** contain full length portraits of historical figures and the **painted decoration** includes heraldic symbols and a frieze of crouching hounds. The chief decoration of the **Grand Staircase** is its **heraldic stained glass**. The arms of the major textile manufacturing towns of both Lancashire and Yorkshire are depicted together with those of countries supplying raw materials. There are also depictions of **technological developments**. The **Great Hall** is a spacious room, modelled upon medieval examples such as Westminster Hall. A series of **carved angels** terminate the **hammerbeams** of the magnificent roof; these originally held chandeliers suspended from their hands. **Benches** are built into the **oak panelling** that runs round the lower part of the walls. The rest of the wall space is filled by a stencilled **floral pattern**, and a **mural** at the east end of the hall depicts 'The Signing of the Magna Carta' by Henry Holiday (1839-1927), a minor Pre-Raphaelite artist. At the western end, behind a **raised platform**, a triple-arched opening houses the **organ**, installed in 1913. The **stained glass** is particularly fine, and contains **portraits of the Kings and Queens of England**. Local tradition states that Hitler coveted the glass, and planned to remove it to Germany when he had conquered Britain...which he never did.

Exit the Town Hall, and turn left along the **Esplanade** below the park. The pedestrian crossing communicates with **Touchstones** (open daily, café open Mon-Sat 11-4, Local Studies Centre closed Sundays and Bank Holidays; admission free). The Arts and **Heritage Centre** opened in 2002, and is housed in a handsome stone building opened as a Public Library in 1884 and extended in 1903 and 1912. Notice the external **carved frieze**, representing Victory crowning Arts and Crafts. Pass through the **Entrance Hall**, with its **reception desk**. Directly ahead are useful **toilets** and the **stairs** leading to the **Art Gallery** on the first floor. There are several **galleries**, mainly used for temporary exhibitions. To the left of the entrance is an excellent **Tourist Information Centre** with a small **shop**, and beyond lies the **café**. However, the principal attraction is the **Museum** on the right. Some curious **stone heads** are placed at the entrance. These date from the 18th century, and are symbolic of a local tradition that originated with the Celtic tribes in prehistoric times. Museums originated as 'cabinets of curiosities' and we are faced with an **eclectic collection in glass columns** to prove the point... ceramics, shoes, cameras, walking sticks...even ancient Egyptian artefacts...all collected by local people! There is a display relating to the **history of the museum and its building** directly behind. Turn sharp left, pass a case with **fashion items**, and find **displays of medical history**. On the right is a **plaque from the old Workhouse** (workhouse infirmaries were the origin of many local hospitals), while on the left is a strange little **hand operated ambulance**, used to transport children between wards at Birch Hill Hospital, and perhaps making illness seem like part of a game for frightened children. There is also an antique **dentist's chair**. Note the contemporary **model of the Town Hall**, and souvenirs of its construction and opening. There follows a series of

John Bright

John Bright, the son of Jacob Bright, a self-made and successful cotton manufacturer, was born in Rochdale on 16th November, 1811. Jacob was deeply religious and sent John to Quaker schools in Lancashire and Yorkshire. This Quaker education helped to develop in Bright a passionate commitment to political and religious equality. Bright joined the rapidly expanding family business, but he also became involved in local politics and joined the campaign to abolish church rates. Richard Cobden, a friend of Bright, suggested he should join the Anti-Corn Law League; Bright agreed and over the next few years he toured the country giving speeches on the need to reform the Corn Laws. He proved to be an outstanding orator and he drew large crowds wherever he appeared. In his speeches Bright attacked the privileged position of the landed aristocracy and argued that their selfishness was causing the working class a great deal of suffering. He cleverly appealed to the working and middle classes to join together in the fight for free trade and cheaper food. In 1843 Bright was elected to represent Durham, and campaigned in parliament for the repeal of the Corn Laws, and he also supported those Whigs advocating universal suffrage and the secret ballot. However, unlike most Radicals, Bright was opposed to Parliament regulating the hours of factory workers, fearing that factory legislation would lower wages and threaten Britain's export trade. After the repeal of the Corn Laws was obtained in 1846, Bright was regarded as a national hero, and he used his high standing to campaign for other progressive causes. He was opposed to the aggressive foreign policy of Lord Palmerston, and campaigned against the Crimean War. Although totally opposed to slavery and a passionate supporter of Lincoln, Bright was shocked by the outbreak of the American Civil War. His religious views stopped him from arguing in favour of Britain sending troops to help the Union forces against the Confederacy. He was happier supporting the extension of the vote to working men in 1867. Gladstone appointed Bright as President of the Board of Trade, but ill-health forced him to retire from the Cabinet. Although he later returned to government as Chancellor of the Duchy of Lancaster, Bright objected to the Liberal government's foreign policy; when the British fleet attacked Egypt in 1882, he resigned from the Cabinet. John Bright remained MP for Birmingham until his death on 27 March, 1889.

displays concerning **famous people associated with Rochdale**. A large case contains a **display cabinet** presented to **John Bright**, a chair used by the **Anti-Corn Law League**, and a **barrel** used to transport flour to Rochdale as a gift from Federal American sympathisers during the Cotton Famine. By pressing a button, you can listen to extracts from some of **Bright's speeches**.

There are relics of **Samuel Bamford**, something of a radical firebrand in his youth. He headed the Middleton contingent to Peterloo, and a brave soul seized the **Yeomanry plume** that is on display. In old age he wrote an autobiography, betraying an interest in local history and folklore. There are **recorded extracts** from his writings. **John Collier (Tim Bobbin)** (p179) is the next personage. You can **listen to his verse**, but note his (reputed) **hat**! The last figure is perhaps the most famous of all. There is a fine **bust of Gracie Fields**, and a variety of mementoes. Sit on the **old cinema seats** and watch **extracts from her films** and **newsreel clips of her visits to Rochdale**.

There follow displays of **local folk customs** and **sport**. The leisure theme is continued by a case full of **old television sets** and a recreated **pub interior**. These surround a **children's dressing up area**. There are sections devoted to **marriage, birth**, and **childhood**. There are displays of **food items** and **trades**, but do not omit the **market**

'Our Gracie'

Grace Stansfield was born over a fish and chip shop owned by her grandmother in Molesworth Street. She made her first stage appearance as a child in 1905, joining children's repertory theatre groups such as 'Haley's Garden of Girls' and the 'Nine Dainty Dots' (she was a half-timer, spending part of the day in the mill and the rest at school.) Her professional debut took place at the Rochdale Hippodrome theatre in 1910, and she soon gave up her job in the local cotton mill (she was billed as the 'singing mill girl' and assumed the stage name of 'Gracie Fields' about this time.) After meeting comedian and impresario Archie Pitt, they began working together. Pitt would come to serve as her manager and the two married in 1923. Their first revue in 1915 was called Yes I Think So and the two continued to tour Britain together until 1924 in the revue Mr Tower of London. Fields came to major public notice when this show came to the West End. Her career rapidly accelerated from this point with straight dramatic performances and the beginning of a recording career. "Sally," her most famous song, and which became her theme, was worked into the title of her first film, Sally in Our Alley (1931), which was a major box office hit. Many people preferred her comic songs such as The Biggest Aspidistra in the World, Walter, and My Little Bottom Drawer. (She was a very accomplished comedienne.) She went on to make several films initially in Britain and later in the United States (for which she was paid a record fee of £200,000 for four films). Regardless, she never enjoyed the process of performing without a live audience, and found the process of film-making boring. Ironically, the final few lines of the song "Sally" were written by her husband's mistress, Annie Lipman, and Fields sang this song at nearly every performance she made from 1931 onwards...claiming in later life that she wanted to "Drown blasted Sally with Walter with the aspidistra on top!" In 1939, she became seriously ill with cancer. The public sent over 250,000 goodwill messages, and after she recovered, recorded a very special 78rpm record simply called Gracie's Thanks, in which she thanked the public for the many cards and letters received while in hospital. Her charitable work was extensive; during World War Two, she paid for all servicemen and women to travel free on public transport within the boundaries of Rochdale. In March 1940, Gracie married Italian-born film director, Monty Banks. However, because Banks remained an Italian citizen and would have been interned in the United Kingdom, she was forced to leave Britain for North America during the war, at the instruction of Winston Churchill, who told her to "Make American Dollars, not British Pounds," which she did in aid of the Navy League and the Spitfire Fund. Gracie occasionally returned to England to show she was not indeed a traitor, performing in factories and army camps around the country. Parliament offered her an official apology about comments that had been made. Gracie Fields travelled to France to entertain the troops in the midst of air-raids, performing on the backs of open lorries and in war-torn areas. She was the first artist to play in captured Berlin. She performed many times for troops in the Far East, travelling as far as New Guinea, where she received an enthusiastic response from Australian personnel. Late 1945 saw her tour the South Pacific Islands. Her career was somewhat quieter after the war, but she was never out of the public spotlight. As an old lady, Gracie was entertained by the children of a local junior school, who enacted their version of her life story. She ended up joining them on the floor and (much to their delight) joining in their songs. That was the kind of person she was. She died in September 1979. To ordinary northern working men and women, she was always 'Our Gracie'.

cross, said to be over 800 years old! There follows an area devoted to **communications**. Notice the model of the **passenger fly-boat** that operated on the Rochdale Canal and the **controller handle** from the first electric tram driven in Rochdale. (The Wheel is about to turn full circle!) The **textiles** area includes a **power loom** and a model of a typical **spinning mill** (p188). **Mining** and **farming** are also represented, with a relief model of the district. But seek out the easily missed annex before you leave, containing **military** displays. Listen to the letter from a recruit who is writing to a girl for the first time, tongue-tied and not knowing what to say...prior to being plunged into an unimaginable hell and being taken prisoner. The **Local Studies Library** is entered through the museum.

Exit Touchstones and walk left along the **Esplanade**. There are glimpses of the River Roch on the left, progressively covered over in the town centre, giving rise to the claim that Rochdale has the **widest bridge in Britain**! The **War Memorial** was designed by

Lutyens and unveiled by Lord Derby in 1922. It stands on the site of Orchard House the residence of the Dearden Family (p182), who acquired the title of Lords of the Manor. The present **Post Office**, to the side of the memorial gardens, was designed before 1914, but (delayed by start of the Great War) it was not opened until 1927. Walk further on till you come to the *Royal Bank of Scotland* on the left. Note the red brick building adjoining it, for it was the home of Rawson's Bank in 1819, and sold to the Royds family in 1827. By 1879, a new stone extension faced Butts Avenue, but Clement Royds sold the

The old Library Building, now Touchstones

enterprise to the Manchester and Salford Bank in 1881. Remember that at this point you are probably standing on the arched over river! (But see p170) Directly ahead, you may be able to make out the **site of the new tram terminus** beyond the Drake Street junction. Retrace your steps and turn right, up **Yorkshire Street**. *Yates's Wine Lodge*, on the left, was the town house of the Stead family, built in 1745. *Lloyds Bank,* on the same side, was another town house, originally the residence of the Vavasour family. As the Union Flag Hotel, it was the intended rendezvous of the local Jacobites in 1745. But, as the **plaque** on the wall relates, they came to a rather sticky end in a confrontation with the authorities. A little further up the hilly street, also on the left, may be found the entrance to the modern **Rochdale Market** (daily, except Tuesday and Sunday), with a **sheep sculpture** at the entrance. Look out for an easily missed little street on the left, called by a strange name...**The Baum**. Upon reaching the main road, cross with care, and proceed to the left along **Hunters Lane** until you reach the **Toad Lane** conservation area. (The name is derived from 'T'owd Lane', or 'The Old Lane'.)

Here may be found the **Rochdale Pioneers Museum** (open Monday to Saturday, 10-5, Sunday 12-4, admission free). The museum opened in 1931, and has just reopened after a major refurbishment, which includes **new educational facilities** and a **new access tower** (incorporating a **lift**). The building itself dates from 1791, and the ground floor was rented by a society of twenty-eight working men in 1844 for £10 per annum. The front room was converted into a **shop**, and this has been recreated as the first successful co-operative enterprise. One is struck by its simplicity; the whitewashed walls, the rudimentary furniture, and the basic goods on offer, for only sugar, butter, flour, and oatmeal were sold in the first instance. Tobacco and tea were soon added, and **Victorian tea containers** can be seen in the Museum. The **scales** near the window are thought to be contemporary, while the ornamental crossbar of the other pair is dated to 1860. Prospective customers waited on the **wooden bench** to be served, while a clerk carefully registered each purchase at the **desk** in the corner (so that a customer's dividend could later be calculated). The room in the rear was used as a stockroom, but also to hold meetings in the early days. Nowadays there are **displays** about the ideas behind co-operation and the development of the **Rochdale Equitable Pioneers Society** and the co-operative movement. The society took over the upstairs part of the building and first used it as a library and classroom, later adopting it for the drapery section and shoe repair. The **middle floor** now contains **displays** depicting **co-operation in the modern era** and the **worldwide influence of the co-operative movement**. The **top floor** is fitted out as a **cinema**, and a number of **films** may be selected. 'Men of Rochdale' (1944), an ambitious drama documentary for its time, tells the story of the Rochdale Pioneers. 'Song of the People' (1945) has an early appearance by Bill Owen, better known as 'Compo' in 'Last of the Summer Wine'. 'Co-operette' (1938) is an amazing early colour film, complete with dancing vegetables and a monologue by Stanley Holloway! **Computers** can access the **archive collection**, but children may like to play the **'dividend game'** with scenarios set in 1910, 1960, and 2010!

The Baum public house, next door, is well worth a visit. The former hardware store is now a mini shrine to Rochdale's heritage, with **pews** from the old Jarvis Street Methodist Church, **panelling** from Rochdale Public Toilets and a **mirror** from the old Rochdale theatre, together with old theatre posters. It is currently CAMRA's 'national pub of the year, and good food is also available. Turn right into **Park Lane**, and ascend the **steps** to visit **St. Mary in the Baum** (there is a **level entrance** from **St. Mary's Gate** at the top of **Toad Lane**). The present church (designed by Ninian Comper, and the only example of his work in the North of England) was consecrated in 1911, replacing a previous Georgian structure dating to 1742. (The church can usually be visited by prior arrangement Wed-Sun, by ringing 01706 352604. Concerts are sometimes held on Wednesday lunchtimes.) The interior is unusual, in that there is a **main aisle**, **choir** and **sanctuary** on the south side, and a **centre aisle** and **Jesus Chapel** on the north side. The **pillars** dividing the chapel from the centre aisle are from the original church, as are the **roundel windows** in the chapel itself. The **altar** is surmounted by **gilded angels**, and the **picture** above is a copy of 'The Holy Family' by Murillo. The great **East Window** portrays the history of God's revelation of Himself to Man from creation to ascension. The striking **screen** is perhaps the finest in the diocese; the figures on the lower part depict the apostles, each one bearing their due symbol. As the dedication is to Our Lady, the church has a Jesus Chapel instead of a Lady Chapel. The **north aisle**, of which the chapel is part, contains the unusual **Jesus Windows**, taken from the original church. Each contains three roundels set in bottled glass representing scenes from the life of Christ.

Co-operation

Robert Owen (1771-1858) was a living paradox, for the owner of the New Lanark Mills by the falls of the Clyde was the first English socialist. He was convinced that character was largely formed by environment, and as master of a practically self-contained mill community, he was able to put his ideas into practice. His new management methods, his provision of good housing and social facilities, and his school, the 'Institution for the Formation of Character', made New Lanark a mecca for visitors from all parts of Europe. He publicised his ideas in his book 'A New View of Society', and later established a model community in America. He was an idealist, but one of his ideas survived him, the idea of co-operation. Think of a community in which the means of production, distribution, and exchange were owned by everybody, and whatever profit that was made was distributed equally! Impractical! But, wait! Suppose a business like a shop was owned by the customers. The more they purchased at the shop, the more they shared in the profits. And if it was run on sound business lines, there was no reason why it should not succeed. There was a sound imperative why co-operation ought to be tried. Working men and women were at the mercy of profiteering shopkeepers who often adulterated the food and drink that they sold: sand found its way into sugar, water into milk, and iron filings into recycled tea leaves. And so twenty-eight Rochdale men, many of them weavers, and fifteen of them Owenite socialists, formed a co-operative society with a capital of £28. Membership was open to anyone, with shares of £1 each. Profits were to be distributed at a fixed rate of 3.5% per share, but any surplus after that would be distributed in due proportion to what a member spent in the shop. This proportionate dividend or 'divi' became the secret of the movement's success. As it expanded, anyone could afford to become a member. The individual co-operative shops created the Co-operative Wholesale Society (CWS). It bought nationally in bulk, and soon owned its own factories. Every co-op member's child was sure to go to the co-op branch if a neighbour sent them on an errand, and knew by heart their parent's 'divi' number that was to be quoted. 'Divi-day' was eagerly anticipated. Neighbours saw new clothes being bought with it, but in one instance when (so the story goes) a piano was delivered, the whole street was down the next morning at the branch, ready to join! The worldwide co-operative movement has over 850 million members in over ninety countries, all stemming from the humble seed sowed in this place.

The Rochdale Pioneers Museum, the birth place of the Co-operative Movement
(photograph courtesy of Alan Hamer)

The original church was built on a field that was locally known for its 'baum' (a Lancashire corruption of 'balm', perhaps) a medicinal herb. The field was also famous for a spectral rabbit that many claimed to have seen there, and about which many stories are told.

The Baum Rabbit

At the time when the Black Death stalked the land, the Earl of Oxford resolved to save his beloved, Blanche, the sister of Thomas de Boulton, Vicar of Rochdale. He lay down by a stone on Whitworth Moor, and there was surprised by two Rochdale lads. He asked if there was any sickness in these parts, and was told "none that they knew of." Consequently, he slept, but when he awoke, he found elves circling the stone in a merry dance. "Cease," said the Fairy Queen, "have you no care for the fate befalling Rachedall?" She gave the Earl a wish. He was to write upon the stone the name of one to save; perhaps himself? He scratched the letters Blanche with his diamond ring. In the twinkling of an eye, a white rabbit sat on the stone, a gold band round its neck. And strange playing cards were lying by its side. There were four suits; rabbits, roses, pinks and columbines, and the face of Blanche appeared on the Queen of Rabbits card! What did it all mean? Perhaps Blanche must have the rabbit to protect her from the plague. He made his way on foot to Rochdale, his horse being lame. He found the girl weak and fevered from the plague. Yet when she took the rabbit from the Earl, it was as if a surge of health ran through her, and she survived to help her brother tend the sick, the rabbit always at her side. The Earl helped too, but when he caught the disease, his life was spared. Thomas de Boulton died, and the rabbit disappeared the day the plague ceased. But some people say that the rabbit does return...and can sometimes be seen in the Baum churchyard by the light of the moon....

The East Manchester and Ashton Line

Piccadilly Station to Holt Town

The tram leaves the Piccadilly Station **undercroft**, crosses **Sheffield Street**, and enters a **stretch of private right of way**. Both tracks splay out to accommodate a central **turn back and storage siding**. The private right of way cuts through two streets and passes through a decaying industrial area (still used by the 'rag trade'), ripe for regeneration. To the left is a glimpse of the edge of **Piccadilly Village**, astride the Ashton Canal. In no time, we pass down the **ramp** and into the **subway**, ascending to a section of **reserved track** on the other side. This subway spares a flat crossing of the busy **Great Ancoats Street**, a grand name dating from 1788. Prior to that date, it was just Ancoats Lane. The name of Ancoats is thought to be Saxon in origin, meaning "gifted cottages or enclosures." It was situated in a rural area, the roadway being utilised by cattle drovers to avoid the narrow streets leading to the butchers' 'shambles' in the market place. However, some drovers took their cattle from the Pennine hills southwards, and the lane connected with a drovers' highway now known as Ashton Old Road. Nowadays, it performs a similar function for vehicles instead of cattle, pigs, and sheep, as part of an **inner ring road**,

The New Athens

Ancoats was the world's first industrial suburb. The first water powered cotton mills were established in country districts, and there were two such mills in and around the town by 1782. Richard Arkwright installed a steam engine at his mill (near the present C.I.S. building) in the same year, but this only pumped water to power the wheel. Another water powered mill was opened in 1785 by David Holt near the confluence of the Medlock and Shooter's Brook, the surrounding settlement being called Holt Town. However, Arkwright went on to successfully adapt the Watt steam engine to directly power the machinery, and cotton manufacture consequently became an urban phenomenon. Manchester had fifty-two steam powered cotton mills by 1792. Many mills were later concentrated in the former green-field site of Ancoats, particularly after the first section of the Rochdale Canal had been cut in 1799. Visitors came in the early 19th century to gaze with a horrified fascination at the evidences of a new industrial civilisation. For why, one of Disraeli's characters asked, should he go to Athens? "The age of ruins is past. Have you seen Manchester? Manchester is as great a human exploit as Athens." Vast wealth was created in the midst of a slum. Ancoats became one of the city's problem districts, but the residents began to disappear in the post-war prosperity, the mills closed, and it seemed that the entire area might become a wasteland of dereliction. A large part of Ancoats is now a conservation area, and some of the major on-going re-development projects can be seen from the tram window. The upmarket denizens of Piccadilly Village are rapidly spilling over into Ancoats, and it is suggested that the consequent gentrification will destroy whatever remains of the character of the old place. Only time will tell.

The Plug Plot Rioters

The second Chartist Petition was presented to Parliament in April 1842, and after its rejection a general strike began in the coal mines of Staffordshire. Stalybridge had contributed 10,000 signatures, so it was no surprise that the second phase of the strike originated there. On 13 August, 1842, there was a strike at Bayley's cotton mill, and roving cohorts of operatives carried the stoppage first to the whole area of Stalybridge and Ashton, then to Manchester, and subsequently to towns adjacent to Manchester, using as much force as was necessary to bring mills to a standstill. It rapidly became a general movement of resistance to the imposition of wage cuts in the mills, spreading to involve nearly half a million workers throughout the country and representing the biggest single exercise of working class strength in 19th century Britain. The tactic was simple. Roving gangs of strikers removed the wash-out plugs from the boilers of the mill engines. As the water ran away, the fusible plug cores in the fire boxes melted, causing the remainder of the water to extinguish the fires. The mass movement thus became known as the 'plug plot' strike or riots. A large force of strikers, marching into Manchester, were intercepted and dispersed by the military at Holt Town.

avoiding the city centre. The **reserved track** runs alongside **Pollard Street**, to the right, and after the track curves slightly in that direction, the tram makes its first stop.

New Islington Station is situated on the southern side of **Ancoats**, and is the starting point for a suggested excursion through the district (see p194). There are **two platforms**, linked by **pedestrian crossings** at either end, communicating with both **Pollard Street** and **Munday Street**.

Notice the avant-garde façade of **'Chips'** (Will Alsop, 2008), across the **canal** to the left, an apartment block seemingly assembled from random chips of wood and emblazoned with the names of the waterways that were connected with this district.

Upon leaving the station, we cross the approach road to the **Milliner's Wharf** development. One hopes that the former **mock-Tudor structure** on the right will survive the developers. The owner refused to sell, but there was plenty of room to take the line past it, obviating the need for a compulsory purchase order. It dates from 1889, and was built to serve as private dining rooms for John Hetherington & Sons of Vulcan Works, Pollard Street. The Dining Rooms were not the works canteen, but would have been for the use of directors and the entertaining of customers. The dining room itself occupied the raised ground floor, above a semi-basement, and had large windows; the diners would have been able to keep an eye on comings and goings at the works! The top storey was a flat for the caretaker, and the first floor was probably the kitchen, with the basement being used for storage. There was a hoist serving all floors. The line slowly curves to the right and crosses the junction of **Pollard Street** and **Carruthers Street** before passing down **Merrill Street**. The **Mitchell Arms**, to the left, stands astride Frost Street, the main traffic artery, and **Beswick Street** (now only accessing Holt Town). **Every Street**, to the right, joins with **Ashton New Road**, which commences at this point. The line crosses **Beswick Street** (at the site of the old Don Picture House, the local 'flea pit'), and descends into **Holt Town Station**.

The station is in a curious position. The **River Medlock**, largely culverted, flows sluggishly on the right, beyond a grassed area reclaimed from dereliction, and Holt Town itself (see p192) is on the left. After passing some side streets it is a cul-de sac for vehicles, but (at **Cavalier Street**) it then becomes the starting point for the **City Link**

footpath that parallels Metrolink all the way to the Etihad Stadium'. Although (as a result of bureaucratic procrastination and shortage of funding) this stretch of Metrolink could not be built in time for the Commonwealth Games, much of the infrastructure was included in the Games construction programme, including this pathway to and from the stadium. There is access to and from the station by **steps and a ramp**, communicating with the **Droylsden platform**, which is also linked with the **Piccadilly platform** by **pedestrian crossings**.

An Excursion through Ancoats

Leave the tram at **New Islington Station** (p193). It was intended that access to the canal towpath would be obtained by a path from the **New Islington Metrolink Station** to the **pedestrian bridge** over the **lock**. At the time of writing (2014), this has not yet materialised. In its absence, exit the Station by the path to **Munday Street**, exiting on to **Pollard Street** by a left turn. Turn left again into **Carruthers Street** by the *Bank of England* pub and cross the road. There is a **path** on the right, beyond the **canal bridge**, that leads to the **tow path**. Double back under the **bridge**, and follow the **tow path** past **Chips** (p193) and the **lock** towards the Dutch style **lifting bridge**.

The **lifting bridge** spans a new **canal arm** that stretches to **Old Mill Street**; a series of newly constructed **basins** continue from that street to the **Rochdale Canal** at **Redhill Street** (see p200). There are developments planned around this series of **boat marinas**, along with the planned network of footpaths and bridges, a new **north-south axis** through the heart of Ancoats. The **towpath** now passes a charming **lock keeper's cottage** by the next **lock**, and spans an original disused **basin**. Ahead is the striking angular tower of **Islington Wharf**; look out for the **Tourist Information Point** on the towpath, detailing the history of the area with a pictorial reconstruction. We emerge on to **Great Ancoats Street** by the side of another **lock**. Turn right, and walk along the road, crossing **Old Mill Street** on the right (notice the **wooden paving** and the curious **lamp standards**), and passing the large **retail park** on the same side, we arrive at the **Rochdale Canal**. It is spanned by a bridge, of which the **iron parapet** is original on this side of the (widened) road. **Brownsfield Mill** (1825) is visible on the other side of Great Ancoats Street. This was a 'room and power' mill, where tenants paid rent to the mill owner for space and power from the steam engine. One of the later occupants was A.V. Roe, the aviation pioneer, who established an **airplane factory** here in 1910 for the manufacture of biplanes and triplanes. The wings were covered with cotton cloth made in Manchester. Turn right into **Redhill Street** by the lock.

The **view alongside the Rochdale canal in Redhill Street** (formerly Union Street) is a classic one, showing a scene that is still essentially the same as it was in the

The Ashton Canal

The original Ashton Canal scheme was completed in 1796, running from a large basin behind what is now Piccadilly Station in Manchester, and climbing gradually eastwards via eighteen locks to Fairfield, Droylsden. From there a level section continues eastward to Whitelands Basin, Ashton under Lyne. Here, a junction is made with the recently re-opened Huddersfield Narrow canal, a Trans-Pennine waterway. Another canal runs from the basin to Buxworth in the Peak district, and a branch from this, the Macclesfield Canal, links with the Trent and Mersey Canal. (Consequently, the canal forms part of the celebrated 'Cheshire Ring'.) Some of these waterways may be read on Chips to the right of the towpath.

The Rochdale Canal

The Rochdale Canal was the second waterway to be built through Ancoats, opening in 1804. The Committee sailed to Manchester in two boats, accompanied by the band of the Manchester and Salford Volunteers. After a major restoration programme, it was officially re-opened by the late Fred Dibnah in 2002, and once more communicates with the Aire and Calder Navigation across the Pennines. It now forms part of the new 'Pennine Ring', enabling (like the old established 'Cheshire Ring') boaters to make a circular excursion of Lancashire and Yorkshire without once doubling back on themselves.

The Rochdale Canal at Redhill (formerly Union) Street (Graham Beech)

19th century (see p196). The old mills are now undergoing restoration and conversion to apartments and retail units.

James McConnel and John Kennedy erected the first large mill that we come across. **Old Mill** was first built in 1799, as the **date stone** proudly recalls, though the mill was

Enterprising Scotsmen

New Galloway was (and still is) a small town in Kircudbright. In the second half of the 18th century, the parents of Adam and George Murray (who were shopkeepers) and James McConnel and John Kennedy (who were small farmers) did not see much of a future for their sons. Fortunately, William Cannan, an uncle of young James had set up a machine making business in far off Chowbent (near Atherton) in bustling and booming Lancashire. Off the boys were sent, to become his apprentices and seek their fortunes. Early textile pioneers, such as Arkwright, had to rely upon the skills of Lancashire clockmakers to perfect and install their inventions, but Cannan was one of a new generation of textile machine makers, who installed and maintained this new technology as well as manufacturing it. Kennedy is a good example of what happened next. Not only did he go into business on his own account, but he specialised in the production of 'Mules' (a cross between Hargreave's 'Jenny' and Arkwright's 'Water Frame'), a machine that Samuel Crompton, its inventor, had obligingly left unpatented. Kennedy's Mules incorporated a number of his own improvements, and were much in demand. A combination of frugal living, re-invested profits, and judicious financial partnerships produced sufficient capital to go into the cotton spinning business. In 1790, Adam Murray had leased a plot of land on Union Street (now Redhill Street) along the line of the projected Rochdale Canal. A few years later, McConnel and Kennedy, now in partnership, followed suit, and erected a large mill powered by a Boulton and Watt steam engine in 1797. Kennedy resided at Ardwick Hall, and was one of the principal promoters of the Liverpool and Manchester Railway. The new partnership of Adam and George Murray commenced construction of their mill on Union Street the following year.

*Cotton Mills in Union Street (Redhill Street). An iconic image of the Industrial
revolution, largely unchanged today*
(From Edward Baines: 'History of the Cotton Manufacture' (1835))

entirely rebuilt in 1912. It was re-christened **Royal Mill**, to celebrate a wartime visit by
King George VI in 1942. Next door, the partnership constructed **Sedgewick Mill** (1818-
20,) the earliest surviving of their mills. Beyond Murray Street, Adam and George
Murray, erected a **complex of four buildings** around a **yard** between 1798 and 1806.
A brief detour down Murray Street can be made as far as the **entrance arch** on the right.
Here, inserted in the wall, may be glimpsed the **monumental slab** belonging to Adam
Murray, who died in 1818. It was originally in the churchyard of St. Mark's, Cheetham
Hill, but the late Georgian church was demolished in 1998, and this was thought the
best place for it! The six-storey **Old Mill**, fronting Redhill Street, was opened by the
brothers in 1798. It is the earliest surviving structure of its kind in the city, and is still
very much in its original condition; perhaps the oldest steam powered cotton mill in
existence. In the course of a recent restoration, an original 'builder's sacrifice' (to bring
good luck) in the form of a woman's shoe was found in the rafters. The **Decker Mill**
next door dates from 1802; the six-storey **New Mill**, on the **Jersey Street** side of the
yard, 1804; and the **rest of the complex** was intended as warehousing. The **central yard**
became a reservoir after the opening of the Rochdale Canal, with which it
communicated by a tunnel under Redhill Street. Coal was later shipped in containers
by barge through the tunnel, which is now blocked up. By 1818, the Murrays
masterminded a commercial empire employing 1,300 workers. (A workforce of fifty
signified a large concern at the time.) The complex has been secured for restoration,

and is being converted to a mixed leisure, retail, and accommodation use, including the **central water feature**! The recently restored **Doubling Mill**, also known as Waulk Mill (1842), lies beyond **Bengal Street**. Turn left down this street, noticing the **courtyard** of the Murray's Mills complex with its **recreated basin** on the left, with the **mill counting house** in the background. We now turn left along **Jersey Street**, and eventually pass **two 1911 houses** (built for electricity workers, next to the **substation** that once served the Royal Mill complex, and perhaps reflecting 'arts and craft' influence). Notice the rebuilt **Coates School building** (with plaque), on the left, almost opposite. Henry Coats, "one of the best penmen in town and a headmaster" opened the school in 1821, and it lasted until the 1860s. Unfortunately, the building fell down before it could be restored, and the **date stone** is all that is left.

We turn right into **Great Ancoats Street** once more. There follows an interesting sequence of buildings on the right. First we pass the new **Nuovo Apartments**, with its **thirteen story tower**, followed beyond **Blossom Street** by a 19th century structure with a **patterned brick façade** and an **electricity station** with a 1927 date stone. **Hudson Buildings** is situated a little further onwards, a fine (refurbished) **terracotta frontage** in which late Art Nouveau influences can possibly be detected (with a 1924 **date stone**). Adjacent is a recently restored **strange little building** (with a 'mock-Tudor' attic) that opened originally in 1899. It was built by W. R. Sharp as a Methodist Women's Night Shelter, which also contained a coffee shop and other community facilities. Known as the 'Derros Building', it has now been converted into flats. We now reach the finest facade on the street. The **Daily Express Building** (Sir Owen Williams, 1939) is an almost exact copy of the newspaper's building on Fleet Street. It makes a stunning use of glass and black 'vitrolite' for, under the energetic leadership of Lord Beaverbrook, the

The restored Express nuilding in Great Ancoats Street (Graham Beech)

Express was then a power in the land, and a very progressive undertaking. At one time, it was possible to see the great printing presses behind the glass sheeting, but the whole complex now has a strange deserted aspect. After the preliminary refurbishment, the usual flats are proposed, together with a restaurant.

The corner of **Oldham Road** is marked by the **'Crown and Kettle'**, standing on the site of an earlier pub, with the odd name of 'Iron Dish and Cob of Coal'. The 'Crown and Kettle' is a strange building, with neo-gothic windows and good quality stonework. One story suggests that it was intended as a Court House for magistrates' sessions, but was found surplus to requirements. The old pub was a haunt of the Daily Express print workers, with its statue of Churchill and a fireplace surround made from the timbers of the R101 airship. Some of these features remain. The wide junction of **Oldham Road** with **Great Ancoats Street** is known as **New Cross**. The long vanished 'New Cross' (presumably to distinguish it from the 'old' Market Cross) was placed here in the 18th century. Perhaps someone wanted to start a rival market. It replaced the earlier 'Barlow's Cross' about which little is known. The site must have had some significance, since the bodies of suicides were buried there, one in 1753 with "a stake driven through the body." Human remains were discovered in the course of road works in 1846. In 1812, a group of starving labourers intercepted a cart en route to Shudehill here and appropriated fourteen sacks of oatmeal and other grains for 'distribution' to the crowd. New Cross is, by tradition, one of the three places in Manchester where the accession of a new monarch is proclaimed.

Stroll down **Oldham Road**, noticing glimpses of the new **Co-operative Headquarters** (p55) through side streets to the left. Straight ahead, across Oldham Road, is a part of the **Forbidden City of Old Peking**! The ancient Chinese Roof and the Pagoda at the street corner betoken a new development by *Wing Ip*, a very large Chinese supermarket. (Members of the public are cordially

Martin Marprelate

Oldham Road was originally known as Newton Lane. Somewhere near this point stood a cottage, a place that played a humble part in English history. The puritans (who, at this stage, had the reform of the state church as their objective) had been forced underground in the later years of Queen Elizabeth's reign. They hit back by attacking the bishops, their principal enemies, in a series of scurrilous (but very amusing) pamphlets. The 'Martin Marprelate' tracts "printed in Almayne (Germany), over the sea, five leagues from a bouncing priest," were very much a home grown product. In 1588, when London became too hot, Robert Waldegrave (the printer and publisher) removed the press to the cottage on Newton Lane. He had just completed a batch of the latest instalment, entitled "Ha' ye anymore work for the Cooper?" (This was a pun on Bishop Cooper's name, imitating the street cry of barrel makers!) Lord Derby, then residing at Chetham's College, sallied forth and raided the premises. Waldegrave escaped, but the press was destroyed. The irony was that, in the year of the Armada, the puritans were amongst the Queen's most loyal subjects. But she could not conceive of a state church without those inconvenient Bishops. Interestingly enough, in changed times, our hero became printer to King James, Elizabeth's successor.

invited to join the restaurant proprietors, busily laying in their weekly provisions.) Although there is a very useful cash machine on the Oldham Road side, entrance to this mysterious and blank-walled domain is obtained by the path from the corner of **Thomson Street**, skirting the **Fire Station** and Brigade Training School (notice the **Lancashire and Yorkshire Railway memorial** on the left, all that remains of the large goods yard that occupied this site. The *Wing Ip* complex also contains a Chinese restaurant (what else!) rather curiously called *'Glamorous'*; perhaps something was lost in the translation. The great forbidding bulk of **Victoria Square** looms on the right. This housing complex, intended to benefit the 'working classes', was erected in a vague Queen Ann style round a large courtyard in 1889. The corner towers contained laundries and drying rooms. The architect seems to have thought that he was building for an alien race; wooden skirting boards were not provided, since these might be ripped out and burned! Take a right turn into **Sherratt Street**. The 'model' workers' housing (1898-9), on the right, are in the form of much kinder, and rather pretty, terraces. However, the city fathers celebrated their progressive ways in the street names. This was all very well, but everyone (certainly by the 1960s) was too posh to live in Sanitary Street! The council dropped some letters to change the name to Anita Street. **St. Peter's Church** (see p199) is clearly visible directly ahead. But pause at the point where **George Leigh Street** cuts across, and glance to the left to see the **old elementary school building** (1912). It was necessary to place the boy's playground on the roof in such a crowded district. George Leigh Street is named after the original owner of the land in the area. It was largely sold to Thomas Bound, a builder, who commenced erecting cheap houses as early as 1775. The man made a fortune. Turn right down the street, passing a fine row of houses with a **pavement sculpture**. **St. Michael's Church** to the left, was (and still is) the home of the

St. Peter's Church, Ancoats (Graham Beech)

Italian community in Ancoats. The sight of the men of the religious fraternity carrying the great statue of the Madonna, accompanied by the girls in colourful national dress, is familiar to generations of Mancunians at the Whit walks.

The way is now to the left, along **Cotton Street**, then left again down **Blossom Street**. The impressive refurbished building on the left is the former **ice plant**, which, amongst other things, serviced the needs of the district's Italian ice cream vendors. We arrive at a new **civic square** distinguished by large **illustrated slabs**. Across the square, to the right is a view of **Jactin House**. It was the Male Methodist Mission (1903-5) and is being redeveloped. If you didn't mind the preaching, good beds might be had for a pittance. If you had no money...well, a bit of labouring work in an adjacent yard earned the right to a bed and a hot meal. Blossom Street passes in front of **St. Peter's Church**. Although Ancoats was a poor district, the Bishop wanted a fine Anglican church built in what was then a place full of Roman Catholic Irish immigrants. Consequently, he insisted that the necessary economy (a budget of £4,200) should be combined with some grandeur, hence the odd combination of a medieval 'Romanesque' design in brick, married to a cast iron internal structure. It was consecrated in 1859, but fell out of use in the 1960s. Fortunately, it has been saved from demolition, and the first phase of restoration concentrated on the unusual campanile tower. Additional funding stabilised the rest of the building. A textile museum has been projected, but it is now a rehearsal space and music store for the Halle Orchestra (p235). A right turn into **Murray Street**, past the east end of the church, brings us back to **Jersey Street**. We retrace our steps to Bengal Street, and then continue on, past **Beehive Mill**, on the left, with its name carved on a stone, and dating from 1820. One day, all the historic mills in the area may be restored to this standard. Like Brownsfield Mill, it was originally a 'room and power mill' where entrepreneurs with 'one foot on the ladder' could rent space and power from the steam engine. It currently houses a number of organisations working for the conservation of the area, together with a recording studio and *Sankey's Soap*! The large attic, with its iron roof trusses, makes an ideal performance area, and is a venue for a variety of bands and performers from time to time, and takes its name from a (restored) painted advertisement, (probably executed in the 1920s) on the side of the water tower. Beyond the **cross roads**, notice the **former 'British and Foreign Flint Glass Works'** on the right hand side of Jersey Street. Cotton was not the only industry in Ancoats; there was also William Fairbairn's engineering works off Canal Street and the Soho Foundry by the Ashton Canal. However, the way is now to the right, along **Radium Street** (formerly Germany Street, the name being changed in the First World War). We have now reached **Redhill Street** once more.

The old **canal road bridge** can be seen to the left. Note the parallel **horse bridge** leading to the curious **spiral ramp**. This enabled 'dobbin' to cross to the towpath on the opposite bank without entangling the tow rope! It is usually possible to cross the **new footbridge** to the right and walk through this complex to **Old Mill Street**. (However, if this way is blocked by future construction operations, cross the **canal road bridge**, and pass the housing development on **New Union Street**, known locally as the **Dutch houses**, and continue to the right, along **Weybridge Street**, to reach **Old Mill Street**.) The new **perforated iron bridge**, to the right, is a curious affair, for it is actually revealed as two bridges in a 'V' shape, the opposite ends straddling the entrance to the **basin** on the far bank. The **right-hand bridge** communicates with the **right side of the basin** and the **towpath in the Manchester direction**; the **left hand bridge** with the **towpath towards the road bridge and spiral**, together with the **left side of the basin**. Cross the former, and walk up to the **right side** of the basin, past the **boater's facility**, to inspect the **attractive water feature** with its curious little island. Turn left and cross the **pedestrian bridge** to the opposite bank, and continue to the end of the **side basin**. Here there is a good view of the housing development with its distinctive gables, known local as the **'Dutch Houses'**; surely something that Prince Charles would approve of! We retrace our steps and turn left crossing the bridges that span the entrances to two as yet **unexcavated side basins**. However, as the two existing basins are already filling up with canal and small boats, they will doubtless soon be needed. (Children may be interested in the **ducks** and **swans** that have also colonised the area.) The main basin (and the footpath) ends at the point where **Old Mill Street** passes it.

A glance down this reveals once more the **wooden paving** and angular lamp standards, but look out for the traditional brick building. This is the **Ardwick and Ancoats Dispensary**, opened in 1829, though this façade is later. It became Ancoats Hospital, an important institution for this poor district, with a waiting room that Lowry painted. All that is left of the hospital is currently (2014) under threat. We walk to the left, turning right at the crossroads into **Beswick Street** and crossing the **Ashton Canal**. At the end of the street we arrive at **Holt Town Station**.

Holt Town to Etihad Campus

Beyond the station, the line descends into the **valley of the River Medlock**, and passes under **Cambrian Street**, which is carried over track, footpath, and river by means of a **brick viaduct**. The **footpath** is now on the right side of the line and both cross the

A Useful Connection

The Lancashire and Yorkshire Railway had opened a branch from their main line at Miles Platting to Ashton and Stalybridge in 1846. A further branch opened in 1848, connecting with the Stalybridge line by what eventually became a triangular junction at Philips Park. After passing to the east of Ancoats, it then joined the former Manchester and Birmingham (now London and North Western) line by a junction facing London Road (Piccadilly) Station at Ardwick. This line, called the Ardwick Branch or Goods Loop, was primarily used for the exchange of goods traffic between the two systems, particularly transporting ceramics from the Potteries to Hull and Goole for export. However, a second curve from the loop line also accessed the Manchester, Sheffield, and Lincolnshire Railway's main line in an easterly direction at Ashbury's. After the opening of a connection from Gorton through to the Midland Railway's main line, this gave the Lancashire and Yorkshire Railway a through passenger route to the south, though, curiously, not for their trains. Instead, the Midland Railway (who worked in partnership with them) operated through coaches from Blackburn and Bolton to Marple this way, where they were united with the St. Pancras expresses. In the days of British Railways, the Manchester to Harwich Boat Train was routed via the loop line. It is still used (though only to Ashbury's, as the Ardwick connection was removed by Beeching) for freight and the occasional special working. Interestingly enough, a rail interchange station has been proposed here, largely to serve Eastlands. It has also been suggested as a means of running Calder Valley line services into Piccadilly Station (by reinstating the Ardwick curve.)

Etihad Campus?

One might think that a tram operating upon a special football working, and turning back at this station, would have 'Eastlands Stadium' or 'City Stadium' on the destination indicator. Instead, football fans will scratch their heads for a time. Of course, the stadium itself is now officially called 'Etihad Stadium'...so why use the word 'campus'? It all boils down to the fact that Etihad Airways, the, Emirates Airline, involved in a major sponsorship deal with Manchester City Football Club, prefer this designation. The latest project involves the construction of a 7,000 seat stadium, seventeen pitches, and a state of the art sports rehab centre, all within eighty acres of land and catering for over 400 youngsters on the cusp of excellence. This 'Etihad Campus' has been designed and approved as a major development in Eastlands, and as a key cog in the machine that is Manchester City's "quest for global dominance." The project, intended to rival Barcelona's famed La Masia training facility, is currently (2014) under construction. Unfortunately, the actual campus (see p206) is situated on a site opposite Velodrome Station, and that name cannot be altered. In any case, the sponsors wanted the new brand name linked with the main Stadium, thus emphasising the new 'campus' concept. So the whole sporting area has been designated a 'campus' and 'Etihad Campus Station' it is!

Medlock by means of two hundred foot steel beams weighing thirty-two tonnes, before we pass under **New Viaduct Street**. Notice that the line is now spanned by the **Ardwick Goods Loop**. The tram now climbs an extremely **steep incline** to reach **Etihad Campus Station**. The **Ashton Canal** can be glimpsed on the left, with a **gasometer** in the background.

The station itself is situated in a cutting with **staggered platforms** astride **Joe Mercer Way**, which spans it. The station is accessed from the stadium side, where a **holding**

The Commonwealth Games

The 2002 Commonwealth Games were held from 25 July to 4 August. It was, at the time, the largest multi-sport event ever to be held in the UK, eclipsing London's 1948 Olympics in numbers of teams and athletes participating. Manchester had twice attempted to obtain the Olympic Games...much to the scorn and ridicule of members of the Metropolitan elite who ought to have known better. The Commonwealth Games was seen as a kind of consolation prize, but the doomsayers suggested that this was a poisoned chalice. Sheffield had lost considerably in hosting international student games, and it was even suggested that Britain lacked the ability to organise successful international sporting events. But Manchester was determined to succeed. Indeed, after the 1996 IRA bombing, the Games helped form the catalyst for the widespread regeneration and heavy re-development of Manchester. Five-time Olympic champion Sir Steve Redgrave inaugurated the two-and-a-quarter-hour opening ceremony by banging a large drum, which initiated a co-ordinated dance and fireworks act. England football captain David Beckham helped chaperone Queen's Baton final runner Kirsty Howard, assisting the terminally ill six-year-old to hand the baton to the Queen. Everything went like clockwork. Pubs and restaurants in Manchester reported a threefold increase in takings during the Games, and local tourism board Marketing Manchester estimated that some 300,000 more visitors would come to the city each year as a result of its increased profile. It has since been estimated that, by 2008, £600m had been invested in the region as a result of the Games, and that about 20,000 jobs had been created. More to the point, the Games clearly bolstered Manchester's international reputation as a European and Global city. It has since been claimed that the success of the games was a major factor in reassuring the UK's sporting authorities and the government that the country could successfully stage major successful international sporting events and that, without them, London's successful bid for the 2012 Olympics would not have come about.

area, with **gates** and **turnstiles** under a **covered entrance** is situated (there is direct access for ordinary passengers, avoiding the holding area outside of match times). This communicates by **lift, steps,** and **ramps** with a **footpath** parallel to the tracks. This leads in one direction to the **Manchester platform,** which is situated beyond **Joe Mercer Way.** The **City Link footpath,** running back towards Holt Town, is also accessed by this path. Notice that access to and from the **Ashton platform,** placed before **Joe Mercer Way,** is by **pedestrian crossings** at both ends. There is currently no access from the canal side of the station.

Joe Mercer (1914-1990) was, of course, the famous English football player and legendary manager of Manchester City. On the road there are two **mosaics** by renowned Manchester artist Mark Kennedy of Mercer; one shows his smiling face lifting the League Championship trophy; the other is a version of a famous photograph showing the back of him as he looks out over the old Maine Road pitch towards the Kippax Stand.

Eastlands

Eastlands was once a large area of derelict land that once included the former Bradford Road Gasworks (a **gasometer,** converted to storing North Sea Gas, remains in the background) and also Bradford Colliery. The Commonwealth Games organisers were mindful that the resulting infrastructure must provide some kind of legacy long after the games were over. Consequently, the area now hosts the regional base for the English

Institute of Sport (with an academy of excellence, and state of the art sports science and medical unit), benefiting from athletics tracks, indoor athletics hall, the Manchester Regional arena, the National Squash Centre, the Regional Tennis Centre (with indoor tennis courts), the Manchester Velodrome, and the Etihad Stadium.

The view from the **bridge** over the station is rather fine. To the west is a panorama of the **central Manchester skyline**; to the north, the **gasometer**, a relic of the industrial past of the area; to the east, the entrance to the **tram subway**, and the distinctive **Velodrome** in the distance; and to the south, the great **Stadium**. A short walk northwards across the **bridge**, passing over the **Ashton Canal** (steps and ramp down to the **towpath**) leads to the **Tennis Centre** on the left. A right turn then eventually communicates with the **Alan Turing Way** exit. However, the **principal route** lies towards the **stadium** in the opposite direction. Immediately to the right is the **Manchester Regional Squash Centre**, containing the **English Institute of Sport** (employing staff from more than ten disciplines to provide sports science and medicine support to world class athletes in over twenty-five Olympic and Paralympic sports) and the **Sportcity Fitness Centre**. Directly ahead is a building containing the **Manchester City Store** (where all manner of souvenirs may be purchased from the **shop** on the ground floor), with the **Ticket Office** upstairs.

Walk to the right, round the side of the stadium. Originally designed as part of Manchester's failed bid for the 2000 Olympics, the **Etihad Stadium** was built for the 2002 Commonwealth Games at a

Blue Moon Rising

It is widely accepted that Manchester City F.C. was founded as St. Mark's (West Gorton) in 1880 by Anna Connell and two churchwardens of St. Mark's Church, in Gorton, a district in east Manchester. Prior to this, St. Mark's played cricket from 1875 and the side evolved out of that cricket team; the key organiser was Churchwarden William Beastow. In 1887, they moved to a new ground at Bennet Street off Hyde Road in Ardwick, and were renamed Ardwick Association Football Club to reflect their new location. Ardwick joined the Football League as founding members of the Second Division in 1892. Financial troubles in the season led to a reorganisation within the club, and Ardwick were reformed as Manchester City Football Club. With Billy Meredith as Captain, the side was soon promoted to First Division. (Meredith was an early football superstar, who played with a trademark toothpick in his mouth!) A fire at the ground resulted in a move to a new Maine Road Stadium in 1923. (The old ground was purchased by Manchester Corporation Tramways for use as a permanent way yard; it was latterly used as a skid pan for training bus drivers!) After a somewhat chequered history, including relegation and subsequent glory days with Joe Mercer, the club was purchased by Abu Dhabi United Group in 2008, and is now one of the richest in the country. One wonders what those Victorian founders would have thought! The City fans' song of choice is a rendition of "Blue Moon", which despite its melancholic theme is belted out with gusto as though it were a heroic anthem. City supporters tend to believe that unpredictability is an inherent trait of their team, and label unexpected results "typical City".

cost of £110 million. To ensure economic value and avoidance of a white elephant, it was decided that Manchester City would inherit the stadium after the games and it was ultimately converted for football use. The stadium is bowl-shaped, with **two tiers** all the way around the ground and a **third tier** along the two side stands. In February 2004,

The Etihad Stadium
(copyright Manchester 2002 Ltd)

following a vote by fans, the West Stand was renamed the **Colin Bell Stand** in honour of the former player. As of the beginning of the 2010/11 season, it is the fifth largest stadium in the Premier League and the twelfth largest in the United Kingdom, with a seating capacity of 47,726. The **stadium roof** is toroidal in shape, and is suspended from steel cables attached to eight towers, which provide access to the upper tiers of seating via spiral ramps. The areas without seating in each corner have moveable louvres to allow for the ventilation of the pitch. Entry is gained by **smart card** rather than the traditional manned turnstile, and this system can admit up to 1,200 people per minute around all entrances. A **service tunnel** running under the stadium provides access for emergency vehicles, and allows the visiting team's coach to enter the stadium directly. Inside the stadium are six **themed restaurants**, two of which have views of the pitch, and a number of **conference facilities**. It is also licensed for marriage ceremonies. In addition to athletics, the stadium has also hosted the 2008 UEFA Cup Final, England Football Internationals, Rugby League Inter-nationals and numerous **music concerts**. Artist appearing have included U2, Rod Stewart, Bon Jovi, and George Michael. The Club signed an agreement with Manchester City Council in March 2010 to allow a **£1 billion redevelopment** led by architect Rafael Vinoly of land around the stadium and possible stadium expansion to over 60,000. Preliminary work on land around the stadium started the same year, and the Club are exploring alternative **leisure attraction** proposals to replace the abortive 'Supercasino' proposal, which was originally planned to be built in the area. The award-winning **Manchester City Experience** is a tour of the stadium, including the directors' box, corporate lounge, dressing rooms, players' tunnel, press section and dugouts. The Manchester City Experience is available daily, including match days; advance booking is recommended (ring 0161 444 1894 option 4, charge).

Notice the **Memorial to the Games Volunteers,** and the sculpture of the **'Running Man'** to the right, in front of the **National Squash Centre**. Costing approximately £3.5m, the facilities include six courts and one glass-walled show court (this alone cost £110,000). The show court is moveable; it floats on air like a hovercraft and can be positioned in the athletics hall for all major tournaments. All of the courts are 'state of the art', with the ability to convert into either singles or doubles courts at the touch of a button. Next is the **Commonwealth Games Winners Memorial**, with a view to the right of the

Manchester Regional Arena, a multipurpose stadium primarily used for athletics and Association Football. It was originally developed as the warm-up track for the Commonwealth Games, and has since hosted the AAA Championships and Paralympic World Cup. It is the current home of the Manchester City ladies' side. **Citizen's Way**, to the right, leads to **Ashton New Road**. But we continue the **circuit of the stadium**, passing the **Memorial Garden**, followed by the **'Past, Present, and Future'** exhibit. We now arrive at a road junction. **Commonwealth Way**, to the right, leads, past the Visitor Centre (open Mon-Fri; ring bell), to the corner of **Alan Turing Way** and **Ashton New Road**, opposite the **Eastlands-Velodrome Station**. But if you wish, you can continue the walk round the stadium to arrive back at the **shop and museum**, thence to **Etihad Campus Station**.

Etihad Campus to Droylsden

The line now runs through a kind of **concrete canyon** braced by concrete spacers before entering a tram **subway**. This was constructed on the 'cut and cover' principle, passing under **Alan Turing Way,** and. curving to the right, emerges alongside that roadway. Evidence of a medieval moated site, including stone walls and timbers, was unearthed during its construction; they were thought to be the remains of Bradford Old Hall, dating to the 14th century. Notice that the track on the exit ramp includes a **central turn back and holding siding**. This is to accommodate up to four empty trams (or two double units) to cater for the crowds on match days, and at times when other events are held in the stadium. No sooner is the top of the long ramp reached, than the tram turns left, passing over the pedestrian entrance to the large *Asda* supermarket on the corner of **Ashton New Road**.

It then enters **Velopark Station**. The two **platforms** are linked by pedestrian crossings; a path from the **Droylsden platform** leads to the *Asda* entrance and the crossing communicating with the road junction. The **Manchester platform** communicates with **Ashton New Road**.

We can see **Ashton New Road** to the right of the **Manchester platform**, and the hangar-like **supermarket** to the left of the **Droylsden platform**, but where is the

The Baby and the Bomb

Alan Turing (1912-1954) was a tragic genius. As a schoolboy, he was much affected by the death of a close friend, and wondered whether a simulation of the electronic activity of the brain, a kind of 'artificial intelligence', might go some way towards proving the possibility of the survival of human personality. Although he never resolved this question, as a gifted mathematician, he did embrace this concept of 'artificial intelligence' as a research path. In a pre-war paper he conceived the idea of a 'universal machine', a theoretical concept from which modern computing is derived. He was able to put his ideas into practice by constructing 'The Bomb', a code breaking machine based at Bletchley Park during the last war. It enabled the allies to read the German 'Enigma' codes, and was a key factor in the resulting victory. After the war, Turing and his team developed 'The Baby', the first modern programmable computer, at Manchester University. Unfortunately, he began to encounter problems with the authorities relating to his homosexuality. After being pressured into an ill-advised course of hormone treatment, a life of great potential was terminated by suicide (Turing's choice of method of release from his personal agony was an apple laced with cyanide). Such was the reward of a grateful country. Manchester has chosen to honour him by erecting a statue in the 'Gay Village' and naming this new road after him.

Velodrome? Actually, it is well to the rear of *Asda*, beyond the Canal. Vehicular access is from **Gibson Street**, off Alan Turing Way. But never fear! There is **direct access** round the right-hand side of the supermarket, by a **path** from the service road at the end of the platforms, which goes on to cross the Canal by a **new pedestrian bridge** that also accesses the **Ashton Canal** towpath.

The **Velodrome** and the new **National BMX Centre** are directly ahead; there is a **common entrance** to the left, opposite the *cycle shop* on the right. (The complex is usually open daily, 7.30-10.30, and the **public galleries** are usually open, except for some special events ; free admission most days.) Enter the **main concourse**, and enquire at the **information desk** as to what is happening (Details of events, and information about public bookings to use the BMX Centre, may be obtained by ringing 0161 223 2244). There is a useful **café** to the right, but go to the left-hand **door**, and ascend the lift to the **public gallery**. **Manchester Velodrome** is an indoor cycle-racing track, opened in September 1994 (thus predating the Commonwealth Games); it is the leading indoor Olympic-standard track in Britain. The Velodrome houses the National Cycling Centre and British Cycling, hosting the track cycling events in the Games, and the UCI world championships in 1996, 2000 and 2008. The **track** is 250 metres long and its **bankings** reach 42 degrees in the middle (the track is as steep at the top as it is on the 'black' or racing line). In 2007 the Velodrome closed to be re-surfaced with Siberian pine, reopening the same year. There are usually cyclists practicing on the track, but do not fail to notice the **statue of Reg Harris** (1920-1992), the cycling champion from Bury, the **ceramic mural** of 'The Race' by Mark, Kennedy, and the **collection of cycling sporting memorabilia**. Back at the **concourse**, go through the entrance on the opposite side, and ascend the **stairs** leading to the main entrance (labeled 'C') to the **BMX public gallery**. British Cycling and Manchester City Council, in partnership with New East Manchester, worked together to deliver the 110,000 square foot **National Indoor BMX Centre** at Eastlands. With the existing Manchester Velodrome, and improved public spaces, the new £24 million complex forms the **National Cycling Centre**. It includes this 2,000-seater capacity BMX arena, and offices for the headquarters of the British Cycling Federation. Designed by Ellis Williams Architects, the work was carried out by contractors Sir Robert McAlpine. The **surface of the arena** is contoured to reproduce all sorts and conditions of terrain, and on a Saturday morning you may see the children's club in full swing.

Across **Ashton New Road**, is the site of the actual **Etihad Campus** (see p201). Construction was delayed by the removal of contaminated subsoil from a considerable depth. The new training complex is based on AC Milan's training facility, which is understood to be one of top training complexes in world football. The £50m million training facility houses the youth academy (removed from the site in Platt Lane), and thus includes a home for up to four hundred young players who will train and study alongside senior players, with a clear development pathway to the first team. This requires a campus containing one half size and eleven full size youth development pitches; one half size and four full size first team pitches; on site sleeping accommodation and a classroom facility for forty young players to allow them to train and study in a safe and secure environment; a first team facility with changing rooms, gym, refectory and injury and rehab centre; a seven thousand capacity stadium for youth matches; and staff offices together with dedicated media centre. The site is linked with the main Etihad Stadium site by an oblique bridge adjacent to the junction of Alan Turing Way with Ashton New Road.

The track continues alongside Ashton New Road for a short distance and crosses the **Ashton Canal by a new bridge**, parallel to the road bridge. The tram now executes a sharp right turn, and crosses Ashton New Road, to run on to a section of **private right of way** (the area was cleared and businesses re-located to create the alignment). There is a brief sighting of the **canal** to the right, before we curve round to the left and pass over **Croft Street** and **Clayton Lane**, arriving at **Clayton Hall Station**, sited at an angle to **Ashton New Road**.

This stop, in the corner of **Ashton New Road** and **Clayton Lane**, comprises two stepped and ramped **platforms** connected by a **pedestrian crossing** at the east end, with an **inclined approach** linking the **Ashton platform** to **Ashton New Road**. There is also access to **Eccleshall Street**.

We alight here to inspect Clayton Hall. Cross to the other side of Ashton New Road, and have a look at the church of **St. Cross**, a fine Victorian piece of neo gothic. It first appears deceptively plain, but a closer inspection reveals an exterior of **polychromatic (multi-coloured) brickwork**, decorated with brick string coursing, and noted for its pencil like rectangular **tower**. The architect, William Butterfield, thus introduced his partiality for coloured brick design (or 'streaky bacon', as his critics referred to it) to Manchester. Butterfield was the darling of the Tractarian (or 'High Church') party, and the Bishop had trouble with both the interior decoration and the dedication;

St. Cross Church, Clayton

although completed in 1866, it was not consecrated until 1874! The **interior** is simply but finely decorated, and there is a **good reredos** behind the **altar**, incorporating a marble cross and arcading. (The church is usually open on the same days as Clayton Hall.) Next to the church is a **small park**, with a **war memorial** in the corner.

Walk through the park to reach **Clayton Hall**. The Hall is a rare survival, a **moated manor house** dating back to the 15th century. It was the ancestral home of the Byron family (who later numbered the famous "mad, bad, and dangerous to know" Lord Byron among their descendants). Robert Grelley, Lord of the Honour of Manchester, granted Robert de Byron property between 1194 and 1212, to be held by the service of half a knight. Sir John de Byron, a descendent, took part in the battle of Crecy and the siege of Calais. After 1540, Newstead Priory, Nottinghamshire, became the chief seat of the family, and the manor of Clayton, with the Hall and lands in Droylsden and Failsworth, was purchased in 1621by the brothers George and Humphrey Chetham (who were 'nouveau riche' cloth merchants). The celebrated Humphrey Chetham (p52) seems to have lived there for some years, and died unmarried at Clayton Hall on 20 September 1653.

The Hall was entirely surrounded by a **moat**, enclosing an area about two acres, and (hopefully) to be restored to its former aquatic glory. The approach is from the south by a **stone bridge** of two arches across the moat, with a cut-water pier in the centre (notice the angular recesses in the low parapet), and on the side next the house a tall

Clayton Hall, a moated residence

iron **entrance gate** between two well-designed stone piers. The bridge was originally very narrow, but was widened at the beginning of the 19th century, when it assumed its present appearance. The current building is but a fragment of the original house, and consists of a **two-story block of timber construction** to the right, to which has been added a **brick building**, probably of early 18th century date, to the left. There are no traces of the rest of the building, which must have been considerably larger than at present, probably quadrangular, and forming the principal residential part of the house. It is said that the **north-west corner** of the enclosed area was the **site of the chapel**, which was standing till the beginning of the 18th century. (A licence for an oratory dated 1400 probably gives the date of its erection, and fragments of masonry said to belong to it have been discovered from time to time.) Notice the stone **mounting block** (with the date 1686) and the Victorian **horse trough** (now full of plants). On the front of the **surviving timber portion** is a corridor with an overhanging staircase and gable, which appears to be of 17th century date. The façade of the corridor is of timber and plaster on a lower stage of brick, the **gable of the staircase** being filled in with half-timberwork, while on the roof is a **cupola containing a bell**. The **bell** bears the inscription: 'Je atende meleor' ('I anticipate the moment'...of the elevation in the mass?), together with a rose and crown, and is said to be from the old parish church of Manchester before its rebuilding in 1422. This part of the Hall consists of two rooms on each floor, divided by timber partitions which are not at right angles to its outer walls; this may be accounted for by the supposition that the vanished south wing of the building (which contained an arched entrance opposite the bridge), was not set at a right angle to the east wing, and that the divisions followed the lines of those which adjoined it. However, the brick **south wall**, facing the moat with its **central stone chimney**, is at right angles to the outer walls, having superseded a timber end which followed the line of the partitions. The **rear of the present structure** is the most interesting portion of the building, with its projecting wooden bays forming an almost continuous line of **mullioned and transomed windows**. A very thorough restoration of the hall was made in 1900, and it is now owned by Manchester City Council.

The very active 'Friends of Clayton Park' have created a **'Living History Museum'** for both the public and school parties in the Hall, which is open to the public every third Saturday of the Month (Admission free, but donation appreciated.) We enter a **hallway** or **lobby** that terminates in a **staircase**. A door to the right leads to the **dining-room (parlour)** of the 18th century portion. It has a large projecting stone **fireplace**. (The fireplaces in the older part of the house are of stone, but have been rebuilt.) Notice the **original beams forming an over-mantel**. The room has been recreated as a **Victorian Dining Room**. Another lobby door on the right accesses (mind the step!) a **sunken cold store room**, the 19th century equivalent of a refrigerator. The first door on the left is the entrance to the **kitchen** (with real food being prepared on open days). Note the original **roof beam**. The second left-hand door opens into a corridor with useful modern toilets. An ascent of the **stairs** will be rewarded with a glimpse of a **Victorian child's bedroom**, complete with some toys. In addition, the Friends have set up a **Clayton Hall History and Memory Room**. The Hall was supposed to be **haunted** by 'boggarts', the Lancashire name for an annoying kind of poltergeist. It was exorcised by the local clergyman...the charm states that "whilst ivy climbs and holly is green, Clayton Hall's boggart shall no more be seen." There is also the 'White Lady', a daughter of the Byron family who died of unrequited love, and a tradition of the ghost of a small child, burnt to death at some unspecified period. Back in the **lobby**, turn right, past the toilets, and exit the house. We then find ourselves in a **small yard**, where the wash house (complete with possers, dolly tub, and a mangle) is situated. There is also a small **café and shop**.

The tram now swings right into **Ashton New Road**, for the line as far as the Audenshaw, runs mainly **on the street**. Many of the terraced houses that we pass also witnessed the passage of the red and cream doubled decked Manchester Corporation trams, and the blue and cream Ashton Corporation ones, followed by the trolleybuses of both operators after 1938. Now the wheel has turned full circle! Notice the **shopping centre** (with an *Aldi* supermarket) on the right; this marks the site of the former Maynes's bus garage. This private company introduced a bus service between a part of Droylsden not served by the trams and Manchester city centre in the 1920s, and remained the only private timetabled bus service within Manchester for many years (despite repeated attempts by the municipality to buy them out). Oddly enough, the brave new world of bus deregulation did not suit them, though they remain as a charter company. The line passes the **Tameside boundary**. (This was once marked by six 'gateway flags', signifying the road number, local legends, crafts, and geographical features! Perhaps they will return at a future date.), The tracks cross **Edge Lane**, and enters the station.

The road here divides and **Edge Lane Station** is placed between the outward and inward lanes, the central **island platform** being accessed by **ramps** linked to **pedestrian crossings** from both sides. A small **car park** (with some **disabled parking places, bicycle storage**, and a **taxi rank**, is situated to the left, beyond the Ashton bound lane. (It is mainly intended as a dropping off and picking up point, termed 'kiss and ride' by transport planners!)

The tram then briefly resumes **street running** along what is now **Manchester Road**. Notice that the outward **track runs for a short distance alongside the pavement** just before the station, in order to create a 'waiting pocket' for traffic turning into **Martins Way**.

We now turn right into **Cemetery Road Station** (the road itself is on the left and leads to **Droylsden Cemetery**). The station has the usual **double platform arrangement**, with **steps, ramps** and a **pedestrian crossing** at each end, communicating with both **Manchester Road** and **Kershaw Street**.

Passengers should alight here for a **short excursion to Fairfield Moravian Settlement**. Walk along **Manchester Road** in the Ashton direction a short distance to the Victorian **police station** (with the inscription 'County Constabulary-Station' on the façade), noticing the next door shop which sells nothing but pigeon corn! Notice the memorial on the wall of the Droylsden Sports and Social Club opposite. It is derived from an earlier building, and commemorates the men of the township who "assisted H.M. Forces in the South African War 1899-1902." One was killed at Spion Kop, a battle in which many Lancashire lads lost their lives through the incompetence of their generals. The police station is situated on the corner of **Mellor Street**, which should be followed beyond the left turn where it becomes **Maddison Road**. The latter terminates in a **turning circle**. Look out for the **sign posted footpath** directly ahead. It **forks** to the right and passes a **lock keeper's cottage**, now used as a **'Water Adventure Centre'** (children can sometimes be seen bobbing about in kayaks on the canal.) The path crosses the **Ashton Canal** by a humped **stone bridge**, from which there is a view of the **lock** and its associated basin. Continue into **Wood Square**, and the large **children's play area** in the middle of a housing estate. Take the **path** through the middle of the **grassed area**, which, in turn, leads to a **path** accessing **Fairfield Road**. Cross the road to the **cobbled way** opposite. There is a charming **garden** to the left, with a recent **statue** (2009) of a Moravian Sister with a schoolboy and his books. Notice also the

The First Protestants

The Moravian Church or *Herrnhuter Brüdergemeine* is an evangelical Protestant denomination. Its religious heritage began in 1457 in Kunvald, Bohemia (modern Czech Republic), and its official name is *Unitas Fratrum*, meaning 'Unity of the Brethren'. Moravians place a high premium on Christian unity, personal piety, missions, and music. The church's emblem is the Lamb of God, with the flag of victory, surrounded by the Latin inscription: *Vicit agnus noster, eum sequamur* (or in English: "Our Lamb has conquered, let us follow Him"). The movement that was to become the Moravian Church was started by Jan Hus in the late 14th century. Hus objected to some of the practices of the Church and wanted to return it in Bohemia and Moravia to what had been common in these territories when they had been Orthodox; liturgy in the language of the people; having lay people receive communion in both kinds (bread and wine); married priests; and eliminating what he considered superstitious ideas, such as indulgences and the idea of purgatory. He was also greatly influenced by John Wyclif, the English religious reformer. Jan Hus can be said to have adopted a doctrine of justification by grace through faith alone; in doing so, the Moravians arguably became the first Protestant church. There was a great revival in the 18th century, and Moravian missions went to several European countries and the American colonies. A community settled here in Droylsden in 1785, in what was then open country. They were much respected in England, and it is said that John Wesley was greatly inspired by the Moravian church. The most famous Moravian is perhaps John Amos Comenius (1592-1670), the great Czech philosopher and educational pioneer.

(reproduction) Victorian **post box**. Directly ahead is **The Square**, forming the **main east-west axis of the settlement**.

A religious community still exists, and everyone is welcome to services in the church. (Guided tours of the settlement and church buildings are available; ring 0161 370 5199. The museum is open Saturday 1-4, May to August: admission charge.) The **residential area**, with its wide cobbled streets, 18th century houses, and mature trees, is a nice place to live. It was a feature of Moravian settlement life in the eighteenth and early nineteenth centuries that members were grouped into three choirs (i.e. communities): married; single brothers; and single sisters. The single brethren would occupy shared accommodation and also work together within the settlement as would the single sisters in their house. However, sons and daughters could choose to live with their parents.

In the Moravian Settlement (Graham Beech)

Walk to the left down **The Square**, and pause in front of the larger house with the **blue plaque**. This was briefly the home of Charles Hindley (1796-1857), a member of the community who achieved both local and national significance. He was the son of a Moravian family who owned a cotton mill, and was active in social reform (serving as Liberal MP for Ashton from 1835 until his death in 1857). He supported the Chartist movement and the reduction of working hours. In late November 1857 he fell ill and his doctor, Robert Bentley Todd, prescribed "six pints of brandy to be drunk in 72 hours" as a cure. The patient consequently died. Doctor Todd also died through an excess of alcohol some three years later! Turn down the street to the right to reach the main **pedestrian terrace**, which forms a symmetrical frontage of the **Church**, flanked by a **High School** and a **College**. In the 18th century, the **Church** was called the 'hall'. It was small rectangular barn-like building, on a north-south axis, unlit and unheated. Hard benches surrounded a pulpit and communion table in the centre of the north wall. The sisters sat on the east side of the hall, near their House, and the brethren on the west side, next to theirs. When the Married group came to church, the men sat with the single brethren and the women with the sisters. This practice continued until late in the 19th century. On the wall opposite the pulpit, there was a gallery with an organ in it; and a musical choir assembled there to sing the responses in the liturgy. The church was extended to the west in 1908, and the interior re-modeled to produce the current east-west axis, with larger windows to create more light. The building has a fine **cupola** as a bell tower (it housed musicians and a small choir on Easter morning). If you are facing the front of the **Church**, walk to the right to reach the **College**, situated beyond the street. This was originally the **Single Sisters House**, but they were moved out to reside in the pleasant Georgian house on the opposite corner, to the right of the Church. Here they passed some of their time making beautiful lace which was sold outside the community. They were replaced by the Moravian Theological College, which moved here from Fulneck in Yorkshire in 1875. When the College shut in 1958, the future of the building was in doubt, but it has been restored for use as a community centre and Sunday school. It contains a very interesting **museum**, with **relics** of the settlement and examples of Moravian Brethren **costume**. There is a large **three-storey building** to the left of the **Church**. This started life as the **Single Brethrens House** (for men), but became a boy's boarding school in the 19th century. The boy's school became a girl's school in 1891, and is now part of Fairfield High School and College. The other side of the terrace is occupied by a **burial ground** known as 'God's Acre', surrounded by quickset **hedges**. The congregation provided small **uniform gravestones** which lay flat on the earth, bearing only the name and age of the departed. This was an expression of the equality of brothers and sisters. Initially, the two sexes were buried separately in a post mortem continuation of the group system. In the female section, for example, SS carved on a stone means 'single sister', and MS 'married sister'. The **sundial** in the graveyard bears the motto, 'I die today, I live tomorrow'. Mourning was not encouraged and corpses were led to the grave by a choir of brass instruments as well as the Minister. At a sunrise service on Easter Sunday the congregation would meet in 'God's Acre' to rejoice in the Resurrection. This remains the custom of the Moravian Church. You can, if you wish, return to the tram route by following **Fairfield Road** to the right, crossing the Canal, and continuing along **Market Street** to the centre of Droylsden.

It is now just a short ride further down **Manchester Road** to reach Droylden, passing the **police station** on the right, and the **memorial** opposite (p210). A large *Tesco* supermarket is to the left, and, opposite, the squat brick **Droylsden Library**, a nice building with Art Deco features and a 1937 date stone. Notice that the pavement beyond the library is carried over the **Hollinwood Branch Canal** (see p213), alongside the **road bridge**, by a new **pedestrian bridge**. The road opens out into **Villemoble Square** (named after the place with which Droylsden is 'twinned') at the centre of the town. Notice the claret painted **clock tower**, with the legend 'Our Town – Droylsden'.

A little beyond the **crossroads**, we finally reach **Droylsden Station**. It is situated in the middle of **Ashton Road**, and comprises an **island platform** that is curiously partly staggered at both ends. There is a **ramp** at the Manchester end and **steps** at the Ashton end; both access either side of the roadway by **pedestrian crossings**.

Droylsden grew as a mill town around the cotton mills established in the mid-19th- century, and the Ashton and other canal links. Beginning in the early 1930s, Droylsden's population expanded rapidly, as it became a housing overflow area for neighbouring Manchester.

Droylsden Clock

Droylsden Wakes

In the 19th century, Droylsden was associated in the popular mind with its famous 'Wakes'. The old Lancashire wakes custom (a survival of medieval ritual and festival celebrations, usually upon the local saint's day) was imported to Greenside in Droylsden in about 1814 from Woodhouses across the Medlock Valley, where it had been associated with rush-cart celebrations for about thirty years.

It's Droylsden Wakes, an' we're comin' to town,
To tell you of sommat of great renown;
An' if this owd jade'll let me begin,
Aw'll show you how hard an' how fast Aw can spin,
So it's three-dy-well, three-dy-well, dan dum dill doe,
So it's three-dy-well, three-dy-well, dan dum dill doe.

Two men would perform a comical play (of which this song was a part) in fancy dress; one would be dressed as a woman. They rode in a ceremonious manner on top of a rush cart, and each would be spinning flax on a wheel. Both would sing the verses alternately, showing the progress and amicable winding up of a domestic dispute, and demonstrating their relative skills. The word "threedywheel" may mean either 'tread the wheel' or 'thread ye wheel'. The chorus line was only repeated twice much later in the 19th century. By then, the tradition of 'Wakes Weeks' had merely become a fixed holiday in most towns, when the mills and factories closed, and everyone who could afford it went off to Blackpool! Droylsden was popularly referred to by Mancunians as "The Silly Country". One suggestion as to the source of that nickname is that some of the town's folk used to watch the annual Wakes celebrations by bringing a pig and sitting it on a wall to watch the passing entertainment with them. The Pig on the Wall pub in Greenside Lane, converted from a farm in 1978, takes its name from that story.

The centre of the town is distinguished by a **crossroads**, where the main road is intersected by **Market Street**, and dominated by a new **shopping centre**, though the old **Co-operative building**, opposite, is worth a glance. **Market Street** (particularly the south side) retains something of the old spirit of the place, with traditional shops and cafés. However, the most significant recent development is that of the adjacent **marina**, opened in September 2008. Situated on the **Hollinwood Branch Canal**, a short distance from the **Ashton Canal**, and visible behind the library, this is a £100 Million redevelopment scheme that will eventually have 92 three and four bedroom houses, and 291 one and two bedroom apartments, as well as waterside offices, restaurants, and shops. About 190 yards (175m) of canal from the junction with the Ashton Canal have been refurbished, and new **waterside facilities** for boaters are available near Lock 18. The original plans would have blocked further restoration of the canal, but were changed after representations were made by the Hollinwood Canal Society, and the canal will now pass under a building which will span the route. Eventually, it is hoped that the Canal will reopen through **Daisy Nook Country Park** (owned by the National Trust) and **linked to the Rochdale Canal**. The **marina** itself is already popular as a **mooring site** with leisure boaters. The **Droylsden Little Theatre** is situated in a former Methodist chapel, located on **Castle Close**, a five minute walk along the northern part of **Market Street** (turn left down **Hart Street** and right along **High Street**). The dramatic society has a history dating to 1929, but the present facilities are very much up to date! The society produce about six plays a year, and have an excellent reputation (ring 0161 370 7713 for further information).

Droylsden became a separate Parish in 1844. **St. Mary's** was erected at a cost of £3500, and consecrated in1848 by James Prince Lee, the newly appointed first Bishop of Manchester. (Ring 0161 370 1569 to arrange a visit.) The **stone wall** that surrounds the Church and grounds was erected in 1857 to celebrate the end of the Crimean War. Enter the Church by the **Southwest door** (the red door) into the **outer porch** which was the former Baptistery, indicated by the **Dove window** above the inner porch door. To the immediate left is a **blue plaque** commemorating a former Rector of the church, the Revd A. H. Procter who was awarded the Victoria Cross in the First World War. Below is the **stone cross**, which fell from the eastern end of the church during a severe storm. Enter the main body of the church (the **Nave**). The **carved head** on the left side (north) below the **chancel arch** represents Archbishop Cranmer; the **matching head** on the right side (south) represents Bishop Ridley, both martyred for their Protestant beliefs in the 1500s. (Perhaps they were intended as a warning to the then current 'High Church' faction.) The **reredos** below is in memory of Maurice Livingston, a Lancashire Fusiliers officer who was killed in France a week before the armistice. It depicts the final hours of Christ in the Garden of Gethsemane. "I prayed my cup might pass." The **panels** each side of the communion rail record the names of those parishioners who gave their lives in the Great War of 1914-1918; a memorial for World War two has been added. The **stained glass** repays inspection. The stained window on the south side of the chancel is in memory of Joseph Hadwen, a great benefactor of both church and school. One of his donations in 1857 was to purchase the instruments for St Mary's Church Sunday school brass band, later to become Droylsden reed band. The magnificent **Lectern** has a much travelled history. It was first placed in St John's Church, Byrom Street, Manchester in 1878 by Edward Byrom in memory of his granddaughter Eleanora Atherton. In 1928 it was removed to St Matthew's church, Liverpool Road, Manchester. When this church closed in 1942 the Lectern was presented to St Mary's; the Eagle has flown about quite a bit! The **Font** is an exact copy of a very ancient Font dated from 1400 in All Saints church Leicester.

Droylsden to Ashton-under-Lyne

Upon departing Droylsden station, notice the **facing crossover** leading to the **'trambahn'** on the right. This is a white concrete apron in the 'up' line, isolated from the incoming traffic by a curb, and affording a refuge to reversing trams while the driver changes ends. We resume street running along **Ashton Road**, passing the recently refurbished 19th century *Moss Tavern* on the left. After **Williamson Lane**, the name changes to **Droylsden Road**. Notice that both tracks have been slewed over to the left, with the down or Ashton line hugging the pavement. This is to allow the up or Manchester line to become a **'tram only lane'**, with space for the ordinary inward traffic beyond it. Indeed, enough space to create a **special lane** to permit inward traffic to queue for a right turn into **Kershaw Lane**. Look out for the **blue plaque** on number 122, on one of the terraces to the right (opposite the end of the row of bungalows). It commemorates John Henry Code (1869-1934) Up until 1910, the family lived here; John was employed as a carpenter for Clayton Gas Works He enlisted in the 5th (Ardwick) Volunteer Battalion, Manchester Regiment in1886, and had risen to the rank of Colour Sergeant by 1902 In September 1914, despite his age, he accompanied what had become the Eighth (Ardwick) Battalion to Egypt and participated in the bloody Gallipoli campaign. As Regimental Quartermaster Sergeant he was a constant inspiration to his comrades, and his work at Gallipoli gained him the Distinguished Conduct Medal.

Audenshaw Station is situated just before the former point of junction of **Droylsden Road** and **Manchester Road**, but with the addition of **Lumb Lane**, it is actually on the northern edge of a large **gyratory traffic system**. The track swings across **two turn-offs** from **Lumb Lane**, accessing **Droylsden Road** in each direction from the south (the first one also continuing **Lumb Lane** northwards), before arriving at an **island platform**. The **ramped island platform** is connected by **pedestrian crossings** to the pavement on the south side of **Droylsden Road**. There are **pedestrian crossings** all over the place, and great care should be exercised in crossing these busy roads.

The name Audenshaw is a corruption of its earlier name Aldwinshagh which derives from Aldwin, a Saxon personal name, combined with the Old English suffix *shagh* meaning woodland. (The famous local rugby team are called the 'Old Aldwinians'!) The Nico Ditch, an early medieval linear earthwork runs through the area (p219). Audenshaw's urbanisation and expansion largely coincided with developments in textile manufacture during the industrial revolution and the Victorian era. In the 1870s, many of Audenshaw's inhabitants were employed in hat-making, cotton-spinning, calico-printing, and silk-weaving. In 1894 this area became Audenshaw Urban District in the poor law union of Ashton-under-Lyne. In 1974 it became part of the Metropolitan Borough of Tameside. It was the birthplace of Frank Hampson (1918-85), the creator of Dan Dare (and Digby and the Mekon!) in the 'Eagle' comic.

Ryecroft Hall is situated to the south of the station across Manchester Road. If you have time to spare walk past the original **stone lodge** and have a wander around the pretty **grounds**, admiring the exterior of one of the best preserved cotton baron's mansions in the Manchester area. The large 'L' shaped house is of two storeys (plus attic) and built of ashlar with a slate roof. It hides an asymmetrical former **carriage house**, built in the 'Tudor-Gothic' style, behind it. The eastern and entrance fronts feature both

Ryecroft Hall

bay windows and pretty oriels; the transomed windows are covered with hood moulds. The main entrance porch has enriched doors beneath a Tudor style arch, diagonal buttresses, and a pierced parapet. Much of the fine interior has survived, particularly the great hall, with its traceried plasterwork and central octagonal gallery with a lantern over it. Many of the rooms still have the original wood paneling and very ornate ceilings. Nowadays, the Hall is available for a variety of functions, including weddings (some Coronation Street stars have held their wedding receptions here!) A small café (currently open Tuesday and Thursday, 12-4) can be frequented. The Hall does have 'open days' from time to time (ring 0161 370 4351 for information about room booking etc.).

A Fine Mansion

Ryecroft Hall is built on land purchased from the Earl of Stamford and Warrington in 1849 by James Smith Buckley. Buckley and his brother were cotton manufacturers, owning Ryecroft and Oxford Road Mills near St Peter's Church in Ashton. Although the Hall took several years to build, it contained all the necessary comforts of a Victorian gentleman, including a library, a large dining room, study, billiard room, and a ball room, as well as sitting rooms, bedrooms, and servant's quarters. James Buckley died in 1851 with the hall still unfinished, and it passed through the family until, in the 1880s, it came into the hands of Abel Buckley, a Liberal MP and a Mayor of Ashton. He lived at Ryecroft Hall for twenty-two years and was an extremely rich man, having interests in collieries, hotels, and banks as well as retaining interests in cotton mills, the mainspring of his wealth. As a devout Congregationalist, he gave large amounts of money for the building of the Albion Chapel in Ashton (making sure that his chapel was taller than the nearby Parish church!). Abel was also an art collector; he owned a Turner, a Gainsborough, and a Reynolds. In 1908, Abel died and the Hall was owned by his sons until February 1913, when it was sold to Austin Hopkinson. The new owner was another rich man, this time making his money from engineering. He built the Delta works in Audenshaw to produce coal cutting machinery which he had invented and developed. Austin served as a local Councillor and was MP for the area from 1918 until 1945 (with just one short break). He was a generous man and was very innovative and liberal in dealing with his work force at the Delta works. During the First World War, the Hall became a Red Cross hospital, and in 1922, Austin gave the house and grounds to Audenshaw. The Hall served as the administrative and social centre for the Urban District until the formation of Tameside MBC in 1974. The Hall has the reputation of being haunted.

There are two **blue plaques** at the Hall. One is to Austin Hopkinson (see above) and the other commemorates Harry Schofield (1865-1931). Schofield was involved in a dramatic action in the Boer War for which he was awarded the Victoria Cross. He originated from Audenshaw, the son of a chemist who had a store on Ashton New Road, Clayton. The young Schofield went to the Royal Military Academy at Woolwich and in 1899 he was sent to South Africa as Aide-de-Camp to General Buller, who commanded the forces of Ladysmith which was under siege by the Boers. Some batteries were rather stupidly placed in the open a thousand yards from the enemy. Boer rifle fire rained down on them and soon many of the drivers and teams serving the guns had been killed or wounded. Captain Schofield rallied a number of men, limbered up two teams and gave the order to gallop towards the guns. The Boers opened fire on them again, but after several attempts they managed to limber up two of the guns belonging to the 66th Battery and saved them from capture. During this action a total of six bullets passed through Captain Schofield's clothes.

The tram crosses the eastern part of the gyratory system, a **roadway** connecting **Droylsden Road** and **Manchester Road**, followed by a crossing of **Assheton Avenue**. At a short section of **central reservation**, look to the right to pick out a building currently (2014) sporting a *Novem* sign (opposite *Wheelchair Centre*). This computer business currently occupies the **former street level booking hall of Audenshaw Railway Station**. (The **cottage** to the right was utilised as the stationmaster's house.) The station opened in 1882 on a London and North Western Railway branch that ran from the long-vanished Droylsden Station (on the still existing Ashton line) to Denton

216

junction; it passed over the road by a bridge at this point, and there are traces of the embankment behind the building. There is an apocryphal story that the Manchester Racecourse, threatened by the proposed Ship Canal, might have been relocated to a site adjacent to the *Snipe* (but see below), and the railway were hedging their bets! The service operated from Manchester to Stockport via Audenshaw and Denton, but was little used, for local people preferred Hooley Hill Station on the London and North Western line from Stockport to Stalybridge. The station closed as long ago as 1905, and it is amazing that the building has survived! (The line itself was used by troop trains in World War Two, and some older residents can remember as children waving at the soldiers, and being thrown candy and gum from American G.I.'s. The line finally closed in 1968.) **F. & S. Scale Models** opposite, can be recommended (open daily except last Sunday of the month).

The track now swings to the left across the start of **Manchester Road**, to run on the left-hand side of that highway. Beyond the **Gainsboro Road** crossing, we curve to the left, passing to the back of the *Snipe*. The rear of the building incorporates part of the toll bar that stood here on the Manchester to Mottram turnpike, converted to a hostelry in 1814 (and boasting of its fruit trees). Betty Berry kept it in 1849, and an 1854 advert boasts of a 'Bowling Green, and Pleasure Gardens' (complete with a dancing stage and quadrille band). Foot races were run in the 19th century, and a cinder race track opened in 1913, taking the former extensive bowling green and garden 'Audenshaw Race Course' was used for trotting and athletics, becoming a noted speedway venue before closure in 1936. The present structure probably dates from the late 19th century; with the coming of Metrolink it has been refurbished, along with the beer garden (which we pass). The pub gave its name to a colliery that once stood across Manchester Road. It was officially called Ashton Moss, but locals (and the workforce) always called it 'Snipe

The Snipe pub

Colliery'. The first shaft was sunk in1875, and a second (reputed to be the deepest in the world at the time) in 1882; the colliery was linked to the LNWR railway and the canal. It experienced a long-drawn death between 1959 and 1968. Nothing remains. The way now lies alongside **Lord Sheldon Way**, which can be seen on the right.

Lord Sheldon Way is a new road, intended to act both as a by-pass and alternative access to the town centre. It is graced with a number of **statues** along its left-hand side, intended to represent the pastimes of Ashton citizens. They were created by Chris Butler, and unveiled on 26 November, 2008; their positions are noted in the text for those passengers (particularly children) who may be inclined to 'spot' them. We pass the *Travelodge Hotel* and the *Sheldon Arms*, the latter a modern pub rather tastefully designed in brick. **Nexus House** is opposite, across the road, one of the newest buildings to come into use by Greater Manchester Police, and home to many of the Force's specialist units. The tram crosses an **access road** to the *Ashton Park Garden Centre* before running past it on the left. Opened in 2007, it is the newest of all the Notcutts Garden Centres.

Ashton Park boasts a large outdoor plant area, with a year round selection of top quality plants. A large range of gardening accessories will be found indoors, together with wild bird care items, a pet centre, a selection of suitable gifts, and a convenient cafeteria. Beyond a path leading to **Rayner Lane** we now arrive at **Ashton Moss Station.**

There is a centre **ramped island platform**, accessed by **pedestrian crossings** at the Manchester end (utilising the existing path) and at the Ashton end, the latter accessing both **Lord Sheldon Way** and (by a footpath) **Alexandria Drive**. There is a small **reservoir or pond** (not visible from this point) to the left of the station.

The track crosses **Alexandria Drive** and swings out to the right at its junction with **Lord Sheldon Way**, entering a **central reservation**. This is called in transport terms a 'median strip', and is maintained for most of the way to Ashton. Note the **statue of a parent and child**, seemingly engaged in shopping, near the bus stop. A **large warehouse** belonging to *Office Depot* is opposite, on the right. Another statue, this time a **cyclist**, is situated at the start of a **curve to the right**. It is followed by a **female runner**. The road and the tramway now cross over the **M60 Motorway**. AMEC and Alfred McAlpine Joint Venture started construction in 1996 (the tender price for the contract was £101.9 million), but progress was not completely smooth. It was found that the peat extended to a depth of about fifteen feet in places, and the contract was extended by thirty seven weeks. Work was completed in 2000. Before being opened for traffic, it was used as a film location for Granada TVs medical drama, 'Always and Everyone'. A Trident aircraft was transported to the site to create a scene of an air crash. Towards the close of the first era of tramways in this country, traffic islands were introduced. Drivers had to get used to the fact that trams were sometimes routed right through the middle of them! Here history repeats itself. The line curves to the left to pass through the **middle of a traffic island**, at a point where access roads to the **Ashton Moss Leisure Development** join **Lord Sheldon Way**. Note the **statue of a trumpeter** to the left (a reference to Ashton's brass band tradition) and a first sight of the **radio masts** looming behind. The Ashton Moss transmitting stations are two independent facilities for medium wave broadcasting; they are approx-imately ¾ mile (1.28km) apart. The stations were constructed and owned by the BBC and IBA for the use of local radio stations. Over time, (1974-2007), by a series of asset sell offs, and mergers, both sites are now owned and operated by *Arqiva*. There is a **statue of a sweeper**, together with a **cricketer** (hobbies and handicrafts? do-it-yourself?) at the point where the line curves to enter **Ashton West Station**.

There are two **platforms**, with **ramps** and **steps**, together with **pedestrian crossings** at both ends. However, the Ashton end of the station is linked by similar **crossings** across **Lord Sheldon Way** with the **leisure park** on one side, and with both sides of **Richmond Street** on the other.

Lord Sheldon

Robert Edward Sheldon, Baron Sheldon, PC (born 13 September 1923) was educated at Burnley Grammar School, various technical colleges, and the University of London. He combined the directorship of a textile firm with a political life in the Labour Party, firstly as Manchester City Councillor and then as Member of Parliament for Ashton under Lyne (being elected at the 1964 general election), serving until the 2001 general election.. He served on the Public Accounts Committee 1965-1966, later holding its chairmanship 1983-1997, and was also Financial Secretary to the Treasury 1975-1979. Upon retiring from the House of Commons, he was created a life peer as 'Baron Sheldon of Ashton-under-Lyne in the County of Greater Manchester'.

This station is destined to be one of the busiest on the line, for it serves the **leisure park** section of *Ashton Moss*, a leisure, commerce, and industrial park development. The leisure park element features a *Cineworld* cinema and a *Hollywood Bowl* bowling alley. Places to eat and drink include the *Eat Inn Chinese Buffet*, *Nando's*, *Frankie and Benny's*, *KFC*, *Chiquito*, and a *Harvester* pub. In addition, there is the *Village Hotel* (120 rooms, swimming pool, and restaurant), and (behind the leisure park) a *Sainsbury's* supermarket. As the tram departs, notice a **footballer statue** to the left, before crossing Richmond Street. Immediately after, look out for the

"They also serve..."

Ashton Moss

Lancashire was once famous for vast tracts of peat bog. Chat Moss is the most famous, spanned by George Stephenson's railway, and Lindow Moss is celebrated for its Iron Age bog figure. Ashton Moss, formerly much more extensive, is less well known. In the middle Ages, it was virtually impenetrable, as it had been for centuries before. Indeed, it was the starting point of the Nico Ditch, a medieval earthwork that ran six miles westwards to just east of Stretford. According to legend, it was completed in a single night by the inhabitants of Manchester, as a protection against Viking invaders in 869-870, and that it was the site of a bloody battle between Saxons and Danes (Gorton and Reddish are supposedly derived from "Gore Town" and "Red-Ditch"). Despite the legend, the U-shape of the ditch (as opposed to the usual V-shape of military earthworks) and the absence of an associated bank indicated that Nico Ditch was probably a boundary marker. The best preserved sections are probably at Platt Fields, Manchester, and Denton. Evidence of prehistoric activity in the area comes from Ashton. A single Mesolithic flint tool was discovered in the bog, along with a collection of nine Neolithic flints. There was further activity in or around the bog in the

Ashton Moss

Bronze Age. In about 1911, an adult male skull was found in the moss; it was thought to belong to the Romano-British period (similar to the Lindow Man bog body) until Radiocarbon dating revealed that it dated from 1,320-970 BC. Consequently it predates the era of bog 'sacrifices' and the local 'cult of the head', though there is still some dispute about that. This area of low lying, deep, peaty bog was drained in the mid 1800s to grow some of the best crops. It was world famous for its celery, but also grew good cabbage, cauliflowers, and lettuce, with cucumbers and tomatoes grown in glasshouses. The ground was apparently fertilised by marl dug from local banks or pits, and by dung brought by horse and cart from the elephant and tiger enclosures at Belle-Vue Zoo, down the road. The Moss is also where Bill Sowerbutts, of Gardener's Question Time fame, learnt his trade. Nowadays all that is left of the Moss is a large tract of land glimpsed to the left of the line.

bridge parapets, indicating that we are crossing a railway line (which is not visible from the tram, see information box below).

The descent from the bridge reveals a large **Sainsbury's supermarket** to the left, and a fine view of the Ashton skyline to the right; the towers of **St. Peter's** and **St. Michael's** churches are prominent, together with the tower-like chimney of the former baths. The great rectangle of blue and yellow, directly ahead, is the *IKEA store*. *IKEA* is a privately owned international home products company that designs and sells ready-to-assemble furniture such as beds and desks, appliances and home accessories. The company is the world's largest furniture retailer, and was founded in 1943 by 17-year-old Ingvar Kamprad in Sweden; it is named as an acronym of the initials of the founder's name (Ingvar Kamprad), the farm where he grew up (Elmtaryd), and his hometown

The Joint Line

The Oldham, Ashton and Guide Bridge Junction Railway connected Oldham and Ashton with Guide Bridge (and thus the Manchester, Sheffield, and Lincolnshire Railway). In 1856, a deputation from Oldham and Ashton project approached the MS&LR for its support for the line. Initially, the MS&LR had hoped that the other lines would support the scheme, but they showed little interest, and the board members had to put up the initial finance privately. Once incorporated in 1857, the MS&LR prevailed upon the London and North Western Railway to join in, making a junction at the south end, thus creating a through route from Oldham and Ashton to Stockport. The Oldham and Ashton railway was eventually leased to the MS&LR and the LNWR, becoming a joint line from 30 June 1862. The section between Guide Bridge and Oldham (together with the junction with the Lancashire and Yorkshire Railway there) was completed in March 1860. On 26 August 1861, the first MS&LR trains ran from London Road through Guide Bridge to the line's new Clegg Street Station in Oldham. Beyond this point, the joint railway connected end-on with the LNWR near Oldham Glodwick Road (see p124) and later with the L and Y extension to Rochdale (p124). The Manchester, Sheffield and Lincolnshire Railway became the Great Central Railway (GCR) on 1 August 1897; as a consequence, the Great Central & London & North Western Joint Committee was set up in 1905, to administer various undertakings jointly owned by those two railways, including the OA&GB. Services on the line ran between Rochdale, Oldham, Ashton, Guide Bridge, and Stockport, including a through coach from these towns to London Euston! The passenger services finally succumbed to the competition from road transport and were withdrawn in May 1959. When the parcels depot at Oldham Clegg Street closed, the section between Oldham and Ashton was closed completely in 1967. The remainder of the original railway route, leading to Reddish and Stockport, remains open for freight, though the connection to Guide Bridge has been severed. Interestingly enough, some steam-hauled excursions are routed this way from time to time.

(Agunnaryd, in Småland, South Sweden). Many people travel to Ashton just to shop at this IKEA branch, and, like other branches, it has a restaurant. The line swings to the right to cross the inbound lane to access a **side reservation** on the right hand side of the road. The **traffic island** on the left, in front of *IKEA*, marks the end of **Lord Sheldon Way**. The line crosses the end of **Portland Street**, prior to it curving to the right and crossing the end of **Cavendish Street**. The way now lies alongside **Wellington Street**, an improved extension of the previous road. *IKEA* is on the left, and an *Aldi supermarket* on the right, before the junction with **Oldham Road** is crossed and the tram enters **Ashton-under-Lyne Station**, the terminus.

The station consists of a **central island platform**, with ramps at each end communicating with **footpaths**. (Passengers will note that trams can arrive and depart at either platform facing by means of a crossovers situated on the station approach.) The ramp at the Manchester end accesses **pedestrian crossings**, one over the northern track exiting at **Wellington Street** and the other over the southern line to **Oldham Road**. The large **paved area at the terminal end of the station** accesses the large **bus station**, which is immediately to the right.

A glance along **Wellington Street** will be rewarded with a glimpse of the **railway station** in the distance. This was opened by the Lancashire and Yorkshire Railway in 1846, and is currently used by trains that serve Manchester Victoria, Stalybridge, and Huddersfield. However, this railway is not the only one passing through Ashton, for the original Manchester, Sheffield and Lincolnshire Railway branch from Guide Bridge to Stalybridge still survives. This line is now used by the Trans-Pennine expresses to and from Leeds, York, and Newcastle, but no-one has thought fit to reopen Ashton (Park Parade) station so that they can stop! **Stalybridge Station** hosts the famous independent **buffet bar**, with its real ales, folk music, and other good things. However, visitors should walk through the bus station which leads to the *Arcades Shopping Centre*. A further stroll through this shopping mall leads to the **Market Place**.

Ashton-under-Lyne

Ashton-under-Lyne once formed a parish and township centred on Ashton Old Hall which was held by the de Asshetons, the Lords of the Manor. The origin of the name is a mystery, but some have suggested that the 'lyne' in question was the great fence surrounding the Royal Forest, high on the Pennine moors. Ashton Old Hall was the administrative centre of the manor; with three wings; it was "one of the finest great houses in the North West," and "a building of great antiquity," and one of the few halls influenced by French design in the country...if only it still existed! Granted a Royal Charter in 1414, the manor spanned a broad rural area consisting of marshland, moorland, and a number of villages and hamlets. It later descended to the Booth family, Earls of Stamford (p263) Until the introduction of the cotton trade in 1769, Ashton was considered "bare, wet, and almost worthless," but the industrial revolution, triggered a process of unplanned urbanisation in the area, and by the mid-19th century Ashton had emerged as an important mill town at a convergence of newly constructed canals and railways. Ashton-under-Lyne's transport network allowed for an economic boom in spinning, weaving, and coal mining, which led to the granting of honorific borough status in 1847. During the mid-20th century, imports of cheaper foreign goods led to the decline of Ashton's heavy industries, but the town has continued to thrive as a centre of commerce, and is now "considered the hub of Tameside, providing the perfect setting for the town hall, council offices and 19th century market hall". (A number of former boroughs were amalgamated in the 1970s to produce 'Tameside'.) Ashton Market is one of the largest outdoor markets in the United Kingdom and attracts many visitors to the town.

Mr. Wroe's Virgins

Johanna Southcott, a Devonshire prophetess, was born in 1750. (Most of her prophecies were kept in a sealed box, to be opened at some future unspecified date.) Her followers were called Southcottians and there were a number in Ashton. John Wroe was born in Yorkshire in 1782, the son of a worsted manufacturer. In his early life, during periods of illness, he would enter into trance like states and developed the ability to prophesy. During one of these periods he was prompted to join the Southcottians, and soon rose to fame as their new prophet. When visiting for the first time in 1822, he found a thriving group and several wealthy sponsors. In a well-publicised event, Wroe was baptised in the River Medlock at Park Bridge; afterwards he was publicly circumcised, and declared that from this date all male members of the Society were also to be circumcised. The following day, Wroe prophesied that a light should break forth which would enlighten the town from the spot on which he stood. A year later Ashton Gas Works was built on the site; not quite the spiritual enlightenment that he had envisaged! Wroe felt that Ashton was particularly well-favoured, and it was here that he intended to build his New Jerusalem. A Sanctuary for his followers was built on Church Street, a sumptuous mini 'Solomon's Temple' in design, with the only form of light entering the building via two large domes in the roof. Four gatehouses were built at the four corners of the town, which he planned to link with city walls, but this madcap scheme was never finished. Wroe prescribed all aspects of the religion. They were to observe Mosaic Law for a period of forty years, followed by forty years of Christian observance, and the 'Second Coming' would follow the end of these two periods. There would be strict Sabbath observance, all men were to be circumcised, and only 'Kosher' produce was to be eaten. Several shops existed for this purpose, reputed for honest trading and fair weights and measures. The signs above the doors said 'Israelite Shops', but the locals called them 'Johanna' shops, not having made the distinction between the followers of Johanna Southcott and John Wroe. Every item of clothing and jewellery had to follow an exact pattern, men were not allowed to shave or cut their hair and he intended that his followers should keep apart from the rest of the population. This was not a poor religion; everything was of the most opulent, so that when they paraded through town in their white linen robes followed by their band of musicians they really did stand out against the grime of a cotton mill town. Wroe persuaded his followers to build him a house, a magnificent, Doric, pillar fronted mansion, which once stood facing the river Tame next to Portland Basin Heritage Museum. He then announced that he had a message from God that they should provide him with Seven Virgins from amongst their number to cherish him and accompany him on his missionary tours. It was after one of these tours in 1830 that rumours circulated that at least two of the said virgins were pregnant. A sham trial took place at one of gatehouses (now the Odd Whim Pub on Mossley Road) where, after six days' deliberations, he was merely admonished for 'lax principles'. Riots followed in the town and Wroe escaped; first to Bradford, where he was trampled underfoot, and then to Wakefield. After this his followers in Ashton declined, from approximately five hundred in their heyday, to one hundred and fifty at the time of the religious census in 1851. There are still six Christian Israelite Churches in New South Wales, one in Poland and one in Indiana USA.

Ashton **town centre**, which is the largest in Tameside, developed in the Victorian period. Many of the original buildings have survived, and as a result, the town centre is protected by Tameside Council as a conservation area. The **Market Place** is the heart and soul of the town. On the west side is located the 140,000-square-foot (13,000 m²) two-floored **Ashton Arcades** shopping centre opened in 1995. Nevertheless, the real attraction is the large **outdoor market** which was established in the medieval period. It is made up of about 180 stalls, and is open daily, except Sunday (Saturday is the busiest day). The **farmer's market** (held on the last Sunday of each month) with over 70 stalls, is the largest in the region. The **flea market** (held on Tuesdays) is said to be the biggest and busiest in the region, and second hand goods, collectables and craft together with consumables are available on over 140 stalls. There is often a **special Sunday Market**, complete with entertainment and stalls hosted by local organisations. **Ashton Market Hall**, a magnificent Victorian building, is situated to the rear of the Square. It underwent a £15 million restoration after it was damaged by fire.

Ashton Market

The former Town Hall

It contains a **display** relating to the market's history, and some useful new public **toilets**. The third side of the Square is dominated by the imposing **Town Hall**. The earliest parts of the building, which was the first purpose-built town hall in what is now Tameside, date to 1840. It has an imposing **façade of Corinthian columns,** flanked by **19th century canons**. After the Ashton-under-Lyne municipal borough was abolished in 1974, the town hall was no longer required and became the home of a museum, and the function rooms are sometimes open for tea on market days (perhaps you might wander into a tea dance!).

However, first seek out the **ground floor** entrance to the left. In the midst of a **modern concourse** is a fine **statue of the famous Black Knight** (Marjan Wouda, 1995).

After inspecting the statue, exit back into the square, and ascend the steps of the **old town hall** (there is an entrance for wheelchairs round the right-hand corner). Here is the entrance to the **Museum of the Manchester Regiment**. (Open Monday-Saturday 10.00-4.00, admission free.) This regiment had its depot in Ashton, and was the only regiment in the British army to use a municipal coat of arms as its badge. The **Ladysmith Gallery** was re-opened in November 2002 by HRH Prince Charles following a major refurbishment. The gallery tells the stories of some of the men, women and children that have been involved with the Regiment from when it was raised in 1756

Riding the Black Lad

One of the local curiosities of Ashton under Lyne is the Black Knight Pageant. This custom is more than 200 years old and has recently been revived after an absence of around 45 years. The "Black Knight" is usually thought to be based on the character of Sir Ralph de Assheton, who for a time resided at Ashton Old Hall in the 15th century. He was said to have been a cruel tyrant and the local inhabitants feared the sight of him riding around the area, on his black horse, looking for hapless peasants to persecute. It is said that he was shot dead one Easter Monday by a relative. His death was celebrated by a custom called 'Riding the Black Lad', where his effigy was paraded around the town on horseback, had lumps of earth thrown at it, and then possibly burnt.

The 'Black Knight' statue

The first written account of the Riding of the Black Lad dates from 1795, although the Court Leet accounts for 1758 refers to the usual five shillings for making the 'Black Lad'. During the 19th century, the custom became rather chaotic, with rival Black Lads and processions that stopped for refreshment at every public house. In 1909, it developed into the Black Knight Pageant, where a horseman dressed up as the knight and was accompanied by a Pageant Queen and other figures. The pageant was traditionally held on Easter Monday and attracted crowds of up to 100,000. It was later combined with a local shopping festival, and an illuminated tramcar toured the town. (One year, Ashton borrowed Liverpool's celebrated illuminated car, which was driven across Lancashire...all the tramway networks connected then). After the war, the dates of the pageant moved around between Easter and September. Fewer people were prepared to undertake the job of organisation, and the pageant stopped suddenly after 1954. The Black Knight was resurrected in 1995 to celebrate the opening of The Arcades shopping centre in Ashton and became the focus of Ashton carnival organised by the Tameside Lions Club for charity. In recent years the fair has been replaced by a street festival and the proceeds from the collection during the parade go to Willow Wood Hospice.

> Sweet Jesu, for thy mercy's sake,
> And for thy bitter passion,
> Save us from the axe of the Tower,
> And from Sir Ralph de Assheton.

through to Regimental life today. The displays also cover all the major campaigns that the Regiment was involved with including the Seven Years War, American War of Independence, New-Zealand War, Crimean War, South African War, and both World Wars through to the Malayan Emergency. The museum's **collection of over 2000 medals** earned by over 650 men of the Regiment are also on display, and includes six **Victoria Crosses**, the highest award for gallantry. You can also experience the sights, sounds and smells of life in a **reconstruction of a First World War trench**. The **Forshaw Gallery** contains an **original army Jeep** on display, of the type used by the Regiment in the Second World War. The gallery was re-opened on July 1 2006, and hundreds of new objects are now on display for the first time. In this gallery you can learn about how a soldier occupied his time when not on duty, about his daily routine, what he wore through the ages, which sports he played, and what he collected as he travelled around the world with the Manchester Regiment. The Gallery also includes a **reconstruction of a Barrack Room** from Ladysmith Barracks in the 1950s which should bring back memories for those that experienced National Service first hand. There is also a **reconstruction of a mortar team in action in Holland in 1944**.

Leave the **Market Place by Warrington Street**, and walk almost to the end before turning left down **Church Street**. Notice the **'Station' pub** on the corner; Warrington Street once continued to access the vanished Park Parade Station (see p221) and the pub is the sole reminder of this (along with the railway signal in its garden). **The Parish Church of St. Michael and All Angels** is now visible at the end of Church Street. (The church is usually closed except for services, though it is generally open for inspection after the Thursday morning communion service; ring 0161 308 279 to arrange a visit.) The site is an ancient one; the church stands at the east end of the town in what was formerly a picturesque situation on rising ground on the north side of the River Tame, and may be the 'St. Michael' mentioned in the Domesday Book. The present church is the direct descendant of a building which appears to have been erected at the beginning

St. Michael and All Angels, Ashton's parish church

of the 15th century (c. 1413), which was repaired by Sir Thomas Assheton or Ashton (died 1514), who added a new tower. In January 1791 this tower was struck by lightning, and it was clear that major repairs and alterations were necessary. Despite the erection of a new tower in 1818, and the reconstruction of the north side of the church, what remained was seriously damaged by fire in 1821. Consequently, a general rebuilding took place in 1840-4, and the **whole fabric underwent a complete restoration and reconstruction**, assuming its present aspect. Nevertheless, some of the medieval fabric survived externally, and it is suggested that the outer **vestry door**, elements of the **south porch**, and some **carved heads** on south facing window-arch corbels may be 14th century work. The **tower**, which was in a dangerous state, was pulled down and a new one built (1886-8). The new tower, the total height of which is 139 feet 6 inches, is 19 feet higher than the former one. There is a **ring of twelve bells**, six belonging to the year 1779, one to 1790, and three dating to 1818. The other two were added after the completion of the new tower in 1888.

The **north porch** (a memorial to the dead of the Great War), is the usual entrance to the church, but, before entering, notice the **grave stone** opposite. It commemorates John Leech of Hurst, who died in 1689, aged ninety-two. Not only had he been born in the reign of Elizabeth I, but he left twelve children, seventy-five grandchildren, ninety two great grandchildren, and two great-great grandchildren at the time of his death! Once inside, look for the **monument** by the side of the **north door**. It is "in memory of John Postlethwaite who sustained the highest orders of masonry without becoming proud, and died 2 February 1818, aged 70 years, preserved from indigence by the bounty of his friends." The stone is replete with masonic symbolism. The **interior of the church** comes as a revelation, for it is largely in its early 19th century state. This is what an Anglican church looked like before the influence of the Tractarian Movement was felt; it is an auditory, a box for preaching, where everything is focused upon the pulpit. Needless to say, the **pulpit** is a fine 'three-decker' in a perfect state of preservation, dating from the reconstruction of the church in the 19th century. The Rector (when he bothered to attend, for he paid a curate to undertake most of his duties) would preside over the service from the **middle desk** (which is older), only ascending to the pulpit itself to preach the sermon. The **bottom seat** was reserved for his poor assistant or, in some years, the parish clerk. The fine **carving of an angel** holding a book is probably 17th century. The **pelicans** on the Rector's Desk are symbolic of Christ; the pelican was thought to feed its young with its own blood. The Earl of Stamford would occupy a prime position in the south gallery (his coronet is still on the **Earl's pew** door), while around him and below him sat his 'loyal tenantry'. Most of the pews were rented by the richer inhabitants of the town, for the lesser beings had to crowd into whatever 'free' seats were available under the galleries. The churchwardens sat in state under the **west gallery**, where their **staves of office** can still be found. Thus was the interior of the church a perfect microcosm of the hierarchical structure of bygone Ashton.

The interior work is of a very elaborate description, with rich ornamentation in wood and plaster, and is a **good specimen of the florid neo Gothic of the period** in the perpendicular style (although some think that the plasterwork hides traces of the original medieval work). The **arcade** is of seven bays with a **clerestory**, and a highly-placed **arch** structurally separates the two eastern bays from the others, but true to its 'low church' inspiration, the ritual arrangement of the chancel is confined to the parts of the church east of the seventh bay, in the fashion of the time in which the building was erected. The oak **roof** is flat and paneled, richly decorated with the arms of those who have identified themselves with the building or patronage of the church. Look for the 'R.A.' signifying Ralph Assheton, a popular candidate for the 'Black Knight'. The regimental flags belong to local units of the Manchester Regiment, whose depot was at Ashton. This was their garrison church. The **chancel arch bears the royal arms**, and the **east end of the chancel** was rebuilt in 1883. Seek out the **display case** to the right of the chancel arch, by the **south gallery steps**. It contains a 16th century copy of the Geneva Bible, sometimes known as the **breeches bible** (which is what Adam and Eve make out of fig leaves to hide their nakedness!).

However, the great glory of the church is the **unique medieval stained glass**. The earliest pieces may date from 1460, and the latest additions from 1517. They probably comprised the original East Window, but have been moved many times, and a quantity of it was removed by parishioners after the fire of 1821. The remaining portions were placed in the north aisle in 1872, and it is now located in windows in the **south aisle**. Obviously, the donors are commemorated in the windows. We start with the **lower lights** of the **three-lighted window** to the left of the **south door**. From left to right we see, firstly, the **children of Sir John Assheton** (died 1428), a soldier with connections at court; **Sir Thomas Assheton** (died 1516) who fought on the Lancastrian side and the last of his line; and **Sir John Assheton** (died 1508) and his wives, also a fervent Lancastrian. Now follows the **lower lights** of the **four lighted window** to the right of the **door**. Again, from left to right we see **Sir Thomas Assheton (wearing the badge of his king) and his wife Elizabeth** (he was one of the boys depicted in the first window, and an alchemist granted a licence by Henry VI to search for the 'philosophers stone'); **Lawrence Assheton**, Rector of Ashton from 1458-86; and **Gervase Assheton**, the Rector who succeeded him. The final light contains a **female figure**, possibly representing Saint Helen. The subject of the principal windows **is the life of St. Helen and the legends connected with her history**, and though much mixed up in places, and with many pieces missing, the story is tolerably clear. It is a very fine piece of 15th century work, the colours being particularly rich. The **window at the end of the north aisle** has medieval fragments in the form of **figures of Kings Henry VI and Edward IV**.

The Legend of Saint Helen
Saint Helen did exist, though much of her story is legendary. She was the mother of Constantine the Great, the first Christian Emperor, and in the course of a pilgrimage to the Holy Land, she rediscovered (and marked by churches) the holy sites. The surviving glass starts by depicting her birth, supposedly the daughter of 'King Cole' (of nursery rhyme fame!). After going to convent school (in what was then contemporary dress), she is depicted visiting prisoners (one of the Seven Acts of Mercy in medieval Christianity). She is next shown betrothed to Constantius Chlorus (a historical fact), who was a deputy to Diocletian. The marriage is illustrated, but he divorced her for political reasons when he became Emperor. The birth of Constantine the Great (at York) is pictured. Constantine is shown becoming Emperor, and a number of minor stories are introduced. The Jewish magician challenges the Pope in front of Constantine. He slays a bull with a whisper, but the Pope restores the bull back to life again, and Helen is converted to christianity! One of the windows depicts the Council of Niceae, settling controversies and creating the Niceaen Creed. Helen travels to the Holy land after seeing a vision. In yet another window she goes

as a penance after Constantine murders his wife and son. One window tells of a Jew who warns his brethren that if Helen finds the True Cross, the Church will triumph. On their refusing to tell her where to dig, she threatens to burn them! Judas discloses where it is hidden (anti-semitism was rife in medieval England, and the Jews had been officially expelled in 1290). Three windows depict the actual discovery, but three crosses are found! Judas, seeing the funeral of a young man, lays the crosses upon his corpse, and the last cross brings him to life again! (The resurrected corpse has a most delightful grin!) St. Helen is shown erecting the Church of the Holy Sepulchre. Finally, Constantine is shown being baptised on his deathbed...he certainly kept his options open!

Retrace your steps to **Warrington Street**, but turn left into **Old Street**. The **Library and Art Gallery** is worth a visit. This recently restored Victorian building (opened in 1893) with many features is home to Tameside's main library, providing extensive lending and reference services. Tameside Central Art Gallery is situated on the first floor with all-year-round temporary exhibitions, workshops and events. Disabled access is available. (The library and art gallery are usually open Tuesday to Saturday at varied times, though the gallery is closed Saturday afternoon; admission free.) Continue down **Old Street**, noting the interesting inscriptions on the old **Drill Hall** and pass through the new **St. Petersfield business district** beyond. We emerge into **Henry Square**, with the **Victorian Baths** to the left and the new **Magistrates' Courts** opposite. The **Corporation Baths** at the Henry Square end of Stamford Street were opened in 1870 at a cost of £16,000, and was one of the first and largest municipal swimming baths. The building is constructed almost entirely of brick, with some stone decoration in a Byzantine style and has a 120 feet high tower which housed the flues from the steam boilers and heaters. Sixty per cent of the building was occupied by the main Swimming Bath; the pool was 100 feet long and 40 feet wide and was used mainly by male bathers, with a three hour period on Thursdays for ladies. In the eastern section of the building was a smaller pool, 27 feet long and 15 feet wide, for the use of female bathers. There were also private bathrooms and Turkish baths. Part of the building was used as a police station and a station for a fire engine! Between November and March each year, the main pool was covered over with a wooden floor, built on wooden supports placed on the bottom of the pool. The room was then used as a skating rink, concert hall and meeting room. The building was closed when the newer baths were opened in the 1970s, since when the building has been vandalised and allowed to deteriorate. As part of the re-generation of this part of Ashton (the St Petersfield development), it is hoped to re-furbish the building and use it for a new purpose. Head directly down **Stamford Street** towards the tower of **St. Peter's Church**.

> *"Have you seen St Peter's Church*
> *In Ashton-under-Lyne?*
> *'Tis a Gothic edifice*
> *Of excellent design."*

The foundation stone of this "Gothic edifice" was laid by Dr Law, Bishop of Chester, on 24 October, 1821. It is one of the "Waterloo" churches. The Napoleonic Wars following the French Revolution had ended in 1815, and to show their gratitude for victory, the Parliamentary Commissioners voted one million pounds to the Church of England.

The former baths

Large, imposing churches were to be built with this money, so that English people might see how grateful the country was for peace at last. (There was an ulterior motive, as the ruling class wanted to counter the ideas of the French Revolution, especially in the new industrial areas.) St Peter's received £12,000 from the Parliamentary Commissioners, leaving only £2,000 to be raised locally. A medal struck in 1821 states that "the area of the church will be 142 feet long by 65 feet wide and will be capable of containing 1,800 persons. The height of the tower will be 128 feet." It was consecrated in 1824, and is noted for its **Rose Window** (1853) and **Belfry**. (Ring 0161 339 0665 to arrange a visit.)

The **pedestrian crossing** leads to the **churchyard**, replete with several ponderous Victorian tombs and a **boulder** commemorating a local who was buried at sea (the inscription includes the co-ordinates!). However, bear left in negotiating the **crossing** to arrive on the **opposite side of the Park Parade by-pass**, which commences at this point. Turn left and head back **towards the Baths**. Look out for the **brown sign** inscribed 'Portland Basin Museum' and turn right down **Welbeck Street South**. It might seem that you have entered a rather grim backwater, but it hides a real gem, so follow the cobbles! After the Ashton Canal was revived, it was decided to turn the **Portland Basin** into a heritage area. The **basin** next to the warehouse is the point at which the **Ashton Canal**, the **Huddersfield Narrow Canal** and the **Peak Forest Canal** meet. (It has been used several times as a filming location for Coronation Street, including a scene where the character Richard Hillman drove into the canal.) An annual Waterways Festival is held here, and boat trips from the museum waterfront are usually available (ring 07807 262170).

The **Portland Basin Museum** (open Tuesday-Sunday 10-5, admission free) is a new development at the Portland Canal Basin. Curiously, a genuine canal warehouse was all but demolished and a pastiche erected in its place. The museum is on two levels. Visitors enter on the **upper level**, and pass through the **entrance area** (containing an **information desk**, **shop**, and **toilets**) to find themselves in a **representation of a 1920s street**. We start with the ground floor of a **typical terraced house**, with a kitchen, yard (complete with mangle dolly tub, and posser) and outside toilet. Round the corner is a view of the parlour. There follows a **school yard** (children can practice hopscotch) and a re-created **schoolroom**. Next comes a **chip shop** (note the bill of fare includes tripe) and a **pawnbroker's**. The corner is distinguished by a **grocer** and a **chapel interior**. The pub includes a diorama with voices, and there is a **doctor's surgery** next door. The newest displays are adjacent, in a balcony area. A portion of **Setantii – Tales of Tameside** has been relocated here from the town hall. (The Setantii were a local Celtic tribe, probably in confederation with the powerful Brigantes.) Notice the **diorama illustrating how the Celts lived**, the **Roman archaeological finds** and **costume** (including armour and weapons) and the **Norman chain mail** and weapons. There is a diorama of a 15th century market. Look out for the famous **Longdendale Longbow** (the type used at the Battle of Agincourt), and the **15th century suit of armour**. In contrast, notice the pageant suit of armour worn by the 'Black Knight' (p223). Go back to the entrance area and **descend the steps** (a **lift** is also available). The lower floor deals with industrial history, with displays of agriculture and coal mining, together with a **model illustrating transport history** and a **cinema** in the next room. The main room has a mock-up of a **canal boat** (complete with living quarters) and **displays relating to local industries**, including the manufacture of **'donkey stones'**.

The Portland Basin

Donkey Stones

Donkey stones were made from a mixture of pulverised stone, cement, bleach powder and water. The mixture was ground up into a thick paste and then formed into a rectangular slab on a bench. The slab was then cut up to form the individual stones. The finished stones were then placed on racks to dry, usually for several days, although sometimes the drying process would take longer if the weather was cold and damp. Donkey stones were made in three different colours; brown, using a type of sandstone called cotta stone from Northampton; white, using a type of stone from a quarry near Wigan; and cream, using a blend of the two. The last manufacturer of the stones was a company called Eli Whalley, founded in the 1890s, in Ashton, which ceased trading in 1979. They were usually obtained from 'rag and bone men', in exchange for old clothes, waste paper, kitchen bones, or anything else that could be recycled (though small children preferred the balloons that were also on offer!). They were used by housewives to clean and scour the steps (and a large part of the pavement too) leaving it a pristine colour. Woe betide anyone who did not match the standard that her neighbours expected, or anybody who did not step on the matting provided!

Walk out into the **basin** itself. There is a **café**, and **boat rides** are usually available at weekends. If there is time, walk along the towpath and inspect the **aqueduct** over the river.

You can return by walking back towards the **church**, but turn left instead of crossing the road. Here is the **stop opposite the churchyard** for the 216 bus to Droylsden Metrolink Station.

The Altrincham Line

Piccadilly Station to St. Peter's Square

This section of the route will be found on the following pages; Piccadilly Station p23; Piccadilly Station to Piccadilly Gardens pp26-28; a description of Piccadilly Gardens p28; Piccadilly Gardens to St. Peter's Square pp32-36; and St. Peter's Square itself p36.

St. Peter's Square to Cornbrook

The tram leaves the station, crosses the west end of the Square, and passes alongside the **Midland Hotel** (p39) on a section of reserved track. The hotel itself stands on the site of a cottage and extensive gardens owned by a Mr. Cooper. He is said to have walked there and back to Doncaster, every year for forty years, to see the St. Leger horse race! At the crossing of **Windmill Street**, notice the rear of the hotel, with the remains of the grand entrance. At a time when most guests arrived and departed by rail, a covered way extended from it across the street and up the forecourt to the station! Windmill Street is named after a windmill that lay in the vicinity, grinding logwoods for dyestuff.

Midland Hotel (from Windmill Street) (Graham Beech)

'The Fields of Peterloo'

The period after the Napoleonic Wars was a hard time, with a combination of economic depression and high food prices. The poor lived off potatoes and a stew made from nettles and dock leaves called 'Waterloo porridge'. But something was very different. The first period of industrialisation had created an industrial working class, a group that was starting to flex its muscles and organise. The cause of political reform had fallen into their hands, for groups of workers had become convinced that the times would only mend when a reformed parliament was achieved. Henry 'Orator' Hunt was to address a great reform demonstration at St. Peter's Fields on 16 August 1819. The immense crowd was augmented by contingents marching in from the surrounding towns. This was no mob. It was more frightening than that, as far as the establishment was concerned, for the crowd was orderly and disciplined, even dressed in their Sunday clothes. (Reports of secret drilling on the moors around Manchester were probably connected with organising the marching contingents.) Unfortunately, as Manchester had no proper local government at the time, legal jurisdiction lay in the hands of unelected magistrates. This panic stricken reactionary group, watching the proceedings from Mr. Cooper's cottage, ordered the military force at their disposal to arrest Hunt. This force was the Manchester Yeomanry, a volunteer cavalry regiment left over from the wars, and officered by the sons of local landowners and merchants. They had to force their way through the crowd to reach the stand with Hunt and his fellow speakers upon it. They lost control, and started lashing out in all directions with their sabres. Some reports state that many of the Yeomanry were drunk. In other cases, individual officers sought out local radicals for retribution in an early form of class warfare. The officers of a detachment of Hussars (regular army) were appalled, and spent as much time trying to control their fellow military as dispersing the crowd. "Fie, gentlemen, for shame!" a Hussar officer cried, as he knocked up some Yeomanry swords. "What are you at? The people cannot get away!" Some of the crowd fought back, and gave as good as they got. Altogether, sixteen people died, and over six hundred were injured. But this is a conservative estimate, for many were no doubt spirited away by their family and friends. Interestingly enough, the authorities had not crushed the political movement. The out of town contingents marched back in good order, and a mood of defiance emerged. Manchester did not explode into anarchy, for not only the town, but the greater part of the country, were united in an expression of universal disgust and loathing at what had happened. The event was christened 'Peterloo' for "Waterloo (in which one of the dead had fought) had been a battle, but St. Peter's Fields was bloody murder." Peterloo was a turning point, and an alliance was forged between the middle and working classes to achieve parliamentary reform. Unfortunately, the urban working class were cheated in the Reform Act of 1832, and had to wait until 1867 to obtain the vote.

These soldiers mow'd folks down like flies,
Thi' sabres drip'd wi' blood.
Thi' heeded man nor woman's cries,
But slew them where thi' stood.

Salute we now these men o' yore,
Who were t'concience true.
An' gave thi' blood for t'common good,
On't fields o' Peterloo!

As the name of nearby **Mount Street** testifies, this was the highest piece of land to the west of the city. We pass through an area that was once known as St. Peter's Fields, the site of the 'Peterloo Massacre'.

The tram now climbs up the ramp at the side of **Manchester Central**, a large exhibition and conference centre, formerly Central Station; the old forecourt and train shed is clearly visible. Look up at the **clock**. In the course of its restoration, a time capsule left by the original workmen was discovered. The Midland, Manchester, Sheffield and Lincolnshire (later Great Central), and Great Northern Railways decided to break the monopoly of the London and North Western between Manchester and Liverpool. They formed a joint company, which (since it would also include a line to Chester) would be called 'The Cheshire Lines Railway'. (It was the only railway in Britain with carriages and wagons, but no locomotives, for the constituent companies provided the latter.) The new route was an instant success, especially the punctual expresses that ran every hour to Liverpool in forty minutes. Other trains ran to Chester Northgate Station (via Northwich), and Southport; there were even holiday season through carriages (via the Cambrian Railway) to Aberystwyth and Pwllheli! Such an undertaking needed a grand terminus, and Central Station opened in 1880. The impressive arched girder frame is the second widest unsupported train shed span after St. Pancras, upon which it is modelled. However, unlike St. Pancras, horizontal beams do not secure the

Manchester Central (Graham Beech)

thrust of the arch. Instead, the great girders run straight through the under croft to anchor themselves in the underlying rock. The **undercroft**, intended as a goods station, used over 34 million bricks in its construction. In addition to Cheshire Lines trains, the constituent railways transferred the great majority of their express services here from London Road, together with some of their local trains. It was intended to build a grand station entrance block, but the companies could never agree on the allocation of the costs. Consequently, the (temporary) wooden buildings, with few alterations, lasted until the station closed!

The Exhibition Hall

For many years, Central station lay derelict, until the old Greater Manchester Council decided that the city needed a good exhibition hall. The Greater Manchester Exhibition and Event Centre (G-Mex), now called Manchester Central, was the consequence of a unique public and private sector partnership, and is definitely an asset to the city. The large hall is 10,000 metres in extent, although it can be subdivided into smaller exhibition halls by moveable screens. You can usually enter the foyer, and take a peep through the hall doors. The Centre hosts a mixture of trade and public exhibitions, and has staged concerts and sporting events, though the latter now faces stiff competition from the Manchester Evening News Arena. It is joined to the new sandstone walled International Convention Centre. In addition to the 2000 square metre hall and an 800 seat auditorium, the convention complex includes banqueting and seminar rooms, translation facilities, and a range of media and catering services. The Centre attracts over 50,000 extra visitors per year to the city, and the entire complex, including the exhibition hall, has been used for both Labour and Conservative Party Conferences.

Look across **Lower Mosley Street** in the direction of **Barbirolli Square**, a fine viewpoint over the restored **canal basin**. The square is paved in York stone, with bands of granite, and a few plane trees. The most conspicuous object is the **'pebble'**, an eighteen ton piece of polished marble (said to have cost £200,000!) by the Japanese sculptor, Kan Yasuda. Steps lead down to the basin, which is graced with the inevitable **water feature**. (It would be nice if some narrow boats actually tied up here. Perhaps some concert goers might arrive by barge!) Notice the large **bronze head** of Sir John

Barbirolli Square (Graham Beech)

Barbirolli (by Byron Howard, 2000). To the rear of the basin is a good view of **Chepstow House** (Sam Mendel's Warehouse, with surviving chimney).

The Rise and Fall of Sam Mendel

Chepstow House was Sam Mendel's warehouse, and has a strange story to tell. Sam was born in Liverpool, and was brought to Manchester by his father, who had set himself up in the business of rope manufacturer. The young lad entered the service of a local merchant, and travelled extensively on his behalf in Germany and South America. After setting up on his own account, Mendel developed a great business empire, and erected this large warehouse in 1874, when he was at the height of his powers. He was a phenomenon. His dealings in 'grey' goods (unprocessed cotton fabric), for export to India and China, took the form of orders so huge that his dealings sometimes seriously affected the market. Yet he was a "gentleman from top to toe," always ready to courteously receive the humblest salesman. As Manchester's greatest 'merchant prince' at that time, he lived in great splendor at Manley Park on the south side of the city. The Suez Canal opened the year after this warehouse, transforming the cotton market. In the vastly changed commercial conditions, Sam lost everything. The contents of his mansion were auctioned, and the pictures (including works by Turner and Constable), silver plate, furniture, and Sevres and Chelsea porcelain, featured in a catalogue of 209 pages. (It took six days to sell his wine collection!) Poor old Sam died in poverty at Balham, London, in 1884. One hopes that the thrice married gentleman had consoled himself with some happy memories. The old warehouse has been converted into seventy-six flats, though the boiler room chimney remains. And over the door is a symbolic carving relating to the eternal quest for the elusive 'golden fleece'.

The chief function of the **Square** is to act as an introduction to the **Bridgewater Hall** (Nicholas Thompson, 1996). The old Free Trade Hall had been the principal concert and performance venue, the home of the Halle Orchestra. Changing circumstances necessitated a move to a new venue. The result is the Bridgewater Hall, the first purpose built musical auditorium in Britain since the Royal Festival Hall of 1951. The B.B.C. Philharmonic and the Manchester Camerata orchestras joined the Halle here. However, it must not be thought that the new place is purely a temple to orchestral classical music. A wide programme is offered, from popular music to stand-up comedy. The entire building is mounted on 270 giant bearings, which act as shock absorbers. No vibration is transmitted to the auditorium. The exterior is placed on a

Bridgewater Hall (Graham Beech)

The 'Halle Band'

Manchester, from the 18th century onwards, has always been a centre for the performing arts, particularly music. This resulted from two diverse traditions that, over the years, have cross fertilised each other and achieved a creative synergy. There is the 'classical music' tradition. In the last century, the cosmopolitan nature of the city encouraged this trend. Charles Halle, a brilliant German musician, settled in a place with a thriving and cultured German community, and created the world famous orchestra that bears his name. The orchestra made the Free Trade Hall its home, and is usually associated with Sir John Barbirolli, the legendary conductor after whom the square is named. However, a working class music tradition developed in the form of brass bands and (to a lesser extent) choirs. Most communities and work places had (and often still have) their band. These were not just marching bands, for classical pieces were transposed for them to be played in parks and the many competitions that they entered. Similarly, it became a tradition for choirs to perform oratorios (particularly Handel's Messiah) from time to time. It was not for nothing that working men sometimes referred to the 'Halle Band'!

plinth of sandstone blocks, supporting angular walls of glass and metal cladding. A **suspended glass curtain** of four levels of foyers and bars is focussed on the Square, with views of the canal basin on one side, and the box office, shops, and offices against Mosley Street. It is best seen illuminated at night, for some have compared it to the prow of a great liner, with people at various levels gazing at the reflections in the water. The **exterior of the auditorium** is encased in Jura limestone, terminating in a **stainless steel roof**. Enter and explore the outer area, noticing the **carpet**, inspired by Monet's Water Lilies, and the inclined auditorium wall. Tours of the Complex are available (charge), but you can usually inspect the **auditorium** if no rehearsals or performances are taking place. It is finished in natural materials; the veneer colours were inspired by some autumn leaves collected by the architect. Notice the **fine organ**, and the fact that the tipped up empty seats reflect the sound back to the performance area. (The Bridgewater Hall is usually open Monday to Saturday from 10am)

Notice the great **bowstring bridge** spanning **Great Bridgewater Street** that the tram crosses after climbing the **ramp**. The *Britons Protection Hotel* is situated on the corner of this street and **Lower Mosley Street**. This old pub dates from 1806, and the name indicates an association with the local volunteers, determined to resist an invasion by Bonaparte. It is worth a visit for its panelled interior, military murals, beer garden, and a collection of over 150 malt whiskies. The upstairs room is a venue for a wide variety of local societies. As the tram **turns sharp right**, there is a **fine panoramic view** to the left, encompassing the **junction of Lower Mosley Street with Whitworth Street** (with the distinctive *City Road Inn* on the far corner) and the **Albion Street arch**, through which some **futuristic buildings** may be glimpsed. The route now follows the **great brick viaduct** approach constructed by the Cheshire Lines Railway to access Central Station. Although not really visible, a **section of the Rochdale Canal** runs alongside Whitworth Street, at the foot of the viaduct. It is the location of *Deansgate Locks*, an interesting development in which retail units have been created in a series of railway arches under the viaduct, accessed by continuous balcony connected with the street by a series of bridges across the canal. The tenants include a number of bars and clubs. A **lock keeper's house** is visible at the end of the street. A rival form of transport is marked by **Deansgate Station**, across the road. It was opened (as Knott Mill) by the Manchester, South Junction, and Altrincham railway (see p242) in 1849, and was rebuilt in its present form in the last quarter of the 19th century, incorporating **mock battlements and a fake portcullis (**in tribute to the nearby Roman Fort), along with the company arms. (The station yard entrance has a 'pun' in the form of a **carving of a reef knot!**) The station is joined to the Metrolink Station by a **futuristic footbridge**.

Deansgate-Castlefield Station is rather clumsily titled Metrolink creation, but reflects the fact that its **staggered platforms**, linked by a **pedestrian crossing**, are located near the end of **Deansgate**, and that it is the nearest stop to **Castlefield**, perhaps Manchester's premier tourist attraction. The **Altrincham platform** is accessed by a **path from steps** situated at the corner of **Lower Mosley Street** and **Whitworth Street**, and the path continues to **steps** at the corner of **Deansgate**. There is also the **footbridge** to the railway station, mentioned above. The **inbound platform** communicates with the **car parks** adjacent to Manchester Central, but a **path** also leads back to a **flight of steps** down to the area containing the **reconstructed Roman Fort**. This station is currently (2014) being remodeled; the incoming platform will be repositioned opposite the Altrincham one, and a loop line will run round the rear of it.

Leave the station by the **Altrincham platform**, but do not venture on to the bridge!

Instead, turn to the right and descend the **flight of steps** to the street below. Walk to the **corner of Whitworth Street and Deansgate**. Notice the so-called **bicycle sculpture** by the railway station corner; it is really meant to symbolise 'ecological balance'! It marks the start of the **lower section of Deansgate**, through the left-hand railway arch, now little more than a backwater since the construction of the **Bridgewater Viaduct** to the right of it. Continue under the bridge, past the *Pack Horse Inn* (noting the slope to the river) down to **Knott Mill Bridge**. This is the third on this site. Only the **left-hand parapet** survives, distinguished by an **old boundary stone** indicating the border between Manchester and Hulme

Roman fort gate (reconstructed)
(Graham Beech)

townships. The **Bridgewater Basin** (p238) commences to the right. There may have been a ford over the Medlock here in Roman times, but the bridge is certainly medieval in origin, on the main route into the town from the west. The 'mill' in question ground corn in the vicinity from an uncertain date, though some local historians think 'Knott' refers to King Canute. Everyone remembers him as the foolish king who placed his throne on a beach, tried to command the tide not to come in, and thus got his feet wet. The whole point of the story is misunderstood. He was actually trying to demonstrate to his sycophantic Witan (Council) that there were strict limits to the power of a king. Knut (to give him his proper name) was a Dane who had seized the English throne. However, he maintained order, made wise laws, and was a great friend to the church. In short...not a bad chap.

> *Merry sungen the monkes of Ely,*
> *When Knut Kyng rowed thereby.*
> *"Row Knichts, nearer to the land,*
> *That we may hear these monkes sing!"*

He may even have visited Manchester, for the town then lay within the Royal Manor of Salford, much used as a kingly hunting lodge.

Sir Tarquin

In olden times, none other than Sir Lancelot, upon a knightly quest, came by this place. Here lived the giant Sir Tarquin, who hung a basin on the bough of a tree. None might pass unless they struck the basin with their lance, thereby challenging the wicked knight to a fight. Sir Lancelot vanquished the giant and freed the local people from his tyranny. A large part of the Arthurian Legend (Sir Gawain's exploits with the Green Knight, for example) is set in the North West of England. Since they largely derive from Celtic oral tradition, this is not surprising, as this border area lay on the edge of the Anglo-Saxon kingdoms and was the last to retain its original culture. Some scholars think that the 'giant of Knott Mill' is a faint echo of some bardic propaganda for a Pennine Dark-Age chieftain. However, some amateur local historians will tell you that Camelot lay in Salford!

Walk back to the **road junction**, and cross **Deansgate**. Directly opposite, **Castle Street** passes alongside the **canal** and under a fine **iron railway bridge** to access the **Bridgewater Canal Basin** and the heart of Castlefield. Alternatively, turn right along **Deansgate** to pass under the **Metrolink viaduct** to reach **Liverpool Road** on the left. This leads directly to the **Museum of Science and Industry** (including **Liverpool Road Station**) and the **Roman Fort**. (There is **a detailed walking tour of Castlefield**, together with **a guide to the Museum of Science and Industry**, in the author's *Discovering Manchester*, also published by Sigma.)

There is a **good view** from the tram, to the right, over the centre of Manchester, dominated by the soaring **Beetham Tower**. The line crosses **Deansgate** and enters **Castlefield**. The **campanile tower**, rising above the other viaduct to the left, belongs to a former nonconformist chapel, once used as a recording studio by Pete Waterman!

As the tram continues along the **viaduct**, the view to the right is somewhat obscured by the **girder box** that once carried a duplicate set of tracks into Central Station. However, you may

Museum of Science and Industry
(Jean Mostall)

be able to catch a glimpse of the **Stafford Canal Basin**, once used by the boats operating on the Trent and Mersey Canal. The view to the left is much clearer. The **Manchester, South Junction, and Altrincham Railway viaduct** curves in to run alongside the Cheshire lines viaduct, albeit at a lower level. You may be able to spot **Castlefield Junction**, where a line branches off under our viaduct to connect with the original Liverpool line at Ordsall Lane. (We are here crossing the **site of the Roman Fort**.) Since the construction of the modern Windsor Link, trains to and from the north now run

Beetham Tower

Manchester's tallest building, Beetham Tower (Ian Simpson Associates, 2006) contains a five star 285 bedroom Hilton Hotel up to level twenty-three, where Cloud 23 (the city's only 'sky bar') is to be found. Apartments are situated in the section from level twenty-five up to the triplex glass penthouse on level forty-seven (purchased by the architect for £3 million). There are also two basement levels, which contain resident's car parking. The tower is reckoned to be the tallest residential development in Europe, with views including Liverpool and Snowdon on a clear day. Cristiano Ronaldo was one of the first people to move in. It dominates the skyline to the right of the line.

this way. There are **good views** on the left, starting with the **terminus of the Rochdale Canal**. After noting the **Lock Keeper's Cottage**, which was also used for levying tolls on barges entering the canal, look across the stone bridge to *Dukes 92* (it is by the ninety second lock). *Duke's*, like a lot of the buildings in the area, is one of Jim Ramsbottom's projects. The popular bar is situated in the former Merchants' Warehouse stables with a yard turned into an **outdoor performance area**, fully equipped with a stage. It has seen everything from rock to Shakespeare, and has a resident theatrical company. There is now a fine view of the barge entrances to the **Merchants' Warehouse** at the start of the **Duke's Canal** (which is usually wrongly referred to as the Bridgewater). It is the oldest surviving canal warehouse in the city, and was built of handmade bricks and timber beams in the traditional way in 1827-28 (the **round headed windows** are typical), though (strangely) at a time when iron girder frames and brick fireproof floors were being installed in local cotton mills. The goods were lifted in and out of the barges by a hoist. Although part of the building was damaged by fire in 1971, it was purchased by Jim Ramsbottom (a local bookmaker turned property developer) for the scrap price of the bricks in 1983. Jim had a vision for the area when few people paid it any notice, and was prepared to play a waiting game. In this case, funding (some of it from the European Union) was not obtained until 1996, when the warehouse was restored and converted into office accommodation. This

Canals and Castlefield

The name, of course, means 'castle in the field', and refers to the Roman Fort, abandoned at some stage in the Dark Ages, visible for many centuries in the countryside outside the small market town, and utilised as a quarry for building materials until it almost disappeared. Nothing much happened after that until Francis Egerton came on the scene. As the third Duke of Bridgewater, he was already heir to a sizable inheritance when (so the story goes) our hero was crossed in love. He turned his back on the amusements of society and decided to develop the resources of his estate, which, in this case, comprised the colliery at Worsley. It was difficult to transport the coal overland to Manchester, but Francis and John Gilbert, his agent, thought they had the answer...a canal! Improved rivers (known as 'navigations') were then quite common, but they decided to employ a continental invention in the form of an artificial waterway or 'cut'. Fortunately, they had the services of James Brindley, an unconventional engineer of genius from a very humble background. The parliamentary committee considering the Bill were sceptical about the principle of the proposed aqueduct over the Irwell at Barton (p292), so Brindley made a hurried model out of the only material to hand...cheese! Construction started in 1759, and the barges arrived at Castlefield in 1764. The work was undertaken by a new kind of labourer, who got the name 'navigators' or 'navvies' for short.

> *That's the rule of the bold navigators,*
> *For we are jovial banksmen all.*

Castlefield was chosen for the Manchester terminus because the Medlock could be used as a feeder for the canal and the terminal basin. Thus Castlefield "had become a sort of Maratime (sic) town, or Dutch Seaport." The canal produced coal in such cheap quantities in Manchester that it was a key factor in the critical mass that produced the first industrial revolution in the history of the world. Over 35,000 tons of coal was carried between 1773 and 1775 alone. The good Duke made an even greater fortune, but some accounts say that he was never happier than when dressed in old clothes, drinking, swearing, and smoking pipes with Gilbert, Brindley, and the navvies. As the national canal system expanded, Castlefield became a major transportation centre, full of wharves and warehouses. It proved the means of supplying the growing manufacturing town with fuel, foodstuffs, potatoes, salt, 'Baltic' timber, stone, slate, lime, and raw cotton. This was why it was finally chosen as the terminus of the Liverpool and Manchester Railway, which opened in 1830. This was the first public railway, with scheduled locomotive hauled passenger and goods trains. By the mid-19th century, the last open fields had disappeared, and the area became full of labourers, warehousemen, watermen, and all manner of transients. This end of Deansgate, and parts of Castlefield, were also noted for wretched housing (including cellar dwellings), crowded lodging houses, rowdy drinking dens, and all manner of vice, drunkenness, and disorder. (Cholera and typhus were also not unknown in the area.) Most of this was swept away by railway developments, particularly from the 1870s onwards. Eventually, the focus of Manchester goods traffic began to move away, although Castlefield remained important in terms of transport. But the decline of the area accelerated in the 20th century, and by the 1960s there was a lot of derelict land and run-down buildings. Four things proved to be Castlefield's salvation. Firstly, the revival of the canals as a leisure facility, particularly the reopening of the 'Cheshire Ring' in the 1960's, brought an

Viaduct from Potato wharf (Graham Beech)

increasing number of pleasure boaters through the area. The 'ring' constituted a regional circuit of canals that enabled boaters to embark on a cruising holiday without repeating any of the mileage sailed. Next, excavations on the Roman Fort site in 1972 and 1979 resulted in some exciting discoveries, and suggested that a reconstruction of the North Gate might prove a useful exercise. The release of a lot of derelict railway land for development purposes (including the historic 1830 station) happened at about the same time. Lastly,

Stafford basin (Graham Beech)

the celebration of 'Rocket 150' (the anniversary of the opening of the Liverpool and Manchester Railway) in 1980 was instrumental in the decision to re-site the then 'Greater Manchester Museum of Science and Industry' in the old railway complex. The end result has been the creation of "Britain's first urban history park," and Castlefield is now the jewel in Manchester's tourism crown. Its attractions include the Roman Fort, the Museum of Science and Industry (perhaps the largest of its kind in Europe), and the Canal Basins.

is followed by the unusual new **Merchants' Bridge** (RHW Architects, 1996), something of a shock in these surroundings, yet perhaps in keeping with the great tradition of civil engineering. It connects **Catalan Square** with the **canal towpath**. Follow the **towpath** past the residential **Slate Wharf** to the **Egerton Street Bridge**. Here, in the distance, is a view of the neo gothic form of **St. George's Church**, consecrated in 1828.This was formerly the garrison church (amongst other things) for the old Hulme Cavalry Barracks, but has now been now been converted into flats. Somewhere near here was the site of Hulme Hall. The owners supported the wrong side in the English Civil War, and buried a large amount of 'treasure' in the grounds. Unfortunately, after the Restoration, no-one could remember its location. But don't try looking for it; one version of the legend says that the finder will be cursed, while another states that the treasure is guarded by demons!

The line now passes a large **high-rise apartment development** to the left, part of it on a kind of **island** between the canal and the railway. The **cow sculptures** are a somewhat incongruous feature! **Woden Street Footbridge** (also popularly known as 'Mark Addy's Bridge', see p285) might be glimpsed to right, where the **River Irwell** is now visible. The bridge is the official starting point for the Manchester Ship Canal (p267). The name refers to Woden's Den, a lost cave (built over in Victorian times) that was considered holy, and full of mysterious Norse carvings. Near this point, the **Duke's Canal** turns under both railway viaducts, but notice that the **old Altrincham viaduct** is now level with ours. There is a **fine view** over Salford to the right.

The tram now arrives at **Cornbrook Station**, another Metrolink creation, and named after one of the lost rivers of Manchester that flows into the Irwell here. Although now covered over here, it still rises on the Ardwick and Gorton boundary. In medieval times it powered at least one corn mill, hence the name. The station is a Metrolink creation on the existing **viaduct**, the **interchange** for the Altrincham, Didsbury, and Eccles/Media City lines (and, in the future, the Airport line), and the intended terminus for the peak Media City shuttle trams. There is an **island platform** accessed by **stairs** and **lift**. As the nearby Pomona Docks development is currently (2014) in abeyance, and the location and approach (leading to **Bridgewater Way**) is rather isolated, foot passengers using the station should exercise caution at night. There is a view over the former **Pomona Docks** (p266) to the right, perhaps best seen on the return journey. A glance to the left reveals a **curious arch** erected in the middle of a traffic island. It comes from an old confectionary factory that once stood in the area, and marks the **boundary of Trafford Metropolitan Borough.**

Cornbrook to Trafford Bar

There were originally two sets of junctions at Cornbrook. Firstly, the viaduct lines converged. Next, the tracks diverged. Those to the left comprised the Altrincham line, also used by Cheshire Lines trains for Chester, and the London North Western Trains for Warrington (Arpley) and Liverpool Lime Street. Those to the right comprised the Cheshire Lines route to Liverpool Central. There was a locomotive shed on the canal side. Nowadays, there is no junction at all. The Liverpool line trains pass from the old MSJR route to the Cheshire lines Liverpool route by means of a **bridge over Metrolink**, so that there is no physical connection between the two. The Altrincham and Chorlton bound trams pass from the Cheshire Lines viaduct to the Altrincham line by diving under the bridge. But there is a **junction**...a rather new Metrolink one! Before we pass down the **incline,** notice the track that diverges to the left. It **parallels the railway line** over the bridge before branching off, for it is used by the outward trams to Media City and Eccles. At the foot of the **incline**, before passing under the bridge, you might spot the **line coming in from the right**, used by the inbound Eccles trams. Beyond the **bridge**, we are now running on the former metals of the Manchester, South Junction, and Altrincham Railway, which opened in 1849.

After passing under the **Liverpool line** and **Bridgewater Way**, followed by an old **occupation bridge**, the line runs into a **shallow cutting**, before curving to enter a **short tunnel**. This carries the line under the **junction of Chester Road, Stretford Road, and Talbot Road**, and into **Trafford Bar Station**.

This is an original station, and was called Old Trafford, but it was decided by Metrolink to give this title to the next station. The 'bar' refers to a nearby toll gate that once stood on the turnpike road into Manchester. Much of the old station remains, including a particularly fine Victorian **street frontage building**, now disused. Note the **urn balustrade**, the mansard **roof** topped with **wrought iron**, and the elaborate carved stone **entrance door** (now blocked up). One wishes that a new use might be found for

The Little Branch that Could...

The Manchester, South Junction, and Altrincham Railway originated in a proposal to link London Road Station (now Piccadilly Station), and the main line to the south, with the Liverpool and Manchester line at Ordsall Lane by means of a loop line across the south side of the city. The joint railway was vested in the London and North Western Railway (LNWR) and the Manchester, Sheffield, and Lincolnshire Railway (MSLR); there were no private shareholders. The details of the land purchasing in the heart of Manchester were so complex that two solicitors were employed full time for over a year (the pressure of work gave one a breakdown). The loop line runs on a continuous brick viaduct of 224 arches containing 50 million bricks. However, almost as an afterthought, a branch from Castlefield Junction to the Cheshire market town of Altrincham was also built, opening in 1848. This ran in a virtually straight line across flat open country, and so was comparatively cheap to build. The loop line, though useful for goods traffic, soon lost its passenger trains (except for a few through coaches between Bolton Great Moor Street and London Euston), but the branch line traffic started to grow. This was due to two reasons. Firstly, it did not long remain a line to nowhere. A line to Warrington, connecting at Timperley, opened in 1853. This became part of the LNWR system, and later enabled trains to be run this way from London Road to Liverpool Lime Street. The first section of the Cheshire Lines network (of which the MSLR was a member of the owning group) opened between Altrincham and Knutsford in 1862. This soon extended to Chester (Northgate), and hourly forty minute expresses between Manchester and Chester were pounding along the line by the turn of the century. The second important feature was the impact of the branch upon housing patterns. Land prices soared along the line as Manchester merchants (or anyone who could afford it) built residences in what was then still countryside. By the turn of the century it was an important commuter line. The development of housing estates in the 1920s resulted in the London, Midland, and Scottish Railway electrifying the line in 1931 at 1500 volts DC as far as the through platforms at London Road Station. New suburban stations were opened. British Railways converted the entire line to 25kV 50HzAC in 1972, enabling suburban trains to be run to and from Crewe and Stafford. Finally, the line was chosen to become part of the Metrolink system from Cornbrook, and this involved a conversion to the Metrolink voltage.

such a fine building. Nowadays, access is by **ramps** and **steps** directly communicating with both platforms, linking the **Altrincham platform** with **Seymour Grove**, and the **Manchester plat**form with the corner of **Seymour Grove** and **Talbot Road**. The latter ramp follows the course of the road which led to the former goods yard (situated to the right of the line beyond the station), and is still supported by a fine **brick retaining wall**.

Traces of the former middle class suburb that once surrounded the station still exist, particularly along **Seymour Grove**. In the 19th century, the people of Chorlton called it Trafford Road, and the people of Old Trafford called it Chorlton Road. Neither name was appropriate, as other nearby roads already had those names. So the richest inhabitant, a millionaire grocer called Sir Thomas Seymour Mead, decided the road should be named after himself! A left turn, down **Talbot Road**, leads to the *Trafford Hall Hotel*, an imposing Victorian building with a rich history. The former home of Trafford Council, the hotel boasts an original **period staircase**. Notice the **stone** over the entrance inscribed 'Trafford Public Hall' with the date 1887. Continue towards **White City Way** on the right, and follow this road, passing the large **Greater Manchester Police Headquarters** on the right. The road now curves to the left into **Chester Road**. There is a **fine view** at the point of junction...to the east (right) is a distant panorama of the **towers of Manchester** city centre; in front lies **Salford Quays** and re-developed Ordsall; and to the left a distant view of the **United Ground**, the 'Theatre of Dreams'. Continue down **Chester Road**, and search out the **White City Gate**, which has an interesting story to tell. The Botanical and Horticultural Society was formed in Manchester in 1827. They purchased this sixteen-acre site, laid out gardens and constructed a large glasshouse. The gardens proved a popular public attraction, but had declined by the turn of the century, prompting a company to step in and acquire the site for the 'White City Amusement Park'. Opening in 1907, this 'refined' attraction was not above advertising itself at night by 25,000 electric lights. The White City is remembered by older Mancunians in its final incarnation as a Greyhound Racing Stadium. Nowadays, it is the home of the **White City Retail Park**. You can continue this walk to the **crossroads** ahead, and combine it with the exploration of the **United Ground** (p245), perhaps returning by the **Old Trafford Station**.

Trafford Bar to Sale

Immediately after starting from the station, the tram negotiates the **junction with the Chorlton line.** The **Chorlton incoming track**, after passing under our line, joins it in the Manchester direction to the right. The **outward track** branches off to the left. From the **bridge**, both lines are observed coming together to the left at the start of the route to Chorlton. The **bridge** that we are passing over formerly spanned a line from junctions on the Cheshire Lines Liverpool route to Chorlton junction and beyond. (p241) It conveyed Midland expresses from Manchester Central to St. Pancras. We pass the **new depot complex** on the left, accessed from both the Altrincham and Chorlton lines. It has repair facilities, though heavy overhauls and rebuilds are still undertaken at Queens Road.

The tram now arrives at **Old Trafford Station**. This was originally called Warwick Road, and has had a rather complex history. A temporary station opened near here in 1857 to serve the Manchester Art Treasures Exhibition, and again in 1887 to serve the Royal Jubilee Exhibition. The section of line between Old Trafford and Sale was **quadrupled** in 1897, and evidence of this can be seen here on the right and along the line. The station became a permanent feature as the 'Cricket Ground Station', before the name was changed upon electrification in 1931 to associate it with the nearby street. In its present incarnation, there are now **staggered platforms** with a **crossing** in between, leading to **Brian Statham Way** and the **Cricket Ground** to the right, and the corner of **Ayres Road** and **Warwick Road South** on the left. Note the **crash barriers** to handle large crowds on match days. (The station is currently used for the **Manchester United Ground** as well as the **Cricket Ground**.)

The **Cricket Ground**, to the right, has been the home of Lancashire County Cricket Club since its foundation in 1864, having been the ground of Manchester Cricket Club

Exhibitions

Manchester became a city in 1853, and immediately started to question its identity. Although it was the primary manufacturing centre in Britain, if not the world, critics satirised the boorishness of the new industrial class. The answer was to promote an art exhibition, the like of which the world had never seen before. It must be remembered that, at that time, most great works of art were largely held in private collections, usually inaccessible to the general public. This exhibition would bring as many of these together as possible. C.D. Young & Co., of London and Edinburgh (already engaged as builders of the new art museum in South Kensington, the precursor of the V&A) were appointed as contractors to build a temporary iron-and-glass structure similar to the Crystal Palace in London, 656 feet (200 m) long and 200 feet (61 m) wide, with one central barrel vault 56 feet (17 m) wide, crossed by a 104 feet (32 m) transept towards the western end. The exhibition comprised over 16,000 works split into ten categories; Pictures by Ancient Masters, Pictures by Modern Masters, British Portraits and Miniatures, Water Colour Drawings, Sketches and Original Drawings (Ancient), Engravings, Illustrations of Photography, Works of Oriental Art, Varied Objects of Oriental Art, and Sculpture. The collection included 5,000 paintings and drawings by "Modern Masters" such as Hogarth, Gainsborough, Turner, Constable, and the Pre-Raphaelites, and 1,000 works by European Old Masters, including Rubens, Raphael, Titian and Rembrandt. The exhibition was opened by Prince Albert on 5 May 1857, and was visited ceremonially by Queen Victoria on 29 June, during her second visit to Manchester, followed by the Queen and her entourage privately on 30 June. The exhibition attracted more than 1.3 million visitors; about four times the population of Manchester in 1857. Prominent visitors included the King of the Belgians, Louis Napoleon, Disraeli, Gladstone, and Charles Dickens. The gross receipts were £110,588 9sh. 8d, from which the exhibition made a small profit of £304 14s. 4d!

The Royal Jubilee Exhibition of 1887 was held to celebrate the Golden Jubilee of Queen Victoria's reign and mark the centenary of the granting of the town's first charter. It was opened by Princess Alexandra, wife of Edward, the Prince of Wales, on 3 May 1887, and remained open for 166 days, during which time there were 4.5 million paying visitors, 74,600 in one day alone. The site chosen for the construction of the purpose-built exhibition halls was the present-day White City Retail Park, formerly the Royal Botanical Gardens. The buildings were constructed from cast iron gas pipes (!), and had large glazed areas. The main building was in the shape of a cross, with a 150-foot (46 m) high central dome 90 feet (27 m) in diameter, from which radiated four long galleries. In addition to a worthy exposition of Manchester's cultural and technological achievements, there were amusements such as tobogganing slides and a sports arena, together with a recreation of 'Old Manchester' complete with costumed figures!

from 1857. International Test matches have been played there since 1884. Very unusually in a test match ground, the Old Trafford wickets are laid along an East-West axis. This has often caused problems for batsmen at the **Brian Statham End** as the sun sets. In 1999, the *Old Trafford Lodge* was opened, bringing to fruition a concept from 1981. The hotel has sixty-eight rooms, thirty-six of which command unobstructed views of the playing surface; an unusual use of space, but one which has proved to be extremely successful, generating income all year round.

After alighting from the tram, **Brian Statham Way** leads past the ground to **Talbot Road**. Notice the **Town Hall** on the corner of **Talbot Road**, to the left, with its impressive **clock tower**. It was designed by architects Bradshaw, Gass, and Hope of Bolton, and the contractors were Edwin Marshall & Sons. Building work began 21 August 1931, and it opened as Stretford Town Hall. It is now the town hall for Trafford Metropolitan Borough, an amalgamation of the former boroughs of Stretford, Sale, and Altrincham. The way continues directly ahead past the town hall, along **Warwick Road** to **Chester Road**. We cross this wide and busy highway with care, continuing along **Sir Matt Busby Way**, and crossing the **railway bridge** to arrive at **Manchester United Stadium**.

The 67,000 seat **Old Trafford Stadium** has always been a special place as it was one of the few grounds where the stands envelop the corners. Although more stadiums are now also totally enclosed, Old Trafford's sheer size still makes it a bewildering sight. Both east and west ends, which look almost identical, are large **two tiered stands**; the latter comprises the famous '**Stretford End**', the home of the most die-hard supporters.

Each comprises a **steep slope**, with a **large lower tier** and **smaller upper tier**. The three tiered **Sir Alex Ferguson Stand**, situated on the north side of the ground, is the largest capacity stand of any League Ground in England. The **corners** on each side of the **stand** are also filled with seating and extend around to meet both ends. These re-developed stands dwarf the older **Main (South) Stand** on the opposite side. This stand is single tiered, with a **television gantry** suspended below its roof. All the stands have a row of **executive boxes** at the back of the lower tier. The ground looks a little imbalanced with the smaller older **Main (South) Stand** looking somewhat out of place with its larger newer neighbours. However, the **best views of the ground** are probably from the front of this stand and from the away (east) section, as one gazes out upon the three newer, larger sides. (The **ticket centre** is located in a separate building.)

The first thing that we see, affixed to the side wall of the East Stand, is a **wall plaque** in remembrance of the Munich

Brian Statham

John Brian "George" Statham, CBE (1930-2000) was one of the leading English fast bowlers in 20th century English cricket. Initially a bowler of a brisk fast-medium pace, Statham was able to remodel his action to generate enough speed to become genuinely fast. This, together with unflagging accuracy and the ability to make the ball break back, made Statham a consistent force both for Lancashire in the County Championship and in Test Cricket, where his strike power helped give England perhaps its strongest attack of the 20th century during the 1950s and early 1960s. Statham was remarkably gentlemanly for a fast bowler and would rarely bowl a bouncer (and would warn the batsmen beforehand if he did), but his straight, full-length bowling could easily hit a batsman on the foot. Statham was also a brilliantly athletic out-fielder who was well suited to the one-day game when it emerged in the latter part of his career. On 30 August 2009, Brian Statham was inducted into the ICC Cricket Hall of Fame.

The Busby Babes

The name inspires memories in a lot of people, and not just football fans. Manchester United is probably the most famous football team in the world. But the rise to a global position had very humble beginnings in an amateur side formed by the workers of the Lancashire and Yorkshire Railway Carriage and Wagon Works at Newton Heath in 1878. (It was then known as 'Newton Heath'.) There is a charming story concerning the early years of the club. In 1901, the financial position was so desperate that a fund-raising bazaar was held. The team captain's St Bernard dog wandered the stalls with a collecting box tied to its neck. One day the dog seemingly disappeared, but ended up in the hands of a rich brewer who sought out the owner. Interestingly enough, the brewer gave the team a financial donation covering the deficit. The club became 'Manchester United' in 1902. The glory days began with the fondly remembered Matt Busby. The 'Busby Babes' were an incomparable football team, but many perished in the terrible Munich crash in 1958. United soon bounced back to its former position, and the rest is too well known to be repeated here. Curiously enough, the majority of supporters come from anywhere but Manchester! Ordinary Mancunians will often state a preference for Manchester City, the other local team. Indeed, it has been argued that United's super star status has removed it from its working class local roots. It is very difficult to obtain tickets at short notice, as every match tends to be sold out, and the cost of a season ticket (after joining a waiting list) might deter all but the most die-hard supporter, someone whose entire life revolves around the club. And there are many people like that.

disaster. Fronting the impressive **green glassed façade of the East Stand** is the **Sir Matt Busby Statue**. The **Megastore** (selling official merchandise) is located at the base of the façade. Opposite, across the **paved area** that terminates **Sir Matt Busby Way**, is the recently erected **United Trinity Statue** of three of the 1968 European Cup winning team; George Best, Denis Law and (now Sir) Bobby Charlton. Walk round the right-hand corner of the main façade to arrive at the entrance to the **North Stand** named for **Alex Ferguson**, the second of the two legendary managers in the team's history. There is a **statue** of the man himself positioned above the entrances to the **Manchester United Museum** (open daily, 9-5 except match days; admission charge), which will interest visitors who do not normally follow the game, and the **Red Café** (you can eat while watching soccer highlights on a television 'wall'). A visit to the former may be combined with a (pre-booked) **stadium tour**, which includes the changing rooms, players' lounge, and (wait for it!) a walk down the historic tunnel on to the sacred turf (stadium Tour bookings, ring 0161 868 8000).

Gary Rhodes, the television chef, is a Manchester United supporter, and one of the reasons why he opened the nearby ***Rhodes and Co*** at **Waters Reach** (not as expensive as you might think).

As the tram leaves **Old Trafford Station**, there is an excellent view of the **Cricket Ground** on the right. The line now passes through **suburbia**, exemplified by the appearance of the 'semi-detached house' a peculiarly British invention. Some distance beyond **Great Stone Road**, it curves to the left, and after passing the **spire of St. Ann's** on the right (p247) enters **Stretford Station**.

This is an original station, though briefly known as Edge Lane when it opened in 1849. It was once a substantial place with four platforms, and there still remains a fine **street frontage building** (now used as a shop), spanning the site of the disused lines to the right, and facing the **road bridge**. The **Altrincham Platform** communicates with **Edge Lane** by **stairs** and a **ramp**, and the **Manchester Platform** accesses the low level **car park** (the former goods yard) and its **approach** (by direct **stairs**). There is a regular **shuttle bus** from this car park to the **Trafford Centre** (p293).

Passengers alighting here can follow **Edge Lane** to the right over the **canal bridge** towards **Chester Road**. The easily missed access to the **towpath** (on the left) is the start of a pleasant walk along the **canal** to the **Watch House** (p248) and (by a continuation of the path) to **Sale Water Park** (p314).The sadly disused **Longford Cinema**, situated on the right-hand corner of the crossroads, is perhaps the most visually striking building in the town. Designed by the architect Henry Elder, it was the height of Art Deco fashion when it was opened by the Mayor

The Longford Cinema, Stretford

of Stretford in 1936. Its unusual "cash register" frontage was intended to symbolise the 'business' aspect of show business, and was once picked out in neon. Opposite, and reached by an **underpass**, is the fine **Stretford Public Hall**, with an impressive **clock tower**. The building has a curious history. It was constructed in 1878, the gift of John Rylands (p248) to the local population (or perhaps an example of his megalomania). Although it housed the Overseers Office, it also contained lecture rooms (in which Mrs. Rylands and her maid taught sewing!); a temperance coffee room; and a lending library to improve the tone of the district. The Local Board purchased it after his death, but, although referred to as the 'Old Town Hall', it was never used as such. It was converted into a Civic Theatre in 1933, but after a period of decline and disuse was restored in 1994. It is now occupied by the Children and Young Persons Services. An extension of the subway system leads to the **Stretford Mall Shopping Centre** on the opposite corner to the former cinema. A short stroll past the **street frontage shops** towards the distant **tower block** leads to **St. Matthews Church**, the parish church of Stretford. The De Trafford family erected a chantry chapel that served as the local church in medieval times, though probably not on this precise spot. A new chapel was erected in 1718, but the current brick structure dates from 1841-2. The **chancel**, with its patterned brickwork, was added in 1860. It is a typical 19th century gothic revival church with **galleries** on three sides. (Saturday coffee morning; otherwise ring 0161 865 2535 to visit.)

A short walk from the crossroads down **Chester Road**, in the Manchester direction, passes **St. Ann's Roman Catholic Church**, with its distinctive **spire**. Like All Saints, Barton (p292), it was the gift of Sir Humphrey De Trafford (as a wedding anniversary present for his wife Lady Annette) and designed by Pugin the younger. It was begun in 1863 and consecrated in 1867. This fine example of the gothic revival is well worth a look. (The church is open at all reasonable hours; but if the main body is closed off, it is usually possible to view it from the west end through a glass screen.) Continue onwards across the **canal**, arriving at **Gorse Hill Park**. Here will be found the fine **entrance gate**, much too grand for the open space beyond. This is because the gate in question once formed the entrance to Trafford Hall, the ancient seat of the De Trafford family. The house and deer park was sold for development in 1897, and the gate removed here. The deer park became the present industrial estate, and what remained of the house was demolished in 1939. Notice the **war memorial** and search out a **mysterious plague stone**. It is probably a glacial erratic, but during the Great Plague of 1655-6 the holes in the top of the stone were filled with vinegar or holy water, through which coins were passed in the belief that this would halt the spread of the disease. The holes are probably too deep for that to have been the stone's original purpose though; consequently, it may originally have been a marker on the Roman road between Northwich and Manchester, or some other kind of boundary marker. Another theory suggests that the stone may have been the base of an Anglo-Saxon cross shaft. A local legend had it that the stone was slowly sinking into the earth, and that its final disappearance would mark the end of the world!

A left turn from the **station entrance** will lead to **Longford Park**, the largest park in Trafford, at 54 acres (22 ha). It includes a **pet's corner**, **botanical garden**, **bowling greens** and **children's play areas**, and is the finishing point of the annual Stretford Pageant. Longford Park was the home of John Rylands, an industrialist, philanthropist, and Manchester's first multi-millionaire, from 1855 until his death in 1888. (The John Rylands Library in Deansgate, Manchester, is his abiding legacy.) The house he constructed in the park, Longford Hall, was unfortunately demolished in 1995. Today only the **front porch**, **coach house**, and the **stable buildings** remain.

Upon leaving the station, it will be noticed that the **canal** has joined the railway to the right. A tall **1960s tower block** is a conspicuous landmark to the right, but look out for the white painted **Watch House** (p247) by the canal towpath. It is the oldest building in Stretford, and was used as a farm house before the canal was constructed. It then became a staging post (where the horses were changed) for the passenger 'fly boats' that plied between Manchester and Runcorn on the Bridgewater Canal. Now it is the headquarters

The historic Watch House on the canal

The Bridgewater Canal

Although the Dukes's Canal was the pioneer 'cut', it was primarily a private affair, intended to bring coal from the Worsley mines to Manchester. However, its success resulted in the Duke thinking that he could better the inadequacies of the Mersey and Irwell Navigation by constructing a canal that accessed the Mersey Estuary near Runcorn. The Bridgewater Canal ran from a junction with the Dukes Canal near Trafford Park at a place called Waters Meeting. The first section opened in 1767, and the canal was complete by 1776. It was an unusual canal, for it passed through flat country, and was more or less straight with virtually no locks. It was thus cheap to build and easy to operate. Long after the railways arrived, it gave its competitors a run for their money by moving bulk cargoes cheaply and efficiently. It is now part of the celebrated 'Cheshire Ring' and you will see lines of pleasure craft moored along its banks at several places.

of a cruising club. **Stretford Cemetery** can be seen to the left; it was designed by John Shaw and opened in 1885. The elaborate **chapel** is in the decorated style, designed by architects Bellamy & Hardy. After passing **Hawthorne Road**, the line runs on to a shallow **embankment** as it traverses the **flood plain of the River Mersey**. As we cross the **River Mersey** by a **girder bridge**, notice the parallel **stone canal aqueduct**.

The **flash** (small lake) in **Sale Water Park** (p314) is visible to the left, before the tram passes under the **M60 Motorway**. A short distance further onwards, and **Dane Road Station** is reached on the other side of the **road bridge**.

This station dates from the electrification of 1931, and the surviving **footbridge** and **booking office** remain largely unchanged. There are stairs from both **platforms** to the **footbridge**, which now extends to link with a **lift** on the **Manchester platform**, and also boasts a new **station entrance** on to **Dane road**. A new **path** also runs from the **Altrincham platform** under the steel **supports** of the (disused) **former booking office** to access **Dane Road**. Notice the (closed) **former footbridge** leading to this building. This station was the scene of a poltergeist manifestation in the 1970s!

The station can be used to access both **Priory Gardens** and (by a pedestrian bridge over the Motorway) **Sale Water Park** (p314). Turn right upon exiting the station, and walk down **Dane Road**. Look for the **main entrance to Priory Gardens** on the left.

Sale Station, in almost its original condition

The line passes through more **suburbia**, though some blocks of **recent apartments** are to the fore.

The tram now arrives at **Sale Station**, an absolute delight to the eye! Although it dates from the opening of the line, the **structures** are somewhat later. There are fine **wrought iron and glass canopies**, and platform buildings (sadly closed up) of superb **polychromatic** (multi-coloured) **brickwork**. **Stairs** access **School Road/Northenden Road** either side of the fine (disused and closed off) **street frontage building** astride the tracks. Two **side exits** from the **Altrincham platform** exit to an **approach road** leading to the corner of **Northenden Road** and **Hope Road**. A **side exit** from the **Manchester platform** accesses a **lift.**(There was a goods siding on this side of the station, alongside the canal.)

Turn left out of the station, and walk down **School Road** across the **canal** to arrive at the tasteful **town hall** (built 1914, damaged by an incendiary bomb in 1940, and rebuilt 1952) and **fine war memorial** (1925) with a **statue of St. George**. Situated next to the town hall, the **Waterside Arts Centre** built around

Sale Town Hall

a **waterside plaza**, houses a **library**, the 320 seat **Robert Bolt Theatre**, the **Lauriston Gallery**, and the **Corridor Gallery**. Robert Bolt the playwright (1924-1995) was born in Sale. He is mainly remembered for writing 'A Man for All Seasons', but he also wrote the screenplays for 'Lawrence of Arabia' and 'Dr. Zhivago'. The centre, which was opened in 2004, regularly hosts concerts, exhibitions and other community events. In 1973, the **shopping precinct** in the town centre, which had grown up in the mid-19th century, was redeveloped and **pedestrianised** in an attempt to increase trade. There are some good **shops and cafés** here. Alternatively, turn right out of the **station** and walk down **Northenden Road**, keeping a look out for **Cheltenham Drive** on the left. This is the entrance to **Worthington Park**, a popular area for recreation since the late Mrs. Worthington donated the land in 1900. The park has many original features including the **bandstand**, a **bronze bust** of Dr J P Joule (1818-1889), the famous local physicist who lived nearby in Wardle Road, and attractive entrance **feature gates**. The **lodge** contains the **date stone** from Sale Old Hall (p315).

Sale to Brooklands

The **canal** parallels the line beyond Sale, through **leafy suburban development** where some fine Victorian houses can be seen. The **cemetery,** with its **chapel spire** (p252), appears to the right, and we pass under **Marsland Bridge** to arrive at the station.

Brooklands Station, a listed structure, remains in its 1859 condition. Note the attractive combination of red brick with blue brick dressings, and the roof of welsh slate. The (disused) **street entrance** is single storey building with a central entrance, framed by blue brick pilasters. The **brick road bridge** formerly

Brooklands Station

The Ambitious Banker

Samuel Brooks was born in 1793 at Whalley. His family had originally been yeoman farmers, but his father developed a business in trading cotton yarn. Almost as a side-line, he opened a bank at Blackburn, and, in partnership with Roger Cunliffe, the firm of Cunliffe Brooks became one of the most important banks in the region. The young Samuel was sent to Manchester, where he became a partner in a calico printing business. However, he opened a branch of the bank in the mill premises and was very successful. He eventually took over the entire banking business and moved the headquarters to Manchester. His eventual fortune exceeded £1million and he was considered to be "one of the wealthiest commoners in the country." 'Old Stink o'Brass' (as Brooks was jokingly called, for he was a tough but friendly Lancashire man with a liking for repartee) had many other interests besides banking. He was, for example, the first Deputy Chairman of the Manchester and Leeds Railway, though his real love was property development, seemingly a desire to transform derelict and often marshy tracts of land into residential suburbs. Having thus transformed large parts of Sale, and created a garden suburb at Whalley Range (named after his Lancashire birthplace), he entered upon a new project with equal vigour in his retirement. In1856, he purchased a large area of ground (about 800 acres in total) alongside the recently opened Manchester to Altrincham railway from Lord Stamford. He successfully drained the marshy ground and built a road running southeast across it for one and a quarter miles as straight as an arrow. Trees lined the road, presenting a green avenue of pine, beech, lime and poplar, framing the stately mansions to be built on each side by wealthy businessmen. He also guaranteed the financial costs of a new railway station, to be called Brooklands (he named both the station and district after himself!). It opened for traffic in 1859, and soon proved that a financial guarantee was unnecessary. Sadly, he died in 1864, and never saw his grandiose scheme come to fruition; indeed, part of it remains unspoiled countryside to this day.

carried a glazed iron footbridge to the **Manchester platform**, now accessed from **Marsland Road** by **stairs** and a **lift**. (The **road bridge** probably predates the station.) The **Manchester platform** has a three bay hipped **roof canopy** on cast iron columns, each carrying four filigree brackets. The canopy has been truncated on the rail side because of the electrification and has a timber fascia. **The Altrincham platform** has the base of the **former staircase entrance** and a three bay **station house**, now *The Brook* pub. Station access here is by way of the **approach road**. There was a small goods yard on this side.

To the left of the **railway bridge**, **Marsland Road** crosses the **canal**. A short walk to the left, down **Walton Road**, brings the visitor to **Sale Cemetery** and **Walton Park**. The latter contains a **miniature railway** that usually operates most Sundays (weather permitting). On 3

Ready to depart on the miniature railway!

A Victorian Valhalla

Sale/Brooklands Cemetery lies on both sides of Marsland Road, near Brooklands Station. The north (right-hand) side is the older, houses a chapel complex, and boasts a large number of large and ornate tombs. Because the cemetery, which opened in 1862, predated Manchester's Southern Cemetery, many wealthy Manchester families were buried in Sale. The Cemetery Chapels, designed by local architects, were built around 1865. They form a H-plan complex, with a tower and spire (visible to the right from the tram, just before Brooklands Station) rising from central archway, and tall gabled flanking cross-wings with linking lower ranges extending to form outer entrance porches. The whole is formed of coursed thin sandstone rubble with ashlar

Sale Cemetry

dressings, coped gables with cross finials, and a Welsh slate roof covering of decorative bands. The cemetery's most famous occupant is perhaps James Joule, the scientist, but the cemetery also contains the graves of John Dancer, a Manchester scientific instrument maker; John Knowles, Master Cotton spinner and friend of Friedrich Engels; Richard Pankhurst, the husband and father of the famous suffragettes; Samuel Lord, an American department store tycoon; and John Brogden, the railway contractor who built the Altrincham line and (amongst other things) Manchester Victoria Station! The two parts of the cemetery are connected by a tunnel under the road. In the newer southern section the newer plots include a number of military graves from World War II.

August 1943, at 11:50 pm, a Wellington Bomber on a training exercise crashed in Walton Park, and the pilot and the bomb-aimer were killed. Spare them a thought before you leave.

If there is time, it is worth a short walk to the right from the station, to the junction with **Brooklands Road.** The block of offices on the opposite corner stands on the site of the Brooklands Hotel, built in 1872. In addition to catering for wedding and masonic banquets, it advertised its suitability as a base for gentlemen hunting with the North Cheshire Hounds, indicating the still rural nature of the area. However, it was also the site of the signing of the 'Brooklands Agreement' on 24 March 1893, the first agreement between capital and labour in the cotton industry. It ended a twenty week lockout, but also uniquely provided for a conciliation and arbitration process that actually worked in the ensuing decades. The Hotel was demolished in 1972. Turn right into **Brooklands Road.** As at Whalley Range, Brooks built this street as a private road in 1862, with plots of land available for superior residences. The original private road was four miles long in its entirety, and this part is wide and tree lined, constructed with a sound stone foundation. The mock Tudor **Arden Hall**, on the right, is typical of the second generation of residences that, sadly, Brooks never lived to see. The Grade II listed structure was built in 1904, and is now used as offices. The ***Belmore Hotel***, on the left, is earlier, and is thought to be one of the few surviving first generation residences that Brooks himself built in 1861. It was extended in later years, and after 1875 was used for a time as the country home for the daughter of a wealthy coal merchant.

We soon reach **St. John the Divine**, a rather fine church on the right (the church is best visited when the Thursday coffee morning is held; otherwise ring 0161 9735947 to arrange access). Amongst other things, Samuel Brooks was a churchman, and he knew that to make a district into a community it needed a church. He had already built a church at Whalley Range and now he looked around for a suitable design for his Brooklands church. He decided to employ a young Manchester architect called Alfred Waterhouse, who had recently won renown with his plans for the Manchester Assize Courts. Brooks gave 8,500 square yards of land and granted £10,000 for the building and endowment of the church, which was to be 'the centrepiece of a respectable suburb' (at a time when churches in Manchester were being built for £2,000!). Work began in 1864, but was delayed by his death later that year. Completed in 1868, it is built of good Yorkshire stone with **two fine facades** to the east and west (the former with a **dedicatory inscription**, and prefaced by a **war memorial**). The **interior** is lined with cream and brown brickwork in horizontal stripes and diaper work ('Bristol Byzantine' some called it). There is some good 'Arts and Craft' movement **stained glass**.

A Hike to Hale

If you want a good long country walk along (mostly) metalled roads and paths, come and follow in the footsteps of Samuel Brooks himself! Continue down **Brooklands Road** to what was the old turnpike road between Stockport and Altrincham (now the **A560**), marked by a large **traffic island**. The road beyond this important junction was not used for development. It may have been made for Samuel's own convenience in travelling around his estate, and it is thought that it comprised part of an intended great driveway that was to communicate between Brooklands Station and his residence at Hale Barns (p255). The original intention was to construct the driveway as far as **Warburton Green**, though it never got that far. Parts of it survive, double hedged and tree-lined with plantations eight yards wide on both sides. The estate was sold and broken up in 1917, but, since World War II, development has been restricted by planning laws and a large part of the road still passes through **greenbelt agricultural land**.

Cross **Stockport Road** and **Shaftesbury Avenue**, and follow the signpost (indicating a path to Manchester Airport) along **Brooks Drive** (which is signed); Brooks was careful to erect a toll house in the vicinity. The road crosses the **Altrincham-Stockport railway line**. Baguely Station was situated to the left of the bridge, adjacent to Shady Lane; it opened in 1866 and closed in 1964. There is a proposal to reopen the station at a site further down the line so it might act as an interchange with the Metrolink station on the intended Airport Line. A little beyond the **bridg**e, the path becomes a little entangled with a **housing estate. Dunmaston Avenue**, a suburban road, joins us from the left by the gate, and we follow it a short distance to where the path resumes, directly ahead. Pass down the **tree- lined path**. Beyond the **gate** the **wooded drive** is now quite straight for some distance, and starts to parallel **Greystoke Avenue** to the right. After crossing **Redbrook Road** (where the path narrows), notice the wooden **sculpted bench** and **sign**. Beyond **Dee Avenue** (opposite the **Youth Centre** and **sports pitches** on the right) we arrive at **Ridgeway Road.** Here we **pass into open country**, following the drive along a **finely wooded stretch** to the road junction with **Dobbinetts Lane.** Go round the **gate** to the left of the **model estate cottages**, and the Drive continues as straight as an arrow, to **Whitecarr Lane.**

This is as far as Samuel got. His son continued the Estate Road by adapting the quaintly named **Roaring Gate Lane** to his purposes. So pass over the **crossroads** and follow this

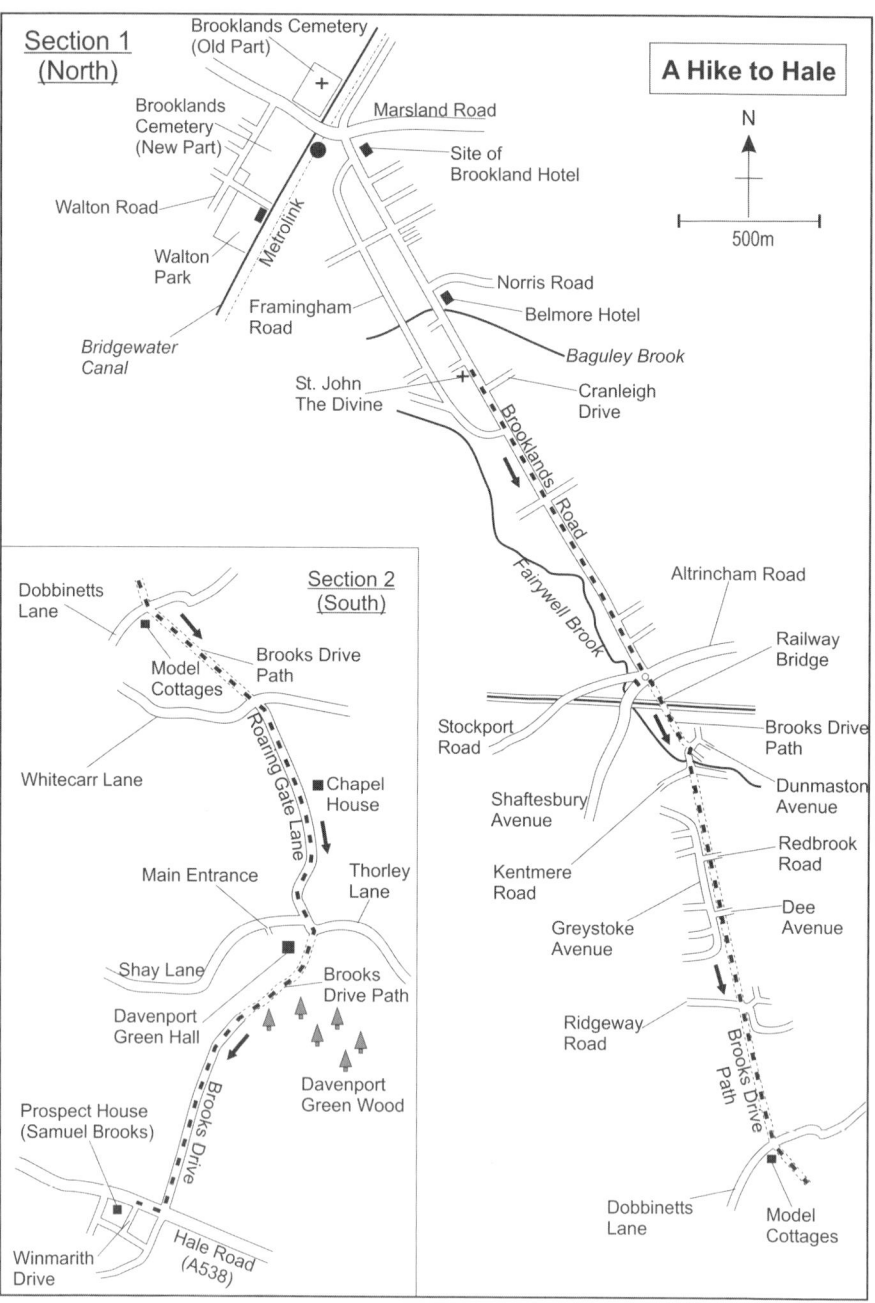

A Hike to Hale

Section 1 (North)

Brooklands Cemetery (Old Part)
Brooklands Cemetery (New Part)
Marsland Road
Site of Brookland Hotel
Walton Road
Metrolink
Walton Park
Framingham Road
Bridgewater Canal
St. John The Divine
Norris Road
Belmore Hotel
Baguley Brook
Cranleigh Drive
Brooklands Road
Fairywell Brook
Altrincham Road
Railway Bridge
Stockport Road
Brooks Drive Path
Shaftesbury Avenue
Dunmaston Avenue
Kentmere Road
Redbrook Road
Greystoke Avenue
Dee Avenue
Ridgeway Road
Brooks Drive Path
Dobbinetts Lane
Model Cottages

Section 2 (South)

Dobbinetts Lane
Brooks Drive Path
Model Cottages
Whitecarr Lane
Roaring Gate Lane
Chapel House
Main Entrance
Thorley Lane
Shay Lane
Brooks Drive Path
Davenport Green Hall
Davenport Green Wood
Prospect House (Samuel Brooks)
Brooks Drive
Winmarith Drive
Hale Road (A538)

254

Lane. (This is a road without pavements so please exercise caution!) We pass **Roaring Gate Farm** on the left, and, beyond a curve to the right, **Davenport Green Farm** (dating from the 18th century). Beyond **Shay Lane**, on the right, the road turns left and becomes **Thorley Lane** (which eventually leads to Manchester Airport). However, we turn right through the gap to the left of the **green gate**, and find ourselves upon a surviving section of **Brooks Drive** once more! There is a glimpse of **Davenport Green Hall** to the right (the house and complex is entered by a driveway off **Shay Lane**). It was built in 1617, and was part of the Davenport Estate, owned by Richard Grantham, who commanded a company in the parliamentary army in the Civil War. In the late 19th- Century Sir William Cunliffe-Brooks MP (Samuel's son) owned the estate and grounds. There is a date stone with "1617 ET," surviving timber framing, and a later brick wing. However, the house was much altered in the eighteenth and nineteenth centuries, though a half-timbered gable is clearly visible through the trees. The Hall is now used for weddings, conferences, and other functions. The path here is unmetalled and can be muddy in wet weather. It leads to a **gate** where a metalled driveway commences. We shortly pass the pretty **Davenport Green Wood** on the left, through which flows **Timperley Brook**. **Housing** soon starts to re-appear (and one can start to study how the 'other half' live!), before the Drive reaches the **Altrincham-Wilmslow road** (now the A538) in the village of **Hale**.

The earliest documented reference to Hale is in the Domesday Book, although the name of the settlement is probably as old as 7th- or 8th century; Hale grew during the medieval period, and **Hale Barns** (the part that we have entered) was created as a separate settlement. It is historically part of Cheshire, and was mostly used for agriculture until the opening of the railway between Altrincham and Knutsford transformed it into a residential area. Hale and Hale Barns encompass some of the wealthiest parts of England, and the district has some of the **most expensive house prices in the country**. It is worth a brief detour to the right as far as **Winmarith Drive** on the left. The third property after this road is **Prospect House**. Samuel Brooks resided in an earlier house on this site, and fragments of it are incorporated into the present structure. (Private property, please respect.) He only stayed here from time to time while he supervised work on his estate, lunching at the local Unicorn Inn. However, he breathed his last at his house in Whalley Range, Manchester. A distance back along **Hale Road** leads to the *Manchester Airport Marriot Hotel*, the **M56** and the **World Freight Terminal**. At some point in the future, it will be possible to return via the Metrolink Airport Line, but, for the time being, there are frequent bus services to **Manchester Airport**, enabling the walk to end here (children may wish to see some aircraft!). The same bus, in the opposite direction, returns the walker to **Altrincham Interchange**.

The recently published (2014) proposals for 'High Speed Line Two' will carry the railway right through this district, with unimaginable consequences. Only time will tell.

Brooklands to Altrincham

Beyond **Brooklands Station**, the line continues through suburban greenery. The **shed** belonging to Trafford Rowing Cub comes into sight after **Sale Cemetery** on the right, and walkers and cyclists can be seen on the canal **towpath**. There are even **allotments** to the left. The tram passes under **Park Road**, and enters **Timperley Station**.

This is another original station, and the attractive **brick main building** and **footbridge** survive. The **platforms** are accessed by **stairs** and **lifts**. The former booking office contains a very useful (and recommended) **café**. The impact of the railway to Altrincham can be seen in Timperley's growth between 1851 and 1871, the population more than doubling from 1,008 to 2,112. The middle classes migrated from the centre of Manchester, and this is reflected by the increase of numbers in domestic servants in Timperley in the census. Many visitors seek out the new **Frank Sidebottom statue**, the persona (with the papier-maché head) of the late Chris Sievey, a performance artist with a cult following. It is to be found at the confluence of **Stockport Road** and **Park Road**, about ten minutes walk to the left of the station.

Immediately after the station, the **canal** parts company with the Altrincham line, and the tracks spread out to accommodate a long **central turn back and storage siding**. The long vanished junction for the LNWR line to Warrington and Liverpool was to the right, before the **bridge** that once carried the Cheshire Lines route to Glazebrook Junction and on to Liverpool Central, the path of the St. Pancras expresses. **Deansgate Junction**, to the left, is very much still alive. Actually, this no longer a true junction; there is no physical connection between the Metrolink line, which is reduced to single track before the junction site, and the railway line, which comes in from the left to run alongside it after also becoming single track. The **second bridge** was used by LNWR trains to Warrington and Liverpool. Beyond **Deansgate Lane level crossing**, the section of line as far as **Navigation Road Station** is very curious. The track formation is not wide enough to permit four tracks, so the old **down** (left-hand) line is used by trains operating the Manchester-Chester service, and the **up** (right-hand) line by the Metrolink trams.

Thus, the **old Manchester platform** (accessed from the **level crossing end**) at **Navigation Road Station** (of 1931 vintage, serving new housing) is for Metrolink trams,

A Maze of Railways

The railway history of the line beyond Timperley Station is complex, and a great deal of the system still survives. The Warrington and Stockport Railway opened in 1854 from Timperley Junction, just beyond Timperley station. The junction was situated to the right of the present three track layout, but nothing now remains. Money ran out, and the line never reached Stockport; it became part of the London and North Western Railway (LNWR) in 1859, and was subsequently used by trains between London Road Station and Liverpool via Warrington (Arpley). The Stockport, Timperley, and Altrincham Junction Railway revived these ambitions at a later date. It linked with the existing LNWR line at Broadheath Junction, passed over the Altrincham line by the second bridge after Timperley Station, and opened through to Stockport in February 1866. A curve ran from Skelton Junction on this line to link with the Altrincham line at Deansgate Junction, and was mainly used by goods trains and a local passenger service via the junction between Altrincham and Stockport. The 'Timperley' curve was built in 1879 by the Manchester, Sheffield and Lincolnshire Railway (MS&LR) linking Skelton Junction with Timperley Junction, enabling rail traffic to run from Godley Junction to Manchester this way. It was a short lived venture, and the site of the curve disappeared before 1914.Lastly, the Cheshire Lines Joint Committee built a link (often referred to as the West Timperley line) from Skelton Junction to Glazebrook on their Manchester to Liverpool line. It opened in 1873, and was later used by the Liverpool-St. Pancras expresses in order to avoid Manchester. It crossed the Altrincham line by the first bridge after Timperley Station, the one that has lost its embankment on the right-hand side. Alas, the link to Glazebrook is no more. The last section of the Warrington line remained open as far as Partington Power Station until the 1980s. However, since the Metrolink conversion, the Chester to Manchester (via Northwich) service has been diverted via Deansgate and Skelton Junctions to Stockport and on to Piccadilly, once more linking Altrincham with Stockport!

while the **former Altrincham platform** is reserved for the train passengers. This can cause some confusion.

However this is resolved beyond the **Navigation Road level crossing**. The track bed widens out so much to permit **four tracks**, two each for both Metrolink and the railway line. The **A560 road bridge** marks the site of a former level crossing and the first Altrincham Station. The latter was replaced by the present station in 1881.

Altrincham Station is very much in its original condition, dating from 1881. The Metrolink trams terminate in the former MSJR platforms, though, in practice, only the **Manchester platform**, with its delightful **glass and wrought iron can**opy is used. Here will be found a **newsagent** and a refurbished **café**. There is also a **booking office** for the trains on the way out to the **bus station**. The **footbridge** accesses an **island platform**, the far side of which is used for train departures to Stockport and Manchester, and then continues to the **departure platform** for the Chester trains. This platform has another fine **canopy**. There was a goods yard (now a **car park**) on this side of the station, and a short branch served the local gasworks. The **footbridge** is now also accessed by **lifts**, but the island platform can be reached by a **pedestrian crossing** beyond the Metrolink tracks. The Altrincham line once continued beyond this point to terminate at Bowdon Station, but the re-siting of Altrincham station made this further stop impractical. Bowdon station became a carriage shed after 1881 (it possessed a fine overall wooden roof), but now no longer exists. Altrincham Station and Interchange are subject to a £19 million redevelopment and refurbishment project. A new footbridge with lifts will link all the platforms, but the original platform canopies will be retained. The booking office will be joined by the 'travel shop'. The bus station will be completely rebuilt, though the (listed) **clock tower** will be untouched.

Altrincham

Altrincham is an old market town, with a long history dating to medieval times and beyond. Many of the inhabitants were engaged in agriculture, and worked on the Earl of Stamford's estate. The opening of the railway transformed large tracts of Altrincham and Bowdon into a residential suburb. First came the Manchester merchants, with their grand houses, followed by the middle class, who resided in tasteful villa style residences. Little has changed over the years, and the district is still a very desirable place to live.

Leave the station and walk to the left of the **bus station** in order to cross Stamford New Road by the **pedestrian crossing**. Notice the **clock tower**, a listed structure contemporary with the station. Follow this street to the right, past the **library** and **Railway House**, turning left up **Stamford Street** by the little **garden** at the corner. If you are a modeller, it is well worth making a short detour by following the street round to the left at the *Victoria* pub to reach *Walton's Model Shop* (closed Wednesday and Sunday). It stocks a wide range of model railway items, and has an excellent reputation. **Victoria Street** diverges at the *Victoria* public house to reach the **Old Market Place**. This is marked by the façade of the *Old Market Tavern* at the top of the street. The principal part of this structure was the Old Town Hall, with its **clock tower** and belfry on **Church Street**, which cuts across the top of **Victoria Street**. It was built by the Earl of Stamford in 1849 and is a listed building. The **oriel window** below the tower is in the Council Chamber where the Court Leet (Manorial Court) met. The **bell tower** itself is a copy of the original 1684 Buttermarket bell tower, and the original bell was re-hung here, but is now in the possession of the Court Leet. The Old Town Hall was merged with the 'Unicorn' public house about 1910. The latter was originally a mail coaching inn; it had livery stables and was used as an Excise Office. The stagecoach from Manchester to Chester used to call each morning and deliver the post and newspapers (newspapers were more than £10 each at today's prices). 'The Unicorn' later became the *Old Market Tavern*. On the wall of the *Old Market Tavern*, round the corner, is a **Plaque** commemorating the lighting of the hotel in 1844 from the first gasworks in the Altrincham area (the gas plant was at the rear of the hostelry). We are now in the area, to the left of the *Old Market Tavern*, known as the **Old Market Place**.

It was possibly the site of the original Saxon settlement and became the medieval trading centre (Hamo de Masci issued a Market Charter in 1290, possibly to help his military finances). It is now a Conservation Area.

A number of the buildings have medieval timbers and were built on narrow burgage plots which existed around **Church Street**, **Old Market Place**, and **Market Street**. The Market Place Traders erected the replica **cross**, **stocks** and **whipping post** in 1990. The **lintel** from the Police Lock-ups of 1838 in George Street, which were closed in 1866, was incorporated into the stocks' seat. Although considered historic medieval market boroughs, the pretensions of these 'antient' Cheshire towns were often mocked.

> "The mayor of Altrincham,
> The Mayor of Over,
> One's a Thatcher,
> T'others a dober (dauber)!"

The *Orange Tree*, to the rear of the cross and stocks, and some of the adjacent structures, contains fragments of 16th and 17th century buildings. The *Orange Tree*, which has been a pub only since the 1880s, consists of two ancient timber buildings which had an alley on the left and has wattle and daub remains in a back room. Notice the **former Cunliffe Brooks**

Butter and Wives for Sale

The three-day 'Sanjam Fair' (a corruption of St. James' Fair, held around the Feast of the Assumption on15 August) was held in Old Market Place from 1319 to 1894, but ordinary trading took place every market day. The Buttermarket hall of 1684 was in the middle of it until about 1850; all sellers of butter and cheese were compelled to bring their wares there. Until 1838 there was a courtroom over the Buttermarket, with a lock-up at the side. There were also stocks and a whipping post, for public floggings took place here until the early 19th century. The Market Cross was located in front of the Buttermarket, where proclamations were made and intending brides and grooms had to declare their intentions! In 1823 a man sold his wife here for 18 pence (7.5p), which he believed was legal if he provided a halter to put over her neck! Thomas de Quincey, in his 'Confessions of an English Opium Eater' described the Old Market Place in 1814 as he travelled by stage coach from Manchester to Chester: "fruits and flowers were scattered about in profusion; even the stalls of the butchers, from their brilliant cleanliness, appeared attractive; and bonny young women of Altrincham were all tripping about in caps and aprons coquettishly disposed."

Altrincham Market Place

258

Bank (p251), to the left, now used as offices, a spectacular essay in mock-Tudor 'black and white' style, with copious sandstone, a tall banking hall illuminated by stained glass, and incorporating accommodation for managers. Return, via the **market**, to the **station**.

Altrincham Ice Dome is an ice rink with 2,000 seats and up to 500 standing places. The Ice Dome hosts the home matches of the Manchester Phoenix and Trafford Metros ice hockey clubs, as well as junior ice hockey, public skating sessions, birthday parties, private events, and skating lessons. It is located in Oakfield Road, which can be reached from the station car park.

An Excursion to Dunham Massey

Altrincham's most famous attraction can be reached by a frequent **bus service** Both the number 5 (daily) and number 38 (not Sunday) deposits the visitor at the **Dunham Massey main gate** (p260); the 38 passes **Bowden** Church en route, and the 5 stops at the foot of **Church Brow**. However, if it is a fine day, and you have the leisure time to do it, the following **walk** is suggested. Leave the **station** and proceed to the left down **Stamford New Road** and **Railway Street**. At the **fork** in the road, go right, along **The Downs**. Note **Victoria Terrace**, a row of what appear to be Regency houses, followed by similar residences to the right. The way is now left along tree lined **Delamer Road**, typical of late 19th century suburbia, with **villa style residences** in light stock brick. The design of these houses is nearly always the same. They are set back from the roadway, sometimes with a small carriage drive. Their gables are capped with barge boarding and the small attic dormer windows indicate servant's quarters. Even a middle class family of the time would possess a butler (who valeted for the master) a cook, a maid, and probably a scullery maid. These would live in, but the family would avail themselves of the services of a jobbing gardener and a laundry woman as required. The **Baptist Chapel** on the left served a business community with pronounced nonconformist leanings. The highway leads to **St. Mary's Road**. Do not be deceived. This is indeed a 'private road', but that only really relates to vehicles. So walk along it, and go to the left along the footpath round the side of a **hedge like barrier**. The street beyond emerges on to **Stamford Road**. Turn right into it, and walk down until you reach the old centre of **Bowdon**. This is marked by two establishments. The *Griffin* is a traditional pub, with a reputation for good food and a beer garden. The *Stamford Arms*, next door (or rather, round the corner) is a Grade II listed building, being over 200 years. It has a whitewashed exterior and there are low beamed ceilings inside. Food is available, and there is a small picnic area overlooking the small **village green**. The **fountain** on the green was erected "in memory of Francis Marriot."

St. Mary the Virgin, Bowdon

Across the road is a sandstone **war memorial** dating from around 1920 by Arthur Hennings. It stands in front of the **church of St. Mary the Virgin**. (The church is usually open 2-4 on Sundays. At other times, enquire at the adjacent Parish Office, or ring 0161 929 1537.)

A church on this site was recorded in

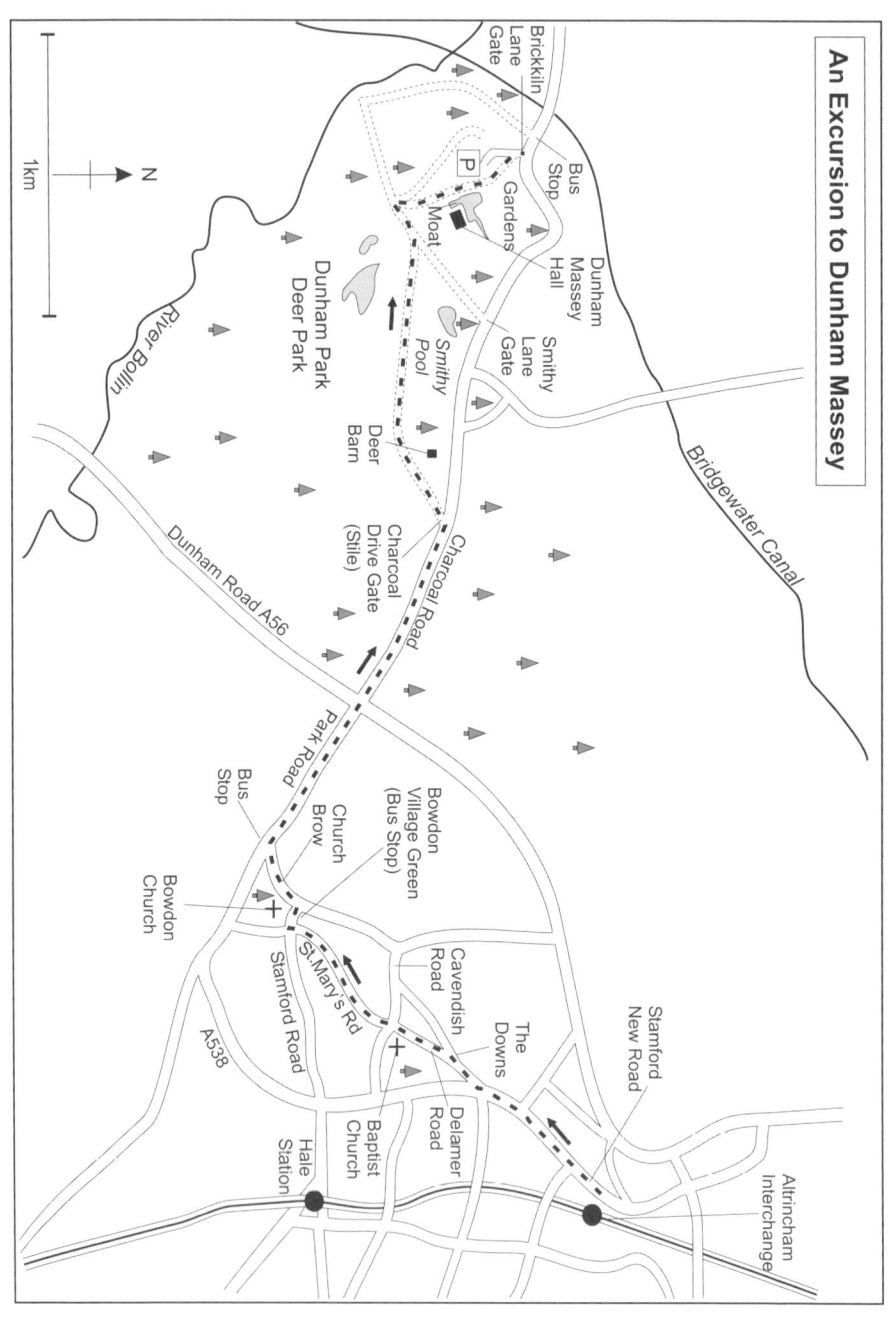

An Excursion to Dunham Massey

the Domesday Book, and it is probable that a new church was built in the 14th century and remodelled in the 16th century. However, as often is the case, the Victorians 'improved' the church by completely rebuilding it between 1858 and 1860, although the **16th century roofs** of the aisles were retained and incorporated into the new structure. The **exterior** is rendered in pink sandstone with a slate roof, and comprises a west **tower**, a six-bay **nave** with **clerestory**, north and south **aisles**, **transepts**, and a **chancel** with an organ loft and **vestry** on the north side, and a **chapel** on the south. The **tower** is in four stages and has diagonal buttresses, ornate **clock faces**, four-light belfry openings, **gargoyles**, and **battlemented top**. The peal is of eight bells, cast in 1964 by Taylor & Co. The aisles and clerestory are also castellated. The transepts have corner pinnacles.

The oldest surviving parts of the **interior** are the **16th century roofs of the aisles**. They are camber beam in type, and are elaborately carved with **bosses and coats of arms**. The **nave roof** is hammer beam in type. In the **north transept** is an **altar table** from the early 18th century and a **chest** dated 1635. The **sanctuary chairs** are Jacobean, and a **15th century octagonal font** has been placed in the north aisle. The most interesting feature of the church is the collection of **tombs and monuments**. Some of the original **medieval tombs** have found their way into the present church, and the oldest are a pair of damaged reclining effigies in the **north transept**, one of which is of **Sir William Baguley** who died in about 1320. The other figure is said (by local tradition) to be a '**Saxon knight**', though this is unlikely. Also in the **north transept** is the **Brereton monument**, with recumbent effigies of William Brereton who died in 1630 and his wife Jane, under a canopy. On the side of the tomb are kneeling figures of their seven children. In the **Stamford Chapel** are two memorials by André Carpentière. One is to **Henry Booth, First Earl of Warrington** who died in 1694, and his wife Mary and their family. The elaborate monument includes the figures of Wisdom and Vanity. The other is to **Langham Booth** who died in 1724, and to **Henry Booth** who died in 1727. A **mural tablet to the Asshetons** is by Richard Westmacott. In the north transept is a **collection of loose carved stones** some of which are from the Norman period. There is also a **Saxon cross**. In the church is **stained glass** by Kempe and by Clutterbuck. The **pulpit**, dating from around 1910, is by Temple Moore.

The **organ** was built in 1875. The silver communion plate includes an alms dish dated 1705-06 and chalices, patens, and flagons dated 1775-76.

Church Brow, a picturesque winding lane with **18th century cottages**, leads to **Park Road**. Turn right, and a short distance along this leafy road (with some **very grand mansion houses**) we come to a **crossroads**. Go directly ahead, and along **Charcoal Ro**ad will be found **Charcoal Gate** on the left, the first entrance to **Dunham Massey**. (The **Deer Park** is open at all reasonable times.)

The **Charcoal Gate** is usually locked, so entrance is obtained by the **stepped stile** by the side of it. (Although children

Church Brow

The Revolutionary

Henry Booth seemed to be an unlikely revolutionary. An aristocrat, set to inherit both a title and an estate, he had seen the chaos of the short lived republic, and believed that a constitutional monarchy was in the best interest of everyone. Yes, he was a Puritan and a Presbyterian, but so long as Charles II more or less adhered to the restoration settlement, he was not one to rock the boat. But Charles had no heir. The next monarch would be his brother James, and he was a very different proposition. James was a Roman Catholic. His ambition was to turn Britain into a Catholic absolutist monarchy modelled on the France of Louis XIV. Booth, and most of the political and mercantile elite, could not stomach that, and tried to exclude James from the succession by constitutional means. When that failed, Booth turned to cultivating a suitable protestant heir, the Duke of Monmouth, one of Charles's numerous illegitimate offspring (though the Duke's supporters claimed to have proof that Charles had secretly married his mother). Booth entertained Monmouth at Dunham Massey in an attempt to gather support for this claimant to the throne, meeting his cavalcade and going ahead of him "well mounted and armed, finely habited with rich furniture on his horse, several led horses and servants going before." It all ended in imprisonment in the Tower, and a period of lying low afterwards. James succeeded to the throne, and his reign was the disaster that many had predicted. Monmouth was dead, but William of Orange could claim the throne in the right of his wife Mary, James's eldest daughter. Booth, now Lord Delamer, secretly met the Earls of Devonshire and Danby at Whittington in Derbyshire to concert action. When William landed in the West Country, Delamer assembled his tenants on 'Boaden Downs' on 16 November, 1688. He told them that the protestant succession was the only guarantee of the liberties of an Englishmen, and that he supported William and Mary's just claims (one of the few to do so openly at this juncture). He then led all that could furnish a horse and a weapon to Derby, then on to Nottingham, the headquarters of the rising in the north. Rather impatient, he then set off for the West Country with a select group of followers, eventually meeting William on the road to London. His probity was such that he was one of a deputation sent to James to persuade him to abdicate and leave the country. After the 'Glorious Revolution' William rewarded him with office and the title of Earl of Warrington, but he was no placeman, for he "was fit to pull a tyrant down, but not to please a prince that mounts the throne." He went into political exile, content to repair the family fortunes and rebuild Dunham Massey before dying at an early age.

love to scramble over the stile, the **main gate**, the third along the road, is user friendly for those with large buggies and wheel chairs.) On the other side of the stile, follow the **metalled drive** that bends slightly to the right, through the parkland. The curious old building to the right is the **Deer Barn**, used to store winter feed for these animals. Dunham Massey has a fine **herd of fallow deer**. They mostly live in the **area to the left**, and far beyond the **main drive** in the **deer sanc**tuary. (Parts of the sanctuary are closed during the rutting and breeding season.) However, they do wander, and depending on the time of year, you may be lucky enough to see some of them. They are shy creatures, so do not approach them too closely, and please do not try to feed them! There are a number of **old fallen trees** along the path, often used as natural climbing frames! We eventually arrive at the **South Lawn**, in front of the house. (See p265 for route from main entrance.)

The former **stable block**, to the left, contains a **shop** (in which admission tickets are obtained) and an **upstairs restaurant**. (The House is open daily except Thursday and

Fallow Deer at Durham Massey

The Earls of Stamford

The Booth line died out with the death of the Second Earl of Warrington in 1758. His daughter had married Harry Grey, the Fourth Earl of Stamford, and so Dunham Massey passed to the Grey family. One of their ancestors was Henry Grey, who had been ennobled as Duke of Suffolk. His wife, Lady Frances Brandon, was the daughter of Mary Tudor, and a grand-daughter of Henry VII. Consequently, Lady Jane Grey, their daughter, had a rather tenuous claim to the throne. Upon the death of Edward VI, an attempt was made to make her Queen. It all ended in tears, and both she and her husband were executed. However, the Grey family bounced back, and a descendent, Henry Grey, became the First Earl of Stamford in the 17th century.

Friday 11-5, from the end of February to the end of October; admission charge. The Gardens are open daily 11-4 or 5.30; admission charge.) There are nearby **toilets**. The present house was initially built in 1616, but was later remodelled between 1732 and 1740, and again between 1905 and 1908. The last refurbishment was for the homecoming of the Ninth Earl, and exemplifies a great country house on the eve of the First World War and a way of life that was about to pass away for ever. We enter by the **great door** on the south front, where the ticket is checked in the **entrance hall**. Before commencing the tour, take a peep at the **pretty little cou**rtyard with its **fountain**. The **south** corridor gives access to **Lady Stamford's Parlour**, an Edwardian room where the wife of the Ninth Earl would write letters and deal with household matters. The foot of the **Crimson Staircase** (notice the **portrait of Henry Booth**) leads to the **Saloon**. This was used for weekend house parties, something of an Edwardian institution. Notice **the fine portraits by George Romney**. The **Great Hall** recreates the proportions of the original hall where, on 14 September, 1682, the Duke of Monmouth was entertained. Many of the **portraits** evoke the personalities of that era. The **Chapel** was created in 1655, and owes its present appearance to the 18th century. Here, family prayers were held regularly, servants and guests alike being summoned by a bell over the kitchen. The **curious little room** the other side of the **garden entrance** is called the **Stone Parlour**. It contains **pictures of Tudor personalities**, recalling that the ancestors of the Earls of Stamford included **Lady Jane Grey**, the 'Nine Days Queen'.

After glimpsing the **Dining Room**, return via the **Great Hall** to the **Grand Staircase**. Before ascending it, take a quick look at the **Billiard Room**. This game had been introduced from India, and was remarkably popular in the 19th century. The stairs lead to a top **landing**, from which the **Green Silk Room** is accessed. The Seventh Earl fell in love with, and married, Catherine Cocks, a bareback rider in a circus. This room was furnished for her, but she had little joy of it. The inverted snobbery of the Dunham tenants caused the pair to flee the estate and they never came back. The **Summer**

Parlour, opposite, was a favourite place to take tea. Notice the **photograph of the Emperor Haile Selassie**; the Tenth Earl espoused his cause after the Italian invasion of Abyssinia, and entertained him here. However, the grandest room is the **Great Gallery**. There are **fine views from the windows** and some **interesting pictures of Dunham Massey** in the seventeenth and 18th century. Note **Guercino's oval 'Allegory with Venus, Mars, Cupid and Time'**, probably the finest picture in the house. Sadly, the old gentleman who used to play the **piano** is no longer with us, but you can play it if you have a mind to! At the end of the Gallery is the **Queen Anne Room**. It houses the magnificent **state bed**. It dates from the 1680s, and was inherited by the Second Earl of Warrington. Such beds were not for everyday use; they were used for the rituals of power and life, such as marriage, receiving visitors to congratulate a new mother, and lying in state. Proceed by way of the **stair land**ing to the **Tea Room**. Serving tea was a ritual in the 18th century. The commodity was so rare and valuable that only the mistress had the key to the caddy! The **Rose Gallery** accesses the Rose Room, containing a fine collection of **Huguenot Silver**. (Huguenots were French protestant refugees fleeing the intolerance of Louis XIV. Many were excellent craftsmen and silk weavers.) After the next **staircase**, round the corner, is the **Stamford Gallery**. Walk to the end and examine the rooms working backwards. The **Blue Chintz Room** contains furniture by Gillows of Lancaster, and the adjacent **Dressing Room** has prints and illustrations reminiscent of the **life and times of Lady Jane Grey**. Then we pass the **St.**

Dunham Massey Hall, from the moat

Thomas Bedroom and the Stamford Bathroom, an interesting period piece. The Oak Bedroom was originally the Second Earl of Warrington's room for reading and transacting business, and some of the bookshelves remain. The final room at the corner of the two corridors, is a rather fine Library. It is little changed since the 18th century, and still houses the Second Earl's book collection. The fine orrery (a popular 18th century mechanical 'toy' demonstrating the planetary system) should be noticed, but the most important feature is the Grinling Gibbons carved panel inserted into the wall. This is the earliest known work by Gibbons, and he was working on it when John Evelyn discovered him in a cottage in Deptford. There are some fragments of 17th century Flemish stained glass in the windows. The Grey Stairs descend back to the ground floor (look out for the Tenth Earl's bicycle, used by him to travel to the Estate Office in Altrincham, at the bottom!). The Study contains more mementoes of Haile Selassie. The Ante Room was used by the Earl's secretary. The west part of the South Corridor leads to the White Room, so called because the pictures in it relate to the White family. We now exit into the Kitchen Courtyard. The kitchen, scullery, dairy, and laundry, together with other domestic rooms have been restored, and are sometimes staffed by costumed interpreters. We exit into the stable yard. We can pass out under the bell turret, and cross the moat. To the left is the 16th century old mill, but turn to the right, and following the path alongside the moat to reach the entrance to the car park. Then you can pick up the driveway to the main gate. However, the best plan (if there is time) is to return towards the South Lawn and proceed to the east side of the house, where the garden entrance is located. The gardens include a lake and a curious mound, said by some to be the remains of a Norman castle. It is preserved in the form of a 17th century 'snail mount'; it was once taller, with a spiral path reaching a summer house at the top. After following the directions to the main gate, it is a simple task to return to Altrincham Station by catching a bus from the stop across the road.

The Eccles Line (Media City, Salford Quays and the Trafford Centre)

Piccadilly Station to Cornbrook

This section of the route is described on the following pages; Piccadilly Station p23; Piccadilly Station to Piccadilly Gardens pp26-28; a description of Piccadilly Gardens p28; Piccadilly Gardens to St. Peter's Square pp32-36; St. Peter's Square itself p36; and St. Peter's Square to Cornbrook pp231-241.

Cornbrook to Broadway

The tram departs from **Cornbrook Station**, and takes the left-hand track, running alongside the Liverpool railway line, while the Altrincham line drops below on the right. The track used by the returning Eccles trams can be seen descending an incline on the extreme right. After crossing the Atrincham line, we diverge from the railway, and, joined by the Manchester bound track, the line now swings to the right to cross the **Duke's Canal** by a **skew bridge**. From the bridge, there is a view on the right of the remaining unfilled basin of **Pomona Docks** and the **modern lock** that communicates between the Duke's Canal and Manchester Ship Canal. The **Pomona Docks** were used by coastal shipping, many of them sailing ships (still widespread in this trade in the 1890s when the Ship canal first opened). The site is scheduled for redevelopment.

Beyond the **bridge**, the line swings left to run along an **elevated viaduct**. To the left is the **Duke's canal**, with the **railway** on its far bank. To the right, there is a glimpse of **Ordsall Hall** (p268) across the **Ship Canal** in the distance.

The name of both the Gardens and the Docks that replaced them is recreated in **Pomona Station**. It was perhaps the first Metrolink purpose built elevated tram stop, constructed with exposed concrete supports similar to much of the Docklands Light Railway. The **island platform** is connected with both the **approach road** and the street

'Way Down to Pomona'

The name comes from Pomona Gardens, a Victorian pleasure resort frequented by (as the locals would say) "mucky women". The grounds were purchased and developed by James Reilly in 1868 and included many attractions such as a ballroom and agricultural halls. The gardens were closed in the 1880s as a result of the land being acquired for the extension of the docks. Reilly was eventually paid £70,352 in compensation for the twenty one acre site.

> T'was down in Albert Square, I never shall forget,
> The day it was fine, but the evening, it was wet.
> She hid behind a veil, but seemed a real flash rover,
> So we rode at night in the pale moonlight,
> Way down to Pomona!

Of course, when the 'lady' removes her veil, it turns out to be his wife...intent on stopping his "mashing!"

level **esplanade** alongside the Ship Canal by **stair** and **lift** (situated at different ends of the platform). It is perhaps under used at present, but this may change when the area of the docks is re-developed (see p266) and when it becomes an interchange for the proposed line to the Trafford Centre and Port Salford.

Just beyond the station is the site of the **junction for the projected line to the Trafford Centre** (p293), and part of the configuration is already in position; notice the concrete bed disappearing into space as the tram curves to the right. In its latest incarnation, the proposed line will extend beyond the Trafford Centre to serve the new Salford Reds Rugby Ground, before terminating at the intended Port Salford container depot and interchange. After the bend, the line crosses the **Ship Canal**, with a fine view up the Canal and Irwell towards Manchester on the right (perhaps best seen on the return journey). The **Swing Bridge**, on the left, was erected in 1893, but is now fixed in position with the new **road bridge** alongside it. It formerly divided **Pomona Docks** from the main **Salford Docks** (now Salford Quays).

Plunging down a **ramp** like a roller coaster, we pass between the former Colgate-Palmolive plant to the right and the maze of glass office blocks, constituting **Exchange Quay**, to the left. The former is embarking upon a new lease of life as the *Soapworks* residential development complex (as the illuminated letters on the **chimney** testify.)

The tram turns to the left to pass along part of **Colgate Lane** before turning right and arriving at **Exchange Quay Station**. There are two **platforms**, both commun-icating by ramps with **Ordsall Lane** and the adjacent **pedestrian crossing**, though the arrangements at the opposite end are rather different. The **Manchester platform** is linked by **ramp** with the end of **Taylorson Street** in one direction, and a

The Big Ditch

The 1870s and 1880s were decades of industrial depression. Perceptive observers realised that it was not just a matter of the operation of the trade cycle, and they searched for underlying structural causes. In Manchester, the culprit was identified as the 'Liverpool toll bar', for the handling charges and dues charged by the Mersey Docks and Harbour Board made Manchester goods uncompetitive. The answer seemed to be the construction of a ship canal that would turn Manchester into an inland port. The initiative in this bold venture is usually ascribed to Daniel Adamson, but a whole cohort of local businessmen held similar views. The canal project became a kind of crusade in which a variety of organisations were involved, embracing all sections of the community including the trade unions. After a great deal of opposition from a variety of vested interests, an Act of Parliament was obtained in 1885. Over 16,000 navvies (assisted by steam shovels) laboured six years to dig the 35 mile long waterway. At one point, the project almost collapsed through lack of funding, but Manchester City council stepped in and saved the day. Queen Victoria eventually opened the Manchester Ship Canal in 1894. The docks were established on the Salford side. Pomona catered for coastal vessels and the remaining sailing ships. The large Salford Docks dealt with ships from all over the world, including transatlantic traders. It was home to Manchester Liners, which operated to America and Canada. The De Trafford family sold their estate, a former deer park, for conversion into Britain's first large scale industrial estate. Westinghouse was one of the first occupants, erecting a reproduction of their American head offices. Metropolitan Vickers, and other famous companies of the time, followed. Economic historians have calculated that the canal did indeed revive Manchester's fortunes prior to the First World War.

Ordsall Hall (Graham Beech)

crossing to the foot of the **Eccles platform** in the other. Note also the **alternative crossing** leading to a kind of **plaza**, which is directly linked with the **Eccles platform** by **steps.** The plaza performs a multitude of functions. It is a turning circle for cars, accesses the adjacent office block, and communicates with both **Colgate Lane** and **Trafford Road**. (It is also graced by a rather nondescript public **sculpture**.)

It is a good idea to leave the tram at Exchange Quay Station for a short while, and turn right down **Ordsall Lane**. It seems to be just an ordinary road. We pass a housing estate, round a bend, and suddenly find an ancient manor house in the shape of **Ordsall Hall**, set back in its own grounds on the left.

There was probably a house here when William de Ferrers, Earl of Derby, exchanged the Manor of Ordsall with David de Hulton (for some land in Pendleton) in 1251. It was eventually bequeathed to Sir John de Radclyffe in 1335. Sir John distinguished himself in the wars of Edward III, being present at the victories of Caen, Crecy, and Calais (which he used as a heraldic motto). Sir John rebuilt most of the house by 1380, and parts of this structure still survive. The Radclyffe family were in possession of the house until the 17th century. After the reformation, they remained loyal to the old faith. Although they retained a chapel at the Collegiate Church in Manchester, and attended services there once in a while, they also retained the services of a 'massing priest' (who doubled up as the family tutor) for saying mass at their private chapel. Nevertheless, they were equally loyal to the monarchy, fighting for Elizabeth I in the Irish Wars and for Charles I in the Civil War.

By the time of the Restoration, the family were bankrupt, and the Hall and its estate were sold in 1662. After many years use as a farmhouse, and a brief tenancy by Frederic Shields, the Pre-Raphaelite painter, the property was rented to the owner of nearby Haworth's Mill for use as a working men's club! Earl Egerton of Tatton then restored the property for use as a Clergy Training School, and it was purchased by Salford Corporation in 1959. The Hall has recently undergone a major £6.5 million restoration programme, reopening in May, 2011. (Open Mon-Fri 10-4, Sunday 1-4, admission free.)

We enter at the **main gate** on **Ordsall Lane**, from which there is a fine view of the **south front**. The **outline of the moat** is clearly visible. The original timber framing is hidden behind a **brick and terracotta façade** dating from Earl Egerton's restoration of 1896. The **Egerton coat of arms** may be seen between the two large windows. The projecting **bays with timber gables** are part of the **Great Hall**. To the left are **service rooms** dating from the 16th century, while the range to the right are the surviving private rooms of the **1360s structure**. Walk past the **east end** and turn left, noting the **recreated 16th century formal gardens**. Stand back a little to inspect the **north front**. The central **brown and white timber framing** constitutes the **Great Hall and service wing** of Sir Alexander Radclyffe's (died 1549) great house, erected around 1510-12, probably in celebration of his first appointment as High Sheriff of Lancashire. Note the distinctive **quatrefoil shape**; the house was one of the first to introduce this fashion. The recent restoration has restored the natural colour of the oak (black painted beams were a Victorian affectation). The **brick wing** to the right was built by another Sir Alexander Radclyffe (died 1654) in 1639, probably as accommodation for a bailiff. The central **chimney stack** is of the same period. The **date** was part of a vanished carved armorial panel that was placed on the projecting **stair tower**. The **Egerton Arms** were later added.

We enter an area currently occupied by the **shop** and **café**. It was originally part of the **service wing** and housed the buttery, pantry, and a corridor leading to the kitchen. The large **bay window** dates from the 1600s. Pass through into the **Great Hall**. Analysis of the timbers suggests a construction date of circa 1512; it remains one of the most impressive examples of a timber framed hall in the North West. The **south wall** of the Hall, to the right, dates from Earl Egerton's restoration (note the **'churchy windows'** suited for a Clergy School). At the **west end** of the Great hall, between the **entrance doors** and the **elaborate archway** supporting the roof, there would have been a 'screens (or cross) passage', a typical medieval arrangement. The passage was created by placing a heavy moveable screen in the **archway** area, and the position of the passage was aligned with the two principal doors. The **great south door** had been blocked up, but was re-opened in the latest restoration. There is now a clear view of the **three doorways** in the

The Maid of Honour

Margaret Radclyffe (1575-1599) was very close to her brother Alexander, and he took her with him to the Court Of Queen Elizabeth. 'Gloriana' seemed to surround herself with beautiful women (in the hope that it 'might be catching', the malicious said), and she certainly took to this pretty girl from Lancashire. Margaret soon became a favourite Maid of Honour. Alexander was killed whilst on campaign in Ireland in 1599. Margaret was inconsolable and Elizabeth insisted that she be brought to Richmond Palace and personally attended to her. But despite the attentions of the royal physicians, she wasted away and died. She was buried as a nobleman's daughter at the London church of St. Margaret, and at the funeral service, twenty four poor women were given gowns (one for each year of her life). At the Queen's command, the poet Ben Johnson wrote an epitaph.

> Rare as wonder was her wit,
> And like nectar ever flowing...
> ...earth thou hast not such another.

A post mortem revealed 'strings about the heart'. It has been pointed out that this could describe fatty deposits resulting from starvation. She really had died of a 'broken heart'!

western wall. The **central one** would have been the start of the kitchen passage. The **left-hand door** accessed the buttery (drinks store) and the **right hand one** the pantry (food store). As was the custom, there was no fireplace, for a log fire would blaze away merrily in the centre of the room (the **outline is marked on the floor**) and the smoke found its way out of a louver in the roof. Note the **dais** at the east end of the Hall. This was where the Lord of the Manor, his family, and honoured guests sat. The **line of a timber canopy** that protected them from soot and drafts is still visible. The current **high table** is 17th century in origin, and the **carving** (roses of Lancaster and York, together with the Welsh Dragon) depict the triumph of the Tudor Dynasty. It would have had a symbolic salt cellar proving that those who sat there were 'worth their salt', the traditional offering to guests. There is a lovely **oriel window** (a bay window) on the left. There are seven sides with a **carved grapevine decoration** (a possible secret symbol of their faith). The heraldic **stained glass** dates from the 1550s, depicting the shields of the Radclyffes and the Stanleys, Earls of Derby. Look upwards to inspect the **Minstrel's Gallery**. It was probably reached by a bridge from the vanished east wing, and the present **staircase** is Victorian. Pass through the **door** beside the dais into the **Star Chamber**, so called from the **lead stars** affixed to the ceiling (one of which concealed a spyhole). The original room timbers date from the 1360s, for this is in the **oldest part of the house**. It is reconstructed as the main **business room** of Sir Alexander. Here he would write letters, meet people, and hear court petitions. Here also, **armour** would be kept, and you can try some modern reproductions on! The **bible box** (1677) and a composite **19th century bed** (with a re-used **headboard** dated 1585) are the principal items of furniture.

Guy Fawkes and the Ghosts!

A popular story features Ordsall Hall as the location for Guy Fawkes and Robert Catesby to plot the overthrow of King James in what was to become the Gunpowder Plot. This legend developed such credibility that the street directly adjacent to the hall has been named 'Guy Fawkes Street'. In fact, such speculations mainly derive from a novel published in 1861 by Harrison Ainsworth (he also invented Dick Turpin's celebrated ride from London to York!) In his romantic novel of Guy Fawkes, Ainsworth introduces us to one Viviana Radclyffe, the sole representative of her family at Ordsall during the absence of her father, Sir William Radclyffe (who is away attending a meeting of Catholic gentry at Holt in Cheshire....as one does!). Viviana is represented as a fair maiden of eighteen, whom Catesby comes in secrecy to woo, but at Ordsall he encounters Guy Fawkes, who has come to secure the support of the Radclyffes in the Plot. When the hall is raided by men in search of the family priest, Viviana, Catesby, Fawkes, and the priest are all rescued by the timely intervention of the celebrated Humphrey Chetham, who conducts them by a secret passage running beneath the moat to a summer house in the grounds, and thence through Old Trafford to Chat Moss. Why does this famous Puritan do this? Well, he is portrayed as being in love with Viviana, but differences of religious faith make their marriage impossible. The story closes with Humphrey left solitary, his life "tinged by the blighting of his early affection ... true to his love, he died unmarried". This hokum proved to be a best seller!

Ordsall Hall is famous for its resident spirits, most often spotted in the Great Hall, including the mysterious White Lady seen near the portrait, and the figure of a young girl often seen on the stairs...There is a web-cam to record these manifestations, and it can be accessed on the Ordsall Hall official website!

`Continue through the **modern fire door** and ascend to the **upper floor**. It is only possible to view the **Italian Plaster Ceiling Room** through the glass screen, for the state of the ceiling is too delicate. The rare **lozenge pattern ceiling** is 16th century in origin, and predates the rest of the room with its 17th century **panelling** and 15th century **medieval stone fireplace**. There is a small **landing** or lobby, which visitors sometimes mistake for the entrance to the next room. However, it is worth a detour to examine the **two stained glass windows**, dating from around 1500, and probably from the (demolished) family chapel. They depict the **Virgin Mary** and **St. Catherine**. The end of the **carved pew** is early 15th century. Enter the **Great Chamber**, thought to be the **oldest part of the hall**. The room is restored as the **bed-chamber of Alice Radclyffe** in 1510. The rare **paintings on the beams** may date to 1360, including a pomegranate (a symbol of unity and fertility). A modern recreation may be found on the opposite side of the beam.) The **portrait of a lady** is believed to be by Marcus Gheeraerts the Younger, painted in 1590. Notice the reproduction 16th century **bath** and the original **coffer** (in which clothes and valuables were kept). Children may enjoy **dressing up** in this room. A **steep staircase** leads to the **Coat of Arms Room**. This was added sometime in the 17th century, and contains (in lime plaster) the **arms of John Radclyffe** (1582-1627). It looks pretty much as it appeared in the time of the Clergy Training School, and the **reproduction wallpaper** is based on an early 19th century design. Notice the **viewing panel** in the roof upon descending the staircase.

Retrace your steps to the **Hall entrance**, and enter the **kitchen**. You are now in the **17th century brick wing**, and this kitchen probably replaced an earlier one. It depicts **preparations for the wedding feast** of Sir John Radclyffe to Ann Asshawe in 1572. The 17th century **rotating spit** was powered by hot air, one of the first to be installed in the area! The **wall ovens** are Victorian. Notice the **original well**, and perhaps drop a coin in it! The adjacent **smoke corridor** was used to hang and cure meat. Ascend the **main stairs** to the **Frederic Shields Gallery**. In addition to commemorating the work of this painter (who lived here between 1872 and 1875) there are **displays relating to the history of the Hall** and its inhabitants down the years. There is also a **viewing panel** into the Great Hall. The adjacent **Egerton Gallery** is used for temporary exhibitions, though there is some **16th century stained glass**. These galleries, and the **roof space** above them, can be accessed by **stairs** and **lift** from the **north end of this wing**. It should be noted that there are a number of 'living history' performers who are 'in residence' from time to time.

Beyond **Exchange Quay Station**, the tram crosses **Ordsall Lane** before curving to the left on a **section of grass track**. The *Ibis Hotel* is passed on the right, before **Trafford Road** is crossed, and the line enters **Salford Quays**.

Salford Quays

The tram runs alongside part of **Merchants Quay**, and immediately swings right, passing the end of **Saint Peter Basin** on the left, to call at **Salford Quays Station.**

This comprises two **platforms** accessed by **stairs** and **ramps**, and linked by **crossings** at either end. The **Eccles platform** is adjacent to the end of the **basin**, and the **Manchester platform** also accesses *The Matchstick Man*, a pub making a reference to the career of L.S. Lowry (p283). This end of the station is a short walk from the start of **Merchants Quay**, while the opposite end leads to **Waterfront Quay Road**.

Saint Peter's Basin, one of three created from a former dock is glimpsed to the left (the other basins are St Louis and St Francis). A whole **range of eating places** (*Frankie*

Salford Quays

The Manchester Ship Canal went on to play an important part in the economic life of the city until the advent of the container revolution. The new ships were just too large, and the docks and headwaters were closed to all except small boats in 1982. (But there is still a ship repair business visible from the Lowry!) The canal was acquired by Peel Holdings, a property development company anxious to exploit the opportunities along its banks, and Salford City Council purchased the derelict Salford Docks in 1983. The two went on to develop the area in partnership with each other (the municipality provided the infrastructure, largely financed by grant aid, for the private developers), and the redevelopment process commenced in 1985. Salford Quays is often compared with London Docklands, but there are important differences. In the first place, it is a distinct area, with no enclaves or parts not included within the project. No local people were displaced or even affected by the development. Secondly, the decision was taken to completely rebuild the docks themselves. Consequently, there are no rats. The water is constantly purified, and bathing or water sports are forbidden for periods following the opening of the gates to the basins (in connection with boat movements). A danger flag is flown until the water is considered pure again. The Quays are a sought after address, both for businesses and house or flat hunters, and are now seen as a symbol of Salford's regeneration.

However, the pattern of trade is now changing once more. Smaller container vessels are now being used to distribute containers from 'entrepot' destinations to smaller ports, and goods traffic upon the Ship Canal is again growing. Hence the project to develop Port Salford!

Salford Quays (Graham Beech)

and *Benny's*, *Chiquito*, and *Arbuckles*) slides past on the right, indicating certain assumptions as to the (transatlantic?) culture of the people who work around here. After crossing **Waterfront Quay Road**, we continue past the end of the **Ontario Basin**, with a number of forlorn **cranes** (moved here from elsewhere in the dock area, but temporarily removed for restoration). Cotton was once unloaded in this dock. We cross the junction of **The Quays**, to the left (with an impressive **canal side walkway**, see p284), with **Furness Quay**, on the right. Beyond the latter, adjacent to Trafford Road, is a large white building, the old **Dock Office (**1927**)**. Dock work was a casual occupation, and the men were hired to help load or unload particular ships. The dockers would congregate here, and the list of work available was chalked on a slate in one of the ground floor windows. The line now swings left before a right turn, ascending an odd little **viaduct section**, as if we are traversing a roller-coaster.

Descending from the short viaduct, the tram now pauses at **Anchorage Station**. The **Eccles platform** is the principal access to **Anchorage building**, on the left, by means of **steps** at both ends and two back to back **ramps** descending from the middle. The rather isolated **Manchester platform** is reached by **pedestrian crossings** at either end, leading to steps, but there is also a **ramp** near the viaduct end.

The great bulky **Anchorage Building** on the left is perfectly hideous, seemingly designed by the team responsible for Ceaucescu's palace in Bucharest. And it is little better round the other side, the part facing **Eerie Basin** (though this is distinguished by an interesting sculpture, executed by Wendy Taylor, of an enormous **anchor**). Over 2000 people work in this monstrosity.

After departing the station, the line crosses the **Anchorage Quay access road** and turns left to cross and run alongside **The Quays** on a **grassy reservation**. There is, on

Ontario Basin (Graham Beech)

the left, a good view of the **Eerie Basin**, once used for the discharge of grain in bulk.

We pause at **Harbour City Station**, with its **staggered platforms**, to the rear of the great building of that name (p284). The **Eccles** platform is the first, alongside the **The Quays**, and accessed by **ramps** at both ends. We cross two pedestrian crossings. The first links with the **multi-story car park** to the right, but the second accesses the end ramp of the **Manchester platform**. The **ramp** at the opposite end of this platform communicates with both a **crossing** to the **The Quays**, and a **footpath** along the right-hand side of the tracks, which eventually leads to **Broadway Station**.

Look out for the **Detroit Bridge**, a little beyond the station on the left.

There are good views of the **Lowry**, **Media City**, and the surrounding area in the distance. At the **junction** the Eccles trams usually diverge to the right, and stop at **Broadway Station**

This is typically composed of two **platforms,** accessed by **ramps** and **steps** at both ends, and linked by **crossings.** The crossing at the southern end is linked to a **dedicated footpath** back towards **The Quays.** The first turn on the right is for **Media City,** and the second is a **crossing** providing access to the **Manchester platform** from **The Quays.** The path itself continues to **Harbour City Station.**

However, the morning and the evening Eccles bound trams run directly ahead down the **short branch,** terminating at **Media City** before reversing and continuing their journey (these vehicles show 'via Media City' on their destination indicator). This also applies to the reverse service at these times. During the greater part of the day, there is a **dedicated shuttle service between Cornbrook and Media City** and vice-versa. (If you are on the wrong service, note that it is a short walk from either Harbour City or Broadway to Media City!)

Media City

Media City UK is a £500 million development managed by Peel Media, a division of the Peel Group, in partnership with the public sector. It comprises a number of distinctive components. The BBC have relocated BBC Children's (including C-Beebies), BBC Learning, BBC

The Bridge that Became a Ship

Salford Docks developed on the north bank of the Ship Canal, but ships also berthed along Trafford Wharf on the south bank. Moreover, the former park of the Trafford Estate was sold off and soon became a vast industrial estate in the decades after 1900. Both developments were served by extensive private railway systems, but these needed to be linked. The answer was a railway swing bridge, situated near the Trafford Road Swing Bridge (the stone column supporting the pivot is still visible), allowing rail traffic access to Trafford Park and Trafford Wharf from the Salford direction. However, the first bridge soon proved inadequate. Replacing the earlier single track bridge, the so-called 'Detroit Bridge' was built by Dorman Long in 1942. Long after the Docks had closed, and railway traffic in Trafford Park had almost disappeared, it was decided to preserve it. The bridge was removed to its present position in 1988, an operation requiring its flotation on pontoons down a section of the Canal. For this, bureaucracy required that it be registered as a ship! It now divides the Eerie Basin from the Huron Basin, and acts a fixed link for pedestrians between the northern and southern halves of the Salford Quays development.

Sport, Radio Five Live, and parts of BBC Future Media and Technology (including a small number from BBC R&D) there, involving about 2,300 staff, as well as all local and network broadcasting formerly based in Oxford Road in Manchester. The move marks a major de-centralisation of the corporation's operations, and represents the BBC's largest presence outside of London. Granada Television's operations moved near here from the site in central Manchester. Most of what was at Quay Street is situated in the Orange Building. This new location includes ITV Studio's production and management teams, ITV regional news, and support staff from across the business. However, most of the filming takes place at a new site across the river. (This involved the long running soap *Coronation Street* moving to a new external set at Trafford Wharf, next to Imperial War Museum North.) There are also facilities targeted at independent production companies. In addition, Salford University and local Colleges have an educational presence, and there are shopping, eating and drinking establishments, a hotel, and apartments.

Media City is approached by a **single track branch line** that runs for a short distance along the side of the road. It passes the **Pie Factory** development on the right (distinguished by two large signs stating 'Media City Studios' and 'Sound Stage'). Once a 'fresh-bake' pie bakery, the extensive on-site facilities provide a practical working environment; the three sound stages offer a total of 15,000 square feet of practical and sound-proofed space, complete with ventilation and all the necessary production facilities, ready to be utilised by independent entrepreneurial media companies.

The line curves off to the right to terminate in the two track terminus at **Media City Station**. There are two **platforms**, ending in a paved **concourse** at the **Piazza** end. A long range of **steps**, also curving round to the left, lead down to the **Piazza,** and a level **path** leads off to communicate with the right-hand side of it. The **left-hand platform** parallels the **dockside terrace,** which is accessed by two short fights of **steps**. The **right-hand platform** accesses the **esplanade** in front of the **north range of buildings** by **two passages**, and passes the **Blue Peter Garden** (p276), which can sometimes be directly accessed by a **gate** from it. Both **platform**s end with **ramps** that communicate with a **pedestrian crossing** at the opposite end to the Piazza.

The principal buildings in Media City are all centred round a five-acre **public area** roughly twice the size of Trafalgar Square, part **paved area** and part **garden,** which gently shelves down on one side towards the Ship Canal. To the left of the station is a fine **lookout point** at a **terrace** beside the **former entrance to the dock basin**. This entrance area was part of 'Nine Dock' (built 1905) and stands on the site of the original Manchester Race Course. The whole area could hold ten ocean liners and (including the section beyond the roadway leading to the Lowry) was once half a mile in length. There is a **fine view** across the water to the **Lowry** (which is built on a tongue of land between the old dock entrance and the Ship Canal) and, further to the right, across the **Ship Canal** to **Imperial War Museum North,** and then towards the **new pedestrian swing bridge.** Walk to the end of the station to enter the **paved Piazza,** specially designed to

Media City, U.K!

provide an outdoor arena capable of accommodating a whole range of different happenings. With enough room for more than 5,000 people, and access to a **huge screen** (mounted on the large **pencil-like columns** dividing it from the gardens), it is suitable for everything from concerts to winter markets. Opposite the end of the station, across the paved square, is **Quay House**, the first block of BBC Offices. The **BBC sports staff** can be observed through the **ground-floor windows**, but the building is also home to 'Radio Five Live', 'BBC Breakfast', and 'North West Tonight'. Between **Quay House** and **Bridge House**, to the right of the former, you will see the **start of the ramp** leading to the **pedestrian bridge** (see p277). **Bridge House** is currently the home of 'C-Beebies' (children's programmes) and 'Dragon's Den' (a sort of business based game show).

Turn right, and walk along the **esplanade** on the **other side of the station** (this description reads from left to right). But first, take a short detour down the street beside **Bridge House** (distinguished by a branch of *Costa Coffee*), with the **accumulator tower** (p277) in the distance and a view across the **Ship Canal** to the left. After returning, notice **The Studio** (distinguished by large roof signs only visible if you step back), on the opposite corner of the street. There is a **reception area** at the front (with a branch of *W.H. Smith* and *Booths Café*) leading to the **audience entrance**, four **studios**, and the home of the **BBC Philharmonic**. The **paved passage** to the right of The Studio leads to a 218-bed *Holiday Inn*, equipped with a bar and lounge, restaurant (with private dining), meeting rooms, and gym. Notice, to the right, a distant view of the **Greenhouse**, a refurbished building within a giant **wooden frame** (it contains a number of small businesses, mostly connected with the media industry).There is a branch of *Booths* supermarket (two floors of produce aimed at an upmarket clientele) beyond the hotel. Back on the **esplanade**, across the paved passage, may be found **Dock House**. A substantial part of **BBC Radio** is located here, together with 'Songs of Praise'. Finally, the **last building** constitutes an out-station of the **University of Salford**, comprising the Media Studies Department (what else?), with *Prezzo* (an Italian restaurant) and a branch of *Wagamama* on the ground floor.

Organised tours of the BBC complex at media city are available. There are a number of options, all lasting about one and a half hours and usually including the chance of interactive participation in a TV Studio. Perhaps the most popular is the **CBBC Interactive Tour**, aimed at children aged between 6 and 11. (They can practice at being an announcer and see themselves on the television screen!) Tours usually take place on Monday, Tuesdays, Wednesdays, and Saturday and Sunday, several times a day, and must be booked in advance (admission charge with a family ticket option). All children must be accompanied by an adult. For further information and to book a tour, ring 0370 901 1227. You can also book tickets for the shows and programmes that feature a **live audience**.

In front of this range of buildings, between them and the tram station, is a fine **garden and grassed area** that is worth exploring. The **Blue Peter garden** was opened by the Princess Royal on 23 February, 2012 in an event tied in to the Jubilee Woods Project. Princess Anne, as patron of the project, also planted a tree. The original garden at the London Television Studios was designed by Percy Thrower, the first 'television gardener'. (The garden was targeted by vandals in a famous episode in1983; they stamped on plants, poured oil into the pond and smashed the stonework. The former members of a rock group publicly confessed years later!) The new garden was landscaped by current Blue Peter gardener Chris Collins, but includes a number of the original features that have been re-located here. Notice the **bust of Petra**, the show's first ever dog, and the ornamental **fishpond**. There are also hand, foot and paw **prints**

Blue Peter

Blue Peter is the world's longest-running children's television show, having first aired in 1958. During its history there have been many presenters, often consisting of two women and two men at a time; the most remembered are perhaps John Noakes and Valerie Singleton. (The current presenters are Helen Skelton and Barney Harwood.) The Blue Peter pets are the animals regularly appearing on the programme. These include dogs, cats, parrots and tortoises. The most famous were Petra, Shep, and Mabel, all dogs. The show uses a studio for the main format of the presenting, but there is also a garden, often referred to as 'The Blue Peter Garden', that is used during the summer months or used when they are showing any outside activities. Children (and adults) who appear on the show or achieve something notable may be awarded the coveted Blue Peter badge. The badge allows holders free entry into a number of visitor attractions across the UK. On 29 March 2011, Blue Peter became the first programme in the UK to

Blue Peter Garden

broadcast an entire show in 360 degrees on the web. Viewers were able to watch the programme via their TVs and simultaneously interact with the television studio in front and behind the cameras on the website. In October 1998, Richard Bacon became the first presenter to have his contact terminated in mid-run (after he admitted to taking cocaine, following reports in a tabloid newspaper). The then Head of BBC Children's programmes, apologised on air in one of the most grovelling, toe curling sequences ever broadcasted!

of the presenters and animals appearing on the show in 1978, when the garden was originally created. A statue of Mabel (another of the show's longest-serving pet dogs) was moved to the reception area in the appropriate building, along with a sculpture of the Blue Peter ship logo.

Now retrace your steps to the **bridge approach**. The £11 million, eighty-five metre long, **pedestrian swing bridge,** funded by the North West Regional Development Agency, was officially opened by the Archbishops of Canterbury and York. So feel quite safe to cross it! Walk up the ramp, and start to cross the bridge, but be sure to stop in the middle of it to admire the **view.** To the right, you can see **Mode Wheel Locks,** the first on the Ship Canal. They were hydraulically operated, and the **brick accumulator tower** is visible to the right of them. An anti-clockwise view encompasses the **dry docks,** followed by the **Granada Television Complex,** and then the **Imperial War Museum North.** The **Granada TV site** (usually closed to the public) is based around a new *Coronation Street* set, an exact replica of the previous one, but increasing the scale of the buildings so they match the size of those in the real world. The focus is still on the main Coronation Street cobbles, but some areas of the fictional *Weatherfield,* such as Victoria Street, have been slightly extended. In addition, there are two studio 'sound stage' buildings, a three storey Studio Production Support Building, and a Set Storage Building (with an integral workshop). The street (with end viaduct and warehouse wall) can be best glimpsed across the Canal from the walkway to the right of the bridge on the Media City side.

Coronation Street

Coronation Street is a British soap opera set in Weatherfield, a fictional town in Greater Manchester, based on Salford. Created by Tony Warren, Coronation Street was first broadcast on 9 December 1960, and has been on the air for over 51 years. It is produced by Granada Television and shown in all ITV regions. It has been filmed in Manchester at the Granada studios since inception, but filming moved to a new set at Media City in 2013. Since first being aired, it has been one of the most financially lucrative programmes on commercial television, underpinning the success of its broadcaster ITV and its franchise Granada Television. On 17 September 2010, it became the world's longest-running TV soap opera. Since 1960, Coronation Street has featured many characters whose popularity with viewers and critics has differed greatly. The original cast was created by Tony Warren, with the characters of Ena Sharples (Violet Carson), Elsie Tanner (Patricia Phoenix), and Annie Walker (Doris Speed) as central figures. These three women remained with the show for 20 years or more, and became icons of British soap opera, often being emulated by other serials. Ena was the street's busybody, battleaxe, and self-proclaimed moral voice. Elsie was the 'tart with a heart', who was constantly hurt by men in the search for true love. Annie Walker, landlady of the Rover's Return pub, had delusions of grandeur. Consequently, the series became known for the portrayal of strong female characters, and Sharples, Walker and Tanner were later joined by Hilda Ogden. (Hilda's best-known attributes were her 'pinny', hair curlers, and the "muriel" in her living room, with three 'flying duck' ornaments.) Conversely, the show has a long tradition of hen-pecked husbands, most famously Stan Ogden and Jack Duckworth, husbands of Hilda and Vera, respectively. Bet Lynch (Julie Goodyear) first appeared in 1966, before becoming a regular in 1970, and went on to become one of the most famous Corrie characters. Bet stood as the central character of the show from 1985 until departing in 1995, often being dubbed as "Queen of the Street" by the media, and indeed herself. Only one character from the first episode remains; Ken Barlow (William Roach) entered the storyline as a young radical, reflecting the youth of 1960s Britain. Though the rest of the original Barlow family were 'killed off', Ken has remained the constant link throughout the entire series of Coronation Street. The programme has evolved over the decades. Some of the early programmes reflected the radical views of Jim Allen, a scriptwriter, but a great deal of the writing came to reflect a mixture of comedy and personal clashes. In many ways, the 'street' continues to characterise the vanished ambience of a Salford terrace in the 1960s. Like other soaps, there have been a number of 'disasters' over the years. The latest involved a Metrolink tram falling off the 'viaduct' at the end of the street!

Continue, to take in the view from the left side, with the **Ship Canal** spanned by the **Lifting Bridge**, followed by the **Lowry** on the opposite bank, and, finally, the former entrance to **Nine Dock**. Continue across the bridge and turn left on to the **esplanade** in front of the **Imperial War Museum North**.

The IWMN and the Lowry

The entrance to **Imperial War Museum North** (open daily, 10-6, admission free) is on the right. This is an out-station of the Imperial War Museum in London, opened to the public in July 2002. The building was designed by Daniel Libeskind, and is intended to represent a world shattered by conflict. It consists of a 29 metre high **'air shard'** (a lift ascends **the tower**; the viewing gallery is not recommended for those subject to vertigo), from which there is a particularly fine view; a domed **'earth shard'**; and a **'water shard'** with views across the Canal to the Lowry. It is worth noticing that the Museum is not intended to give a detailed history of Britain's involvement with the wars of the modern era (that is the purpose of the Imperial War Museum in London), but only deals with aspects of the conflicts.

The **entrance** leads to an **information and security point** (from which tickets for the viewing platform are available), beyond which is a **ground floor area** comprising a well-stocked **shop, toilets,** and **lockers**. There is also a **computerised information area**, which is useful for those interested in the military aspects of genealogy. A **canalside restaurant** is located in the 'water shard' part of the building, and can be accessed directly from the concourse by a **stair** (main access is from first floor level). Note that it is possible to exit the shop area to the **lift for the viewing area**. (It is worth a short detour beyond the lift, outside towards the **old street entrance** to view the **T55 tank**, captured in Iraq.)

Lifts ascend to the **upper floor** from the concourse, but it is best to ascend a **flight of stairs** to the **landing on the main level**. The entrance to the right accesses a **Special Exhibitions Gallery**, but most visitors go straight through into the main exhibition area...where they come face to face with a **Harrier V.T.O.L. 'Jump Jet'**, seemingly mounted just like a model. This highly successful fighter and ground attack aircraft entered service in 1969, fitted with an unusual engine that could be 'vectored' into a downward thrust mode. This meant that it could vertically take off and land in a confined space, yet still perform as a normal jet aircraft. (It could also engage in some pretty unorthodox moves in a dogfight too, even avoiding missiles!) Its flexibility proved a godsend in the Falklands War, and it remains the only post-war British military aircraft purchased for use with the American armed forces. We now **traverse the displays in a clockwise direction**, starting with the wall to the left of the entrance. The **introductory case** sets the scene with a **potted history of the Imperial War Museum**, an institution that has evolved and changed since it was first set up. Around the corner, we are immediately plunged into the **'Great War'. Case (i)** displays uniforms and equipment associated with trench warfare on the Western Front; search out the **'hardtack'** biscuit and read the comment inscribed on it... Linger in front of the **video of the Battle of the Somme**. Some of the scenes are posed in training areas, such as the wild rush 'over the top', but others are authentic. The wounded man being carried down the trench died a few minutes after the cameraman finished filming. **Case (ii)** deals with the Air War, something that no-one (apart from a few visionaries and enthusiasts) expected. Notice **the tail rudder of a shot down German albatross fighter**, no doubt kept like a sporting souvenir. **Case (iii)** reminds us that it was a truly global war, fought in the **Balkans**, the **Middle East**, and on the **Eastern Front**. And it is clear that the campaign on the **Eastern front** was every bit as horrible as that in Flanders. **Case (iv)** deals with the War at Sea. Of course, everyone expected a great naval battle, but the German high seas fleet only once ventured out in force. The result was the inconclusive battle of Jutland, marked by the **ship's bell from HMS _Iron Duke_**, the British flagship. The scene changes, with the new angle of wall, to life and times on the **home front in Britain**, shown in **case (v).** It was the first war in which Britain was bombed from the air, and there are relics of the great hydrogen filled **Zeppelin airships** (the Manchester area was twice attacked by the 'gasbags') and the twin-engined **Gotha bombers**. (Look up at the **Gotha propeller** mounted on the wall.) The war fundamentally altered the lives and

Imperial War Museum North (Graham Beech)

status of women, and there is a selection of **videos relating to women workers**. The last case in this section **(vi)** details events leading to the **Armistice**.

An enclosed area, the **first of the 'silos'**, is situated in the angle of the walls. It is devoted to the theme of the **experience of war**, and contains a curious display in the manner of a **series of filing cabinets** of personal effects and letters. There are mementoes of the recruits in both wars and the period of 'national service'; **badges of the 'pals battalions'** (p66); and a most poignant exhibit...a **letter from a nine year old boy to Lord Kitchener**, pleading to be allowed to enlist and take part in the game that older boys looked forward to. Other material relates to the **experiences of prisoners** (including those in Japanese camps); **internees**; and **evacuees** who were labelled like luggage. The **ship's bell of the Lusitania** is exhibited. This liner, sunk by a U-Boat off Ireland in 1915, had a dramatic effect upon public opinion in America, and sparked off anti-German riots up and down the country.

The next set of displays, enclosing **Silo two**, is devoted to the **inter-war period**. **Case (vii)** contains artifacts relating to **Fascism** and **Communism**, the two ideologies arising out of the Great War. The relics of the **Spanish Civil War**, in which many local men fought as volunteers in the International Brigade, are noteworthy. **Case (viii)** traces the rise of **Hitler**. A **1932 German ballot paper** reminds us that the majority of the German people did not vote for Hitler; he was invited to form a government (as the Nazis share of the vote was declining!) by the leaders of other right-wing parties, in an arrangement that they thought they could control ...**Video film** illustrates such charming activities as organising **boycotts of Jewish shops** and **book burning**. "Where one burns books, one later burns men."

Silo Two contains displays about **women and war**. Contrasting **videos** reveal all manner of **participation by women in armed conflict** and a variety of **female peace**

campaigns. Look for the **pair of wire cutters** used at the Greenham Common protest. The next wall area contains a long section about a variety of aspects of **World War Two**. A **sea mine** is surrounded by a display in **case (ix)** concerning the **war at sea**. **Case (x)** relates to the War in Europe; notice the army **'bren' gun** (a conflation of the Czech town of Brno, the location of its inventors, and Enfield Lock, the ordnance factory in England where it was first manufactured). There is a sad little item in **case (xi)** dealing with air attack and its effects; a **'mickey mouse' gas mask** intended for children. However, notice the **target map of Hamburg** (the centre was destroyed by a fire storm created by allied bombing). Of course, this was seen at the time as Nazi Germany "reaping the whirlwind" of what they had sown. Indeed, the **video film** of the **Battle of Britain** and the **'Christmas Blitz'** on Manchester are worth a glance. **Case (xii)** tells the story of the **Desert** and **Jungle** wars. The former was a rather unique affair. The Eighth Army and the Afrika Korps fought each other in a harsh landscape almost completely bereft of 'civilians'. It was thus a 'soldiers' war'…each side learned to respect the other, and thought of themselves as a group of professionals who just happened to be in a position where they had to kill each other. It was one of the few instances (perhaps the only one) where a degree of chivalry prevailed. Both sides tuned in to Belgrade radio to hear Lale Anderson sing Lilly Marlene, and, sadly, sometimes advanced into battle against each other singing this song. The Eight Army did not adopt any form of conventional dress code, as might be seen in figures illustrating **Jon's cartoon of 'Two Types'**!

Explore **Silo Three** before continuing with the wall displays. This Silo deals with **impressions of war**, including **myths, propaganda**, and **children's war toys**. However, the material relating to the **liberation of the concentration camps** (which created a profound impression in Britain at the time) in **case (xiii)** is real enough, though, and introduces the displays about the post-war world.

Inevitably, various episodes of the **'cold war'** are dealt with in the next section, including the **Cuban missile crisis** (which brought the world to the closest point it has ever been to a nuclear war), the **invasion of Czechoslovakia in 1968**, and the **implosion of the Soviet Empire** in the 1980s. There is an introductory **video of Cold War highlights**. Notice the **piece of the Berlin Wall** and the **AK47 assault rifle** in case **(xiv)**, both icons of the era. (The latter featured in liberation struggles in the Third World, a process somewhat overlaid and distorted by Cold War preoccupations.) **Case (xv)** provides a useful corrective to the international scene with **British and Northern Ireland** developments.

Silo Four looks at the **contribution of the Commonwealth** in the last war. The video of the almost forgotten **exploits of the East African troops** in Burma is particularly interesting. **Silo Five** is unusual, in that it is not as isolated, and we walk directly through it. Display cases deal with the **role of science and technology in modern war**. Individual displays relate to **medicine in war; poison gas; communications**; and the atom bomb. Look for the **'Protect and survive' leaflets** issued by the Thatcher government in the 1980s. These were mercilessly satirised at the time and feature in 'When the Wind Blows' (a cartoon book and film) by Raymond Briggs. There is a 1976 **government instructional film** about how to survive a nuclear attack. God knows what people made of this…market research revealed that some thought that fall-out actually made the curious noise designed to draw attention to it in the sound track!

The final wall display deals with the **post-cold war era**, and features (amongst other things) the **break-up of Yugoslavia**. The **last silo** concludes with **the effects and impacts of war**. It is all summed up by the **three-wheeled invalid carriage**, but the

1945 plan to rebuild Manchester is interesting. Of course, there was no money to carry it out; and a good thing too, for the place would have ended up looking like downtown East Berlin.

The **main exhibition space** contains a number of exhibits. In perusing this display, we pass a **Russian T34 tank**. The allied nations contributed in a variety of ways to the defeat of the Nazis. The Soviets tied down a large part of the Nazi land forces and more or less ripped the heart out of the elite Panzer (tank) regiments at the Battle of Kursk in 1943. The principal instrument of victory was the T34, simply designed, rugged, and manufactured in enormous quantities by emergency factories set up beyond the Urals, out of range of the German bomber force. Fortunately, drivers and mechanics could be recruited from the former inmates of the machine tractor stations, set up under the auspices of the Five Year Plan. Many people are drawn to the **thirteen pounder field gun**; it fired the first British artillery round of the First World War, near Binche in Belgium. Do not neglect the **fire brigade pump trailer** and the **Trabant Car**. The former saw great service in the 'blitz'; there was such a shortage of proper fire appliances that many of these pumps were towed by requisitioned taxicabs. The latter remains, of course, the icon of the collapse of the Berlin Wall; a two-stroke fibreglass bodied chariot of freedom.

Last, but not least, search out the **'time stack'** situated in the rear wall of Silo One. Here, a kind of dumb waiter arrangement summons a selection of artefacts that can be personally handled and inspected.

You are in the midst of a **large arena**. In the course of your progress around the displays, concentration will have been interrupted at least once by an audio-visual presentation. The **'Big Picture Show'** utilises most of the wall space in the arena, using sixty projectors. The shows are usually given at hourly intervals and last around fifteen minutes. Current subjects are 'Why War?'; 'Weapons of War'; and 'Children and War'. Please be advised that these shows **contain loud noises and flashing lights**, so you should retreat into a Silo or leave this area when a show is announced if you feel it will affect a medical condition or frighten small children.

Return to the **Esplanade**, and continue towards the shining pink glass of the **Peel Estates** offices directly in front, turning left to reach the **Lowry Lifting Bridge** This marvellous pedestrian bridge was designed by Casado of Madrid, and fabricated by Parkman's of Salford. The view from it is impressive. Downstream are the new **swing-bridge** and **Mode Wheel Locks.** The view upstream runs to the former **Trafford Road Swing Bridge** in the distance, with the **Quays** to the left and **Trafford Wharf** to the right. The *former Samuel Platt* public house (partly perched in the Canal) is visible at the end of the latter, named after one of the pioneers of the Canal saga (his steam yacht, 'The Norseman', headed the opening day procession).

Cross the bridge, noting The **Lowry**, designed by Michael Wilford, a major new arts complex comprising an **art gallery**, two **theatres**, a **restaurant**, corporate **hospitality suite**, a **bookshop**, **publishing house**, and **study centre**. It cost £94million, of which £64.3million came from the National Lottery. The building is perhaps best seen from this bank of the Ship Canal, and at sunset, when the light catches the glass and polished metal. Otherwise, it seems a mass of sharp geometric forms, cones, cubes, and circles. The tall **drum tower** (housing the archive and study centre) is meant to reflect Salford's industrial past. The Lowry has been compared with the Guggenheim in Bilbao. (The galleries are open Sunday to Friday 11-5, and Saturday 10-5. Admission to the Lowry is free, though some temporary exhibitions may have an entrance charge.) Walk through

The impressive entry to the Lowry Centre (Graham Beech)

L.S. Lowry is much misunderstood. He was not from the working class, as his family was quite well off (he worked, for a time, as a rent collector). Nor was he a genuine 'primitive'. He had art lessons at the Art School at All Saints, where he was taught by (amongst others) Adolphe Valette. He lived a curious, almost solitary, life. He was mother fixated and never married. As is clear from the words you will hear, he never developed a rational philosophy of life or art. His paintings were a mere extension of his own complex personality and its inner demons. Most people think of his 'matchstick figures', and in the Lowry Galleries you will find them in profusion. But his paintings are much more complex. They reveal an obsession with loneliness, and spiritual and physical deformity. The face with the staring red eyes is quite terrifying. Most of the pictures here originated in the Salford museum collection. Interestingly enough, Manchester City Art Gallery has the contents of his studio and sitting room, removed from the modest terraced house that he occupied at the time of his death. These rooms were recreated for a short period at the Art Gallery, and became one of its most popular attractions. There are no plans to reconstitute the exhibit in the new display areas there, so it might be a nice idea if they came here.

the entrance doors to the **foyer**. There is a very useful **Tourist Information Centre** for Salford to the left, adjacent to the **Terrace Bar** (good view over the Ship canal), but most people turn right and towards the **escalator** to the **galleries**. (There is a **shop** and small **café** to the right, at their foot.) Before looking at the paintings, view the excellent **video** in the **'Meet Mr Lowry'** display.

The **main gallery** always contains a **selection of Lowry's paintings and drawings**. (Admission is free, but a minimum donation of £3 per person is requested.)**Temporary exhibitions** are to be found in a **side gallery** to the right. The **stairs** to the left of the main gallery lead to the **Deck Gallery**, containing a **children's activity area** (where they can draw, read and play) with a **special space for under-fives**. On Saturday mornings families can enjoy a range of **Playhouse** activities and there are lots of other things to look out for including **Family Talks, Art Detective** and **Hide and Seek Trails**.

The Lowry has two theatres. The **Lyric Theatre**, with 1,750 seats, has the largest stage outside London. The **Quays Theatre**, with 460 seats, offers the intimacy of smaller venue.

An Excursion through Salford Quays

Upon leaving the Lowry, stand on the **paved piazza** between it and the *Lowry Outlet Mall*. To the left of the mall is the **Digital World Centre**, while the tall apartment block on the right is **'Waterside@the Lowry'**. Walk up the steps and enter the *Lowry Outlet Mall*, obtaining a store guide and plan from the **information desk**. The Mall is a two-storey shopping centre, intended to house the upmarket equivalent of 'factory shops', selling designer labels at discounted prices (in some of the designer outlets, a minimum of 30% is discounted from the ordinary shop price). It contains such 'names' as *Nike*, *Austin Reed, Trespass,* and *Antler,* together with eateries such as *Limes* and *Café Rouge.* The upper floor contains the **Vue multiplex cinema** (nine screens). The cinema and eateries are open till late (an interesting package that includes a classic film in the morning, a packed lunch, and a tea dance is sometimes available; ring 0161 848 1847).

Exit the Mall on to the **Centenary Walkway,** opened by Princess Anne in 1994, and celebrating the anniversary of the opening of the Manchester Ship Canal by Queen Victoria. (The **ducks** often waddle across it in search of discarded tit-bits!) Look out for a series of **embedded steel discs;** these are engraved with words and pictures depicting the history of the docks and the area. This is also the departure point for the **Ship Canal Cruises** to Liverpool. They are performed by Mersey ferries, and the price includes return to Manchester by coach. (There are usually cruise leaflets at the Tourist information Centre at the Lowry during the operating season, or access the Cruise website.) Even if you are not sailing, it is worth turning up to see the bridges open! There is a **good view** across **the widest stretch of water,** once used by ocean-going ships for turning movements utilising the Canal tugboats. We have soon reach **Welland Lock,** the entry point from the Canal to three enclosed docks. Adjacent to the lock is the **Watersports Centre,** offering courses in canoeing, kayaking, sailing, and windsurfing at a variety of levels. Pass in front of the centre, noticing the **Salford Quays Operations Tower** on the right. Ascend the **steps** and pause on the **footbridge** over the new **Mariners Canal** (intended for small boat owners), which cuts through the housing development to the **Eerie Basin**. The canal is centred on the main frontage of **Harbour City** to the left, another piece of Bucharest transplanted to Salford. One can almost imagine the Roumanian dictator fleeing in his helicopter; but it actually grows on you, and you end up feeling that it is an impressive vista (and thousands of postcards can't be wrong). The way now lies alongside **Ontario Basin**, past a *Beefeater Inn* and a *Premier Inn* to the **Four Corners Sculpture**. This work of art (by Noah Rose) echoes the shapes of propellers, hulls, and sails, whilst the weather vane represents Pomona and Salford Docks. From here, it is a short walk to the **main road**. Cross the tram tracks to the pavement, and turn right, walking past the **cranes** (see p273) to arrive at **Salford Quays Station** to resume the journey to Eccles.

Media City to Eccles

The routing can be resumed at **Salford Quays Station** or other stops, but, to avoid duplication, the description resumes at **Broadway Station**. The tram departs from **Broadway Station**, crosses **Broadway** itself, and runs past the industrial estates in **Langworthy Road**. Note that the track is near the pavement, termed 'gutter running'. At the top of Langworthy Road, it turns left into **Eccles New Road**, and stops at **Langworthy Station**.

Again, there are the usual two **platforms**. The **Manchester platform** is accessed exclusively by **ramps** at both ends, but the isolated **Eccles platform**, reached by **pedestrian crossings,** can also be accessed from the **Langworthy Road** end. Here both **steps** and a **ramp** are provided.

From now on the route runs **almost entirely through the street**. This was the first section of Metrolink (apart from Mosley Street in the City centre) where this happened. Notice the former 1920s **Salford Corporation tram depot** (the building has been adapted to other uses, but the original façade remains, see p286) with its **clock tower** on the left, near **Weaste Station**.

The tram swings to the right, before stopping at **Weaste Station**, situated to one side of **Eccles New Road**. The station comprises **two platforms** linked by **pedestrian crossings** at either end. The **Eccles platform**, adjacent to the main road on the left, is reached by **ramps** at both ends. However, the **Manchester platform**, opposite, has **steps** at each end and **two exits** on to the **pavement** (which is on the same level as the platform at these points) and is adjacent to the housing on this side.

Cross the road, and walk back in the Manchester direction. The second turning to the right is **Cemetery Road**, leading to the main lodge of **Weaste Cemetery**. This was Salford's first municipal cemetery, and something of a historical landmark. Before it opened in 1857, most burials took place in local churchyards, which were full to overflowing. Salford Corporation was one of the first municipal authorities to recognise that private cemeteries alone could not solve the problem, and it was a pioneer in proposing a municipal solution.

Let us now praise famous men...

A spare hour can be usefully spent in inspecting the tombs and monuments of some of the more famous burials. Joseph Brotherton (1783-1857) is considered to be the founding father of the Borough of Salford (helping to obtain its charter of incorporation), and was also its first M.P. He was a deeply religious man, acting as minister of the Bible Christian Church for 40 years. This was the wellspring of many of his principles and political achievements; he consequently (in 1847) helped to establish the Vegetarian Society, and, in politics, he was a reformer. He campaigned for the 1832 Reform Act and the repeal of the Corn Laws, and advocated improved working conditions and the abolition of both slavery and the death penalty. The causes of public education and beneficial leisure activities were particularly dear to his heart, and, with his help, Salford became the first municipal authority to provide a free lending library, museum and art gallery. He also supported the provision of municipal cemeteries. Ironically, he was the first person to be buried here, and his striking monument is the largest and most elaborate in the cemetery.

Mark Addy (1838-1890), known as 'The Salford Hero' was famous for rescuing over fifty drowning people from the Irwell. The famous rescues began when Mark was only thirteen and unable to swim, but he later went to Greengate Baths and became a proficient swimmer. Mark received many medals for his bravery, including the gold medal of the Salford Hundred Humane Society and the Albert Medal First Class, which was presented by Queen Victoria. He died of tuberculosis, possibly enhanced by the inhalation of polluted water. Donations poured in from a grateful public and a large monument to Addy was erected. It is an unusual obelisk, and is Grade II listed.

Charles Halle (1819-1895) was the founder of the famous Manchester Halle Orchestra, the longest established symphony orchestra in Britain. Born in Hagan, Westphalia, he was the son of a church organist. By the age of nine he was an accomplished pianist and gave his first public performance. In 1836 he moved to Paris and spent twelve happy years there, but the 1848 Revolution forced him to move to England. In 1853 he became director of Gentleman's Concerts in Manchester, and was determined to improve the quality of music in the town, forming his own orchestra in 1857. Halle attracted leading musicians from all over Europe to play in the North West. By insisting on lower priced tickets he brought orchestral music to a wider audience than ever before. He was knighted by Queen Victoria in 1888. He is buried with his first wife.

The Cemetery also contains the graves of Crimean War veterans, including at least one who took part in the Charge of the Light Brigade'.

In the Victorian age cemeteries were considered to be amenities like parks and gardens, and were usually designed in a similar way. Weaste Cemetery was no exception. The cemetery once boasted four chapels and a glazed summer house, indicating that the intention was to offer a beautiful landscaped garden of rest where the visitor could escape the bustle of city life. The beautiful design made Weaste Cemetery a most desirable final resting-place for well-to-do Mancunians and Salfordians, as is evidenced by the large ornate monuments in 'Rich man's plot'. Since 1857 over 330,000 interments have taken place at the cemetery, and it is now also valued for its historical and ecological significance. A heritage trail can be downloaded from the Cemetery's website. (Tours can sometimes be booked by ringing 0161 748 3123.)

Back at the **former tram depot**, there is **a section of original tram track** still in situ in the cobbles of a side street to the right of the main facade.

Upon leaving **Weaste Station**, the tram continues down the road and crosses the **bridge** over the (disused) railway track that once connected the Lancashire and Yorkshire Railway's main line with the Ship Canal system. Note the refurbished housing development before arriving at **Ladywell Station**.

This is a **'park and ride'** station, with a large **car park** on the site of a former hospital, behind the **flats** to the left.

The former Weaste tram depot

Tramway Resurrection

Under the direction of Henry Mattinson, a far sighted General Manager who had built upon the foundations of his mentor and predecessor, James McElroy, Manchester Corporation Tramways was a progressive undertaking. It was the third largest network in Britain, at the heart of an even wider network within what is now Greater Manchester, one that included Salford Corporation Tramways. But one sad summer in 1929, Mattinson went on holiday to Devon...and died there. His successor took the fateful decision to start substituting buses for the trams, and the surrounding towns took their cue from Manchester. The process was delayed by the need to conserve energy in World War Two, but the last Manchester tram ran in 1949, only twenty years after his death. As for the Salford trams...the remaining part of the system was badly neglected, and the surviving trams were almost falling apart when the system closed in 1947. However, in 1992, forty-two years after the last tram ran, trams once again appeared in Manchester streets. But it was not as things seemed. In this first phase, apart from a short central section through the streets of Manchester (albeit mostly on reserved track), it was mainly a conversion of two former railway lines. However, the Eccles line was a completely new 'greenfield' route, built from scratch. It opened in two phases. The first, to Broadway was completed in 1999, and ran mostly on reserved track and private right of way. But the second, to Eccles itself, introduced a section of almost continuous street running when it opened the following year. This time it might truly be said that the wheel had come full circle. If you stand on the old track beside the former Weaste depot and contemplate the new in Eccles New Road, remember Henry Mattinson.

There are **two platforms**, with both **stairs** and **ramps** at either end, and linked by **pedestrian crossings**. The station is a short walk from **Salford Royal Hospital**, which is accessed from nearby **Stott Lane**.

At the approach to Eccles, we dive under the major **road junction** with **Gilda Brook Road** in an **underpass**, and terminate at **Eccles Station** adjacent to **Regent Street**.

The station is unusual, in that it consists of a **single terminal track** with a **platform** (used for both arrivals and departures) adjacent to **Regent Street** to the right. There are **ramps** at both ends, and **steps** leading to the **street**. It is adjacent to a small **bus station** at its west end, where the entrance to *Morrison's supermarket* is also situated.

Eccles

Eccles (the name is perhaps Celtic in origin, and probably indicates an early church) was a settlement that predated the arrival of the Saxons in the area. It was a small weaving village in the 18th century, but was then transformed...firstly by the opening of the Mersey and Irwell Navigation; then by the cutting of the Dukes Canal; and latterly by the construction of the Manchester Ship Canal and associated industrial premises. Now it is more or less a suburb of Salford.

The row of property in **Regent Street**, opposite the tram station is worth a look. There are interesting shops and cafés, including the former Regent Picture House (the first 'talkie' in Eccles was shown here in 1929), a fine terracotta confection that is now the *Eccles Cross*, a *Weatherspoons* pub. A short distance down the street, towards the underpass, is another pub. The *Lamb Hotel* was re-built in 1906 by a Mr Newton of Hartley, Hacking & Co., for Holt's

Eccles Cakes

An Eccles cake is a small, round cake filled with currants and made from flaky pastry with butter, and can sometimes be topped with Demerara sugar. It is not known who invented the recipe, but James Birch is credited with being the first person to sell Eccles cakes on a commercial basis in 1793. He sold them from his shop at the corner of Vicarage Road and St Mary's Road (now known as Church Street) in the town centre. There are accounts of hawkers carrying the cakes on trays up and down the trains that stopped at the Eccles 'road station' when the Liverpool and Manchester Railway first opened.The original shop is no more, but Parker Bradburn Bakers are supposed to make them to the original secret recipe. Nicknames for the Eccles cake include Squashed Fly Cake, Fly Cake, Fly Pie or even a Fly's Graveyard owing to the appearance of the currants that it contains.

Eccles Cross

Brewery. It is an excellent example of an Edwardian public house or 'gin palace'; its interior has been little altered and contains many well preserved fittings of an elaborate and ornate nature, including rich wood paneling and a **well preserved billiard room**. Walk past the **tram terminus** towards the **bus station** to the *National Westminster Bank* on the corner. It still has "Manchester and County Bank" carved into its façade. Opposite is the site of **Eccles Cross**. The **cross** itself, a 19th century replacement (with an **older section** incorporating a basin), has been moved a short distance from its original position to become the centrepiece of a **pedestrianised area** (the former Church Street). Turn right and walk along **Church Street**, passing two interesting pubs. The ***Nag's Head*** was once known as the Fox Vaults, after hunters brought the last fox to be killed in the locality here. The ***Grapes*** dates to 1772. Its claim to fame is that Friedrich Engels (the companion and patron of Karl Marx) popped in here when he came to Eccles to visit his father's mill. However, as the name implies, the street is the location of the historic **parish church**.

The **Parish Church of St. Mary the Virgin** is the only Grade I listed building in Eccles. A local legend tells of a visit by St. Germanus (accompanied by St. Patrick) who set up an altar on the site of the present church. Nevertheless, there is no trace of a pre-Conquest church, although there is a **fragment of an ancient cross**, said to date from the tenth to eleventh centuries (see p290), excavated during the construction of the Ship Canal. A church was mentioned by implication in a document referring to "Helias,

St. Mary the Virgin, Eccles

clerico de Eccles" in 1180, and Norman fragments have been found during building work. It is conjectured that north and south aisles were added to the original structure at some stage, a chancel created, a chapel possibly added at the east end of the north aisle, and a tower constructed. The Chantry Chapel of St. Catherine was added at a date before 1368. In that year, Thomas Del Bothe, of Barton Hall, instructed that he should be buried before the Chapel altar, and that £6 13 s. 4d should be paid for chaplains to say masses for his soul, his parents, and his feudal lord. (He also left money to repair the bridge at Manchester.) William Booth, a descendent of Thomas, was Chancellor to Margaret of Anjou (Henry VI's Queen)

and Bishop of Lichfield. A person of some importance, he later became Archbishop of York, and re-founded his grandfather's chapel, widening the south aisle. A second chantry was established in 1453 by Sir Geoffrey de Massey of Worsley. William added the final chantry in 1460. The nave was rebuilt at about this time (making the tower out of centre), and the roof was raised by the construction of a clerestory. Work continued into the 16th century, but a rebuilding of the chancel was never finished, for the reformation intervened. The church was then stripped of its ornaments and fittings, and the chantries suppressed.

Galleries were erected (along with a 'three-decker pulpit) in the 18th century. The church was restored to something approaching its original medieval appearance in the course of the 19th century and the last galleries disappeared in 1926. Today, it is a welcoming place, with a well-used the **meeting centre** in the church. (The church is usually open Tuesdays, Thursdays, and Saturdays, from about 10.30 to 12 or 1.30; coffee is served in the meeting centre, and a light lunch is sometimes available at midday.)

The church is usually entered by the **west door** under the **tower**. Notice the two **medieval gravestones**, discovered during 19th century alterations and placed either side of the **inner door** of the **porch**. One bears a cross and shield, and the other a cross and cup (probably signifying a priest). Enter the church, and examine the **nave**. This was enlarged around 1400 by the provision of side **aisles**, and was completely rebuilt around 1500, when the aisles were probably widened. The **clerestory**, designed to create more light, was probably added at the same time together with the **magnificent timber roof**. The **carved bosses** show "the sunne in splendour," the badge of the Yorkist King Edward IV. "Now is the winter of our discontent made glorious summer by this son of York." (One of the smaller carved bosses is said to depict a '**green man**', an ancient fertility symbol.) The **nave pillars** contain **niches for the statues of saints**, removed in the course of the reformation. They face the **south door**, then the main entrance. The **marks in the piers** on the **south side** show where the 18th century gallery was fixed. Notice the **brass plates** in some of the **pews**; most indicate that they are 'free', but some state that they are reserved for important people and local families. The latter would pay a 'pew rent', a useful source of income to the church. (Poorer members of the congregation were confined to the gallery.) Turn and inspect the **west end**. (The **outline of the steeply pitched 15th century roof** is faintly visible on the west wall, mainly in the angular line to the left. Evidence of the **extension of the north aisle** is clearly visible in the masonry to the right.) The present **tower** was constructed in the 15th century to house the peal of bells, and the **west end** was converted to become the principal entrance around 1861-2, when the **window** was inserted.

The Hall that Went to America

For hundreds of years, Agecroft Hall was the distinguished home of the Langley and Dauntesey families. At the end of the 19th century, however, Agecroft fell into disrepair, and in 1925 it was sold at auction. Hearing of this tremendous opportunity, Thomas C. Williams (Junior), a native of Richmond, Virginia, purchased the structure, and had it dismantled, crated, and shipped across the Atlantic. It was then painstakingly reassembled in a Richmond district known as Windsor Farms. Today, Agecroft Hall still stands, beautifully re-created, as a major tourist attraction in a setting reminiscent of its original site on Lancashire's Irwell River (though without the encroaching industrial developments). This curious saga was probably the inspiration for the Rene Clair film 'The Ghost Goes West' (1935), starring Robert Donat. In it, an American buys a decaying Scottish baronial castle from its impoverished laird and ships it to the States...only to find that his purchase includes the ghost of the laird's ancestor!

The **Royal Coat of Arms** (which is placed over the door) dates from 1816, and was originally placed at the Church Street gate as a remembrance of the Battle of Waterloo, fought the previous year. The two curious **carved wooden heads**, either side of the modern font, were once attached to the galleries. Note the **brass memorial**, to the right of the **font**, to the **Dauntesey family** of Agecroft Hall. (See infomation box on p289.)

The **Churchwardens Pew**, to the left of the west door, has a canopy commemorating the centenary of the Diocese of Manchester (1947).

We now arrive at the west end of the **south aisle**, which was widened in 1450. A lovely **Palm Sunday window** depicts the entry of Christ into Jerusalem, and has an interesting history. It is said to have been brought from a French convent at the time of the Revolution, installed in St. John's Church, Manchester, and brought here when that church was demolished. The **studded south door** perhaps dates from the 14th century, and still operates on its original hinges. However, the **south porch** is modern and comprises a **memorial to those local men who gave their lives in the First World War**, mostly in the 'Salford Pals' (p66) It now also commemorates the dead of the Second World War, too. The bricked up **circular window** is a relic of the gallery. The **niche** on the **south pillar of the chancel arch**, at the **east end** of this aisle, once held a statue of Saint Catherine, and it formerly faced the site of the chantry chapel founded by Thomas Del Bothe. **Carvings of the implements of her martyrdom** (the hammer, pincers, and the celebrated wheel) have survived.

The original **chantry chapel**, to the right, was first built in 1368, and the present **entrance arch** is 14th century in origin, and may be original. The chapel was re-founded in 1450, but the present structure largely dates from the 19th century rebuilding. The area was converted into its present guise, a **heritage centre**, in 1997. It contains the Jacobean **Brereton Tomb**, commem-orating Richard Brereton (died 1598), his wife Dorothy (died 1639), and their infant son Richard (died 1575). It was moved here from the Bridgewater Chapel in 1996. Perhaps the most interesting exhibits were recovered by archaeologists from the **Duke of Bridgewater's family vault** (under the Bridgewater Chapel). Evidently, the good Duke thought that it might not see much future use, and assigned it to John Gilbert, his talented agent (see p239). The remains of John's **coffin**, and those of other family members are displayed (there is a **picture of Gilbert** on the wall). The former **Bridgwater Chapel**, where these finds originated, was located at the end of the south aisle, and is now converted to a **community meeting room** (where tea, coffee, and perhaps lunch, may sometimes be obtained). It was originally established as a chantry by Sir Geoffrey de Massey of Worsley in 1453, before passing to the Egerton family by marriage.

On either side of the **chancel arch** are **plaques commemorating the Vicars of Eccles**. The incumbent of 1830 had the dying William Huskinson brought to his door, the victim of Stephenson's 'Rocket' on the opening day of the Liverpool and Manchester Railway (see p291) The **chancel** was left uncompleted by the reformation, and was only really finished in 1862. On the wall behind the **high altar** are 19th century **pictures of the four evangelists**. The **reredos** was installed against the wishes of the congregation, who thought it too 'high church' at the time. The **Victorian East Window** was damaged in the Christmas Blitz of 1940; the missing pieces were never replaced as a reminder of what war can do. Examine the **carving on the pulpit**. Can you spot the snail among the flowers? The fragment of the **Saxon cross** (p288) is preserved here, beside the pulpit, though recent analysis has suggested that the cross betrays Norse or Viking influence in the style of carving. On the **nave arch to the left of the pulpit**, a close inspection will reveal **medieval mason's marks** (to the left of the crown of the arch).

The **Pitcairn Chapel**, to the left of the chancel, was at one time the Jesus Chantry, founded in 1460 by William Booth when he was Archbishop of York. It later passed to the De Trafford family, and now stands as a memorial to Canon Pitcairn, a leading light in the restoration of the church in the 1860s.

The tour concludes in the **north aisle**, enlarged around 1480. The **Air Training Corps Window**, at the east end, commemorates former local members who died in the Second World War. At its foot (and partly obscured by carpet!) is the **grave of Ralph Robinson**, who served both James I and Charles I. Finally, at the west end notice the 1674 **hatchment of George Legh**, probably carried at his funeral. Americans may be interested by the **Mayo Window**, installed by the sons of locally born William Worrell Mayo, the founder of the famous Mayo Clinic in Rochester, Minnesota.

Upon leaving the church, take a brief detour towards to the right, past the **north gate of the churchyard**, to seek out *The Cross Keys*. (Main entrance round the corner) This rambling pile is the oldest pub in Eccles, being mentioned in a register of 1629. Appropriately for a location next to the church, the sign represents the emblem of St. Peter, who holds the keys to heaven! John Bradburn, the landlord, something of a local jack-of-all-trades, is reputed to have supplied Huskisson's coffin. It must have brought ill luck, for his wife committed suicide by plunging her head into a vat of boiling liquor in the brew house the following year! Continue walking to the station, past the site of the old cholera cemetery (**plaque** on the left). **Eccles Railway Station** was an original 'road station' on the Liverpool and Manchester Railway.

The Diligent Curate

At this station, on 15 September, 1830, the opening day of the railway, the 'Northumbrian' engine (conveying one carriage) made an unscheduled stop. It brought William Huskisson, President of the Board of Trade, and people soon learned that the 'Rocket' locomotive had run over his leg and mangled it at Parkside. Huskisson was travelling on the official train with the Duke of Wellington, but not in the Duke's ceremonial carriage. The plan was for the other trains to pass the Duke's in procession on the northernmost track at Parkside, while the locomotive took on water. There was a delay, and people got off to stretch their legs. Huskisson was estranged from the Duke, and people wanted to bring about a political reconciliation. As the two opponents chatted, someone saw the 'Rocket' approaching. Huskisson panicked, and the rest is history...The wretched man was carried to the rectory. The Vicar was absent, but his curate fervently exhorted Huskisson to make his peace with God and man. In great pain, he dictated codicils to his will, took the sacrament, and promptly expired. Lord Wilton was so impressed with the curate's performance (so the story goes) that he offered him the vacant living of Prestwich. 'Every cloud has a silver lining'!

The station has recently undergone restoration work by the 'Friends of Eccles Railway Station', including clean-ups, renovation of the station garden, and the creation of a mural.

An Excursion to the Trafford Centre

It is only a short bus ride from the bus station to the Trafford Centre, and several services perform it by more or less the same routing. The bus leaves the stop, and passes the **cross**. To the left is the recently restored **Old Town Hall**, an imposing brick building with stone facings and an impressive **clock tower**. It was originally designed by John Lowe in 1881, and built on the site of the old cockpit by the Local Board of Health, the forerunners to the local council. For many years the whole of the former town hall was devoted to magistrates' courts, and it has even featured for a court scene in an episode of Coronation Street! A little further on, again on the left, is the town's fine **War Memorial**. Local sculptor John Cassidy was commissioned to design the structure. Built from Portland Stone and topped with a **bronze figure**, it was unveiled by Lord Derby in August 1925, and is now a Grade II listed building. **Eccles Library**, behind it, was built on a slum clearance site in the town centre. The building was funded by Andrew Carnegie, designed by Edward Potts, and opened on 19 October 1907. Designed in the Renaissance style, it is also a Grade II listed building. Potts had hoped that the building would become "the Eccles University", where inhabitants might educate themselves. After passing along **Liverpool Road** (though one service runs via Barton Lane), we cross the **Duke's Canal** (see p239), turn left into **Barton Road**, and follow it to the Ship Canal. The **Duke's Canal bank** appears to be one long row of boats of all shapes and sizes, largely belonging to members of the Worsley Cruising Club. In addition to this mooring, look out for their small **private marina**, where boats may be hired.

We cross the **Ship Canal Swing Bridge**, while the **canal** crosses the **Ship Canal** on the left. This area was the site of James Brindley's stone aqueduct over the River Irwell, the feature that gave him so much trouble before the parliamentary committee (and led to

Pugin's Masterpiece

The De Traffords were an ancient family, owning vast estates to the south of the Mersey. They remained loyal to the old faith, and this had two important consequences in the Victorian era. Catholic emancipation meant that their religious opinions were once more respectable, and it became possible to have a personal chantry chapel once more at this spot. But, with the growing Roman Catholic population in the area (many were Irish immigrants), a parish church was clearly needed...a mission church, in fact, to preserve and perhaps extend the Roman Catholic faith. Money was no object, and Sir Humphrey De Trafford engaged Edward W. Pugin (the son of the famous G. A. W. Pugin, the great architect of the Gothic revival) to construct a fine church alongside the equally imposing de Trafford chantry. The edifice erected in 1865-8 was hailed by Pevsner as 'Pugin's masterwork', rivalling his father's achievements. Indeed, this richly finished Grade I listed church demonstrates his powers in designing articulated spaces and surfaces, both externally (with a characterful western gable sporting a prominent rose window and bellcote), and internally (where the coursings of piers and arches alternate with striking brilliance between red Runcorn and white Painswick sandstones). The figurative details of the carvings are attributed to Richard Boulton, Pugin's favourite sculptor, who also carved the surviving, angel-laden polychrome marble reredos behind the altar. The murals flanking the chancel are by J.A. Pippett, and include a rare portrait of Pugin the younger kneeling before the Agnus Dei, and holding a ground plan of the church. The statue of Saint Maximilian in the North Chapel sports a shirt denoting Auschwitz concentration camp. The modern world was not kind to either the family or church. The estate was sold off, the deer park becoming a large industrial estate, and the church became isolated from its congregation by the new Ship Canal. The church is now in the care of a small community of Grey Friars. (Intending visitors should write to the Custodian at the Friary, Redclyffe Road, Urmston, M41 7LG)

The Trafford Centre galleria
(Trafford Cemtre)

Xanadu

"In Xanadu, did Kublai Khan, a stately pleasure dome decree..." Well, not quite like the fabled Xanadu, but in a similar fashion to Kublai Khan's Pleasure Palace, the glittering glass domes of the Trafford Centre are perhaps the next best thing. Here Peel Estates decreed not a palace, but a major shopping centre. People get the wrong idea about the Trafford Centre. It is not an out-of-town hypermarket, for shopping in bulk. It is not even an ordinary mall, like the Metrocentre at Gateshead or Meadowhall at Sheffield. Instead, the company undertook a great deal of research into upmarket malls and shopping trends in the United States. Consequently, two things are apparent. With few exceptions, it is aimed at a customer interested in brands, labels, and more specialised shopping. And it is based on the assumption that a shopping mall can be turned into an attraction in its own right, with themed areas, leisure and entertainment facilities, and event based attractions. Wandering down the great galleries, reminiscent of Brussels or Milan, and tastefully decorated in the neo-classical manner; exploring the themed areas; and comparing the quality with other leisure attractions; and one rapidly comes to the conclusion that the designer has successfully walked the tightrope above what could have become a mass of Las Vegas style kitsch. Note that the leisure section and food court can be isolated from the shopping area, and remains open until long past midnight. Like many such developments, the Centre is currently geared to the car, but a stop is projected on the proposed Metrolink line to Port Salford.

the model hastily carved from cheese, see p239). The Ship Canal virtually obliterated the course of the old river, sweeping away the original aqueduct. But the Duke's Canal still had to cross at the same level without impeding the passage of ocean-going ships and the sailing ships that were still in use at the time. The solution was the unique **Barton Swing Aqueduct** on the left. When the aqueduct is required to open, gates seal off each end, so that a box of water can be swung clear of a passing ship. It is still operational, but rarely used these days. Notice **All Saints Roman Catholic Church and Friary** on the banks of the Ship Canal to the right.

Do not miss the view, on the right, of the spectacular **viaduct** in the distance, carrying the **M60** over the Ship Canal. The domes of the **Trafford Centre** now appear.

After quitting the bus (and noting the shuttle service to Stretford Metrolink Station) in the immense **bus station**, it is best to proceed into the **covered car park** by the pavement at the end next to the Centre. A sign directs to the **escalator**, by which we find ourselves at Gate One. This leads to the **first floor gallery** at the end of the Centre adjacent to *Debenhams*. Procure a floor plan at this stage, either from one of the many racks or one of the red uniformed staff. The décor is a kind of 19th century baroque revival, reminiscent of the galleria of Milan or Leeds. People have claimed to see local personalities (including soccer stars) in the faces along the frieze, but they represent people involved in the design and construction of the building. Cross over by one of the many **bridges** to the **right-hand**

balcony, and walk towards the first major **intersection.** A right turn leads into the first themed area, representing the **French Quarter of New Orleans.** We then reach a **classically themed concourse,** with a view over the ground floor **food court,** reached by stairs, lifts and escalators. The food court is designed to represent the **deck of a great ocean liner.** Descend to explore it, and briefly exit through the great hall to admire the **Greek temple façade** with its gigantic statuary. Retrace your steps into the court (noticing the **children's play area** and **crèche** on the right) and return to the **first floor concourse.** Take another detour up to the landing of the spectacular **central dome,** admiring the view. This is also the entrance for the *Odeon Multi-Screen Cinema, Laser Quest, Namco Funscape* (bowling alley and games) and *Paradise Island Adventure Golf.* Back at the **concourse,** exit via the themed area of **Chinatown.** Cross to the left-hand side of the galleria in order to inspect *Selfridges,* before walking to the last **dome,** adjacent to *John Lewis.* This is the home of a **fountain** that, at intervals, shoots an enormous jet of water as high as the roof, to the accompaniment of the 'oohs' and 'aahs' of the spectators. Retrace your steps to the right hand turn-off for **Barton Square,** along a corridor decorated with Greek statuary. **Barton Square,** built around a piazza, is dedicated to domestic furnishing, fixtures and fittings. The exceptions are *Legoland Discovery Centre* (admission charge), demonstrating that almost anything can be constructed from these small plastic bricks, and *Sea Life Manchester* (admission charge) with over 5,000 creatures, including sharks, seahorses, octopus, jellyfish and rays. If you can drag yourself away from the **giant singing bears,** go and inspect the **fountain.** Here, the designer has come to the end of his balancing act, and fallen into a positive riot of kitsch. But the effect is glorious…it is as if Hugh Hefner's greatest fantasy (or worst nightmare) has been conjured forth… Leave Barton Square and follow the signs for **Event City.** This large aircraft hangar of a building acts as an **exhibition centre** (admission charges); recent exhibitions have ranged from a reconstruction of the Tomb of Tutankhamen (and its contents) to a large display of model engineering.

The **Trafford Quays Leisure Village** has developed adjacent to the Trafford Centre, and is located across Trafford Boulevard. It is about five minutes' walk from the bus station, and the route is signposted. *Airkix Indoor Skydiving* suspends participants on a high speed column of air! (Advance booking recommended; ring 0845 331 6549 for further information and charges.) *Trafford Golf Centre* includes 62 driving bays, boasting four state of the art teaching studios, personal tuition from the academy, an American golf store, café and licensed bar. (Call 0161 749 7000 for further information.) The *Powerleague Soccerdome* offers 19 indoor and 4 outdoor pitches, organised matches, five-a-side leagues and football camps, providing a safe environment where the visitor can refine their skills under the watchful eye of experienced, registered referees. Ring 0161 755 9720 for further details) *David Lloyd Leisure* offers members the very best in racquet, fitness and health facilities for adults and children. DW Fitness has recently invested over £350,000 in new equipment. (For membership enquiries, ring 0845 129 6806.)

Last, but not least, the village includes **Chill Factor,** a large indoor ski slope (complete with snow). There's great family fun to be had, whizzing down the slope on the tubing track or even taking on the only ice slide in the UK! Catering for the little ones too is the magic of *snowplay* with soft play and mini tubing. Those with a head for heights can take on the 12 metre high climbing wall in the authentic Alpine street. (Activities start from £4 per person.) Off the slopes, visitors can enjoy an authentic après ski experience with a sit down meal in the Mont Blanc restaurant or in well-known favourites like *Nando's, Wetherspoon* and *Costa*. There is a wide range of leading shops, including *Snow & Rock, The North Face, Subvert* and *Quicksilver*. (Pre-booking is recommended: call 0161 749 2222 for information and bookings.).

Aerial Extreme's High Ropes Adventure Courses at Wilderspool Wood (off Regent 13 car park), adjacent to the Trafford Centre, offer a family fun day out involving a series of challenging obstacles set at varying heights above the ground, including rope bridges, scramble nets, zip wires, swinging logs and balance beams etc. (Advance booking recommended; ring 0845 652 1736 for information and charges.)

You can now return, either to Eccles or by the shuttle bus to Stretford Metrolink station.

The South Manchester and Didsbury Line

Piccadilly Station to Trafford Bar

There is a description of the line from Piccadilly Station to St. Peter's Square on pp26-36; from St. Peter's Square to Cornbrook on pp231-241; and from Cornbrook to Trafford Bar on pp241-243.

Trafford Bar to St. Werburgh's Road

The Chorlton Line proper commences at the **junction** situated immediately after **Trafford Bar Station** (p242). There was no physical connection with the original railway line to Chorlton at this point, which passed directly under the Altrincham line. It was built by the Midland Railway, and opened in 1880, connecting the new Central Station with their main line to St. Pancras, via Stockport. The opening of the Fallowfield Loop (p303) in 1891 resulted in the purchase of over a mile of track as far as Chorlton Junction by the Cheshire Lines Railway (p233). The last passenger train ran on 2 January 1967, although there were freight services (using the Wilbraham Road Loop, see p303) until the late 1980s. In re-opening this section of railway, the Passenger Transport Executive worked closely with 'Natural England' to protect wildlife along the new route; they pledged to plant at least five new young trees for every tree they needed to remove.

In order to create a point of junction with the Altrincham line, and provide access to the **new depot**, the former railway cutting has been partially filled with hard-core to the Altrincham line level (formed from crushed concrete from former building floors and hard standing areas on the depot site). The tram diverges to the left, joining the **inward line** (which has a depot connection at this point), and connecting with it by a **trailing crossover**. Of course, the alteration of the levels did not solve the junction problem completely, since inbound trams had to cross the Altrincham line. This was done by providing an access **ramp** to the former level at the Altrincham line end of the in-filled area. On the return journey, the trams descend this to run alongside the **piled diaphragm wall** between outbound and inbound lines at this point, allowing a grade-separated junction. They then pass **under the Altrincham line**, and this **bridge** or underpass is original. Notice that the railway line once continued onward on the other side, through the (backfilled) **tunnel entrance**, and under both Talbot Road and Chester Road to connect with the Cheshire Lines Liverpool route by vanished junctions facing east and west. However, inbound trams swing to the right, and up the **new Metrolink slope** to connect with the **Altrincham line** in the Manchester direction, by means of a **trailing junction** before the **Manchester platform** at **Trafford Bar Station**. As the outward bound tram runs on the **raised route section**, there is a fine view (to the right on the outward journey) of the **new Metrolink Depot**. It has a total capacity for forty trams (fifty-five at maximum), and contains workshop facilities for routine maintenance, offices, and a control centre. The outdoor **track fans** for the storage sidings are particularly noticeable. The line descends to its original level by a **steep incline** just before **Ayres Road Bridge**. As we are now in a cutting, with little visibility

The Blue Pullman

The Blue Pullman was a class of luxury train used from 1960 to 1973 by British Railways. Unlike the locomotive-hauled luxury trains pioneered by the Pullman Car Company, and the 'Brighton Belle' electrical multiple units, the Blue Pullmans were the first diesel-electric multiple units designed for high-speed Pullman train services, incorporating several novel features and sporting a bright blue livery. The entire train set was air-conditioned with automatic humidity control. Consequently, the power cars contained a large primary diesel engine and generator for motive power, while a secondary diesel engine and auxiliary generator provided electrical power for the air-conditioning, fridges and ancillary equipment (an onboard technician monitored the supply of services). The passenger areas were provided with armchair type table seating, in a 2+1 formation, each with a table lamp and steward call button. The cabins were protected from track noise by extra insulation in the bodywork and double glazed windows with Venetian blinds contained within the panes. How very different from the home life of our own dear tram! London Midland Region operated the "Midland Pullman" from 1960 to 1966 from Central Station to St. Pancras via this line and Cheadle Heath in the morning, and an evening return to Manchester

at this point, thoughts may return to those who have passed this way long before us, and we shall see evidence of their presence at Chorlton.

We pass under **Rye Bank Road** to arrive at **Firswood Station**. This stop is located between the **St. John Vianney School** and **Firs Avenue**. **Stairs** and **lifts** from both **platforms** access a **new footbridge**, which communicates by a **pathway** with **Rye Bank Road**. There is also a **pedestrian crossing** at the south end of the station.

If there is time, alight here and walk to the right along **Rye Bank Road**. This tree-lined suburban street was farm land as late as the last quarter of the 19th century, though housing had begun to reach **Seymour Grove** (p243), with its fine houses for the Manchester business elite. Turn right into the latter, walking a short way to the **junction with Upper Chorlton Road**. Once known as 'West Point', it was a fashionable area, and the large houses offered rich pickings for the criminal fraternity. One of these, owned by Samuel Gratrix, stood on the site of the **modern block of flats** (with balconies) on the opposite side of the road. Here, on the night of the 1 August, 1876, the notorious Charles Peace was disturbed while 'casing' the property in question. He shot P.C. Nicholas Cock, an atrocious murder that was, for many years, Chorlton's chief claim to fame. The house later became the Seymour Hotel. While it still stood, locals used to point

Charlie and the Little Bobby

Nicholas Cock was a baby-faced new recruit to the Lancashire Constabulary, affectionately known by the local inhabitants as "the little bobby." On the fateful night in question, he was conversing with a fellow constable and a civilian passer-by at West Point when he observed a figure behaving rather oddly for the time of night. After he went off to investigate, the others heard a shot. Cock was discovered lying by the house wall. He had been shot in the chest, and was losing a lot of blood. After being removed to the house of a local doctor, he promptly expired. Suspicion immediately fell upon the Habron brothers, rough Irish labourers employed locally as market gardeners. They were also poachers, and Cock had tried to convict them of this activity. Indeed, one of them had boasted in the 'Royal Oak' pub that he would "get the little bobby." Although the evidence was circumstantial, William Habron (18) was convicted of murder, though this was remitted to life imprisonment.

Although forgotten today, Charles Peace was once as notorious as Jack the Ripper. 'Charlie' was a 'Jekyll and Hyde 'character; by day a family man, a picture framer who liked to play the violin, even (at one point) a Sunday School teacher; and by night a burglar, and (despite an unprepossessing appearance) a notorious womaniser. His crimes were not particularly sensational, but some of the incidents of his life were...the Banner Cross Murder, and his attempted escape from a moving train featured in the sensational press. He was the subject of the first real crime film made in Britain, "The Life and Death of Charles Peace," filmed by the Sheffield Photographic Company. While awaiting execution for another murder, he confessed to the shooting of P.C. Cock. It had not been intentional, he said. Cock refused to be warned off, and in the struggle, Peace had tried to shoot him in the arm (to loosen his grip) and shot him in the chest instead. Habron was released on the understanding that he went to Ireland immediately, and never came back. When the Old Parish Church burial ground finally closed in 1956, Cock's headstone was removed to the County Police Headquarters near Preston. Here the memorial to "the little bobby" remains to this day.

out a blue painted brick in the boundary wall, supposedly marking the impact point of the fatal bullet! (However, some local historians think that the incident occurred in the garden of a house across the road, owned by another member of the Gratrix family.)

After leaving the station, the tram passes under **Manchester Road**, and continues between buildings on **Albany Road** and **Buckingham Road**. The cutting is much shallower at this point, and the **piling** to the right is particularly noticeable. Beyond **Brantingham Road**, the ground opens out to the right, and there is a glimpse of a **Victorian terrace** on Albany Road. The **modern brick buildings** that obscure the view are mostly on the **site of the old railway goods yard**. You might just pick out the remains of the far end of the **old Manchester platform** of the **previous Chorlton-cum-Hardy railway station**, just before *Morrisons Supermarket.*

The tram now arrives at **Chorlton Station**. The **outward platform** accesses **Wilbraham Road** to the south by **stairs** and **lift**. It also connects with the **inward platform** by a **pedestrian crossing** at the Manchester end. The **inward platform** is situated alongside *Morrisons Supermarket*, with which it communicates. It is also linked with **Wilbraham Road** by **stairs** (though passengers can also reach **Wilbraham Road** via the **supermarket car park**).

(Chorlton Station is the starting point for a short **tour of Chorlton-cum-Hardy**, described on p300).

The line now commences a long curve in an easterly direction. After passing under **Wilbraham Road,** it continues behind the houses on south-western side of **Egerton Road South**. The long wooden plank fence to the right conceals a paved walkway and cycle path, which crosses the line just before **St. Werburgh's Road Station,** adjacent to **Sidbury Road**. This **crossing** for pedestrians and cyclists communicates with a fenced off **pathway** running along the left-hand side of the line (linked with **St. Werburgh's Road** by a **doubled-back ramp**). From Manchester to Didsbury the original railway was double track. At Chorlton Junction, immediately east of **St. Werburgh's Road**, a double track line diverged left towards Guide Bridge. This is now the **Fallowfield Loop footpath/cycleway**. The old railway companies acquired enough land for four track lines. Widening the cutting, within existing boundaries on both sides of **St. Werburgh's Road Bridge**, has therefore allowed the **footpath/cycleway** to be diverted through the previously unused **northern bridge span**. Metrolink tracks go through the **southern bridge span**.

The Gospel Train

The original Chorlton Station had a strange history. In 1873, the Manchester South District Railway obtained an Act to construct a railway from Manchester to Didsbury and Alderley, with an eye to obtaining commuter traffic from developing residential districts on the south side of the city. It varied the route the following year, intending a connection with the projected Cheshire Lines route (between Woodley and Skelton Junction) at Heaton Mersey. This, of course, made it a strategic link within the context of the new Central Station proposal. Consequently, the Cheshire Lines Committee toyed with the idea of purchasing the company, but the Manchester Sheffield and Lincolnshire Railway (one of the joint owners of Cheshire Lines) pulled out of the deal. However, the Midland Railway still wanted an independent route into Manchester, and obtained parliamentary authority to purchase the Manchester South District and build the line in 1877. The line, together with Chorlton Station, was opened in 1880. The original station was situated on the north side of Wilbraham Road, accessed by ramps from the platforms. The main station building was located on the Manchester Platform, and there was a large goods and coal yard on the west side. Ownership of the station, and the track to the north of it, was transferred to the Cheshire Lines in 1891, coinciding with the opening of the Fallowfield Loop by the Manchester, Sheffield and Lincolnshire Railway the following year; this provided a link between Manchester Central and Guide Bridge. Thus, in addition to the local services, expresses thundered through without stopping. The Midland trains ran to St. Pancras, and the Manchester, Sheffield, and Lincolnshire (later Great Central) trains ran via the loop line and the Woodhead Tunnel to St. Marylebone. In later years, one might spot the Harwich Boat Train passing through the station. Chorlton closed in 1967, but that was not the end of its curious saga. Granada Television used the derelict site as the venue for a music programme entitled 'Gospel Train'. The cast was amazing: it featured the legendary Muddy Waters, with Rosetta Tharpe, Country Joe Pleasants, Rev Gary Davis, Otis Spanne, Brownie McGhee, and Sonny Terry. Or so it was thought! In fact, Granada used Wilbraham Road Station on the Fallowfield loop line. They didn't like the name and erected signs for 'Chorltonville'. (The station also had a similar architectural style to Chorlton.) Consequently, the old station lives on, vicariously under another identity, in a classic piece of musical history.

St. Werburgh's Road Station is the second in Chorlton. Beyond the road bridge, it comprises an **island platform**, linked with the footpath/cycleway by means of **pedestrian crossings** over the outbound track at either end. **Cycle parking** is provided alongside the diverted footpath/cycleway, which communicates by a **ramp** with **St. Werburgh's Road**. The tracks continue to the east of the station, where a trailing crossover is provided near the new Airport Junction (p318).

(The station is the starting point for walks on described on p303.)

Saint Who?

The dedication of the local church (after which both the street and station are named) is an unusual but interesting one. Werburh or Wærburh (also known as Werburgh and Werburga) is an English saint and the patron saint of Chester. She was born at Stone (now in Staffordshire), and was the daughter of King Wulfhere of Mercia, the Christian son of King Penda of Mercia, and his wife Ermenilda. Mercia was a Saxon kingdom in the Midlands, in an important strategic position, with a northern boundary stretching to the Mersey and influence further than that. Penda (after whom the penny is named) was a wily and far-sighted ruler. Although a pagan, he married the daughter of the Christian King of Kent for political reasons. Ermenilda ensured that Wulfhere, her son and Penda's successor, and Werburgh, her granddaughter, were both brought up in the Christian faith. As was the practice at the time, Werburgh became a nun in later life and Abbess of Ely. She was instrumental in convent reform across England, and became the great patroness of the church and monastery at Chester. Werburgh died on 3 February 699 at Trentham, and was buried at Hanbury in Staffordshire. Her remains were later transferred to Chester, where the magnificent shrine survived until the 16th century. As patron saint of that city, pilgrims flocked there hoping for miracles. "St Werburg lies at Chester, about whom, among the many things said of her, one is outstanding and unheard of, which I cannot avoid mentioning. For it is written that a large flock of wild geese were destroying her growing corn by feeding on it: she had them confined in a certain house, as if they were domestic geese. In the morning, when she called them, ready to send them out, she saw that one was missing. On enquiry, she heard that it had been eaten by the servants. "Bring me," she said, "the feathers and bones of the bird that has been eaten." When they were brought to her, this bride of the high God commanded that it should be whole and should live. And it was done. Then she instructed the geese, which were cheering and crying out at the return of their lost companion, that no other of their kind must ever, in all eternity, enter that field. They all departed in safety. And what the virgin commanded has been observed up to the present day." (Henry of Huntingdon: Historia Anglorum.) Yes, the pilgrims who visited her shrine sported a badge depicting geese in a basket! Indeed, her relics were once carried in solemn procession through the streets in order to assuage a serious fire that threatened to burn down the city. Perhaps the old girl did enough to have a station named for her!

Chorlton-cum-Hardy

In medieval times the district formed part of the Manor of Withington, an area stretching from Longford Park to Debdale Park, and south to the Mersey. The character of the district was agricultural and the rural village benefited from the growth of Manchester in the 19th century by supplying it with food, fruit in particular. The construction of Wilbraham Road in 1869 (intended to connect Lord Egerton's holdings in Withington to Edge Lane in Chorlton) established the nucleus of a residential area at the intersection with Barlow Moor Road, away from the old village centre. The opening of the Midland Railway line to Stockport and beyond in 1880 (p296) led to considerable residential and commercial development centred on this crossroads. After the Great War came a period of residential development to the east of the new village either side of Wilbraham Road and a council housing estate at Merseybank. From the 1980s, a new kind of resident arrived; these were people who had studied in Manchester, and had fond memories of the city's southern suburbs. The high salaries available in the upper reaches of a growing public sector were available to them and they brought a particular sensibility. This has rejuvenated the area's cultural life, and transformed some of its shopping areas. The influx of a large number of musicians, artists in all media, and others, and has given the area a significant 'vibe'.

Leave the station and turn right into **Wilbraham Road** (this was a popular Christian name in the Egerton family, who were Lords of the Manor.) *The Bar*, almost opposite the station entrances, is a local institution, but notice that the *Metro Café* has also adopted the new Metrolink colour scheme for its sign board! Turn right at the junction with **Barlow Moor Road** and cross the latter. We soon come to an interesting group of three buildings on the left at the former junction with **Manchester Road**. The dreadful reception block of the *Co-operative Funeral Parlour* cannot hide the former cinema behind it; indeed the history of this site is interesting and complex. The opening of Chorlton Station attracted the Booth family, who owned a packing warehouse in Manchester to the area. They built an eleven room house in the midst of what was then open fields and called it 'Sedge Lynn'. The house was demolished around 1920, and a cinema entrepreneur constructed a fine picture house with a façade of twin domes and a wrought iron colonnade in its place. This was acquired by the Savoy cinema chain before it was completed, and opened as the 'Savoy Cinema' in 1921. Passing through the hands of the ABC chain, it became a 'Gaumont cinema' in 1946, but closed (after showing 'The Pyjama Game') in 1962. In addition to adding the reception block to the façade, the Co-op extended the circle to the proscenium arch to form an upper floor for the storage of coffins. What Doris Day might have thought is anyone's guess! The building next door is an absolute gem. The *Sedge Lynn*, a *Weatherspoons* pub, has been called after the former house. It was, however, built in 1907 as a Temperance Billiard Hall, one of several designed by Norman Evans. Notice the charming hexagonal **porch** with its little dome, and the semi-circular **bay window** with a **long window** of glass with Venetian motifs above it (influenced by the 'art nouveaux' style). Once inside, the magnificent **barrel roof**, with its dormers and wooden trusses, is the main feature. The establishment has a reputation for its food. The final building in the group is **Chorlton Library**, an imposing confection in brick and Portland stone. It is one of a set (Withington Library has a similar design), and was financed to the tune of £5000 by Andrew Carnegie. It opened in 1914. Retrace your steps to the **funeral parlour** and notice the angle of the frontage; here, **Manchester Road** once diverged to the right. However the brick carbuncle (as Prince Charles might say) of **Graeme House**, and its shopping centre, now stands in the way. Turn right by the side of the funeral parlour before bearing left across the **car park** to the rear of Graeme House. We soon come to a detached part of **Manchester Road**, here reduced to a cul-de-sac. Look out for the pair of houses on the right (the one next to the *Pizzeria* is called **Orchard House**). Built in red and grey brick to a design by Henry Goldsmith, they are illustrated in his 'Economical Homes' (1895) and priced at £500 each! Turn right into the continuation of **Wilbraham Road** and cross over.

The junction with **another Manchester Road** on the left (this can be confusing!) is marked by two imposing buildings. The first is **Lloyds Hotel**, dating from 1870. It was originally called the 'Lloyd Platt Hotel (Lloyd was the landowner and Platt the developer); notice the sandstone dressings amidst the brick and the **masonic insignia**! The **Conservative Club**, opened in 1891, is on the opposite corner, with a brick and terracotta façade set off by blue painted **half-timbering** and a **corner clock turret**. The club formerly also served as a village hall, and still has a large auditorium that is available for functions. Non-members are welcome, and there is often music in the evenings. Now turn left into **Manchester Road**. The **Methodist Church** is immediately visible to the right, a neo-gothic structure opened in 1873 and designed by the architect of the Southern Cemetery mortuary chapels (telephone 0161 860 4681 for further information and access). The former schoolroom, to the rear of the church, now houses *The Edge*. This new Theatre and Arts Centre is run by the registered charity *Waters Edge Arts*, producers of high quality participatory and mainstream theatre, and is a cultural partner with Manchester City Council. The Centre provides the area with a new seventy seat theatre for use by amateur, community and professional companies. As well as a theatre space, the building also houses workshop, rehearsal and meeting rooms; there are plans to open a café with both indoor and outdoor seating areas in 2014. The centre runs a variety of projects, including an arts club for unemployed people and an in-house theatre company for actors with learning disabilities. (For further information about the Centre or forthcoming productions, telephone 0161 282 9776, or log on to their website.) **Manchester Road** leads to the junction of **High Lane** and **Edge Lane**. It is worth a short detour to the right along the latter to Number Twelve, the site of the **former Masonic Hall**. It is currently (2014) in a very sad condition, virtually derelict, although conversion into housing is planned. This unusual building was created by joining two houses (dating from the 1860s) together by an upper storey (containing the masonic hall itself) in the 'Italian Gothic' style. Retrace your steps to **St. Clement's Parish Church**, situated on the corner of **Edge Lane** and **St. Clement's Road**. The history of this Victorian church is a tale of factions, intrigue, and petty jealousy that might have come straight from the pages of Trollope. By 1860, the original parish church (see below) was in a poor condition. Lord Egerton offered this site, together with some financial help, provided that the original endowment of the old church was transferred to the new. A local faction (led by William Cunliffe-Brooks, the banker, and Sam Mendel, the cotton magnate) opposed this, and proposed a re-development of the old church. By 1865, the endowment had not been transferred and funding had dried up. Only the **nave** and **chancel** were anything like complete, allowing the first service to be held in 1866. But the majority of the parishioners persevered, and funding came from the influx of rich inhabitants in the 1880s. The **north transept** was finished in 1883 and the south transept in 1896, allowing the building to be consecrated in the same year, about thirty-six years after the project began! Meanwhile, the old church that it was designed to replace was still in business down the road! The church is constructed in the 'Decorated' style, though the arrangement of the interior has been altered in recent years. The caretaker can usually be found in its vicinity on Monday to Friday, nine to twelve; otherwise ring (0161) 881 3063 to arrange admission. The Roman Catholic church of **Our Lady and Saint John** will be found almost opposite, on the corner of **High Lane** and **St. Clement's Road**, with the main frontage along the former. Constructed of red brick and terracotta in the 'Decorated' and 'Perpendicular' styles, it was consecrated in 1927.

Our path now lies along **St. Clement's Road** to what is perhaps Chorlton's best kept secret. The first sight of **Chorlton Green** is something of a surprise; one might be in some rural backwater instead of in the middle of suburbia. This amazing survival of the original village is a wedge shaped area of grass, fenced off and adorned with a replica gas lamp in the centre. At one end is the ***Horse and Jockey***, with its 'olde worlde' half timbering. This is a modern pastiche, grafted on to a 19th century public house. However, the brick structure underneath was probably a farm house, and has parts that may date to 1520! The name is said to be derived from the horse races that were held on nearby Scaffold Field. This was a convenient location, as illegal gamblers could slip across the Mersey into Cheshire to avoid arrest! We now head towards the **brick arch** at the opposite end of the Green. Chorlton was a Chapelry of the Parish of Manchester. Around 1512, a Chapel of Ease was erected, to save the residents the long trek to the Collegiate Church in Manchester. Here they could hear mass and be buried, though the Collegiate Church reserved the right to marry and baptise to themselves, since such services were lucrative. This chapel was probably half timbered and may have lasted until the 18th century. A plain brick church was erected in 1779, and the growing local population resulted in the addition of aisles in 1837. This may have weakened the church and eventually resulted in its "poor" condition. We last left the parishioners squabbling about its replacement (p302). William Cunliffe-Brooks decided to ignore the new project, and restored the old church at his own expense. In 1888, to celebrate the Royal Jubilee, he provided the brick **Jubilee Lych Gate**, with the **bellcote** above. The old church finally closed in 1940 as a result of frost damage, and was finally demolished in 1949. Pass through the **gateway** into the **old churchyard**, noticing the remains of part of the **foundations** at the far end. Here will be found the **oldest surviving gravestones** from the 18th century. We exit the churchyard opposite the *Bowling Green Hotel*, reputedly first licenced in 1693. The 1780 incarnation of the hostelry was rebuilt in 1908, but the adjacent **bowling green** has antecedents dating back to the 15th century! The road to the right of the Bowling Green Hotel leads to the **bridge** over the **Chorlton Brook**. It flows from the confluence of Platt Brook and Shaw Brook (or Red Lion Brook), and heads westward through Chorlton-cum-Hardy, and Chorlton Ees into the River Mersey upstream of Sale Water Park (p315).

There is an entrance to **Ivy Green Nature Reserve** on the right, just before the **bridge**. Although there are several walks, this will be found the most useful (see map on p314). Follow the **path** commencing on the side of the **car park** nearest the bridge, keeping **Chorlton Brook** on the left hand side. Turn left across the **footbridge** which leads to **Chorlton Ees Car Park**. We now follow the **car park road** on the left a short distance before turning right on to the **path** that leads to the River Mersey. The way now lies to the left, along the river to the **Jackson's Boat Bridge** (p313). From this point both **Sale Water Park** (p315) and **Chorlton Water Park** (p308) may be reached.

Retrace your steps to the *Horse and Jockey*, bearing to the right before turning right at the *Beech Inn* into **Beech Street**. The road has been transformed in recent years, and now contains a wide selection of **niche** or speciality shops, cafés, and restaurants. After passing the pretty little **park** on the left, we arrive at **Barlow Moor Road**. A left turn here, and a short walk past the small **bus station** brings the visitor back to the crossroads with Wilbraham Road. The **Metrolink Station** lies to the right.

Excursions to the Country

Until the Airport line opens, the Chorlton line can be used by as a starting point for forays into the nearest countryside. The area of land stretching from Barlow Moor Road towards the Mersey and the M60 Motorway was transformed by the construction of the latter. Large gravel pits were excavated; two were flooded, forming the central focus of what became **Sale Water Park** and **Chorlton Water Park**. The rest were used as landfill sites, now reclaimed and landscaped. The two Water Parks, together with their associated woods and meadows, constitute the nearest accessible countryside for many of the residents of South Manchester. Consequently, **two excursions** are given for the energetic, to be undertaken on a fine day. Both start from **St. Werburgh's Road Station**, and both can, if desired, **be combined**. However, the **Sale Water Park** excursion can also be extended to terminate either at **Stretford** or **Dane Road** Stations, permitting the option of returning to Manchester by the Altrincham line. **(It must be noted that these excursions will eventually be accessed from stations on the Airport Line.)**

There is a common starting point. To reach it, leave the **station** by the **walkway/cycle path** to the left where it diverges away from the Metrolink line. As already stated, this is the trackbed of the Fallowfield Loop, which opened in two stages; firstly from Chorlton Junction to Fallowfield in September, 1891, and from there to the Manchester, Sheffield, and Lincolnshire Railway's main line the following year. There were two curves at the point of junction with the Sheffield line, one in the direction of Manchester and the other joining the main line just before Fairfield (for Droylsden) station in the direction of Guide Bridge and Sheffield. The entire loop line was over seven miles long, with stations at Alexandra Park (later Wilbraham Road), Fallowfield, Levenshulme, and Hyde Road. The local service, from Central Station to Guide Bridge, was used by commuters and also travellers wishing to access this important junction on the main line. There was also a curious (and short lived) local train that ran backwards and forwards between Central and London Road (now Piccadilly)! But we are really walking on the path of former expresses to St. Marylebone Station in London that roared through the suburbs without stopping! At the second turning to the right (distinguished by a **signpost** for Hough End and Chorlton Water Park) follow the **path** and the **short street** that it leads to. Another **signpost** (with a bicycle symbol) points to the left down the winding **Chelsfield Grove**. We follow this street to emerge on to **Maudeth Road West**, constructed as an interwar 'improvement' with a central reservation intended for a tramway that never materialised due to a change of policy (p286). However, in an interesting twist of fate, it will soon have a tramway (albeit for a small part of its length) as was originally intended! So, turn right, and walk along the road to the former **railway bridge**, from where the Metrolkink line can be seen. The **junction** for the intended line to Wythenshawe and Manchester Airport is visible on the right. After leaving the Chorlton/Didsbury line at this point, it joins **Mauldeth Road West** adjacent to **Chorlton High School**.

Beyond the bridge, there is a glimpse of the rear of **Hough End Hall** on the right. To inspect this property, take a short detour to the right, down **Nell Lane** (with Chorlton Park on the opposite corner). Unfortunately, the view is marred by a crass planning decision in the 1960s to put **Mauldeth House** in the way. So continue onwards, and turn right, down the **fenced off road** by the side of the offending building, arriving at the forecourt in front of the Hall. **Hough End Hall** is said to have been built by Sir Nicholas Mosley shortly after he bought the Manor of Manchester in 1596, on the site of an older house which is known to have existed in the middle of the 15th century. (An account of this family is given on p33). It is a picturesque brick building of three stories on a stone base three feet high, consisting of a **centre portion** with a wing at **each end**. The **principal doorway** is central, opening to a central passage with another door (now blocked) on the north side. The total length of the chief or **south front** is about 94 feet, the central or recessed portion measuring 42 feet, and the wings projecting 6 feet 9 inches. The **windows** are all square-headed and with stone mullions; those on the top floor, however, extend across the whole length of the front. The **wings** are **gabled** and ornamented with **balls**, and the centre portion is surmounted with a **parapet** in the form of three smaller gables with similar finials. The **chimneys** are square shafts set diagonally on square bases. The **original hand-made bricks** are 2¼ inches in thickness, laid in alternate courses of headers and stretchers. The house has had a very unhappy history. After the Mosley family left, it was used in the 19th century as a farmhouse. The interior of the building was 'modernised' and stripped of its old oak, including a handsome staircase at the cast end (removed by Lord Egerton to Tatton Lodge). By the time Pevsner inspected it, the house was in a semi-derelict condition. Fortunately, the City Council was shamed into doing something by his publication, but the subsequent restoration cannot be said to be sympathetic. Some **original windows** do survive, however, and the **brickwork on the right-hand side** appears to be original. The house has been used in recent years as a restaurant. Retrace your steps, and continue along **Mauldeth Road West** and arrive at the junction with **Barlow Moor Road**, the site of the intended **Barlow Moor Road Station**, after which the trams will pass through to **Hardy Lane** by means of a level crossing. This is the starting point for both of the walks.

Chorlton Water Park via Southern Cemetery

Turn left, and walk down **Barlow Moor Road**. The great expanse of **Southern Cemetery**, to the left, is introduced by the **crematorium complex**. The oldest part, beyond the low brick modern construction, was created by the Manchester Cremation Society, founded in 1888.

The founders were deeply concerned about two related issues. Firstly, the appalling living conditions of workers in the then rapidly developing industrial Manchester put a premium upon open spaces for healthy relaxation. Secondly, the growing population seemed to make the acquisition of land for more and more cemeteries a greater priority. The society would have none of this. It believed that they should 'Save the Land for the Living' and that Manchester should open its own crematorium. The first such establishment had opened at Brookwood Cemetery, Woking, and Manchester's crematorium was the second in the country. The **Crematorium Chapel** (designed by Edward Salomons and A.Steinthall) was built in1892, on a rectangular plan with an **entrance** at the south-west end and a **chimney tower** at the north-east corner. It is in

The Crematorium Chapel

the 'Basilican Lombard' style. The **gabled facade** has a projecting **gabled porch** with a Lombard frieze and a tall round-headed **entrance arch** on coupled columns; and, above the porch, **blind arcading** with slender columns. The **sides** have **arcaded cloisters** (in effect, aisles turned inside out), with round-headed arches on circular columns, the **inner walls** lined with memorial plaques. There is a pilastered **clerestory** with a Lombard frieze and three round-headed clerestory windows to each bay. The tall **chimney-tower** is square, with pilastered corners, a short top stage with arcaded three light windows, a Lombard frieze to the cornice, and steeply-pitched **mansard roof**. The **interior** has a barrel roof.

A **Jewish chapel** is passed beyond the crematoria, followed by the **first gated entrance** to the cemetery proper. The north-western corner of the cemetery, with its memorials to war and disaster (see below) can also be accessed by following the direct path that commences here, running past the Muslim section.

The **main entrance** to **Southern Cemetery** may be found a little further on. In 1872, Manchester Corporation purchased about forty hectares of land at a cost of £38,340 for the purpose of a cemetery, in open country to the south of the city. The architect for the cemetery was H J Paull, who was responsible for Phillips Park Cemetery. The plaque in the Registrar's Office records that Southern Cemetery was opened on 9 October 1879 by the Mayor, Alderman Charles Sydney Grundy and lists the names of the Parks and Cemeteries Committee together with the Town Clerk, Joseph Heron. The design for the layout of the cemetery has been attributed to James Gascoigne Lynde, the City Surveyor from 1857 to 1879. The original plan created an elliptical drive linking the Church of England, Nonconformist, and Roman Catholic chapels, centred on a main

Ashes to Ashes

The cremation society was formed in 1874. Interestingly enough, its Declaration was signed by (amongst others) John Everett Millais, John Tenniel, and Anthony Trollope. It encountered much difficulty and prejudice until a catalyst for action resulted from a bizarre episode. In 1883, the eccentric Doctor William Price attempted to cremate the body of his five months old son (christened Jesus Christ) and born to him at the age of eighty three! He was at once arrested and put on trial in Cardiff. Doctor Price claimed to be a Druid High Priest (he performed the rites dressed in a white tunic over green trousers while sporting a fox-fur). The result of the trial was the breakthrough the Cremation Society had been waiting for. Mr. Justice Stephen delivered his all-important pronouncement that cremation is legal provided no nuisance is caused in the process to others. Following this, Doctor Price tried to claim £3,120 damages against the police for preventing the completion of his son's cremation. He was, however, awarded the nominal sum of only one farthing. Meanwhile, on 26 March, 1885, the first official cremation at Brookwood Cemetery, Woking, took place. Mrs. Pickersgill, a well-known figure in literary and scientific circles, was the first of three cremations that year. During the year 1888, in which twenty-eight cremations took place, the Council of the Cremation Society issued a special appeal to the public for funds to carry out a plan to provide a chapel, waiting rooms and other amenities at the Woking Crematorium. The subscription list was headed by the Dukes of Bedford and Westminster. The buildings were constructed in the character of English 13th century Gothic, and were available for use at the beginning of January, 1891. In 1892 over a hundred cremations were carried out at Woking, and the Cremation Movement may at this stage be considered to have been successfully launched.

axis leading north-north-east from the principal entrance to the Church of England chapel and beyond to the north-east boundary. A symmetrical, radial path layout within the elliptical drive overlies a rectilinear pattern, which extends beyond the drive. The cemetery expanded beyond the driveway, with paths in a rectangular grid pattern. In 1926, a further thirty-six hectares of land was purchased to the north-east of Nell Lane for future expansion of the cemetery, but some of this was later used for housing and allotments. The cemetery is open for visitors from 9am on weekdays and from 10am on Saturday, Sunday, and public holidays, until dusk. The office and Memorial Room are usual open Monday to Friday, closing at 4.30. All other enquiries, ring 0161 227 3205. Please note that the cemetery registers may be researched on both microfilm and computer at Manchester Central Library.

The **principal entrance** lies at the centre of the south-west boundary of the main section of the cemetery. It is set back between curving sandstone walls, topped with Victorian wrought-iron railings, with stone piers marking the junctions between the curved sections of wall and the boundary wall. Further piers flank two pedestrian entrances and a central, larger pair of stone piers marks a carriage entrance, all with wrought-iron gates. Immediately north-west of the entrance stands the **Registrar's Office**, and to the south-east a **Lodge** (both listed grade II), dating from 1879. They are two-storey stone buildings in the Gothic style, with steeply pitched gabled roofs, complete with a **tower and short spire**. Immediately south-east of the lodge a small, single-storey **sandstone building** adjoins the south-west boundary. This is a former public convenience now used by a cable television company. Seek out the (recently restored) wooden building opposite the Registrars Office, across the driveway. This contains a **Memorial Room**, containing some displays on the history

Southern Cemetry gates

of the cemetery, and files about the famous burials that may be perused. Walk towards the **elliptical driveway**. There are three **mortuary chapels**, again all dating from 1879. The **Anglican chapel** is sited 240 metres north-north-east from, and on an axis with, the principal entrance. On a cross-axis, 240 metres north-north-west and 210 metres east-north-east of the principal entrance, are sited the **Nonconformist** and **Catholic** chapels respectively. The **chapels** vary in design but all are in Gothic style and are built of sandstone with steep slated roofs, each with a tower below a short spire. The Nonconformist chapel is now unused. The **grass circle within the ellipse** is laid out with formal beds, and a number of **large monuments** are set around, facing the encircling drive. One of these, 140 metres north-north-east of the principal entrance, is the **Alcock monument** (listed grade II), a white marble Celtic cross of circa 1920, commemorating Sir John Alcock (1892-1919), pilot of the first non-stop Trans-Atlantic flight (tragically killed in a flying accident shortly afterwards). The **paths** within the elliptical drive are lined with a wide variety of monuments, many from the late nineteenth and early 20th century in polished granites and marbles; this was the **most prestigious part of the** cemetery. Amongst these, about forty metres south-east of the Nonconformist Chapel, is the **grandiose marble tomb of John Rylands** (1801-88), the wealthy cotton merchant, who is also commemorated by the John Rylands Library in Manchester (parts of the original tomb structure are missing). In the north-west corner of the cemetery, a rectilinear plot is subdivided by hedging to enclose **two war memorials** (there were several military hospitals in Manchester in both conflicts), and a **memorial to the Tenerife Air Disaster of 1979.** (Two aircraft collided on the ground when one attempted to take off; it remains the worse loss of life ever recorded in an air crash, and involved many Manchester holidaymakers.) The remainder of this plot is reserved for commemorating possible future disasters. The **mass grave of the victims of the Manchester 'Christmas Blitz'** of 1940 is also in this area. In addition to Alcock and Rylands, the **famous burials** include Philip Baybutt, who fought in the American Civil War and was awarded the Congressional Medal of Honour; Sir Matt Busby; Leslie Ann Downey, a sad victim of the Moors Murderers; L.S. Lowry; Billy Meredith (p203); Ernest Marples, a controversial Conservative Minister of Transport; Wilfred Pickles, the first BBC broadcaster with a (Yorkshire) accent; John Prettyjohns, the Crimean V.C.; and Anthony H. Wilson, guru of the 'Madchester' music scene.

Almost opposite the main gate, seek out **Maitland Avenue**. The entrance to **Chorlton Water Park** lies at the bottom of it. Chorlton Water Park stands on what was the site of Barlow Hall Farm. Up until the 1950s the farmer flooded the field to increase the fertility of the land. He recalled that 'the sluice gates were never opened for the first flood as this brought down the rubbish: the second flood brought down rich mud'. Gravel was

The Alcock Monument

The remains of the Ryland Monument

The 'Christmas Blitz' memorial

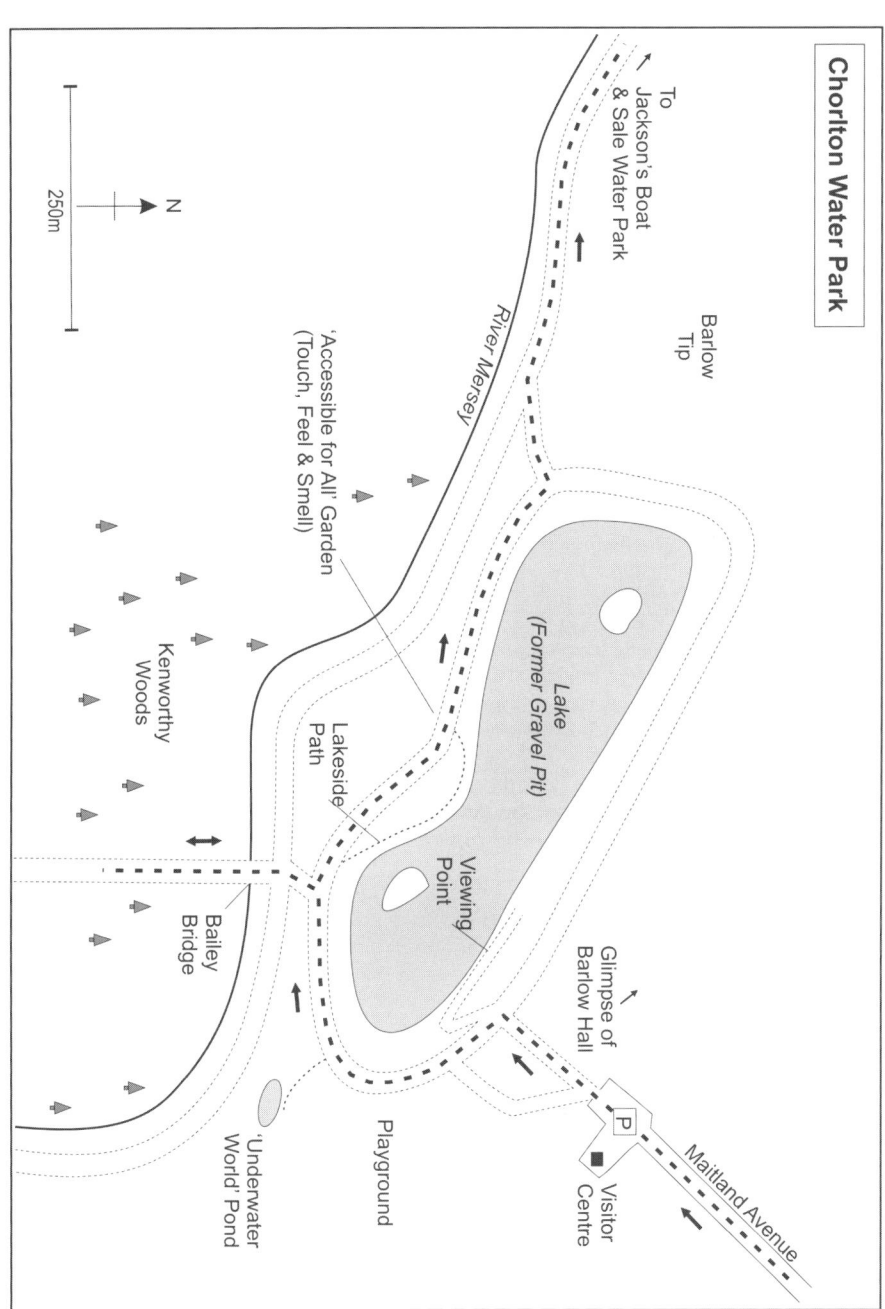

Choriton Water Park

N

250m

To
Jackson's Boat
& Sale Water Park

Barlow
Tip

River Mersey

'Accessible for All' Garden
(Touch, Feel & Smell)

Kenworthy
Woods

Lake
(Former Gravel Pit)

Lakeside
Path

Viewing
Point

Bailey
Bridge

'Underwater
World' Pond

Playground

Glimpse of
Barlow Hall

P

Visitor
Centre

Maitland Avenue

excavated from the site and used in the construction of the M60 motorway in the 1970s. The gravel pit was subsequently flooded, creating the lake that is central to the Water Park today. As the trees have grown and the grasslands developed, the Park has become increasingly valuable for wildlife. Until Salford Quays was redeveloped, large numbers of pochards roosted on the lake during the day, heading to the Quays to feed on bloodworms (a type of midge larvae) at night. Although many of the pochards have found new places to feed further afield, the lake remains a nationally important wintering site for water birds. The lake is well stocked with coarse fish and well-spaced fishing platforms are situated around the water's edge. The fishing season runs from May to December and fishing permits can be obtained from the Wardens. They are cheaper to buy from the Office or Information point than the bank side (contact 0161 8815639 for further details).

Pass the **information office** and **car park**, taking the **direct path** towards the lake shore, visible directly ahead. On the right, through the **railings**, is a glimpse of **Barlow Hall**. The house perhaps dates to the 16th century, though an earlier building may have stood here in the reign of Henry VI. It has had a very chequered history, being substantially altered at various dates. A disastrous fire in 1879 destroyed the remaining historical part, and few original features are left, none of which are visible from this vantage point. The mostly two storey brick structure formerly enclosed a courtyard, but the east range has disappeared. The principal features of interest now include a surviving north-east **oriel or bay window** of the Great Hall in the west range (facing on to the courtyard), which is timber-framed, jettied and gabled, and standing on a sandstone plinth. It contains a twelve light wooden mullion-and-transom window at ground floor (with much original glass) with carving, and an altered three light casement window at first floor level. The roof bargeboards have pierced quatrefoils, typical of the 16th century. There are **two timber-framed panels** at first floor level on the south side of the north range, which also have quatrefoil panelling. The former brick **entrance porch** on the north side of this range has a cambered timber lintel to the former waggon entry (now blocked, re-using a carved bargeboard as a lower lintel). Nothing remains of the original interior except some **stained glass** shields in the oriel window, and one pane lettered "1574". The house is now private property, being used as the clubhouse of Chorlton Golf Club.

After admiring the view and the waterfowl, follow the **main path** to the left to commence a **clockwise perambulation** around the lake. Beyond the wooded area, pass the **playground** and note the easily missed path on the left, leading to the **'underwater**

A Saint in the Family

The Barlow family, the owners of the Hall until the 18th century, were recusants. That is to say that they adhered to the old faith after the reformation, suffering for their beliefs. Alexander Barlow, probably the builder of the house, was a marked man. A search was made of the new house for both priests and hiding places, and he was hauled off to Manchester for questioning, an ordeal that probably brought about his death in 1584. He had three grandsons, one of whom was baptised Edward at Didsbury Church on 30 November, 1585. Edward later changed his name to Ambrose and travelled to Douai in France to study at the English College (an institution for training missionary priests to work undercover in England) before attending the Royal College of St. Alban in Valladolid, Spain. In 1615, he returned to Douay where he became a member of the Benedictine Order and was ordained as a priest in 1617. He returned to Barlow Hall, before taking up residence at the home of Sir Thomas Tydesley at Astley. Sir Thomas's grandmother had arranged for a pension to be made available to the priest which would enable him to carry out his priestly duties amongst the poor Catholics within his parish. To avoid detection by the authorities, he devised a four week routine in which he travelled throughout the parish for four weeks and then remained within the Hall for five weeks. He would often visit his cousins, the Downes, at their residence of Wardley Hall, and conduct Mass for the gathered congregation. He was noted for "his great zeal in the conversion of souls and the exemplary piety of his life and conversation." On the eve of church festivals, Catholics resorted to where he happened to be, and spent the night in prayer watching, and 'spiritual colloquies'. In the meantime, he would spend the night hearing confessions. The next day he would treat them all to a dinner, the rich waiting upon the poor, and everyone received a groat in alms before they departed. Unfortunately, this was happening at a time when religion was once more politicised, and mixed up with foreign politics. 'Papists' were once more seen as a threat. On 25 April 1641, Easter Day, the Vicar of Leigh received a 'tip off' during the morning service. Ambrose and his congregation of around a hundred people were surrounded at Morleys Hall, Astley by the Vicar (still wearing his surplice!) and his armed congregation of some four hundred. After a trial and imprisonment at Lancaster Castle, Ambrose was drawn on a hurdle to the place of execution, hanged, dismembered, quartered, and boiled in oil. His head was afterwards exposed on a pike. On 15 December 1929, Pius XI proclaimed Father Ambrose as Blessed, and on 25 October 1970 Paul VI canonised a number of people who were to be known as the Forty Martyrs of England and Wales, of whom Ambrose was one. His skull is said to be the one preserved at Wardley Hall.

world' pond. Here, supervised small children can observe all manner of pond life. We soon reach a major junction, and it is worth while walking a short distance to the left, down the **path to the Mersey**. It is here spanned by a **Bailey Bridge**.

If you have the time and inclination, the walk can be extended by crossing the bridge to explore **Kenworthy Woods**. A web of footpaths and bridle routes crisscross through Kenworthy Woods, making it a great place to explore. A patchwork of woodlands, grasslands and secluded ponds encourages a diverse range of wildlife. Listen out for the chirruping of grasshopper warblers in spring in the grassland or look out for redpoll and siskin eating seeds in winter from the alder trees on Kenworthy Lane. The area was originally farmland that was subject to regular flooding from the **River Mersey**, which flows around the Northeast perimeter. Gravel was extracted from the land in the 1960s and it became a landfill site, used mainly for bomb debris after World War Two. The site was capped with a thin layer of soil and the first patches of woodland were planted in the 1970s. In 1997 the Co-operative Bank funded a huge project under the Co-operative Bank Community Woodland Scheme to plant native trees on the site, creating 13 hectares (32 acres) of new woodland. The plantations include a **community orchard**, a **coppice trail** and a collection of over twenty varieties of poplar.

Back on track, so to speak, continue to follow the **main path along the shore of the lake**, though a **lower path** runs nearer the water's edge. Both come together adjacent to an '**Access for All Garden**' on the left, which is wheelchair and stroller accessible, and offers opportunities to 'see, touch, and smell'. Towards the end of the lake, take the left hand **fork** to find the **main, metalled path** along the **banks of the River Mersey**,

Mr. Bailey's Bridge

Donald Bailey was a civil servant in the War Office who tinkered with model bridges as a hobby. He presented one such model to his chiefs, who saw some merit in the design. The Bailey bridge is a type of portable, prefabricated, truss bridge. They were developed by the British during World War Two for military use and saw extensive use by both British and American engineering units. A Bailey bridge had the advantages of requiring no special tools or heavy equipment to construct. The wood and steel bridge elements were small and light enough to be carried in trucks and lifted into place by hand, without requiring the use of a crane. The bridges were strong enough to carry tanks. After the war, the stockpiled components were temporarily used to restore transport links in many parts of Europe. They continue to be extensively used in civil engineering construction projects, and to provide temporary crossings for foot and vehicle traffic.

One of the last Bailey Bridges

and continue in the same direction. It seems strange that this river, here a winding stream once prone to flooding, should terminate in a great estuary by a major port. We pass **Barlow Tip** (also known as Barlow Eye) on the right. It is neither owned nor managed by the Mersey Valley Countryside Warden Service, but is the responsibility of the Greater Manchester Waste Disposal Authority Ltd., who have established a methane extraction plant at the west end of the site. During the mid to late 1970s the site was used for gravel extraction, then the tip was capped, seeded and planted. Nowadays the site comprises young woodlands, grasslands and scrub and is **one of the highest points of altitude** within the Valley. Our walk ends at the **bridge** leading to *Jackson's Boat* (p313). You can now commence the **walk to Sale Water Park**, or return via **Hardy Lane** to **Barlow Moor Road** (p305). Or perhaps just adjourn to the pub across the bridge for a pint and a (recommended) meal!

Chorlton Ees, Sale Water Park, and Priory Gardens

This excursion offers a number of options. You can return to the starting point at **Barlow Moor Road**, or **extend the walk** to terminate at either **Stretford** or **Dane Road** Station (p249), returning to Manchester by the Metrolink Altrincham line.

Cross **Barlow Moor Road** and walk down **Hardy Lane** which is directly ahead. This is the route that the Metrolink Manchester Airport line will take. Bear to the right at the end of the road, passing through the **stile** where the **signpost** directs to 'Sale Water Park'. The winding metalled path passes the **Hardy Farm** site to the left, and leads to the **bridge over the Mersey**. Again, time and inclination might suggest a diversion by following the path to the right, along the north bank of the river to **Chorlton Ees**. A brick walkway betrays the history of Chorlton Ees. For over a century, the site was the old Withington sewage works; and the walkway was once one of the sewage channels. When the sewage works were closed in 1972, the site was restored under a government scheme called 'operation eyesore', which was set up to reclaim derelict land. The mosaic of different habitats supports a diverse range of bird species, which makes the area an established **bird watching spot**. Flocks of goldfinch, linnet, greenfinch, redpoll and siskin flit between the trees on the grassland, whilst herons, reed bunting, whitethroat, blackcap, chiffchaff and goldcrest are all known to breed at Chorlton Ees. One of the Mersey Valley's Health Walks takes you through the **woodlands** at Chorlton Ees. Follow the **signs**, which will take you on a **circular route of about a mile in length**. The well-surfaced paths are accessible to wheelchairs and push chairs; and there are no unexpected steep hills. You will find benches situated at intervals along the route should you need to rest a while, or you just want to sit and enjoy the countryside. (The **riverside path** continues to **Chorlton Ees Car Park**, and thence by a further **path** through **Ivy Green Nature Reserve**, terminating at the car park by Chorlton Brook. See p303.)

The **footbridge** across the River Mersey was originally erected in 1816 and at that time there was a halfpenny toll to cross it. The bridge was built to replace a local farmer called Jackson and his boat, who had provided a ferry service across the river. The boat was hauled from bank to bank by a chain fastened to posts on either side. The present bridge dates from 1881. The corporation bought it in the 1940s, and abolished the toll. From it, there is a fine view of the **new viaduct** carrying the Metrolink Airport Line over the Mersey and its flood plain. Cross the **bridge** and find a delightful hostelry. The River Mersey is the traditional boundary between Cheshire and Lancashire. However, the *Jackson's Boat Inn* is in Lancashire, in spite of sitting on the Cheshire side of the river. This anomaly is due to natural changes in the course of the river over many centuries. During the Jacobite uprisings of the 18th century, Stuart sympathisers met secretly at the inn. According to local tales, they drank to the health of the Pretender Prince Charles 'across the water' in France, symbolising this with a bowl of water placed in the centre of the table. The present building is 18th century in origin, and the pub is comparatively unspoiled. 'George' the ghost has been known to put in an appearance, sometimes wearing highland dress! The **food** can be recommended, and the pub offers a **beer garden**, and a **children's play area**. **Rifle Road** commences at the pub entrance, with a **bicycle hire and repair** facility opposite the pub. Continue along **Rifle Road**, noting the future Metrolink line to the left, alongside the **golf course**. The **site of Sale Water Park Station** is a little beyond the **road junction**, before the Airport line turns left to follow the Motorway.

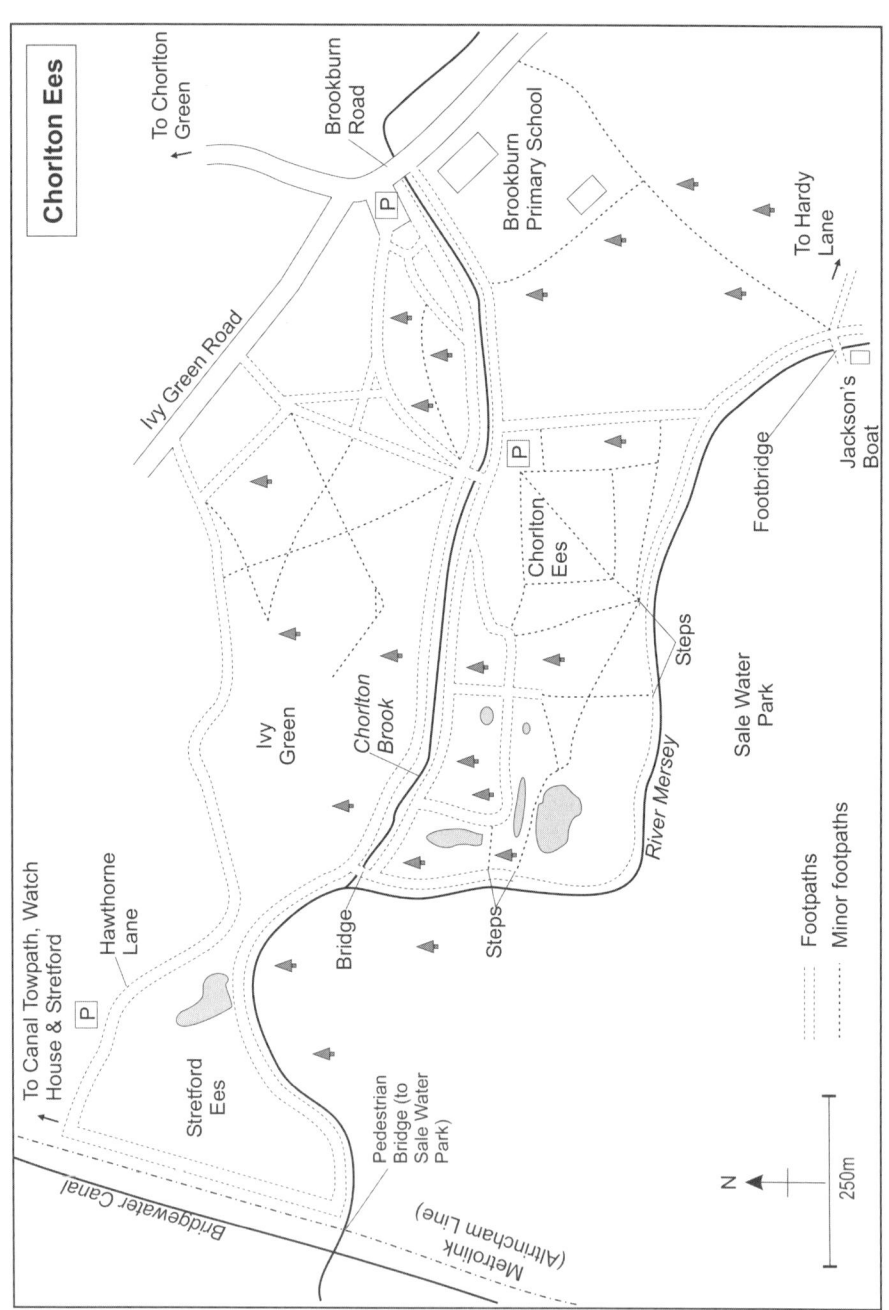

Chorlton Ees

To Chorlton Green

Brookburn Road

Brookburn Primary School

To Hardy Lane

Jackson's Boat

Footbridge

Ivy Green Road

Chorlton Ees

Steps

Sale Water Park

River Mersey

Chorlton Brook

Ivy Green

Steps

Bridge

Hawthorne Lane

To Canal Towpath, Watch House & Stretford

Stretford Ees

Pedestrian Bridge (to Sale Water Park)

Bridgewater Canal

Metrolink (Altrincham Line)

N

250m

Footpaths

Minor footpaths

Sale Water Park

A right turn at the road junction leads to the **Mersey Valley Visitor's Centre**, along an **approach road** that curves to the left. The **Visitor Centre** (opening times vary, **toilets** and **picnic area** available, recommended **café** open Wed-Sun) overlooks a small **marshland area** full of reed mace and reed sweet grass. A network of ditches is important for ten types of spined sticklebacks and a variety of insects (especially dragonfly nymphs). The area is rich in wildflowers, including the regionally rare great yellow-cress, water forget-me-not, and skullcap. There is a **viewing platform** over the marsh that allows you to get closer to this habitat without getting your socks soggy! The **bank of wildflowers** below the Visitor Centre is awash with colour during summer months and bumble bees and hoverflies buzz around feeding on nectar and collecting pollen. It is also a good place to spot butterflies. Local community groups have planted corn-poppy, birds foot trefoil, yellow rattle, toad flax and meadow cranesbill, amongst others to create this beautiful **wildflower meadow**. Leave the **Visitor Centre** by the **steps** down from the picnic area by the café, and turn left along the metalled path in the direction of the Motorway. The way is now down **Cow Lane** to the right. This is a broad metalled roadway, but it is paralleled by a **wooded walk** to the left. The Lane passes through a pleasantly **wooded area**; note the **viewing area** (comprising wooden staging with seats) over the wetland pond and marsh to the right. We see our first view of the lake directly ahead near the point where the parallel track re-joins the Lane. It crosses the **water course** that feeds the **lake** to the left.

Like the lake at Chorlton Water Park, the lake at Sale was a gravel pit, flooded after the extraction of gravel for the M60 in the 1970s. Previously the land belonged to Sale Old

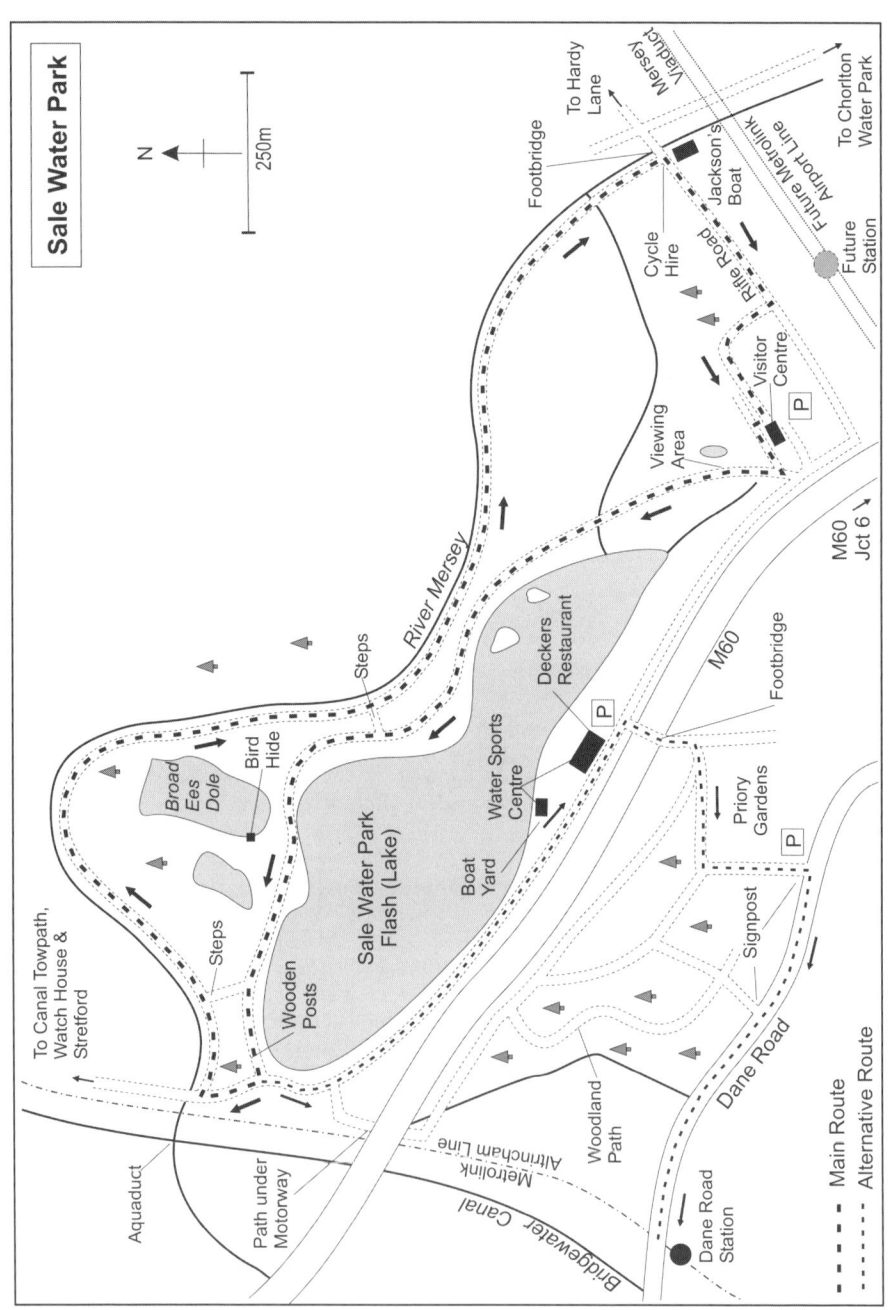

Sale Water Park

N

250m

To Hardy Lane

Mersey Viaduct

Footbridge

Jackson's Boat

Cycle Hire

Rifle Road

Future Metrolink Airport Line

To Chorlton Water Park

Future Station

Visitor Centre

P

Viewing Area

M60 Jct 6

M60

River Mersey

Deckers Restaurant

P

Steps

Water Sports Centre

Boat Yard

Footbridge

Bird Hide

Broad Ees Dole

Priory Gardens

P

Steps

Sale Water Park Flash (Lake)

Signpost

Wooden Posts

To Canal Towpath, Watch House & Stretford

Dane Road

Woodland Path

Aquaduct

Path under Motorway

Metrolink Altrincham Line

Bridgewater Canal

Dane Road Station

- - - Main Route
······· Alternative Route

Hall, which stood close to the site of Junction Six. The Motorway Junction is also the spot where volunteers stood in days gone by to watch for potential invaders during the Napoleonic Wars. As the path passes around the **shore of the lake**, notice that, during summer, it is busy with everything from sail boats to jet skis. Nevertheless, there is a pair of mute swans resident on the lake; they have bred successfully since 2002. We pass **between the lake and the Mersey** (either by the **main path** or along the **lakeshore**, with several opportunities to return to the **main path** through **gaps in the trees**), heading in the direction of **Broad Ees Dole**. Note the **embankment** on the right, part of the flood defence scheme. Cormorants are prominent visitors to Sale Water Park and can often be seen perched on the electricity pylons on the Broad Ees Dole side of the lake. You are well advised to be cautious when walking underneath them, or carry an umbrella; their guano makes a substantial mess!

Broad Ees Dole is an important wildlife refuge in the busy Sale Water Park site. Although there are no footpaths leading through the Dole, the **footpaths around the perimeter** of the site provide excellent viewpoints to watch the **bird life** for which the site is so important. The unusual name of this site explains its past use: Ees is a word to describe a wetland, whilst Dole originally referred to a plot of land allotted to the poor. Until the 1970s, this flood meadow was used as pasture. In times of heavy rain, sluice gates were opened and the area would be submerged in water that came gushing out of the swollen river. During the excavation of the lake at Sale Water Park in the 1970s, the site was used for parking construction vehicles and for washing gravel. The weight of heavy machinery compacted the soil making it prone to waterlogging, whilst the gravel washing created areas of fine silt. As a result, Broad Ees Dole became an area of marshland. In the 1980s, a major project took place to radically redesign Broad Ees Dole, creating a wetland area that could be managed to improve the wildlife value of the site for bird life in particular. Although there is a lake just a short distance away, it is too deep to provide food for many bird species. In contrast, the wetland created at Broad Ees Dole has shallow sloping sides. The water levels can be controlled in order to expose mud banks to the beaks of wading birds, who probe the silt for invertebrates. The path passes **between the lake and Broad Ees Dole**, and there are fine views to the right over the marshy bird sanctuary. A **brick public hide** (always open) is passed on the right, giving a concealed viewing point over a **sheet of water**, and a nearby **information panel** details gives details about the bird life.

Ignore the first path to the right. At the **second junction**, near the end of the lake and beyond the **wooden posts**, a decision must be made. If you wish to return via **Stretford** or double back **to Jackson's Boat**, turn right and proceed to the **fork**. The **right-hand path** follows the **bank of the Mersey**, and we can return by this to **Jackson's Boat bridge** (p313), passing round the other side of **Broad Ees Dole**. The **left-hand path** (unsuitable for buggies and wheelchairs owing to stiles at the far end) crosses the **Mersey** by a **bridge parallel to the Metrolink Altrincham line** (p249), and continues alongside **Stretford Ees** before turning left and passing under **Metrolink** and the **Bridgewater Canal** (this section can be muddy!). Double back after the **metal stile**, and follow the **row of cottages** named **Hawthorne Road** to the **canal bank**, which is accessed by a short flight of **steps**. Turn left along the **towpath** past the historic **Watch House** (see p248) to the **Edge Lane Bridges**. A **path** to the left, before the first bridge, leads to the corner of **Edge Lane** and **Stretford Road** (p247) not far from **Stretford Metrolink Station**.

However, if you wish to **prolong the walk**, carry on the perambulation of the lake by bearing left at the junction, following the path round the **end of the lake**. Here, the pathway again forks, resulting in another choice of route. That to the right (unsuitable for wheelchairs and large baby buggies, owing to steep inclines/steps towards the end) is perhaps the most picturesque. It runs alongside the Metrolink line and under the motorway before curving to the left and running alongside the latter. Look out for the non-metalled path diverging to the right, into the woods. It turns to the left, and then right, passing through fine stands of trees. It finally curves round to the left to reach a kind of crossroads. The way is to the right, straight on to emerge on to Dane Road. (Turn right for the Station, p249.)

Otherwise, back at the fork, take the left hand path, and continue around the edge of the lake. This soon becomes a narrow footpath that skirts to the right to pass behind a fenced boatyard. You can inspect the sailing dinghies and other craft before the path emerges at the car park and Trafford Water Sports Centre. Facing the main building there is (from left to right) Deckers Restaurant, useful public toilets, and (round the right hand corner) the entrance to the Centre itself. The restaurant is usually open daily between 12 and 2.30 and 6 and 9; a three course meal can be obtained for around £25 (2014) and a children's menu is available. The Water Sports Centre offers sailing, windsurfing, canoeing, hire of boats and equipment, and even facilities for model boating. (For information on Water Sports on the lake at Sale Water Park, contact the Trafford Water Sport Centre on 0161 962 0118. The Centre also sells fishing permits for the lake.)

There is a spectacular ramped footbridge adjacent to the Centre that crosses the Motorway. It leads to Priory Gardens. Beech and Yew trees shade the grass beneath their branches in the remains of the formal gardens that belonged to Sale Hall Priory. Paths dip down into old woodland and, beyond the slopes to the opposite side of the Gardens, where the woods open out onto a meadow area. Newly created ponds in these meadows have become important for dragonflies, where emperors, common and brown hawkers and common darters have been spotted. In the 18th century, the property belonged to Dr Thomas White, who practised medicine in Manchester, and then to his son Dr Charles White, who wrote a treatise on forestry and probably planted many of the trees on the site. The latter is associated with the infamous 'Mummy of Birchin Bower' (p127). Indeed, there is a local tradition that Hannah Beswick's mummy rested on the roof of the Priory for many years! Her ghost is said to walk the gardens at night. The estate was sold to Sale Urban District Council for £1,000 in 1920 on the death of the last owner, Mr A H Megson, and the house was demolished in 1932. Take the right-hand broad pathway from the end of the bridge, which curves left to a triangular area where paths fork. Walk along the track to the left of this (not sharp left!), the bridleway that runs alongside a fringe of trees. At the junction with the broad path, make a left turn, and follow the pathway through the wood, negotiate the stile, and proceed past the car park. It emerges on to Dane Road. Turn right, and follow the road to Dane Road Metrolink Station (p249).

St. Werburgh's Road to West Didsbury

The tram continues onwards in shallow cutting, and passes the site of the future junction for the Airport Line (see p299), where the tracks will curve away to the right across Chorlton Brook. Beyond the Mauldeth Road West bridge, inter-war and post-war housing sprawls to the right, followed by allotment gardens. However, the view to the left is mostly taken up by Hough End Fields, a council-owned facility with twenty-four full-size pitches and three rugby pitches. You may catch a glimpse of the skyscraper of Owen's Park student residence and campus in the distance. As we near Princess Road, the tower of St. Bernadette's (p319) may be seen.

The Vanished Airport

The playing fields were the site of Manchester's second airport. Following the closure of Trafford Park in 1918, Alexandra Park Aerodrome was constructed and opened in 1918 for the assembly, test flying, and delivery of aircraft for the RAF. These were built in the Manchester area by A. V. Roe & Company (Avro) at Newton Heath and the National Aircraft Factory No. 2 (NAF No.2) at Heaton Chapel. The airfield took its name from the nearby Alexandra Park (later Wilbraham Road) railway station on the Great Central Railway line. Many aircraft sections arrived by rail at this station, while other aircraft parts came by road. When peace came, the Avro Transport Company operated the UK's first scheduled domestic air service from Alexandra Park via Birkdale Sands (Southport) to South Shore (Blackpool) in 1919, mainly using Avro 504 three-seat biplanes. From 1922 until 1924, the Daimler Airway operated daily scheduled passenger flights to Croydon Airport near London, later followed by a regular extension to Schiphol Airport Amsterdam. However, on the merger of Daimler with other airlines to form Imperial Airways in April 1924, the new airline terminated the service. In any case, the terms of the land lease, laid down by Maurice Egerton, Baron Egerton of Tatton, stipulated that flying from the site would cease within five years of the war's end. The hangars and ancillary buildings were demolished, and the aerodrome closed on 24 August 1924. In any event, the site would have been unable to cope with the increasing size and weight of airliners by the mid-1930s.

Withington Station is situated immediately before the bridge carrying **Princess Road** over the line. It comprises **two platforms**, connected by a **pedestrian crossing** at the west end. The **Didsbury platform** is connected with **Princess Road** by both **steps** and a **lift**; the **Manchester platform** by **steps** and a **ramp**

Princess Road was built in 1924-5, and was a rather fine piece of municipal town planning that also did something to help the unemployment situation. It contained a reservation down the middle, upon which a sleeper track tramway extension was constructed as far as Barlow Moor Road, opening in 1925. It was intended to be part of a new route to Wythenshawe, but the far-sighted tramway manager died, and his policies were abandoned (p286). The route itself was abandoned in 1947. The new road brought semi-detached suburbia to the area. On the other side of the bridge, **St. Bernadette's Roman Catholic Church** (built 1959-63, and typical of the design of that period) is at the top of the bank to the left (but not visible from the platform level). It was built in brick around a rectangular steel 'cruck' system, with the church entered at the upper level from the bridge approach, and a parish hall placed under it; the **campanile tower** is a prominent

What's In a Name?

Technically, we are within the old township of Withington. But most people associate the name with 'Withington Village' or 'Withington Hospital', and we are nowhere near these places. It could, perhaps, be called 'Princess Road'...but that is a very long stretch of highway. However, if you turn to the right at the entrance, and walk past the allotments, Southern Cemetery is reached. Well, not quite...just the cemetery annexe beyond Nell Lane. The main part of the cemetery is further on. Anyway, some people might find 'Southern Cemetery' a trifle depressing (though it isn't "the end of the line!"). So 'Withington' it is. But the station does serve a lot of nearby housing, and is useful as a bus interchange.

feature. (The interior is decorated with a list of 'family virtues'...starting with 'self-control'!)

The line passes between suburban housing in a cutting to arrive at **Burton Road Station**. Again, there are two **platforms**, linked by a **pedestrian crossing** at the Manchester end. **Burton Road** is accessed by **steps** or a **lift** from the **Didsbury platform**, and by **steps** or a **ramp** from the **Manchester platform**.

A **right turn** from the station exit (via the recommended *Metro Café*) obtains the junction with **Cavendish Road** and **Lapwing Lane** (p322). *The Metropolitan*, on the corner of the latter, is a huge mock-Tudor building that used to be the 'Midland', pub (named after the railway). Once famed for bikers and hard rock, it is now rather upmarket, transformed into a café-bar which offers food, Sunday Lunch, and decent wines, and catering for families. There is even a conservatory! The shopping area on **Burton Road** appeared in the Edwardian era, and now is locally famous for its range of independent eateries (which are going upmarket in response to the gentrification of the neighbourhood), interspersed with some rather quirky **niche shops**. Continue along **Burton Road** and turn right into **Nell Lane**, noticing the new **Withington Community Hospital** on the corner. Despite being named as the Withington Community Hospital, due to local border modifications the hospital is now situated in West Didsbury! It replaces the former Withington Hospital (see below) and acts as a primary care base, providing specialist care to those who are awaiting diagnostic treatment, and day surgery appointments. Walk further along **Nell Lane** to reach the **remains of the original hospital** on the right. Originally known as the Chorlton Barlow Moor Work House, the hospital was purpose-built in 1854-55 as a workhouse for the poor of the Chorlton Poor Law Union, which covered most of south Manchester. Three of the former buildings are Grade II listed. The **frontage of 1854-55**, with a **gateway** and **offices**, is showy, and the **chapel** is Italianate in style: behind were the original (surviving) **workhouse building** and the (demolished) seven pavilions of the hospital of 1864-66, with many later buildings all over the site. The whole site is being developed for housing.

A **left turn** from the station exit gives on to the part of the road that stretches northwards, before swinging to the right in the direction of Palatine Road. Notice the *Old House at Home* public house on the right, developed from a row of five cottages.

We now pass **Withington Leisure Centre** to the left (open daily), an institution run by Manchester City Council, with a large pool, sauna, and gym. As Withington Baths, it was built by Manchester Corporation in 1911 (foundation stone), and was designed by the architect of the celebrated Victoria Baths in Manchester. Although smaller than the latter, there are similarities in the design features and decorations. Shortly afterwards, **Old Moat Lane** diverges to the left, a reminder of the moated manor house that once stood to the west of the original Withington Village. Ten thousand houses were built in the area of

The old Workhouse entrance

'The Poor are Always with You'

The problem of 'pauperism' (or rather its growing expense) greatly exercised the political elite in the early 19th century. The result was the 1834 Poor Law Amendment Act, which grouped parishes into 'Unions'. Each Union levied a rate (based on property values) for the purpose of dealing with pauperism; the definition extended to everyone who could not support themselves (including unwanted children, the aged, and the sick). Nowadays, we ascribe poverty to external factors, such as economic depression, structural unemployment, and personal situation (such as lack of education or skills). In contrast, the 19th century utilitarian philosophy suggested that an able-bodied pauper was largely the result of a lack of individual motivation. Consequently, the Act was intended to compel all paupers to enter a workhouse. These institutions enshrined the principle of 'less eligibility'; the workhouse provided the barest minimum to keep someone alive and acted to deter applications for assistance by the poor in other ways (husbands and wives were separated). Of course, it was impossible to provide for all the poor using the workhouse, and 'outdoor relief' (as it was termed) could never be eliminated. But, for those who went there, the workhouse remained a place of dread, especially for old people, until the last vestiges of the system were abolished in the 1930s. The Chorlton Union, like similar progressive unions, began to construct separate institutions for the sick and other categories that it had to deal with, and these were located in Withington. In 1859 the new Withington Workhouse and Infirmary had as inmates 458 adults (including minors of seventeen and upwards) and 195 children. In the 1880s conditions were improved at the instigation of Dr J. Milson Rhodes (p328) one of the board members; the removal of the children to Styal was one of his reforms. In 1864-66, it was converted into a hospital for the poor. Florence Nightingale told Thomas Worthington, the architect, that "... your hospital plan will be one of the best, if not the best, in the country." In the later years all the old buildings were taken over by the hospital and a new smaller workhouse was built on the opposite side of Nell Lane (this closed in 1928). The name was changed to Withington Hospital in 1910. The hospital was used by the military in the First World War, and German prisoners of war were kept there. In 1929, it had beds for 1,300 patients, twelve pavilions, and eleven visiting consultants. The site developed considerably under the National Health Service until the 1990s, when the hospital faced closure. Its fate was sealed when the doors finally shut in 2002.

the former hall and its park between1919 and1928. However, the way lies along the last stretch of Burton Road, which emerges alongside the **former 'White Lion'**. (The Withington Walk can be joined here, see p323).

We now resume our journey. The tram passes under **Burton Road** and runs along a shallow cutting, passing the **site of Withington and Albert Park Station**. It was the second station on the Midland line from Central Station (p299) and opened on 1 January, 1880. It was intended to serve the new housing developments (the area was promoted as 'Albert Park') and, upon opening, was served by fourteen trains in each direction between Central Station and Stockport (Tiviot Dale). Passengers could also access St. Pancras expresses by changing trains at Stockport and (by 1902) Cheadle Heath. Two canopied platforms were connected by an iron footbridge (with a roof!). The main station building, built in the 'gothic' style was situated on the Manchester platform, and accessed by an approach from Lapwing Lane (p322). The station closed on 3 July, 1961, and nothing now remains.

The line now passes, by means of a **short tunnel,** under the crossroads that mark the intersection of **Lapwing Lane** and **Palatine Road,** and the tram enters **West Didsbury Station.** The station follows the usual pattern, with **platforms** connected by a **pedestrian crossing** at the Didsbury end. The **Manchester platform** accesses **Palatine Road** by **steps** or an **extended ramp,** while the **Didsbury platform** accesses **Lapwing Lane** by **steps** or a **lift.**

Withington

In the middle of the 19th century the area was occupied by fields and farmsteads in the townships of Didsbury and Withington. Wilmslow Road was then a turnpike crossing the Ball Brook on its way to Didsbury. Lapwing Hall was located on the south side of Lapwing Lane. Then the mercantile class began to migrate to the area. Palatine Road was authorised by Act of Parliament in 1861, opening in 1862 (briefly) as a toll road. It was so named because it linked Lancashire and Cheshire, both of which were county palatines, a medieval title signifying that the counties were virtually autonomous. Large mansion houses with extensive grounds were built along it. Where the rich migrated, the middle class was sure to follow, particularly after the opening by the Midland Railway of the Manchester South District line on 1st January 1880. Withington and Didsbury became incorporated into the City of Manchester in 1904, together with three other townships in South Manchester. Today, the residents of Withington comprise a mixture of families, university students and "young professionals"....often themselves former students. This is in a large part due to its education links; particularly the proximity to Manchester University, which has the largest student population in the United Kingdom. As a consequence, Withington is predominantly an area of mixed affluence. It is also a medical centre, with the Christie Hospital, one of the largest cancer treatment centres in Europe, and Withington Community Hospital.

Outside the station is the **junction of Palatine Road and Lapwing Lane.** From 1897 to 1902, the frontages to Wilmslow Road and Lapwing Lane were developed with mostly three-storey Victorian villas, the majority of which can still be seen today. The western pat of the latter runs towards Burton Road, and it is worth a brief detour (by crossing Palatine Road) along this part of the Lane to admire the **former Withington Town Hall** on the left. Following the Public Health Act, 1875, Withington Town Hall was built in 1881 on Lapwing Lane, originally to house Withington Local Board of Health, and later occupied by the Withington Urban District Council. It is an imposing structure of buff brick with dressings of red brick and red terracotta A **gable** over the central section contains a **terracotta roundel** with a shield and console supporters, under a semi-circular band with raised lettering 'Local Board Offices'. Notice the carved **Mosley family** (p33) **crest**; they were the Lords of the Manor. Behind this is a short **pyramidal turret** supporting a **square clock** with swept copper-clad fleche roof finished with a weathervane. It has now been converted into private apartments. A little further along, on the right hand side, may be found traces of the **cobbled approach** to the long-vanished Withington Station (p321).

Retrace your steps, noticing the Edwardian **terrace of shops** with a cast-iron and glass canopy on the continuation of Lapwing Lane across the junction. Turn left along **Palatine Road.** The former mansion of **Holly Royde,** on the left, was given by its owner to Manchester University for use as an external residential centre, but is now converted into flats. **St Cuthbert's Roman Catholic Church** on the corner of **Palatine Road** and

Marriott Street, to the right, was established in 1874 and the nave opened in 1881. Originally dedicated to "The Holy Ghost and St. Cuthbert", the church was extended in 1902. It is constructed of red brick and terra cotta, with much moulded decoration around the **rose windows** on the gables.

The building alongside (1891) was a catholic school until a new school was built on Cotton Lane.Turn right down **Marriott Street** to arrive at **Wilmslow Road**. The **Red Lion Inn,** the earliest surviving building in the area, is situated on the corner, facing Wilmslow Road. The Inn dates from the 17th century (it was once the meeting place of the Manorial Court Leet), but what survives is incorporated in many later additions. The horizontal sliding-sash windows are of particular interest. A short walk beyond this pub in the Didsbury direction leads to the **Christie Hospital** on the right. This institution originated as an indirect recipient of the will of Joseph Whitworth, the famous Manchester inventor and industrialist.

The Red Lion

Richard Christie, one of the legatees, financed a Cancer Pavilion and Home for Incurables on Oxford Road in 1892 It was renamed the Christie Hospital in honour of himself and his wife Mary in 1901 An initial contribution of £2000 from local brewer Edward Holt resulted in city-wide fund to establish a 'Radium Institute', and both the Institute and hospital moved to the Withington site in 1934 (merging in 1946). The Christie registers around 12,500 new patients and treats about 40,000 patients every year, and is the lead cancer centre for the Greater Manchester and Cheshire Cancer Network (covering a population of 3.2 million) and runs clinics at 16 other general hospitals. Around 15% of patients are referred from outside Greater Manchester and Cheshire, and there is also a private patients unit. The Christie is now the largest cancer treatment centre of its kind in Europe, and an international leader in research and development. As of 2010, it is also home to the largest clinical trials unit of its kind in Europe.

Continue in the opposite direction, crossing the road. Next to the **fire station**, on the right, notice **Withington Old Forge**. Built of brick in 1881, it is a symmetrical building with a large **central coach-and-horse entrance** (it was also a carriage works), and accommodation on either side. The floor above would have been the blacksmith's residence. The **Parish Church of St Paul** (Hayley & Brown) is set back beyond a **churchyard**. The brick church was built in 1841, and extended in 1864, in a simplified Norman style with a tall, square tower with large pinnacles forming small spires. Wilbraham Egerton, the lord of the manor of Withington, gave the land and £400, or possibly £800, towards the cost of the construction. We now arrive at a **major road junction** of **Wilmslow Road**, **Palatine Road**, and **Burton Road**, commanded by the impressive **former White Lion Public House**. It is a most striking building, on account of its **clock tower**, and thus forms a focus at the southern end of the 'village'. The structure was built in 1881, in a mixed Gothic-style, of brick with stone dressings. The forecourt is separated from the highway by railings supported on stone piers. The original railings have been replaced by plain steel horizontal poles, but the piers remain. The ground floor is now a *Sainsbury's* supermarket. Next door is the **site of the much-missed Scala Cinema** (1912-2008), the first purpose built cinema in Manchester (the third cinema to open in Britain). Later renamed Cine City, the cinema eventually closed despite heroic attempts to save it. Independent to the last, it once sported a large poster proclaiming "Emily, Starring Koo Stark (Prince Andrew's Latest)!" The area beyond is usually referred to as **'Withington Village'**,

The former White Lion

though little, if anything, of the original settlement remains (but notice the narrowing roadway and the odd building lines). The area to the east of Wilmslow Road here was developed between 1910 and 1914. At the northern end of the village, the *National Westminster Bank* is a stone building with much decoration, including a finely carved frieze and balustrade parapet wall at roof level. It was originally built as the Manchester and County Bank Ltd in 1890, as **inscribed in the stone carving** over the entrance. Adjoining the bank is the **Methodist Church**, a stone building in Gothic style. At the northern extremity of the area is the **Withington Public Library**, opened in 1927, and admirably constructed of stone to suit its corner site.

West Didsbury to East Didsbury

The line continues in **cutting**, spanned by **Elm Road** and **Parkfield Road South**. The bridge carrying **Wilmslow Road** over the line has been extended into a **short tunnel** on the opposite side by means of the construction of a concrete platform (a far sighted way of preserving the track-bed some years before Metrolink arrived). The greater part of the new tunnel is supported by a central concrete wall, creating a portal for each track. It supports *Slug and Lettice* pub (if you happen to like that kind of thing!) and a car park behind a retail and housing development fronting Wilmslow Road. The tunnel, and the area immediately beyond it, was the **site of Didsbury Station**, which opened in 1880 and closed in 1967. As at Withington, a covered footbridge connected the two canopied platforms, and the main station building was situated on the Manchester platform, this time accessed from Wilmslow Road. Unusual features included lengthened platforms and stabling facilities incorporated into the main building, anticipating a high volume of commuter traffic and local deliveries. A goods yard was located to the south east of the station; the passenger services provided were the same as at Withington.

The train now runs through the **canyon like cutting**, with retaining wall either side, before passing under **School Lane** and entering **Didsbury Village Station**.

The modern Metrolink Station consists of two **platforms**, connected by a **pedestrian crossing** at the East Didsbury end. An inclined **footpath** runs from the **East Didsbury platform** to **School Lane**, while the **Manchester platform** accesses **Olive Shapley Avenue**, which is on the same level as the station. This street leads via **William Street** to connect with **School Lane**.

(A detailed descriptive walk around Didsbury Village, commencing at School Lane, will be found on p327.)

The line is paralleled by **Olive Shapley Avenue** on the right, and is crossed by a footbridge, an extension of **Sandhurst Road**.

The **cycle way** crosses to the left here, and follows the line to the terminus. Notice that part of it is raised on a kind of kerb.

The tram passes under **Parrs Wood Road**, with **playing fields** beyond on the left. The line is then crossed by what is known as the **Styal Loop**, opened by the London and North Western Railway in 1910. It left the main line at Slade Lane Junction and re-joined it at Wilmslow, and was intended for suburban or commuter traffic, a function that it still performs, though, as then, main line services are sometimes diverted this way.

The Great Air Race

The loop line had its moment of glory in 1910. On 28 April, the French pilot Louis Paulhan landed his Farman biplane in Barcicroft Fields, Pytha Fold Farm, on the borders of Withington, Burnage and Didsbury. This completed the first ever powered flight from London to Manchester, with a short over-night stop at Lichfield, (195 miles/298 km), and he won a £10,000 prize offered by the Daily Mail, beating the British contender, Claude Grahame-White. Two special trains were chartered to Burnage Station, a short distance to the north of this point, to take spectators to the landing, with other spectators waiting through the previous night. Paulhan was followed throughout by a train carrying his wife, Henri Farman, and his supporting mechanics. Today, a blue plaque recording Paulhan's achievement is displayed on a house in Paulhan Road, which forms part of the site where he landed.

'Let the People Sing'!

Olive Mary Shapley (1910-1999), though born into a lower-middle-class family, saw for herself the squalor and poverty of the homeless poor and the plight of people sleeping under railway arches. Her concern for the underprivileged, her belief in the potential of the ordinary person, and her abhorrence of injustice and inequality were to be a driving force for the rest of her life. She went up to Oxford in 1929 and began a rocky but creative association with the BBC in 1934 as Children's Hour organiser, becoming a postwar presenter of Woman's Hour. The association with the latter was to last for twenty years, during which time she helped shape its reputation for tackling sensitive issues and pushing boundaries. She was one of the first radio broadcasters and producers to take the microphone (sometimes accompanied by the seven-ton recording van) to people in the streets, in their homes, and at work: a startling departure from the studio-based broadcasting which was the norm. When Shapley first broadcast Yorkshire and Lancashire accents and took the unmistakable sound of the Scouser and the burr of the Bolton mill worker into the nation's parlours and front rooms, the reaction was mixed. The debate she helped start still continues. Living in a huge rambling mansion called Rose Hill with its own orchard and stables in the leafy and cosmopolitan Manchester suburb of Didsbury, she formed the Rose Hill Trust for Unsupported Mothers and Babies (she refused to use the expression "unmarried mothers"), providing mothers and babies with accommodation, food and clothing. Olive Shapley never lost her interest in broadcasting and one of the last posts she held was membership of BBC Radio Manchester (GMR)'s Radio Council. While in her seventies she was a frequent broadcaster with the station.

After a **pedestrain crossing, Kingsway** (see below) now crosses the line, and the cycle path passes through an original **subway** to the left.

The tram now arrives at **East Didsbury Station**, the present terminus. The arrangement of the station is unusual. Trams terminate either side of a central **island platform**, accessing either platform face or reversing by means of a **crossover** the other side of **Kingsway**. A **platform ramp** at the **terminus end** accesses a kind of **crossroads**. The (un-metalled) **footpath** directly ahead carries the **Trans-Pennine Cycle Way** (which parallels the north side of the station) along part of the remainder of the **old railway trackbed**, through a former **arched bridge**. (One day, the line may continue on this route to Stockport!) The **path** on the right, leads to the **large station car park**. That to the left swings across the **bicycle way**, with which it communicates before leading, by a choice of **ramp** or **stair** to **Burnage Lane**. The **platform ramp** at the **Manchester end** accesses **pedestrian crossings** of both lines. That to the right communicates with the **cycle way**, and a left turn along it, under the **road** by the **pedestrian subway** , leads to **steps** accessing the supermarket side of **Kingsway**. The **pedestrian crossing** a little further on, leads to a path alongside the supermarket, emerging on to the **supermarket car park** and **main entrance**. However, by keeping the car park on the left, the footpath emerges opposite the entrances to **East Didsbury Railway Station** (see p327). (Please note that this route should only be used in office hours, and ought not to be attempted at night.) The left-hand **crossing** leads to the **main station access point**, affording a choice of route. **Steps** or a **lift** access the level of **Kingsway**, but the **pathway** to the left runs along a slight incline to reach **Parrs Wood Lane**, opposite the *Bell Tower* restaurant and the **hotel** (p327).

Leave the station by the main entrance. **Kingsway,** one of the earliest purpose-built roads especially for motor vehicles, was constructed as a dual carriageway in stages, from 1926 to 1930. (This period just predated effects of the Wall Street Crash on Britain, sending unemployment to record levels, so the construction project would prove a godsend to many.) However, the actual purpose was to provide relief for the congested Wilmslow Road to the west; it was named after King George V and was originally numbered A5079. Like Princess Road, a new tramway extension with sleeper track ran down the middle, predating the road surface by opening in stages during 1926. Sadly, the line closed in 1947. In 1959, Kingsway was extended south across the river Mersey to bypass Cheadle and later renumbered to A34 in 1967. As with Princess Road, Kingsway proved to be the catalyst for suburban development in the area. Turn left, and

The former bus garage Clock Tower

walk down **Kingsway** to the junction with **Parrs Wood Lane,** noticing the *Tesco* supermarket complex to the right. Cross the Lane to arrive at *Bell House.* The **restaurant and bar** is aimed at a family audience, with entertainment and activities for children. The *Travel Lodge* hotel is part of the *Bell House* complex. The name refers, no doubt, to the **clock tower** across the road. This is all that is left of the former Parrs Wood Bus Depot, opened in 1926 with accommodation for fifty motor buses, and extended in 1932. The supermarket stands on the site, and *Tesco* preserved the clock tower, which had become a local landmark. The **pyramid motif** on its top is repeated on the store. We continue down Kingsway to reach the *Parrs Wood Entertainment Centre.* Following a deal with the council to build a new school in exchange for land, the complex was completed in 2001. The centre is owned by X-Leisure, a company that has created a number of similar sites across the U.K, including the *Xscape* brand. Attractions and businesses in the Entertainment Centre include **Tenpin Bowling**, a **Lazer Game Experience**, an **American pool and arcade area**, a *Cineworld Multiplex Cinema*, and the **Grosvenor Casino**! **Catering outlets** include *Burger King, Frankie & Benny's American Italian restaurant, Nando's, Chiquito,* and *Pizza Hut.* The site also includes a *Virgin Active Health Club.*

East Didsbury may one day develop into a travel interchange; at the time of writing, **East Didsbury Railway station** (frequent trains to Piccadilly Station and Manchester Airport) is reached by following the road to the left side of the **parkland area** opposite the entertainment complex...in all, about ten minutes' walk from the Metrolink Station. (Airport trains are accessed by the slope just before the bridge; for Manchester trains, walk under the bridge and turn left.) In office hours, try the short cut on p326.

Didsbury Village

Didsbury derives its name from the Anglo-Saxon *Dyddi's burg*, probably referring to a man known as Dyddi whose stronghold or township it was, situated on a low cliff overlooking a place where the river Mersey could be forded. The earliest reference to Didsbury is in a document dating from 1235, recording a grant of land for the building of a chapel. Didsbury was one of the few places between Stretford and Stockport where the River Mersey could be forded, which made it significant for troop movements during the English Civil War. Prince Rupert stationed himself at Didsbury Ees, to the south of Barlow Moor, en route to Lathom and the attempted relief of York, and it is also likely that Charles Edward Stuart crossed the Mersey at Didsbury in 1745, in the Jacobite march south from Manchester to Derby, and again in the subsequent retreat. During the Victorian expansion of Manchester, Didsbury developed as a prosperous merhant's suburb; a few mansions from the period still exist on Wilmslow Road between Didsbury Village and Parrs Wood to the east and Withington to the north, but they have now been converted to nursing homes and offices. The opening of the Midland Railway line in 1880 contributed greatly to the rapid growth in the population of Didsbury, with stations at Didsbury and Withington offering easy rail connections to Manchester. Nowadays, Didsbury has been colonised by professional people, many connected with the local universities, and there is a growing student population. Didsbury Village, the central shopping area along Wilmslow Road, has developed a European-like café-culture over recent years, with the opening of many new bars, cafés and delicatessens. The original site of Didsbury Village is in the conservation area now known as Didsbury St James, about half a mile (1 km) to the south of what is today's village centre.

There is a **path** from the new **East Didsbury platform** to **School Lane**. From the Manchester platform, follow **Olive Shapley Avenue** and **William Street** to School Lane.

Look out for **Ogden Street** (by the *Milson Rhodes* pub). It runs alongside the Metrolink line before turning into **Warburton Street**, on the left, a delightful cobbled by-way, with pretty cottages and *Morton's Bookshop*. This is an old fashioned establishment, a bookshop for exploring and rummaging, with very helpful staff. Turn right into **Wilmslow Road**, and walk towards the **clock tower**. It stands in front of what was the **site of the original Didsbury Station**. It opened in 1880, and closed in 1967, and nothing now remains. The **clock tower** and adjacent **fountain** are memorials to Doctor J Milson Rhodes (1847-1909), who both professionally, and as a social

Milson Rhodes clock tower

worker, did much for the poor, particularly the young people assigned to the Nell Lane Workhouse (p321) and those suffering from TB. He was responsible for the founding of a colony for epileptics at Langho, near Whalley in Lancashire, to which the epileptics from the Workhouse were transferred. At his suggestion children were removed from the workhouse to cottage homes at Styal. The clock is inscribed with the words: 'A Friend to Humanity'. These distinctive landmarks mark the start of Didsbury's **café and shopping area**. Almost opposite, **Didsbury Library** is set back from the road, a Carnegie Trust endowment of 1915, and resplendent in a vaguely Jacobean style, brick edged with stone. There are **two blue plaques** on the side wall of the Library. One commemorates Prince Rupert of the Rhine, who was the nephew of King Charles I. Prince Rupert was a soldier who was appointed commander of the Royalist cavalry during the English Civil War and he stationed himself in the building which formerly stood on the site of the library. He surrendered after the Battle of Naseby and was banished from England. The other plaque commemorates Sir William Brereton (1604-1661). Brereton was the MP for Cheshire and was also a soldier, politician and writer who was stationed at Didsbury for a time when on campaign in the English Civil war. He was appointed Commander in Chief of Parliament's forces in Cheshire, Shropshire, Lancashire and Staffordshire. Brereton developed a network of spies and conducted a relentless military campaign against the Royalists in the region. The adjacent **War Memorial** is worth inspection. Retrace your steps back down **Wilmslow Road**, but continue beyond the junction with **School Lane** and **Barlow Moor Road**. The entrance to the pretty **Didsbury Park**, on the left, is marked by a fine **tree sculpture** of 'The Owl and Her Children'. **Ford Lane**, almost opposite leads to the **Mersey** and a

The 'Gates of Hell'

pleasant riverside walk to **Northendem** (with an old village centre and an interesting church).

We pass the **Didsbury Campus of Manchester Metropolitan University.** Notice the fine **classical façade** originally belonging to a house from c.1790, altered with extensive additions during its tenancy by a Wesleyan Theological College about 1842 It is now part of the Met's School of Education.

The **main road** swings sharply to the left, but turn right, where the cobbles denote the entrance to **Stenner Lane.** Until last century this area used to be the centre of village life, with the **village green** (now reincarnated as a beer garden) outside what is now *The Didsbury* pub, (formally The Ring O' Bells). The adjacent pub, *The Olde Cock*, was the coaching inn and originally called simply The Cock, probably because cock fighting used to take place in the upper rooms.   Incorporated into this pub was formerly a Post Office/Store, and nearby was the village well. One of the most iconic images of Didsbury is the **main gateway to the parsonage gardens**, to the right. The great **stone eagle** was formally part of the Spread Eagle Hotel, on Corporation Street, Manchester, where Fletcher Moss (see below) had once been proprietor. The magnificent eagle and gate was bought by Mr. Moss as a souvenir for ten pounds when the Hotel was demolished in 1902. (The Didsbury Civic Society logo carries a representation of the 'Eagle Gate'.) Though the **Old Parsonage** was in the midst of what was then the busy village centre, it must have been the secluded haven of peace and tranquility that it still is today. This small, but atmospheric garden, allows you to step back to a quieter, gentler time when the olde-worlde garden was tended for so many years by Alderman Fletcher Moss and his family.

The Passionate Pilgrim

It is impossible to write about the Old Parsonage and its Gardens without remembering Alderman Fletcher Moss. He was born into a local family in July 1843, and spent most of his life as both a country landowner and proprietor of the Spread Eagle Hotel in Manchester. He originally moved into the Old Parsonage House in the early 1860s and stayed for 50 years until his death in 1919. He never married. One suspects that he was the main domestic support, not only to ageing parents, but numerous relatives, and, as he grew older, he developed a variety of preoccupations and leisure pursuits into which his spare energies were directed. Upon retirement, the transformation was complete as he became a gentleman of independent means. His passions, so to speak, were two-fold. Firstly, he engaged in public work and philanthropy, serving on Withington Local Board (which later became a Council) and Manchester City Council. He was an independent, always standing in the ratepayer's interest. Although he hardly ever spoke in debates, he became very influential behind the scenes. He interested himself in municipal libraries, museums, parks and allotments, and issues relating to leisure. He was a valued Councillor, and became an Alderman of Manchester (a kind of unelected ex-officio Council Member). His public life extended into philanthropy, and he was instrumental in persuading Andrew Carnegie to provide the money to build Didsbury's wonderful library in 1915. He had a great love for Didsbury, especially the Old Parsonage, and it was he who gave us the beautiful Gardens named after him. In 1915, in his own words, he had "determined to offer all that part of my property extending from the Fletcher Moss Playing Fields to Stenner Lane to the corporation if I could retain the use of it for my life". His other, more private, passions extended to embrace natural history, gardening, folklore, and antiquarianism. Over the years, the Old Parsonage was the rendezvous of the members of various Manchester societies visiting Didsbury at the invitation of simple Mr. Moss (for he did not stand on ceremony, and had a natural empathy with whoever he met, whatever their background). On these occasions he dispensed his hospitality to the company assembled on the lawn, if the weather permitted, or in his dining room as circumstances required. In later life, he took to a bicycle, and he and a friend (who took the photographs) journeyed mainly in Lancashire, Cheshire, and the Welsh Border, in search of 'ancient homes' and other objects of antiquarian interest. After summarizing these wanderings in pieces in Manchester City News (he was already a prolific freelance writer) he published a series of books entitled 'Pilgrimages to Old Homes'. They not only describe the historical places, but also adventures associated with each 'pilgrimage' and people who were encountered along the way, all in a very witty and very idiosyncratic style.

The Old Parsonage, Didsbury

The **Old Parsonage** is largely as its most famous resident left it. The exact date of the building is not known, but references were made to it in 1650 as a "tenement assigned to the use of the minister". It has been added to and improved over the years but, with the exception of the church, it is still thought to be the oldest building in Didsbury. In the early 1860s, the Rev W J Kidd hastily left the property complaining of 'ghosts and troubles', and as no-one else seemed to want to live there, Fletcher Moss took a lease on the otherwise desirable property. After 20 years, in 1884, he eventually bought the house and gardens (which included the Cock Inn and the Post Office adjoining it) for approximately £3000. He is quoted as saying "considering all things it was probably the best purchase I ever made; its influence on my life and work has been great, and indirectly on the history of the village." In 1902, he installed wrought iron gates at the entrance to the parsonage's garden, which, because of the building's reputation, became known locally as "the gates to Hell". (Others say that the flanking public houses constitute the real explanation!) Since Mr Moss's death the building has been used for many things including an art gallery which was devoted entirely to depictions of scenes and events concerning Manchester. It is now in the care of the Civic Society, and they are in the process of developing it as a community centre, and organise exhibitions and open days. (The building is usually open daily, 9.30-5.30; admission free, but donations appreciated.) However, if it is closed, one may still enjoy the extensive **gardens**. The **front of the house** is dominated by several **magnificent old trees**, and the **tall palms**, especially, give the house a 'colonial' feel. Walk along the **main path** past the **entrance to the house**. Directly ahead is the entrance to an **adjacent garden**, comprising a **tree lawn**, with a great variety of **interesting small trees** including a very rare, yet unremarkable, surviving **specimen of an early bio-engineered tree**. The lawn is surrounded by **herbaceous borders**, and there are many benches to encourage the visitor to sit a while and enjoy the surroundings and the view towards the church and beyond. There are the **greenhouses** where orchids were grown, and one is now an **alpine house**. Now retrace your steps back into the main garden and turn right towards the **secondary entrance** (sometimes locked). Here may be found a **milestone** which was originally situated at the Parrs Wood turnpike toll bar (approximately where the junction of Wilmslow Road and Kingsway is now), together with the **foundation stone** of the (demolished) Didsbury Mill. Return to the main path by way of the central clump of trees, which shelter the **graves of several of Mr. Moss's dogs**. Even a favourite horse is reputed to be buried there!

St. James's Church, Didsbury

Almost opposite the **Eagle Gate** may be found the **lych-gate** of the **church**. The **Parish Church of St. James** stands on high ground, to the south-west of the village, the land sloping down on the west side of the site towards the River Mersey. The view from the churchyard on that side, towards Cheshire, is very extensive. It is uncertain when the first chapel was built in Didsbury, but it is thought to have been before the middle of the 13th century. (When the plague reached the village in 1352 the chapel yard was consecrated to provide a cemetery for the victims, it being "inconvenient to carry the dead all the way to Manchester".) Of the original building which stood on the site nothing is known, as the ancient chapel is said to have been entirely rebuilt of stone in 1620. In 1770 the chancel was declared to be "very old, ruinous, and decayed," and was taken down and rebuilt on a large scale. In 1855 the building underwent a thorough restoration, in the course of which the outside walls (with the exception of the tower) were cased in new stone, new traceried windows inserted, and the roof raised over the aisles. By these alterations the building lost any traces that remained of its original appearance, and assumed more or less its present aspect. A new chancel was added in 1871. The **external walls** are built of red sandstone and have **plain parapets**, the **buttresses** marking the ends of the old nave and the old chancel, the new chancel being marked by **pinnacles**. The **chancel roof** is slightly lower than that of the nave, and is separated from it externally by a **stone gable surmounted by a cross**. The **nave roof** is continued at a slightly lower pitch over the aisles, and all the roofs are slated. A portion of the exterior walling on the **south side** between the **vestry** and the **extension** shows an **old rubble facing**, having apparently been left untouched in the restoration of 1855.

The **tower** is of three stages with a vice (staircase) in the south-west angle, with diagonal **buttresses** of unequal projection on the west side. The two **entrances** on west and north sides are modern, and above the west door is a modern pointed **window** of four lights, lighting the **ringers' chamber**, the floor of which is on a level with the springing of the tower arch. Externally a string-course runs round the tower at about mid-height above the west window, and the **belfry stage** has a two-light pointed window with stone louvres on each face, above which is a string-course. The **original embattled parapet** is now on the old south vestry, the tower finishing with a nondescript **parapet** of four **semicircular arches** on each side, with angle and intermediate **pinnacles**, erected in 1801. There is a **clock dial** in front of the parapet on the east side facing the village. On the **north side of the tower are three inscribed stones** in a line. The **initials** are those of Sir Edward Mosley, knight, and Ann Mosley (Sutton), second wife of his elder and deceased brother Rowland of Hough End Hall, who are named as the founders. 'E. M. Esq. Patron' is Edward Mosley, son of Rowland Mosley of Hough End, and afterwards first baronet, and 'Sir G. B. K. Baronet' is supposed to be Sir George Booth, of Dunham Massey (knighted 1595, baronet 1611), but this is uncertain. The **inscription** on the third stone is partly obliterated ... 'DOMNI 16/20,' alone being visible. The tower is said generally to have been built in 1620, but more probably an older tower was refaced in stone, as there appear to be traces of older work inside. There are **six bells** all cast by Abraham Rudhall of Gloucester 1727. (The church is usually closed; to arrange a visit, ring 0161 446 4150.)

The **chancel** has a **five-light window** at the east end and **two windows** of two lights on the north. The south side has **two pointed arches** opening respectively to the **organ chamber** and **vestry**. The **nave** consists of **six bays**, the **two easternmost** of which **formed the 18th century chancel**. These have **four centred arches** on octagonal piers and responds, which appear to be of later date than 1770. The **old nave arcade** consists of **four semicircular arches** resting on circular columns. They have the appearance of 18th century work, but may possibly belong to the previous century, and may be part of the rebuilding of that date. A portion of the **old wall** behind the old nave arcade still stands, and the **former chancel arch** divides the nave into two unequal parts. The **windows** to both north and south aisles are all modern, and are placed without regard to the position of the piers. They are mostly of three lights, with a single light window at the west end of each aisle. The **south-west vestry** is built in front of the south doorway, and appears to be modern, never having been intended as a porch.

The fittings are all modern. The present **font**, near the Mosley Monument, dates from 1881, but the whereabouts of the original (in which St. Ambrose Barlow was baptised, (see p310) are unknown. The **lectern** was presented in 1905, by a Mr. Gledhill, and represents the Angel of the Book of Revelation, rather than the traditional eagle. Another donor, Mr. William Heald, presented a Chancel Screen, but the Rector rather foolishly cut a hole in it so that he could more easily reach the lectern from his seat! The donor, quite naturally, was outraged, and after mediation by the Bishop, removed the screen to a church in Ormskirk, where he had retired. It has been replaced by a charming **low wall** of marble, topped with onyx. The **pulpit** is made of the same materials, though the **sounding board** is English oak. The stained glass in the **East Window** (1856) was partly donated by John Moss, the father of Fletcher.

Between the windows of the south wall of the extension of the south aisle (sometimes called the **Mosley Chapel**) is a **fine marble and alabaster monument** to **Sir Nicholas Mosley, knight**, 1612, sometime Lord Mayor of London, with three lower compartments containing the kneeling figures of his two wives and three sons. Above is a figure of Sir Nicholas in mayoral robes. Over the figure are his arms, and below on either side over the figures of his wives are two shields in oval frames. The first has the arms of the Mosley family impaling those of Elizabeth Rookes (his second wife, who survived him), widow of (?) Hendley. The second has the Mosley arms impaling those of Margaret Whitbroke, his first wife. There are four male figures in the lower central compartment,

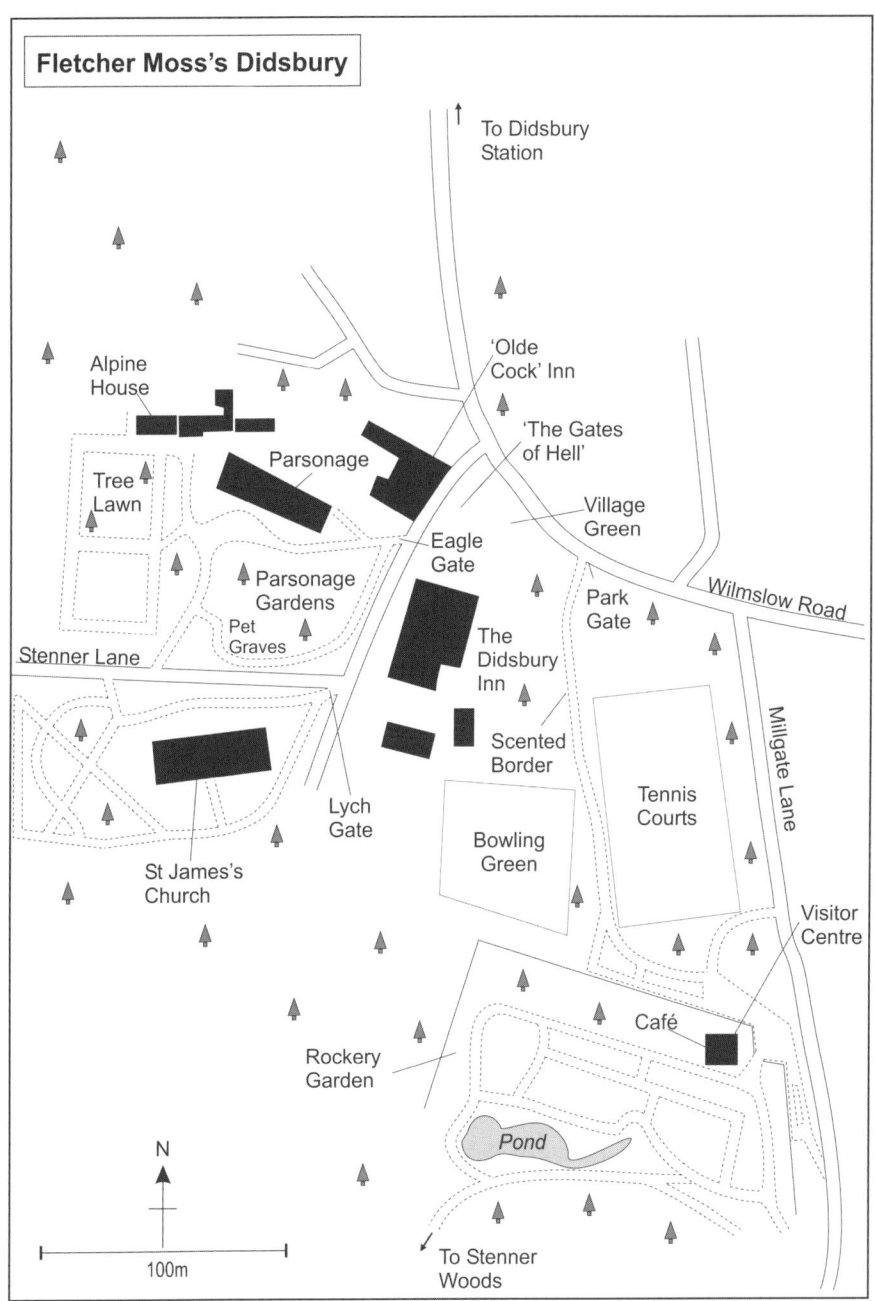

Fletcher Moss's Didsbury

To Didsbury Station

'Olde Cock' Inn

Alpine House

'The Gates of Hell'

Parsonage

Village Green

Tree Lawn

Eagle Gate

Wilmslow Road

Parsonage Gardens

Park Gate

Pet Graves

Stenner Lane

The Didsbury Inn

Scented Border

Millgate Lane

Lych Gate

Tennis Courts

Bowling Green

St James's Church

Visitor Centre

Rockery Garden

Café

N

Pond

100m

To Stenner Woods

being probably those of Rowland Mosley (died 1616), son and heir of Sir Nicholas, with his eldest son; Anthony Mosley; and Sir Edward Mosley, the two latter still living when the monument was erected (see p33). At the east end of the north aisle is a **mural tablet** with good plaster ornament to **Ann, Dowager Lady Bland** (died 1734), erected by her son "in memory of one of the best of women" with a lozenge over bearing the arms of Bland, impaling the quartered arms of Mosley, as on Sir Nicholas Mosley's monument (the Mosley coat is repeated an escutcheon). Lady Anne inherited the Manor of Manchester, and was responsible for St. Ann's Church in the the city, a fact curiously omitted in the inscription. (A posy of flowers is placed on the monument each 17 July, the date of her death, by the congregation of St Ann's.) There is also a mural monument on the west wall of the Mosley Chapel to Sir John Bland (died 1715).

Walk back to Wilmslow Road, and go past *The Didsbury* to the entrance to **Fletcher Moss Park**. **Fletcher Moss Park** is part botanic gardens and part wildlife habitat. Spanning to the River Mersey in one direction and **Stenner Woods** in another, there is potential for long walks through pleasant surroundings as well as the more obvious educational aspect of the botanic garden. The **path** from the gate is **signposted** for the 'café' and 'rockery', and passes the **tennis courts** on the left to arrive at the **entrance to the rockery** to the right. Part of the garden consists of a **rockery** created by Robert Wood Williamson, which was sold to Alderman Fletcher Moss, together with his house called The Croft, in 1912. The **rock and heather gardens,** complete with **water features,** tumble down a picturesque slope that is negotiated by both steps and a winding path.

'The Towers', the finest mercantile mansion in the Manchester area

This garden feature, now so common, was perhaps one of the first in the country. The former **house** is situated just beyond the rockery garden entrance. The Croft lays claim to a niche in history as the birthplace of the Royal Society for the Protection of Birds. In 1889 Emily Williamson (Robert's wife) formed a group called the Plumage League, with the aim of stopping the wholesale slaughter of birds in the cause of making women's hats. This grew in support and eventually joined forces with Mrs. Phillips' 'Fur and Feather League' in Croydon, to become the RSPB. Today, in recognition of this, this organisation holds events in the park with the intention of educating people about birds and eliciting more support for their valuable conservation work. At this level, it now contains a good **café** (with outside tables for fine weather). However, a **curving path** that runs behind and around the house descends to the **lower level of the gardens**. Here, in the lower part of the house, is located a **visitor centre**, adjacent to the lower entrance to the rockery. From here, paths also lead to **Stenner Woods** and **Millgate Fields** (the Mersey Valley Warden service produce a map of these, which can also be downloaded from their website). **Meadows,** edged by pleasant **woodland**, extend from the gardens to the quarter-mile distant **River Mersey**, offering some interesting walking potential to the more energetic visitor. Warden-led wildflower planting by school groups regularly takes place in the meadow, and the subsequent growth of biodiversity in the area is proving of interest to the naturalist as well as the gardener. Fletcher Moss Botanical Gardens has held a Green Flag Award since 2000. This is the national standard for parks and green spaces in England and Wales and a benchmark of excellence in recreational green areas. However, our perambulation continues through the **nearby gate** on to **Millgate Lane**. Turn left into the Lane and pass the **picturesque cottages** to arrive back at **Wilmslow Road**.

Between **Kingston Road** and the **Cricket Ground**, on the right, is the **Tower Business Park**, called after '**The Towers**'. The house itself (private property, please respect) is situated in the heart of the park, which can be accessed at all reasonable times. If Didsbury is overwhelmingly a product of the 19th century, architecturally speaking, the crown must be the 'grossly picturesque' Victorian mansion called 'The Towers', off Wilmslow Road. The architectural historian Sir Nikolaus Pevsner called it "the grandest of all Manchester mansions". Thomas Worthington, architect of the Albert Memorial in Albert Square, Manchester, designed it. (It was popularly known after it was built as the 'Calendar House' since it was said to have 12 towers, 52 rooms and 365 windows.) It was built originally for John Edward Taylor, founder of the Manchester Guardian, and was sold in 1874 to the engineer, Daniel Adamson. The decision to build the Manchester Ship Canal was taken in the drawing room of the house by Adamson and a group of associates in 1882. The house and its estate were bought in 1920 for the use of the newly established British Cotton Industry Research Association. One of the cotton spinners, W. Greenwood, met a large part of the costs and asked that the place be named after his daughter Shirley, hence it being named the 'Shirley Institute'. Purpose-built laboratories were subsequently opened on the site. Even though much of the fourteen and a half acre estate has been developed as a business park with some striking modern architecture, the BCIRA's successor, the British Textile Technology Group, still retains a presence.

Conclusion

The principal task of a conclusion in a work of this nature is to look ahead, and speculate upon the future expansion of the Metrolink system. Of course, the conclusion of the present phase, excluding the future Airport Line, is dealt with in the first chapter. Consequently, we must first briefly outline this future route. Ccommencing at a junction just beyond St. Werburgh's Road Station, the line runs via Mauldeth Road West and Hardy Lane to cross the Mersey Valley flood plain, and the River Mersey itself, by means of a low viaduct. After paralleling the M60, it crosses it to serve Wythenshawe Park, prior to passing along Moor Road and Southmoor Road. A new bridge carries Metrolink over the railway line at Baguley (where an interchange may eventually be created). The route continues along Southmoor Road, with a station to access Wythenshawe Hospital, before running along Hollyhedge Road (crossing the M56), Brownley Road, Crossacres Road, and Poundswick Lane, to reach Wythenshawe Town Centre. The way then lies along Fleming Road and proceeds via Simonsway and Shadowmoss Road to access the existing Airport Station. The latter is intended to be part of the Ground Transport Interchange.

The link between the existing construction phases and the notional future Phase Four comprises the 'Second City Centre Crossing', already mentioned in the Central Manchester chapter. A indicated in the introduction, the first phase has already commenced. The Metrolink Second City Crossing commences at Deansgate-Castlefield Station, (formerly G-Mex), and continues through St. Peter's Square (the station will be resited, together with the Cenotaph, as detailed on p36), along Princess Street, Cross Street and Corporation Street, before rejoining the existing Metrolink line just outside Victoria Station. There will only be one station, situated at Exchange Square, servicing the Exchange Square shopping quarter, Printworks, the Arndale Centre, and the Millenium/Medieval Quarter (containing the Wellington Inn, Hanging Bridge, Manchester Cathedral, and Chetham's College, see p51). It would be preferable to have a station in Cross Street, near to Albert Square, but it is doubtful if the siting problems can be solved in this case.

However, the bulk of this notional Phase will comprise two extensions and a completely new line. The first extension is part of an original proposal to link Stockport town centre to East Didsbury and the Metrolink network. The former railway from Didsbury to Stockport Tiviot Dale station was not protected after closure. Mostly built on an embankment, in cuttings or in tunnel, access to adjacent areas would not be good even if the route were still available. Nevertheless, the then GMPTE applied for Transport and Works Act powers but the process came to a halt in 2004 when the 'Big Bang' expansion was halted, and is currently in abeyance.

The proposed extension commences at the East Didsbury terminus, and largely follows the old railway track bed as far as Heaton Mersey Junction. The River Mersey and M60 would be crossed at the same place with a single bridge. Because Brinksway is narrow, has sharp bends and carries a large amount of traffic, the Metrolink line will cross back to the north bank of the river. The route then crosses back onto the south bank of the Mersey and joins Brinksway just before the junction with Hollywood Way. Then the trams would run in both directions along Chestergate into Stockport town centre. Metrolink would go under the railway viaduct to terminate alongside Stockport Bus Station. Bus connections here serve a wide area of Stockport. The East Didsbury terminus is planned to enable an eastward extension of Metrolink at some future date.

The second possible extension once featured in the original Airport Line proposal. It forms a loop in the form of a direct routing between Roundthorn Station and the Manchester Airport terminus, with stations at Wythenshawe Hospital, Newall Green, and Davenport Green. This variant was abandoned in 2005 for reasons of economy, but Transport for Greater Manchester will continue to retain and protect powers for this section.

There already exist powers to build a completely new line from Pomona Station to the Trafford Centre (the existing junction track formation at Pomona is noticed on p267). Total private sector funding was required before the line was included in the TIF (congestion charge) bid proposals; these were rejected and this line now requires funding beyond the existing Greater Manchester Transport Fund proposals. However, funding will probably be made available under a new 'Earnback Scheme' by which up to £30 million per annum may be claimed back in lieu of previous infrastructure investments. Outline Planning Permission for the proposed stations was renewed by Trafford MBC in June 2008, and, at the time of writing, the funding was said to be in place.

The (revised) 5.5km route will leave the existing tram stop at Pomona, descending to ground level and passing under the old Swing Bridge approach. From here it will run alongside the Ship Canal, before following Trafford Wharf Road and Warren Bruce Road to pass through the Village area of Trafford Park. The new route will then cross Parkway Circle and the Bridgewater Canal before obtaining the Trafford Centre. While station names have not yet been decided, it is likely there will be tram stops close to key destinations such as Old Trafford Stadium, The Imperial War Museum North, Trafford Park Village, Parkway Circle, Event City and finally Trafford Centre. The current proposal includes an extension from the Trafford Centre to Port Salford.

The route now continues beyond the Trafford Centre. A station is proposed at Trafford Quays, before it passes over a new opening low level bridge across the canal alongside the M60. Another proposed stop is at the Salford Reds Stadium, prior to the terminus at Port Salford, a massive container depot development situated on the north bank of the Manchester Ship Canal.

The future of the Metrolink system is also seen as being bound up with the development of tram-trains. A tram-train is a light rail system where trams run both on an urban tramway network and on main-line railways to combine the tram's flexibility and availability and the train's greater speed. The Karlsruhe model pioneered this concept in Germany, and it has since been adopted on projects in the Netherlands and France. In March 2008, the UK Department for Transport released details of a plan to trial diesel tram-trains on the Penistone line for two years starting in 2010, but the proposal was withdrawn. Instead, single-voltage electric tram-trains will be trialled between Rotherham and Sheffield. It is proposed to apply this concept to Metrolink, where a hybrid vehicle, perhaps utilising a diesel-electric transmission system (with an on-board 'clean' diesel engine) for the railway sections, and a normal overhead electric feed direct to the motors on Metrolink itself might be used.

The 'Tram Train Strategy' was considered by the Capital Projects and Policy Committee of TfGM in November, 2013, and a number of options were examined.

The first was that section of the old Cheshire Lines route between Altrincham and Chester. The train service from Manchester Piccadilly to Chester by this routing was diverted via Stockport as a consequence of the conversion of the Altrincham line to

Metrolink operation, with the trains joining the original route at the former Deansgate Junction, and running parallel to Metrolink through Navigation Road Station to reach the railway platforms at Altrincham Station. Although the diversion suits passengers wanting connections at Stockport, it is inconvenient for many Manchester commuters, who already change to the tram at Altrincham. Consequently, it would be a simple task to restore a rail connection at Deansgate Junction once more, and operate tram-trains between Piccadilly Station Metrolink Station, via the city centre, to Knutsford, Northwich, and Chester, and vice versa, tapping into the large commuter traffic between these places and Manchester. However, the Committee thought that such a plan would not offer sufficient value in return for the capital investment, though an extension as far as Hale, and greater flexibility in the Navigation Road area might be worthwhile objectives.

Glossop might be part of a 'second generation' tram-train phase, provided the four track alignment between Ashburys and Guide Bridge (shared with Trans-Pennine trains) was preserved by Network Rail.

Conversion of the Manchester-Atherton-Wigan line to tram-train operation was also favourably received, perhaps as part of the second phase. Consideration was also given to routes to Hazel Grove and between Stockport and Atrincham in the long term; the latter depending upon developments involving the HS2.

However, the lead candidate for tram-train operation was a Manchester to Marple service via Bredbury. The tram-train would follow the existing railway route from Marple/Rose Hill, via Romiley, to a point short of the junction at Ashbury's East. In order to avoid crossing the 25KV Guide Bridge line (also used by Trans-Pennine expresses), there might be a section of street running along Gorton Lane and Gorton Road. This would access the Ardwick Loop, which the tram trains would follow to the point where it crosses the East Manchester Line (p201) Presumably, the tram-trains would reach the Metrolink system proper by means of an inclined curve. Alternatively, the route could access the rear of Piccadilly Station at Sheffield Street by extending the street running a short distance along Ashton Old Road.

The 2001 Greater Manchester Strategic Rail Study by the Department for Transport included an indicative route through inner South Manchester, which although drawn approximately on the report map as heading down Kingsway, more likely, utilising the Oxford Road-Wilmsow Road corridor. This route has also been raised as a potential Bus Rapid Transit Route, where work is currently underway to restrict part of the route to buses only. It might be a future Metrolink line, linked with the Styal Loop railway line to enable tram-trains to run to Wilmslow, and perhaps Crewe.

With the completion of the Phase 3b, Metrolink will be the largest tram network in Britain. Taking account of the proposals outlined in this conclusion, there is no possibility of this proud title ever being lost.

Bibliography

A large part of the *Central Manchester* and *Salford Quays* chapters were sourced from the author's *Discovering Manchester* (also by Sigma). The *East Lancashire Railway* chapter is based on notes created by the author for the railway company, but not hitherto published in this form.

It would be impossible to detail all the many and varied sources used in researching and compiling this book, but the following publications were particularly useful:-

Dr. Peter Arrowsmith: *Bury Castle* (1999)
Philip Atkins: *A Guide Across Manchester* (1983 Edition)
Ian Beesley and Peter de Figuarido: *Victorian Manchester and Salford* (1988)
L.D. Bradshaw: *Origins of Street Names in the City Of Manchester* (1985)
Derek Brumhead and Terry Wyke: *A Walk Round Manchester Statues* (1990)
Rev. Arthur J. Dobb: *Like a Mighty Tortoise- A History of the Diocese of Manchester* (1978)
Frank Dixon: *The Manchester South Junction & Altrincham Railway* (Second Edition, 1994)
K.H. Dixon: *Top o' th' Steps - History of St. Chad's Parish Church, Rochdale* (Revised Edition, 2004)
Dunham Massey National Trust Handbook (2000)
Ian Goldthorpe: *Further Rossendale Rambles* (1991)
Clare Hartwell et al: *The Buildings of England – Lancashire: Manchester and the South East* (2005)
Clare Hartwell et al: *The Buildings of England – Cheshire* (2011)
A History and Guide of Ashton Parish Church (2010)
Geoffrey Howard: *The Parish Church of St. Mary and St. Bartholomew, Radcliffe – A Guide and Brief History* (2000)
John Marshall: *The Lancashire and Yorkshire Railway* (Vols. One and Two, 1969-70)
Oldham Town Trail (No date)
Ordsall Hall Guide (2011)
John Parkinson Bailey: *Manchester – An Architectural History* (2000)
Ian Pringle: *St. Mary's Church, Prestwich* - A History (No date)
Michael Rose et al: *Ancoats - Cradle of Industrialisation* (2011)
Peter Riley: *Heaton Hall and the Egerton Family* (2007)
Rossendale Museum – A Brief History and Guide (1993)
St. Mary in the Baum, Rochdale – A Short History (No date)
Jonathan Schofield: *City Life Guide to Manchester* (Various Editions)
T.Swindells: *Manchester Streets and Manchester Men* (1910)
Victoria County History of Lancashire (1907 – 1911)
Jeffrey Wells: *The Oldham Loop Part One - Victoria to Shaw and Crompton* (No date)
Jeffrey Wells: *The Oldham Loop Part Two - New Hey. Milnrow, and Rochdale* (No date)
Barry Worthington: *Discovering Manchester* (Revised Edition, 2011)
Ian Yearsley and Philip Groves: *The Manchester Tramways – 90 Years of Progress* (Revised Edition, 1991)

Index

Also from Sigma Leisure:

Discovering Manchester
2nd Edition
Barry Worthington

This stylish walking guide doubles as a detailed account of the city's architecture, its history and tourism attractions. There are walks throughout Manchester including such major entertainment and cultural centres as the Bridgewater Hall, Urbis, the Museum of Science and Industry, the Lowry and many more. Explore the entire city – from the Corn Exchange to G-Mex, from the Cathedral to Affleck's Palace.
£10.99

Peak District Walking
On The Level
Norman Buckley

Some folk prefer easy walks, and sometimes there's just not time for an all-day romp. In either case, this is definitely a book to keep on your bookshelf. Norman Buckley has had considerable success with "On The Level" books for the Lake District and the Yorkshire Dales.

The walks are ideal for family outings and the precise instructions ensure that there's little chance of losing your way. Well-produced maps encourage everybody to try out the walks - all of which are well scattered across the Peak District.
£8.99

Rocky Rambles in The Peak District 2nd Edition
Fred Broadhurst

"The Peak District has a dramatic story to tell and Fred Broadhurst is just the guide we need." – Aubrey Manning, presenter of the BBC TV series 'Earth Story'.

You don't have to be an expert or even an amateur geologist to enjoy these 'rocky rambles'! Where better than in and around the Peak District would you find geology right there beneath your feet - all you need to know is where to look.

The comprehensive glossary of terms, which covers the identification of Peak District Rocks, forms an invaluable supplement and provides 'at a glance' information for the reader.

£8.99

Dark Peak Hikes
Off the Beaten Track
Doug Brown

Here are 30 walks in the Dark Peak - the legendary northern part of the Peak District that covers some of the best hill country of Derbyshire, Yorkshire and Greater Manchester. Renowned for its unique peat ecology and striking gritstone scenery, the Dark Peak is a paradise for adventurous walkers intent on exploring the remoter parts of the moors.

Includes lots of helpful information for each walk – starting point, distance and estimated time, a general description including level of difficulty, and a very detailed route description.

£8.99

Peak District Walks
starting from train stations
Peter Naldrett

Two types of train station walks are covered in this book: there are those from existing train stations that still have passengers bustling about them, and there are those from platforms that fell silent in the infamous closures of the 1960s. Whether you are wanting to reach your starting point via train or delve into the history of transport in the Peak District, this book has something for you. One thing all the train station walks have in common is that they enjoy a fabulous route into some breath-taking countryside. Gorges, woodland, moors, farmland, rivers, glacial valleys and some tremendous hills are all included in this series of 20 walks, linked together by the transport routes that, today and in the past, dissected the Peak District.
£8.99

High Pub Walks
In the Peak District
Martin Smith

The Peak District National Park is noted for more than just its scenery. It also has a wealth of real ale pubs, many of which lie above 1000 feet (304 metres). It's these pubs that feature in this book. What better way to visit them than on foot? The book describes 30 walks and also has lots of information about the areas through which the various routes pass. The walks vary in length from a mere 2½ miles to 12¾ miles, so there's something suitable for everyone here. The walks generally start from the pub and with certain rare exceptions, can be reached by public transport, so you can leave your car at home and savour the liquid products on offer.
£8.99

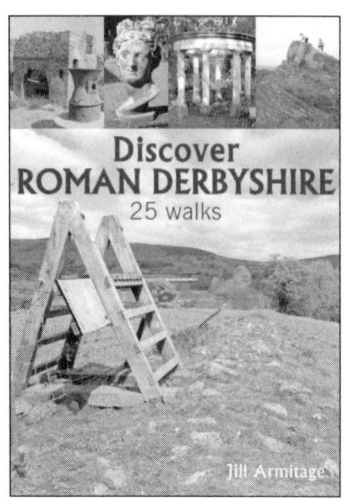

Discover Roman Derbyshire
25 walks
Jill Armitage

The Romans have been credited with giving Britain a network of roads that still has a profound effect on our road systems, so Discover Roman Derbyshire, 25 walks sets out to trace those roads on foot in the same manner that the Roman soldiers did when they occupied the region between the 1st and 5th centuries. The roads linked forts with their accompanying vici, busy trading centres where industry prospered similar to our present day towns. The walks not only include the roads, forts and vici, they also trace localities where finds have been discovered.

£8.99

Discover Celtic Derbyshire
25 walks
Jill Armitage

Discover Celtic Derbyshire follows the Portway from the key Celtic Hillfort of Mam Tor in North Derbyshire to the Derbyshire/Nottinghamshire border at Stapleford and the southern river ports. Along the route, you will encounter the hermitages and industries, visit tribal hillforts, those iconic symbols of the age, and through megalithic mysteries, ancient feasts and festivals, discover the lifestyle of these people the conquering Romans considered barbaric. They were not. They had their beliefs and their gods and the Roman conquest of Britain did not signal the immediate death of Celtic culture. That is why this area has a treasure trove of early curiosities and customs, showing that pre-history is not quite dead in this ancient heart of England. Of the 25 walks in this book, 15 are circular, however, the route of the ancient Portway has been divided into ten manageable walks ranging from 3½ -7 miles.

£8.99

Peak District Walking Natural History Walks
Christopher Mitchell

An updated 2nd Edition with 18 varied walks for all lovers of the great outdoors — and armchair ramblers too! Learn how to be a nature detective, a 'case notes' approach shows you what clues to look for and how to solve them. Detailed maps include animal tracks and signs, landscape features and everything you need for the perfect natural history walk. There are mysteries and puzzles to solve to add more fun for family walks — solutions supplied! Includes follow on material with an extensive Bibliography and 'Taking it Further' sections.

£8.99

Best Tea Shop Walks in the Peak District
Norman and June Buckley

A wonderful collection of easy-going walks that are ideal for families and all those who appreciate fine scenery with a touch of decadence in the shape of an afternoon tea or morning coffee —or both! The 26 walks are spread widely across the Peak District, including Lyme Park, Castleton, Miller's Dale, and The Roaches and — of course — such famous dales as Lathkill and Dovedale. Each walk has a handy summary so that you can choose the walks that are ideally suited to the interests and abilities of your party. The tea shops are just as diverse, ranging from the splendour of Chatsworth House to more basic locations. Each one welcomes ramblers and there is always a good choice of tempting goodies.

£8.99

Exploring the North Peak & South Pennines
25 rollercoaster mountain bike rides
Michael Ely

This book will inspire you to pump up the tyres and oil the chain for some excitement, exercise and a feast of rollercoaster riding as you join Michael Ely on some great mountain biking in these Pennine hills. Over 500 miles of riding for the adventurous off-road cyclist that explore the tracks and steep lanes in the Pennine hills. There are twenty-five illustrated rides - with cafe stops half way round - to provide both a challenge and many hours of healthy exercise in classic mountain biking country.
£8.99

Archaeology Walks in the Peak District
Ali Cooper

Put on your walking boots, enjoy the superb scenery of the Peak District and enjoy a roller-coaster ride through history with Ali Cooper. Routes ranging from 3 to 12 miles explore Peak District sites where there are visible features in the landscape. Brief descriptions of the major finds on the walks are included, plus a bibliography for those who want to delve deeper.

"... a new authoritative book ... for a spot of time travel while out walking" – Derby Evening Telegraph
£8.99

All of our books are all available online at www.sigmpress.co.uk or through booksellers. For a free catalogue, please contact:

SIGMA LEISURE, STOBART HOUSE, PONTYCLERC, PENYBANC ROAD, AMMANFORD, CARMARTHENSHIRE SA18 3HP
Tel: 01269 593100   Fax: 01269 596116
info@sigmapress.co.uk   www.sigmapress.co.uk